A Restorative Justice Reader

A Restorative Justice Reader

Texts, sources, context

Edited by

Gerry Johnstone

WILLAN
PUBLISHING

Published by:

Willan Publishing
Culmcott House
Mill Street, Uffculme
Cullompton, Devon
EX15 3AT, UK
Tel: +44(0)1884 840337
Fax: +44(0)1884 840251
e-mail: info@willanpublishing.co.uk
website: www.willanpublishing.co.uk

Published simultaneously in the USA and Canada by:

Willan Publishing
c/o ISBS, 5824 N.E. Hassalo St,
Portland, Oregon 97213-3644, USA
Tel: +001(0)503 287 3093
Fax: +001(0)503 280 8832

ISBN 1-903240-81-6 Paperback
ISBN 1-903240-82-4 Hardback

British Library Cataloguing-in-Publication Data
A catalogue record for this book is available from the British Library

Project management by Deer Park Productions
Typesetting by TW Typesetting, Plymouth, Devon.
Printed and bound by T.J. International Ltd, Padstow, Cornwall.

Contents

Preface

Amongst the most important developments in contemporary crime policy and criminal justice is the emergence of a vibrant international campaign promoting restorative justice as an alternative to conventional ways of viewing and responding to crime. Proponents of restorative justice contend that, in responding to crime, our main concern should not be to punish offenders; rather, it should be to ensure that offenders account for and repair the harm they bring about. They also maintain that, rather than entrusting the task of dispensing criminal justice entirely to state officials and professionals, modern societies should create processes in which ordinary people, including the perpetrators and victims of an offence, resolve collectively how the harm created by the offence should be repaired and how reoffending is to be prevented.

Restorative justice policies and programmes are usually offered as a progressive alternative to the increasing use of imprisonment and other exclusionary measures to control crime and dispense justice. Many penal reformers and professionals interested in developing constructive ways of dealing with people whose lives are somehow affected by crime have found restorative justice appealing. Moreover, the idea has recently started to influence government thinking and policy, especially but not exclusively in the realm of youth justice. With official encouragement and support, restorative justice schemes are now proliferating rapidly around the world.

Such has been the success of the restorative justice movement that, today, anybody interested in the future of crime policy and criminal justice – indeed anybody interested in the development of more constructive forms of conflict resolution and crime control – has to understand what it is about. One problem they may encounter is simply getting access to the diverse international literature on restorative justice. However, even if this difficulty is overcome, there is the problem of knowing where to start and how to work one's way through a rather bulky, diverse, international literature. Nor is this simply a problem of separating the wheat from the chaff. As numerous commentators have pointed out, restorative justice is not a single coherent theory or perspective on crime and justice, but a loose unifying term which encompasses a range of distinct ideas, practices and proposals. The danger with a random browse or trawl through the literature is that one could spend a lot of time reading repetitive materials on a few aspects of restorative justice, whilst failing to encounter other aspects of restorative justice thought and practice which are of equal or greater importance. An even greater danger is that one will encounter literature advocating and supporting restorative justice, or evaluating it in terms of its effectiveness in achieving its declared goals, but not encounter the extremely important critical literature which highlights the limitations and potential dangers involved in developing restorative justice.

It was partly in order to address such problems that I wrote my recent book *Restorative Justice: Ideas, Values, Debates* (Willan, 2002). However, those whose interest in the subject has been whetted (either by reading that book or in other ways) will want to read some of the key 'original writings'. But, for the busy student or practitioner, constructing an appropriate reading list – one which will enable him or her to encounter a range of key writers and a range of key ideas, processes and critiques in a manageable way – remains a daunting task. Hence, this book contains an edited selection of key literature on restorative justice, encompassing a range of authors and topics from a number of continents. The hope is that the reader will benefit from the effort I have put into: (1) *selecting* a suitable range of writing on restorative justice; (2) *editing* the selected material, so that the most important ideas and topics are covered and so that repetition is, if not entirely avoided, at least reduced considerably; (3) *organising* that material so that one can work through it in a systematic, logically structured way; and (4) introducing the material so that the contexts in which it was produced and some of its most significant features can be better understood. The readings are preceded by my own introductory essay, in which I explain a range of different ways in which restorative justice has been envisaged and present some of my views on how we should think about the task of evaluating the case for restorative justice.

I would like to record my thanks to Brian Willan, for suggesting this book and for once more being patient and constructive. I also wish to thank a number of people who made extremely valuable comments, concerning both the structure and content of the book. Inevitably, I have not been able or willing to incorporate all their suggestions, but a significant number of them have been taken on board. Thanks, therefore, to John Braithwaite, Kathleen Daly, David Miers, Paul McCold, Lynette Parker, George Pavlich, Daniel Van Ness, Lode Walgrave, Brian Williams, Howard Zehr and two anonymous reviewers whose willingness to share their expertise has been of enormous benefit. None of the above are responsible for any limitations or defects of this book. Thanks are also due to the authors and publishers whose work is reproduced here, for their prompt and helpful responses to my requests, and for allowing their work to be used in edited form. Finally, thanks are again due to my wife, Brigid, and our children Eleanor and Pierce, for their constant support and encouragement.

Acknowledgements

The editor and publisher would like to thank the following for their kind permission to reproduce copyright material:

Part A

The extract from 'Restorative Justice: An Overview' by Tony F. Marshall is reproduced with permission of the author. The full text was published and distributed in 1998 by The Center for Restorative Justice and Peacemaking (University of Minnesota) and the Restorative Justice Consortium (UK). It is available online at http://ssw.che.umn.edu/rjp/Resources/Resource.htm.

The extract from 'Restitution: A New Paradigm of Criminal Justice' by Randy E. Barnett is reproduced with permission of The University of Chicago Press and the author. The full text was published in *Ethics*, Vol. 87 (1977), pp. 279–301.

The extract from 'Conflicts as Property' by Nils Christie is reproduced with the permission of Oxford University Press and the author. The full text was published in *The British Journal of Criminology*, Vol. 17:1 (Jan. 1977), pp. 1–15.

Retributive Justice, Restorative Justice by Howard Zehr is reproduced with the permission of the Mennonite Central Committee, Office on Crime and Justice. It was published as an Occasional Paper (number 4 in the series *New Perspectives on Crime and Justice*) in September 1985 (MCC Canada Victim Offender Ministries Program and the MCC US Office on Crime and Justice).

The extract from 'Restorative Justice and a Better Future' by John Braithwaite is reproduced with the permission of the author. It was published in the *Dalhousie Review*, Spring 1996, 76:1, pp. 9–32.

Part B

The extract entitled 'The Background of the Western Legal Tradition' by Harold J. Berman is reproduced with permission of Harvard University Press. It is taken from Berman's book, *Law and Revolution: The Formation of the Western Legal Tradition* (Cambridge, Massachusetts: Harvard University Press, 1983), pp. 77–9. The copyright belongs to the President and Fellows of Harvard College.

The extract from 'The History of Restorative Justice' by Elmar G.M. Weitekamp is reproduced with permission of Richard Allinson (Willow Tree Press/Criminal Justice Press). The full version is published in Bazemore, G. and Walgrave, L. (eds) *Restorative Juvenile Justice: Repairing the Harm of Youth Crime* (Monsey, NY: Criminal Justice Press, 1999), pp. 75–102.

The extract from Rupert Ross's book *Returning to the Teachings: Exploring Aboriginal Justice* (copyright © University of Saskatchewan, 1996) is reprinted by permission of Penguin Group (Canada), a Division of Pearson Penguin Canada Inc.

The extract from 'Navajo Restorative Justice: The Law of Equality and Justice' by Robert Yazzie and James W. Zion is reproduced with the permission of Richard Allinson (Criminal Justice Press). The full text is published in Galaway, B. and Hudson, J. (eds) *Restorative Justice: International Perspectives* (Monsey, NY: Criminal Justice Press, 1996), pp. 157–73.

The extract 'The Maori Restorative Tradition' by Jim Consedine is reproduced with permission of the author and Ploughshares Publications. It is taken from Chapter 6 of Consedine's book, *Restorative Justice: Healing the Effects of Crime* (revised edition) (Lyttleton, New Zealand: Ploughshares Publications, 1999).

The extract from 'Christianity: The Rediscovery of Restorative Justice' by Pierre Allard and Wayne Northey is reproduced with permission of State University of New York Press. The full text is published in Hadley, M. (ed) *The Spiritual Roots of Restorative Justice* (Albany, NY: SUNY Press, 2001), pp. 119–41.

Part C

The extract from 'The Kitchener Experiment' by Dean E. Peachey is reproduced with the permission of the author. The full text is published in M. Wright and B. Galaway (eds) *Mediation and Criminal Justice* (London: Sage Publications, 1989), pp. 14–26.

The extract 'Justice without Lawyers: Enabling People to Resolve their Conflicts' by Martin Wright is reproduced with the permission of the author. It comes from Chapter 4 of his book, *Justice for Victims and Offenders: A Restorative Response to Crime*, 2nd edn (Winchester: Waterside Press, 1996).

The extract from 'Restorative Justice in New Zealand: Family Group Conferences as a Case Study' by Allison Morris and Gabrielle Maxwell is reproduced with permission of the editors of the *Western Criminology Review*. The full text is published in the *Western Criminology Review*, 1(1), 1998, and is available online at: http://wcr.sonoma.edu/v1n1/morris.html.

The extract from 'Family Conferencing in Wagga Wagga: A Communitarian Model of Justice' by D.B. Moore and T.A. O'Connell is reproduced with permission of the Australian Institute of Criminology, Canberra. The full text is published as Chapter 3 of Alder, J. and Wundersitz, J. (eds) (1994) *Family Conferencing and Juvenile Justice: The Way Forward or Misplaced Optimism* (Canberra: Australian Institute of Criminology), pp. 45–86.

The extract from 'A Comparison of Four Restorative Conferencing Models' by Gordon Bazemore and Mark Umbreit is reproduced with permission of the Office of Juvenile Justice and Delinquency Prevention (OJJDP), of the US Department of Justice. The full text is published in the *OJJDP Juvenile Justice Bulletin* (February 2001). The full version is available online at http://www.ncjrs.org/html/ojjdp/.

Part D

The extract from 'Restorative Justice for Juveniles: Just a Technique or a Fully Fledged Alternative?' by Lode Walgrave is reproduced with permission of the author and Blackwell Publishers. The full text is published in *The Howard Journal of Criminal Justice*, 34:3 (1995), pp. 228–49.

The extract from 'Creating Restorative Systems' by Daniel Van Ness is reproduced with permission of Willan Publishing. The full version is published in Walgrave, L. (ed.) *Restorative Justice and the Law* (Cullompton, Devon: Willan, 2002).

The extract from 'The Function of Forgiveness in the Criminal Justice System' by John R. Gehm is reproduced with permission of the author and Kluwer Academic Publishers. The full text is published in Messmer, H. and Otto, H. (eds) *Restorative Justice on Trial* (Netherlands: Kluwer, 1992), pp. 541–50.

The extract from 'Justice for Victims of Young Offenders: The Centrality of Emotional Harm and Restoration' by Heather Strang is reproduced with permission of the author. The full text is published in Morris, A. and Maxwell, G. (eds) *Restorative Justice for Juveniles: Conferencing, Mediation and Circles* (Oxford: Hart Publishing, 2001), pp. 183–193.

The extract from 'Community is not a Place: A New Look at Community Justice Initiatives' by Paul McCold and Benjamin Wachtel is reproduced with permission of Taylor & Francis Ltd. The full text is published in *Contemporary Justice Review*, 1:1 (1998), pp. 71–85. The Taylor & Francis Journals website is at http://www.tandf.co.uk/journals.

The extract from 'What is Relational Justice?' by Michael Schluter is reproduced with permission of Waterside Press and the Relationships Foundation (Cambridge). The full text is published in Burnside, J. and Baker, N. (eds) *Relational Justice: Repairing the Breach* (Winchester: Waterside Press, 1994), pp. 17–27.

'In the Hands of the Public?' by Adam Crawford is reproduced with permission of the author and the Relationships Foundation. It was originally published in the *Relational Justice Bulletin*, Issue 13, January 2002, pp. 6–8. It draws on a longer paper 'Public Matters', published by and available from the Institute of Public Policy Research (IPPR).

'Does Restorative Justice Work?' by John Braithwaite is a slightly abridged version of Chapter 3 of his book, *Restorative Justice and Responsive Regulation* (Oxford University Press, 2002). It is reproduced with permission of the author and Oxford University Press.

Part E

The extract from 'Restorative Justice: The Real Story' by Kathleen Daly is reproduced by permission of Sage Publications. The full article is published in *Punishment and Society*, 4:1 (2002), pp. 5–79.

The extract from 'Restorative Punishment and Punitive Restoration' by R.A. Duff is reproduced with permission of the author and Willan Publishing. The full version is published in Walgrave, L. (ed) *Restorative Justice and the Law* (Cullompton, Devon: Willan, 2002).

The extract from 'Just Cops Doing "Shameful" Business?: Police-led Restorative Justice and the Lessons of Research' by Richard Young is reproduced with the permission of the author and Hart Publishing. The full version is in Morris, A. and Maxwell, G. (eds) *Restorative Justice for Juveniles: Conferencing, Mediation and Circles* (Oxford: Hart Publishing, 2001), pp. 195–226.

The extract from 'Reconsidering Restorative Justice: The Corruption of Benevolence Revisited? by Sharon Levrant, Francis T. Cullen, Betsy Fulton and John F. Wozniak is reproduced with permission of Sage Publications Inc. The full version is published in *Crime and Delinquency*, Vol. 45, No. 1, Jan. 1999, pp. 3–27.

The extract from 'Responsibilities, Rights and Restorative Justice' by Andrew Ashworth is reproduced with permission of the author and Oxford University Press. The full version appears in a special edition of the *British Journal of Criminology* (42:3, 2002), on 'Practice, Performance and Prospects for Restorative Justice', edited by Kieran McEvoy, Harry Mika and Barbara Hudson. Ashworth's paper is at pp. 578–95.

The extract from 'Restorative Justice: The Challenge of Sexual and Racial Violence' by Barbara Hudson is reproduced with permission of Blackwell Publishers. The full version is in the *Journal of Law and Society* (25:2) 1998, pp. 237–56.

The extract from 'Deconstructing Restoration: The Promise of Restorative Justice' by George Pavlich is reproduced with permission of the author and Willan Publishing. The full version is available in Weitekamp, E. and Kerner, H.-J. (eds) *Restorative Justice; Theoretical Foundations* (Cullompton, Devon: Willan, 2002), pp. 90–109.

The extract from 'Critiquing the Critics: A Brief Response to Critics of Restorative Justice' by Allison Morris is reproduced with permission of Oxford University Press. The full version appears in a special edition of the *British Journal of Criminology* (42: 3, 2002), on 'Practice, Performance and Prospects for Restorative Justice', edited by Kieran McEvoy, Harry Mika and Barbara Hudson. Morris's article is at pp. 596–615.

Appendix A

The Declaration of Leuven on the Advisability of Promoting the Restorative Approach to Juvenile Crime is reproduced, with minor abridgments, with permission of Lode Walgrave. The full version is published in Walgrave, L. (ed) *Restorative Justice for Juveniles: Potentialities, Risks and Problems for Research* (Leuven University Press, 1998).

Appendix B

The *Statement of Restorative Justice Principles* is reproduced with permission of the Restorative Justice Consortium, an organisation formed in 1997 to bring together a wide range of organisations with an interest in restorative justice. See www.restorativejustice.org.uk.

Introduction: restorative approaches to criminal justice

Crime is perceived by many as a growing social evil. Its existence gives rise to public demands: that crime be brought under control and that, in the aftermath of a crime, justice be done.

In contemporary society, these two tasks – controlling crime and dispensing justice – tend to be seen as jobs for the criminal justice system. Its main tool for performing these tasks is judicial punishment, often and increasingly in the form of imprisonment. Punishment in general and imprisonment in particular are used in efforts to deter criminal lawbreakers from reoffending, to discourage others tempted to commit crime, to keep troublesome people out of circulation or subject them to intense supervision, and to express society's disapproval of criminal behaviour. Judicial punishment is also the method of choice, in contemporary society, for doing justice in the wake of a crime. By inflicting 'a just measure of pain' (Ignatieff, 1978) on those who violate the basic rights of others, and in the process intimidate the community, the criminal justice system seeks to satisfy the needs of victims and the public for justice.

In recent decades, however, an increasingly significant and influential social movement has emerged which questions both the idea that dispensing justice and controlling crime are jobs for the criminal justice system and the notion that the best tool for performing these tasks is judicial punishment. Advocates of restorative justice suggest that, instead of relying entirely upon the criminal justice state and its professional employees to handle crime, ordinary people affected by crime should participate in defining and handling their own crime problems. The role of criminal justice agencies and officials should be to facilitate processes whereby ordinary people do justice, rather than to take over complete responsibility for the task.

However, according to proponents of restorative justice, if people are to dispense justice and control crime, they need to reject punitive interventions, which are of questionable effectiveness and morality. In place of punishment, they need to use restorative interventions. Experiments with restorative justice demonstrate, it is claimed, that it is highly effective in diverting offenders – especially young offenders – from criminal habits and that it satisfies the needs of crime victims for justice. Moreover, it achieves these goals whilst treating offenders with respect.

Envisaging restorative justice

So what is the restorative approach to criminal justice? Answering this question is not as straightforward as we might suppose (Hoyle and Young, 2002: 527–33). One reason for this is that the term 'restorative justice' has been applied to a range of seemingly quite diverse modes of intervention into the lives of offenders and victims (Zehr and Mika, 1998). Indeed, it seems more accurate and fruitful to refer to restorative *approaches* to justice rather than to *the* restorative approach. The picture is complicated further by the fact that some leading promoters of restorative justice contend that many forms of intervention represented as restorative are really not good examples of restorative justice at all (ibid.; Morris and Gelsthorpe, 2000; Sullivan and Tifft, 2001; Zehr, 2002).

However, there is another reason why defining restorative justice is far from simple. It is often unclear how we should *envisage* restorative justice. For instance, Braithwaite and Strang (2001: 1–2) suggest that restorative justice is conceived in the literature in two quite different ways. They distinguish a 'process conception' from a 'values conception'. Their view is that 'it is best to see restorative justice as involving a commitment to both restorative processes and restorative values' (ibid.: 2). Yet, as they readily admit, these two ways of envisaging restorative justice are in tension with each other. Moreover, there may be other ways of envisaging restorative justice, including as a 'set of principles that may orientate the general practice of any agency or group in relation to crime' (*Marshall*);[1] as a distinctive paradigm of justice (*Zehr*); as a normative social theory (Sullivan and Tifft, 2001); and as a lifestyle (Sullivan, 1998).

In what follows I will briefly explain some of these ways of envisaging restorative justice.[2] My aim is not to provide a comprehensive account of all the existing ways of envisaging restorative justice, but to explain a *range* of conceptions. Hence, I will include some of the more extreme versions of restorative justice which, although they exist on the margins of the restorative justice movement, are important in that they reveal something important about its character. In the subsequent section I will *supplement* these accounts with an analysis that – developing an idea that is present but under-developed in the restorative justice literature – seeks to clarify the idea of restorative justice by showing how it blends features of traditional criminal law with modified versions of certain principles of private or civil law. In the final section of this Introduction, I will draw attention to just a few important questions relevant to our assessment of the strengths and weaknesses of the case for restorative justice.

Restorative justice as a process

A common way of explaining restorative justice, used especially by practitioners, is to describe it as a distinctive *process*. For instance, restorative justice is often contrasted with conventional criminal justice processes in which victims and offenders are positioned as adversaries, discouraged from communicating directly with each other, and expected to remain passive whilst all the key decisions are made by professionals. In restorative justice, victims and offenders take part in mediation sessions designed to help both of them. In these sessions, offenders and victims communicate directly with each other and participate in decision-making.

At such meetings, victims tell 'their' offenders about how the crime affected them. One claimed advantage of this direct communication is that it brings offenders to recognise fully that their behaviour does harm people and it helps them understand the extent of this harm. Offenders then have an opportunity to account for themselves, answer any questions the victim has and to offer something by way of apology and reparation. Advocates of the process report that many offenders – shocked at hearing first-hand how extensively their behaviour has harmed real people – show deep remorse, apologise to their victims and offer to make amends for their misdeeds.

Such a process, according to its advocates, has a positive effect on the future behaviour of offenders, because it confronts them with the full implications of what they have done. It also, it is claimed, meets important needs of victims which are not met by conventional criminal justice processes. For instance, it meets their need to be involved in the process by which their crime is handled and their need for answers to questions such as why the offender targeted them and whether the offender intends them further harm.

An important variant, within this 'process conception' of restorative justice, is to describe it as a process in which *all* 'stakeholders' – i.e. all people affected significantly by a criminal offence – meet in a circle to discuss the harm caused by the offence and to decide, collectively, how the harm should be repaired. On this view, important features of a fully restorative process are that conflicts and problems are discussed and resolved within a family or community context. Rather than delegating important decisions to professionals, ordinary people affected by a crime work together to handle their own crime problems, devising solutions that meet their own 'local' needs. Restorative justice is characterised by a constructive meeting between law-abiding members of the community and those members of the community who commit harmful acts.

Such descriptions capture a great deal of what restorative justice is about. However, on their own, they do not convey the full meanings and implications of the term. In particular, they do not tell us enough about how restorative interventions differ in their goals and methods from more conventional penal interventions. Hence, these descriptions of the processes of restorative justice need to be supplemented by explanations focusing on the outcomes which proponents of restorative justice argue we should strive to achieve, as well as the methods they recommend and reject as useful or appropriate for achieving these outcomes. Moreover, I suggest, once we start thinking of restorative justice primarily in terms of outcomes, the tendency to over-identify restorative justice with particular processes such as victim–offender meetings is rendered problematic.

Goals and methods of restorative justice

Most proponents of restorative justice accept that the ultimate purpose of criminal justice interventions must be to ensure that justice is done and to make people safer. They argue, however, that judicial punishment is neither necessary nor sufficient to achieve these goals. The 'retributive justice' that is achieved through the .punishment of offenders is not the only form which justice can take and is in fact an impoverished and thin conception of justice. Justice in the aftermath of a crime can take the richer form of 'restorative justice'. Also, the use of punishment as a deterrent or incapacitating device is not necessary to control crime, nor is it particularly effective. Rather, crime can be controlled best by interventions which open the eyes of offenders to the harm their behaviour causes, instil empathy in them and strengthen their bond to, and stake in, the law-abiding community. So, according to advocates of restorative justice, what is required to achieve such ultimate ends as justice and security is a process designed to achieve outcomes such as:

- offenders repairing the harm resulting from their criminal acts;
- offenders experiencing and expressing repentance for their misdeeds;
- offenders being fully reintegrated into communities of law-abiding citizens; and
- victims being healed of the trauma resulting from their experience.

Punishment, they argue, hinders rather than promotes such outcomes. It does little to encourage, and much to discourage, reparation and remorse on the part of offenders. It tends to result in the social exclusion, rather than reintegration, of offenders. This renders offenders more rather than less of a threat to the community. And state-imposed punishment of offenders tends to aggravate rather than heal the trauma suffered by crime victims.

Hence, to accomplish restorative outcomes – such as reparation of harm, reintegration of offenders, a restored sense of security and recovery of victims from psychological trauma – we need to reject the use of state punishment. In its place should be interventions that:

- encourage offenders to undertake appropriate reparative acts;
- instil repentance within offenders and facilitate its communication;
- facilitate the social reacceptance of offenders who have expressed repentance and made serious efforts to repair the damage they caused;
- assist ex-offenders who are making serious efforts to refrain from further offending; and
- promote the healing of victims and survivors of crime.

Processes described above – such as mediated meetings between victims and offenders or the broader-based family or community conferences – are usually recommended as useful in that they can make a crucial contribution to the achievement of these outcomes. For instance, by promoting respectful and constructive dialogue between victims and offenders (and between offenders and the community), such encounters bring offenders to appreciate the harmful consequences of their behaviour and enable victims and offenders to come to a better understanding of each other. Also, by giving victims an effective voice within the criminal justice process, and giving them the opportunity to see and hear their offender, these processes contribute to the recovery of victims from their traumatic experience.

However, if we think of restorative justice in terms of outcomes, it is arguable that such encounters will seldom in themselves be sufficient. Moreover, in some cases they may not be necessary or may even be inappropriate. Depending on the circumstances of a case, other measures may be required in addition to or instead of processes such as victim–offender mediation and restorative conferences. For example, if a victim is unwilling to meet with an offender, other ways might be found of bringing offenders to appreciate how their criminal behaviour damages the lives of people. More controversially, some supporters of the idea of restorative justice are of the view that, in many cases, in order to reassure victims and the public that they *genuinely* repent their misdeeds, offenders may have to agree to undergo some 'punishment' for them (cf. *Duff*). Also, if offenders are to be fully reintegrated into the community, it seems clear that much more than gestures of reacceptance by victims will often be required. Methods will have to be found whereby the social stigma of being an offender is reduced or avoided, which means that members of the community will have to adjust their attitudes towards ex-offenders. To make such an adjustment, they in turn may need various forms of reassurance and education. As a final example, whilst victim–offender mediation and the like may contribute to the healing of crime victims, for many deeply traumatised victims and survivors much more will need to be done if they are to recover fully. Indeed, in some cases, victim–offender meetings – even if skilfully organised and facilitated – may be counterproductive for the healing of victims.

I argue then, that if we think of restorative justice primarily in terms of outcomes, it is necessary to reject the tendency to over-identify it with a particular set of processes. Moreover, it is equally mistaken to think that restorative justice must exclude any process. Processes such as victim–offender mediation and restorative conferencing may well, if skilfully organised and facilitated, prove to be of immense value in *contributing* to the achievement of restorative outcomes. But their value should always be something to be demonstrated rather than assumed. And, it should be recognised that different types of case may require different types of process.

Restorative justice as a set of distinctive values

For some advocates, descriptions of restorative goals and processes, for all their worth, miss what is most important and distinctive about genuinely restorative interventions: the values which guide them. A typical statement is that conventional criminal justice responds to the hurt of crime with the hurt of punishment, whereas restorative justice is guided by the value of healing (Braithwaite and Strang, 2001: 1–2). Other values in which restorative justice is grounded are said to include 'democracy', 'social support', 'caring', 'love' and 'non-dominated speech' (ibid.: 12). In the discourse of restorative justice one regularly comes across other terms which feature much less often, if at all, in more conventional criminal justice discourses, such as 'compassion', 'redemption', 'forgiveness' and 'reconciliation'. The militaristic manner of conventional criminal justice is to be replaced with the peaceful co-operative dialogue of restorative justice. The attitude of indignation which fuels the practice of punishment is to be exchanged for an attitude of censuring in a spirit of respect and solidarity. Whereas punishment involves the use of power to achieve our goals, restorative justice, on some accounts, eschews power and relies instead on 'time, patience and a loving attitude' (Sullivan *et al.*, 1998: 10). Also, the stiff, distant formality of the conventional criminal trial is contrasted with the warmth, humanity and informal communication of the restorative healing circle.

We should not, of course, accept such representations of restorative justice as accurate descriptions. For one thing, they tend to present us with a one-sided picture of the values that underpin conventional criminal justice. This is not to deny that the practice of judicial punishment is motivated to a considerable extent by some rather unsavoury values. The rampant brutality of modern penal systems surely reflects a callous willingness to hurt and destroy the lives of others in order to secure our own comfort or simply to vent our frustrations (Cayley, 1998; Garland, 2001). However, the practice of punishment is supported in principle by many as necessary for the protection of more decent values, such as respect for victims or even respect for offenders (see Moberly, 1968; Duff, 2001). Also, an examination of the discourses of imprisonment will reveal a much wider range of values, including compassion and love for offenders, than one would guess from reading the works of restorative justice advocates (Ignatieff, 1978; Johnstone, 1996; Van Ness and Strong, 2002: 11–12).

Further, it is important to distinguish between the values espoused by many restorative justice proponents and the values actually embodied in the discourses and practices of restorative justice. For instance, most proponents of restorative justice continue to use the language bequeathed to them by the system of state punishment which they purportedly oppose in its entirety (Hulsman, 1986). Many continue to talk of 'crimes', 'offenders' and 'victims' as if these terms were value-free – i.e. neutral descriptions of a reality which one can approach either punitively or restoratively. It seems more adequate to regard these terms as a product of a particular (and contestable) way of *constructing* 'troublesome behaviour': the criminal law model (ibid.; cf. Shearing, 2001). A more radical break with the values of conventional criminal justice would seem to require the rejection of such language and the adoption of different terms, such as 'conflicts' and 'parties in dispute'. This is not, of course, to say that such a radical break with conventional criminal justice values would be justified. My point is simply that restorative justice is, in many ways, much more committed to the values of conventional criminal justice than its proponents sometimes acknowledge.

Nevertheless, any attempt to understand or assess restorative justice needs to attend to its self-understanding as a practice motivated by radically different values from those which underpin conventional penal practices. The restorative justice movement draws upon and attempts to put into practice a definite set of ethical ideas about how we should relate to other human beings and in particular to those who cause us trouble. For instance it suggests that instead of severing relationships with troublesome people we should seek to strengthen our relationship to them; instead of trying to intimidate them into better behaviour we should seek to awaken and appeal to their conscience, a task which does require more patience and perhaps a more loving attitude; and instead of regarding and treating them as people essentially different from and inferior to ourselves, we should see and treat them as people like ourselves, people with whom we have almost everything in common.

It is of course true that many 'restorative' practices – or perhaps many practices calling themselves restorative justice – fail to reflect such values. The importance of the values conception of restorative justice is precisely that it provides a standpoint from which such practices can be criticised as falling short of a richer notion of restorative justice.

Restorative justice as the application of spiritual teaching to criminal justice

Whilst most advocates describe the distinctive values of restorative justice in secular terms, some understand and represent restorative justice as an application of faith-based principles of reconciliation, restoration and healing to the handling of criminal behaviour (see Hadley 2001; *Allard and Northey*). In making this point, I should make it clear that most proponents and practitioners of restorative justice – whatever their religious beliefs – clearly think that the approach can be described, explained and justified in purely secular terms. Indeed, a few feel that the use of spiritual language in the discourse of restorative justice can hinder the movement by putting off many potential supporters.[3] Nevertheless, many proponents and practitioners of restorative justice make it quite clear that their commitment to it is intricately bound up with their commitment to religious doctrines, stemming from Aboriginal spirituality, Buddhism, Chinese religions, Christianity, Hinduism, Islam, Judaism and Sikhism (Hadley 2001; see also Ross 1996; Van Ness and Strong 2002: 116).[4] This is an aspect of the restorative justice movement which must be taken into account in any attempt to understand its character and potential.

Restorative justice as a theory of social justice

For a few restorative justice campaigners, a commitment to the values of restorative justice requires much more than a programme for the radical reform of society's response to crime; it also requires a plan for the transformation of *social arrangements* so that they take into account the basic human needs of all and so that 'violence' is eradicated (Sullivan *et al.*, 1998: 15). Hence, restorative justice is conceived not simply as an alternative way of handling 'crime'; it is also understood as an alternative vision of a just and non-violent society.

  This way of envisaging restorative justice has been promoted by, among others, Dennis Sullivan and Larry Tifft (2001). They maintain that in everyday life (e.g. families, schools, workplaces), people are constantly subjected to 'violence' and exercises of power that are equally if not more harmful to them than are acts officially labelled as 'offences'. Moreover, these 'harms' are not confined to those emerging from conscious acts of individuals. Many result from the very structure of social arrangements, in which benefits and burdens are allocated by reference to people's supposed rights or deserts rather than on the basis of their needs as they define them. Hence, to regard crime, as officially defined, as a major social evil for which some more effective solution is required, whilst ignoring the much more pervasive and damaging harm caused to people by 'power-based' social arrangements, is itself inconsistent, or so it is insinuated, with fundamental goals and values of restorative justice, such as preventing harmful behaviour and opposing the use of violence.[5]

Restorative justice as a lifestyle

Closely related to the above is a conception of restorative justice as an alternative lifestyle (Sullivan, 1998; Sullivan and Tifft, 2001: ch. 8). Those who conceive of restorative justice in this way insist that, if we are committed to the idea, we should do more than adopt a restorative approach to problems we encounter in our professional lives. Moreover, we should do more than campaign for the transformation of criminal justice or protest about social injustice. It is suggested that, whilst such activities are very important, we must also apply the principles and values of restorative justice in our everyday interaction with other people.

What precisely is meant by this depends, of course, on our conception of what the principles and values of restorative justice are and, in particular, on our understanding of how deep they go. It would be fairly uncontroversial to suggest that somebody committed to a restorative approach to crime ought to apply its principles when he or she encounters troublesome behaviour in his or her personal life. For instance, a restorative justice campaigner who is also a parent arguably should regard and respond to his or her child's naughty behaviour through a restorative rather than a punitive lens.

However, some have more radical views on what is involved in living a lifestyle of restorative justice. According to Sullivan and Tifft (2001), we must confront our view of our own worth and recognise that it is unjust to assume the existence of a social hierarchy in which the needs of some (including ourselves) are thought to be more important than the needs of others. Ultimately, we must 'dissolve the power-based self' (ibid.: 169) and allow the boundaries between our selves and others to disintegrate (ibid.: 174). For such writers, exemplars for those who wish to lead a lifestyle of restorative justice include Fred Boehrer and his family who live in 'a house of hospitality for the homeless. To show its solidarity with the poor, the family lives in voluntary poverty. In all aspects of their lives, they live day to day the principles that reside at the core of the restorative justice movement' (Sullivan, 1998: 149).

'Civilising' the law

Having set out various ways of envisaging restorative justice, I now aim to clarify the concept, analysing it as an attempt to break with the traditional criminal law model by applying (in modified form) certain principles of civil law to the handling of 'crime' (cf. Zehr, 1990: 215).[6] Many proponents of restorative justice have presented it in such terms. Often, however, the idea is not developed in detail and it is not made clear precisely how principles of civil law are to be applied to crime (but see *Barnett*).

Analysing restorative justice in this way brings out certain aspects of the idea which are often neglected or made insufficiently clear in other ways of explicating the concept. Another advantage of looking at restorative justice in this way is that it enables us to identify certain unresolved tensions within restorative approaches to justice. However, it must be understood that what proponents of restorative justice envisage is anything but a straightforward application of a civil law model to the problem of crime. Advocates of restorative justice clearly want to retain core elements of the criminal law model. Also, the restorative approach is shaped by ideas and values which owe nothing to the civil law model.

The criminal law model

When we respond to a harmful act as a crime we bring into play a set of interdependent assumptions about how we should regard and handle it. Taken together, these assumptions form a model which we might call the criminal law model. In this context, the most important assumptions are these:

- The focus of official attention is squarely upon the harmful *act* and the perpetrator of it.

- This act is construed as a transgression of society's fundamental laws – the perpetrator has done something which society forbids people to do because it deems it harmful and/or immoral.

- The state initiates legal action against the perpetrator of the act, on behalf of society. The state also has the exclusive power to decide to discontinue the action, and may in theory continue it even though the person directly harmed wants it discontinued.[7]

- If the state's legal action is successful – i.e. if the alleged perpetrator is found guilty of having committed a criminal act – the offender is punished (i.e. has some loss or suffering imposed upon him or her). If the crime is deemed serious, the punishment may take the form of imprisonment.

- There is considerable social stigma attached to being convicted and punished for a criminal offence (and perhaps even to being suspected). More specifically, convicted offenders suffer a considerable loss of moral reputation. In reality, this stigma lingers long after the formal penalty for the crime has been paid, especially if the offender has been imprisoned. Convicted offenders, and especially ex-prisoners, may find it very difficult to get a job and impossible to obtain certain forms of employment. They may be shunned by members of the community. In some places, they may be permanently denied rights such as the right to vote.

- Because of the extremely harmful effects of criminal conviction and punishment upon the person, many people maintain that those suspected of crime should receive a very high level of procedural protection to prevent them being wrongfully convicted and punished. For instance, they regard it as fundamentally important to our way of life that the onus is on the state to prove its case against a person accused of a criminal offence. To discharge this burden, the state must persuade the court beyond a reasonable doubt that the accused person is guilty; the state must prove every fact necessary to constitute the offence; a finding of guilt must take place in public in a court of law; the trial of accused persons must be governed by very strict rules of procedure and evidence; accused people are facilitated, and not hampered, in their efforts to rebut the charges against them; etc.

The 'civil law' model

When a 'harmful act' is responded to as a civil wrong, the response is structured by a quite different set of assumptions:

- Attention is focused on both the harmful act and *the damage or loss resulting from it*.

- The harmful act is construed as an injury by one (private) person to another.

- The injured party initiates legal action against the perpetrator on his or her own behalf. The injured party can decide to discontinue the action. As we shall see, this is quite common where an out-of-court settlement is reached.

- If the injured party's action is successful – i.e. if the perpetrator is found to be liable for the damage or loss resulting from the harmful act – the perpetrator is ordered to compensate the injured party. This may be very onerous; the perpetrator will have to make good the losses for which he or she is deemed legally responsible.[8] However, the perpetrator cannot be imprisoned.

- There is relatively little social stigma attached to being found liable for a civil wrong. Being found liable has relatively little and often no negative consequences for the moral reputation of the person.[9] The person found liable in civil law completely avoids the social stigma attached to being imprisoned.

- Because being found liable in civil law is perceived as much less damaging to the person than being found guilty in criminal law, there seems to be less concern to provide strong procedural protection for those accused of civil wrongs. The injured party must show that the alleged perpetrator is liable only by a preponderance of evidence. In civil law, the rules of evidence and procedure are less strict than in criminal law. Crucially, cases can be, and often are, settled out of court as a result of negotiations. Indeed, out-of-court settlement tends officially to be regarded as desirable and is encouraged in various ways.

The restorative justice model

Advocates of restorative justice sometimes suggest that the civil law model of dispute settlement provides a better model for doing justice in the aftermath of an offence than does the criminal law model. Hence, the restorative approach to criminal justice might be understood as an alternative to the pure criminal law model, an alternative which incorporates certain features of the civil law model. Looked at in these terms, we can identify some distinctive features of restorative approaches to justice along the following lines:

- The restorative approach focuses attention on both the harmful act and the damage or loss resulting from it. Unlike the pure criminal law model, it does not restrict its gaze to the offender and his or her act. As in the civil law model, it directs our attention on the loss or damage suffered by the direct victim(s).

- As in the civil law model, the harmful act is construed as *essentially* the wronging of a *person* by another person. The restorative approach does not deny that which the pure criminal law model emphasises: that there is a larger social dimension to crime (Zehr, 1990: 182). However, in restorative justice, the emphasis is on harm done to society rather than the fact of law-breaking and it tends to be insisted that the *harm* crime does to society, whilst important, is of secondary importance to the harm it does to its direct victims.

- As in the criminal law model, the state initiates action against the perpetrator. However, in the restorative approach, *the state's action seems to be initiated on behalf of the victim* as well as on behalf of society. What is unclear in most accounts is how much weight, if any, might be attached to a victim's wish to discontinue the action. For instance, what happens if the victim receives and accepts an apology and offer of reparation before a formal victim–offender mediation session is held, and indicates a wish that no further action be taken? Under the criminal law model, the victim's wish would be largely irrelevant. Under a civil law model, it would be decisive. In practice, most restorative justice programmes would veer towards the criminal model here, and continue the action. However, the rationale for this is rarely articulated.

- In restorative justice, if a person is found guilty of a criminal act or admits involvement in a criminal act to the police, he or she may be offered the option of taking part in a process designed to repair the harm resulting from the act.[10] As part of this process, the offender may offer the victim some compensation. In one respect, this makes restorative justice much closer to the civil law model than to the criminal law model. However, there are some crucial differences between reparation in restorative justice and compensation in the civil law model.

  In civil law, the tendency is to attempt to place a monetary value upon the injury or loss suffered by the injured party and to order the liable party to pay the amount. That is, the emphasis is on monetary compensation. In restorative justice, there is seldom any attempt to place a precise monetary value upon the victim's injury or loss. Indeed, those elements of the victim's loss which would be easiest to express in monetary terms often receive least emphasis. The focus tends to be on the psychological trauma or emotional harm suffered by the victim (see *Strang*) and there is usually little attempt to determine how much money would be required to compensate the victim for this suffering. This is because, in restorative justice, unlike in the civil law model, full monetary compensation is often regarded as either impractical or (for various reasons) inappropriate.

  In restorative justice, payment of a small amount of compensation (seldom anywhere near the amounts awarded in civil law cases) is often encouraged for its purely symbolic value – i.e. as a sign that the perpetrator accepts responsibility for the harm caused and repents his or her actions. However, monetary compensation is often regarded as insufficient for reparation and is sometimes seen as not even necessary. Reparation also consists, and in some cases can consist entirely, of non-monetary ways of making amends. These can include offering a verbal apology and/or written apology, offering to do some service for the victim or offering to do something about oneself that will render one less likely to reoffend (e.g. if the perpetrator committed an assault in anger, participating in an anger management class). These mechanisms are obviously examples of symbolic reparation rather than acts of reparation in any concrete sense.

  Importantly, some of the preferred ways of *symbolically* repairing harm within restorative justice may overlap with ways in which one can undergo punishment in conventional criminal justice (cf. *Walgrave*). Indeed, there has been some discussion of whether one could symbolically repair harm, in a restorative justice sense, by voluntarily undergoing something painful such as imprisonment or indeed corporal pain (cf. Ivison, 1999). This seems to blur the distinction, which is of crucial importance to most (not all) restorative justice proponents, between punishment and reparation (compare *Barnett* with *Duff* and *Daly*). In the light of this debate, it is important to raise a few issues which need to be addressed by supporters of restorative justice.

  First, in restorative justice, as in the civil law model, reparation is usually burdensome for the perpetrator. However, in civil law, it is not *essential* that paying compensation be *experienced* as burdensome. A millionaire ordered to pay somebody £100 compensation is unlikely to experience this as a significant burden. But this would not be a reason for increasing the amount ordered. Provided £100 is sufficient to make up for the harm done, it is an appropriate amount of compensation. In criminal law, on the other hand, we seem to require the perpetrator to suffer. For instance, one of the complaints made when a rich individual or corporate body is fined for some fairly serious crime is that paying the fine does not cause any pain. In this context, it is important to be clear about the reason for demanding that the offender repair harm in restorative justice. Is our main concern that the harm be repaired, as in the civil law model? Or, is our main concern that the perpetrator be made to suffer some burden, as in the criminal law model? (cf. *Barnett* on pure vs. punitive restitution).

Secondly, to the extent that one attempts symbolic reparation by undertaking some burden, the reparation is *indirect*. However, some restorative justice writing emphasises the need for *direct* forms of reparation, or at least a close link between the 'reparative act' and repair of the actual harm done. An example might help make this point clear. If a youth has deliberately caused serious damage to a neighbour's garden fence in an act of anger, and does not have the money to compensate the owner or the skill to rebuild the fence, how might he or she repair the harm? Doing some service for the neighbour can clearly be reparative in a restorative justice sense. Taking part in an anger management course might contribute to reparation. However, doing something else burdensome, such as washing police cars, is likely to contribute little to reparation. Such an act is undertaken more as a punishment than as an act of direct reparation. It seems too far away from the civil law model, too close to the criminal law model, to constitute a good example of restorative justice.

- The restorative justice approach to crime usually operates through the criminal justice system. To this extent, much of the stigma of being a criminal justice case attaches itself to those who are dealt with by restorative approaches to criminal justice. Moreover, restorative process are often designed to 'shame' perpetrators of harm (i.e. to expose their wrongdoing in contexts, such as family meetings, which are likely to make them experience the painful feeling of shame over what they have done). To this extent, restorative justice seems much closer to the criminal law model than the civil law model, in which there is little stigma attached to being found liable. Indeed, in some restorative approaches, one of the goals appears to be to instigate and intensify social processes of shaming which are felt, by some proponents, to be too weak in contemporary society (Johnstone, 2002: ch. 6; cf. Braithwaite, 1989).

  There are, however, some crucial differences between restorative justice and conventional criminal justice in this respect. In restorative justice, any shaming that occurs usually takes place in a relatively 'private' context. The offence is shamed not in front of the entire public, but in a conference attended by a relatively small group of people. Moreover, shaming is supposed to take place in such a way that the perpetrator of harm is not entirely or permanently stigmatised. Offences are shamed before people who also care about the offender and are therefore likely to recognise and draw attention to the good as well as the bad side of their characters. And, crucially, in restorative justice, there is an emphasis on terminating stigma once it has served its purpose of making offenders aware of and repentant of the harmful effects of their misdeeds. Whereas conventional criminal justice shames offenders, but provides them with no opportunity to recover their moral reputation, the emphasis in restorative justice is upon creating means whereby the perpetrator of harm can regain the respect and even esteem of the community. Through expressing remorse and shame, offering a genuine apology and undertaking burdensome acts of reparation, offenders can regain the respect they lost by committing an offence. Moreover, in the discourse of restorative justice, there is considerable emphasis on developing ways of reintegrating offenders into the community. Instead of being permanently shunned, offenders who acknowledge and repent wrongdoing and make serious efforts at reparation are to be welcomed back into the community and helped to become active and valued members of it. One of the most powerful and important features of restorative justice (sometimes lost sight of when it is envisaged as a mere process) is the attention it gives to the goal of reinstating offenders to full membership of the law-abiding community.

• Restorative justice is frequently understood and represented by its advocates as a non-punitive mode of intervention. Indeed, for advocates such as David Moore (1993), restorative interventions remove the offending behaviour of young adults from a 'criminal framework' and place it within an educational and/or health framework. That is to say, restorative justice is conceived by Moore and others as a form of moral education and healing rather than as a method of punishment. For some, the logical implication of this is that restorative interventions should not be accompanied and hampered by the painstaking procedural safeguards which surround and limit punitive interventions. Such safeguards would serve only to limit the capacity of restorative interventions to achieve the beneficial effects for offenders and victims that they are designed to bring about. In this respect, the more relaxed procedures of the civil law model might be thought more appropriate than the strict procedures of the criminal law model.

The crucial question here is, of course, whether restorative interventions are a form of punishment (*Ashworth*; *Daly*; *Duff*; *Levrant* et al.). What if, despite the benevolent intentions of its proponents and practitioners, restorative justice is experienced as punishment, or falls within the field of punishment once that concept is adequately defined? Then the argument that the procedural safeguards we deem appropriate for those who are candidates for criminal punishment are not required for those subjected to restorative interventions collapses. Moreover, the attempt to define restorative interventions as non-punitive begins to take on a more sinister and dangerous aspect. It can be used as a way of dispensing with procedural safeguards for suspects and offenders, thereby leaving them exposed without legal protection to the power to punish.[11]

In response to criticisms that, despite the benevolent intentions of restorativists, restorative interventions can result in serious breaches of the rights of suspects and offenders, advocates of restorative justice, many of whom are also active in human rights movements, have begun to pay serious attention to the question of how the rights of suspects and offenders are to be protected in restorative processes (see, for example, Walgrave, 2002). Efforts are now being made to devise authoritative guidelines for the practice of restorative justice, designed partly to ensure that the rights of suspects and offenders receive proper protection. However, the underlying issues have yet to be adequately addressed. Many restorative justice proponents seem to have simply conceded the 'liberal-legal' case that procedural safeguards are important, rather than thinking the issue through more seriously from within a restorative justice framework.[12] Until restorative justice proponents take seriously the fact that restorative justice, no matter how beneficial its intentions and even its outcomes, involves an exercise of considerable social power, they will be unable to address the important question of how that exercise of power should be controlled and limited. If they are to be consistent with their premises, the answers should perhaps be sought within the realm of democratic theory rather than in liberal jurisprudence (*Crawford*; Braithwaite, 1994; Johnstone, 2000).

Assessing the case for restorative justice

I have suggested that it is no simple matter to explain what restorative justice is. Not only is the term applied to a quite diverse range of interventions, it is also used in quite different senses. The term has been used to indicate, *inter alia*, processes, criminal justice goals, 'penal' methods, values, theories of social justice and lifestyles. Moreover, on certain key matters, proponents of restorative justice are, on the whole, quite vague. For instance, it is still unclear what the *core* purpose of restorative interventions is meant to be. Are they intended *primarily* as means of crime prevention, peacemaking, calculating and dispensing justice, moral education or therapy? Many proponents would respond, no doubt, that they are intended to achieve all these things. This is acceptable up to a point, but problems arise when these purposes conflict, as they invariably do.

There is also a great deal of divergence, amongst campaigners for restorative justice, on what the ultimate goal of their campaign is. Is it to abolish or at least marginalise judicial punishment and replace it with restorative interventions? Is it to provide an alternative to the use of judicial punishment, to which some 'appropriate' cases can be diverted? Is it to end 'professional justice' and to revive community justice? Is it to end professional crime control and revive moralising community control? Is it to sensitise us to richer conceptions of justice found, for example, in aboriginal societies and in the Bible? Is it to transform society, creating arrangements in which the needs of all people as defined by them are met?

My point, in emphasising the haziness surrounding the concept of restorative justice, is *not* to criticise it as impossibly vague and to call for greater clarity. Rather, it is to establish that assessing the case for restorative justice is far more complicated than it is often assumed to be.

It is often supposed that evaluating the case for restorative justice is a relatively simple affair. There are certain outcomes which any criminal justice intervention should seek to achieve; the question is whether restorative interventions achieve these outcomes more effectively (and perhaps more cost-effectively) than more traditional forms of criminal justice intervention. For instance, criminal justice interventions should seek to prevent reoffending by the offender, satisfy victims and be perceived as fair. If restorative justice outperforms conventional criminal justice in achieving such goals, then – provided it is also cost-effective – the case for it is made out.

One thing that is often not appreciated is that, even within these limits, assessing the case for restorative justice is extremely difficult. Here I will mention only a few problems. First, even if these were the only goals that mattered in criminal justice interventions (they are not), there would still be the problem of comparing like with like. Criminal justice interventions can be carried out under various conditions, with diverse subjects, and with various degrees of sophistication, skill, resources and organisational efficiency. For a comparison of the effectiveness of conventional criminal justice interventions with restorative interventions to have much value, one would have to eliminate virtually all the significant variables that can affect the capacity of a criminal justice intervention to prevent reoffending, satisfy victims and create a perception of fairness – a difficult if not impossible task.

Even if this problem could be overcome, there would still be the problem of devising satisfactory ways of measuring reoffending behaviour, victim satisfaction and perceived fairness. At what stage, and by what criteria, does one decide whether an intervention has made a difference to an offender's future behaviour? How does one actually determine whether a victim is satisfied? Is it simply a matter of asking him or her whether he or she is very satisfied, satisfied or unsatisfied? Or do we need to probe more deeply into his or her expectations and use more sophisticated techniques to draw out his or her 'real' attitude towards the process he or she has been through? Similarly, how do we really determine whether an offender thinks the process he or she has been through was fair?

Added to this is the problem that some commentators would dispute whether these are appropriate measures of success or failure at all. For instance, some might dispute whether a suspect's or offender's perception of fairness is what really matters. Such perceptions will depend on what they expect, and these expectations will be shaped by all sorts of factors. Hence, for some, the question is whether a process is fair when measured against some objective, rationally defensible conception of what fairness in criminal justice is (Ashworth, 1998). Similar arguments could apply to victim satisfaction. And, of course, some would question whether *victim* satisfaction is an appropriate measure at all. Why victim satisfaction rather than public satisfaction?

This is simply to skirt around some of the enormous complexities involved. Dozens more difficulties could be raised. The key point is that evaluating any criminal justice process involves a number of things. First, one must devise an appropriate framework for evaluation (Ashworth, 1998: ch. 2). Secondly, one must justify that framework. Thirdly, one must develop highly sophisticated ways of assessing a process in terms of that framework. The first two of these tasks involve considerable engagement with an enormously complex body of legal, ethical and political theory. The third requires considerable engagement with a very complicated body of thought about methods of social inquiry. Anybody with an adequate appreciation of the complexities involved would surely be very cautious in making strong claims about the relative effectiveness or otherwise of restorative interventions.

However, the difficulty in assessing the case for restorative justice does not end there. So far, I have tried to show that the project of assessing the effectiveness of restorative processes is fraught with difficulty. However, as we have seen, some want to define restorative justice primarily in terms of its values. What is important for them is not this or that process, but the values that guide us in our dealing with those who perpetrate and those affected by harmful acts. Should we seek to hurt those who hurt others? Or should we respond to them by emphasising the fact that we care deeply for them, whilst also communicating to them that we do not care much for what they have done and would like them to apologise for it and repair the damage caused? The choice between these two approaches cannot be made simply by asking which would be most effective in preventing them committing further harmful acts, which they would perceive as most fair, and which would most satisfy their victims. Knowing these things might help us in making a choice between the two approaches. But, ultimately, this is an ethical issue. In choosing between the two approaches we need to be guided, less by the results of empirical studies of the effectiveness of restorative interventions, more by ethical studies which discuss, although rarely resolve, the question of which attitude is most appropriate. And, of course, those studies themselves have to be firmly grounded in psychological and sociological studies which might tell us something about why we adopt certain approaches to wrongdoing, about the possibility of changing our approach and about the conditions in which a change of approach might be possible.

Evaluating restorative justice, then, is anything but the straightforward, technical task it is all too often taken to be. It is an extremely complicated affair, which requires a multidisciplinary and interdisciplinary approach. We need to approach the task from the perspectives of empirical criminology and penology, legal studies, ethics, psychology, sociology and history (at least). And we need studies which integrate the findings and insights from multiple studies carried out from such perspectives. The readings in this volume have been selected on the basis that, taken together, they amount to a very significant contribution to this incredibly difficult but also important undertaking.

Notes

1 References in italics are to readings in this volume.
2 In doing so I draw upon, but also revise and develop, analyses presented in my earlier book *Restorative Justice: Ideas, Values, Debates* (2002). I will avoid detailed referencing here, referring readers instead to the more extensive analysis in my earlier book and to the readings in this volume which deal, in different ways, with the same territory.
3 A number of proponents have expressed such sentiments in personal communications.
4 Conventional criminal justice is, of course, also deeply rooted in theological concepts and reasoning and has numerous links with religious institutions; although, in its case, the theological roots of its concepts tend to be forgotten or denied (see Johnstone 2002a: 172–4).
5 For a very brief discussion of this argument, and associated positions, see Johnstone (2002b).
6 In using the term 'civil law' I am referring to the distinction drawn in the Anglo-American legal tradition between criminal law and civil law. A conventional way of stating this distinction is to say that criminal law defines the duties which a person owes to society, whereas civil law is primary concerned with the rights and duties of individuals among themselves (Card, 2001: 1). This distinction should not

be confused with the quite different distinction drawn by legal scholars between common law traditions (found, for example, in England and North America) and civil law traditions (found, for example, in continental Europe).

7 This issue is coming to the fore in the UK in domestic violence prosecutions. The solicitor general, Harriet Harman, has recently urged crown prosecutors to press ahead with domestic violence prosecutions, even if the victim insists on the case being dropped (*Guardian*, 22 October 2002: 2). Harman's reasoning is that domestic violence is a crime – an offence against the public interest – and not a private matter for its direct victim. She stated: 'She might want to forgive him, but the next time he assaults her she could be killed. Even if she has left him and wants to move on in her life and put it all behind her, he is likely, unchecked, to just go on and assault his next partner and she might end up dead' (quoted in the same place).

8 In practice, many people will be insured for damage which they cause. In such cases, the burden of compensating those they harm is reduced considerably; but it is by no means eliminated as they will usually have to pay more for future insurance.

9 Where they caused harm through negligent performance of some professional task, their professional reputation may suffer and they may find their career blocked. But, this is due more to assessments of their professional competence than to assessments of their moral character.

10 Currently, whether this option will be offered depends upon whether the case is considered *appropriate* for restorative justice. However, as yet, there is little agreement either about what cases are appropriate for restorative justice or about who should make such a determination (see Crosland, forthcoming). If a case is not deemed appropriate, then it is dealt with in the conventional criminal law way.

11 Similar issues arise, of course, with regard to therapeutic approaches to offenders (see Johnstone, 1996).

12 John Braithwaite is one of the more notable exceptions. For one of the most sustained efforts at placing restorative approaches to justice within a broader political theory, see Pettit and Braithwaite (1990).

References

Ashworth, A. (1998) *The Criminal Process: An Evaluative Study* (2nd edn) (Oxford: Oxford University Press).

Braithwaite, J. (1989) *Crime, Shame and Reintegration* (Cambridge: Cambridge University Press).

Braithwaite, J. (1994) 'Thinking Harder about Democratising Social Control', in Alder, J. and Wundersitz, J. (eds) *Family Conferencing and Juvenile Justice: The Way Forward or Misplaced Optimism* (Canberra: Australian Institute of Criminology), pp. 199–216.

Braithwaite, J. and Strang, H. (2001) 'Restorative Justice and Civil Society', in Strang, H. and Braithwaite, J. (eds) *Restorative Justice and Civil Society* (Cambridge: Cambridge University Press), pp. 1–13.

Card, R. (2001) *Criminal Law* (15th edn) (London: Butterworths).

Cayley, D. (1998) *The Expanding Prison: The Crisis in Crime and Punishment and the Search for Alternatives* (Cleveland, OH: Pilgrim Press).

Crosland, P. (forthcoming) *50 Appropriate Cases for Mediation within the Criminal Justice System* (London: Mediation UK).

Duff, R. (2001) *Punishment, Communication, and Community* (Oxford: Oxford University Press).

Garland, D. (2001) *The Culture of Control: Crime and Social Order in Contemporary Society* (Oxford: Oxford University Press).

Hadley, M. (ed.) (2001) *The Spiritual Roots of Restorative Justice* (State University of New York Press).

Hoyle, C. and Young, R. (2002) 'Restorative Justice: Assessing the Prospects and Pitfalls' in McConville, M. and Wilson, G. (eds) *The Handbook of the Criminal Justice Process* (Oxford: Oxford University Press), pp. 525–48.

Hulsman, L. (1986) 'Critical Criminology and the Concept of Crime', *Contemporary Crises*, 10:1, pp. 63–80.

Ignatieff, M. (1978) *A Just Measure of Pain: The Penitentiary in the Industrial Revolution* (London: Macmillan).

Ivison, D. (1999) 'Justifying Punishment in Intercultural Contexts: Whose Norms? Which Values?', in Matravers, M. (ed.) *Punishment and Political Theory* (Oxford: Hart Publishing), pp. 88–107.

Johnstone, G. (1996) *Medical Concepts and Penal Policy* (London: Cavendish).

Johnstone, G. (2000) 'Penal Policy Making: Elitist, Populist or Participatory?', *Punishment and Society*, 2:2, pp. 161–80.

Johnstone, G. (2002a) *Restorative Justice: Ideas, Values, Debates* (Cullompton: Willan).

Johnstone, G. (2002b) 'Book Review (Sullivan and Tifft)', *Howard Journal of Criminal Justice*, 41:3, pp. 302–3.

Moberly, W. (1968) *The Ethics of Punishment* (London: Faber & Faber).

Moore, D. (1993) 'Shame, Forgiveness and Juvenile Justice', *Criminal Justice Ethics*, 12:1 (also at http://www.lib.jjay.cuny.edu/cje/html/sample2.html).

Morris, A. and Gelsthorpe, L. (2000) 'Something Old, Something Borrowed, Something Blue, but Something New? A Comment on the Prospects for Restorative Justice under the Crime and Disorder Act 1998', *Criminal Law Review*, Jan., pp. 18–30.

Pettit, P. and Braithwaite, J. (1990) *Not Just Deserts: A Republican Theory of Criminal Justice* (Oxford: Clarendon Press).

Ross, R. (1996) *Returning to the Teachings: Exploring Aboriginal Justice* (Toronto: Penguin).

Shearing, C. (2001) 'Transforming Security: A South African Experiment', in Strang, H. and Braithwaite, J. (eds) *Restorative Justice and Civil Society* (Cambridge: Cambridge University Press), pp. 14–34.

Sullivan, D. (1998) 'Living a Lifestyle of Restorative Justice: An Interview with Fred Boehrer', *Contemporary Justice Review*, 1:1, pp. 149–66.

Sullivan, D. and Tifft, L. (2001) *Restorative Justice: Healing the Foundations of our Everyday Lives* (Monsey, NY: Willow Tree Press).

Sullivan, D., Tifft, L. and Cordella, P. (1998) 'The Phenomenon of Restorative Justice: Some Introductory Remarks', *Contemporary Justice Review*, 1:1, pp. 7–20.

Van Ness, D. and Strong, K.H. (2002) *Restoring Justice, 2nd edn.* (Cincinnati, OH: Anderson Publishing).

Walgrave, L. (ed.) (2002) *Restorative Justice and the Law* (Cullompton: Willan).

Zehr, H. (1990) *Changing Lenses: A New Focus for Crime and Justice* (Scottdale, PA: Herald Press).

Zehr, H. (2002) *The Little Book of Restorative Justice* (Good Books).

Zehr, H. and Mika, H. (1998) 'Fundamental Concepts of Restorative Justice', *Contemporary Justice Review*, 1:1, pp. 47–55.

Part A

Overviews and early inspirations

Introduction

The pieces in Part A are intended to provide the reader with a general idea of how the idea of restorative justice arose, the sorts of practices with which it is associated, and the theories and discourses which have attempted to make sense of it and which have provided the restorative justice movement with inspiration and some sense of direction. The section opens with an excerpt from Tony F. Marshall's much cited and admired overview of restorative justice, published in 1998. Whilst written primarily for a UK audience, the extract focuses mainly upon those parts which are of broader interest.

Marshall makes the important point that restorative justice is a set of *principles*, not a particular practice. He then goes on to describe a range of practices which illustrate and apply the principles of restorative justice. It is worth noting how broadly he casts the net. When ideas such as restorative justice are developed in practice, there is a danger that the idea can become over-identified with a particular practice or set of practices. For example, there is some tendency to think of restorative justice as being mainly or even exclusively about processes such as victim–offender mediation or family group conferencing, or to associate the idea wholly with reparation schemes. Marshall offsets such tendencies not only by surveying a wide range of processes informed by the idea of restorative justice, but also by showing how a range of more traditional criminal justice practices and forms of community action can and must be part of a broad programme of restorative justice.

A very important feature of Marshall's overview is the way he presents the relationship between theory and practice in restorative justice. Marshall presents restorative justice as a set of principles which were developed in practice and remain grounded in practical experience. Restorative justice is not the practical outgrowth of any particular 'academic' criminological or justice theory. Rather, it was developed by practitioners frustrated with traditional ways of doing things, exploring alternatives and assessing them pragmatically in terms of their success in reforming offenders, satisfying victims and solving crime problems. Nevertheless, restorative justice proponents have drawn upon (and inevitably been influenced by) a wide range of 'academic' theories in order to make sense of their practice, to develop it and to promote it. In turn, some criminologists and justice theorists have been attracted to restorative justice as a practical illustration of their ideas. The final part of Marshall's essay is a survey of such theories, which is correctly cautious about over-identifying restorative justice with any of them.

The second extract in this section is from a paper by American legal and political theorist, Randy E. Barnett, published in 1977. Barnett suggests that the paradigm of punishment has ceased to solve our problems and should be replaced by a new paradigm: restitution. Barnett did not propose 'restorative' justice, in the sense that the term is now understood. His focus was on *financial* restitution from offenders to victims; today, restorative justice proponents tend to see 'restoration' as much broader than financial restitution and, indeed, in many schemes financial restitution plays little or no role.[1] It is also worth mentioning that few if any of Barnett's practical proposals (such as the creation of something analogous to the medieval Irish system of *sureties*) have figured seriously in subsequent restorative justice discourse.[2] Nevertheless, there are very good reasons for including Barnett's work among the key early inspirations of the restorative justice movement, and for recommending it as still relevant to anybody interested in restorative justice.

Barnett introduced the idea, later taken up by Howard Zehr (see Chapter 4 of this volume), that the failures of our criminal justice system could be analysed in Kuhnian terms as a crisis of an old paradigm: punishment (cf. Kuhn, 1970).[3] This implied the need for a *radical* shift of perspective. Most other reforms of criminal justice could be understood as attempts to salvage the old paradigm (i.e. to improve the customary way of constructing the problem of crime and its solutions). For Barnett, the system was beyond salvaging in such fashion. It needed to be discarded and replaced by an entirely new paradigm. Many proponents of restorative justice would now say that, although he was on the right track, Barnett's proposed new paradigm was not quite what is required. What we need is not restitutive justice, in the narrow sense proposed by Barnett, but restorative justice. However, the idea that 'punishment' or 'retributive justice' can be understood as a paradigm, and that restorative justice is an alternative paradigm (as opposed to a mere reform), continues to influence the thinking and political strategies of many supporters of restorative justice.

Like many contemporary proponents of restorative justice, Barnett opens the case for restitution by criticising the traditional way of responding to crime (i.e. punishment). All too often, proponents of restorative justice are vague about what 'punishment' or 'retributive justice' is. Barnett, however, presents a relatively clear account of what it is that he rejects. Hence, I have included his account of the paradigm of punishment and its problems here, even though it will sound very familiar to many readers. It is interesting to note that Barnett uses many of the arguments which retributivists use to question whether the practice of punishing offenders can be justified by reference to the utilitarian benefits which it might bring about. However, he then goes on to question (all too briefly and all too vaguely) whether retributivists can themselves justify the forceful imposition of punishment on anyone, before listing other defects of the punishment paradigm. He suggests that those who support forceful punishment have failed to come up with convincing justifications for the practice. He proposes a complete refocusing: the criminal's debt is not to society but to the victim and what he or she owes the victim is restitution.[4]

In his description of restitution, Barnett draws a crucial distinction between 'punitive restitution' and 'pure restitution' and argues for the latter. It is very interesting to ask to which of these types current restorative justice schemes are closest, and to which they should be closest. If, as I suspect, most schemes are closer to the idea of 'punitive restitution' than to 'pure restitution' then, according to Barnett, they would fail to constitute a break with the old paradigm of punishment. If this were accepted, it could still be argued that, in dealing with crime, punitive restitution is more appropriate than pure restitution. However, those making such an argument should do so in awareness that it may be inconsistent with the notion that restorative justice is a new *paradigm* in criminal justice. They need to engage with Barnett, rather than neglect his important essay.

Chapter 3 is a slightly abridged version of Nils Christie's renowned essay 'Conflicts as Property', which was presented as the Foundation Lecture on the opening of a Centre for Criminology at the University of Sheffield (UK) in 1976. Christie's paper is about our attitude towards *conflicts* and the way we handle them. Although he does not quite spell this out, Christie's concern is to propose an alternative to a more conventional way of thinking about conflicts or disputes. There is a tendency to think of conflicts as 'pathological'; as departures from a normal and healthy state of harmony between people (cf. Marshall, 1988). Hence, it is commonly supposed that conflicts ought to be solved and that what is needed is a speedy solution that will terminate the conflict and restore harmony. In order to obtain such a solution, it is thought, we should delegate the task of solving conflicts to professionals and we should give them the power to impose their solutions on the conflicting parties. One of the reasons professionals will be effective in solving conflicts is that they are trained to narrow down a dispute to a few 'relevant' issues, leaving out of the picture much that the parties to the conflict would want to discuss (matters which might be irresolvable).

Christie uses the example of 'conflict-handing' in the Arusha province of Tanzania to show that other attitudes towards conflict are possible and in many respects preferable. He suggests that we might see conflicts as valuable things. For instance, they provide people with opportunities to clarify, elaborate and refine the norms by which they live co-operatively with each other. However, if we are to harvest these benefits, we need to cease searching for the most speedy and effective solutions. We have to be prepared to engage in lengthy and perhaps unending 'political' discussion of the issues in conflict, unconfined by 'legal' rules or relevance and other 'external' stipulations of what matters. Above all, to benefit from conflicts we must cease handing them over to professionals to solve. The parties directly involved must be at the centre of any search for solutions, surrounded by their families, friends and neighbours; professionals should remain on the periphery. By handling their own conflicts, people gain in various ways. As we have seen, there are opportunities for norm clarification. Also, victims of harm benefit from the opportunity to participate in discussing and deciding issues of vital importance to them and from having their anxieties reduced. Perpetrators of harm also benefit from having an opportunity to explain themselves to people whose evaluation of them might matter and from having the possibility of being forgiven.

Such ideas have had enormous influence on proponents of restorative justice. It is important, however, to point out that the views presented in 'Conflicts as Property' differ in some significant respects from the orthodoxies of the contemporary restorative justice movement. One important difference is that, whereas many contemporary proponents of restorative justice insist that it must be a voluntary process for all involved,[5] Christie maintained that offenders should be 'forced' to assume ownership of their conflicts. Many offenders will want to give their conflicts away, as this is the 'easy option'. But, according to Christie, they have no right to do so. They *must* participate in the handling of their own conflicts. Another difference is that Christie does not rule out the possibility that participatory conflict handling will conclude with a decision to punish the offender. What he does propose is that questions of punishment should be raised only after the victim's situation is considered and decisions made about what the offender (and others) should do for the victim. Then, the question of punishment is *transformed*. The question is: what, if any, suffering should be imposed '*in addition* to the constructive sufferings the offender would go through in his restitutive actions vis-à-vis the victim'?

Christie's paper is rightly regarded as essential reading for anybody wishing to understand the restorative justice perspective. I suggest that it is essential *re*-reading for those involved in the development of restorative justice programmes. While the paper lends support to much that happens in the name of restorative justice, it also provides important challenges.

Whilst Barnett's and Christie's essays might be regarded as 'precursors' of restorative justice, Howard Zehr's 'Retributive Justice, Restorative Justice' (Chapter 4) can be seen as one of the first attempts to propose a new approach explicitly called 'restorative justice'. Perhaps more important, Zehr's essay, unlike the previous two, was an attempt to think through the wider significance of a new practical experiment in criminal justice which Zehr was instrumental in starting: the Victim Offender Reconciliation Programs (VORPs) which sprang up in North America and elsewhere in the late 1970s and 1980s (see also *Peachey*). Zehr's essay sets out the ideas which would be later developed in his hugely influential book, *Changing Lenses* (1990).[6]

Zehr argues that the criminal justice system is failing to meet the needs of both victims (for restitution and an experience of justice and forgiveness) and offenders (for genuine accountability). Like *Barnett*, Zehr claims that these failures are due to our adherence to a particular paradigm (the state/punishment or retributive para-digm). Hence, he argues, we need a new model of crime and justice, one with roots in ordinary people's needs and experiences. One place we can look, for elements with which we can construct a new restorative paradigm, is our own history. Zehr contends that, throughout most of Western history, state punitive justice has had to compete with an alternative: community justice. It is only in recent centuries that state punitive justice has come to dominate, indeed monopolise, understandings of crime and justice in the West. Before that, community justice was more the norm. Communities tended to resolve their own disputes through informal negotiation models, in which the normative outcome was compensation and the central focus was the vindication of victims (cf. *Daly*).

However, Zehr does not propose a simple revival of the principles of community justice. He also proposes that we look to biblical justice or 'covenant justice' for concepts with which to rethink what crime and justice are. Here, Zehr argues that the Old Testament concept of justice has been gravely misunderstood. We tend to assume that the Old Testament mandates a harsh, retributive response to crime. This assumption, Zehr claims, is based on misreadings and on overlooking the themes of restoration, forgiveness and reconciliation that appear regularly in the Old Testament (cf. Gorringe, 1996). Such themes, Zehr suggest, were then developed in the teachings of Jesus, who proposed a radical notion of 'relational justice', informed by an ethic of love and forgiveness and focusing on restoration and the healing of relationships damaged by 'crime'.[7]

Zehr suggests that VORPS are a practical demonstration that such an approach to crime and justice can work in contemporary Western societies. However, he concludes with a theme which occurs repeatedly in his subsequent writings. Throughout the history of criminal justice, efforts to bring about radical changes have been co-opted, and made to serve interests and goals quite different from those originally intended. Zehr warns that VORPS may share this fate and, in subsequent writings, has argued that as restorative justice is 'hitting the big time' it is in danger of being diverted more and more from its original vision. Programmes designated 'restorative justice' are being made to serve retributive rather than restorative goals and values (Zehr and Mika, 1998; Zehr, 2000). Hence, for Zehr, it is of crucial importance to ensure that restorative justice retains its integrity and remains true to its original vision. To do this, it may often be necessary to resist pressures for 'premature practicality' (Zehr, 1990: 221).

John Braithwaite entered the debate about restorative justice much later than Barnett, Christie and Zehr. His hugely influential book, *Crime, Shame and Reintegration* (1989), made no explicit mention of restorative justice. In this book, the harmful disintegrative shaming (stigmatisation) typical of criminal justice interventions was contrasted with the constructive reintegrative shaming found, among other places, in loving families, in oriental societies such as Japan and in some regimes for regulation of corporate wrongdoing. Braithwaite's core thesis was that societies which engage in reintegrative shaming tend to have lower crime rates than others, and that a radical shift in crime policy – away from over-reliance on state punishment towards promoting and facilitating informal and moralising social control – was required. It was only later that Braithwaite began to depict restorative justice practices, such as family group conferences, as examples of reintegrative shaming at work and began to promote reintegrative shaming as a core aspect of restorative justice (for an account of how this connection was made, see *Moore and O'Connell*).

In the essay reprinted here, Braithwaite attacks Western criminal justice systems as not only humiliating and stigmatising, but brutal, vengeful and hypocritical. Despite their harshness, these systems fail to prevent crime (as the theory of stigmatisation predicts). The solution, for Braithwaite, is to replace stigmatic punishment with restorative justice, in which evil acts are condemned, but those who commit them are treated as essentially good people who, with love and social support, can be helped to turn away from crime and be restored to the community as responsible and valued citizens. For Braithwaite, restorative justice should be understood as an institutionalisation of certain processes which take place informally within communities (such as the practice of a gathering around of friends in times of crisis). However, at least in the sphere of crime, these processes have been weakened due to our excessive reliance on state professionals to control crime through punitive and therapeutic interventions. Hence, these informal processes may need to be strengthened.

Braithwaite is unfashionably optimistic (in this, as in much else, he seems to take pride in being unfashionable). Developments which others lament, such as the growth of conservative imperatives for fiscal frugality, are regarded by him as opportunities for the development of restorative justice. However, he is also well aware that proposing an idea is one thing, but getting from here to there is an entirely different matter. Hence, in this essay, as elsewhere in his work, he pays due attention to the question of how restorative processes can be nurtured and developed so that public support for them can be built up to the level where politicians and policy-makers find it politic to associate themselves with the restorative justice movement.

Braithwaite's writings have energised and in some ways redirected the restorative justice movement with remarkable effects. Without wishing to overstate his influence, it is probably fair to say that the take-off of restorative justice in the UK and elsewhere since the mid-1990s has been assisted considerably by the attractiveness of his ideas (mediated by others) to senior, forward-thinking practitioners and policy-makers in the police and other criminal justice agencies. Some would argue that this success has been bought at a price. Braithwaite's *original* interest was in crime control rather than other aspects of restorative justice, such as the empowerment of crime victims (see *Marshall*). And, although Braithwaite by no means ignores the wide range of restorative goals, including that of 'restoring victims', this goal sometimes seems less central in his writings than it is in those of some other key advocates of restorative justice, such as *Barnett* and *Wright* (Chapter 13). In short, as well as contributing enormously to the development and promotion of restorative justice, Braithwaite has subtly, for better or worse, shifted the emphasis, giving crime control a higher priority than it has in other versions of the ideal.

Notes

1 In a subsequent paper, Barnett (1980) himself explored other ways by which offenders could make good the loss or harm they caused.
2 It is interesting to think about the reasons for this. The neglect of such proposals might be due, largely, to the fact that they are closely tied to Barnett's focus on financial restitution. Arguably, however, their neglect is due in part to the 'failure' of the restorative justice movement to make as sharp a break as Barnett proposes with the paradigm of punishment.
3 For Kuhn, paradigms (in science) are 'universally recognized scientific achievements that for a time provide model problems and solutions to a community of practitioners' (1970: viii).
4 What is unclear from this particular account is why we are not entitled to impose punishment upon offenders but are entitled to *force* them to pay restitution.
5 Although the offender's 'voluntary' participation may be due to his or her knowledge that the alternative may be coercive penal interventions.
6 Zehr's choice of metaphor owes much to the fact that he is a photographer as well as a writer. We should note here that Zehr has subsequently accepted that the sharp contrast he drew between Retributive and Restorative justice fails to take account of what both have in common (see Zehr 2002: 29–30). I have suggested that, despite its limitations, this contrast, carefully used, is useful and should not be rejected entirely (Johnstone, 2002: 87–93).
7 One need not, of course, adhere to any religious faith to recognise that the Bible and other sacred books might have much to teach us about how we might view and respond to wrongdoing, and may even contain some quite radical ethical and political ideas (cf. Gorringe, 1996).

References

Barnett, R. (1980) 'The Justice of Restitution', *American Journal of Jurisprudence*, 25, pp. 117–32.
Braithwaite, J. (1989) *Crime, Shame and Reintegration* (Cambridge: Cambridge University Press).
Gorringe, T. (1996) *God's Just Vengeance* (Cambridge: Cambridge University Press).
Johnstone, G. (2002) *Restorative Justice: Ideas, values, debates* (Cullompton, Devon: Willan).
Kuhn, T. (1970) *The Structure of Scientific Revolutions* (2nd edn, enlarged) (Chicago, IL: University of Chicago Press).

Marshall, T. (1988) 'Out of Court: More or Less Justice?' in Matthews, R. (ed.) *Informal Justice?* (London: Sage), pp. 25–50.

Morris, R. (1995) 'Not Enough!' *Mediation Quarterly*, 12:3, pp. 285–91.

Zehr, H. (1990) *Changing Lenses: A New Focus for Crime and Justice* (Scottdale, PA: Herald Press).

Zehr, H. (2000) 'Restorative Justice Hits the Big Time: But will it Remain True to its Vision?' (available online at http://www.restorativejustice.org/conference/RJhitsbigtime.html).

Zehr, H. (2002) 'Journey to belonging' in Weitekamp, E. and Kerner, H.J. (ed.) *Restorative Justice: Theoretical foundations* (Cullompton, Devon: Willan).

Zehr, H. and Mika, H. (1998) 'Fundamental Concepts of Restorative Justice' *Contemporary Justice Review*, 1:1, pp. 47–55.

1. Restorative justice: an overview

Tony F. Marshall

What is restorative justice?

Restorative justice is a problem-solving approach to crime which involves the parties themselves, and the community generally, in an active relationship with statutory agencies.

It is not any particular practice, but a set of *principles* which may orientate the general practice of any agency or group in relation to crime.

These principles are:

- making room for the *personal involvement* of those mainly concerned (particularly the offender and the victim, but also their families and communities)
- seeing crime problems in their *social context*
- a forward-looking (or preventative) *problem-solving* orientation
- *flexibility* of practice (creativity).

Restorative justice may be seen as criminal justice embedded in its social context, with the stress on its relationship to the other components, rather than a closed system in isolation (see [Figure 1.1]).

A commonly accepted definition used internationally is: *Restorative justice is a process whereby parties with a stake in a specific offence resolve collectively how to deal with the aftermath of the offence and its implications for the future.*

Restorative Justice Pyramid

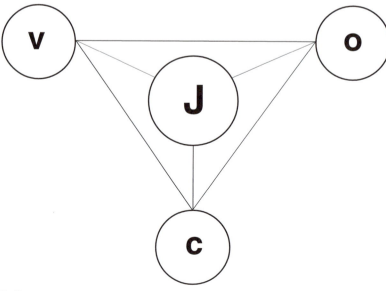

Figure [1.1]

What is restorative justice for?

The primary *objectives* of restorative justice are:

- to attend fully to *victims' needs* – material, financial, emotional and social (including those who are personally close to the victim and may be similarly affected)

- to prevent re-offending by *reintegrating offenders* into the community

- to enable offenders to assume active *responsibility* for their actions

- to recreate a *working community* that supports the rehabilitation of offenders and victims and is active in preventing crime.

- to provide a means of *avoiding escalation* of legal justice and the associated costs and delays.

These all might also be said to be objectives of the current criminal justice system, but that system only achieves such aims partially and haphazardly. It is not centrally concerned with victims and does not address most of their needs. Only limited action is taken to encourage the reintegration of offenders, and the evidence is that this is largely unsuccessful. It requires only the passive acquiescence of offenders, who are not expected to take the initiative in making good what they have done, but only to suffer their punishment. It is distant from the community and does little to encourage any role for the latter in the prevention of crime. Despite various programmes intended to divert offences from the full process and reduce costs and delays, these have had only a minor effect and also encourage the criticism that much crime is not taken sufficiently seriously.

Restorative justice is based on the following *assumptions*

- that crime has its origins in social conditions and relationships in the community

- that crime prevention is dependent on communities taking some responsibility (along with local and central governments' responsibility for general social policy) for remedying those conditions that cause crime

- that the aftermath of crime cannot be fully resolved for the parties themselves without allowing their personal involvement

- that justice measures must be flexible enough to be able to respond to the particular exigencies, personal needs and potential for action in each case

- that partnership and common objectives among justice agencies, and between them and the community, are essential to optimal effectiveness and efficiency

- that justice consists of a balanced approach in which a single objective is not allowed to dominate the others.

Why is it called restorative justice?

Restorative justice is concerned centrally with 'restoration': restoration of the victim, restoration of the offender to a law-abiding life, restoration of the damage caused by crime to the community. Restoration is not solely backward-looking; it is equally, if not more, concerned with the construction of a better society in the present and the future.

  [. . .]

How did the idea of restorative justice arise?

The first use of the term is generally ascribed to Barnett (1977) referring to certain principles arising out of early experiments in America using mediation between victims and offenders (see Wright, 1991, for more on the early history of the idea). These principles have been developed further over time, as commentators have thought them through further and as other innovative practices have been taken into account, but their basic justification is still *grounded in practical experience*. Innovation in criminal justice has mainly been in response to frustrations that many practitioners have felt with the limitations, as they perceived them, of traditional approaches. In the course of their normal work these practitioners started to experiment with new ways of dealing with crime problems. Practice developed through experience of 'what worked' in terms of impact on offenders, satisfaction of victims, and public acceptability. In particular, it was realised that the needs of victims, offenders and the community generally were not independent and that justice agencies had to engage actively with all three in order to make any impact. For instance, public demands for severe punishment, which those working to reform offenders found to be counter-productive, could only be relieved if attention was paid to victims' needs and healing the community, so that offender rehabilitation could only occur in parallel with the satisfaction of other objectives. Similarly, the overloading of courts and other justice agencies was due to the increasing lack of capacity of local communities to manage their indigenous crime problems, so that escalating costs could only be prevented by agencies working in partnership with communities to reconstruct the latter's resources for crime prevention and social control.

  Restorative justice is not therefore a single academic theory of crime or justice, but represents, in a more or less eclectic way, the accretion of actual experience in working successfully with particular crime problems. Although contributing practice has been extremely varied (including victim support, mediation, conferencing, problem-oriented policing and both community- and institution-based rehabilitation programmes), all these innovations were based on recognition of the need for engagement between two or more of the various parties represented in the diagram [Figure 1.1]. Coming from very different directions, innovating practitioners found themselves homing in on the same underlying principles of action (personal participation, community involvement, problem-solving and flexibility). As practice is refined, so is the concept of restorative justice.

In the course of this development, there has been much inspiration from examples of 'community justice' still in use (or recently so) among other non-western cultures, particularly among the indigenous populations in such New World countries as North America (Native American sentencing circles) and New Zealand ('Maori justice'). These practices have particularly contributed to the development of 'family (or community) group conferencing' (see below), and were effective in moving restorative justice ideas away from the excessive individualism of victim/offender mediation practice, providing a new community-oriented focus. (A communitarian theme, however, was also evident in the early development of mediation in the form of Victim Offender Reconciliation Projects, or VORPs, which initially represented an attempt by close-knit religious communities in North America to decrease reliance on formal justice.)

Relationship of restorative justice to legal justice

One of the prominent concerns both within and outside restorative justice has been the boundary between negotiatory practices and the workings of the criminal justice system. There are concerns that the due process safeguards for rights, equality and proportionality could all be lost. There are also concerns that the power of judicial agencies might undermine and convert the aims of restorative practices (Messmer and Otto, 1992). Some have argued for completely separate and parallel systems, neither interfering with the other. Others have countered that this would not lead to restorative justice at all, because all that it gained would be destroyed by the alienating and negative effects of adversarial justice.

It is in fact impossible to conceive of two systems side-by-side and entirely independent. There is bound to be some influence each way, and therefore the problem cannot be avoided. Even though restorative justice involves a greater or lesser degree of devolution of control to individual citizens and communities, it is now generally accepted that restorative justice can, and should, be integrated as far as possible with criminal justice as a complementary process that improves the quality, effectiveness and efficiency of justice as a whole. It is this concept of *integrated or 'whole' justice* (Marshall, 1997) which underlies the concept of restorative justice that was outlined [earlier]. It is not just a matter of new and different practices, but of traditional practice, too, informed by the same underlying principles. In this way the two processes reinforce one another to mutual benefit, and evolve towards a single system in which the community and formal agencies cooperate. It is in this context that issues of legality and control must be resolved.

[. . .]

Examples of restorative justice practice

[. . .]

Victim–offender

Victim–offender meetings are organised to give offenders a chance to take active steps to make voluntary reparation to their victims. Such reparation extends much wider than financial compensation. It includes an apology and an explanation of how it came about, and the offender has to listen to the victim's own story and respond to it. The exchange can be therapeutic for victims and usually has a visible impact upon the offenders, who have to face up to the reality of what they have done. Offenders can restore their own reputations, to some extent, through reparation, and can be better prepared for reintegration into mainstream society by having resolved their guilt in this way. Reparation may take the form of:

- financial payments,
- work for the victim,
- work for a community cause selected by the victim,
- specific undertakings (e.g. to attend a counselling course), or
- a mixture of these.

The context of personal negotiation allows flexible adjustment of agreements to the parties' needs and capacities and a greater level of creativity than court processes. Some victims find it helpful to themselves to be able to offer forgiveness in return for the offender's atonement. Any unresolved difficulties between them can also be settled – e.g. how to behave should they meet one another in the street, any remaining bad feelings or fears, or continuing relationship problems (if, as often happens, they already knew each other). Such meetings deal with victims' emotional needs as much as their material ones. After a successful meeting both parties can effectively draw a line under the experience. In many cases the victim also experiences satisfaction from influencing the offender away from crime – transforming a negative experience into something positive.

The social benefits of victim–offender mediation are that:

- victims' needs are more comprehensively served, including the need to be consulted,
- victim and offender are able to see each other as persons rather than stereotypes (a learning experience for both), and
- offenders are more affected by the experience than by formal prosecution and punishment, while being given a positive motivation to reform and a feeling that society is ready to offer re-acceptance.

Such meetings have to be carefully facilitated by a skilled, specially trained, mediator, whose prime tasks are to ensure a safe and comfortable environment, and firm ground-rules for a fruitful exchange which is re-affirming and a positive learning experience for both parties. The mediators may be employed by the body offering the service, or they may be lay volunteers. Both staff and volunteers require the same training programme which is specific to the task of mediation with victims and offenders. The skills required are not the same as those of counselling, social work, legal negotiations, arbitration, or any other profession.

In this country, victim–offender mediation is usually offered by specially constituted programmes that are run semi-independently from criminal justice agencies, although they are often managed by such agencies (probation or social work services, police services, or inter-agency panels). Some programmes are community-based, and victim–offender mediation may be offered as a special service by community mediation programmes whose other main caseload is comprised of neighbourhood disputes. Whatever the managing agency, there is usually a steering committee composed of representatives of community groups, victim support and criminal justice agencies. As mediators have to be respected and trusted by both victims and offenders it is crucial that their impartiality is protected.

[. . .]

As well as direct meetings between victims and offenders, mediation services may negotiate between the two, even if they do not want to meet, or are unable to do so. This is usually described as 'indirect mediation'. It enables flexible negotiation to suit both parties, but the agreement is usually limited to practical reparation and the transmission of an apology. Compared to a meeting, indirect mediation is less personal, does not allow victims' more emotional needs to be satisfied, is less effective in breaking down stereotypes and increasing understanding, and may be less influential in reforming offenders. On the other hand, for many victims not desiring a direct encounter, it may be preferable to no involvement at all.

Victim–offender mediation may be offered in conjunction with a police warning or caution, with deferred prosecution, in parallel with prosecution (before court or between conviction and sentence), in the place of a court, or after sentence. It is relevant to any offence, however serious, as long as there is an identifiable victim (which may be a corporate body) and as long as the defendant admits causing the harm. Participation in mediation is always entirely voluntary for both parties. Mediation may be initially suggested by an agency, the offender (or his/her legal representative), or the victim.

Apart from specific programmes, it sometimes happens that criminal justice officers have a chance to mediate between a victim and an offender in the normal course of their work. This may, for instance, be a police officer at a call-out to a domestic dispute, or a probation officer in the course of normal casework. While formally-offered mediation services should be professionally organised and conducted by qualified staff or volunteers, such incidental or extempore mediation still has its place as long as officers are aware of the limitations on what they can attempt with little time and experience, and from a position that may not be entirely impartial (or not perceived as such). An example of where this sometimes occurs and can be valuable is in social work with incest offenders, in which a meeting with the victim can help resolve remaining emotional problems when both parties have reached the necessary stage in therapy and emotional adjustment.

As well as negotiation between victims and their offenders, there have from time to time been programmes for groups of offenders who have committed similar offences to meet with a group of victims who have suffered from the same type of crime. It is a way of being able to provide a service to victims whose own offenders are not caught or are unable to meet them. They get the same chance to express their feelings and to ask questions of the offenders. For offenders it is also a chance to gain some insight into the personal effects of what they have done. Group meetings lack the immediacy and personal relevance of the one-to-one victim/offender meeting, but may still perform a useful communication function. Such programmes are carried out usually with groups of prison inmates or probationers. One is currently running in Long Lartin prison. The programmes have so far always been short-lived, partly because they only appeal to a small minority of victims.

Victim–community

Community support for victims most often occurs through the victims' own personal acquaintances or relatives, and this is the most natural source of assistance and usually the most valued. Such assistance may, however, be less available to some individuals than others. The voluntary organisation *Victim Support* exists to fill this gap by offering practical help, support and consolation to victims on a local basis, using trained lay volunteers available to visit those who request it. By showing community concern, Victim Support helps to overcome the social distrust and sense of alienation that afflict many victims as the result of a crime. It helps restore the victim materially, psychologically and socially. Moreover, volunteers' specialist knowledge of psychological reactions to crime may facilitate better support, in some cases, than friends and relations who may fail to understand the victim's real needs (or have their own problems coming to terms with what has happened).

Other community groups are also engaged in helping particular kinds of victim. These may, for instance, be women victims of domestic violence (e.g. Women's Aid), or children victims of abuse (Childline). There also exist self-help support groups for parents of murdered children, victims of drunk drivers, and so on. These voluntary organisations play a crucial part in restoring victims and are an essential part of a functioning community.

Yet other groups may be concerned with helping to prevent victimisation, such as the *Suzy Lamplugh Trust*, which offers training in how to deal with violence and prevent its escalation.

Offender–community

There are a multitude of [*sic*] projects in different communities which attempts to help offenders of various kinds, whether it is trying to find jobs, retraining, literacy education, relationships counselling, drug or alcohol counselling, mentoring, accommodation for the homeless, support for the isolated, or the provision of activities to release energies or encourage social integration. Other services support families to improve their parenting skills. Such provision is unsystematic and variable, but it is an expression of communities' feelings of responsibility for reincorporating their deviant members and supporting those that have been damaged by their experiences. Many organisations, such as youth clubs or adventure playgrounds, perform a preventative function by their very existence. [. . .]

A special group of programmes, rather than helping individuals or groups, is concerned with helping communities as a whole become less crime-prone. NACRO's Safe Neighbourhoods work is an example of these: attempting to improve the physical and social fabric of crime-prone neighbourhoods. They are a special example of economic and community development programmes generally which, by encouraging communal action and responsibility, and providing the resources for this (including the skills), enable communities to prevent and contain crime, as well as improving the quality of life generally.

Another group of programmes is engaged in *schools*. These are mainly concerned with incipient offending – programmes for bullying, truants, misbehaviour or school exclusions, for instance. They are often concerned with improving the capacities of schools to deal with their internal problems themselves – such as dispute resolution training for pupils, which enables them to avoid trouble escalating from disputes or even to provide their own mediation services for fellow pupils (Marshall, 1987). School mediation programmes exist in a number of British schools and even more in America and other countries, such as Norway. Group meetings of family members, pupils, other parents, teachers, and community members are being facilitated in some schools to develop programmes for supporting disruptive pupils who would otherwise have to be excluded. Other programmes are concerned with making children aware of their coming responsibilities as adults and citizens – parenthood training, drugs and sex education, and citizenship. An example of the latter focussed more specifically on crime is the *Howard League*'s 'Citizenship and Crime Project', in which conferences are held in secondary schools, led by volunteers from a variety of agencies to facilitate discussion among young people. [. . .]

Yet other programmes are concerned to help *imprisoned offenders* before they are released or on release, including work with prisoners' families, which may help to keep their social networks intact. Some programmes help violent offenders learn how to control their own violence and channel their aggression in a positive way (e.g. the *Alternatives to Violence Project*, AVP, which began in America and has been introduced into Britain). Some projects work specifically with wife-abusers. Other programmes help in a more general way to prepare for release in order to avoid the prisoner facing extreme social pressures of isolation and social rejection, or overwhelming feelings of inadequacy (e.g. *Inside Out*).

Similar programmes providing a wide range of interventions are operated in the community for persistent offenders in danger of being sent to prison, participation in which may be assigned as part of a community sentence by the court. There have been a large number of 'intermediate treatment' programmes of this sort over the years, run by community organisations (such as *Save the Children* or *Barnardos*) or by multi-agency teams (e.g. the Kent Intensive Support and Supervision Programme, or Repeat Offender Project, which also offers community conferencing [. . .].

The relationship does not have to be all one way. Offenders in some programmes carry out work for their own communities, which can help give the offenders a sense of social responsibility and an experience of social acceptance and recognition. Prisoners, for instance, may be allowed to carry out work on behalf of the community or make produce for sale in order to provide the profits to Victim Support (a kind of indirect reparation).

Victim, offender and community

In traditional victim–offender mediation the community has a minimal role, except that the mediator may be a local community member, although sometimes victims assume this kind of role, exploring with the offender how they might keep out of trouble in future or, on rare occasions, offering personal support. (In some cases the offender may be more obviously suffering than the victim.)

The community is given a more direct role in the case of 'group conferencing', which is essentially an extension of victim–offender mediation to include more parties – the offender's family, the victim's family or supporters (or several victims together), and community contacts of the offender who may be able to offer support or help (a teacher, employer, neighbour, youth worker, church contact, etc.). While the emphasis in victim–offender mediation is on the victim's suffering and how the offender may make reparation for this, the conference allows the offender's family (especially in the case of younger people) to share the blame and directly witness the harm caused, and, most importantly, allows an exploration not only of how the offender can atone, but also how they can keep out of trouble in the future. It is equivalent to a case conference where the offender's social network replaces the formal agencies and takes responsibility for exploring what has gone wrong, what steps the offender can take to reform, and how others can support him/her in doing this. As a force for social reintegration of offenders, conferencing is potentially a more powerful tool than one-to-one mediation, because it allows social resources to be brought to bear to ensure that the offender's change of heart is more likely to continue. While still addressing victims' needs, it also addresses those of the offender – and of society, that would benefit from his/her rehabilitation.

The first use of conferencing in New Zealand (Brown and McElrea, 1993; Hudson *et al.*, 1996) demonstrated the possible problems – especially the difficulty of maintaining the focus on the victim when most of the participants were there because of their relationship to, and interest in, the offender (see Morris *et al.*, 1993). 'Empowerment' is also resisted by many families only too happy to leave responsibility for their wayward children to the 'system'. Large groups of this kind also require even more skilful mediation than one-to-one encounters. While the mediator in the New Zealand system is a youth justice worker, and in the Australian version is a police officer (a model emulated by

Thames Valley Police in this country in their 'restorative cautioning' experiment; see Alder and Wundersitz, 1994), more independent observers have inclined towards a neutral person with specific professional qualifications for such a role. The skills required, in fact, are very similar to those required for other kinds of multi-party mediation utilised in this country and America for environmental, land-use and planning conflicts, and training is available in these skills. This would help avoid some of the procedural problems to which conferencing can give rise (as pointed out by Marshall, 1997 and Wright, 1997).

Like victim–offender mediation, conferencing can be used at different stages of the criminal process. In New Zealand it is used in conjunction with either a caution or a court appearance. In the latter case the offender and his/her family are charged with proposing a package of measures to compensate the victim and undertakings that will help prevent a repetition of the behaviour. If acceptable to the victim(s), this package is put before the court for ratification as a sentence. However, this involves the victim with a degree of responsibility for the sentence which Victim Support in this country has considered an unfair burden.

Used in conjunction with a caution the resulting agreement is not enforceable, and more emphasis tends to be placed, as a result, on the process itself – especially (in the Australian version and in restorative cautioning) on the 'shaming' of the offender. This process of shaming is based on the ideas of John Braithwaite (see below) and is meant to be 'reintegrative' and not negative, but Braithwaite's theory held that shaming was only positive in its effects if it occurred within and by a community of people that the shamed person was attached to and respected. The artificial imposition of a shaming experience by agents of a statutory power does not seem to accord with that proposition, so it is doubtful whether such a process would be beneficial in its effects on future behaviour.

Given the greater resources needed to set up conferences, there may be arguments for prioritising them in terms of their likely usefulness (e.g. where there are indications of family dysfunction or of continued offending), and victims who are not related to the offender may prefer to take part in a simple one-to-one meeting which focuses more clearly on their own needs, either instead of attending a conference (which could still proceed with the other members) or preceding it. [. . .] Conferencing is still a new technique in criminal justice and more experimentation is required. The inclusion of the victim in particular makes it very different from the kind of family conference with which social workers in this country are more familiar. [. . .] In its combination of victim restoration, offender reintegration, individual participation and community involvement, conferencing might be seen as a restorative justice process *par excellence*, but it needs to be questioned whether it is either practical or desirable to meet all these ends at one time in the majority of cases.

[. . .]

In Canada a model of conferencing has been developed explicitly modelled on native Canadian customs, which includes an even higher level of community involvement and control. This is known as 'circle sentencing' and places the highest value on 'healing' the community after crime (Assembly of Manitoba Chiefs, 1989). It is only likely to be relevant, however, to communities with a strong identity and a tradition of operating in this way. Similar practices occur as an alternative to legal procedure in many other countries that have indigenous populations with strong ancient traditions of managing their own concerns. One problem that these approaches encounter is the proclivity of many of their younger members to loosen their communal ties and become 'Westernised', so that the procedures have little power over them. This has happened with respect to traditional Maori clan-based practice in New Zealand.

Another strand of development has been Neighbourhood Justice Centres, which do not exist in this country, but are well established in North America, Australia and Norway (Municipal Mediation Boards) in particular. These receive referrals of cases involving disputes between parties from the police, courts, etc. Mediation is carried out by trained independent mediators or a community panel. If successful, it allows for prosecution to be dropped. A good example is provided by the Community Justice Centres of New South Wales, which received over 5,500 referrals during 1996–97, of which 45% resulted in direct mediation. Over 86% of the latter ended in agreement. Referrals from courts were the most likely to be resolved (59% of all referrals). They have over 300 active mediators at any one time. (See Community Justice Centres, 1997.)

Justice agencies and victims

The Victims Charter already embodies responsibilities on the part of all criminal justice agencies on behalf of victims, and represents a step towards the assumption of certain restorative ends. It is focused more at present on avoiding secondary victimisation (not making the victim feel even worse) than on providing positive help, although the latter is not entirely missing (e.g. providing information on victim support services). A stumbling-block, at least in the context of prosecution, is that the victim has no standing as such, as against being a reporter or witness of a crime, until there is a conviction. Measures exist for awarding compensation to be paid by convicted offenders on behalf of their victims and could be more widely used. The new reparation order will extend the capacity of courts to ensure that victims' material needs are served.

Probation services have recently been charged with victim enquiry work in the case of offenders serving longer prison sentences for personal crimes, helping to avoid further trouble on release. In this context some services with established mediation programmes have charged these units with victim contact work, so that they can offer mediation with the offender if relevant. This work extends the job of probation from its traditional offender-focus to include more general responsibility for preventing trouble.

Justice agencies and offenders

The main thrust of criminal justice has been to assign responsibility for criminal acts and allot proportionate punishments. It has not therefore been centrally concerned with reintegration of the offender. Attempts at reintegration are largely confined to the probation and social work services. Their work is essentially restorative, effecting a link between offenders and the community through their work with families, help in gaining employment, referral to treatment facilities, encouraging community programmes for offenders, and so on. These important efforts, however, remain marginal to the main processes of justice, which may conflict with reintegration (for instance, incarceration, unless accompanied by a structured programme for release into the community).

Other agencies can, however, assist reintegration. [. . .]

Justice agencies and communities

While criminal justice as a whole has been traditionally remote from the community, this has never wholly applied to the police forces, which have always had a major peacekeeping and public assistance role in support of the community. Public surveys have shown that this is still highly valued. In the context of restorative justice, police Community Relations divisions would take on a more significant central role, because active responsibility for developing good public relations would not rest with a small number of designated officers but would be part of the duties of every officer. [. . .]

Probation services, too, have sometimes been seen as a link between criminal justice and the community, but the demands of casework have never allowed a major expansion of the probation community development role, which could be given higher priority within a restorative system. While police community work is more directly related to physical crime prevention, probation services could usefully encourage means for social crime prevention.

Opportunities for volunteering in relation to criminal justice agencies provide another community link – lay visitors to police stations, boards of prison visitors, probation volunteers, special constables, prison visiting, mediators for victim/offender programmes, etc.

Interagency partnerships can extend to collaboration between criminal justice agencies and community groups. This often happens now when agencies make use of community agencies for rehabilitation programmes, or in problem-oriented policing. It occurs on a wider scale in Community Safety Partnerships, organised at local authority level to bring together justice agencies, local authority departments and community groups in order to establish priorities that accord with local needs and to use a problem-solving approach to crime prevention. In this context there are possibilities for effective mediation between community groups (e.g. youth groups and householders). Such collaboration is similarly seen in the new Young Offender Teams. Probation services have often formed partnerships with community agencies to deliver reintegrative programmes for offenders (such as *The Prince's Trust* schemes to help offenders get work, learn skills or even start their own businesses). [. . .]

Community involvement has long been a feature of juvenile justice in Scotland, since the introduction of the Children's Hearings under the 1968

Social Work (Scotland) Act. Hearings are conducted before a lay tribunal of community representatives and include attendance by the offenders and their parents. Their remit is the best interests of the child rather than punishment (McAra and Young, 1997). There is, however, no role for victims in this system.

An innovative practice has been in operation in Vermont since 1995, the reparative probation programme, where 'non-violent offenders are sentenced by the court to a hearing before a community reparative board (RB) composed of local citizens' (Bazemore and Griffiths, 1997). Victims, however, are rarely consulted at present, and the idea might be more applicable as a supplement to other practices (like victim/offender mediation) for victimless crimes.

Partnerships explicitly focused on restorative justice are increasingly under consideration, with examples in the US (especially Minnesota and Maine, and, with respect to juveniles, Pennsylvania, Florida, New Mexico and Montana) and in this country (particularly the Milton Keynes Youth Crime Reduction Project, incorporating a number of interlocking initiatives).

[. . .]

Theories related to restorative justice

The first writer to create a really integrated and comprehensive model of restorative justice was Howard Zehr, firstly in a small pamphlet called 'Retributive Justice, Restorative Justice' (1985) [see Chapter 4 of this volume], and subsequently in his book *Changing Lenses* (1990). He represented restorative justice as an 'alternative justice paradigm', opposed in all principal respects to the principles underlying legal or retributive justice. His work placed particular stress on benefits to victims and enabling offenders to assume active responsibility for putting right the harm they had caused (both as a matter of natural justice and as having a more profound impact on the offender than simply receiving punishment from the court). The interaction between victim and offender, involving personal reconciliation, atonement and, potentially, forgiveness, was presented as entirely compatible with religious notions (especially, but not only, Christian) and given justification in those terms. The drawbacks of Zehr's work were an excessive attachment of restorative justice ideas to a single practical innovation, mediation (and a particular manifestation of such practice as represented by the VORPs), and its individualistic emphasis, largely neglecting public interests in crime in favour of the more or less private concerns of the victim and the offender (an unintended but still significant bias).

Zehr's work was widely influential among the growing cohort of converts to such ideas, being particularly evident in the works of Mark Umbreit (1985) in America and Martin Wright (1991) and John Harding (1992) in Britain. These authors treated restorative justice as virtually synonymous with victim/offender mediation and continued the emphasis on private negotiation as a sufficient response to crime. Wright, for instance, presented restorative justice as a shift from criminal to civil law. This argument is traditionally backed by reference to an earlier paper by Nils Christie (1977) [see Chapter 3 of this volume] which treated crimes as conflicts between the parties that had been 'stolen' out of their hands by the State and should be returned to the parties. Christie's ideas were particularly influential in his home country, Norway, where they formed the ideological foundation for the unique Municipal Mediation Boards (Fjaerem, 1996). European theory itself developed predominantly in the direction of 'abolitionism' (Bianchi and van Swaaningen, 1986), a radical rejection of state intervention, under the influence of academics like Christie, Bianchi, and de Haan (1990) and has only recently embraced the more Anglo-American ideas of restorative justice, with the influence of restorative justice practitioners in Europe (particularly pioneers like Christa Pelikan in Austria, Ivo Aertsen in Belgium, Bonafe-Schmidt in France, and a number of people in Germany, some of whom directly imported personal experiences in the USA and elsewhere – e.g. Thomas Trenczek, Elmar Weitekamp, and Heike Jung).

Wright was also much exercised by the problem of reconciling restorative justice procedures (i.e. in his case, victim/offender mediation) with the traditional justice system. This issue was made particularly clear by emerging research, such as that in Britain published by the Home Office (Marshall and Merry, 1990), and in America and Europe (e.g. Messmer and Otto, 1992, papers from an international NATO conference in Italy). The relationship between the two approaches was made particularly difficult by the apparent opposition between their underlying principles as represented in Zehr's two paradigms, and by the denial in restorative justice of the public interest dimension. It was at about this time that criticism of the 'over-individualised' nature of restorative justice thinking also began to emerge, particularly from Harry Mika (1992) in the US and Tony Marshall (1994) in the UK. As early as 1987, however, Shonholtz in America was advocating community-based justice (with some influence from the European abolitionism movement, which was always chary of the ease with which victim–offender mediation could become incorporated by traditional legal values).

The social dimension of restorative justice was given a boost by ideas associated with the group forum approaches of indigenous cultures in North America and Pacific nations (e.g. Consedine, 1995) and formal cultural practices of apology and forgiveness in Japan (Haley, 1988). While there is a large literature on 'community justice' (summarised in Marshall, 1985) which was important in the early days, largely in support of 'neighbourhood justice centres' in America and elsewhere, more recently these ideas became associated, almost by accident, with a quite separate thread of criminological thought initiated by John Braithwaite (1989) in Australia. His work had developed the idea of 'reintegrative shaming', a theory of social control that argued that potential offenders were positively influenced by being shamed by their circle of acquaintances or their own community, but were negatively influenced by the alienative shaming of the State in the form of criminal punishment. He favoured locating social control in the community as far as possible. Several writers saw parallels with restorative justice thinking in Braithwaite's work (see especially Dignan, 1994). At about the same time Braithwaite himself began to make the same connections. In more practical terms, Braithwaite reinterpreted the New Zealand family group conferences in terms of reintegrative shaming, and this innovation was introduced experimentally in Australia with an explicit justification in terms of his 'shaming' theory. The 'shaming' idea gained further currency and was introduced even into probation and social work practice with offenders on an ad hoc basis, confused with notions of meeting the victim and mediation.

'Reintegrative shaming' is by no means universally accepted as part of restorative justice theory. Many people are unhappy with its overtones, as 'shaming' can easily be misapplied in a negative way. For instance, it goes entirely against the grain of Braithwaite's original ideas for agents of the state to apply 'reintegrative' shaming, as is happening when it is applied in social work contexts or even in family group conferences run by youth justice workers or the police. There is a basic contradiction in state agencies attempting to engineer a community-based process. While they might go as far as to set up the circumstances, through community involvement in which reintegrative shaming might occur, whether or not it happens will depend on the individuals involved and so it cannot be used as a rationale for state intervention. In any case, Braithwaite's theory is only one of crime control and prevention, and does not encompass the victim-interests and justice-issues that are primary components of restorative justice as a whole (Bazemore, 1997).

As it currently stands, restorative justice still lacks a definitive theoretical statement, although works continue to be written that take thinking forward, such as Cragg (1992) and Bianchi (1994). The latter casts prisons in a restorative role (as much for the support and protection of the offender as for public protection). Dignan and Cavadino (1996) have made an attempt to integrate different models of restorative justice action. The most comprehensive statement and the one that most recognises the community role in restorative justice is contained in a number of brief papers by Kay Pranis (e.g. 1997), which attempt to encapsulate the essence of the more 'socialised' conception of restorative justice. Marshall (1991) represented an early attempt to present restorative justice in the context of holistic changes in the structure of community, society and political organisation, a line also followed by Weitekamp (1992).

Whether or not it is capable of becoming more than just a model of practice and becoming a complete theory of justice remains to be seen. The academic development of such a theory is still in the early days of development, particularly in terms of the formulation of a philosophy or 'ethics' of restorative justice, in which a number of commentators are currently engaged, such as Rob Mackay at Dundee (e.g. Mackay, 1992), and the Penology and Victimology research group at Leuven in Belgium (e.g. Deklerck and Depuydt, 1997).

To practical developments this matters very little, and it may be advantageous that it remains an open model able to accept innovations as they occur, rather than a closed system of thought that might restrict options. It is its ability to absorb many different concerns that gives it appeal, and it is its grounding in successful practice that gives it persuasive justification. In this lies its strength and weakness. There is a grave danger that restorative justice may end up being all things to all men and women, concealing important divergences of practice and aim. Marshall (1996) identifies one such major rift between social work-oriented practice and the professional mediation stance.

Although no other criminological or justice theory can be held to underpin restorative justice, many academic theories and approaches have been incorporated in, or associated with, it at different stages. Perhaps the most fully compatible, although it is not often referred to in this context (with the exception of Marshall and Merry, 1990, and Haines, 1997), is Hirschi's (1969) 'control theory', which argues that state intervention cannot replace the power of community ties and community acceptance to control misbehaviour. In many ways Braithwaite's ideas are a re-working of Hirschi, and the latter is similarly restricted in its applicability to restorative justice because of its lack of concern with justice per se and victims.

Matza's theory of 'neutralisation' has also been applied to victim/offender mediation (e.g. Mackay, 1988; Marshall and Merry, 1990; and Messmer, 1992). Matza argued that a major element in enabling offenders to commit crime while maintaining a positive self-image was that they employed a number of 'techniques of neutralisation' to dismiss or minimise the effects of what they do ('they can afford it', 'they'd never miss it') or to justify their actions ('they asked for it'). A confrontation with the victim makes it difficult to maintain such fictions and makes the offenders face up to the reality of the harm they cause.

Other strands of thought that have impacted on restorative justice include abolitionism (Bianchi and van Swaaningen, 1986), which advocates community control in place of state control; feminist criminology (e.g. Heidensohn, 1986; Pepinsky and Quinney, 1991), which emphasises personal relationships and community; peace-making (Pepinsky and Quinney, 1991) and conflict resolution theory (Kennedy, 1990; Scimecca, 1991), which both treat crime as a conflict better resolved through participation and voluntary agreement than by dictate.

These extracts are taken from Restorative Justice: an Overview, *by Tony F. Marshall (Centre for Restorative Justice and Peacemaking, University of Minnesota, and Restorative Justice Consortium, UK), 1998.*

References

Alder, C. and Wundersitz, J. (eds) (1994) *Family Conferencing and Juvenile Justice* (Canberra: Australian Institute of Criminology).

Assembly of Manitoba Chiefs (1989) *Final Submission to the Aboriginal Justice Inquiry* (Manitoba: Department of Justice).

Barnett, R. (1977) 'Restitution: A New Paradigm of Criminal Justice', *Ethics*, 87:4, pp. 279–301.

Bazemore, G. (1997) 'After Shaming, Whither Reintegration: Restorative Justice and Relational Rehabilitation', in Bazemore, G. and Walgrave, L. (eds) *Restoring Juvenile Justice* (Amsterdam: Kugler).

Bazemore, G. and Griffiths, C.T. (1997) 'Conferences, Circles, Boards, and Mediations: The "New Wave" of Community Justice Decisionmaking', *Federal Probation*, 61:2, pp. 25–37.

Bianchi, H. (1994) *Justice as Sanctuary: Toward a New System of Crime Control* (Bloomington, IN: Indiana University Press).

Bianchi, H. and van Swaaningen, R. (eds) (1986) *Abolitionism* (Amsterdam: Free University Press).

Braithwaite, J. (1989) *Crime, Shame and Reintegration* (Cambridge: Cambridge University Press).

Brown, R.J. and McElrea, F.W.M. (eds) (1993) *The Youth Court in New Zealand: A New Model of Justice* (Auckland: Legal Research Foundation).

Community Justice Centres (1997) *Annual Report 1996–97* (New South Wales: CJC).

Consedine, J. (1995) *Restorative Justice: Healing the Effects of Crime* (Lyttelton, NZ: Ploughshares Publications).

Cragg, W. (1992) *The Practice of Punishment: Towards a Theory of Restorative Justice* (London: Routledge).

de Haan, W. (1990) *The Politics of Redress* (London: Unwin Hyman).

Deklerck, J. and Depuydt, A. (1997) 'An Ethical Approach to Crime Prevention', *European Journal on Criminal Policy and Research*, 5:3, pp. 71–80.

Dignan, J. (1994) 'Reintegration through Reparation: A Way Forward for Restorative Justice?', in Duff, R.A. *et al.* (eds) *Penal Theory and Practice* (Manchester: Manchester University Press).

Dignan, J. and Cavadino, M. (1996) 'Towards a Framework for Conceptualising and Evaluating Models of Criminal Justice from a Victim's Perspective', *International Review of Victimology*, 4, pp. 153–82.

Fjaerem, A. (1996) 'The Norwegian System of Mediation Boards.' Paper to Council of Europe Committee of Experts on Mediation in Penal Matters (Strasbourg: Council of Europe).

Haines, K. (1997) 'Some Principled Objections to a Restorative Justice Approach to Working with Juvenile Offenders.' Paper to the First International Conference on Restorative Justice for Juveniles, Leuven, 14 May.

Haley, J. (1988) 'Confession, Repentance and Absolution', in Wright, M. and Galaway, B. (eds) *Mediation and Criminal Justice* (London: Sage).

Harding, J. (1982) *Victims and Offenders: Needs and Responsibilities* (London: Bedford Square Press).

Heidensohn, F. (1986) 'Models of Justice: Portia or Persephone?', *International Journal of the Sociology of Law*, 14, pp. 287–98.

Hirschi, T. (1969) *Causes of Delinquency* (Berkeley, CA: University of California Press).

Hudson, J., Morris, A., Maxwell, G. and Galaway, B. (eds) (1996) *Family Group Conferences: Perspectives on Policy and Practice* (Monsey, NY: Willow Tree Press).

Kennedy, L.W. (1990) *On the Borders of Crime: Conflict Management and Criminology* (London: Longman).

Mackay, R. (1988) *Reparation in Criminal Justice* (Edinburgh: SACRO).

Mackay, R. (1992) 'A Humanist Foundation for Restitution.' Paper to Fulbright Colloquium, University of Stirling.

Marshall, T.F. (1985) *Alternatives to Criminal Courts* (Aldershot: Gower).

Marshall, T.F. (1987) 'Mediation: New Mode of Establishing Order in Schools', *Howard Journal*, 26.

Marshall, T.F. (1991) 'Criminal Justice in the New Community.' Paper for British Criminology Conference, York.

Marshall, T.F. (1996) 'The Evolution of Restorative Justice in Britain', *European Journal on Criminal Policy and Research*, 4:4, pp. 21–43.

Marshall, T.F. (1997) 'Criminal Justice Conferencing Calls for Caution', *Mediation* (2 parts).

Marshall, T. and Merry, S. (1990) *Crime and Accountability* (London: HMSO).

McAra, L. and Young, P. (1997) 'Juvenile Justice in Scotland', *Criminal Justice*, 15, pp. 8–10.

McElrea, F.W.M. (1994) 'The New Zealand Youth Court: A Model for Development in Other Courts?' Paper for the National Conference of District Court Judges, 6–9 April.

Messmer, K. (1992) 'Communication in Decision-making about Diversion and Victim/Offender Mediation', in Messmer, K. and Otto, H. (eds) *Restorative Justice on Trial* (Rotterdam: Kluwer).

Messmer, K. and Otto, H. (eds) (1992) *Restorative Justice on Trial* (Rotterdam: Kluwer).

Mika, H. (1992) 'Mediation Interventions and Restorative Justice: Responding to the Astructural Bias', in Messmer, K. and Otto, H. (eds) *Restorative Justice on Trial* (Rotterdam: Kluwer).

Morris, A., Maxwell, G. and Robertson, J. (1993) 'Giving Victims a Voice', *Howard Journal*, 32:4.

Pepinsky, H. and Quinney, R. (eds) (1991) *Criminology as Peacemaking* (Bloomington, IN: Indiana University Press).

Pranis, K. (1997) 'Communities and the Justice System – Turning the Relationship Upside Down', *VOMA Quarterly*, 8:1, pp. 7–10.

Pranis, K. (1997) 'Rethinking Community Corrections: Restorative Values and an Expanded Role for the Community', *ICCA Journal on Community Corrections*, 8:1, pp. 36–9.

Scimecca, J.A. (1991) 'Conflict Resolution and a Critique of "Alternative Dispute Resolution" ', in Pepinsky, H. and Quinney, R. (eds) *Criminology as Peacemaking* (Bloomington, IN: Indiana University Press).

Shonholtz, R. (1987) 'The Citizen's Role in Justice', *Annals of the American Academy of Political and Social Science*.

Umbreit, M. (1985) *Crime and Reconciliation* (Nashville, TN: Abingdon Press).

Umbreit, M. (1994) *Victim Meets Offender* (Monsey, NY: Criminal Justice Press).

Weitekamp, E. (1992) 'Reparative Justice: Towards a Victim Oriented System', *European Journal on Criminology, Policy and Research*, 1:1, pp. 70–93.

Wright, M. (1991) *Justice for Victims and Offenders* (Milton Keynes: Open University Press).

Wright, M. (1997) 'Some Questions Answered about FGCs', *Family Group Conferences and Youth Justice*, 2, pp. 2–3.

Zehr, H. (1985) *Retributive Justice, Restorative Justice* (Elkhart: Mennonite Central Committee, US Office of Criminal Justice).

Zehr, H. (1990) *Changing Lenses* (Scottdale, PA: Herald Press).

2. Restitution: a new paradigm of criminal justice

Randy E. Barnett

[. . .]

In the criminal justice system we are witnessing the death throes of an old and cumbersome paradigm, one that has dominated Western thought for more than 900 years. While this paper presents what is hoped to be a viable, though radical alternative, much would be accomplished by simply prompting the reader to reexamine the assumptions underlying the present system. Only if we are willing to look at our old problems in a new light do we stand a chance of solving them. This is our only hope, and our greatest challenge.

The crisis in the paradigm of punishment

'Political revolutions are inaugurated by a growing sense, often restricted to a segment of the political community, that existing institutions have ceased adequately to meet the problems posed by an environment they have in part created . . . In both political and scientific development the sense of malfunction that can lead to crisis is prerequisite to revolution.'[1] Kuhn's description of the preconditions for scientific and political revolutions could accurately describe the current state of the criminal law. However, simply to recognize the existence of a crisis is not enough. We must look for its causes. The Kuhnian methodology suggests that we critically examine the paradigm of punishment itself.

The problems which the paradigm of punishment is supposed to solve are many and varied. A whole literature on the philosophy of punishment has arisen in an effort to justify or reject the institution of punishment. For our purposes the following definition from the *Encyclopedia of Philosophy* should suffice: 'Characteristically punishment is unpleasant. It is inflicted on an offender because of an offence he has committed; it is deliberately imposed, not just the natural consequence of a person's action (like a hangover), and the unpleasantness is *essential* to it, not an accompaniment to some other treatment (like the pain of the dentist's drill).'[2]

Two types of arguments are commonly made in defense of punishment. The first is that punishment is an appropriate means to some justifiable end such as, for example, deterrence of crime. The second type of argument is that punishment is justified as an end in itself. On this view, whatever ill effects it might engender, punishment for its own sake is good.

The first type of argument might be called the *political* justification of punishment, for the end which justifies its use is one which a political order is presumably dedicated to serve: the maintenance of peaceful interactions between individuals and groups in a society. There are at least three ways that deliberate infliction of harm on an offender is said to be politically justified.

1. One motive for punishment, especially capital punishment and imprison-ment, is the 'intention to deprive offenders of the power of doing future mischief'.[3] Although it is true that an offender cannot continue to harm society while incarcerated, a strategy of punishment based on disablement has several drawbacks.

Imprisonment is enormously expensive. This means that a double burden is placed on the innocent who must suffer the crime and, in addition, pay through taxation for the support of the offender and his family if they are forced on to welfare. Also, any benefit of imprisonment is temporary; eventually, most offenders will be released. If their outlook has not improved – and especially if it has worsened – the benefits of incarceration are obviously limited. Finally, when disablement is permanent, as with capital punishment or psychosurgery, it is this very permanence, in light of the possibility of error, which is frightening. For these reasons, 'where disablement enters as an element into penal theories, it occupies, as a rule, a subordinate place and is looked upon as an object subsidiary to some other end which is regarded as paramount. . . .'[4]

2. Rehabilitation of a criminal means a change in his mental *habitus* so that he will not offend again. It is unclear whether the so-called treatment model which views criminals as a doctor would view a patient is truly a 'retributive' concept. Certainly it does not conform to the above definition characterizing punishment as deliberately and essentially unpleasant. It is an open question whether any end justifies the intentional, forceful manipulation of an individual's thought processes by anyone, much less the state. To say that an otherwise just system has incidentally rehabilitative effects which may be desirable is one thing, but it is quite another to argue that these effects themselves justify the system. The horrors to which such reasoning can lead are obvious from abundant examples in history and contemporary society.[5]

[. . .]

3. The final justification to be treated here – deterrence – actually has two aspects. The first is the deterrent effect that past demonstrations of punishment have on the future of others; the second is the effect that threats of future punishment have on the conduct of others. The distinction assumes importance when some advocates argue that future threats lose their deterrent effect when there is a lack of past demonstrations. Past punishment, then, serves as an educational tool. It is a substitute for or reinforcement of threats of future punishment.

As with the goals mentioned above, the empirical question of whether punishment has this effect is a disputed one.[6] I shall not attempt to resolve this question here, but will assume *arguendo* that punishment even as presently administered has some deterrent effect. It is the moral question which is disturbing. Can an argument from deterrence alone 'justify' in any sense the infliction of pain on a criminal? It is particularly disquieting that the actual levying of punishment is done not for the criminal himself, but for the educational impact it will have on the community. The criminal act becomes the occasion of, but not the reason for, the punishment. In this way, the actual crime becomes little more than an excuse for punishing.

Surely this distorts the proper functioning of the judicial process. For if deterrence is the end it is unimportant whether the individual actually committed the crime. Since the public's perception of guilt is the prerequisite of the deterrent effect, all that is required for deterrence is that the individual is 'proved' to have committed the crime. The actual occurrence would have no relevance except insofar as a truly guilty person is easier to prove guilty. The judicial process becomes, not a truth-seeking device, but solely a means to legitimate the use of force. To treat criminals as means to the ends of others in this way raises serious moral problems. This is not to argue that men may never use others as means but rather to question the use of force against the individual because of the effect such use will have on others. It was this that concerned del Vecchio when he stated that 'the human person always bears in himself something sacred, and it is therefore not permissible to treat him merely as a means towards an end outside of himself'.[7]

[. . .]

It is not my thesis that deterrence, reformation, and disablement are undesirable goals. On the contrary, any criminal justice system should be critically examined to see if it is having these and other beneficial effects. The view advanced here is simply that these utilitarian benefits must be incidental to a just system; they cannot, alone or in combination, justify a criminal justice system. Something more is needed. There is another more antiquated strain of punishment theory which seeks to address this problem. The *moral* justifications of punishment view punishment as an end in itself. This approach has taken many forms.[8] On this view, whatever ill or beneficial results it might have, punishment of lawbreakers is good for its own sake. This proposition can be analyzed on several levels.

The most basic question is the truth of the claim itself. Some have argued that 'the alleged absolute justice of repaying evil with evil (maintained by Kant and many other writers) is really an empty sophism. If we go back to the Christian moralists, we find that an evil is to be put right only by doing good.'[9] This question is beyond the scope of this treatment. The subject has been extensively dealt with by those more knowledgeable than I.[10] The more relevant question is what such a view of punishment as a good can be said to imply for a system of criminal justice. Even assuming that it would be good if, in the nature of things, the wicked got their 'come-uppance', what behavior does this moral fact justify? Does it justify the victim authoring the punishment of his offender? Does it justify the same action by the victim's family, his friends, his neighbors, the state? If so what punishment should be imposed and who should decide?

It might be argued that the natural punishment for the violation of natural rights is the deserved hatred and scorn of the community, the resultant ostracism, and the existential hell of *being* an evil person. The question then is not whether we have the right to inflict some 'harm' or unpleasantness on a morally contemptible person – surely, we do; the question is not whether such a punishment is 'good' – arguably, it is. The issue is whether the 'virtue of some punishment' justifies the *forceful* imposition of unpleasantness on a *rights violator* as distinguished from the morally imperfect. Any *moral* theory of punishment must recognize and deal with this distinction. Finally, it must be established that the state is the legitimate author of punishment, a proposition which further assumes the moral and legal legitimacy of the state. To raise these issues is not to resolve them, but it would seem that the burden of proof is on those seeking to justify the use of force against the individual. Suffice it to say that I am skeptical of finding any theory which justifies the deliberate, forceful imposition of punishment within or without a system of criminal justice.

[...]

Punishment, particularly state punishment is the descendant of the tradition which imparts religious and moral authority to the sovereign and through him, the community. Such an authority is increasingly less credible in a secular world such as ours. Today there is an increasing desire to allow each individual to govern his own life as he sees fit provided he does not violate the rights of others. This desire is exemplified by current attitudes toward drug use, abortion, and pornography. Few argue that these things are good. It is only said that where there is no victim the state or community has no business meddling in the peaceful behavior of its citizens, however morally suspect it may be.[11]

Furthermore, if the paradigm of punishment is in a 'crisis period' it is as much because of its practical drawbacks as the uncertainty of its moral status. The infliction of suffering on a criminal tends to cause a general feeling of sympathy for him. There is no rational connection between a term of imprisonment and the harm caused the victim. Since the prison term is supposed to be unpleasant, at least a part of the public comes to see the criminal as a victim, and the lack of rationality also causes the offender to feel victimized. This reaction is magnified by the knowledge that most crimes go unpunished and that even if the offender is caught the judicial process is long, arduous, and far removed from the criminal act. While this is obvious to most, it is perhaps less obvious that the punishment paradigm is largely at fault. The slow, ponderous nature of our system of justice is largely due to a fear of an unjust infliction of punishment on the innocent (or even the guilty). The more awful the sanction, the more elaborate need be the safeguards. The more the system is perceived as arbitrary and unfair, the more incentive there is for defendants and their counsel to thwart the truth-finding process. Acquittal becomes desirable at all costs. As the punitive aspect of a sanction is diminished, so too would be the perceived need for procedural protections.

A system of punishment, furthermore, offers no incentive for the victim to involve himself in the criminal justice process other than to satisfy his feelings of duty or revenge. The victim stands to gain little if at all by the conviction and punishment of the person who caused his loss. This is true even of those systems discussed below which dispense state compensation based on the victim's need. The system of justice itself imposes uncompensated costs by requiring a further loss of time and money by the victim and witnesses and by increasing the perceived risk of retaliation.

[...]

Outline of a new paradigm

The idea of restitution is actually quite simple. It views crime as an offence by one individual against the rights of another. The victim has suffered a loss. Justice consists of the culpable offender making good the loss he has caused. It calls for a complete refocusing of our image of crime. Kuhn would call it a 'shift of world-view'. Where we once saw an offence against society, we now see an offence against an individual victim. In a way, it is a common sense view of crime. *The armed robber did not rob society; he robbed the victim.* His debt, therefore, is not to society; it is to the victim. There are really two types of restitution proposals: a system of 'punitive' restitution and a 'pure' restitutional system.

1. Punitive restitution. 'Since rehabitation was admitted to the aims of penal law two centuries ago, the number of penological aims has remained virtually constant. Restitution is waiting to come in.'[12] Given this view, restitution should merely be added to the paradigm of punishment. Stephen Schafer outlines the proposal: '[Punitive] restitution, like punishment, must always be the subject of judicial consideration. Without exception it must be carried out by personal performance by the wrong-doer, and should even then be equally burdensome and just for all criminals, irrespective of their means, whether they be millionaires or labourers.'[13]

There are many ways by which such a goal might be reached. The offender might be forced to compensate the victim by his own work, either in prison or out. If it came out of his pocket or from the sale of his property this would compensate the victim, but it would not be sufficiently proportionate for the offender. Another proposal would be that the fines be proportionate to the earning power of the criminal. Thus, 'A poor man would pay in days of work, a rich man by an equal number of days' income or salary.'[14] Herbert Spencer made a proposal along similar lines in his excellent 'Prison Ethics', which is well worth examining.[15] Murray N. Rothbard and others have proposed a system of 'double payments' in cases of criminal behavior.[16] While closer to pure restitution than other proposals, the 'double damages' concept preserves a punitive aspect.

Punitive restitution is an attempt to gain the benefits of pure restitution, which will be considered shortly, while retaining the perceived advantages of the paradigm of punishment. Thus, the prisoner is still 'sentenced' to some unpleasantness – prison labor or loss of X number of days' income. That the intention is to preserve the 'hurt' is indicated by the hesitation to accept an out-of-pocket payment or sale of assets. This is considered too 'easy' for the criminal and takes none of his time. The amount of payment is determined not by the *actual harm* but by the *ability of the offender to pay*. Of course, by retaining the paradigm of punishment this proposal involves many of the problems we raised earlier. In this sense it can be considered another attempt to salvage the old paradigm.

2. Pure restitution. 'Recompense or restitution is scarcely a punishment as long as it is merely a matter of returning stolen goods or money . . . The point is not that the offender deserves to suffer; it is rather that the offended party desires compensation.'[17] This represents the complete overthrow of the paradigm of punishment. No longer would the deterrence, reformation, disablement, or rehabilitation of the criminal be the guiding principle of the judicial system. The attainment of these goals would be incidental to, and as a result of, reparations paid to the victim. No longer would the criminal deliberately be made to suffer for his mistake. Making good that mistake is all that would be required. What follows is a possible scenario of such a system.

When a crime occurred and a suspect was apprehended, a trial court would attempt to determine his guilt or innocence. If found guilty, the criminal would be sentenced to make restitution to the victim.[18] If a criminal is able to make restitution immediately, he may do so. This would discharge his liability. If he were unable to make restitution, but were found by the court to be trustworthy, he would be permitted to remain at his job (or find a new one) while paying restitution out of his future wages. This would entail a legal claim against future wages. Failure to pay could result in garnishment or a new type of confinement.

If it is found that the criminal is not trustworthy, or that he is unable to gain employment, he would be confined to an employment project.[19] This would be an industrial enterprise, preferably run by a private concern, which would produce actual goods or services. The level of security at each employment project would vary according to the behavior of the offenders. Since the costs would be lower, inmates at a lower-security project would receive higher wages. There is no reason why many workers could not be permitted to live with their families inside or outside the facility, depending again, on the trustworthiness of the offender. Room and board would be deducted from the wages first, then a certain amount for restitution. Anything over that amount the worker could keep or apply toward further restitution, thus hastening his release. If a worker refused to work, he would be unable to pay for his maintenance, and therefore would not in principle be entitled to it. If he did not make restitution he could not be released. The exact arrangement which would best provide for high productivity, minimal security, and maximum incentive to work and repay the victim cannot be determined in advance. Experience is bound to yield some plans superior to others. In fact, the experimentation has already begun.[20]

While this might be the basic system, all sorts of refinements are conceivable, and certainly many more will be invented as needs arise. A few examples might be illuminating. With such a system of repayment, victim *crime insurance* would be more economically feasible than at present and highly desirable. The cost of awards would be offset by the insurance company's right to restitution in place of the victim (right of subrogation). The insurance company would be better suited to supervise the offender and mark his progress than would the victim. To obtain an earlier recovery, it could be expected to innovate so as to enable the worker to repay more quickly (and, as a result, be released that much sooner). The insurance companies might even underwrite the employment projects themselves as well as related industries which would employ the skilled worker after his release. Any successful effort on their part to reduce crime and recidivism would result in fewer claims and lower premiums. The benefit of this insurance scheme for the victim is immediate compensation, conditional on the victim's continued cooperation with the authorities for the arrest and conviction of the suspect. In addition, the centralization of victim claims would, arguably, lead to efficiencies which would permit the pooling of small claims against a common offender.

Another highly useful refinement would be *direct arbitration* between victim and criminal. This would serve as a sort of healthy substitute for plea bargaining. By allowing the guilty criminal to negotiate a reduced payment in return for a guilty plea, the victim (or his insurance company) would be saved the risk of an adverse finding at trial and any possible additional expense that might result. This would also allow an indigent criminal to substitute personal services for monetary payments if all parties agreed.

Arbitration is argued for by John M. Greacen, deputy director of the National Institute for Law Enforcement and Criminal Justice. He sees the possible advantages of such reform as the '... development of more creative dispositions for most criminal cases; for criminal victims the increased use of restitution, the knowledge that their interests were considered in the criminal process; and an increased satisfaction with the outcome; increased awareness in the part of the offender that his crime was committed against another human being, and not against society in general; increased possibility that the criminal process will cause the offender to acknowledge responsibility for his acts.'[21] Greacen notes several places where such a system has been tried with great success, most notably Tucson, Arizona, and Columbus, Ohio.[22]

Something analogous to the medieval Irish system of *sureties* might be employed as well.[23] Such a system would allow a concerned person, group, or company to make restitution (provided the offender agrees to this). The worker might then be released in the custody of the surety. If the surety had made restitution, the offender would owe restitution to the surety who might enforce the whole claim or show mercy. Of course, the more violent and unreliable the offender, the more serious and costly the offence, the less likely it would be that anyone would take the risk. But for first offenders, good workers, or others that charitable interests found deserving (or perhaps unjustly convicted) this would provide an avenue of respite.

Restitution and rights

These three possible refinements clearly illustrate the flexibility of a restitutional system. It may be less apparent that this flexibility is *inherent* to the restitutional paradigm. Restitution recognizes rights in the victim, and this is a principal source of its strength. The nature and limit of the victim's right to restitution at the same time defines the nature and limit of the criminal liability. In this way, the aggressive action of the criminal creates a *debt* to the victim. The recognition of rights and obligations make possible many innovative arrangements. Subrogation, arbitration, and suretyship are three examples mentioned above. They are possible because this right to compensation[24] is considered the property of the victim and can therefore be delegated, assigned, inherited, or bestowed. One could determine in advance who would acquire the right to any restitution which he himself might be unable to collect.

[...]

Advantages of a restitutional system

1. The first and most obvious advantage is the assistance provided to victims of crime. They may have suffered an emotional, physical, or financial loss. Restitution would not change the fact that a possibly traumatic crime has

occurred (just as the award of damages does not undo tortious conduct). Restitution, however, would make the resulting loss easier to bear for both victims and their families. At the same time, restitution would avoid a major pitfall of victim compensation/welfare plans: Since it is the criminal who must pay, the possibility of collusion between victim and criminal to collect 'damages' from the state would be all but eliminated.

2. The possibility of receiving compensation would encourage victims to report crimes and to appear at trial. This is particularly true if there were a crime insurance scheme which contractually committed the policyholder to testify as a condition for payment, thus rendering unnecessary oppressive and potentially tyrannical subpoenas and contempt citations. Even the actual reporting of the crime to police is likely to be a prerequisite for compensation. Such a requirement in auto theft insurance policies has made car thefts the most fully reported crime in the United States. Furthermore, insurance companies which paid the claim would have a strong incentive to see that the criminal was apprehended and convicted. Their pressure and assistance would make the proper functioning of law enforcement officials all the more likely.

3. Psychologist Albert Eglash has long argued that restitution would aid in the rehabilitation of criminals. 'Restitution is something an inmate does, not something done for or to him ... Being reparative, restitution can alleviate guilt and anxiety, which can otherwise precipitate further offences.'[25] Restitution, says Eglash, is an active effortful role on the part of the offender. It is socially constructive, thereby contributing to the offender's self-esteem. It is related to the offence and may thereby redirect the thoughts which motivated the offence. It is reparative, restorative, and may actually leave the situation better than it was before the crime, both for the criminal and victim.[26]

4. This is a genuinely 'self-determinative' sentence.[27] The worker would know that the length of his confinement was in his own hands. The harder he worked, the faster he would make restitution. He would be the master of his fate, and would have to face that responsibility. This would encourage useful, productive activity and instill a conception of reward for good behavior and hard work. Compare this with the current probationary system and 'indeterminate sentencing' where the decision for release is made by the prison bureaucracy, based only (if fairly administered) on 'good behavior'; that is, passive acquiescence to prison discipline. Also, the fact that the worker would be acquiring *marketable* skills rather than more skillful methods of crime should help to reduce the shocking rate of recidivism.

5. The savings to taxpayers would be enormous. No longer would the innocent taxpayers pay for the apprehension and internment of the guilty. The cost of arrest, trial, and internment would be borne by the criminal himself. In addition, since now-idle inmates would become productive workers (able, perhaps, to support their families), the entire economy would benefit from the increase in overall production.[28]

6. Crime would no longer pay. Criminals, particularly shrewd white-collar criminals, would know that they could not dispose of the proceeds of their crime and, if caught, simply serve time. They would have to make full restitution plus enforcement and legal costs, thereby greatly increasing the incentive to prosecute. While this would not eliminate such crime it would

make it rougher on certain types of criminals, like bank and corporation officials, who harm many by their acts with a virtual assurance of lenient legal sanctions.[29] It might also encourage such criminals to keep the money around for a while so that, if caught, they could repay more easily. This would make a full recovery more likely.

A restitutional system of justice would benefit the victim, the criminal, and the taxpayer. The humanitarian goals of proportionate punishment, rehabili- tation, and victim compensation are dealt with on a *fundamental* level making their achievement more likely. In short, the paradigm of restitution would benefit all but the entrenched penal bureaucracy and enhance justice at the same time. What then is there to stop us from overthrowing the paradigm of punishment and its penal system and putting in its place this more efficient, more humane, and more just system? The proponents of punishment and others have a few powerful counterarguments. It is to these we now turn.

Objections to restitution

1. Practical criticisms of restitution. It might be objected that 'crimes disturb and offend not only those who are directly their victim, but also the whole social order'.[30] Because of this, society, that is, individuals other than the victim, deserves some satisfaction from the offender. Restitution, it is argued, will not satisfy the lust for revenge felt by the victim or the 'community's sense of justice'. This criticism appears to be overdrawn. Today most members of the community are mere spectators of the criminal justice system, and this is largely true even of the victim.[31] One major reform being urged presently is more victim involvement in the criminal justice process.[32] The restitution proposal would necessitate this involvement. And while the public generally takes the view that officials should be tougher on criminals, with 'tougher' taken by nearly everyone to mean more severe in punishing, one must view this 'social fact' in light of the lack of a known alternative. The real test of public sympathies would be to see which sanction people would choose: incarceration of the criminal for a given number of years or the criminal's being compelled to make restitution to the victim: While the public's choice is not clearly predictable, neither can it be assumed that it would reject restitution. There is some evidence to the contrary [. . .].

This brings us to a second practical objection: that monetary sanctions are insufficient deterrents to crime. Again, this is something to be discovered, not something to be assumed. There are a number of reasons to believe that our *current* system of punishment does not adequately deter, and for the reasons discussed earlier an increase in the level of punishment is unlikely. In fact, many have argued that the deterrent value of sanctions has less to do with *severity* than with *certainty*,[33] and the preceding considerations indicate that law enforcement would be more certain under a restitutional system. In the final analysis, however, it is irrelevant to argue that more crimes may be committed if our proposal leaves the victim better off. It must be remembered: *Our goal is not the suppression of crime; it is doing justice to victims.*

[. . .]

This extract is taken from 'Restitution: a New Paradigm of Criminal Justice', by Randy E. Barnett, in Ethics, *Vol. 87 (1977), pp. 279–301.*

Notes

1 Kuhn, T. (1970) *The Structure of Scientific Revolutions* (2nd edn) (Chicago, IL: University of Chicago Press), p. 92.

2 Benn, S.I. (1967) 'Punishment', in Edwards, P. (ed.) *The Encyclopedia of Philosophy* (New York, NY: Macmillan) p. 29 (emphasis added).

3 Oppenheimer, H. (1913) *The Rationale of Punishment* (London: University of London Press), p. 255.

4 Ibid.

5 See Szasz, T. (1963) *Law, Liberty, and Psychiatry* (New York, NY: Macmillan).

6 See, e.g. Yochelson, S. and Samenow, S.E. (1976) *The Criminal Personality. Vol. 1. A Profile for Change* (New York, NY: Jason Aronson) pp. 411–16.

7 Del Vecchio, G. (1969) 'The Struggle against Crime', in Acton, H.B. (ed.) *The Philosophy of Punishment* (London: Macmillan), p. 199.

8 For a concise summary, see Oppenheimer, p. 31.

9 Del Vecchio, p. 198.

10 See, e.g. Kaufman, W. (1973) *Without Guilt and Justice* (New York, NY: Peter H. Wyden), esp. Chap. 2.

11 This problem is examined, though not ultimately resolved, by Edwin M. Schur in his book *Crimes without Victims – Deviant Behavior and Public Policy, Abortion, Homosexuality, and Drug Addiction* (Englewood Cliffs, NJ: Prentice Hall, 1965).

12 Mueller, G.O.W. (1965) 'Compensation for Victims of Crime: Thought before Action', *Minnesota Law Review*, 50, p. 221.

13 Schafer, S. (1970) *Compensation and Restitution to Victims of Crime* (2nd edn) (Montclair, NJ: Patterson-Smith), p. 127.

14 Ibid.

15 Spencer, H. (1907) 'Prison-Ethics', in *Essays: Scientific, Political and Speculative* (New York, NY: Appleton & Co.), 3, pp. 152–91.

16 Rothbard, M.N. (1972) *Libertarian Forum*, 14:1, pp. 7–8.

17 Kaufmann, p. 55.

18 The nature of judicial procedure best designed to carry out this task must be determined. For a brief discussion of some relevant considerations, see Laster, R.E. (1970) 'Criminal Restitution: A Survey of its Past History and an Analysis of its Present Usefulness', *University of Richmond Law Review*, 5, pp. 80–98; Galaway, B. and Hudson, J. (1975) 'Issues in the Correctional Implementation of Restitution to Victims of Crime', in Galaway, B. and Hudson, J. (eds) *Considering the Victim: Readings in Restitution and Victim Compensation* (Springfield, IL: Charles C. Thomas), pp. 351–60. Also to be dealt with is the proper standard of compensation. At least initially, the problem of how much payment constitutes restitution would be no different than similar considerations in tort law. [. . .]

19 Such a plan (with some significant differences) has been suggested by Smith, K.J. in *A Cure for Crime: The Case for the Self-determinate Prison Sentence* (London: Duckworth, 1965), pp. 13–29; see also Tannehill, M. and Tannehill, L. (1970) *The Market for Liberty* (Lansing, MI, privately printed), pp. 44–108.

20 For a recent summary report, see Galaway, B. (1977) 'Restitution as an Integrative Punishment.' Paper prepared for the Symposium on Crime and Punishment: Restitution, Retribution, and Law, Harvard Law School, March.

21 Greacen, J.M. (1975) 'Arbitration: A Tool for Criminal Cases?', *Barrister*, Winter, p. 53; see also Galaway and Hudson, pp. 352–55; 'Conclusions and Recommendations, International Study Institute on Victimology, Bellagio, Italy, July 1–12', *Victimology*, 1 (1976), pp. 150–1; Goldfarb, R. (1976) *Jails: The Ultimate Ghetto* (Garden City, NY: Anchor Press/Doubleday) p. 480.

22 Greacen, p. 53.

23 For a description of the Irish system, see Peden, J.R. (1973) 'Property Rights in Medieval Ireland: Celtic Law versus Church and State.' Paper presented at the Symposium on the Origins and Development of Property Rights, University of San Francisco, January; for a theoretical discussion of a similar proposal, see Spencer, pp. 182–6.

24 Or, perhaps more accurately, the compensation itself.

25 Eglash, A. (1958) 'Creative Restitution: Some Suggestions for Prison Rehabilitation Programs', *American Journal of Correction*, 40: November–December, p. 20.

26 Ibid.; see also Eglash's 'Creative Restitution: A Broader Meaning for an Old Term', *Journal of Criminal Law and Criminology*, 48, 1958, pp. 619–22; Galaway, B. and Hudson, J. (1972) 'Restitution and Rehabilitation – Some Central Issues', *Crime and Delinquency*, 18, pp. 403–10.

27 Smith, pp. 13–29.

28 An economist who favors restitution on efficiency grounds is Gary S. Becker, although he does not break with the paradigm of punishment. Those interested in a mathematical 'cost-benefit' analysis should see his 'Crime and Punishment', *Journal of Political Economy*, 76, 1968, pp. 169–217.

29 This point is also made by Minocher Jehangirji Sethna in his paper, 'Treatment and Atonement for Crime', in Viano, E.C. (ed.) *Victims and Society* (Washington, DC: Visage Press, 1976), p. 538.

30 Del Vecchio, p. 198.

31 McDonald, W.F. (1976) 'Towards a Bicentennial Revolution in Criminal Justice: The Return of the Victim', *American Criminal Law Review*, 13, p. 659; see also his paper 'Notes on the Victim's Role in the Prosecutional and Dispositional Stages of the Criminal Justice Process' (presented at the Second International Symposium on Victimology, Boston, September, 1976); Kress, J.M. (1976) 'The Role of the Victim at Sentencing.' Paper presented at the Second International Symposium on Victimology, Boston, September.

32 McDonald, pp. 669–73; Kress, pp. 11–15. Kress specifically analyzes restitution as a means for achieving victim involvement.

33 Yochelson and Samenow, pp. 453–57.

3. Conflicts as property

Nils Christie

Introduction

Maybe we should not have any criminology. Maybe we should rather abolish institutes, not open them. Maybe the social consequences of criminology are more dubious than we like to think.

I think they are. And I think this relates to my topic – conflicts as property. My suspicion is that criminology to some extent has amplified a process where conflicts have been taken away from the parties directly involved and thereby have either disappeared or become other people's property. In both cases a deplorable outcome. Conflicts ought to be used, not only left in erosion. And they ought to be used, and become useful, for those originally involved in the conflict. Conflicts *might* hurt individuals as well as social systems. That is what we learn in school. That is why we have officials. Without them, private vengeance and vendettas will blossom. We have learned this so solidly that we have lost track of the other side of the coin: our industrialised large-scale society is not one with too many internal conflicts. It is one with too little. Conflicts might kill, but too little of them might paralyse. I will use this occasion to give a sketch of this situation. It cannot be more than a sketch. This paper represents the beginning of the development of some ideas, not the polished end-product.

On happenings and non-happenings

Let us take our point of departure far away. Let us move to Tanzania. Let us approach our problem from the sunny hillside of the Arusha province. Here, inside a relatively large house in a very small village, a sort of happening took place. The house was overcrowded. Most grown-ups from the village and several from adjoining ones were there. It was a happy happening, fast talking, jokes, smiles, eager attention, not a sentence was to be lost. It was circus, it was drama. It was a court case.

The conflict this time was between a man and a woman. They had been engaged. He had invested a lot in the relationship through a long period, until she broke it off. Now he wanted it back. Gold and silver and money were easily decided on, but what about utilities already worn, and what about general expenses?

The outcome is of no interest in our context. But the framework for conflict solution is. Five elements ought to be particularly mentioned:

1. The parties, the former lovers, were in *the centre* of the room and in the centre of everyone's attention. They talked often and were eagerly listened to.

2. Close to them were relatives and friends who also took part. But they did not *take over*.

57

3. There was also participation from the general audience with short questions, information, or jokes.

4. The judges, three local party secretaries, were extremely inactive. They were obviously ignorant with regard to village matters. All the other people in the room were experts. They were experts on norms as well as actions. And they crystallised norms and clarified what had happened through participation in the procedure.

5. No reporters attended. They were all there.

My personal knowledge when it comes to British courts is limited indeed. I have some vague memories of juvenile courts where I counted some 15 or 20 persons present, mostly social workers using the room for preparatory work or small conferences. A child or a young person must have attended, but except for the judge, or maybe it was the clerk, nobody seemed to pay any particular attention. The child or young person was most probably utterly confused as to who was who and for what, a fact confirmed in a small study by Peter Scott (1959). In the United States of America, Martha Baum (1968) has made similar observations. Recently, Bottoms and McClean (1976) have added another important observation: 'There is one truth which is seldom revealed in the literature of the law or in studies of the administration of criminal justice. It is a truth which was made evident to all those involved in this research project as they sat through the cases which made up our sample. The truth is that, for the most part, the business of the criminal courts is dull, commonplace, ordinary and after a while downright tedious.'

But let me keep quiet about your system, and instead concentrate on my own. And let me assure you: what goes on is no happening. It is all a negation of the Tanzanian case. What is striking in nearly all the Scandinavian cases is the greyness, the dullness, and the lack of any important audience. Courts are not central elements in the daily life of our citizens, but peripheral in four major ways:

1. They are situated in the administrative centres of the towns, outside the territories of ordinary people.

2. Within these centres they are often centralised within one or two large buildings of considerable complexity. Lawyers often complain that they need months to find their way within these buildings. It does not demand much fantasy to imagine the situation of parties or public when they are trapped within these structures. A comparative study of court architecture might become equally relevant for the sociology of law as Oscar Newman's (1972) study of defensible space is for criminology. But even without any study, I feel it safe to say that both physical situation and architectural design are strong indicators that courts in Scandinavia belong to the administrators of law.

3. This impression is strengthened when you enter the courtroom itself – if you are lucky enough to find your way to it. Here again, the periphery of the parties is the striking observation. The parties are represented, and it is these representatives and the judge or judges who express the little activity that is activated within these rooms. Honoré Daumier's famous drawings from the courts are as representative for Scandinavia as they are for France.

There are variations. In the small cities, or in the countryside, the courts are more easily reached than in the larger towns. And at the very lowest end of the court system – the so-called arbitration boards – the parties are sometimes less heavily represented through experts in law. But the symbol of the whole system is the Supreme Court where the directly involved parties do not even attend their own court cases.

4. I have not yet made any distinction between civil and criminal conflicts. But it was not by chance that the Tanzania case was a civil one. Full participation in your own conflict presupposes elements of civil law. The key element in a criminal proceeding is that the proceeding is converted from something between the concrete parties into a conflict between one of the parties and the state. So, in a modern criminal trial, two important things have happened. First, the parties are being *represented*. Secondly, the one party that is represented by the state, namely the victim, is so thoroughly represented that she or he for most of the proceedings is pushed completely out of the arena, reduced to the triggerer-off of the whole thing. She or he is a sort of double loser; first, *vis-à-vis* the offender, but secondly and often in a more crippling manner by being denied rights to full participation in what might have been one of the more important ritual encounters in life. The victim has lost the case to the state.

Professional thieves

As we all know, there are many honourable as well as dishonourable reasons behind this development. The honourable ones have to do with the state's need for conflict reduction and certainly also its wishes for the protection of the victim. It is rather obvious. So is also the less honourable temptation for the state, or Emperor, or whoever is in power, to use the criminal case for personal gain. Offenders might pay for their sins. Authorities have in time past shown considerable willingness, in representing the victim, to act as receivers of the money or other property from the offender. Those days are gone; the crime control system is not run for profit. And yet they are not gone. There are, in all banality, many interests at stake here, most of them related to professional-isation.

Lawyers are particularly good at stealing conflicts. They are trained for it. They are trained to prevent and solve conflicts. They are socialised into a sub-culture with a surprisingly high agreement concerning interpretation of norms, and regarding what sort of information can be accepted as relevant in each case. Many among us have, as laymen, experienced the sad moments of truth when our lawyers tell us that our best arguments in our fight against our neighbour are without any legal relevance whatsoever and that we for God's sake ought to keep quiet about them in court. Instead they pick out arguments we might find irrelevant or even wrong to use. My favourite example took place just after the war. One of my country's absolutely top defenders told with pride how he had just rescued a poor client. The client had collaborated with the Germans. The prosecutor claimed that the client had been one of the key people in the organisation of the Nazi movement. He had been one of the master-minds behind it all. The defender, however, saved his client. He saved him by pointing out to the jury how weak, how lacking in ability, how obviously deficient his client was, socially as well as organisationally. His client could simply not have been one of the organisers among the collaborators; he was without talents. And he won his case. His client got a very minor sentence as a very minor figure. The defender ended his story by telling me – with some indignation – that neither the accused, nor his wife, had ever thanked him, they had not even talked to him afterwards.

Conflicts become the property of lawyers. But lawyers don't hide that it is conflicts they handle. And the organisational framework of the courts underlines this point. The opposing parties, the judge, the ban against privileged communication within the court system, the lack of encouragement for specialisation – specialists cannot be internally controlled – it all underlines that this is an organisation for the handling of conflicts. *Treatment personnel* are in another position. They are more interested in *converting the image of the case from one of conflict into one of non-conflict*. The basic model of healers is not one of opposing parties, but one where one party has to be helped in the direction of one generally accepted goal – the preservation or restoration of health. They are not trained into a system where it is important that parties can control each other. There is, in the ideal case, nothing to control, because there is only one goal. Specialisation is encouraged. It increases the amount of available knowledge, and the loss of internal control is of no relevance. A conflict perspective creates unpleasant doubts with regard to the healer's suitability for the job. A non-conflict perspective is a precondition for defining crime as a legitimate target for treatment.

One way of reducing attention to the conflict is reduced attention given to the victim. Another is concentrated attention given to those attributes in the criminal's background which the healer is particularly trained to handle. Biological defects are perfect. So also are personality defects when they are established far back in time – far away from the recent conflict. And so are also the whole row of explanatory variables that criminology might offer. We have, in criminology, to a large extent functioned as an auxiliary science for the professionals within the crime control system. We have focused on the offender, made her or him into an object for study, manipulation and control. We have added to all those forces that have reduced the victim to a nonentity and the offender to a thing. And this critique is perhaps not only relevant for the old criminology, but also for the new criminology. While the old one explained crime from personal defects or social handicaps, the new criminology explains crime as the result of broad economic conflicts. The old criminology loses the conflicts, the new one converts them from interpersonal conflicts to class conflicts. And they are. They are class conflicts – also. But, by stressing this, the conflicts are again taken away from the directly involved parties. So, as a preliminary statement: Criminal conflicts have either become *other people's property* – primarily the property of lawyers – or it has been in other people's interests to *define conflicts away*.

[. . .]

Conflicts as property

Conflicts are taken away, given away, melt away, or are made invisible. Does it matter, does it really matter?

Most of us would probably agree that we ought to protect the invisible victims just mentioned. Many would also nod approvingly to ideas saying that states, or Governments, or other authorities ought to stop stealing fines, and instead let the poor victim receive this money. I at least would approve such an arrangement. But I will not go into that problem area here and now. Material compensation is not what I have in mind with the formulation 'conflicts as property'. It is the *conflict itself* that represents the most interesting property taken away, not the goods originally taken away from the victim or given back to him. In our types of society, conflicts are more scarce than property. And they are immensely more valuable.

They are valuable in several ways. Let me start at the societal level [. . .]. Highly industrialised societies face major problems in organising their members in ways such that a decent quota take part in any activity at all. Segmentation according to age and sex can be seen as shrewd methods for segregation. Participation is such a scarcity that insiders create monopolies against outsiders, particularly with regard to work. In this perspective, it will easily be seen that conflicts represent a *potential for activity, for participation.* Modern criminal control systems represent one of the many cases of lost opportunities for involving citizens in tasks that are of immediate importance to them. Ours is a society of task-monopolists.

The victim is a particularly heavy loser in this situation. Not only has he suffered, lost materially or become hurt, physically or otherwise. And not only does the state take the compensation. But above all he has lost participation in his own case. It is the Crown that comes into the spotlight, not the victim. It is the Crown that describes the losses, not the victim. It is the Crown that appears in the newspaper, very seldom the victim. It is the Crown that gets a chance to talk to the offender, and neither the Crown nor the offender are particularly interested in carrying on that conversation. The prosecutor is fed-up long since. The victim would not have been. He might have been scared to death, panic-stricken, or furious. But he would not have been uninvolved. It would have been one of the important days in his life. Something that belonged to him has been taken away from that victim.[1]

But the big loser is us – to the extent that society is us. This loss is first and foremost a loss in *opportunities for norm-clarification.* It is a loss of pedagogical possibilities. It is a loss of opportunities for a continuous discussion of what represents the law of the land. How wrong was the thief, how right was the victim? Lawyers are, as we saw, trained into agreement on what is relevant in a case. But that means a trained incapacity in letting the parties decide what *they* think is relevant. It means that it is difficult to stage what we might call a political debate in the court. When the victim is small and the offender big – in size or power – how blameworthy then is the crime? And what about the opposite case, the small thief and the big house-owner? If the offender is well educated, ought he then to suffer more, or maybe less, for his sins? Or if he is black, or if he is young, or if the other party is an insurance company, or if his wife has just left him, or if his factory will break down if he has to go to jail, or if his daughter will lose her fiancé, or if he was drunk, or if he was sad, or if he was mad? There is no end to it. And maybe there ought to be none. Maybe Barotse law as described by Max Gluckman (1967) is a better instrument for norm-clarification, allowing the conflicting parties to bring in the whole chain of old complaints and arguments each time. Maybe decisions on relevance and on the weight of what is found relevant ought to be taken away from legal scholars, the chief ideologists of crime control systems, and brought back for free decisions in the court-rooms.

A further general loss – both for the victim and for society in general – has to do with anxiety-level and misconceptions. It is again the possibilities for personalised encounters I have in mind. The victim is so totally out of the case that he has no chance, ever, to come to know the offender. We leave him outside, angry, maybe humiliated through a cross-examination in court, without any human contact with the offender. He has no alternative. He will need all the classical stereotypes around 'the criminal' to get a grasp on the whole thing. He has a need for understanding, but is instead a non-person in a Kafka play. Of course, he will go away more frightened than ever, more in need than ever of an explanation of criminals as non-human.

The offender represents a more complicated case. Not much introspection is needed to see that direct victim-participation might be experienced as painful indeed. Most of us would shy away from a confrontation of this character. That is the first reaction. But the second one is slightly more positive. Human beings have reasons for their actions. If the situation is staged so that reasons can be given (reasons as the parties see them, not only the selection lawyers have decided to classify as relevant), in such a case maybe the situation would not be all that humiliating. And, particularly, if the situation was staged in such a manner that the central question was not meting out guilt, but a thorough discussion of what could be done to undo the deed, then the situation might change. And this is exactly what ought to happen when the victim is re-introduced in the case. Serious attention will centre on the victim's losses. That leads to a natural attention as to how they can be softened. It leads into a discussion of restitution. The offender gets a possibility to change his position from being a listener to a discussion – often a highly unintelligible one – of how much pain he ought to receive, into a participant in a discussion of how he could make it good again. The offender has lost the opportunity to explain himself to a person whose evaluation of him might have mattered. He has thereby also lost one of the most important possibilities for being forgiven. Compared to the humiliations in an ordinary court – vividly described by Pat Carlen (1976) in [. . .] the *British Journal of Criminology* this is not obviously any bad deal for the criminal.

But let me add that I think we should do it quite independently of his wishes. It is not health-control we are discussing. It is crime control. If criminals are shocked by the initial thought of close confrontation with the victim, preferably a confrontation in the very local neighbourhood of one of the parties, what then? I know from recent conversations on these matters that most people sentenced are shocked. After all, they prefer distance from the victim, from neighbours, from listeners and maybe also from their own court case through the vocabulary and the behavioural science experts who might happen to be present. They are perfectly willing to give away their property right to the conflict. So the question is more: are *we* willing to let them give it away? Are we willing to give them this easy way out?[2]

Let me be quite explicit on one point: I am not suggesting these ideas out of any particular interest in the treatment or improvement of criminals. I am not basing my reasoning on a belief that a more personalised meeting between offender and victim would lead to reduced recidivism. Maybe it would. I think it would. As it is now, the offender has lost the opportunity for participation in a personal confrontation of a very serious nature. He has lost the opportunity to receive a type of blame that it would be very difficult to neutralise. However, I would have suggested these arrangements even if it was absolutely certain they had no effects on recidivism, maybe even if they had a negative effect. I would have done that because of the other, more general gains. And let me also add – it is not much to lose. As we all know today, at least nearly all, we have not been able to invent any cure for crime. Except for execution, castration or incarceration for life, no measure has a proven minimum of efficiency compared to any other measure. We might as well react to crime according to what closely involved parties find is just and in accordance with general values in society.

With this last statement, as with most of the others I have made, I raise many more problems than I answer. Statements on criminal politics, particularly from those with the burden of responsibility, are usually filled with answers. It is questions we need. The gravity of our topic makes us much too pedantic and thereby useless as paradigm-changers.

A victim-oriented court

There is clearly a model of neighbourhood courts behind my reasoning. But it is one with some peculiar features, and it is only these I will discuss in what follows.

First and foremost; it is a *victim-oriented* organisation. Not in its initial stage, though. The first stage will be a traditional one where it is established whether it is true that the law has been broken, and whether it was this particular person who broke it.

Then comes the second stage, which in these courts would be of the utmost importance. That would be the stage where the victim's situation was considered, where every detail regarding what had happened – legally relevant or not – was brought to the court's attention. Particularly important here would be detailed consideration regarding what could be done for him, first and foremost by the offender, secondly by the local neighbourhood, thirdly by the state. Could the harm be compensated, the window repaired, the lock replaced, the wall painted, the loss of time because the car was stolen given back through garden work or washing of the car ten Sundays in a row? Or maybe, when this discussion started, the damage was not so important as it looked in documents written to impress insurance companies? Could physical suffering become slightly less painful by any action from the offender, during days, months or years? But, in addition, had the community exhausted all resources that might have offered help? Was it absolutely certain that the local hospital could not do anything? What about a helping hand from the janitor twice a day if the offender took over the cleaning of the basement every

Saturday? None of these ideas is unknown or untried, particularly not in England. But we need an organisation for the systematic application of them.

Only after this stage was passed, and it ought to take hours, maybe days, to pass it, only then would come the time for an eventual decision on punishment. Punishment, then, becomes that suffering which the judge found necessary to apply *in addition to* those unintended constructive sufferings the offender would go through in his restitutive actions *vis-à-vis* the victim. Maybe nothing could be done or nothing would be done. But neighbourhoods might find it intolerable that nothing happened. Local courts out of tune with local values are not local courts. That is just the trouble with them, seen from the liberal reformer's point of view.

A fourth stage has to be added. That is the stage for service to the offender. His general social and personal situation is by now well-known to the court. The discussion of his possibilities for restoring the victim's situation cannot be carried out without at the same time giving information about the offender's situation. This might have exposed needs for social, educational, medical or religious action – not to prevent further crime, but because needs ought to be met. Courts are public arenas, needs are made visible. But it is important that this stage comes *after* sentencing. Otherwise we get a re-emergence of the whole array of so-called 'special measures' – compulsory treatments – very often only euphemisms for indeterminate imprisonment.

Through these four stages, these courts would represent a blend of elements from civil and criminal courts, but with a strong emphasis on the civil side.

A lay-oriented court

The second major peculiarity with the court model I have in mind is that it will be one with an extreme degree of lay-orientation. This is essential when conflicts are seen as property that ought to be shared. It is with conflicts as with so many good things; they are in no unlimited supply. Conflicts can be cared for, protected, nurtured. But there are limits. If some are given more access in the disposal of conflicts, others are getting less. It is as simple as that.

Specialisation in conflict solution is the major enemy; specialisation that in due – or undue – time leads to professionalisation. That is when the specialists get sufficient power to claim that they have acquired special gifts, mostly through education, gifts so powerful that it is obvious that they can only be handled by the certified craftsman.

With a clarification of the enemy, we are also able to specify the goal; let us reduce specialisation and particularly our dependence on the professionals within the crime control system to the utmost.

The ideal is clear; it ought to be a court of equals representing themselves. When they are able to find a solution between themselves, no judges are needed. When they are not, the judges ought also to be their equals.

Maybe the judge would be the easiest to replace, if we made a serious attempt to bring our present courts nearer to this model of lay orientation. We have lay judges already, in principle. But that is a far cry from realities. What we have, both in England and in my own country, is a sort of specialised non-specialist. First, they are used *again and again*. Secondly, some are even *trained*, given special courses or sent on excursions to foreign countries to learn about how to behave as a lay judge. Thirdly, most of them do also represent an extremely *biased sample* of the population with regard to sex, age, education, income, class[3] and personal experience as criminals. With real lay judges, I conceive of a system where nobody was given the right to take part in conflict solution more than a few times, and then had to wait until all other community members had had the same experience.

Should lawyers be admitted to court? We had an old law in Norway that forbids them to enter the rural districts. Maybe they should be admitted in stage one where it is decided if the man is guilty. I am not sure. Experts are as cancer to any lay body. It is exactly as Ivan Illich describes for the educational system in general. Each time you increase the length of compulsory education in a society, each time you also decrease the same population's trust in what they have learned and understood quite by themselves.

Behaviour experts represent the same dilemma. Is there a place for them in this model? Ought there to be any place? In stage 1, decisions on facts, certainly not. In stage 3, decisions on eventual punishment, certainly not. It is too obvious to waste words on. We have the painful row of mistakes from Lombroso, through the movement for social defence and up to recent attempts to dispose of supposedly dangerous people through predictions of who they are and when they are not dangerous any more. Let these ideas die, without further comments.

The real problem has to do with the service function of behaviour experts. Social scientists can be perceived as functional answers to a segmented society. Most of us have lost the physical possibility to experience the totality, both on the social system level and on the personality level. Psychologists can be seen as historians for the individual; sociologists have much the same function for the social system. Social workers are oil in the machinery, a sort of security counsel. Can we function without them, would the victim and the offender be worse off?

Maybe. But it would be immensely difficult to get such a court to function if they were all there. Our theme is social conflict. Who is not at least made slightly uneasy in the handling of her or his own social conflicts if we get to know that there is an expert on this very matter at the same table? I have no clear answer, only strong feelings behind a vague conclusion: let us have as few behaviour experts as we dare to. And if we have any, let us for God's sake not have any that specialise in crime and conflict resolution. Let us have generalised experts with a solid base outside the crime control system. And a last point with relevance for both behaviour experts and lawyers: if we find them unavoidable in certain cases or at certain stages, let us try to get across to them the problems they create for broad social participation. Let us try to get them to perceive themselves as resource-persons, answering when asked, but not domineering, not in the centre. They might help to stage conflicts, not take them over.

Rolling stones

There are hundreds of blocks against getting such a system to operate within our western culture. Let me only mention three major ones. They are:

1. There is a lack of neighbourhoods.
2. There are too few victims.
3. There are too many professionals around.

With lack of neighbourhoods I have in mind the very same phenomenon I described as a consequence of industrialised living; segmentation according to space and age. Much of our trouble stems from killed neighbourhoods or killed local communities. How can we then thrust towards neighbourhoods a task that presupposes they are highly alive? I have no really good arguments, only two weak ones. First, it is not quite that bad. The death is not complete. Secondly, one of the major ideas behind the formulation 'Conflicts as Property' is that it is neighbourhood-property. It is not private. It belongs to the system. It is intended as a vitaliser for neighbourhoods. The more fainting the neighbourhood is, the more we need neighbourhood courts as one of the many functions any social system needs for not dying through lack of challenge.

Equally bad is the lack of victims. Here I have particularly in mind the lack of personal victims. The problem behind this is again the large units in industrialised society. Woolworth or British Rail are not good victims. But again I will say: there is not a complete lack of personal victims, and their needs ought to get priority. But we should not forget the large organisations. They, or their boards, would certainly prefer not to have to appear as victims in 5,000 neighbourhood courts all over the country. But maybe they ought to be compelled to appear. If the complaint is serious enough to bring the offender into the ranks of the criminal, then the victim ought to appear. A related problem has to do with insurance companies – the industrialised alternative to friendship or kinship. Again we have a case where the crutches deteriorate the condition. Insurance takes the conseqences of crime away. We will therefore have to take insurance away. Or rather: we will have to keep the possibilities for compensation through the insurance companies back until in the procedure I have described it has been proved beyond all possible doubt that there are no other alternatives left – particularly that the offender has no possibilities whatsoever. Such a solution will create more paper-work, less predictability, more aggression from customers. And the solution will not necessarily be seen as good from the perspective of the policy-holder. But it will help to protect conflicts as social fuel.

None of these troubles can, however, compete with the third and last I will comment on: the abundance of professionals. We know it all from our own personal biographies or personal observations. And in addition we get it confirmed from all sorts of social science research: the educational system of any society is not necessarily synchronised with any needs for the product of this system. Once upon a time we thought there was a direct causal relation from the number of highly educated persons in a country to the Gross National

Product. Today we suspect the relationship to go the other way, if we are at all willing to use GNP as a meaningful indicator. We also know that most educational systems are extremely class-biased. We know that most academic people have had profitable investments in our education, that we fight for the same for our children, and that we also often have vested interests in making our part of the educational system even bigger. More schools for more lawyers, social workers, sociologists, criminologists. While I am *talking* deprofessionalisation, we are increasing the capacity to be able to fill up the whole world with them.

There is no solid base for optimism. On the other hand insights about the situation, and goal formulation, is a pre-condition for action. Of course, the crime control system is not the domineering one in our type of society. But it has some importance. And occurrences here are unusually well suited as pedagogical illustrations of general trends in society. There is also some room for manoeuvre. And when we hit the limits, or are hit by them, this collision represents in itself a renewed argument for more broadly conceived changes.

Another source for hope: ideas formulated here are not quite so isolated or in dissonance with the mainstream of thinking when we leave our crime control area and enter other institutions. I have already mentioned Ivan Illich with his attempts to get learning away from the teachers and back to active human beings. Compulsory learning, compulsory medication and compulsory consummation of conflict solutions have interesting similarities. When Ivan Illich and Paulo Freire are listened to, and my impression is that they increasingly are, the crime control system will also become more easily influenced.

Another, but related, major shift in paradigm is about to happen within the whole field of technology. Partly, it is the lessons from the third world that now are more easily seen, partly it is the experience from the ecology debate. The globe is obviously suffering from what we, through our technique, are doing to her. Social systems in the third world are equally obviously suffering. So the suspicion starts. Maybe the first world can't take all this technology either. Maybe some of the old social thinkers were not so dumb after all. Maybe social systems can be perceived as biological ones. And maybe there are certain types of large-scale technology that kill social systems, as they kill globes. Schumacher (1973) with his book *Small is Beautiful* and the related Institute for Intermediate Technology come in here. So do also the numerous attempts, particularly by several outstanding Institutes for Peace Research, to show the dangers in the concept of Gross National Product, and replace it with indicators that take care of dignity, equity and justice. The perspective developed in Johan Galtung's research group on World Indicators might prove extremely useful also within our own field of crime control.

There is also a political phenomenon opening vistas. At least in Scandinavia social democrats and related groupings have considerable power, but are without an explicated ideology regarding the goals for a reconstructed society. This vacuum is being felt by many, and creates a willingness to accept and even expect considerable institutional experimentation.

Then to my very last point: what about the universities in this picture? What about the new Centre in Sheffield? The answer has probably to be the old one: universities have to re-emphasise the old tasks of understanding and of criticising. But the task of training professionals ought to be looked into with renewed scepticism. Let us re-establish the credibility of encounters between critical human beings: low-paid, highly regarded, but with no extra power – outside the weight of their good ideas. That is as it ought to be.

This extract is taken from 'Conflicts as Property', by Nils Christie, in The British Journal of Criminology, *Vol. 17: 1 (Jan. 1977), pp. 1–5.*

Notes

1 For a preliminary report on victim dissatisfaction, see Vennard (1976).
2 I tend to take the same position with regard to a criminal's property right to his own conflict as John Locke on property rights to one's own life – one has no right to give it away (*cf.* C.B. MacPherson (1962)).
3 [. . .] see Baldwin (1976).

References

Baldwin, J. (1976) 'The Social Composition of the Magistracy', *British Journal of Criminology*, 16, pp. 171–4.

Baum, M. and Wheeler, S. (1968) 'Becoming an Inmate', in Wheeler, S. (ed.) *Controlling Delinquents* (New York: Wiley), pp. 153–87.

Bottoms, A.E. and McClean, J.D. (1976) *Defendants in the Criminal Process* (London: Routledge & Kegan Paul).

Carlen, P. (1976) 'The Staging of Magistrates' Justice', *British Journal of Criminology*, 16, pp. 48–55.

Gluckman, M. (1967) *The Judicial Process among the Barotse of Northern Rhodesia* (Manchester: Manchester University Press).

Kinberg, O., Inghe, G. and Riemer, S. (1943) *Incest-Problemet i Sverige*. Sth.

MacPherson, C.B. (1962) *The Political Theory of Possessive Individualism: Hobbes to Locke* (London: Oxford University Press).

Newman, O. (1972) *Defensible Space: People and Design in the Violent City* (London: Architectural Press).

Schumacher, E.F. (1973) *Small is Beautiful: A Study of Economics as if People Mattered* (London: Blond & Briggs).

Scott, P.D. (1959) 'Juvenile Courts: The Juvenile's Point of View', *British Journal of Delinquency*, 9, pp. 200–10.

Vennard, J. (1976) 'Justice and Recompense for Victims of Crime', *New Society*, 36, pp. 378–80.

4. Retributive justice, restorative justice

Howard Zehr

Let's start with what we know.

We know that the system we call 'criminal justice' does not work.

Certainly, at least, it does not work for victims.

Victims experience crime as deeply traumatic, as a violation of the self. They experience it as an assault on their sense of themselves as autonomous individuals in a predictable world. Crime raises fundamental questions of trust, of order, of faith. And this is true for many crimes we consider 'minor' as well as for serious violent crimes.

Victims have many needs. They need chances to speak their feelings. They need to receive restitution. They need to experience justice: victims need some kind of moral statement of their blamelessness, of who is at fault, that this thing should not have happened to them. They need answers to the questions that plague them. They need a restoration of power because the offender has taken power away from them.

Above all, perhaps, victims need an experience of forgiveness. I do not have time here to explore this fully, and certainly I am not suggesting that forgiveness comes easily. I want to suggest, though, that forgiveness is a process of letting go. Victims need to be able to let go of the crime experience so that, while it will always – must always be – part of them, it will no longer dominate their lives. Without that, closure is difficult and the wound may fester for many years.

Much more needs to be said about what victims feel and need than is possible here – this has been only the briefest summary. My point, though, is this: Victims have serious important needs, yet few, if any, of them will be met in the criminal justice process.

In fact, the injury may very well be compounded. Victims find that they are mere footnotes in the process we call justice. If they are involved in their case at all, it will likely be as witnesses; if the state does not need them as witnesses, they will not be part of their own case. The offender has taken power from them and now, instead of returning power to them, the criminal law system also denies them power.

For victims, then, the system just is not working.

But it is not working for offenders either.

It is not preventing offenders from committing crimes, as we know well from recidivism figures. And it is not healing them. On the contrary, the experience of punishment and of imprisonment is deeply damaging, often encouraging rather than discouraging criminal behavior.

Nor is the justice system holding offenders accountable. Judges often talk about accountability but what they usually mean is that when you do something wrong you must take your punishment. I want to suggest that real accountability means something quite different. Genuine accountability means,

69

first of all, that when you offend, you need to understand and take responsibility for what you did. Offenders need to be encouraged to understand the real human consequences of their actions. But accountability has a second component as well: Offenders need to be encouraged to take responsibility for making things right, for righting the wrong. Understanding one's actions and taking responsibility for making things right – that is the real meaning of accountability.

Unfortunately, though, our legal process does not encourage such accountability on the part of offenders. Nowhere in the process are offenders given the opportunity to understand the implications of what they have done. Nowhere are they encouraged to question the stereotypes and rationalizations ('It's no big deal; they deserved it; insurance will cover it') that made it possible for them to commit their offences. In fact, by focusing on purely legal issues, the criminal process will tend to sidetrack their attention, causing them to focus on legal, technical definitions of guilt, on the possibilities for avoiding punishment, on the injustices they perceive themselves to undergo.

The criminal process, then, not only fails to encourage a real understanding of what they have done: it actively discourages such a realization. And it does nothing to encourage offenders to take responsibility to right the wrong they have committed.

I am increasingly impressed at the parallels between what victims and offenders go through.

I have suggested that for victims, crime involves a question of power. Part of what is so dehumanizing about being a victim is that power has been taken away. What is needed for healing is an experience of empowerment.

But offenders also need an experience of empowerment. For many offenders, crime is a way of asserting power, of asserting self-identity, in a world which defines worth in terms of access to power. Crime, for many, is a way of saying 'I am somebody'. My friend, an armed robber, who grew up Black and poor, then spent 17 years in prison for his robberies, said it more clearly than most: 'At least when I had a shotgun in my hand I was somebody.'

Crime is often a way for offenders to assert power and worth, but in doing so they deny power to others. The unfortunate thing is that the criminal justice process compounds the problem by making pawns of both, by denying power to both victim and offender. The victim is left out of his or her own case; the offender's fate is decided by others, without encouragement to take responsibility for righting the wrong.

I have suggested that victims need to experience forgiveness. Offenders, too, need such an experience – how else are they to put their pasts behind them? But they also need opportunities for repentance and conversion. Confess, repent, turn around; admit responsibility, take responsibility for making things right, change directions – this is what needs to happen. But the criminal process has little room, provides little encouragement, for such events.

For offenders, the justice process will encourage anger, rationalization, denial of guilt and responsibility, feelings of powerlessness and dehumanization. As with victims, the wound will fester and grow.

So the system is not working for victims, and neither is it working for offenders.

We have known that for many years and have tried many reforms, and they have not worked either.

This is not to say that 'nothing works', that no 'reform' programs have been without good results for the persons involved. What does seem to be true is that most criminal justice reforms of the past century have not done what was intended. All too often they have been perverted, coopted, coming to serve ends different than those intended. They have not brought about substantial improvements in the process of justice. The system of justice seems to be so impregnated with self-interest, so adaptive, that it takes in any new idea, molds it, changes it until it suits the system's own purposes.

Why? Why are victims so ignored? Why are offenders dealt with so ineffectively? Why do so many reforms fail? Why is crime so mystified, so mythologized, so susceptible to the machinations of politics and the press?

It seems to me that the reasons are fundamental, that they have to do with our very definitions of crime and of justice. Consequently, the situation cannot be changed by simply providing compensation or assistance to victims, by providing the possibility of alternative sanctions for offenders, or by other sorts of 'tinkering'. We have to go to root understandings and assumptions.

Let's look at some of those assumptions and definitions.

When a crime is committed, we assume that the most important thing that can happen is to establish guilt. That is the focal point of our entire criminal process: to establish who did it. What to do with the person once guilt is established is almost an afterthought. The focus is on the past, not the future.

Another assumption we make is that of just deserts: everyone must get what is coming to them. The metaphysical order of the universe has been upset and the balance must be righted.

Everyone must get what is due, and what is due is pain. Nils Christie has been very helpful in teaching us to call a spade a spade: What we are doing is inflicting pain. Penal law would be more honestly called 'pain law' because in essence it is a system for inflicting graduated measures of pain.

Our legal system tends to define justice not by the outcome but by the process itself and by the intention behind it.

As Herman Bianchi has pointed out, it is the intention that matters. The intention of the law is to treat everyone fairly and equally, but whether that is actually achieved is less important than the design, the intention.

Moreover, the test of justice is whether or not the process was carried out correctly. We see justice as a system of right rules. Were the rules followed? If so, justice has been done. I could point to a variety of cases – including death penalty cases – where substantial questions of guilt or innocence remain unanswered but because the rules were followed, appeals have been exhausted and justice is considered to have been done.

So we define justice as the establishment of blame and the imposition of pain all administered according to right rules. But there is something even more basic: Our legal system defines crime as an offence against the state, the government. Legally it is the state which has been violated, and it is up to the state to respond. So it is a professional proxy for the state – the prosecutor who files charges, who pursues the case, who represents the victimized state. And it is a judge, another representative of the state, who decides the outcome.

It is no accident, then that the crime victim, the person who has been victimized is so left out of this process. He or she is not even part of the equation, not part of the definition of the offence. Victims are left out because they have no legal standing, because they are not part of the legal definition of the offence.

No wonder that in spite of our reforms, we have not been able to incorporate victims into the justice process in any integral way. While I think victim compensation and victim assistance are important programs, I am pessimistic about the possibilities for a substantial impact because they do not attack the fundamental issue – the definition of crime which excludes crime victims.

We define crime as an offence against the state. We define justice as the establishment of blame and the imposition of pain under the guidance of right rules.

I think it is essential to remember that this definition of crime and justice, as common-sensical as it may seem, is only one paradigm, only one possible way of looking at crime and at justice. We have been so dominated by our assumptions that we often assume it is the only way, or at least the only right way, to approach the issue.

It is not. It is not the only possible model or paradigm of justice – not logically, not historically.

Some of you may be aware of Thomas Kuhn's *The Structure of Scientific Revolutions*. Using the 17th-century scientific revolution as a model, Kuhn advances a theory of scientific revolutions which may have some bearing here.

Kuhn notes that the way we understand and explain the world at any time is governed by a particular model. A scientific revolution, and by implication an intellectual revolution, occurs when that model comes to be seen as inadequate and is replaced by a different model, a different way of understanding and explaining phenomenon [*sic*]. Scientific and intellectual 'revolutions' represent shifts in paradigms.

The classic scientific revolution of the 17th century is a case in point. Before Copernicus, human understanding of the universe was governed by the Ptolemaic paradigm or model. In this understanding the earth was central with planets and heavenly bodies whirling around in orbits which consisted of some sort of crystalline spheres. While this may seem ludicrous to us today, it seemed to fit what people saw and it meshed with important philosophical, scientific and theological assumptions. It was common-sensical. It was a paradigm which governed understandings and was used to explain phenomena.

For many years this paradigm seemed to fit, adequately explaining what was seen and experienced. But aberrations and dysfunctions cropped up – in fact, some were observed right from the start. At first, these aberrations seemed to offer no real threat to the paradigm. Adjustments could be made. For example, the phenomenon of retrograde motion – the fact that planets seemed to move backward briefly during rotation – was explained by adding 'epicycles' to the model. Apparently planets rotated in smaller orbits or spheres as they moved along in their larger orbits.

In the 16th century, Copernicus suggested a different model, one which put the sun at the center. Few, however, took his suggestion seriously. It flew in the face of too many assumptions, threatened too many theological and philosophical ideas. It seemed nonsensical. But by the early 17th century more accurate observations of the skies (made possible by telescopes and careful observations) began to create increasing problems in the old model. The number of 'epicycles' necessary to make the model work became ridiculous, for example.

Numerous efforts were made to shore up the model. Finally, though, a series of discoveries, synthesized by Isaac Newton in a new paradigm, brought about a revolution in our understanding of the universe. In this model, the sun is central to our galaxy. The 'laws' which govern the movement of planets are one with those which govern forces on the earth.

This understanding made modern science possible, became today's common sense, but is understood now by scientists to also be just one model, and an imperfect model at that. Newtonian physics is useful in everyday life, but it is inaccurate for much scientific work: The Einsteinian paradigm must be used to incorporate the complexity, the plasticity of time and space.

Kuhn's point, in short, is that the way we explain and make sense out of phenomena is governed by paradigms. Our paradigms, however, are often rather incomplete reflections of reality and do not adequately fit every situation. So we make adjustments, build in 'epicycles' to try to make them work. Gradually the number of aberrations grows. At the same time, we make attempts to salvage the model, adding more 'epicycles' until, hopefully, a new paradigm emerges, a new way of putting the pieces together that fits experience better. That is the structure, the pattern, of scientific and intellectual revolutions.

Why this long excursion into the history of science? First, it may help us to be more humble about our understandings, to see our definitions and assumptions as models rather than as absolutes. And second, it may suggest the possibility of a paradigm change in justice.

Randy Barnett has suggested that state-centered and punishment-centered assumptions constitute just such a paradigm and that this paradigm is in the process of breaking down. We may, he suggests, be on the verge of a revolution in our understanding of crime and justice.

As with the Ptolemaic paradigm, problems have been seen right from the start and they have multiplied with time. Thus we had to invent 'epicycles'.

The concept of proportionate punishment, an Enlightenment concept, was an attempt to limit the imposition of pain, to inflict it in measured, 'scientific' doses. It did not question the fact of imposing pain, but attempted to grade it to fit the offence. Prison caught on because it was a way of grading pain. Similarly, the Enlightenment did not question the centrality of the state's role, but concerned itself with limiting the arbitrary power of the state.

But that 'epicycle' did not work very well. Prisons also turned out to be brutal, needing reform right from the start. Even proportionate punishment failed to deter effectively. Proportionate punishment seemed to have its problems.

So the concept of rehabilitation was born, but that too led to problems. It didn't work and it was terribly susceptible to abuse. This reform, like the concept of proportionate punishment, attempted to rescue the paradigm without questioning fundamentals. When it did not work, the pendulum swung back to punishment. The underlying assumption that pain must be inflicted remains unquestioned.

Victim compensation, Barnett notes, can be seen as another such 'epicycle'. It, too, tries to tinker with the model, to correct a problem, but without asking basic questions.

But the dysfunctions are so great and so widely recognized that an intellectual revolution just might be possible. Disenchantment with the state/punishment paradigm with what might be called the 'retributive paradigm' is so great that we may be on the verge of a paradigm change.

There are certain problems in applying Kuhn's pattern of paradigm change. It does not, for example take into account the politics of paradigm change. However, I want to make two points here. First, there are glimmers of hope that change may be coming. And second, it is important for us to step back and realize that our model is only that – one model, one paradigm. Other models can be conceived.

In fact, other models have predominated throughout most of western history. It is difficult to realize sometimes that the paradigm which we consider so natural, so logical, has in fact governed our understanding of crime and justice for only a few centuries. We have not always done it like this.

Let me interject a warning here. What I am going to suggest will be a bit scattered. I am going to jump through centuries, generalizing rather freely. While I have been working on this for some time, I have not yet had time to assimilate all my reading. So my suggestions also must be considered somewhat tentative.

My thesis is that western (and possibly early near-eastern) history has been dominated by a dialectic between what Bruce Lenman and Geoffrey Parker have called 'community justice' and 'state justice'.

State justice reared its head early – you can see it already in the Code of Hammurabi – but it has only come to be predominate in the past several centuries. Instead, community justice has governed understandings throughout most of our history.

Several themes are important in an attempt to develop an historical perspective.

One theme has to do with the modern division between criminal and civil law. Criminal law is characterized by the centrality given to the state: The state is victim, and the state prosecutes. It is dominated by a coercive, punishment motif. Civil law, on the other hand, assumes that two private parties are in conflict, with the state being asked to arbitrate between them, and the outcome focuses largely on making things right, on compensation. The division of law into these two types is quite recent, an important historical development.

A second theme is included in the preceding theme. This is the idea that it is the state's responsibility, even monopoly, to prosecute. That too is new, although its roots go back to perhaps the 12th and 13th centuries.

A third theme is the assumption that punishment is normative. The idea of punishment is old, of course, but some scholars suggest that it is relatively recent that punitiveness became normal and dominant. This is contrary to common images of primitive, vigilante vengeance.

For most of our history in the West, nonjudicial, nonlegal dispute resolution techniques have dominated. People traditionally have been very reluctant to call in the state, even when the state claimed a role. In fact, a great deal of stigma was attached to going to the state and asking it to prosecute. For centuries the state's role in prosecution was quite minimal.

Instead, it was considered the business of the community to solve its own disputes. Even when state-operated courts became available, they were often places of last resort, and it was common to settle out of court after court proceedings had been initiated. Out-of-court settlements were so normal, in fact, that a new French legal code as late as 1670 prohibited the state from getting involved if the parties came to a settlement, even after proceedings had begun.

Most of our history has been dominated by informal dispute resolution processes for conflicts, including many of the conflicts today defined as crimes, and these processes highlighted negotiation/arbitration models. Agreements were negotiated, sometimes using community leaders or neighbors in key roles. Agreements were validated by local notables, by government notaries, by priests. Often parties would go before such a person, once an agreement was made, and make it binding. But it was negotiated rather than imposed.

To what extent these methods were used for the most serious crimes is still uncertain. Herman Bianchi, however, has argued that sanctuaries were a key part of western civilization for just this purpose: a place for those who committed the most serious crimes to run to, to be safe, while they negotiated an agreement with the victim and/or family.

The process emphasized negotiation, therefore, and the expected outcome was compensation. Restitution to victims was common, perhaps even normative, even though violent retribution is our usual picture.

Even an 'eye for an eye' justice focused on compensation. In some cases, it was a way of establishing restitution – the value of an eye for the value of an eye. Limit the response, in other words, and convert it to restitution.

When 'eye for an eye' justice was taken literally, however, it still was seen as compensation. When someone in a collectivist, tribal, clan society is killed or hurt, the balance of power between groups is upset. Balance is restored by repayment in kind. An eye for an eye, taken literally, is both a means of limiting violence and of compensating groups for the loss of, or damage to, one of its members.

Such justice is also a way of vindicating the victim. Both restitution and vengeance may often have been intended less to punish than to vindicate the moral rightness of the victim. In a small, tightly organized community, the victim needed a moral statement to the community that they were right and that the other person was wrong. They needed moral compensation.

So restitution was common. Violent revenge did occur, but it may not have happened as frequently as we often assume. And both restitution and vengeance may have been intended less as punishment than as moral vindication and as a means of balancing power.

Much more work needs to be done, but my point is this: We have had a long history of community justice in our culture. Until recently, it was not assumed that the state had a duty to prosecute most crimes, and certainly not assumed that the state had a monopoly on prosecution.

Through most of our history, two systems of justice have coexisted – state justice and community justice – which both complemented and conflicted with each other. Community justice tended to focus on restitution through a somewhat informal process of mediation and arbitration. State justice tended to be more punitive, more formal, and put the state at the center, although until recently it did not claim a monopoly.

Traditionally, at least on the Continent, when individuals wished to use state courts, individuals had to bring the complaint. The victim had to initiate proceedings and could decide when to terminate them. The state functioned as a kind of regulatory system. It was an accusatorial system: if you were a victim, you came forward and accused someone, and the state could not do anything unless you did this. If you did, the state would locate the accused person, bring them before you, and regulate the dispute. But the victim had to trigger the process and could terminate it as well.

During the 12th century, however, the state began to take a larger role and began to initiate some prosecutions. This process seems to have been tied, at least in part, to the revival of Roman law. It was during this time that Roman law was rediscovered; law schools began to teach it, and the Church picked it up and made it the basis of canon law.

The Inquisition was one outcome of this transformation of Roman law into canon law. In the Inquisition, the Church initiated prosecution, sought evidence and carried the prosecution through. Canon law, therefore, provided a model for state-initiated prosecution.

Evidently the state began to adopt this model which provided for a more aggressive, powerful role for the central authority. This takeover by the state was gradual and much resisted but eventually was victorious.

So this enlarged responsibility and power for the state in the prosecution of crime seems to have been based on the revival of Roman law, which was introduced through canon law, then adopted and secularized by the state.

Many reasons for this trend can be suggested. They may have to do with the breakdown of community or the needs of an emerging capitalist order. They seem to have something to do with Christian theology. They certainly have something to do with the dynamics of emerging nation states: I view the modern state as an exceedingly greedy institution which will keep growing unless we can keep it in check, and criminal law is one of its primary means of expressing power. But I do not pretend to understand how to sort out the roots of this process.

Although this is an oversimplification of reality, I am arguing that history has been a dialectic between two rival systems. Community justice was basically extra-legal, often negotiated, often restitutive. State justice was legal, expressing formal rationalism and rules, the rigidification of custom and principles derived from the Roman tradition into law. It was imposed justice, punitive justice, hierarchical justice.

During the past two centuries this latter model has won, but not without a fight, and not completely. In American history, for example, there has been a long and persistent history of alternative dispute resolution processes. Jerold Auerbach, in *Justice Without Law?*, outlines an amazing variety of examples. The state tried to co-opt them, and often eventually did, but they have been very persistent.

In fact, even in the United States the idea that the state ought to prosecute crimes is relatively new. Until a hundred years ago, it was not assumed that it was up to prosecutors to initiate all prosecutions; many were left to individuals to initiate.

We are beginning to recognize that a legal revolution has taken place in western history, a revolution with tremendous implications but until recently much neglected by historians. Its dimensions have included a separation of law into criminal and civil, an assumption of state centrality and monopoly in conflicts which are legally defined as criminal, a movement from private to public justice, an assumption that punishment is normative, a movement from custom to formal legal structures.

Parallel with the rise of the state as the central actor and the increase in punitiveness was the rise of the modern prison. Many would argue that it is no accident that these developments coincide chronologically.

I have suggested two historical models: state justice and community justice. There is, however, a third way: covenant justice. In some ways it has links with both community and state justice but in covenant justice the patterns are transformed. Millard Lind has outlined this well when he traces 'the transformation of justice from Moses to Jesus'.

Many assume that the primary theme of Old Testament justice is retribution, that an 'eye for an eye' is the central paradigm. This view is inadequate for a number of reasons.

Some have argued, for example, that the words we translate into English as retribution really do not mean that. Also, the phrase 'an eye for an eye' does not occur as often as most of us assume; the phrase is used, I believe, only three or four times. And we often misunderstand its function. An 'eye for an eye' was intended as a limit, not a command. If someone takes your eye, respond in proportion. Limit your response. Do this much, and only this much. An 'eye for an eye' was intended to introduce limits in a society unused to the rule of law.

Some have also argued that the concept was designed as a way of converting wrongs to compensation. As I suggested earlier, it may have been intended as 'the value of an eye for an eye'. And it was designed as way of maintaining a balance of power between groups.

Our understanding of an eye for an eye has often been off base, oversimplified, and has overemphasized its importance. An eye for an eye is NOT the central paradigm of Old Testament justice. Restitution, forgiveness, reconciliation are just as important, perhaps more important. In fact, in many ways the central theme of the Old Testament is a theology of restoration.

I have recently been rereading Leviticus, Exodus and Deuteronomy. I have been struck with how often forgiveness and restoration appear there. We have been so dominated by retributive language that we often overlooked these other themes.

So my first point about covenant law is this: Retribution is not as central to Old Testament justice as is often assumed, and we have often misunderstood the functions of this theme.

My second point is that we must understand that the meaning of law in the Old Testament is much different than ours today. Law certainly does not mean the legal formalism that is integral to today's understanding of law. Bianchi has helped us to understand that in the Old Testament, law is conversation, 'palaver'. Law is a 'wise indication' of the way we ought to go, and we ought to talk about that. Old Testament law does not have the sense of rigidity and formalism that our law does. Law points a direction, and it must be discussed.

We tend to see the Ten Commandments as purely prohibition: 'Do not do these things.' Bianchi suggests, however, that they should be read as promise. God is saying, 'If you walk in my ways, if you are true to my covenant, this is how you shall live. You will not kill. You will not commit adultery.' It's a promise.

The differences in our concepts of law are much more profound than I have outlined here. What is important is that we realize that we cannot simply transfer Old Testament laws to the [21st] century legal milieu.

Furthermore, justice in the Old Testament is not based on a state law model. In fact, a consistent theme is the warning against becoming like other nations with a coercive kingship structure. Israel's kings were to be different, subject to God and God's commandments. They were not to be above the law, not to be the source of law, as was the case in other nations.

Consequently, even when Israel adopted laws with parallels to those of other surrounding nations (for example, the Code of Hammurabi), they were transformed. They were set in a covenant context and did not assume the centrality of the state as others did.

Our information about the structure and administration of Old Testament law is quite fragmentary. However, it seems clear that the law was not administered by police and public prosecution. There was no police force which ran around, arresting people for wrongdoing. There were no state prosecutors to bring charges in formal courts. Instead, as Hans Boecker has described it for us, justice seems to have been done at the gate, at the open place in the city where people met, where things were happening, where the market took place, where people talked. If you had a complaint against someone, you brought it to this place. Here justice was done in a structured but democratic and fairly unbureaucratic way. It involved much negotiation, much discussion, and the focus was on a solution rather than some abstract concept of justice. The idea that justice is an abstract balancing was a Roman, not a Hebrew concept. Covenant justice was making things right, finding a settlement, restoring Shalom.

The key to Old Testament justice was the concept of Shalom – of making things right, of living in peace and harmony with one another in right relationship. Restitution and restoration overshadowed punishment as a theme because the goal was restoration to right relationships.

The test of justice, then, was not whether the right rules, the right procedures, were followed. Justice was to be tested by the outcome, by its fruits. As Bianchi has pointed out, if the tree bears good fruit, it is justice; if not, it is not justice. Justice is to be tested by the outcome, not the procedures, and it must come out with right relationships. Justice is a process of making things right.

Jesus continues and expands this theme of covenant justice. He focuses on the recovery of wholeness in community with one another and with God. In the New Testament as in the Old, justice has a relational focus.

And Jesus raises real questions about some of the central assumptions of today's retributive justice. He seems to suggest real caution about focusing on blame-fixing. He casts doubt on the idea of just deserts. And, his primary focus is on the ethic of love and forgiveness rather than punishment.

It seems to me that the central focus of covenant justice, in both its Old and New Testament forms, is on love, on restoration, on relationships. It is the kind of thing we talk about in VORP (Victim Offender Reconciliation Program). Crime is a wound in human relationships. The feelings that victim and offender have toward one another are not peripheral issues, as assumed by our justice system, but are the heart of the matter. Relationships are central.

Covenant justice also seems to focus more on problem-solving than on blame-fixing. As Bianchi has suggested, it focuses more on liabilities than on guilt. When you commit a crime, you create a certain debt, an obligation, a liability that must be met. Crime creates an obligation – to restore, to repair, to undo. Things must be made right. And the test, the focus, of justice is the outcome, not the process.

So the tension today is between three basic models. State justice is dominant but seriously flawed. Community justice has a long history and many possibilities, but it too has its pitfalls and has been largely co-opted by state justice. Then there is covenant justice. Our problem is to understand and find our way through these models.

But my goal today is quite limited: We must realize that many of the problems in the way we do justice today are rooted in our understanding of justice, and that this particular understanding is only one possible way, one paradigm. Others are possible, others have been lived out, others have actually dominated most of our history. In the long sweep of things, our present paradigm is really quite recent.

Now, if it is true that the problem lies in the way we understand crime and justice, how should we understand them? What would a new paradigm look like?

I would suggest that we define crime as it is experienced: as a violation of one person by another. Crime is a conflict between people, a violation against a person, not an offence against the state. The proper response ought to be one that restores. In place of a retributive paradigm, we need to be guided by a restorative paradigm.

I have tried to sketch out, in table form, the contrasting characteristics of the two paradigms (see Appendix). It is very sketchy and highly theoretical at this point, but might help to clarify the differences.

And the differences are significant.

The old paradigm makes the state into the victim, thus placing the state at the center, leaving out the individual victim, and denying the interpersonal character of the offence. The new paradigm defines crime as a conflict between persons, putting the individuals and their relationship at center stage.

The old paradigm is based on a conflictual, adversarial, model, but sees the essential conflict between individual and state, and utilizes a method that heightens conflict. The new paradigm recognizes that the essential conflict is between individuals and encourages dialogue and negotiation. It encourages victim and offender to see one another as persons, to establish or re-establish a relationship.

The central focus of the old paradigm is on the past, on blame-fixing. While the new paradigm would encourage responsibility for past behavior, its focus would be on the future, on problem-solving, on the obligations created by the offence.

Restoration, making things right, would replace the imposition of pain as the expected outcome in new paradigm justice. Restitution would be common, not exceptional. Instead of committing one social injury in response to another, a restorative paradigm would focus on healing.

Retributive justice defines justice the Roman way, as right rules, measuring justice by the intention and the process. Restorative justice would define justice the Hebrew way, as right relationships measured by the outcome.

As Auerbach has pointed out, modern justice grows out of and also encourages competitive individualism. A restorative, negotiated focus should encourage mutual aid, a sense of mutuality, of community, of fellowship.

In today's justice, all action is hierarchical, from the top down. The state acts on the offender, with the victim on the sidelines. Restorative justice would put victim and offender at the center, helping to decide what is to be done about what has happened. Thus the definition of accountability would change. Instead of 'paying a debt to society' by experiencing punishment, accountability would mean understanding and taking responsibility for what has been done and taking action to make things right. Instead of owing an abstract debt to society, paid in an abstract way by experiencing punishment, the offender would owe a debt to the victim, to be repaid in a concrete way.

Retributive justice as we know it views everything in purely legal terms. As Nils Christie has said, legal training is trained tunnel vision. In law schools, you are taught that only legally defined issues are relevant. Restorative justice will require us to look at behavior in its entire context – moral, social, economic and political.

All this is, of course, very fragmentary and very theoretical. However, as Kay Harris has pointed out, our problem in the past is that we have attempted to provide alternative programs without offering alternative values. We need an alternative vision, not simply alternative sentences.

What such a vision means in practice is still hard to say. Some have suggested that we abolish criminal law – a slightly radical but intriguing idea. Herman Bianchi is suggesting that, historically, it has been good to have competing systems – they provide a useful corrective to one another, and pose a choice for participants. So perhaps we need to work at setting up a separate but parallel justice system without abolishing the old. Perhaps, as Martin Wright suggests, we need to make more use of what we already have by 'civilizing' our legal process – that is, by drawing on and expanding the civil process that already exists.

All this raises many questions, of course, and suggests many dangers. Good intentions can, and often do, go awry; just look, for example, at the history of prisons, which were advocated by Christians with the best of intentions.

Should something like this be attempted on a societal level, or is it something that belongs primarily within the church? And what about the politics of paradigm change? Make no mistake: The criminal justice industry is big business, shot through with all kinds of self-interest and will not be changed.

Can such a model actually work? We know from VORP that it can work, that it does work in many cases, with certain kinds of crime. But are there limits? Where are they? It is our responsibility to find out.

That is our challenge. Will VORP be just another alternative program, an alternative that becomes institutionalized, ossified, co-opted until it is just another program, and perhaps not an alternative at all? Or will VORP be a means of exploring, communicating, embodying an alternative vision? Will it demonstrate that there is another way? Could it even be the beginning of a quiet revolution?

That is, at least in part, up to us. For me that is an exciting dream. But it is also an awesome responsibility.

Appendix: paradigms of justice – old and new

Old Paradigm
Retributive Justice

1. Crime defined as violation of the state

2. Focus on establishing blame, on guilt, on past (did he/she do it?)

3. Adversarial relationships and process normative

4. Imposition of pain to punish and deter/prevent

5. Justice defined by intent and by process: right rules

6. Interpersonal, conflictual nature of crime obscured, repressed: conflict seen as individual vs. state

7. One social injury replaced by another

8. Community on sideline, represented abstractly by state

9. Encouragement of competitive, individualistic values

10. Action directed from state to offender:
    ● victim ignored
    ● offender passive

11. Offender accountability defined as taking punishment

New Paradigm
Restorative Justice

1. Crime defined as violation of one person by another

2. Focus on problem-solving, on liabilities and obligations, on future (what should be done?)

3. Dialogue and negotiation normative

4. Restitution as a means of restoring *both* parties; reconciliation/ restoration as goal

5. Justice defined as right relationships: judged by the outcome

6. Crime recognized as interpersonal conflict: value of conflict recognized

7. Focus on repair of social injury

8. Community as facilitator in restorative process

9. Encouragement of mutuality

10. Victim's and offender's roles recognized in both problem and solution:
    ● victim rights/needs recognized
    ● offender encouraged to take responsibility

11. Offender accountability defined as understanding impact of action and helping decide how to make things right

12. Offence defined in purely legal terms, devoid of moral, social, economic, political dimensions	12. Offence understood in whole context – moral, social, economic, political
13. 'Debt' owed to state and society in the abstract	13. Debt/liability to victim recognized
14. Response focused on offender's past behavior	14. Response focused on harmful consequences of offender's behavior
15. Stigma of crime unremovable	15. Stigma of crime removable through restorative action
16. No encouragement for repentance and forgiveness	16. Possibilities for repentance and forgiveness
17. Dependence upon proxy professionals	17. Direct involvement by participants

This extract is taken from 'Retributive Justice, Restorative Justice', by Howard Zehr, Occasional Paper no. 4, New Perspectives on Crime and Justice series (MCC Canada Victim Offender Ministries Program and MCC US Office on Crime and Justice), 1985.

References

Auerbach, J.S. (1983) *Justice Without Law?* (Oxford University Press).

Barnett, R. (1981) 'Restitution: A New Paradigm of Criminal Justice', in Galaway, B. and Hudson, J. (eds) *Perspectives on Crime Victims* (C.V. Mosby).

Bianchi, H. (1984) 'A Biblical Vision of Justice', *New Perspectives on Crime and Justice* (Mennonite Central Committee).

Berman, H.J. (1975) 'The Religious Foundations of Western Law', *The Catholic University of America Law Review*, Spring, pp. 490–508.

Boecker, H.J. (1980) *Law and the Administration of Justice in the Old Testament and Ancient East* (Augsburg Publishing House).

Christie, N. (1981) *Limits to Pain* (Columbia University Press).

Christie, N. (1984) 'Crime, Pain and Death', *New Perspectives on Crime and Justice* (Mennonite Central Committee).

Harris, K. (1987) 'Strategies, Values, and the Emerging Generation of Alternatives to Incarceration', *New York University Review of Law and Social Change*, 1, pp. 141–70.

Kuhn, T. (1970) *The Structure of Scientific Revolutions* (2nd edn) (University of Chicago Press).

Lenman, B. and Parker, G. (1980) 'The State, the Community and the Criminal Law in Early Modern Europe', in Gatrell, V.A.C. *et al.* (eds) *Crime and the Law: The Social History of Crime in Western Europe Since 1500* (Europa Publications).

Lind, M. (1982) 'Law in the Old Testament', in Swartley, W.M. (ed.) *Occasional Papers* (Council of Mennonite Seminaries).

Lind, M. (undated) 'The Transformation of Justice: From Moses to Jesus' (Mennonite Central Committee).

Wright, M. (1982) *Making Good: Prisons, Punishment and Beyond* (Burnett Books).

5. Restorative justice and a better future

John Braithwaite

Imagine two robbers

A teenager is arrested in Halifax for a robbery. The police send him to court where he is sentenced to six months' incarceration. As a victim of child abuse, he is both angry with the world and alienated from it. During his period of confinement he acquires a heroin habit and suffers more violence. He comes out more desperate and alienated than when he went in, sustains his drug habit for the next 20 years by stealing cars, burgles dozens of houses and pushes drugs to others until he dies in a gutter, a death no one mourns. Probably someone rather like that was arrested in Halifax today, perhaps more than one.

Tomorrow another teenager, Sam, is arrested in Halifax for a robbery. He is a composite of several Sams I have seen. The police officer refers Sam to a facilitator who convenes a restorative justice conference. When the facilitator asks about his parents, Sam says he is homeless. His parents abused him and he hates them. Sam refuses to cooperate with a conference if they attend. After talking with his parents, the facilitator agrees that perhaps it is best not to involve the parents. What about grandparents? No, they are dead. Brothers and sisters? No, he hates his brothers too. Sam's older sister, who was always kind to him, has long since left home. He has no contact with her. Aunts and uncles? Not keen on them either, because they would always put him down as the black sheep of the family and stand by his parents. Uncle George was the only one he ever had any time for, but he has not seen him for years. Teachers from school? Hates them all. Sam has dropped out. They always treated him like dirt. The facilitator does not give up: 'No one ever treated you okay at school?' Well, the hockey coach is the only one Sam can ever think of being fair to him. So the hockey coach, Uncle George and older sister are tracked down by the facilitator and invited to the conference along with the robbery victim and her daughter, who comes along to support the victim through the ordeal.

These six participants sit on chairs in a circle. The facilitator starts by introducing everyone and reminding Sam that while he has admitted to the robbery, he can change his plea at any time during the conference and have the matter heard by a court. Sam is asked to explain what happened in his own words. He mumbles that he needed money to survive, saw the lady, knocked her over and ran off with her purse. Uncle George is asked what he thinks of this. He says that Sam used to be a good kid. But Sam had gone off the rails. He had let his parents down so badly that they would not even come today. 'And now you have done this to this poor lady. I never thought you would stoop to violence,' continues Uncle George, building into an angry tirade against the boy. The hockey coach also says he is surprised that Sam could do something as terrible as this. Sam was always a troublemaker at school. But he could see a kindly side in Sam that left him shocked about the violence. The sister is invited to speak, but the facilitator moves on to the victim when Sam's sister seems too emotional to speak.

The victim explains how much trouble she had to cancel the credit cards in the purse, how she had no money for the shopping she needed to do that day. Her daughter explains that the most important consequence of the crime was that her mother was now afraid to go out on her own. In particular, she is afraid that Sam is stalking her, waiting to rob her again. Sam sneers at this and seems callous throughout. His sister starts to sob. Concerned about how distressed she is, the facilitator calls a brief adjournment so she can comfort her, with help from Uncle George. During the break, the sister reveals that she understands what Sam has been through. She says she was abused by their parents as well. Uncle George has never heard of this, is shocked, and not sure that he believes it.

When the conference reconvenes, Sam's sister speaks to him with love and strength. Looking straight into his eyes, the first gaze he could not avoid in the conference, she says that she knows exactly what he has been through with their parents. No details are spoken. But the victim seems to understand what is spoken of by the knowing communication between sister and brother. Tears rush down the old woman's cheeks and over a trembling mouth.

It is his sister's love that penetrates Sam's callous exterior. From then on he is emotionally engaged with the conference. He says he is sorry about what the victim has lost. He would like to pay it back, but has no money or job. He assures the victim he is not stalking her. She readily accepts this now and when questioned by the facilitator says now she thinks she will feel safe walking out alone. She wants her money back but says it will help her if they can talk about what to do to help Sam find a home and a job. Sam's sister says he can come and live in her house for a while. The hockey coach says he has some casual work that needs to be done, enough to pay Sam's debt to the victim and a bit more. If Sam does a good job, he will write him a reference for applications for permanent jobs. When the conference breaks up, the victim hugs Sam and tearfully wishes him good luck. He apologises again. Uncle George quietly slips a hundred dollars to Sam's sister to defray the extra cost of having Sam in the house, says he will be there for both of them if they need him.

Sam has a rocky life punctuated by several periods of unemployment. A year later he has to go through another conference after he steals a bicycle. But he finds work when he can, mostly stays out of trouble and lives to mourn at the funerals of Uncle George and his sister. The victim gets her money back and enjoys taking long walks alone. Both she and her daughter say that they feel enriched as a result of the conference, have a little more grace in their lives.

I will return to the meanings of this story.

Institutional collapse

Few sets of institutional arrangements created in the West since the industrial revolution have been as large a failure as the criminal justice system. In theory it administers just, proportionate corrections that deter. In practice, it fails to correct or deter, just as often making things worse as better. It is a criminal *injustice* system that systematically turns a blind eye to crimes of the powerful, while imprisonment remains the best-funded labour market programme for the unemployed and indigenous peoples. It pretends to be equitable, yet one offender may be sentenced to a year in a prison where he will be beaten on reception and then systematically bashed thereafter, raped, even infected with AIDS, while others serve 12 months in comparatively decent premises, especially if they are whitecollar criminals.

While I do believe that Canada's criminal justice system is more decent than ours in Australia, all Western criminal justice systems are brutal, institutionally vengeful, and dishonest to their stated intentions. The interesting question is why are they such failures. Given that prisons are vicious and degrading places, you would expect fear of ending up in them would deter crime.

There are many reasons for the failures of the criminal justice system to prevent crime. I will give you just one, articulated in the terms of my theory in *Crime, Shame and Reintegration*.[1] The claim of this theory is that the societies that have the lowest crime rates are the societies that shame criminal conduct most effectively. There is an important difference between reintegrative shaming and stigmatization. While reintegrative shaming prevents crime, stigmatization is a kind of shaming that makes crime problems worse. Stigmatization is the kind of shaming that creates outcasts; it is disrespectful, humiliating. Stigmatization means treating criminals as evil people who have done evil acts. Reintegrative shaming means disapproving of the evil of the deed while treating the person as essentially good. Reintegrative shaming means strong disapproval of the act but doing so in a way that is respecting of the person. Once we understand this distinction, we can see why putting more police on the street can actually increase crime. More police can increase crime if they are systematically stigmatizing in the way they deal with citizens. More police can reduce crime if they are systematically reintegrative in the way they deal with citizens.

We can also understand why building more prisons could make the crime problem worse. Having more people in prison does deter some and incapacitates others from committing certain crimes, like bank robberies, because there are no banks inside the prison for them to rob, though there certainly are plenty of vulnerable people to rape and pillage. But because prisons stigmatize, they also make things worse for those who have criminal identities affirmed by imprisonment, those whose stigmatization leads them to find solace in the society of the similarly outcast, those who are attracted into criminal subcultures, those who treat the prison as an educational institution for learning new skills for the illegitimate labour market. On this account, whether building more prisons reduces or increases the crime rate depends on whether the stigmatizing nature of a particular prison system does more to increase crime than its deterrent and incapacitative effects reduce it.

A lack of theoretical imagination among criminologists has been one underrated reason for the failure of the criminal justice system. Without theorizing why it fails, the debate has collapsed to a contest between those who want more of the same to make it work and those who advance the implausible position that it makes sense to stigmatize people first and later subject them to rehabilitation programmes inside institutions. With juvenile justice in particular, the debate [. . .] has see-sawed between the justice model and the welfare model. See-sawing between retribution and rehabilitation has got us nowhere. If we are serious about a better future, we need to hop off this see-saw and strike out in search of a third model.

For me, that third model is restorative justice. During the past decade a number of different labels – reconciliation (Dignan,[2] Marshall,[3] Umbreit[4]), peacemaking (Pepinsky and Quinney[5]), redress (de Haan[6]) – have described broadly similar intellectual currents. Philip Pettit and I have sought to argue for republican criminal justice (Braithwaite and Pettit,[7] Pettit with Braithwaite[8]). Yet the label that has secured by far the widest consent during the past few years has been that employed by Zehr,[9] Galaway and Hudson,[10] Cragg,[11] Walgrave,[12] Bazemore,[13] Umbreit,[14] Consedine,[15] Peters and Aertsen,[16] Messmer and Otto,[17] Marshall,[18] McElrea,[19] McCold,[20] Maxwell,[21] Carbonatto,[22] Crawford, Strong, Sargeant, Souryal and Van Ness,[23] Denison,[24] Knopp,[25] Mackey,[26] Morrell,[27] Van Ness,[28] and Young[29] – restorative justice. It has become the slogan of a global social movement. For those of us who see constructive engagement with social movement politics as crucial for major change, labels that carry meaning for activists matter. In this spirit, I now wish that I had called reintegrative shaming restorative shaming.

What is restorative justice?

Restorative justice means restoring victims, a more victim-centred criminal justice system, as well as restoring offenders and restoring community. First, what does restoring victims mean? It means restoring the *property loss* or the *personal injury*, repairing the broken window or the broken teeth (see Table [5.] 1). It means restoring a *sense of security*. Even victims of property crimes such as burglary often suffer a loss of security when the private space of their home is violated. When the criminal justice system fails to leave women secure about walking alone at night, half the population is left unfree in a rather fundamental sense.

Victims suffer loss of dignity when someone violates their bodies or shows them the disrespect of taking things which are precious to them. Sometimes this disrespectful treatment engenders victim shame: 'He abused me rather than some other woman because I am trash', 'She stole my dad's car because I was irresponsible to park it in such a risky place'. Victim shame often triggers

Table [5.]1   What does restoring victims mean?

Restoring victims
- Restore property loss
- Restore injury
- Restore sense of security
- Restore dignity
- Restore sense of empowerment
- Restore deliberative democracy
- Restore harmony based on a feeling that justice has been done
- Restore social support

---

a shame–rage spiral wherein victims reciprocate indignity with indignity through vengeance or by their own criminal acts.

Disempowerment is part of the indignity of being a victim of crime. According to Pettit and Braithwaite's republican theory of criminal justice,[30] a wrong should not be defined as a crime unless it involves some domination of us that reduces our freedom to enjoy life as we choose. It follows that it is important to *restore any lost sense of empowerment* as a result of crime. This is particularly important where the victim suffers structurally systematic domination. For example, some of the most important restorative justice initiatives we have seen in Australia have involved some thousands of Aboriginal victims of consumer fraud by major insurance companies.[31] In these cases, victims from remote Aboriginal communities relished the power of being able to demand restoration and corporate reform from 'white men in white shirts'.

The way that Western legal systems handle crime compounds the disempowerment that victims feel, first at the hands of offenders and then at the hands of a professional, remote justice system that eschews their participation. The lawyers, in the words of Nils Christie 'steal our conflict'.[32] The western criminal justice system has, on balance, been corrosive of deliberative democracy, though the jury is one institution that has preserved a modicum of it. Restorative justice is deliberative justice; it is about people deliberating over the consequences of a crime, how to deal with them and prevent their recurrence. This contrasts with the professional justice of lawyers deciding which rules apply to a case and then constraining their deliberation within a technical discourse about that rule – application. So restorative justice restores the *deliberative control of justice by citizens*.

Restorative justice aims to *restore harmony based on a feeling that justice has been done*. Restorative harmony alone, while leaving an underlying injustice to fester unaddressed, is not enough. 'Restoring balance' is only acceptable as a restorative justice ideal if the 'balance' between offender and victim that prevailed before the crime was a morally decent balance. There is no virtue in restoring the balance by having a woman pay for a loaf of bread she has stolen from a rich man to feed her children. Restoring harmony between victim and offender is only likely to be possible in such a context on the basis of a discussion of why the children are hungry and what should be done about the underlying injustice of their hunger.

Restorative justice cannot resolve the deep structural injustices that cause problems like hunger. But we must demand two things of restorative justice here. First, it must not make structural injustice worse (in the way, for example, that the Australian criminal justice system does by being an important cause of the unemployability and oppression of Aboriginal people). Indeed, we should hope from restorative justice for micro-measures that ameliorate macro-injustice where this is possible. Second, restorative justice should restore harmony with a remedy grounded in dialogue which takes account of underlying injustices. Restorative justice does not resolve the age-old questions of what should count as unjust outcomes. It is a more modest philosophy than that. It settles for the procedural requirement that the parties talk until they feel that harmony has been restored on the basis of a discussion of all the injustices they see as relevant to the case.

Finally, restorative justice aims to *restore social support*. Victims of crime need support from their loved ones during the process of requesting restoration. They sometimes need encouragement and support to engage with deliberation toward restoring harmony. Friends sometimes do blame the victim, or more commonly are frightened off by a victim going through an emotional trauma. Restorative justice aims to institutionalize the gathering around of friends during a time of crisis.

Restoring offenders, restoring community

In most cases, a more limited range of types of restoration is relevant to offenders. Offenders have generally not suffered property loss or injury as a result of their own crime, though sometimes loss or injury is a cause of the crime. Dignity, however, is generally in need of repair after the shame associated with arrest. When there is a victim who has been hurt, there is no dignity in denying that there is something to be ashamed about. Dignity is generally best restored by confronting the shame, accepting responsibility for the bad consequences suffered by the victim and apologizing with sincerity.[33] A task of restorative justice is to institutionalize such *restoration of dignity* for offenders.

The sense of insecurity and disempowerment of offenders is often an issue in their offending and in discussion about what is to be done to prevent further offending. Violence by young men from racial minorities is sometimes connected to their feelings of being victims of racism. For offenders, *restoring a sense of security and empowerment* is often bound up with employment, the feeling of having a future, achieving some educational success, sporting success, indeed any kind of success.

Many patches are needed to sew the quilt of deliberative democracy. Criminal justice deliberation is not as important a patch as deliberation in the parliament, in trade unions, even in universities. But to the extent that restorative justice deliberation does lead ordinary citizens into serious demo-cratic discussion about racism, unemployment, masculinist cultures in local schools and police accountability, it is not an unimportant element of a deliberatively rich democracy.

The mediation literature shows that satisfaction of complainants with the justice of the mediation is less important than the satisfaction of those who are complained against in achieving mutually beneficial outcomes.[34] Criminal subcultures are memory files that collect injustices.[35] Crime problems will continue to become deeply culturally embedded in western societies until we reinvent criminal justice as a process that restores a sense of procedural justice to offenders.[36]

Finally, Frank Cullen[37] has suggested that there could be no better organizing concept for criminology than *social support*, given the large volume of evidence about the importance of social support for preventing crime. The New Zealand Maori people see our justice system as barbaric because of the way it requires the defendant to stand alone in the dock without social support. In Maori thinking, civilized justice requires the offender's loved ones to stand beside him during justice rituals, sharing the shame for what has happened. Hence the shame the offender feels is more the shame of letting his loved ones down than a western sense of individual guilt that can eat away at a person. The shame of letting loved ones down can be readily transcended by simple acts of forgiveness from those loved ones.

Restoring community is advanced by a proliferation of restorative justice rituals in which social support around specific victims and offenders is restored. At this micro level, restorative justice is an utterly bottom-up approach to restoring community. At a meso level, important elements of a restorative justice package are initiatives to foster community organization in schools, neighbourhoods, ethnic communities, churches, [and] through professions . . . who can deploy restorative justice in their self-regulatory practices. At a macro level, we must better design institutions of deliberative democracy so that concern about issues like unemployment and the effectiveness of labour market programmes have a channel through which they can flow from discussions about local injustices up into national economic policy-making debate.

The universality of restorative traditions

I have yet to discover a culture which does not have some deep-seated restorative traditions. Nor is there a culture without retributive traditions. Retributive traditions once had survival value. Cultures which were timid in fighting back were often wiped out by more determinedly violent cultures. In the contemporary world, as opposed to the world of our biological creation, retributive emotions have less survival value. Because risk management is institutionalized in this modern world, retributive emotions are more likely to get us into trouble than out of it, as individuals, groups and nations.

The message we might communicate to all cultures is that in the world of the twenty-first century, you will find your restorative traditions a more valuable resource than your retributive traditions. Yet sadly, the hegemonic cultural forces in the contemporary world communicate just the opposite message. Hollywood hammers the message that the way to deal with bad guys is through violence. Political leaders frequently hammer the same message. Yet many of our spiritual leaders are helping us to retrieve our restorative traditions – the Dalai Lama, for example. Archbishop Desmond Tutu in his Forward [sic] to Jim Consedine's new edition of *Restorative Justice*, correctly sees a 'very ancient yet desperately needed truth' as underlying restorative justice processes 'rooted as they are in all indigenous cultures, including those of Africa'. He sees his Truth and Reconciliation Commission as an example of restorative justice.

All of the restorative values in Table [5.] 1 are cultural universals. All cultures value repair of damage to our persons and property, security, dignity, empowerment, deliberative democracy, harmony based on a sense of justice and social support. They are universals because they are all vital to our emotional survival as human beings and vital to the possibility of surviving without constant fear of violence. The world's great religions recognize that the desire to pursue these restorative justice values is universal, which is why some of our spiritual leaders are a hope against those political leaders who wish to rule through fear and by crushing deliberative democracy. Ultimately, those political leaders will find that they will have to reach an accommodation with the growing social movement for restorative justice, just as they must with the great religious movements they confront. Why? Because the evidence is now strong that ordinary citizens like restorative justice.[38] When the major political parties did their door-knocking during our last election in Canberra, they found that the thousands of citizens who had participated in a restorative justice conference mostly liked the justice they experienced.

It is true that the virtues restorative justice restores are viewed differently in different cultures and that opinion about the culturally appropriate ways of realizing them differ greatly. Hence, restorative justice must be a culturally diverse social movement that accommodates a rich plurality of strategies in pursuit of the truths it holds to be universal. It is about different cultures joining hands as they discover the profound commonalities of their experience of the human condition; it is about cultures learning from each other on the basis of that shared experience; it is about realising the value of diversity, of preserving restorative traditions that work because they are embedded in a cultural past. Scientific criminology will never discover any universally best way of doing restorative justice. The best path is the path of cultural plurality in pursuit of the culturally shared restorative values in Table [5.] 1.

A path to culturally plural justice

A restorative justice research agenda to pursue this path has two elements:

1. *Culturally specific investigation of how to save and revive the restorative justice practices that remain in all societies.*
2. *Culturally specific investigation of how to transform state criminal justice both by making it more restorative and by rendering its abuses of power more vulnerable to restorative justice.*

On the first point, I doubt that neighbourhoods in our cities are replete with restorative justice practices that can be retrieved, though there are some. Yet in the more micro context of the nuclear family, the evidence is overwhelming from the metropolitan US that restorative justice is alive and well and that families who are more restorative are likely to have less delinquent children than families who are punitive and stigmatizing.[39]

Because families so often slip into stigmatization and brutalization of their difficult members, we need restorative justice institutionalized in a wider context that can engage and restore such families. In most societies, the wider contexts where the ethos and rituals of restorative justice are alive and ready to be piped into the wider streams of the society are schools, churches and remote indigenous communities. If it is hard to find restorative justice in the disputing practices of our urban neighbourhoods, the experience of recent years has been that they are relatively easy to locate in urban schools.[40] This is because of the ethos of care and integration which is part of the western educational ideal (which, at its best, involves a total rejection of stigmatization) and because the interaction among the members of a school community tends to be more intense than the interaction among urban neighbours. Schools, like families, have actually become more restorative and less retributive than the brutal institutions of the nineteenth century. This is why we have seen very successful restorative conferencing programmes in contemporary schools.[41] We have also seen anti-bullying programmes with what I would call a restorative ethos which have managed in some cases to halve bullying in schools.[42]

More of the momentum for the restorative justice movement has come from the world's churches than from any other quarter. Even in a nation like Indonesia where the state has such tyrannical power, the political imperative to allow some separation of church and state has left churches as enclaves where restorative traditions could survive. Religions like Islam and Christianity have strong retributive traditions as well, of course, though they have mostly been happy to leave it to the state to do the 'dirty work' of temporal retribution.

When I spoke at a conference on restorative justice in Indonesia last month, I was struck in a conversation with three Indonesians – one Muslim, one Hindu and one Christian – that in ways I could not understand as an agnostic, each was drawing on a spirituality grounded in their religious experience to make sense of restorative justice. Similarly, I was moved by the spirituality of Cree approaches to restorative justice when a number of native Canadians visited Canberra [. . .]. There is something important to learn about native American spirituality and how it enriches restorative justice. It seems clear to me that it does enrich it, but I do not understand how. [. . .]

[. . .] Canadian indigenous communities are a cultural resource for the whole world. Because they have not been totally swamped by the justice codes of the West, they are a cultural resource, just as the biodiversity of [the North American] continent supplies the entire world a genetic resource. The very people who by virtue of their remoteness have succumbed least to the Western justice model, who have been insulated from Hollywood a little more and for a little longer, the very people who are most backward in Western eyes, are precisely those with the richest cultural resources from which the restorative justice movement can learn.

Important scholarly work is being done to unlock the cultural codes of restorative justice in [Canadian] indigenous communities. 'Healing circles', what a profound cultural code that is to unlock for the rest of the world.[43] How much we all have to learn from the experience of the Hollow Water community in dealing with an epidemic of child abuse through healing circles. Therese Lajeunesse's report on Hollow Water is already a wonderful resource for the world.[44] Joan Pennell and Gale Burford[45] have done a splendid job in their reports which document the conferences for dealing with family violence in Newfoundland, which are quite distinctive from, and doubtless in some ways superior to, the conferencing models we have applied in the Southern Hemisphere. I have already remonstrated with them about the need to pull all this illuminating research together into a book that can also have a massive effect internationally, as could a book on Hollow Water. So point 1 of the reform agenda of restorative justice is a research programme to retrieve the restorative justice practices of not only native communities, but also of the schools and churches of dominant urban cultures. Scholars like Carol LaPrairie and Don Clairmont are among the Canadian scholars who are doing vital work in advancing point 1 of this agenda.

Point 2 of the agenda is to explore how to transform state criminal justice. In our multicultural cities I have said that we cannot rely on spontaneous ordering of justice in our neighbourhoods. There we must be more reliant on state reformers as catalysts of a new urban restorative justice. In our cities, where neighbourhood social support is least, where the loss from the statist takeover of disputing is more damaging, the gains that can be secured from restorative justice reform are greatest. When a police officer with a restorative justice ethos arrests a youth in a tightly knit rural community who lives in a loving family, who enjoys social support from a caring school and church, that police officer is not likely to do much better or worse by the child than a police officer who does not have a restorative justice ethos. Whatever the police do, the child's support network will probably sort the problem out so that serious reoffending does not occur. But when a police officer with a restorative justice ethos arrests a homeless child in the metropolis like Sam, who hates parents who abused him, who has dropped out of school and is seemingly alone in the world, it is there that the restorative police officer can make a difference that will render him more effective in preventing crime than the retributive police officer. At least that is my hypothesis, one we can test empirically and are testing empirically.

In the alienated urban context where community is not spontaneously emergent in a satisfactory way, a criminal justice system aimed at restoration can construct a community of care around a specific offender or a specific victim who is in trouble. That is what the story of Sam is about. With the restorative justice conferences being convened in multicultural metropolises like Auckland, Adelaide, Sydney and Singapore, the selection principle as to who is invited to the conference is the opposite to that with a criminal trial. We invite to a criminal trial those who can inflict most damage on the other side. With a conference we invite those who might offer most support to their own side – Sam's sister, uncle and hockey coach, the victim's daughter.

In terms of the theory of reintegrative shaming, the rationale for who is invited to the conference is that the presence of those on the victim side structures shame into the conference, the presence of supporters on the offender's side structures reintegration into the ritual. Conferences can be run in many different ways from the story of Sam's conference. Maori people in New Zealand tend to want to open and close their conferences with a prayer. The institutions of restorative justice we build in the city must be culturally plural, quite different from one community to another depending on the culture of the people involved. It is the empowerment principle of restorative justice that makes this possible – empowerment with process control.

From a restorative perspective, the important thing is that we have institutions in civil society which confront serious problems like violence rather than sweep them under the carpet, yet do so in a way that is neither retributive nor stigmatizing. Violence will not be effectively controlled by communities unless the shamefulness of violence is communicated. This does not mean that we need criminal justice institutions that set out to maximize shame. On the contrary, if we set out to do that we risk the creation of stigmatizing institutions.[46] All we need do is nurture micro-institutions of deliberative democracy that allow citizens to discuss the consequences of criminal acts, who is responsible, who should put them right and how. Such deliberative processes naturally enable those responsible to confront and deal with the shame arising from what has happened. And if we get the invitation list right by inviting along people who enjoy maximum respect and trust on both the offender and victim side, then we maximize the chances that shame will be dealt with in a reintegrative way.

[. . .]

Beyond communitarianism versus individualism

Some criminologists in the West are critical of countries like Singapore, Indonesia and Japan where crime in the streets is not a major problem because they think individualism in these societies is crushed by communitarianism or collective obligation. Their prescription is that Asian societies need to shift the balance away from communitarianism and allow greater individualism. I don't find that a very attractive analysis.

Some Asian criminologists are critical of countries like the US and Australia because they think these societies are excessively individualistic, suffering much crime and incivility as a result. According to this analysis, the West needs to shift the balance away from individualism in favour of communitarianism, shift the balance away from rights and toward collective responsibilities. I don't find that a very attractive analysis either.

Both sides of this debate can do a better job of learning from each other. We can aspire to a society that is strong on rights and strong on responsibilities, that nurtures strong communities and strong individuals. Indeed, in the good society strong communities constitute strong individuals and vice versa. Our objective can be to keep the benefits of the statist revolution at the same time as we rediscover community-based justice. Community justice is often oppressive of rights, often subjects the vulnerable to the domination of local elites, subordinates women, can be procedurally unfair and tends to neglect structural solutions. Mindful of this, we might reframe the two challenges posed earlier [. . .]:

1. *Helping indigenous community justice to learn from the virtues of liberal statism – procedural fairness, rights, protecting the vulnerable from domination.*
2. *Helping liberal state justice to learn from indigenous community justice – learning the restorative community alternatives to individualism.*

This reframed agenda resonates with the writings of Canadians such as Donald Clairmont[47] and Marianne Nielsen, who writes that native communities 'will have the opportunity of taking the best of the old, the best of the new and learning from others' mistakes so that they can design a system that may well turn into a flagship of social change'.[48] Together these two questions ask how we save and revive traditional restorative justice practices in a way that helps them become procedurally fairer, in a way that respects fundamental human rights, that secures protection against domination? The liberal state can be a check on oppressive collectivism, just as bottom-up communitarianism can be a check on oppressive individualism. A healing circle can be a corrective to a justice system that can leave offenders and victims suicidally alone; a Charter of Rights and Freedoms a check on a tribal elder who imposes a violent tyranny on young people. The bringing together of these ideals is an old prescription – not just liberty, not just community, but liberté, egalité, fraternité. Competitive individualism has badly fractured this republican amalgam. The social movement for restorative justice does practical work to weld an amalgam that is relevant to the creation of contemporary urban multicultural republics. Day to day it is not sustained by romantic ideals in which I happen to believe like deliberative democracy. They want to do it for Sam and for an old woman who Sam pushed over one day. That is what enlists them to the social movement for restorative justice; in the process they are, I submit, enlisted into something of wider political significance.

This extract is taken from 'Restorative Justice and a Better Future', by John Braithwaite, in Dalhousie Law Review, *spring 1996, 76:1, pp. 9–32.*

Notes

1 Braithwaite, J. (1989) *Crime, Shame and Reintegration* (Cambridge: Cambridge University Press).
2 Dignan, J. (1992) 'Repairing the Damage: Can Reparation Work in the Service of Diversion?', *British Journal of Criminology*, 32, pp. 453–72.
3 Marshall, T.F. (1985) *Alternatives to Criminal Courts* (Aldershot: Gower).
4 Umbreit, M. (1985) *Crime and Reconciliation: Creative Options for Victims and Offenders* (Nashville, TN: Abington Press).
5 Pepinsky, H.E. and Quinney, R. (1991) *Criminology as Peacemaking* (Bloomington, IN: Indiana University Press).
6 de Haan, W. (1990) *The Politics of Redress: Crime, Punishment and Penal Abolition* (London: Unwin Hyman).
7 Braithwaite, J. and Pettit, P. (1990) *Not Just Deserts: A Republican Theory of Criminal Justice* (Oxford: Oxford University Press).
8 Pettit, P. with Braithwaite, J. (1993) 'Not Just Deserts Even in Sentencing', *Current Issues in Criminal Justice*, 4, pp. 225–39.
9 Zehr, H. (1990) *Changing Lenses: A New Focus for Criminal Justice* (Scottdale, PA: Herald Press); Zehr, H. (1985) 'Retributive Justice, Restorative Justice'. *New Perspectives on Crime and Justice. Occasional Papers of the MCC Canada Victim Offender Ministries Program and the MCC US Office of Criminal Justice*, 4, September.
10 Galaway, B. and Hudson, J. (1990) *Criminal Justice, Restitution and Reconciliation* (Monsey, NY: Criminal Justice Press); Galaway, B. and Hudson, J. (eds) *Restorative Justice: International Perspectives* (Monsey, NY: Criminal Justice Press).
11 Cragg, W. (1992) *The Practice of Punishment: Towards a Theory of Restorative Justice* (London: Routledge).
12 Walgrave, L. (1995) 'Restorative Justice for Juveniles: Just a Technique or a Fully Fledged Alternative?' *The Howard Journal*, 34:3, pp. 228–49; Walgrave, L. (1993)

'In Search of Limits to the Restorative Justice for Juveniles'. Unpublished paper presented to the International Congress on Criminology, Budapest, 23–27 August.

13 Bazemore, G. (1993) *Balanced and Restorative Justice for Juvenile Offenders: An Overview of a New OJJDP Initiative* (Washington, DC: Office of Juvenile Justice and Delinquency Prevention).

14 Umbreit, M. (1995) 'Holding Juvenile Offenders Accountable: A Restorative Justice Perspective', *Juvenile and Family Court Journal*, Spring, pp. 31–42; Umbreit, M. (1994) *Victim Meets Offender: The Impact of Restorative Justice and Mediation* (Monsey, NY: Willow Tree Press); Umbreit, M. (1989) 'Crime Victims Seeking Fairness, not Revenge: Towards Restorative Justice', *Federal Probation*, 53:3, pp. 52–7.

15 Consedine, J. (1995) *Restorative Justice: Healing the Effects of Crime* (Lyttleton, New Zealand: Ploughshares Publications).

16 Peters, T. and Aertsen, I. (1995) 'Restorative Justice: In Search of New Avenues in the Judicial Dealing with Crime: The Presentation of a Project of Mediation for Reparation', in Fijnaut, C. *et al.* (eds) *Changes in Society, Crime and Criminal Justice in Europe* (Antwerpen: Kluwer Law and Taxation Publishers).

17 Messmer, H. and Otto, H.U. (1992) 'Restorative Justice: Steps on the Way toward a Good Idea', in Messmer, H. and Otto, H.U. (eds) *Restorative Justice on Trial* (Dordrecht: Kluwer Academic).

18 Marshall, T. (1992) 'Grassroots Initiatives towards Restorative Justice: The New Paradigm?'. Unpublished paper for the Fulbright Colloquium, 'Penal Theory and Penal Practice', University of Stirling, September.

19 McElrea, F.W.M. (1994) 'Restorative Justice – the New Zealand Youth Court: A Model for Development in other Courts', *Journal of Judicial Administration*, 4:1, pp. 33–54.

20 McCold, P. (1995) 'Restorative Justice and the Role of Community.' Unpublished paper presented to the Academy of Criminal Justice Sciences annual conference, Boston, March.

21 Maxwell, G. (1995) 'Some Traditional Models of Restorative Justice from Canada, South Africa and Gaza', in McElrea, F.W.M. (ed.) *Rethinking Criminal Justice. Vol. 1. Justice in the Community* (Auckland: Legal Research Foundation).

22 Carbonatto, H. (1995) *Expanding Options for Spousal Abuse: The Use of Restorative Justice. Occasional Papers in Criminology: New Series* 4 (Wellington: Institute of Criminology).

23 Crawford, T., Strong, K., Sargeant, K., Souryal, C. and Van Ness, D. (1990) *Restorative Justice: Principles* (Washington, DC: Justice Fellowship).

24 Denison, K. (1991) *Restorative Justice in Ourselves: New Perspectives on Crime and Justice* (Issue 11) (Akron, PA: Mennonite Central Committee Office of Criminal Justice).

25 Knopp, F.H. (1992) 'Restorative Justice for Juvenile Sex Offenders.' Paper presented to the National Council of Juvenile and Family Court Judges, Lake Tahoe/Reno, 16 November.

26 Mackey, V. (1990) *Restorative Justice: Towards Nonviolence* (Louisville, KY: Presbyterian Criminal Justice Program, Presbyterian Church (USA)).

27 Morrell, V. (1993) 'Restorative Justice: An Overview', *Criminal Justice Quarterly*, 5, pp. 3–7.

28 Van Ness, D. (1993) 'New Wine and Old Wineskins: Four Challenges of Restorative Justice', *Criminal Law Forum*, 4, pp. 251–76.

29 Young, M. (1995) *Restorative Community Justice: A Call to Action* (Washington, DC: National Organization for Victim Assistance).

30 Pettit, P. and Braithwaite, J. (1990) *Not Just Deserts: A Republican Theory of Criminal Justice* (Oxford: Oxford University Press).

31 See Fisse, B. and Braithwaite, J. (1993) *Corporations, Crime and Accountability* (Cambridge: Cambridge University Press), pp. 218–23.

32 Christie, N. (1978) 'Conflicts as Property', *British Journal of Criminology*, 17, pp. 1–15.

33 On this issue, I find the work of Tom Scheff and Suzanne Retzinger on by-passed shame illuminating. Scheff, T. and Retzinger, S. (1991) *Emotions and Violence: Shame and Rage in Destructive Conflicts* (Lexington, MA: Lexington Books).

34 Pruitt, D.G. (1995) 'Research Report: Process and Outcome in Community Mediation', *Negotiation Journal*, October, pp. 365–77, at p. 374.

35 Matza, D. (1964) *Delinquency and Drift* (New York, NY: Wiley), p. 102.

36 Tyler, T. (1990) *Why People Obey the Law* (New Haven, CT: Yale University Press).

37 Cullen, F.T. (1994) 'Social Support as an Organizing Concept for Criminology: Presidential Address to the Academy of Criminal Justice Sciences', *Justice Quarterly*, 11:4, pp. 527–59.

38 See, for example, Morris, A. and Maxwell, G. (1992) 'Juvenile Justice in New Zealand: A New Paradigm', *Australian and New Zealand Journal of Criminology*, 26, pp. 72–90; Hyndman, M., Thorsborne, M. and Wood, S. (1996) *Community Accountability Conferencing: Trial Report* (Department of Education, Queensland); Goodes, T. (1995) 'Victims and Family Conferences: Juvenile Justice in South Australia.' Unpublished paper; Moore, D. with Forsythe, L. (1995) *A New Approach to Juvenile Justice: An Evaluation of Family Conferencing in Wagga Wagga: A Report to the Criminology Research Council* (Wagga Wagga: The Centre for Rural Social Research); Clairmont, C. (1994) *Alternative Justice Issues for Aboriginal Justice* (Atlantic Institute of Criminology, November).

39 See the discussion of the evidence on this in Braithwaite, *Crime, Shame and Reintegration*, pp. 54–83.

40 Hyndman *et al.*, *Community Accountability Conferencing*.

41 Ibid.

42 Olweus, D. (1994) 'Annotation: Bullying at School: Basic Facts and Effects of a School Based Intervention Program', *Journal of Child Psychology and Psychiatry*, 35, pp. 1171–90; Farrington, D.P. (1993) 'Understanding and Preventing Bullying', in Tonry, M. (ed.) *Crime and Justice: Annual Review of Research. Vol. 17* (Chicago: University of Chicago Press); Pitts, J. and Smith, P. (1995) *Preventing School Bullying. Police Research Group: Crime Detection and Prevention Series Paper* 63 (London: Home Office); Pepier, D.J., Craig, W., Ziegler, S. and Charach, A. (1993) 'A School-based Antibullying Intervention', in Tattum, D. (ed.) *Understanding and Managing Bullying* (London: Heinemann).

43 Melton, A.P. (1995) 'Indigenous Justice Systems and Tribal Society', *Judicature*, 79:3, pp. 12 and 33; Four Worlds Development Project (1984) *The Sacred Tree* (Alberta: Four Worlds Development Press).

44 Lajeunesse, T. (1993) *Community Holistic Circle Healing: Hollow Water First Nation* (Solicitor General Canada, Ministry Secretariat).

45 Burford, G. and Pennell, J. (1995) *Family Group Decision Making: New Roles for 'Old' Partners in Resolving Family Violence* (St Johns, Newfoundland: Memorial University of Newfoundland); Pennell, J. and Burford, G. (1994) 'Attending to Context: Family Group Decision Making in Canada', in Hudson, J. *et al.* (eds) *Family Group Conferences: Perspectives on Policy and Practice* (Monsey, NY: Criminal Justice Press); Pennell, J. and Burford, G. (0000) 'Widening the Circle: Family Group Decision Making', *Journal of Child and Youth Care*, 9:1, pp. 1–11; Burford, G. and Pennell, J. (forthcoming) 'Family Group Decision Making: An Innovation in Child and Family Welfare', in Galaway, B. and Hudson, J. (eds) *Child Welfare Systems: Canadian Research and Policy Implications*.

46 Retzinger, S. and Scheff, T. (1996) 'Strategy for Community Conferences: Emotions and Social Bonds', in Galaway, B. and Hudson, J. (eds) *Restorative Justice: International Perspectives* (Monsey, NY: Criminal Justice Press).

47 Clanmont, D. (1994) 'Alternative Justice Issues for Aboriginal Justice.' Unpublished Manuscript, Atlantic Institute of Criminology, November.

48 Nielsen, M. (1992) 'Criminal Justice and Native Self-Government', in Silverman, R. and Nielsen, M. (eds) *Aboriginal Peoples and Canadian Criminal Justice* (Toronto: Butterworths), p. 255.

Part B

The background: legacies and frameworks

Introduction

One of the problems confronting proponents of restorative justice is that our current manner of viewing and responding to crime is so familiar that it seems natural, obvious and inevitable. We take it for granted that crime is essentially a wrong against the public at large, for which the obvious response is state prosecution and punishment. Proponents of restorative justice argue, often quite persuasively, that much criminal law enforcement today is in fact about advice and assistance, with prosecution and punishment as a last resort, and that restorative justice interventions outperform prosecution and punishment in achieving goals such as prevention of reoffending and victim satisfaction. Yet, it is difficult for us to shake off the assumption that prosecution and punishment are the norm, and therefore require little justification, whereas restorative justice is the 'alternative' which requires strong justification.

Studies from history and anthropology are useful in that they can jolt us into realising that our ways of seeing things and doing things are not natural, but are historical inventions which should be questioned. Our distant ancestors (and people elsewhere today) viewed and responded to 'crime' in a quite different manner. In Europe between the sixth and tenth centuries, and in some 'simple societies' today, restorative justice was and is more the norm, state prosecution and punishment the exception. Recognising this can unsettle our assumptions that offenders must be punished and that the state must take charge of this process. It can make us more amenable to giving the case for restorative justice a fair hearing. Many of us might still conclude that *we* cannot or should not dispense with state punishment, no more than we can and should dispense with myriad other social technologies which our culture has invented. Others, however, may be persuaded that state punishment is a failed Western experiment which should be jettisoned, along with other 'outmoded' institutions such as duelling. Whatever the outcome, we are richer for having such a debate rather than simply taking our existing institutions for granted and assuming that the only viable questions are those of how penal systems can be improved.

Hence, the first four readings in this section are historical and anthropological accounts of how people in other times and other places have survived in an orderly way without law courts and modern penal institutions, relying instead on principles of restorative justice. The section opens (Chapter 6) with a short extract from Harold J. Berman's book *Law and Revolution* (1983). This book is not about restorative justice as such.[1] Rather, its subject is nothing less than the origins and early development of the Western legal tradition. This tradition began to take shape, according to Berman, in the late eleventh and twelfth centuries in Europe. Berman claims that this tradition is now in crisis, and that – to find our way out of our predicament – we need to understand what is distinctive about Western legal institutions, values and concepts and we need to understand the historical context within which they were formed and forged into a tradition.

As part of this long, complex, fascinating and extremely important story, Berman describes the basic positive features of the 'folklaw' of Europe which

101

existed in the centuries prior to the emergence of the Western legal tradition and which continues to exist in many non-Western cultures. In these societies, he writes, law was not a set of rules imposed from above but part of the 'common conscience'. When social bonds were violated, there followed negotiation for restitution and reconciliation. The law was a mediating process designed, not to allocate blame and punishment, but to reconcile conflicting parties. Law was not a separate institution but a diffuse process interwoven with all other aspects of life.

In the second reading of this section, Elmar Weitekamp (in Chapter 7) fleshes out such a picture of olden forms of conflict resolution. Weitekamp challenges the conventional story of the emergence of state punishment, according to which the institution arose from a 'bloody Hobbesian jungle' (cf. Hobbes 1651/1991). The conventional story has it that, in the days before crimes were recognised and punished as public wrongs, those who considered they had been wronged by others pursued private – often violent – revenge. The only mitigating feature of this situation was that those who could afford it sometimes 'bought off' revenge by paying compensation to the injured parties. More often, though, violent retaliation was followed by violent retaliation, so that neither the parties to the conflict nor the rest of the community enjoyed any security or peace. The state stepped into this situation, so the story goes, claiming a monopoly of violence and pacifying society. An implicit message in this historical myth is that the inevitable result of any withdrawal by the state from the realm of conflict resolution will be a return to this 'Hobbesian' predicament.

For Weitekamp, this historical account is quite erroneous. He claims that in acephalous societies (i.e. societies without rulers) negotiated restitution was far more common than blood revenge for all 'crimes' including homicide. Revenge could have disastrous consequences, whereas restitution performed multiple useful functions, including the prevention of conflict escalation, the rehabilitation of offenders and the meeting of the victim's needs. Crucially, Weitekamp implies, there was social pressure upon conflicting parties to resolve their conflicts peaceably – through restitution – since the restoration of peace was of the utmost importance for the rest of society. Restitution was facilitated, on the other hand, by the fact that communities tended to accept responsibility for the deviant behaviour of their members, so that the burden of paying restitution seldom if ever fell upon an isolated individual.

In most early state societies, Weitekamp argues, restitution remained a significant means of conflict resolution. However, as centralised rulers took more and more interest in the resolution of trouble, the needs of the state began to take precedence over the needs of the victim. Correspondingly, the victim's role in settling disputes declined. By the twelfth century, restorative justice was completely eroded in Europe. The humane and beneficial 'sanction' of restitution eventually all but disappeared from Western penal systems. A few isolated voices made occasional calls for its revival. (Some of these are quite surprising, as they tend to be associated with rather different penal philosophies. For example, Weitekamp points to Jeremy Bentham and Enrico Ferri as advocates of restitution.) Towards the end of the nineteenth century, there were some more concerted efforts, through the International Prison Congress, to introduce restitution. But, by the end of the century, this earlier campaign had died out. For Weitekamp, the current campaign for restorative justice, which emerged in the 1970s, can be understood as another

– this time more successful – effort to revive the 'ancient wisdom' that, in the handling of conflict, restorative justice is superior to retributive and purely rehabilitative responses.

The next two pieces in this section shift the focus slightly, from the historical use of restorative justice to practices in contemporary 'traditional' societies – albeit as described by non-indigeous commentators, rather than by indigenous people themselves – which exemplify its principles and methods. Rupert Ross, as Assistant Crown Attorney in northwestern Ontario, was responsible for criminal prosecutions in remote Cree and Ojibway First Nations. In September 1992 he embarked upon a three year secondment with the Aboriginal Justice Directorate of Justice Canada, in which he examined Aboriginal approaches to justice in the context of the wider visions of life of which they form a part. The reading here is from his book *Returning to the Teachings*, his fascinating report on his findings and personal struggle to understand the Aboriginal inclination for healing and peacemaking justice.

Ross shows how the idea of punishing solitary offenders is quite alien to traditional Aboriginal life, in which the proper response to 'crime' is the teaching and healing of all the parties involved. He then illustrates how this healing strategy works with the most serious offences and offenders. He does this through a very disturbing account of widespread sexual abuse – particularly of children – in many Aboriginal communities across Canada. Ross argues emphatically that widespread sexual abuse was not a part of traditional life. Rather, he contends, the 'cancer of sexual abuse' was a result of the destruction and denigration of all things Aboriginal by Western institutions. The journey to healing, then, had to involve a restoration of power to a people who had turned to sexual abuse after being stripped of their centre of life. The Community Holistic Circle Healing Program at Hollow Water, described by Ross, can only be properly understood and assessed in this context. It is not merely a new method, adopted to achieve a particular external goal. Rather, its very existence, as a revival of traditional Aboriginal approaches to justice, is part of the empowerment that is an essential part of the solution to the problems it addresses.

Similarly, the Navajo peacemaker courts were established as part of a broader struggle by Navajos to run their affairs in accordance with their own cultural traditions rather than in accordance with concepts, values and institutions imposed by the surrounding 'Anglo-European' culture. In the early 1980s, Navajo community leaders and judges began a process of reviving Navajo justice principles and methods. The result was a system of handling conflicts which differs radically in its foundational ideas and practices from Western criminal justice, yet which seems successful in resolving conflicts over 'criminal' conduct to the satisfaction of the parties involved and in preventing recidivism. The ideas on which this system is based, the way in which it works and the context in which it works are described here by two practitioners and advocates of Navajo peacemaking: Robert Yazzie and James W. Zion.

One of the most distinctive features of the Navajo court, according to this account, is that there are no judges, in the sense of specialists with the power to make decisions on behalf of others and to use coercive police power to ensure compliance with these legal decisions. In an 'egalitarian' process, the parties to a dispute, with their relatives, assisted by a peacemaker, resolve things themselves. The aim is conciliation rather than to divide disputants into winners and losers.

Importantly, the process seems to deal with much that, in Western criminal justice systems, would be regarded as the 'factual matters' of the dispute, such as the extent of the perpetrator's responsibility for the misconduct. For instance, perpetrators' attempts to justify or excuse their misconduct are assessed by the 'lay' participants in the process. This might serve as a corrective to the assumption, made in many discussions of restorative justice, that it comes into play only at the sentencing stage of the criminal justice process (i.e. after legal guilt has been determined by an impartial court or has been admitted by the perpetrator). The problem with this assumption is not that it is entirely incorrect. Rather, it is that in a fully fledged restorative justice system, such as that described by Yazzie and Zion, the sharp distinction *we* tend to draw between the trial and sentencing stage of the criminal justice process seems to have less of a rationale. Where the focus is not on the allocation of blame for 'criminal wrongdoing' but solving the problems which produced it and which arise from it, where disputing parties are not so sharply demarcated as victims or offenders (see Yazzie and Zion's discussion of the domestic dispute), and where responsibility for misconduct is less individualised/ more communal, the need for a highly legalised form of fact-finding seems less obvious.

Yazzie and Zion do not say, however, how the process would deal with cases where the alleged perpetrator denied committing the offence or denied any responsibility for his or her actions, but failed to convince anybody, including his or her own relatives, of his or her innocence. Presumably, since it is a principle of Navajo justice that people cannot be forced to do something they do not want to do – they must be persuaded to do it voluntarily – the alleged perpetrator could simply ignore all demands for reparation. However, on Yazzie and Zion's account, this would seem to leave the alleged perpetrator alone, outside the community, a position in which he or she could not function. Yazzie and Zion do not address this thorny issue. Perhaps such situations seldom if ever arise among the Navajos (i.e. perhaps false allegations of criminal wrongdoing are themselves largely a product of Western individualism).

One of the main values of this account of Navajo peacemaking is that it demonstrates how far-reaching the implications of restorative justice are. A *radical* shift towards restorative justice would mean more than a shift in our forms of sanctioning criminal misconduct and more than a shift towards a more participatory justice procedure. Taken to its logical conclusion, it would mean a shift in our conception of law itself. As Yazzie and Zion's piece (along with other readings in this section) shows, examples of restorative justice from 'other cultures' are really examples of radically different notions of law. For instance, in the Navajo peacemaking courts, the search for precedents to solve problems is not confined to a search through a narrow, clearly demarcated legal tradition. Rather, in their search for solutions to disputes, the Navajos draw on the full resources of Navajo culture. But, the Navajo courts are clearly not in the business of finding 'legal' solutions to disputes as we in the West understand it. There, much more so than here, the court is in the business of educating all who participate (broadly conceived) and, in the process, maintaining and repairing communal bonds between the individuals and groups that constitute the Navajo Nation.

The next reading presents a rather different type of account of indigenous justice. Jim Consedine (in Chapter 10) describes the Maori system of criminal justice which operates alongside the dominant English-derived system in New Zealand. Although many Maori activists insist that contemporary 'Maori justice' is *not* a modern version of traditional Maori justice, but is a practice influenced by non-Maori (Pakeha) traditions and was established precisely to destroy Maori judicial structures, Consedine presents it as a model of restorative justice. Maori justice, Consedine shows, is primarily about helping and healing, as opposed to retribution. It operates without lawyers, judges or police. Instead, the families of both sides to a criminal conflict come together to resolve collectively how the offender will be dealt with and what will be done for the victim.

Consedine provides some brief accounts of cases to illustrate how the process is informed by restorative principles and often has restorative outcomes. Interestingly, most of these cases involve rape and other sexual assaults. Under Pakeha criminal justice, the perpetrators of these attacks, if proved guilty, would be sent to prison where, according to Consedine, they would sit on all their anger. In contemporary Maori justice, on the other hand, the offenders are made to experience shame. They are expected to acknowledge the wrongness of their acts, show remorse, commit themselves to changing their attitudes and future behaviour, and undertake often quite arduous acts of compensation/reparation. On Consedine's account, many of them do co-operate with this process, never reoffend and become respectable and valuable members of their communities.

What about the victim? Consedine states that, under Pakeha justice, the victim would suffer a degrading court experience and then become a marked woman and have to leave town. Under Maori justice, the victim gets a chance to communicate her pain, distrust, anger, etc., to the perpetrator and others; to hear the perpetrator acknowledge that what he did was wrong and accept full responsibility for what occurred; to receive reparation; and – if she wishes – to forgive the perpetrator thereby ridding her herself of destructive emotions and putting the incident behind her. Victims of rape and other sexual assaults who have been through the process have apparently been well pleased with what it achieves.

One thing left unanswered in this piece, and in many such discussions, is what happens and what should happen when the perpetrator (or alleged perpetrator) refuses to co-operate with the process. Do we then have, and do we then need, Pakeha justice as a backup? But, assuming this issue could be resolved, there may still be concerns about the system of justice described by Consedine. For instance, on his account, rape and sexual assault do not only occur frequently among the Maori; they were once part of what appears to be an initiation ritual in Maori gangs. The Pakeha way of dealing with the problem may, as Consedine claims, have increased rather than reduced the incidence of such rape. The Maori justice approach, on the other hand, appears to have contributed to a reversal of the attitudes which encouraged such rape. Indeed, it seems to have resulted in gangs, formerly committed to rape, enforcing their new moral code against their own members. If we accept all this, then, as a purely practical solution to the problem of rape, Maori justice seems obviously more effective than Pakeha justice. But many, women in particular, would still find some of the 'sanctions' for what seem to have been brutal sexual assaults disturbingly mild. Some may wonder about whether it is right to encourage women to forgive those who committed such acts, even though they have shown genuine remorse and desire to change. Some may question whether, when it comes to rape, the willingness of the victim to be generous towards the attackers is enough to sanction a generous social response. An underlying issue here is that, as in the previous account of Navajo justice, a concept of 'community' is at work in these readings which may distort the reality of social relations – such as gender relations – in the societies they describe.

The final reading in this section (Chapter 11) shifts the focus slightly, from the roots of restorative justice in history and in the customs of Aboriginal peoples to its roots in biblical justice. The Bible is, of course, often interpreted as authorising severe retributive punishment. As Allard and Northey note, there are plenty of passages in the Hebrew Scriptures depicting Yahweh as a severe and even blood-thirsty judge, bent on violent punishment. Moreover, secular rulers have been all too eager to portray themselves as ministers of God's wrath. Church leaders have all too seldom challenged them in this, and all too often endorsed a theology of law and punishment and actively colluded with the secular punitive authorities.

In recent decades, however, the prevailing view of biblical justice has been challenged. A number of biblical scholars, whose key ideas are usefully summarised by Allard and Northey, now argue that the Hebrew Scriptures and New Testament point towards a restorative response to offenders. Support for such a reading is relatively easy to find in the New Testament. Jesus introduced a revolutionary ethic of forgiveness and the acceptance of 'prodigals'. He preached and practised the principle of loving one's enemy and those who are unjust. He taught that God loves us, not because we have earned it, but because we need His love, thereby paving the way for a needs-based – rather than desert-based – model of justice (on needs-based justice, see also Sullivan and Tifft, 2001). However, according to the biblical scholarship described by Allard and Northey, a proper reading of the Hebrew Scriptures reveals that it too authorises restorative rather than retributive justice. To understand this, it is necessary to shift our focus from the specific descriptions of divine punishment towards broader and more pervasive Old Testament themes, such as God's persistence in keeping his promise to his people, despite their persistent failure to adhere to their side of the Covenant (on this see also Yoder, 1987; Zehr, 1990: ch. 8).

So, why has the Christian tradition generally failed (spectacularly) to recognise this? Why has it drawn from the Old Testament an image of a wrathful, violent God? And, why has it interpreted the crucifixion of Christ as meaning that earthly punishment is demanded because God demanded the death of his son (on this, see also Gorringe, 1996)? In Allard and Northey's account, these 'misinterpretations' occurred when the Christian Church moved from being the persecuted to becoming the dominant power in society, itself involved in persecuting Pagans, Jews and other outsiders. A politically powerful church began reading the Bible though a different lens, finding in it a justification for its violent suppression of sin and evil. From then on, the Christian Church became a conservative force, rarely challenging and frequently supporting the state criminal justice system based on the repressive Roman slave law.

Now, though, with new readings available to us, Allard and Northey call for 'a radical reengagement of the Christian faith in criminal justice issues from a restorative justice perspective'. However, those who do not adhere to the Christian faith, and prefer to assess the case for restorative justice in more secular terms, can still learn from the scholarship which Allard and Northey so usefully discuss. In particular, this scholarship presents us with a powerful account of how the ideology of punitive justice has become so deeply rooted in Western cultural sensibilities, and how those who planted this ideology were influenced by the social position and interests of the Christian Church to overlook an earlier understanding of biblical justice as restorative justice.

Note

1 As far as I am aware, its significance to restorative justice was first brought out by Howard Zehr (see Zehr, 1990: 108 ff).

References

Berman, H. (1983) *Law and Revolution: The Formation of the Western Legal Tradition* (Cambridge, MA: Harvard University Press).

Gorringe, T. (1996) *God's Just Vengeance* (Cambridge: Cambridge University Press).

Hobbes, T. (1651/1991) *Leviathan* (Cambridge: Cambridge University Press).

Sullivan, D. and Tifft, L. (2001) *Restorative Justice: Healing the Foundations of our Everyday Lives* (Monsey, NY: Willow Tree Press).

Yoder, P. (1987) *Shalom: The Bible's Word for Salvation, Justice and Peace* (Newton, KN: Faith & Life Press).

Zehr, H. (1990) *Changing Lenses: A New Focus for Crime and Justice* (Scottdale, PA: Herald Press).

6. The background of the Western legal tradition

Harold J. Berman

[...]

As in many non-Western cultures, the basic law of the peoples of Europe from the sixth to the tenth centuries was not a body of rules imposed from on high but was rather an integral part of the common consciousness, the 'common conscience', of the community. The people themselves, in their public assemblies, legislated and judged; and when kings asserted their authority over the law it was chiefly to guide the custom and the legal consciousness of the people, not to remake it. The bonds of kinship, of lordship units, and of territorial communities *were* the law. If those bonds were violated, the initial response was to seek vengeance, but vengeance was supposed to give way – and usually did – to negotiation for pecuniary sanctions and to reconciliation. Adjudication was often a stage in the reconciliation process. And so peace, once disrupted, was to be restored ultimately by diplomacy. Beyond the question of right and wrong was the question of reconciliation of the warring factions. The same can be said also of the law of many contemporary so-called primitive societies of Africa, Asia, and South America, as well as of many ancient civilizations of both the past and the present.

Before the professionalization and systematization of law, more scope was left for people's attitudes and beliefs and for their unconscious ideas, their processes of mythical thought. This gave rise to legal procedures which depended heavily on ritual and symbol and which in that sense were highly technical, but by the same token the substantive law was plastic and largely nontechnical. Rights and duties were not bound to the letter of legal texts but instead were a reflection of community values, a living law which sprang, in Fritz Kern's words, 'out of the creative wells of the sub-conscious'. Kern recognized that the customary law of this early period of European history was often 'vague, confused, and impractical, technically clumsy', but that it was also 'creative, sublime, and suited to human needs'.[1] These characterizations, too, are applicable to the legal concepts and processes of many contemporary nonliterate cultures of Africa, Asia, and South America, as well as to complex, literate, ancient civilizations such as those of China, Japan, and India.

Thus many characteristics of the Germanic folklaw that to Western eyes appear to be weaknesses may to non-Western eyes appear to be strengths. The absence of law reform movements, of sophisticated legal machinery, of a strong central lawmaking authority, of a strong central judicial authority, of a body of law independent of religious beliefs and emotions, of a systematic legal science – are only one side of the coin. The other side is the presence of a sense of the wholeness of life, of the interrelatedness of law with all other aspects of life, a sense that legal institutions and legal processes as well as legal norms and legal decisions are all integrated in the harmony of the universe. Law, like art and myth and religion, and like language itself, was for the peoples of Europe, in the early stages of their history, not primarily a matter of making and applying rules in order to determine guilt and fix judgment, not an instrument to separate people from one another on the basis of a set of principles, but rather a matter of holding people together, a matter of reconciliation. Law was conceived primarily as a mediating process, a mode of communication, rather than primarily as a process of rule-making and decision-making.

In these respects, Germanic and other European folklaw had much in common with certain Eastern legal philosophies. In the Sufi tradition of the Middle East, one of the stories told of the Mulla Nasrudin depicts him as a magistrate hearing his first case. The plaintiff argues so persuasively that Nasrudin exclaims, 'I believe you are right'. The clerk of the court begs him to restrain himself, since the defendant is yet to be heard. Listening to the defendant's argument, Nasrudin is again so carried away that he cries out, 'I believe you are right'. The clerk of the court cannot allow this. 'Your honor,' he says, 'they cannot both be right.' 'I believe you are right,' Nasrudin replies.[2] Both are right, yet both cannot be right. The answer is not to be found by asking the question, Who is right? The answer is to be found by saving the honor of both sides and thereby restoring the right relationship between them.

In the tradition of peoples of Asia who have lived under the strong influence of both Buddhist and Confucian thought, social control is not to be found primarily in the allocation of rights and duties through a system of general norms but rather in the maintaining of right relationships among family members, among families within lordship units, and among families and lordship units within local communities and under the emperor. Social harmony is more important than 'giving to each his due'. Indeed, 'each' is not conceived as a being distinct from his society – or from the universe – but rather as an integral part of a system of social relationships subject to the Principle of Heaven. Therefore in the ancient civilizations of Asia the traditional, collective, and intuitive sides of life were emphasized, and the intellectual, analytical, and legal sides were fused with and subordinated to them.[3]

This was true also of the peoples of Europe before the great explosion of the late eleventh and early twelfth centuries. The folk myths which dominated their thought prior to (and after) the introduction of Christianity did not make a sharp division between magic and logic or between fate and the rules of criminal law. Nor did Christianity – an Eastern religion – make a sharp division between faith and reason.

But is it possible to say that law exists in a society whose social order reflects an 'Eastern' concept of the fusion, or harmony, of all aspects of social life? Does law exist, for example, among the Tiv of northern Nigeria, who have a system of social control which rests on clan and lineage loyalties, clan reprisals, and ritual reparation to avoid punishment by supernatural sources, but who have no distinct governmental institutions, no courts, and no word in their language for law?[4] They accept certain rules as binding upon them, certain decisions as authoritative, and certain procedures for declaring these rules and decisions effective. Does the fact that *they* do not distinguish these procedures and decisions and rules from religion, politics, economics, and family life, and do not call them 'law', mean that *we* should not call them law? May we not say that among the Tiv – and in many other societies – *what we call law* is wholly diffuse, wholly interwoven with religion, political, economic, family, and other social institutions and processes? [. . .]

This extract is taken from Law and Revolution: the Formation of the Western Legal Tradition, *by Harold J. Berman (Cambridge, MA: Harvard University Press, 1983), pp. 77–9.*

Notes

1 Kern, *Kingship and Law*, p. 180. Kern speaks of 'medieval' law, but he is clearly referring to the folklaw of the Early Middle Ages, that is, the period prior to the late eleventh century.
2 The story is told in Robert E. Ornstein, *The Psychology of Consciousness*.
3 On the intuitive (including mystical and poetic) and the analytical as two complementary aspects of consciousness . . . see Ornstein, *Psychology of Consciousness*. [. . .]
4 See Paul Bohannan, *Justice and Judgment among the Tiv* (London, 1957).

References

Bohannan, P. (1957) *Justice and Judgment among the Tiv* (London).
Kern, F. (1939) *Kingship and Law in the Middle Ages* (trans. S.B. Chrimes) (Oxford: Oxford University Press).
Ornstein, R.E. (1972) *The Psychology of Consciousness* (San Francisco, CA: Freeman).

7. The history of restorative justice

Elmar G.M. Weitekamp

[...]

1. Restorative justice in acephalous societies

According to Michalowski (1985), human societies can be broken down into two broad categories: acephalous (non-state) and state. Acephalous societies, the earliest type, did not have rulers and were the only type of human community for some 30,000 years. Acephalous societies can, according to Hartmann (1995), be distinguished as nomadic tribes and segmental societies. The former are constituted by gatherers and hunters, while segmental societies develop if the tribe changes from a food-gathering to a food-producing economy. These societies were small, economically cooperative, and relatively egalitarian, and used simple technology. Toennies' (1940) concept of *gemein-schaft* comes to mind in this regard. That these societal forms were very basic and stable did not preclude instances of deviance or trouble. As Michalowski (1985) pointed out, because of the acephalous society's diffuse structure, kin-based social organization and the concept of collective responsibility, individuals were bound very strongly to the group, thus reducing the likelihood of egoistic interests. These characteristics also minimized the potential for trouble while producing conformity and placing restraints on a potential deviant. If trouble did occur, the acephalous society resolved it without a formal legal system. After evaluating the harm, the society had to regain its lost balance by doing something either for the victim or to the offender. A state of unrest remained until the victim was satisfied; and because collective responsibility was combined with important social and economic ties between the offender's group and the victim, a resolution was important for facilitating a quick return to daily life. Resolutions were usually achieved through: (1) blood revenge, (2) retribution, (3) ritual satisfaction or (4) restitution.
   [...]

Restitution

Restitution was probably the most common form of resolving a conflict in acephalous societies because it also allowed the disputing clans to resume normal relations expeditiously. Since both the offender's clan and the victim's clan were involved in the restitution negotiations, both were to a certain degree in control of the negotiations and their outcome, thus allowing a compromise that satisfied both parties. According to Nader and Combs-Schilling (1977: 34–5), the restitution process in acephalous societies constituted six purposes and functions: (1) to prevent further, more serious, conflicts, particularly to avoid a feud; (2) to rehabilitate the offender back into society as quickly as possible and to avoid a negative stigma; (3) to provide for the victim's needs; (4) to restate the values of the society by addressing the needs of both the victim and the offender, thus indicating that the society desired some type of justice for all its members; (5) to socialize the members about its norms and values; and (6) to provide regulation as well as deterrence for its members. These functions clearly indicate that restitution as a form of sanction had multiple purposes in these societies and that these elements are clearly restorative justice-oriented.

One of the main reasons for the underlying pressure to come to an agreement in kinship networks was the implicit threat of a feud should no settlement be reached. After a crime was committed, a cooling-off period usually took place, during which some safety measures were provided for the offender and after which the case was evaluated. According to Nader and Combs-Schilling (1977), in some societies the offender fled to the household of a sacred leader who provided sanctuary until the conflict was resolved. The sacred leader was often chosen as the negotiator between the victim's and the offender's clans. In the absence of a sacred person, the offender and his clan often had to flee the area for safety reasons or break off communications with the other community groups until a negotiator with ties to both groups initiated the mediating process. This negotiator was frequently a member of the offender's clan who had married into the victim's group.

[. . .]

Negotiated restitution or compensation culminating in some form of payment to the victim was an important mechanism for resolving criminal behavior in acephalous societies; there was no need for either supra-familial authority or state control. As this type of society is brought within a state legal system, it is apparent that severe conflicts will arise, one of which is often the absence of restitution or compensation in the state legal system. As Nader and Combs-Schilling illustrate (1977), this conflict can be observed in countries such as Zambia, Sardinia, Mexico, and Lebanon. Canter (1973) described this process among the Mongule tribe of Zambia as follows:

> Prior to the imposition of state law, cattle-rustling cases were settled by restitution. With state law, people accused and convicted of cattle rustling were sent to jail. To make matters worse, jailing people did not decrease the incidence of cattle rustling. The Mungule measure the competence of the legal system by whether there is a decrease in recidivism, by which they would mean a decrease in cattle-rustling cases. Since they lost confidence in the State legal system, the consequences were 'self-help' and rioting (n.p.; cited in Nader and Comb-Schilling, 1977: 35).

Schneider (1988) described a similar process for the Aborigines in Australia. Originally they formed a peaceful, ecologically balanced, nomadic culture with strong familial and tribal orientations. Following the invasion of white settlers, however, their lifestyle was destroyed, and they were forcibly resettled into three reservations. By imposing upon the Aborigines a white Protestant culture, the Australians created a culture conflict that led to the destruction of the former's culture. Today welfare checks have replaced hunting and gathering. The Aborigines' high crime rate constitutes 1% of the total rate in Australia, yet this group represents 30% of the prison population. Since they view crime as a collapse of relationships rather than as an individual guilt phenomenon, the Aborigines reject the white criminal justice system because its formality makes reconciliation impossible. Imprisonment is not a deterrent; and once they are released on parole they cannot be supervised because of the difficult topographical conditions in which they live. Grabosky (1989) noted that the new approach of the Australian government is to let the Aborigines handle their own problems because all the programs – and there have been many – it has imposed have failed miserably.

As we pointed out earlier, the historical origin of restorative justice has existed since humans began forming communities. It is easy to assume from the literature that punishment is the most universal way of responding to norm violators. However, by expanding the analysis to acephalous societies, we find that restitution to victims and their kin frequently takes precedence over taking action against the offender, and that the reestablishment of peace in society or *gemeinschaft* was of utmost interest. While restitution or compensation takes something away from the offender, it is different in form, purpose and consequences from punishment in the form of revenge or retribution. Human societies seek to resolve problems, but that does not necessarily mean that something must be done to the offender out of a desire for revenge. As Michalowski (1985) concluded:

> It is ironic that modern state societies, with their elaborate institutions for law enforcement (often supported by an array of high-technology crime control devices such as cars, two-way radios, computers, etc.), cannot achieve the degree of social order and long term stability characteristic of simpler societies that have none of these tools. The reason for this seeming irony is that the degree of social peace a society enjoys depends upon the nature of its social organization, not upon its ability to capture and punish those defined as deviant (p. 65).

A number of characteristics contributed to order without a state government in acephalous societies. These societies were more egalitarian; and most of their members had nearly equal access to material consumption and opportunities to develop a sense of personal worth. This might explain why there was little basis for the development of property crimes in these societies. In addition, because every member was necessary for the life of the community, deviant members were neither devalued nor disgraced, nor did they receive a negative label or stigma for even a short period of time as these societies were interested in restoring the peace as quickly as possible. Because these communities were small, all relationships and interactions were personal, thus leading to strong bonds among the members and a reduction in deviant behavior. Usually viewed in these groups as a collective responsibility, deviant behavior constituted both a community problem and a community failure and thus provided motivation for all the members to resolve the conflict – most commonly by means of kin-based restitution and in a restorative justice manner.

[. . .]

These few examples from an abundant literature on primitive and acephalous societies reflect the wide extent of restorative justice in some form, and indicate that 'punishment' – in today's sense – was the exception rather than the norm. It is no surprise that Fry (1951: 124) asked: 'Have we not neglected overmuch the customs of our earlier ancestors in the matter of restitution? We have seen that in primitive societies this idea of "making up" for a wrong done has wide currency. Let us once more look into the ways of earlier men, which may still hold some wisdom for us.' Tallack (1900: 7) argued similarly in comparing ancient forms with more modern forms of punishment: 'For injuries both to person, or property, it enacted restitution, or reparation, in some form, as the chief, and often as the whole, element of punishment. And this was wiser in principle, more reformatory in its influence, more deterrent in its tendency and more economic to the community . . .' Barnes and Teeters (1959: 401) suggested: 'It is perhaps worth noting that our barbarian ancestors were wiser and more just than we are today, for they adopted the theory of restitution to the injured, whereas we have abandoned this practice, to the detriment of all concerned.'

2. Restitution in early state societies

In examining the early literature on restitution and elements of restorative justice, we find that the scholars usually began with state societies rather than acephalous societies (Klein, 1978; Laster, 1975; Schafer, 1970a; Sutherland and Cressey, 1960; Wolfgang, 1965; to name but a few), thus taking for granted the existence of political power and state law. This might explain why, according to Schafer (1970a), many scholars have identified the historical origin of restitution as a key element of restorative justice in the Middle Ages. Schafer (1970a) also pointed out that earlier sources did not offer clear information, and thus he found only sporadic reference to restitution. As we have shown, that is not the case. Overlooking earlier historical facts means that if we change its basic elements, we have limited our ability to understand how a society changes in defining and dealing with trouble.

As in acephalous societies, the norms and laws of early Western cultures provided forms of restitution and elements of restorative justice for the parties involved in a dispute. The Code of Hammurabi (c. 2380 BC) espoused the practice of individual compensation, which, according to Gillin (1935), was related primarily to property offences and in general did not apply to personal injuries; however, in one case it served as a substitute for the death penalty. The Code of Hammurabi is the only source in the historical literature on restitution where the concept of restitution is restricted to property crimes. In all the other sources, this concept is applied to both property and personal crimes. Drapkin (1989) also identifies elements and/or true concepts of restorative justice for almost all societies in the ancient world that included property offences as well as crimes against persons. Therefore, we have been unable to determine why the concept of restorative justice and restitution in today's literature is almost always limited to property offences.

It is interesting to note that all the authors in the 1970s and 1980s have focused on restitution and restorative justice as a concept for property offences without providing a reasonable explanation for the exclusion of personal crimes. They simply take for granted the exclusion of personal crimes, even though an examination of the history of restorative justice elements and forms clearly emphasizes the applicability of a restorative justice approach for personal crimes. In addition, most of the literature on acephalous societies deals with restorative justice elements and forms of personal crimes since property crimes played a minor role in those societies. The limitation of restitution and restorative justice to just property offences [. . .] hampered the movement of restorative justice for the better part of the 1970s and 1980s and has no logical explanation.

The early Hebrews also used restitution and forms of restorative justice for personal crimes. Gillin (1935: 198) described the case of two men involved in a fight that resulted in non-fatal injuries to one of the men. The one who inflicted the injury was required to pay for the employment time the other man lost due to the healing process. Similarly, if an ox was known to be dangerous but the owner did not take proper precautions and the ox gored a person to death, both the ox and its owner were to be killed unless the victim's family was willing to accept a reparation instead. Tyler (1889, cited in Gillin, 1935) reported that the transition from blood vengeance to compensation could be observed in Arabia. While the nomad tribes outside the cities continued to enforce the blood feud rather strictly, the people living in the cities found it necessary to resolve violent conflicts through compensation in order to avoid the blood feud's devastating effects.

Homer, in the Ninth Book of the *Iliad*, referred to the case of Ajax, who reproached Achilles for not accepting Agamemnon's offer of reparation. Ajax reminded Achilles that even a brother's death may be compensated by the payment of money so that the murderer, having paid restitution, may remain free among his people. Tacitus (n.d., as cited in Michalowski, 1985) reported that among the ancient Germans: 'Even homicide is atoned by a certain fine in cattle and sheep; and the whole family accepts the satisfaction to the advantage of the public weal, since quarrels are most dangerous in a free state.'

Diamond's (1935) research on the sanctions imposed for homicide confirmed that monetary restitution was an accepted form throughout the Western world:

> Of fifty to one hundred scattered tribal communities as to which the information available is of undoubted reliability 73 per cent called for a pecuniary sanction versus 14 per cent [that] called for a certain number of persons to be handed over to the family of the victim as a sanction. This too is actually a fine, though not a monetary one. One hundred per cent of the Early and Early Middle Codes, beginning with the Salic code (around 500–600 AD) and lasting through the Anglo-Saxon laws (900–1100 AD), called for pecuniary sanctions for homicide. It was not until the Late Middle and Late Codes that death was established as the exclusive sanction for intentional homicide (p. 148; as cited in Barnett, 1977: 352).

Schafer (1970a) noted that among Semitic nations the death fine was used and continued to prevail under the Turkish Empire. He also described the use of restitution and atonement among Indian Hindus under the theme of 'he who atones is forgiven', where the offender was obliged to pay compensation to the king, the relatives of the deceased or both.

While each tribe had its own set of laws, the contents of these laws were quite similar. The first written laws were the Salic Law of the Franks (about 500 AD) and the Laws of Ethelbert of Kent (about 600 AD), whose main concern was to avoid the blood feud. Every crime was a crime against the family or clan, and the offender's clan was held responsible for crimes committed by its members. The Laws of Ethelbert invented a system of compensation involving the *wergild*, *bot* and *wite* (Jeffrey, 1957). The *wergild* was money paid to a family for the death of one of its members; the *bot* was money paid for injuries not leading to the death of a family member; and the *wite* was money paid to a mediator to cover the costs of overseeing the compensation plan. However, some crimes were considered *botless* crimes, that is, no bot or compensation could be paid, making it necessary for the victim's family to resort to the blood feud. An example of a *botless* crime was a secret murder. The *wergild* was to be paid by the offender, often with the help of friends and family, within 12 months. If the offender failed to pay the compensation, he or she was liable to bear the consequences of a vendetta.

These tribes developed extremely elaborate systems of accounting for the injuries suffered by their members. Under the Laws of Ethelbert, according to Pollock and Maitland (1968: 460, as cited in Barnett, 1977: 351): '. . . the four front teeth were worth 6 shillings each, the teeth next to them four, the others one; thumbs, thumbnails, forefingers, middle fingers, ringfingers, little fingers and their respective fingernails were all distinguished and a separate *bot* [italics added] was set for each . . .' Gillin (1935) reported that similarly, under the early Saxon Laws a man who knocked out the front tooth of another man had to pay eight shillings; if it was an eyetooth he had to pay four shillings, and if it was a molar the price was 15 shillings. In addition, the Saxons had a catalog for almost all types of injuries. Similar provisions can be found in the Salic Laws of the Franks, where compensation rates were provided in detail for all types of crimes. It is interesting to note that compensation was determined by the rank of the injured person. Gillin (1935) further noted that compensation for the murder of a free Frank or a barbarian was 800 dinars, with half the restitution money paid to the sons of the slain father and the other half to the nearest relatives on both the mother's and father's sides. In the absence of relatives, the money went to the 'fisc', or royal treasury. Private revenge by the victims or their clans was sanctioned in this tribal society. However, if offenders refused to pay the demanded compensation they were, according to Schafer (1968), stigmatized as outlaws, and any member of the community could kill them with impunity.

As these examples of early state societies demonstrate, restitution was an important tool for resolving conflicts. As in acephalous societies, the main reason was to avoid the devastating effects of the blood feud. The reported systems of compensation and restitution were applied mostly for crimes against the person rather than property offences. As the form of the tribal organization advanced, the role of a recognized ruler or chief, with the authority to issue commands, increased, Michalowski (1985) describes these early forms of proto-states that were characterized by simple technology, simple division of labor, some form of control over the produced property and limited material inequality. The rulers and chiefs exercised a certain degree of power, but could [not] control or exploit the labor of others by making them work for the former because the state lacked a class of rule enforcers. The rules were enforced by the rulers' kinship members, who had to work for the support of the kinship in the first place, thus limiting the rulers' power.

As centralized rulers emerged and took an increasingly interested and active role in the resolution of trouble, the needs of the victims, as Schafer noted (1968), were replaced progressively by the interests of the state as the basis for settling conflicts. Michalowski (1985) describes a Zulu tribe where people were said to belong to the king. As a result, restitution was no longer paid to the victim and his clan but rather to the king. The king collected monetary restitution from the offender for having killed one of his people, thus denying the victim and his clan compensation for the loss suffered. This decline in the victim's role in settling disputes signified an important change in the nature of social control. As the leader or the state became the central leader for settling disputes, he or it took this role away from the clans or kinship, thus making a restorative justice approach impossible. Responsibilities became increasingly individualized rather than collective, thus making more abstract the obligation to conform to social rules. As historian Maine (1905, as cited in Michalowski, 1985) observed, with the coming of the state power 'the individual is steadily substituted for the family as the unit of which civil laws take account'. [. . .]

In the Anglo-Saxon hemisphere, the increasing power of kingships as trans-local and trans-tribal institutions, uniting large areas containing various people, marked the beginning of a radical change in societal structure: the communitarian tribal society was supplanted by a hierarchical feudal system. After the division of the Frankish Empire by the treaty of Verdun in 843 AD, restitution was replaced by a fine, assessed by a tribunal, which went to the state rather than to the victim and his kinship. Parallel with the rise of the feudal system was the increasing influence of Christianity on legal concepts. According to Barnett (1977), the rise of Christianity influenced ecclesiastical law leading to canon law and an attempt to influence tribal, local and feudal customs in Europe. Using this system as their model and their rival, the kings created their own legal systems that vested legal and political authority in themselves. Previously as Oppenheimer (1913: 162, as cited in Barnett, 1977: 353) noted, the state was concerned only with its own affairs and 'did not include among its functions the repression of wrongs between individual and individual, between family and family, between clan and clan'. The crown began to claim a share of the compensation payment, according to Oppenheimer (1913: 162), as: 'a commission for this trouble in bringing about a reconciliation between the parties, or, perhaps as the price payable to the malefactor either for the opportunity which the community secures for him of redeeming his wrong by a money payment, or for the protection which it affords him after he has satisfied the award, against further retaliation on the part of the man whom he has injured'.

Tallack (1900) referred to the greedy feudal barons and ecclesiastical powers who exacted a double vengeance upon the offender by taking his property instead of giving it to the victim and his kinship, and by applying corporal punishment or imprisonment to the offender while ignoring the victim. By monopolizing the institution of dispute settlement, the kings increased their share of payments and eventually absorbed the entire amount (Schafer, 1975b). Jeffrey (1957) reported similarly that:

> Early Germanic justice was based on a folkpeace, a peace of the community. This idea gave way to the *mund* [italics added]. A *mund* [italics added] was the right of the king or lord had [*sic*] to protect a person or area. At first the *mund* [italics added] was restricted to special persons and areas; gradually it was extended to include the king's court, army, servants, hundredcourt, and finally the four main highways in England. It was now referred to as the king's peace. The kings, lords, and bishops now received the compensation rather than the kinship group. They had a *mund* [italics added] which had to be protected (p. 657).

Wolfgang (1965) pointed out that the state's claim to the exclusive right to inflict punishment was made in the interest of peace but not necessarily of justice. He noted further that:

> It may be argued that an injury to any citizen is an injury to the social whole of which the citizen is a member, but under the feudal system (and as late as Louis XIV who dared to say, 'L'etat c'est moi') the grand seigneurs disposed of the property and persons of the common people on the pretext of their criminality, almost at discretion. Using the principle of composition of public injuries to find [*sic*] offenders, they abused their power until the administration of justice became an act of confiscation, if not outright blackmail (p. 9).

By the end of the 12th century the erosion of restorative justice elements and restitution in Europe was complete; but the system of compensation surrendered only after a struggle. The system was not voluntarily abandoned by the people; it was deliberately and forcibly co-opted by the crown and then discarded. The victim's right to receive compensation directly from the offender and his kinship was transferred to the collective society, where it remains to this day.

As Barnett (1977) pointed out rightly, that criminal punishment by the state emerged from a bloody Hobbesian jungle is pure myth. Monetary payments replaced violence as the means of dispute settlement and have functioned well for most of the time humans have lived together if we include acephalous societies. It was through the violent conquest of most of Europe that state criminal punishment was accepted reluctantly. Michalowski (1985) noted that formal law emerged as a means of controlling property relations in civilizations and that the concept of individual property and the history of law are inseparable or, in Jeremy Bentham's words (cited in Diamond, 1935: 33), 'Property and law are born together and die together'.

Before turning our attention to more recent developments in the area of restorative justice, we must clarify a controversy about restitution as one form of restorative justice in the Middle Ages. As Klein (1978: 383) noted, 'If one is to believe Pollock and Maintland (1968), the state of affairs during what Schafer (1968) has termed the "golden age of the victim" can only be described as brutal.' Geis (1977: 150–2) also called for the dismemberment that surrounds the history of restitution, while others (Jacob, 1970; Laser, 1975; Wolfgang, 1965; Schafer, 1968, to name but a few) have emphasized that restitution was used widely and well in the Middle Ages. While one side of this controversy praises the Middle Ages for its wise use of restorative justice as a humane penal sanction perceived as being beneficial to the offender and his kinship, the victim and his kinship, and society in general, the other side argues that this view is absolutely wrong, that restorative justice in its applied forms was abused by people in power, misused by the rich people as a cheap way out of trouble, and led to chaos in society. The restorative justice advocates argue in addition that restorative justice and restitution disappeared as a penal sanction after the state took over the criminal justice system, thus leading to an inhumane and brutal system of criminal justice where the victim had no place. The other side argues that the state moved in and took control of the criminal justice system because of the public outcry about the horrors of the existing system. While this controversy appears to be unsolvable, we suggest that by looking at the definition of the Middle Ages we might find a reasonable solution to this dilemma. *The Random House Dictionary of the English Language* (1968: 906) defines the Middle Ages as: '. . . the time in European history between classical antiquity and the Italian Renaissance (from the late 5th century AD to about 1350): sometimes restricted to the later part of this period (after 1100) and sometimes extended to 1450 to 1500.'

Because this definition indicates two time frames for the Middle Ages, we think it is worthwhile to examine both in connection with restorative justice and the controversy surrounding these periods. If we talk about the Middle Ages as occurring from 500 to 1350, the advocates of restorative justice and restitution are correct because, for the better part of that period, restorative justice was used in a humane way that benefited the victim, the offender and society in general. According to the advocates, the use of restorative justice declined at the beginning of the 12th century; and it is generally agreed that by the end of that century the erosion of restorative justice was complete. If, on the other hand, the critics of the historical use of restorative justice use the time frame from 1100 to 1500 – as their criticism indicates – they are right as well. Geis (1977) uses historical examples in his critique in which he clearly talks about a time during which kings established their power and took the conflict-solving process away from the parties involved by creating a firm, state-controlled, criminal justice system. Klein (1978: 383–5) writes about the same time frame and the atrocities committed during the decline of restorative justice approaches and the establishment of a state-run criminal justice system.

All the evidence in this controversy indicates that the facts presented by both sides are correct and that the two definitions of the Middle Ages, which are both correct, led to the controversy. However, Geis (1977) and Klein (1978) were incorrect in their historical critiques of restorative justice and restitution because they ignored the 'golden age of the victim', and began their reviews with the decline of the restorative justice approach and restitution as a penal sanction. Their critiques of the decline period were nevertheless correct because restorative justice approaches and elements had prevailed for about 600 years, and both periods took place in what is known as the Middle Ages.

3. Restitution at the turn of the century

By the end of the 12th century the erosion of restorative justice elements was complete, and the state had taken control of the criminal law. Harding (1982) noted that as the rights of the state gradually overshadowed and supplanted those of the victim, the link among restorative justice, restitution and punishment was severed. As Harding (1982) and Schafer (1970a) pointed out, restorative justice and restitution to the victim plays an insignificant role in the administration of criminal law and justice, and, with the disappearance of compensation, a crime was considered an offence against the state while a tort was an offence against individual rights only. The victim, in terms of his or her rights to pursue compensation or restitution for damages suffered, had to pursue his or her claim through the separate body of civil law. Because the victim could not always afford the expense in terms of time and money of bringing a civil action against the offender, Harding (1982) concluded that the civil remedy had not been a very effective measure for obtaining restitution on the victim's behalf, let alone the principles of restorative justice and their benefits for the victim, the offender, their extended families, the communities and society.

In some countries the criminal case was combined with civil action for purposes of procedural processing. In the 16th and 17th centuries the German legal system developed the '*Adhaesionsprozess*' in which the judge of a criminal process was allowed, at his discretion, to decide a victim's claim for restitution within the scope of the criminal proceeding. As Schafer (1970b) noted, the criminal trial still predominates in the German system and takes precedence over hearing the victim's claim. For reasons of convenience, the victim's claim for restitution is heard at the same time as the criminal charges; however, technically, the two hearings are independent of each other. This practice has been adopted by a number of other countries. However, as Schafer (1970a) pointed out, it was almost abandoned only a few years after its invention and was kept alive only by the force of tradition. In general, because victims are ignored by most criminal justice systems, they have been forced to resort to civil law procedures to obtain restitution or compensation.

Despite the increasing interest in reforming the offender, which has been matched by decreasing concern for the victim, some legal philosophers and reformers have reiterated the importance of restitution and compensation and, on a more general level, a restorative justice approach. Among them were Sir Thomas More who suggested in his 17th century *Utopia* that restitution should be made by offenders to their victims and that offenders should be required to work for the public to raise money for the restitution payments. Another philosopher, James Wilson (1985), discusses justice as the protection of rights through restorative justice: 'Every crime, as we have seen, includes an injury: this I consider as a leading maxim in the doctrine of crimes. In the punishment of every crime, reparation for the included injury ought to be involved; this I consider a leading maxim in the doctrine of punishments' (as cited in McCloskey, 1984: 626).

Other advocates of restorative justice and restitution have outlined similar plans of reparation. Despite the widespread adoption of retributive justice throughout Europe, Beccaria (1977) emerged as a brilliant criminal law reformer. Credited with having begun the classical school with its seemingly rigid approach, Beccaria was actually a humanitarian opposed to capital punishment and the often arbitrary and unfair way the law was applied, thus laying the groundwork for advocates of restorative justice. Bentham (1977: 40), for instance, stressed the necessity of taking care of the crime victim by means of restorative justice: '[S]atisfaction is necessary in order to cause the evil . . . to cease, and reestablish everything in the condition it was before the offence; to replace the individual who has suffered in the lawful condition in which he would have been if the law had not been violated.' He argued strongly for a restorative justice approach of punishment and complained that satisfaction is given with grudging parsimony while punishment is meted out with a lavish hand. One of the first advocates of a state compensation plan should the offender be unable to pay satisfaction, he considered satisfaction almost as necessary as punishment and beneficial to the public.

Bonneville de Marsangy proposed in 1847 a compensation plan that combined restitution and compensation:

> Now if it is true that there is no real social security without reparation, the conclusion is that this reparation must take place, cost what it will, and as one of the *sine qua non* [italics added] conditions of the social contract; and that, in consequence, society must rigorously impose it on the culprit, at the same time and under the same justification that it imposes punishment on him; however, by the same token, we must conclude that [if] there is no known culprit, society itself must assume the responsibility for reparation. . . . It would be easy to show, with arguments of an irresistible logic, that, when the authors of a crime are unknown or when the condemned persons are insolvent, the State should repair the harm done to the victim (Normandeau, 1973: 133).

Ferri (1917) argued that the state was negligent in protecting its citizens and must be indemnified for the harm caused them by crimes; the state must take into account the victim's rights. Garofalo (1914) pointed out the benefits of restorative justice to society as a whole: 'If offenders were persuaded that . . . they could in no wise evade the obligation to repair the damage [of] which they have been the cause, the ensuing discouragement to the criminal world . . . would be far greater than that produced by temporary curtailment of their liberty' (p. 419).

Advocacy for restorative justice, restitution and compensation was discussed at a number of International Prison Congress meetings between 1878 and 1900. At the 1878 Congress in Stockholm, it was proposed that all nations return to the ancient concept of restitution; Garofalo raised the same issue at the next Congress in Rome in 1885 (Jacob, 1970). Further Congresses in 1890 in Petersburg, Russia and in 1891 in Christiana, Norway, led, according to Schafer (1970b: 10) to the following conclusions:

1. modern law does not sufficiently consider the reparation to injured parties;
2. in the case of petty offences, time should be given for indemnification; and
3. prisoner's earnings in prison might be used to this end.

At the following Congress in 1895 the question of restorative justice, restitution and compensation to the victim was dealt with intensively. As Schafer (1970b) pointed out, it was felt that (1) modern laws were weak on this point, and (2) in some countries the laws were harder on the victim than on the offender. The final resolutions of this Congress were similar to the conclusions of the Christiana meeting, and, in the absence of sufficient evidence, the problem was adjourned to the next meeting. At the Brussels Congress in 1900, restorative justice and restitution were discussed exhaustively, and, as Barrows (1903) reported, Prins (1895) proposed that restitution be considered a condition of suspension of sentence or of conditional release after imprisonment. The penalists tried to agree upon a resolution that was presented by Garofalo and described by Barrows (1903) in his summary report about the conference as follows:

> In the case of prisoners having property, steps should be taken to secure it, and to prevent illegal transfers. As to insolvent offenders, other methods of constraint must be sought. The minimum term of imprisonment being sufficiently high, its execution should be suspended in the case of offenders who beyond the costs of the process have paid a sum fixed by the judge as reparation for the injured party, exception being made in the case of professional criminals and recidivists. The State Treasury would gain, since it would not only be spared the expense of supporting the prisoner, but would be reimbursed for all other expenses. The delinquent would be punished and the injured party reimbursed. In the case of serious offences in which imprisonment is deemed necessary, Garofalo would make parole after a certain time of imprisonment depend on the willingness of the prisoner to reimburse his victim from his earnings saved in prison. He favors a public fund to assure reparation for those who cannot obtain it in any other manner (pp. 23–4).

Unfortunately, the members of the conference were unable to pass any specific proposal or resolution that would have required restorative justice and restitution in any of its various forms. The members did finally pass a resolution that merely readopted the recommendations of the previous Congress, and called for increasing the rights of the victim of a crime under civil law. As Geis (1977: 160) noted, the Brussels Congress had the effect of 'blatantly misstating both the ingredients and the spirit of the earlier resolutions and effectively managed to bury the subject of victim compensation as a significant agenda topic at international penological gatherings from hence forth to the present time'. The resolution adopted buried not only the subject of victim compensation by the state but restitution by the offender to the victim, as well as any other restorative justice components. [. . .]

Conclusions

As we have shown, humans have used forms of restorative justice for the larger part of their existence. Penal law and the often destructive retributive answer to crime – or, more recently, the failed rehabilitative efforts – have been fairly new. The two latter approaches have led to systems of (in)justice that have to be considered as failures. Forms of restorative justice, as we could find them in acephalous societies and especially early state societies, seem to be the better answer to the crime problem of today's societies. It is interesting to note that [currently] the most promising answers to the ills of society caused by crime are of a restorative justice nature. The family group conferences of New Zealand and other forms of conflict resolution as practiced by indigenous people seem to be in this context the most promising ones, and can look back to an extraordinarily long tradition. The advantage of such programs lie in their healing power for all involved people, and the participation of the enlarged family, social group and community.

This extract is taken from 'The History of Restorative Justice', by Elmar G.M. Weitekamp, in G. Bazemore and L. Walgrave (eds), Restorative Juvenile Justice: Repairing the Harm of Youth Crime *(Monsey, NY: Criminal Justice Press, 1996), pp. 157–73.*

References

Barnes, H.E. and Teeters, N.K. (1959) *New Horizons in Criminology* (3rd edn) (New York, NY: Prentice Hall).

Barnett, R. (1977) 'Restitution: A New Paradigm of Criminal Justice', in Barnett, R. and Hagel, J. (eds) *Assessing the Criminal* (Cambridge, MA: Ballinger).

Barrows, S. (1903) *Report on the Sixth International Prison Congress, Brussels, 1900* (Washington, DC: US Government Printing Office).

Canter, G. (1973) 'Consequences of Legal Engineering: A Case from Zambia.' Paper presented at the annual meeting of the American Anthropological Association, New Orleans.

Diamond, A.S. (1935) *Primitive Law* (London: Longmans, Green & Co.).

Drapkin, I. (1989) *Crime and Punishment in the Ancient World* (Lexington, MA: Lexington Books).

Ferri, E. (1917) *Criminal Sociology* (Boston, MA: Little, Brown).

Fry, M. (1951) *Arms of the Law* (London: Victor Gollancz).

Garafalo, R. (1914) *Criminology* (Boston, MA: Little, Brown).

Geis, G. (1977) 'Restitution by Criminal Offenders: A Summary and Overview', in Hudson, J. and Galaway, B. (eds) *Restitution in Criminal Justice* (Lexington, MA: Lexington Books).

Gillin, J.L. (1935) *Criminology and Penology* (rev. edn) (New York, NY: Appleton-Century).

Grabowski, P.N. (1989) Personal communication to the author.

Harding, J. (1982) *Victims and Offenders: Needs and Responsibilities* (London: Bedford Square Press).

Hartmann, A. (1995) *Schlichten oder Richten. Der Täler-Opfer-Ausgleich und das (Jug-end-) Strafrecht* (München: Willem Fink Verlag).

Jacob, B. (1970) 'Reparation or Restitution by the Criminal Offender to his Victim: Applicability of an Ancient Concept in the Modern Correctional Process', *Journal of Criminal Law, Criminology, and Police Science*, 61, pp. 152–67.

Jeffrey, C.R. (1957) 'The Development of Crime in Early English Society', *Journal of Criminal Law, Criminology, and Police Sciences*, 47, pp. 645–66.

Klein, M. (1994) 'American Juvenile Justice: Method and Madness', *European Journal of Criminal Policy and Research*, 2:2, pp. 24–41.

Laster, P.E. (1975) 'Criminal Restitution: A Survey of its Past History', in Hudson, J. and Galaway, B. (eds) *Considering the Victim* (Springfield, IL: Charles C. Thomas).

Maine, H. (1905) *Ancient Law* (London: J. Murray).

McCloskey, H.J. (1984) 'Respect for Moral Rights versus Maximising Good', in Frey, R. (ed.) *Utility and Rights* (Oxford: Blackwell).

Michalowski, R.J. (1985) *Order, Law, and Crime* (New York, NY: Random House).

Nader, L. and Combs-Schilling, E. (1977) 'Restitution in Cross-cultural Perspective', in Hudson, J. and Galaway, B. (eds) *Restitution in Criminal Justice* (Lexington, MA: Lexington Books).

Normandeau, A. (1973) 'Arbould Bonneville de Marsangy (1802–1894)', in Mannheim, H. (ed.) *Pioneers in Criminology* (Montclair, NJ: Patterson-Smith).

Oppenheimer, H. (1913) *The Rationale of Punishment* (London: University of London Press).

Pollock, F. and Maitland, F.W. (1968) *The History of English Law* (2nd edn) (London: Cambridge University Press).

Prins, A. (1895) *Paris Prison Congress Summary Report* (London).

Random House Dictionary of the English Language (abbrev. ed.) (1968) (New York, NY: Random House).

Schafer, S. (1968) *The Victim and His Criminal* (New York, NY: Random House).

Schafer, S. (1970a) *Compensation and Restitution to Victims of Crime* (Montclair, NJ: Patterson-Smith).

Schafer, S. (1970b) 'Victim Compensation and Responsibility', *Southern California Law Review*, 43, pp. 55–67.

Schneider, H.-J. (1988) 'Leben im gesellschaftlichen Niemandsland: die Kriminalität der Aborigines in Zentralaustralien – Eine empirische Studie der vergleichenden Kriminologie', in Kaiser, G. *et al.* (eds) *Kriminologische Forschung in den 80er Jahren* (Freiburg: Max Planck Institute).

Sutherland, E.H. and Cressy, D.R. (1960) *Principles of Criminology* (6th edn) (Chicago, IL: Lippincott).

Tallack, W. (1990) *Reparation to the Injured and the Rights of Victims of Crime Compensation* (London: Wertheimer, Lea).

Toennies, F. (1940) *Fundamental Concepts of Sociology (Gemeinschaft und Gesellschaft)* (New York, NY: American Book Company).

Tyler, E.B. (1889) *Anthropology* (New York, NY).

Wilson, J.Q. (1985) *Thinking about Crime* (New York, NY: Basic Books).

Wolfgang, M.E. (1965) 'Victim Compensation in Crimes of Personal Violence', *Minnesota Law Review*, 50, pp. 223–41.

8. Returning to the Teachings

Rupert Ross

The Movement Towards Teaching and Healing

> Probably one of the most serious gaps in the system is the different perception of wrongdoing and how to best treat it. In the non-Indian community, committing a crime seems to mean that the individual is a *bad person* and therefore must be punished . . . The Indian communities view a wrongdoing as *a misbehaviour which requires teaching or an illness which requires healing*. (Emphasis added)

That paragraph came from a justice proposal prepared in 1989 by the Sandy Lake First Nation, a remote Oji-Cree community in northwestern Ontario. I quoted it towards the end of my first book, *Dancing with a Ghost*. In the three and a half years since its publication, I have heard almost identical statements in Aboriginal communities from one coast to the other.

I remember, for instance, meeting with a chief, his young council and some elders at a remote Cree First Nation in northwestern Ontario. At one point I asked what the community used to do in traditional times, before the courts came, to those who misbehaved. An old lady (and I adopt that phrase as a term of respect common with Aboriginal people) answered immediately. Through the interpreter she said, 'We didn't do anything *to* them. We *counselled* them instead!' Her emphatic Cree suggested that she couldn't understand why I would ask such a question. At the same time, the hand-covered grins of the councillors told me that they had regularly felt the power of her certainty about the wisdom of the old ways.

For the longest time, I didn't fully believe pronouncements like that. I suspected that people were giving me romanticized versions of traditional justice, with all of the punishments removed to make things look rosier than they really were. The more I looked, however, the more I saw how widespread this preference towards teaching and healing – and away from punishment – really was.

It wasn't until a few years ago, however, in a remote, fly-in Cree community of five hundred people that I understood on an emotional level how deep the commitment to teaching and healing really was. It is a story that will take a while to tell, but it is important that the full setting be understood.

The three Cree women

As the Crown Attorney, I had flown into the community several days before court for what we called our 'Advance Day.' With me was another lawyer, the Duty Counsel, whose job was to act as a public defender of sorts. Together, we were to prepare for the court day by interviewing witnesses and examining how accurate and necessary the charges were. In the majority of cases, such advance work weeds out improper charges, reduces the need for trials and helps all parties come up with sentencing proposals for the judge that seem most realistic in the circumstances.

The community's solitary policeman met us at the gravel airstrip, then drove us into the community over snow-packed roads. The temperature was about −30°C, it was still and sunny, and woodsmoke rose straight up from the hundred or so chimneys of the village. We dropped the Duty Counsel off at the Band Office and carried on to the policeman's office. It was a tiny, plywood-floored hut with a woodstove, a metal desk, a single filing cabinet, a one-bunk holding cell and an outhouse. He had put a fire in the woodstove some hours earlier, so I no longer had to wear my mitts. I unzipped my parka but kept it on.

As he filled me in on the dozen or so cases on the court list, I began to breathe a small sigh of relief. None of them looked serious enough that I would feel obliged to ask the court to impose a jail term. That meant that we were unlikely to have any contested trials, for nothing inspires please of 'Not Guilty' like the news that the Crown is looking for jail. We quickly settled into some small talk, chatting about things like problems in the community, the extent of the drinking, what kind of hockey team was being assembled for the upcoming tournament down in Sioux Lookout, whether the kids here were sniffing gasoline, and so forth. It was at that point, almost casually, that he mentioned that the community had formed a 'Police Committee' of six men and six women, and that they had been working with each of the people charged, as well as their families. In fact, he told me, they had prepared detailed recommendations for all the cases and would appear at court to ask the judge if they could speak. When I asked what kinds of recommendations to expect, he answered something like 'Oh, just probation and counselling, that kind of stuff.'

A few days later, we returned to the community for the actual court.

There is something about northern courts they neglected to tell us in law school: one of the more important jobs of the Crown Attorney involves getting to the local school, hall, gymnasium, church, office or other makeshift courthouse as early as possible, then locating and setting up just the right number of trestle tables and stacking chairs to accommodate the likely turnout. That was how I began that court day, for the police officer was out at the airstrip waiting for Judge Fraser's plane. Both of our local judges, Don Fraser and Judyth Little of the Ontario Court (Provincial Division), prefer putting those tables in a 'circle' shape, hoping that this will reduce the adversarial nature of the process. Instead of having the accused and his lawyer sit directly opposite the Crown and the police like boxers on opposite sides of the ring, they are spread around the circle together with probation officers, translators, alcohol workers and anyone else who might have a contribution to make. My own impression is that such an arrangement does make people feel more comfortable and also contributes to a fuller community participation. Perhaps people feel better joining as equals a group discussion aimed at finding solutions than they do making formal and solitary suggestions to an all-powerful judge.

As time passed that morning, people filed into the gymnasium and milled about, helping themselves to coffee provided by the band. The Duty Counsel was scurrying about doing last-minute checks with various people. When the police officer returned with Judge Fraser, his court clerk and reporter, they took their seats and the court was opened. I advised him of the existence of the Police Committee, and he invited them to come forward. Instead of twelve people, as I had expected, three women emerged from the group at the back of the room. Judge Fraser gave them seats just to his right, directly opposite me. One of them looked to be in her sixties or seventies, another in her forties and the third in her twenties.

I should have said that there were *four* of them, because they had brought an infant along, snugly wrapped in its *tikinagan*, or cradle board. They laid the *tikinagan* flat on the trestle table in front of them, where all three could watch, touch, feed, coo and tickle. The baby stayed there through the entire court, causing no commotion at all. I should mention that in northern courts Judges Fraser and Little not only tolerate but welcome such additions. While we've never really talked about it, I suspect that they too see it as a reminder of something Aboriginal communities always stress whenever we come into them: that we are all assembled to help make life better for the next generation. Having some of that generation actually present often proves to be a valuable reminder when we start to get caught up in our self-important roles!

One of the cases on the list, the one that makes me remember that day, concerned a man who had assaulted his wife. It was not, in strictly physical terms, a serious assault, for it involved 'only' a couple of slaps. There had been no bruising or other injury. The police officer expressed his concern, however, that violence might have been used before and might be escalating. The court shared his concern, for the accepted wisdom in urban Canada is that by the time a woman reports an assault by her partner, it's the thirty-fifth time, on average, that he's done it to her.

The charge of assault was read out. The husband, a man in his twenties, entered his guilty plea. Because of that, I was permitted to 'read in' a short summary of the events, instead of making witnesses give evidence themselves. It sounded like so many other summaries I had read in over the years: he had been drinking that evening, an argument had developed over some minor matter and he had slapped her twice. She had taken their two small children to her family's house overnight, returning in the morning after he had sobered up. End of story. In normal circumstances, this would have been followed by a short lecture on using violence, a sentence imposing a fine or community service work and a Probation Order requiring (I can hear the chant so clearly!) that for six months the accused must 'keep the peace and be of good behaviour and abstain absolutely from the consumption of alcohol or attending at premises where alcohol is sold or dispensed. That means no house parties either. If anyone starts drinking, you leave. Do you understand?'

Except that in this case the Police Committee had their own ideas. They were put before the judge by the Duty Counsel, and they were far more complex than I was expecting them to be.

As the first stage of their proposal, they suggested that the offender go out of the community to attend a thirty-day alcohol treatment program in the distant urban centre of Thunder Bay. It was their understanding, however, that the drinking was just a surface problem that could not be solved on its own. If the reasons for the drinking were not looked at and dealt with, it would continue – course or no course. We were told that certain things had happened to the man as a boy, things he had never talked about until now. They didn't give us any more details, except to say that the elders were once again coming forward to help the young people learn what they needed to know to 'live a good life' and that the young man was beginning to open up to them.

Next, they recognized that there was a serious lack of communication between husband and wife. They felt that both of them were carrying burdens alone, and that neither had really understood what was going on with the other. For that reason, they recommended that they both go the following week to a neighbouring community to attend a three-day series of workshops being held on family violence and family communication. Further, when those workshops were repeated a week later in their home community, they had to attend then as well. In that way, perhaps they could begin to break down the silences that had come between them.

At that point, I felt I was hearing one of the most thorough assessments possible. They were not, however, finished.

They told us that the children still had to be considered. Those children had seen the violence at home and were confused by it. The committee felt that if the children were not involved in understanding things, talking about them and helping to turn them around, they would grow up to repeat their father's behaviour themselves. The last recommendation therefore involved having the whole family attend a month-long family healing program available at another neighbouring community, once all the other steps had been carried through.

After the Duty Counsel finished summarizing the plan and explaining that the offender would be a willing participant, Judge Fraser turned to the three women. He asked them if they wished to speak to the court themselves, instead of through the Duty Counsel. As I recall, it was the woman in her forties who spoke to us, in Cree. The transcript records the interpreter as saying the following (with the real name of the offender removed by me):

> She stated that she feels [the offender] is very sincere in his desire to seek help and treatment, and after deliberations of the other committee members they set a plan for him. That the problems [the offender] has stem from his childhood and are finally surfacing. And also that [the offender] has indicated a desire to seek help. And also that it's a good sign that he included his wife and his whole family in that process. And she feels, you know, that healing will come, that all of them seek help.
>
> In the past this was not the case, but we're getting more organized at the community level. And trying to find ways of trying to help people in our community setting, rather than have the people that are charged be taken away. They come back with the same problems, too, so the band is trying to take a different approach.

Judge Fraser included all their recommendations in the Probation Order. He also reminded the offender that it wasn't just the promises in the Probation Order that were important, but the fact that he had made the promises to his own community and to the Police Committee, which was trying to help him. The offender nodded that he understood.

At the end of the day, when all the cases had been heard, something else happened. The three women turned to Judge Fraser and, through the interpreter, thanked him for giving them the chance to give their thoughts to the court. Judge Fraser seemed to be as moved as I was, not only by the depth of their concern and the thoroughness of their analysis throughout the day, but by the fact that they should be extending their thanks to him at the end of it. As best I recall, he replied that he should be thanking *them* instead. He also said something to the effect that, in his view, their approaches to problems in their community could help show the way to the rest of Canada.

A number of things struck me at the time.

One was the fact of that 'thank you.' I know that very formal expressions of appreciation before and after speaking are common, for respect must always be shown to other people, whether a consensus has been reached or substantial issues remain unresolved. In my view, however, there was something else at work that day, an extra emphasis in that 'thank you,' as if it had been a *special* privilege to be able to give the community's perspective to the court. That, in turn, made me wonder how excluded they must have felt from the court up to that day. When they thanked Judge Fraser for 'giving' them the opportunity to speak, I wondered once again what it must be like to suspect, from past dealings, that the outsiders who possess all the power don't really want to hear a single thing you have to say. For how many decades had they been hearing that kind of a message, and in how many ways?

In the face of that history, I once again marvelled at the immense respect they continued to show us as we kept flying in to do 'our' business with them, using only 'our' ways, then flying back out the very same day. There is one remote community in northwestern Ontario that prepares a feast for the court party each court day, with pots of wild rice, bannock, fish and game stew carried into the schoolhouse where we hold court. Those feasts take place despite the fact that, as I hope to demonstrate in the pages that follow, almost every aspect of our Western approach to justice breaks traditional Aboriginal law.

But it was not just their continuing respect for us that struck me that day. I was also inspired by the thoroughness and sophistication of their analysis. There were no Western Ph.D.'s in that group, but their knowledge of the ways in which dysfunctions – or 'disharmonies' – spread and multiply within families and from generation to generation could have stood up against the best material I have seen come out of Canadian universities. That day, when I compared the sophistication of their recommendations to our usual courtroom response of 'probation, abstention from alcohol, and fine or community service work,' I felt just the way Judge Fraser did – that we should be thanking them instead.

I was also struck by the fact that punishment did not even seem to be an *option* that day, even amongst the women on that Police Committee – despite the fact that the victim was a woman and family violence seemed to be a major concern in the community. Why were they not saying the kinds of angry things I was used to hearing from the victims of family violence elsewhere in Canada? Their position reminded me of the old Cree lady who was so perplexed when I asked what they'd 'done to' people who'd misbehaved in traditional times.

The approach they seemed to take went beyond a belief that punishment wasn't necessary in that particular case, for punishment simply didn't seem to be an option in the first place.

Listening to how they approached the problem was a turning point of sorts for me. I had been hearing Aboriginal people talk about 'justice-as-healing' a great deal, but I still had some doubts about how deep-rooted that approach really was. It almost seemed as if everyone had attended the same lecture somewhere and had decided to dress themselves up in the same philosophical clothes, just to look superior to the Western system. What I saw from those three women in that tiny Cree community ended my doubts about such things. What they offered was not an imported response designed to support some romantic reinvention of traditional approaches. Instead, as I felt it then and know it now, it came from the hearts of all of them and from the accumulated understandings of centuries.

I acknowledge that I shared the scepticism of many observers about how 'traditional' such healing approaches really are. I have found, however, that my scepticism just couldn't survive the eyes and voices of so many old people, men and women alike, speaking only their own ancient languages, all looking dumbfounded (or outraged!) at my suggestion that punishment might be used to make things better. Nor could it withstand sitting in the sexual abuse healing circles at Hollow Water, an Ojibway community east of Lake Winnipeg, where the ancient teachings of the medicine wheel come to life to move victims and offenders forward out of their hurt and anger. As a result, my scepticism has gone into a complete meltdown. I now see teaching and healing as cornerstones of traditional Aboriginal thought.

In saying that, I want to be careful about a number of things.

First, what I have said does not mean that traditional responses to dangerous individuals were so generous in every case. Community welfare had to come first, and if a particular individual resisted (or was beyond) community efforts aimed at healing, then banishment to the wilderness was a viable, if regretted, option. I have never heard an Aboriginal community say that healing can work with everyone; what I have heard, however, is that it is short-sighted to offer healing to no one at all and to rely entirely on deterrence and jail instead.

Second, what I have said does not mean that traditional responses to dangerous individuals cannot contain elements of pain. As I will later explore, some teaching is indeed painful, and some healing is much more painful than simply hiding from the truth in a jail cell. I am saying instead that imposing pain for its own sake, strictly as punishment, unaccompanied by efforts to move people forward out of their problems, seldom seems to be an option. An eye-for-an-eye approach, I am told, leads only to the blindness of all (a phrase which suggests an alternate explanation for why the Statue of Justice is blindfolded as she holds up her scales!).

Third, I don't mean to suggest that healing is the central goal of every Aboriginal community – or even the numerical majority – at this particular point in history. A great many focus on punishment instead, and some propose punishments that are more severe than those of the Western courts. Many traditional people suggest, however, that such perspectives were simply the inevitable result of generations of imposed Western approaches, including the use of corporal punishment in residential schools. They point, for instance, to the fact that the Navajo are now moving away from their once-famous Western-based tribal courts and reinvigorating traditional peacemaking processes instead. Colonization strategies, they say, have touched everything, including dispute resolution, and are making it difficult for many communities to break free of punitive approaches and re-root themselves in restorative approaches instead.

Fourth, I don't mean to suggest that all Aboriginal leaders who now speak the language of healing are doing so out of an honest commitment to the betterment of their communities. Sadly, there are many dysfunctional communities where the groups in power promote 'traditional healing programs' for one reason only: to prevent their abusive friends from being truly called to account in *anyone's* justice system. Western or Aboriginal. It is not the teachings themselves that are responsible for such abuse; it is their misuse by desperate people in desperately ill communities.

After my experience of the last several years, I now hold the view that there is one best way for communities to deal with the problems that show up as charges in criminal courts: the traditional teachings need to be brought back to prominence once again, rather than being discounted as inadequate relics of a simpler past. In a number of communities, this has already been done: the teachings have been brought forward into fully twentieth-century flower by good people determined to replace silence and suffering with honesty, hope and health.

So I offer my own conclusion: the three Cree women were not a fluke or an oddity, or a special case. Instead, they spoke from an ancient conviction shared by a great many Aboriginal peoples, a conviction that the best way to respond to the inevitable ups and downs of life, whether defined as 'criminal' or not, is not by punishing solitary offenders. The focus might be shifted instead towards the teaching and healing of all the parties involved, with an eye on the past to understand how things have come to be, and an eye on the future to design measures that show the greater promise of making it healthier for all concerned.

[. . .]

Healing Inside the Whirlwind of Sexual Abuse

The Community Holistic Circle Healing Program at Hollow Water

Hollow Water is a village of some six hundred people on the east shore of Lake Winnipeg, almost at the end of the physical road – but significantly out in front when it comes to building traditional values and teachings into effective, modern-day justice processes. In tackling the most taboo subject of all, sexual abuse within families, the Hollow Water healing team has had to immerse itself totally in relationships, and in all the illnesses that can pervert them through the generations. It has proven to be a painful, often tortuous, process for all concerned.

It began in 1984, when a group of people got together to discuss community problems, especially concerning youngsters. Many of them were 'social service providers' such as the child protection worker from the Manitoba Children's Aid Society, the community health representative, the nurse in charge and the NADAP (Native Alcohol and Drug Addiction Program) worker, together with people drawn from the RCMP, the Frontier School Division of the Manitoba Department of Education and community churches. The majority of the team members were Aboriginal women from the community, many of whom were volunteers, but the team included non-Aboriginal people as well.

Their concern at the time was the level of substance abuse, vandalism, truancy, suicide and violence involving community children. The more the team worked with them, however, the more their attention turned to the kinds of homes those children returned to each day. Over time, they came to face the reality that those homes were often plagued by high levels of alcohol and drug abuse, as well as family violence. The violence in those homes was seldom acknowledged in the community, much less dealt with.

When the focus shifted from the children to the behaviour of their parents, however, things took another turn, this one more disturbing still. In looking for the causes of the substance abuse and violence among the adults, the team came to confront a frightening possibility – the possibility that underneath everything else lay generations of sexual abuse, primarily within families and involving children, that no one wanted to admit, even to themselves.

One of the first decisions as a group was to break down the professional barriers between them. They found that they each operated in separate chains of command, reporting to separate agencies. Just as importantly, they were each controlled by confidentiality rules that kept them from sharing information with each other, even when they were dealing with the same 'clients' or families. They were all working in isolation, often dealing with separate aspects of each troubled person. As long as that continued, they predicted that the result would be a further splintering of those people – exactly the opposite of their shared goal of creating 'whole' people.

As a result of this discovery, one of their earliest accomplishments was the creation of a true team approach of sharing their information fully with each other. Outside professionals, highly regarded by the team for their knowledge and experience, were seen from the outset as important to the project's success, but they were required to 'sign on' to the team approach. They also had to permit a 'lay' member of the team to be with them at all times, so their skills could be learned by community members. This pairing was also a way for team members to help train the professionals to work within a holistic framework. Partnership was, and remains, the model. Having sat in some healing circles at Hollow Water, I can say that there are no colours or races or genders in those circles – only people committed to helping others.

Team training

They also embarked on a lengthy process of training themselves to work as a team. The more they came together, the more they were surprised to find they had been trained in different, sometimes contradictory, methods of intervening with troubled people. It all depended on whether the issue was defined as 'suicide prevention,' 'substance abuse,' 'mental health,' 'child protection' or whatever. Each 'problem' had its own separate 'solution' in the compartmentalized approach of outside agencies. The more they shared information with each other, the more they realized that the dysfunctional people they dealt with were very good at telling each worker just what they wanted to hear and manipulating all the systems at once to their own advantage!

The need for common training was apparent, and over the course of five years they created over twenty different training programs for themselves. Many of them were based on Western models for intervention and healing, but others included reaching out to Aboriginal communities outside Hollow Water to explore traditional ways and teachings. At every step, they took the best from everything they explored, creating a comprehensive program that reflects both traditional Aboriginal and contemporary Western approaches.

When their attention was inevitably drawn to the issue of sexual abuse, however, they hit a snag. This had to do with the fact that the majority of the team members were members of a severely 'ill' community. As such, they had not escaped the intergenerational chains of sexual abuse that were pulling everyone else down. Many of them were victims too, but they had never acknowledged that fact to anyone. As time went by, their commitment to helping their community forced them to confront their own secrets, first in their own hearts and minds, and then in the presence of other team members. It was a turning point for them, for their program and for their community. The healers came to the open acknowledgment that they too needed healing and that they would have to move some distance along their own healing paths, as individuals and as a group, before it would be safe for them to reach out to others.

I don't know how they accomplished what they did, both with and for each other. I have been with them in their healing circles as they reach out to other people, sharing their own stories of abuse, helping sketch the pathways that lead both victims and abusers out of self-hatred, alienation, anger and despair. I do know that their stories are still accompanied by vibrant pain and tears and that it is understood their healing path will require time and attention, likely for the rest of their lives. I also know that, thanks to many of the teachings they have sought out and restored, they now operate within complex and formal processes designed to take away as much of the pain as possible.

When they began to be honest with each other for the first time, however, they were largely on their own, separated from many of those teachings by generations of Western church workers intent on the complete disappearance of the sweat-lodge, the sacred fire, the shaking tent, the talking circle and all the other cleansing resources developed over the course of centuries. These traditions are coming back to Hollow Water now, for those who choose to use them, but they were not at hand when those first disclosures between team members were made. I marvel at the strength, commitment and determination of all of them in those early days. No army unit in any war has undergone a more daunting trial by fire nor built a greater sense of common spirit and dedication.

Healing strategy

The community strategy the team developed involves a detailed protocol leading all the participants through a number of steps or stages. They include the initial disclosure of abuse, protecting the child, confronting the victimizer, assisting the (non-offending) spouse, assisting the families of all concerned, co-ordinating the team approach, assisting the victimizer to admit and accept responsibility, preparing the victim, victimizer and families for the Special Gathering, guiding the Special Gathering through the creation of a Healing Contract, implementation of the Healing Contract and, finally, holding a Cleansing Ceremony designed, in their words, to mark 'the completion of the Healing Contract, the restoration of balance to the victimizer, and a new beginning for all involved.'

The Healing Contract is similar to the 'sentence' created by Family Group Conferences. Designed by all the parties involved in, or personally touched by, the offence, it requires that they each 'sign on' to bring certain changes or additions to their relationships with all the others. Such contracts are never expected to last for less than two years, given the challenges of bringing true healing in the context of sexual abuse. One of them is still being enforced six years after its creation.

This community healing takes place outside the normal criminal justice process – although links to the system are maintained. When someone alleges that they have been abused, the CHCH assessment team evaluates the complaint as quickly as possible. If it appears to be valid, the team swings into action. I was present at one such organizing session and found myself comparing it to a complex military operation. After selecting two team members to make the initial confrontation with the victimizer (instead of the police, but with full police backup if necessary), other team members 'fanned out' to be with all the others who would be affected by the disclosure. That meant that the non-offending spouse, brothers and sisters, grandmothers and grandfathers, aunts and uncles – everyone affected – would have a helper at their side to explain what had been alleged, the processes that were to be followed and the help that might be made available to everyone. No one would be left either in the dark or in their own painful isolation.

The victimizer is approached by two members of the team at a time and place most likely to permit the best atmosphere for honesty and progress. They communicate the allegations and listen to the response. They do not expect immediate acknowledgment, for their own experience with sexual abuse has taught them to expect denials, minimizations, victim blaming, hostile manipulations and the like. When they tell the victimizer that criminal charges are about to be laid, they also say that they are available to accompany him or her through the criminal justice process as long as sincere efforts are being made to accept responsibility and go through the healing process. If that is not agreeable, the victimizer is on his own. Out of forty-eight cases dealt with through to the spring of 1996, only five have failed to enter into – and stay with – the program.

The victimizer is then accompanied to the police station where he or she is formally charged and asked to provide a statement. While that statement would probably not be admissible in court, it is seen as a first step in the long process of accepting responsibility. The team then requires the victimizer to enter a guilty plea to the charges in court as quickly as possible.

The team then asks the court to delay sentencing for as long as possible. Experience has taught that they need a great deal of time to work with the victim, the offender, the families of each and the community as a whole before they can provide the court with a realistic assessment of the challenges and possibilities each case presents. Ideally, the team would like to see sentencing delayed until the Special Gathering has produced the Healing Contract. Unfortunately, that complex process often takes much more time than the courts permit, and sentencing often takes place before real commitments to sustained healing can be expected.

When the community healing process was first established, the team restricted its in-court activities to the preparation of a Pre-Sentence Report. This was a large document, analysing everything from the offender's state of mind, level of effort and chance of full rehabilitation, to the reactions, feelings, plans and suggestions of all people affected. Special attention was paid to the victim, the non-offending spouse and the families of each. The report also detailed a proposed plan of action, stated whether or not the parties themselves had achieved a Healing Contract and requested that any Probation Order require the offender to continue to co-operate fully with the team's healing efforts. If a jail sentence was imposed, they did what they could to arrange regular work with the offender while in custody and to prepare everyone for the day of release.

More recently, however, the team has moved its processes into the courtroom itself. In December 1993, after months of separate healing circles with all the people affected by the case, a man and his wife came before the Associate Chief Judge of Manitoba's Provincial Court, Judge Murray Sinclair, for sentencing. They had jointly been involved in the sexual abuse of their three daughters, had pleaded guilty and had worked with the team. This was the first time the team had organized its own process to complement that of the court.

Since then, an elaborate sentencing procotol has been established, using a circle format. There are actually two circles, one within the other. The inner circle is for those who wish to speak, the outer one for those who wish to observe and listen. About two hundred people attended that first in-court circle, and over ninety-five attended the second one, held in August 1994.

Before court opens in the morning, the community conducts a pipe ceremony, hangs the flags, smudges or purifies the court buildings with the smoke from smouldering sweetgrass, places the community drum and eagle staff in the courtroom, serves breakfast to people from outside the community and offers an elder tobacco as a request for a prayer to guide the sentencing circle.

The sentencing proceeds according to a number of steps agreed to with the presiding judge: personal smudging (usually with sage or sweetgrass); an opening prayer; court technicalities like confirming the guilty plea; an outline of the ground rules by the presiding judge; a first 'go-round,' where the participants say why they came to be in the court that day; a second go-round, where all the participants are given the chance to speak directly to the victim; a third go-round, where all the participants are allowed to speak to the offender about how the victimization has affected them, the families and the community at large; a fourth go-round, where the participants outline their expectations to the offender and give their views about what needs to be done to restore balance; the passing of sentence by the judge; and a closing prayer. Following that, the participants may stay to use the circle for sharing or 'debriefing' purposes. I will speak later of the rules that govern how each person is required to participate in such circles, for they are integral parts of the healing strategy.

Out of forty-eight offenders in Hollow Water over the last nine years, only five have gone to jail, primarily because they failed to participate adequately in the healing program. Of the forty-three who did, only two have repeated their crimes, an enviable record by anyone's standards. Of those two, one reoffended at a very early stage, before the sentencing had actually taken place. The second reoffended when the program was in its infancy. Since that reoffending, he has completed the formal healing program and is now a valuable member of the team, given his personal knowledge of the ways victimizers try to avoid responsibility.

More recently, after sentencing has taken place, the team requires that the process be repeated publicly at six-month intervals, without the court party, to reaffirm the promises of all, to honour whatever healing steps have been taken and to maintain community expectations of offenders.

At all times, from the moment of disclosure through to the Cleansing Ceremony, team members have the responsibility to work with, protect, support, teach and encourage a wide range of people. It is their view that since a great many people are affected by each disclosure, all of them deserve assistance. Just as importantly, all must be involved in any process aimed at creating healthy dynamics and breaking the intergenerational chain of abuse.

I indicated that many of the team members from the community are themselves victims of long-standing sexual abuse. Even former victimizers who have completed the formal healing process successfully are being asked to join the team. The personal experience of team members in the emotional, mental, physical and spiritual complexities of sexual abuse gives them an extraordinary rapport with victims and victimizers alike. I sat with them in circles as they shared their own histories as a way to coax others out of the anger, denial, guilt, fear, self-loathing and hurt that must be dealt with if health is to be re-established. Their personal experience also gives them the patience needed to stay with long and painful processes, and to see signs of progress that might escape the notice of others. It also gives them the insight to recognize who is manipulating or hiding in denial, and the toughness to insist that they keep moving towards greater honesty. The word 'healing' seems such a soft word, but, as I will show later, Hollow Water's healing process is anything but soft. In fact, jail is a much easier alternative, because it does not require the victimizer to face the real truths about abuse.

Crimes too serious for jail?

While the Western justice system seems to have forged an unbreakable link between 'holding someone responsible for their crime' and sending them to jail, the Community Holistic Circle Healing Program (CHCH) at Hollow

Water fiercely denies the wisdom of that connection. In 1993 they drafted a 'Position Paper on Incarceration,' in which they discuss their objections, as well as their reasons, for choosing the healing and teaching path instead. It stands as the most eloquent plea I have come across thus far.

They described, for instance, two realizations which caused them to abandon their initial support for using jail in cases which were felt to be 'too serious' for a strictly healing approach. To use their words, they realized:

(1) that as we both shared our own stories of victimization and learned from our experiences in assisting others in dealing with the pain of their victimization, it became very difficult to define 'too serious.' The quantity or quality of pain felt by the victim, the family/ies and the community did not seem to be directly connected to any specific acts of victimization. Attempts, for example, by the courts – and to a certain degree by ourselves – to define a particular victimization as 'too serious' and another as 'not too serious' (e.g. 'only' fondling vs. actual intercourse; victim is daughter vs. victim is nephew; one victim vs. four victims) were gross over-simplifications, and certainly not valid from an experiential point of view; and

(2) that promoting incarcertaion was based on, and motivated by, a mixture of feelings of anger, revenge, guilt and shame on our part, and around our personal victimization issues, rather than in the healthy resolution of the victimization we were trying to address.

Incarceration, they concluded, actually works against the healing process, because 'an already unbalanced person is moved further out of balance.' The team also came to believe that the threat of incarceration prevents people from 'coming forward and taking responsibility for the hurt they are causing.' It reinforces the silence, and therefore promotes rather than breaks, the cycle of violence that exists. 'In reality,' the team wrote, 'rather than making the community a safer place, the threat of jail places the community more at risk.'

The position paper goes on to speak of the need to break free of the adversarial nature of Western courts, the barrier to healing that arises when defence lawyers recommend complete silence and a plea of 'not guilty' and the second 'victimization' that occurs when victims are cross-examined on the witness stand. In their view, the 'courtroom and process simply is not a safe place for the victim to address the victimization – nor is it a safe place for the victimizer to come forward and take responsibility for what has happened.'

Noting that this acceptance of responsibility is more difficult yet more effective than a jail sentence, the team concluded:

'Our children and the community can no longer afford the price the legal system is extracting in its attempts to provide justice in our community.'

The need to break the silence is great. The Hollow Water team presently estimates that 80 per cent of the population of their community, male and female alike, have been the victims of sexual abuse, most often at the hands of extended family members and usually for long periods of time. Just as shockingly, they now estimate that a full 50 per cent of the community's population, male and female, has at one time or another sexually abused someone else.

In fact, many knowledgable Aboriginal people tell me that there are hundreds of such communities across Canada, all of them stuck in the silence and denial that characterized Hollow Water only nine years ago. The program director of an Aboriginal treatment program for substance abuse told me that 100 per cent of the people coming to her centre have been the victims of sexual abuse. Another prominent Aboriginal woman told me that she does not have one close Aboriginal woman friend who has escaped sexual abuse.

In the next chapter, I will begin my exploration of where the healing perspective comes from, what sustains it and how it can penetrate even the most pain-filled relationships. First, however, I'd like to tell a story, one which gave me my first clues as to how abuse gets passed from generation to generation, multiplying as it goes, until entire communities become engulfed by it. Of all the stories I know, it gives the clearest picture of the incredible whirlwinds of anger, guilt and denial which communities like Hollow Water must ultimately confront. Until we gain some understanding of how this state of affairs came into being, mapping a way out of it remains almost impossible.

Carl and the cancer of abuse

This story is about a boy from another community, a boy I will call Carl, though that is not his real name. When he first came to the attention of the justice system at age fifteen, Carl stood charged with forcible confinement and with the sexual abuse, both anal and vaginal, of two girls. They were four and six years old.

Carl was one of five children growing up in a remote reserve of some four hundred people. His community had no airstrip, no sewer system, no running water, virtually no employment – and only one telephone.

In his first five or six years, a number of events began to shape him. He saw his Dad repeatedly beat and rape his mother in drunken rages. He, in turn, was regularly beaten by his father, sometimes for trying to protect her. His mother also beat Carl, on orders from his father. She did it, he believed, only to keep from being beaten herself. His Dad also forced him into oral and anal sex with him, then forced his mother to join in or be beaten herself.

While these acts were being repeated, Carl learned a number of things. He learned how his Dad blamed his Mom for his own rages, screaming that it was always her fault. He learned that his father justified his anger by pointing to her 'failures' as a wife, mother, housekeeper, cook and so on. Carl began to see things in the same way, to believe that the violence was all her fault, that she 'deserved' it.

More than that, he learned how to endure all the violence within his family in total silence. In the words of the probation officer, he 'lived in dread of what would happen if he ever told or shared the family secret.' At the same time, Carl began to develop a real anger towards his neighbours and his community because, as he phrased it, 'They didn't see, and thought Dad was so nice.'

Unable to reach outside the family for help, he came to rely on his brothers. On one occasion, they all joined together in attacking their father to rescue their mother from another brutal assault.

It should come as no surprise that they all began to sniff solvents, especially gas. It was the only way to escape.

When Carl was five or six, it became known to outsiders that his Dad was sexually abusing one of his older brothers. As a result, a child protection agency placed Carl with his grandparents in another reserve community. He stayed there until he was eight or nine, separated from his brothers and sisters, his only allies. Unfortunately, living with his grandparents did not result in an end to the abuse. A male cousin some six years older than Carl forced him into oral and anal sex on a regular basis, often bribing him with cigarettes and drugs. That abuse continued sporadically until his final arrest in 1992, at age fifteen.

When he was eight or nine, Carl's Dad remarried and quit drinking. He took Carl home, and for a while things were fine. The new wife was a good person, whom he trusted. Then, in the second year there, his Dad started drinking again, and the violence returned. On one occasion when his Dad struck him, the new wife came to protect him and his Dad turned on her. She was pregnant at the time and lost the baby as a result of that assault. Carl blamed himself for the loss of the baby. Not surprisingly, he began sniffing solvents more frequently.

Then, by his own admission, he started taking his anger out on people less powerful than himself. At age nine, he forced intercourse on a six-year-old girl who was his cousin. In his own words, he did so on 'countless' occasions. At age ten, he forced intercourse on an eight-year-old girl, and did so some four or five times. At age ten, he forced anal intercourse on a five-year-old boy.

Then, when Carl was about ten or eleven, his Dad's new wife arranged for him to return to his grandparents, apparently afraid for him, but unaware of what had happened there before. He stayed with his grandparents until he was nearly thirteen. During that period, the male cousin who had sexually assaulted him resumed his abuse, supplying him with marijuana and hashish as rewards this time. He grew to use them almost daily. Another boy, who was about five or six years older, forced him into acts of oral and anal sex on four or five occasions, pretending to others that he was there to teach him martial arts. At the same time, Carl began to threaten his grandparents and to steal from them to buy drugs. He also continued to abuse others. He forced intercourse on a nine-year-old girl after watching a porno movie. He also forced intercourse on a girl his own age, a girl whom he says he liked. He also began to think about suicide, later telling the probation officer: 'I remember feeling ashamed and wanting to kill myself. I'd tell myself that I was no good and that I should just kill myself.'

In fact, he attempted suicide several times, later saying: 'I was having bad memories of Dad slapping [the new wife] around, and being sexualy victimized as well.' Because of the suicide attempts and threats of violence to others, he was placed in a group home a couple of months before his thirteenth birthday. That, however, changed nothing. While there, he learned that his Dad's new wife had committed suicide. He had now lost the one person who had not abused him, the one person he trusted, and he blamed himself for her suicide.

Then, in the spring of 1991, at age thirteen, he went back to his Dad. He was using hash and marijuana on an almost daily basis, smoking with his brother, his uncles, his cousins – and even his Dad. He also resumed his own abusive behaviour. He again forced intercourse on his younger cousin, sometimes being assisted by one of his brothers. It was also at this time that he committed the offences that brought him to court – forcing anal and vaginal sex on the two girls aged four and six, keeping them imprisoned for several hours. In his words later, it was 'as my father had done to us.' He was charged with those offences.

In the words of the probation officer who prepared the evaluation report for court, Carl had learned a number of things growing up in such conditions: (1) 'He learned as a young child both to lie and pretend, to protect himself from his father's violence.' The primary lie was that his family life was good, while secondary lies involved such things as why he was staying away from home. (2) 'He . . . learned to become a sexual perpetrator. His victimization experiences [led] him to de-value himself and his very existence. It was only a matter of time before he started de-valuing the needs of others. In his own words: 'I told myself that I was no good. I'm a nobody. I'll only end up in jail anyway, so I'll do what I want . . . I victimized to regain the power I lost when I was being victimized.'

In summary, this fifteen-year-old boy was sexually victimized by at least *four* people: his father, his mother, an older cousin and another older boy. At the time of his sentencing, he acknowledged victimizing at least the following *seven* people: a six-year-old girl cousin, repeatedly; an eight-year-old girl some four or five times; a five-year-old boy, once; a nine-year-old girl, once; a same-age girlfriend, several times; and two little girls, aged four and six. Since his sentencing into custody and treatment, he has now acknowledged sexually abusing at least another six people. This boy is only fifteen.

As this one painful story illustrates, the cancer of sexual abuse, as long as it remains hidden, spreads from generation to generation, multiplying as it goes. In many communities, health-care workers estimate that such sexual abuse spans three or four generations. It is considered an illness because it is passed from one person to another as victims try to compensate for their own degradation by degrading others. This was the situation facing the people of Hollow Water, although they didn't know its full horror at the time.

As Hollow Water has learned, however, it is impossible to deal with the Carls of this world simply by prosecuting their abusive fathers. Instead, it is necessary to ask how those abusive fathers got that way, how the illness that erupts as sexual abuse got started. Until that is done, until the factors that first spawned such disharmonies are identified and dealt with, the illness will continue to afflict one generation after another.

The most basic question, then, is: Where did it all begin?

At this early stage there is one thing I would like to make clear: all the evidence I have seen thus far sends me the unequivocal message that such widespread abuse was *not* a part of traditional life. In fact, it appears to have been a very rare occurrence, and the object of strong condemnation.

For instance, many early explorers, like David Thompson, were moved to comment on how much love and protection children were afforded and how much they were the healthy centre of a strong and caring society. At the same time, sophisticated measures designed to prevent such abuse were prominent in traditional society, and these are still used in communities where such traditions have been maintained. In the Medewewin Lodge of the Ojibway, for instance, a place in the circle remains reserved for the Deer Clan, despite the fact that no members of the Deer Clan have existed for centuries. The disappearance of this most gentle, song-filled and poetic clan is traced in Ojibway storytelling to their refusal to heed the Creator's warning against incest, even when their continued misbehaviour sent them afflicted children. As a result, the Creator was left with no choice but to see to the disappearance of the entire clan. The vacant place that still remains within the Midewewin Lodge thus stands as a reminder from those ancient times that incest is abhorrent in the Creator's eyes.

There are a great many other practices and traditions that were clearly established to prevent sexual abuse – including the prohibition of direct communication in some groups between fathers and daughters during adolescence. I leave it to others to present them more completely than my knowledge permits. I only wish to indicate my present view that the plague of sexual (and other) abuse that afflicts so many Aboriginal communities is not a 'natural' event within what the settler nations called a 'pagan' society. On the contrary, I see it as an almost inevitable consequence of historically labelling *everything* Aboriginal as pagan, of declaring at every step and in every way that every aspect of traditional life was either worth less than its European equivalent – or just plain worthless.

Losing the centre

One event in particular began to guide me towards this most uncomfortable conclusion. A few years ago, I heard an Ojibway woman tell her story at a workshop on sexual abuse. She told us that she had been born into a tiny community that survived on its trapping, hunting, fishing and rice harvesting. Then, at age six or seven, she was taken away to residential school, along with all the other school-age children. She stayed there until she was sixteen. Contrary to what I expected, her sexual abuse did not begin at that school. While there were unquestionably many schools where the physical abuse of children, sexual and otherwise, seems to have been commonplace, she was in one where 'only' the children's language, spirituality, culture and worldview were abused – as the priests and nuns tried to train the 'Indian' out of them. This woman was not sexually abused until, at the age of sixteen, she was released from school and went back to her tiny village. First it was an uncle, then older cousins – her own people.

She spoke to the workshop about how she handled the abuse of her 'Indian-ness' by the nuns and priests and the abuse of her body by her relatives. She first went into the predictable downspin of alcohol and drugs, winding up on the streets of a city, abusing herself in virtually every way. Then, to the surprise of many, she did what she calls a 'complete flip.' She got sober, went back to school, graduated from university, got married and had children. She thought everything was fine.

Then, she told us, a day came when one of her daughters returned from school with a straight-A report card. She asked her daughter why there were no A-plus marks on it. The daughter's tearful response was to ask why they had to be *better* than everyone else, and in everything they did. It was at that point that her mother understood that she was still hiding from her sexual abuse, that she had only traded alcohol and drugs for perfectionism. She began to understand that she still had not come to grips with the pain, the guilt and the 'dirtiness' of being a victim of sexual abuse. Needless to say, the fact that she had been abused by her own people did not help.

In the years that followed, she returned to her tiny community and began to speak openly about what had happened to her, about the sexual abuse that had caught so many people in its web. Despite hostility and fear, she persisted. She sought guidance from the elders about how to face up to realities, how to put the pain behind her, how to embark on healing both for herself and for the community. It was, she told us, the elders who helped her understand the reason why it was her own people, her own family, who had abused her that way. 'I began to learn,' she said, 'that the people I came back to at age sixteen were not the same people I had left at age six. The change began on the day we were taken from them.'

I will never forget how powerfully her simple declaration affected the room. I could almost feel everyone being jolted into sharing her realization: her abusers, Aboriginal people all, did not abuse because they were Aboriginal people, but because they were *changed* Aboriginal people. If that was so, then there was something they could do to reverse the downward spiral that had everyone so firmly in its grip: they could look back to see when the changes began, what they were, how they touched people – and how they might be *reversed*. In other words, there was a chance that they could rescue themselves.

As she spoke, it became clear that residential schools were not the solitary cause of social breakdown amongst Aboriginal people. Rather, they were the closing punctuation mark in a loud, long declaration saying that nothing Aboriginal could possibly be of value to anyone. That message had been delivered in almost every way imaginable, and it touched every aspect of traditional social organization. Nothing was exempt, whether it was spiritual belief and practices, child-raising techniques, pharmacology, psychology, dispute resolution, decision making, clan organization or community govern-ance. In time, even economic independence was stripped away as governments built community schools, which made it impossible for families to tend traplines often a hundred kilometres back in the bush. Even the law added its voice to the degradation, making it illegal to possess medicine bundles, vote in Canadian elections, hold a potlach to honour the assistance of others or (difficult as this is to believe) hire a lawyer even to *ask* a court to force governments to honour their treaty obligations.

Taking the children away to residential school was, in a way, just an exclamation mark ending the sentence that declared: All things Aboriginal are inferior at best, and dangerous at worst. When the children were gone, however, so was the centre of life for everyone left behind. I find it impossible to imagine the feelings that must have swamped all those mothers and fathers, aunts and uncles, grandmothers and grandfathers. Some of them thought that such a drastic step was necessary for future generations to gain the skills needed to survive in the non-Native world. Some of them, however, still rage at the arrogance of such a move and lament the loss of social and personal health that followed for everyone concerned. No matter how much the outsider's education was desired, what was left behind for all the adults was a gargantuan hole, out of which many were unable to climb.

Those of us in the criminal justice field are familiar with studies of what happens in one-industry towns where the mine or mill closes. When those jobs suddenly vanish, the unemployed are robbed of one source of self-esteem: the ability to provide adequately for their families. Alcohol and drug use increase measurably, along with the rate of family violence. If the loss of that *one* source of self-esteem can have such a significant effect, what must have been the effect on all of Canada's Aboriginal people as our institutions attacked *every* aspect of their lives?

Try a short exercise in role reversal, imagining a non-Aboriginal mine worker whose job was taken away by all-powerful outsiders. Imagine that he knew he had no realistic chance of ever qualifying for another one. Imagine that he was unable to go for comfort and help to his own churches and his own psychiatrists and hospitals, because those same outsiders had made them illegal. Imagine that, whenever he went to their versions of such helping places, the professionals who staffed them could not speak his language, but demanded that he learn theirs. Imagine, as well, that all those powerful outsiders held him, his language and his culture in such low esteem that they forcibly removed his children, to raise them to be just like them. Imagine, at that point, waking up to silence throughout your entire community, where only the week before there had been the raucous voices of new generations. What reason would there be even to get out of bed?

And what happens when you are told, from every direction and in every way, that you and all your people have no value to anyone, no purpose to your lives, no positive impact on the world around you? No one can stand believing those things of themselves. No one can bear considering themselves worthless, essentially invisible. At some point people brought to this position stand up and demand to be noticed, to be recognized as being alive, as having influence and *power*. And the easiest way to assert power, to prove that you exist, is to demonstrate power over people who are weaker still, primarily by making them do things they don't want to do. The more those things shame and diminish that weaker person, the more the abuser feels, within the twisted logic of victimization, that they have been empowered and restored themselves. Further, nothing is more attractive to those who need to feed off the denigration of others than the road of sexual abuse, and the safest and easiest sexual abuse is of children.

This extract is taken from Returning to the Teachings: Exploring Aboriginal Justice, *by Rupert Ross, chapter 1, pp. 1–15 and 29–48 (Penguin Group Canada, 1996).*

9. Navajo restorative justice: the law of equality and justice

Robert Yazzie and James W. Zion

[...]

Egalitarian conceptions of decision-making process

The process of law flows from conflict to judgment or a final decision. It is important to understand who makes the decision to resolve a conflict and how that decision is made. The very process of decision-making points to the healing component of Navajo justice. State systems use judges to make the decisions. The judges are selected on the basis of their education to hear the facts, apply the law and make wise decisions for others. This is alien to the Navajo concept of freedom and individuality, where one person cannot impose a decision on another. Instead, Navajos are their own judges in an egalitarian process.

What happens when there is a dispute? First, a person who claims to be injured or wronged by another will make a demand upon the perpetrator to put things right. The term for this is *nalyeeh*, which is a demand for compensation; it is also a demand to readjust the relationship so that the proper thing is done. In a simple situation such as theft, confrontation of the thief with a threat of public disclosure is usually sufficient. Women who are wronged by a sexual impropriety have the right to confront the offender in a public place to disclose the insult and demand compensation for it. In situations where individuals are unable to make a direct demand, or do not wish to do so, they will seek the help of relatives. There have been situations where young women herding sheep are sexually wronged; a relative of the woman will approach the man's relatives to talk out the situation and demand some sort of compensation or arrangement to mend it [...].

There are more formal dispute resolution methods to talk out disputes. A victim or a victim's relative will approach a *naat'aanii* to request his or her assistance in talking out a particular problem. A *naat'aanii* is a respected community leader, and often a basis for that respect is the very fact that a civil leader is also a clan leader. The *naat'aanii*-peacemaker will summon the interested parties for a group discussion of what to do. An important difference between state system adjudication and peacemaking is the identity of the participants and their role. Peacemaking is not a confrontation between two particular individuals who are immediately involved in the dispute, but a process that involves the family and clan relations of victims and perpetrators as active participants. They are involved because they have an interest in the matter; what affects their relative affects them. Relatives have an opinion about the nature of the dispute or what should be done to resolve it.

A *naat'aanii* will give notice to everyone affected and designate a place to talk out the problem. The process always begins with prayer, which is essential to the healing nature of peacemaking. Prayer is a process that summons supernatural help; the Holy People are called to participate directly. They are not summoned to be a witness, a custom that is reflected in the giving of the oath in courts. *Naat'aaniis* are called in to help the parties and to answer their demands for justice. The prayer is also an opportunity for the *naat'aanii* to focus the minds of the parties on a process that is conciliatory and healing, not confrontational and winner-take-all. Following prayer, the parties have an opportunity to lay out their grievances. There is venting, as in other mediation processes, where the victim has an opportunity to disclose not only the facts, but their impact. People have an opportunity to say how they feel about the event and make a strong demand that something be done about it. Relatives also have an opportunity to express their feelings and opinions about the dispute.

The person accused of a wrongful act also has an opportunity to speak. Human behavior is such that we often put forward excuses or justifications for our conduct. Many Navajo peacemaking cases involve alcohol abuse. A common psychological barrier where an individual is alcohol-dependent is denial. The person will say, 'I don't have a drinking problem'. In adjudication, a defendant accused of an alcohol-related crime will challenge the court to prove that he or she has an alcohol problem to be addressed in some sort of treatment program. Often, defendants referred to such programs do not wholeheartedly participate, using denial to fool themselves. Another barrier is minimalization, where someone excuses conduct by saying, 'It's no big deal'. We see this in domestic violence cases, where a batterer says, 'It's no big deal for an Indian man to beat his wife'. In some child sex abuse cases, perpetrators (falsely) claim that it is traditional to have sex with a stepchild or a young woman who has barely reached puberty. A third barrier is externalization, the excuse that the offence is someone else's fault. 'It's her fault!' a batterer will say. 'If she didn't nag me all the time I wouldn't have to beat her.' Or, 'It's her fault – if she would do what she is supposed to do, I wouldn't be forced to push her around.' Another facet of externalization is excuses. 'It's not my fault; I'm just a dependent alcoholic and I can't help myself.' Many criminal defendants attempt to excuse their conduct by saying, 'I was drunk'. There is also a systemic excuse that is related to anomie (Greek for without law).

The police model inherited by the Navajo Nation has severe limitations. There are not enough police to patrol a rural nation that is larger than nine states. Limited police officers, who must prepare cases in a system where there is proof beyond a reasonable doubt and a defendant cannot be compelled to testify, limits the effectiveness of adjudication. The Navajo Nation also has an imposed social work model for child welfare which is overburdened. Accordingly, when the police or social work system is overburdened we sometimes hear the institutional excuse, 'we can't do anything'.

How does peacemaking address these excuses; these barriers to solving problems? It confronts them directly. In peacemaking, the person who is the focus of the discussion gets to explain his or her excuses in full, without appearing before a judge to determine whether or not they are true. Instead, judges are the people who know the wrongdoer best – his or her spouse, parents, siblings, other relatives and neighbors. They are the reality check for excuses. In a case involving family violence, a young man related his excuses, exhibiting denial, minimalization and externalization. One of the people who listened was the young man's sister. She listened to his story and confronted him by saying, 'you know very well you have a drinking problem'. She then related the times she had seen him drunk and abusive. Having broken the barrier, she told her brother she loved him very much and was willing to help him if only he would admit his problems. He did. In another case, a young woman went to court to establish paternity for her child. The young man she said was the father denied it. The judge sent the case into peacemaking, where the parents and relatives of both were present. They immediately announced that the purpose of the meeting was to decide what to do with *their* grandchild. The families knew about the couple's relationship and the fact of paternity, so the case was quickly settled. The young man was not employed, so the families developed a plan whereby he would cut and haul firewood for the mother until he got a job. In peacemaking, the people who know the facts directly or know the people in the process very well are the ones who develop the facts of the situation. They are not laid out for a judge to decide, but for the participants to discuss and know. The talking-out process of peacemaking is designed to clarify the situation and, where necessary, get to the root of the problem. Excuses do not prevail in a process that fosters full discussion to solve problems.

Peacemaking is a remedy for the 'we can't do anything' excuse. Most cases in Navajo peacemaking are those brought directly by the people. For example, there was a situation where a couple broke up when their son reached adulthood. The man ran off with another woman, leaving his wife to make the mobile home payment. She had little education and no job. She got a low-paying job in a laundromat, but that was not sufficient to make the monthly payment. She went to the local legal aid program for a divorce to assure the payment, but was told that the program was overburdened and did not take divorce cases. The woman began going to her husband's place of work to demand money. Very soon, the receptionists and fellow employees made it known she was not welcome. One day, the woman confronted her husband in the parking lot and demanded the money for the mobile home payment. When he refused, she hit him. He got a domestic violence restraining order from the court, and the woman sought advice about what it meant and what she should do. She was advised to seek peacemaking. Within a few days, a peacemaking session was scheduled and the husband agreed to make the mobile home payment. The peacemaker set up a follow-up meeting to assure the agreement was carried out. In the meantime, the domestic violence case was dismissed.

The Navajo Nation child welfare program is overburdened with abuse and neglect cases. Accordingly, we see many applications for guardianships of children brought by grandmothers, aunts and other relatives of children. A guardianship is a form of private child welfare action in Navajo practice, and relatives seek court confirmation of arrangements to care for children. Often, relatives seek temporary guardianships to allow parents an opportunity to deal with personal problems or seek employment to create a stable household. In most state systems, child welfare cases are confrontational and challenge adults to explain why they are bad parents. Navajos use peacemaking for guardian-ship cases, and that forum allows relatives to discuss what is best for their children. Parents assert their excuses for the way they deal with their children, but the focus is genuinely upon the best interests of the child. There is no judge or social worker to make the determination of what is best for a child – the people most closely connected with the child make that decision. Direct access to swift justice within the community addresses the 'we can't do anything' excuse, and the process utilizes readily available resources for problem solving. There is no need for a confirming medical statement in domestic violence cases, or for a home study in child welfare cases. The people who have a dispute treat it as a problem to be resolved within families, and take direct action on their own.

In peacemaking, a *naat'aanii* has persuasive authority. Peacemakers are chosen by local units of Navajo Nation government on the basis of their standing in the community and respect for their abilities. Peacemakers can be removed at any time should they lose respect. A peacemaker does not have the authority to make a decision for others or to impose a decision, but his or her power is not merely advisory. A *naat'aanii* has an opinion, and the process prompts him or her to express it. Given that peacemakers are chosen because of their wisdom and planning abilities, the process encourages them to act as guides and teachers. Their opinion will most likely have a strong impact on the decision of the group. The opinion is expressed in something called the lecture – an unfortunate rendering in English because the process is not an abstract exhortation about morality; it is a very practical and concrete process. The peacemaker knows all about the situation given that the parties and their relatives have an opportunity to vent, accuse, exhibit psychological barriers and engage in discussions to clarify things. He or she will then provide reality therapy and perform values clarification in a talk designed to guide the parties. The talk focuses on the nature of the problem and uses traditional precedent to guide a decision.

Navajos have a great deal of respect for tradition, and they recognize both a form of traditional case law and a corpus of legal principles. The case law can be in the form of what happened in the time of creation, e.g. what First Man and First Woman, the Hero Twins or the Holy People did to address a similar problem. The case may involve Coyote or Horned Toad, and the foolishness of what Coyote did or the wisdom of Horned Toad to resolve a similar conflict. There are principles to be derived from ceremonial practice, songs, prayers, or other expressions of Navajo doctrine. The *naat'aanii* draws upon traditional teachings to propose a plan of action for the parties in order to resolve their dispute. Many peacemaking sessions are short, lasting only a few hours, but where emotions are particularly strong or it is difficult to break down the psychological barriers, peacemaking can last longer. The peacemaker may call a halt to the discussions to allow time for reflection and prepare for a resumption of talks on another day.

When the lecture is done, the parties return to a discussion of the nature of the problem and what needs to be done to resolve it. Planning is a major Navajo justice value that is sometimes ignored in state practice. *Nahat'a*, or planning process, is very practical. Non-Navajos sometimes mock traditional practice. For example, there are Navajos who look into the future using a crystal. A non-Navajo might ridicule that, but Navajos explain how it is done. When you hold a crystal in your hand, you see that it has many facets. You examine each closely, and upon a full examination of each side of the crystal you can see it as a whole. That describes *nahat'a*, where the parties closely examine each facet of the dispute to see it as a whole. The talking-out phase fully develops the facts so the parties can fully understand the nature of the problem that lies beneath the dispute. The lecture phase draws upon traditional wisdom for precedent and guidance. The prayer commits the parties to the process. Following full discussion, the parties themselves serve as the judges and make a decision about what to do. It is most often a practical plan whereby people commit themselves to a course of action.

Often, the action is in the form of *nalyeeh*, which also translates as restitution or reparation. Payments can be in the form of money to compensate for actual out-of-pocket loss. There are also payments in the form of horses, jewelry or other goods. The payment can be symbolic only and not compensate for actual loss. The focus is not upon adequate compensation, as in state tort or contracts doctrines, but upon a make-whole kind of remedy. The feelings and relationships of the parties are what is most important. For example, there are cases involving sexual misconduct where the victim demands symbolic compensation, often in the form of horses, cows or sheep. Can a price tag be placed on a rape? The act of delivering cattle as compensation is visible in a rural community. Members of that community will most likely know about the event, and the public act of delivering cattle or horses shows the woman's innocence. It reinforces her dignity and tells the community she was wronged.

Non-Navajo corporate parties have also participated in peacemaking, such as in a wrongful death-products liability case brought before the Navajo Nation courts in 1994. A child got scorched to death in a clothes dryer, and the child's parents brought a standard wrongful death manufacturer negligence suit. The corporate defendants were very nervous about the possible outcome before a Navajo jury. The child's parents were not so much concerned about getting money as they were with dealing with the emotional impact of their child's death. The parties went into peacemaking without their lawyers present, and they fully discussed the problem of what to do about the loss of the child. They addressed the parents' feelings about their loss and what the corporate defendants could and should do about it. The result was a monetary settlement that was within the range of usual rural Arizona state court verdicts. More importantly, the parties discussed what symbolic act the manufacturer and laundromat operator could take to assume responsibility for the death. Negotiated compensation can address the costs of actual loss, but it can also be an agreed resolution with only a symbolic payment. It addresses relationships.

Peacemaking also involves personal commitments to deal with underlying behavior. It can involve agreements to attend a ceremony. For example, the Honorable Irene Toledo of the Ramah District Court recognized that many violent assaults brought before her involved Vietnam veterans and other Navajos who returned from war. Upon examining the cases more closely, she recognized the presence of post-traumatic stress disorder from war. She also recognized that veteran parents were teaching their children violent behaviors. Navajos are familiar with war from many centuries of conflict with Spanish, Mexican and American invaders. There is a Navajo ceremony that addresses post-traumatic stress disorder, and it is quite effective in dealing with the memories of war. Judge Toledo urged some of the defendants to have the ceremony done, as well as to seek treatment through a Veterans Department hospital. Some replied, 'I'm modern and I don't really believe in that tradition'. The judge used peacemaking as a form of counseling for the defendants to urge them to have the ceremony performed. One veteran reported that while he 'did not believe in it', he had the ceremony done and it worked.

Peacemaking is used to overcome psychological barriers and self-imposed impediments to personal responsibility. Parties in peacemaking will often agree to seek traditional ceremonies or modern counseling as part of the resolution of the dispute. When they do, they are fully committed to the process and they cooperate with traditional or modern treatment programs. One pilot project of the Navajo courts was the Minority Male Program. It was designed to offer diversion alternatives for persons charged with driving while intoxicated. Peacemaking proved successful in getting beneath the problem of drunk driving by motivating people to recognize that they indeed did have a drinking problem and should do something about it. Recidivism rates dropped for those who went through peacemaking.

Relationships and relatives are an important distinction that makes peace-making unique. A person who agrees to pay *nalyeeh* may not have the personal wealth or means to do so. It is traditional for family and clan members to make the payment on their relative's behalf. The tradition is not simply that relatives assume obligations for others, although that is fundamental to Navajo society. When an individual commits a wrong against another, it shames the person's relatives – 'He acts as if he had no relatives'. The family will keep an eye on the offender to assure there will be no future transgressions. Where there is a particularly malicious or heinous act, community members will 'kill with the eyes'. That describes a practice where people keep a watch for an offender, and use social pressure to keep him in line with the community's expectations of proper behavior. We recognize this dynamic of Navajo custom for modern adjudication as well. Both the Rules for Domestic Violence Proceedings and the Navajo Nation Sentencing Policy include provisions to require offenders to get family member sureties for bonds to assure future good conduct. We call this the 'traditional probation officer', where we recruit family members to assume supervisory obligations.

What makes peacemaking work? Peacemaking is based on relationships. It uses the deep emotions of respect, solidarity, self-examination, problem-solving and ties to the community. Navajo common law recognizes the individual and individual rights, but it differs from Western individualism in that the individual is put in his or her proper place within community relationships. Western legal thought speaks to 'me' and 'I', but the individual is viewed in the isolated context of individual rights. In Navajo legal thinking, an individual is a person within a community, it is impossible to function alone. They say that Navajos always go home: Navajos who have better potentials to earn a high income in a big city return home to a lesser-paying job because they cannot live outside Navajo society. Navajos responded to recent disclosures that the Navajo Nation has the lowest family and per capita incomes of all Indian nations of the US, and the highest poverty rate, by pointing out that their rural economies and lifestyles are a matter of choice. Yes, there is a great deal of poverty in the Navajo Nation and limited economic opportunities, but Navajos live as Navajos.

An important Navajo legal term is *k'e*, for which there is no corresponding word in English. *K'e* is the cement of Navajo law; it describes proper relationships, and underlies and fuels consensual justice. It is what allows a traditional justice system to operate without force or coercion. It allows people to be their own judges and to enforce binding judgments without jails or sheriffs.

Peacemaking agreements can be reduced to judgment and enforced as any other court judgment. In practice, the people prefer informal agreements and often do not seek court ratification of it in a formal judgment. Relationships and methods designed to build or reinforce them, supported by the strong emotional force of *k'e*, are the underpinnings of peacemaking. It is not a system of law that relies upon authority, force and coercion, but one that utilizes the strengths of people in communities.

Corrective, restorative and distributive justice

Most state law methods are based on corrective justice. That is, the hierarchy of power attempts to maintain social control using state authority. The difficulty lies in abuses of authority, and people tend to resist being told what to do. They respond better when they buy into or accept a decision that they help make. Navajo justice methods are corrective in the sense that they attempt to get at causes that underlie disputes or wrongdoing. They address excuses such as denial, minimalization and externalization in practical ways in order to adjust the attitudes of wrongdoers. The methods educate offenders about the nature of their behaviors and how they impact others, and help people identify their place and role in society in order to reintegrate them into specific community roles. Navajo justice methods recognize the need to implement justice in a community context, because ultimately the community must solve its own problems. Navajo families, clans and communities were stripped of their long-standing responsibility for justice in adjudication and in the police and social work models. There are now more than 250 peacemakers in the Navajo Nation's 110 communities, and they accept that responsibility with a great deal of enthusiasm and energy. Navajo corrective justice can be immediate because it is carried out in communities. People expect an immediate resolution of their problems, and they do not want to wait on the schedules of judges and police officers.

Navajo corrective justice is actually restorative justice. It is not so much concerned about correction of the person as it is about restoring that person to good relations with others. This is an integrative process whereby the group as a whole examines relationships and mends a relationship gone wrong. Navajo justice uses practical methods to restore an offender to good standing within the group. Where the relationship does not exist in the first place (e.g. as with dysfunctional families), peacemaking builds new relationships that hopefully will function in a healthy manner. Another way to describe the result of peacemaking is *hozho nahasdlii*. The phrase describes the result of 'talking things out' and reaching a consensual conclusion. It says, 'now that we have done these things and gone through this process, we are now returned to a state of *hozho*'. The process determines the outcome, and is one of restored mutual and reciprocal relationships with a group functioning as a whole.

Another function of Navajo justice is known as distributive justice. Where there is an injury, the group identifies resources to address it. For example, when a Navajo is arrested and charged for an offence, relatives will collect money to post a money bond or buy a bail bond. When a family member is injured in an accident, others give financial support. It is a form of insurance, also known as *nalyeeh*. In peacemaking, there are practical discussions of the injured person's needs and who has the resources to address it. Need is served with monetary, material and even emotional support. Distributive justice asks, 'what do we have and how can we help?' It is based on reciprocal obligations founded in *k'e* for *hozho*.

Does peacemaking actually work? Is it romantic or practical? Does peacemaking speak to universals of human behavior or is it culture-specific to Navajos? The *Hozhooji Naat'aanii* (Peacemaker Division of the courts) staff report that recidivism rates among wrongdoers are only about 20%. There are reports of people telling of their personal satisfaction with peacemaking and how it has made a difference to their lives. Peacemaking does deal with homicides or murders (without using those classifications), and there are instances of deaths within family groups (and sometimes among strangers) where peacemaking is used to resolve the emotions and hardships that come in the wake of the killing of one person by another. The question of the kinds of cases handled is not as relevant as the result, restorative justice. Navajo cultural perspectives are unique. They are a product of the Navajo language and of the concepts it expresses. Navajo ceremonial practice and the norms, values and moral principles it maintains are perhaps unique to Navajos. However, we believe that we have identified human behavior that is universal and grounded in the norms of many cultures. We use psychological discourse and approaches to explain peacemaking so we can show the outside world what Navajos are doing. They are very practical, pragmatic and concrete in what they do.

This extract is taken from 'Navajo Restorative Justice: the Law of Equality and Justice', by Robert Yazzie and James W. Zion in B. Galaway and J. Hudson (eds), Restorative Justice: International Perspectives *(Monsey, NY: Criminal Justice Press, 1996), pp. 157–73.*

10. The Maori restorative tradition

Jim Consedine

An elderly Far North Maori has been banned from his home marae for a sex offence. A spokesman said the offender was a very active member on the marae, and was very embarrassed and humiliated by his actions. The six-month ban was a suitable penalty.

The case follows recent publicity about marae hearings in the Waikato that have resulted in seven Maori elders being stripped of their kaumatua status. The process, developed by the Hamilton child and protection agency Kokana Ngakau, has resulted in 18 cases of physical and sexual abuse being taken back to various marae.

Maori lore has a way of addressing Maori grievances, with court sessions being held on marae in accordance with tikana Maori, and whanau determining the sentence. Some court sessions had taken up to three days of non-stop discussion to resolve.

NZPA, September 1993

It will have come as a considerable surprise to most New Zealanders to learn that Maori have a traditional integrated system of criminal justice and that in some areas of Aotearoa to a degree it is still being used. The general perception among Pakeha is that such 'quaint customs' died out over a century ago.

Clearly this is not the case. Despite the strongest efforts of the 'one law for all' brigade, there obviously has been a parallel system of justice operating alongside the dominant English-derived system.

Modern case histories

Aroha Terry of Tainui, an expert in sexual abuse cases, claims marae justice is more effective than the traditional Pakeha justice system. In the latter, a person can be locked away for a few years in jail and no-one hears about it. They never have to face their accusers or take responsibility for their actions, and they never have to change. There is no healing for the victim, no healing for the whanau. In the Pakeha system there is no appropriate procedure for the whanau, and no empowerment for them to make decisions.

Under marae justice it is just the opposite. The purpose of marae justice is a healing for all: it is not a battleground. The process is primarily about hearing and helping the victim, healing the whanau, and helping and healing the perpetrator. It works for all three.

Marae justice is set up to meet victims' needs. It is not about squashing the offender into the dirt. It is about recognising who got hurt – to hell with people saying society is the victim: it was *me*, not society, that got hurt.

Marae justice takes the responsibility away from the victim and places it where it belongs – with the offender. It is particularly appropriate for dealing with sexual

152

offences. The offender is the one who puts all the crap on the victim. We're so scared, we're so tidy in our little whares, in our lives, picking on the victim. It's all so wrong. I say go back to the offender and say, 'Hey, this is your problem'.[1]

Waha Stirling of Ngai Tahu and Ngati Porou na Whanau Apanui, in speaking of his youthful days in the 1930s and 1940s on the East Coast, remembers that most cases of wrongdoing involving criminal behaviour were dealt with on the local marae by elders. Cases included all petty offending such as stealing and assault as well as more serious ones of sexual and child abuse. The police were only called in for more serious offending.

The process used was one of bringing the families together and talking it all through in a way that is very similar to the process now used in Aotearoa under the Children, Young Persons and their Families Act.

The whanau of both sides in a complaint were invited to a hui. The accused needed to plead guilty and not hide what had been done. It was up to the accused's whanau to get to the root of the matter before the hearing began, and elicit a guilty plea if this was the case. In a sense the whole whanau was on trial so this usually wasn't hard to do. At the hui the elders would take the offender to task, with the kuia being particularly prominent in shaming the offender and the whole family. Often they were all reduced to tears.

Then, consultation between the parties would take place as to a suitable way of dealing with the matter, so as to heal any hurts and restore things to 'normal' again. Things stolen would have to be recovered or compensation paid. Damage would have to be repaired. The penalty usually also involved some compulsory work – sometimes offenders would be sent off to work on adjacent cattle stations if there was not enough work for them around the marae or village.

Hohua Tutengaehe of Ngai Te Rangi and Ngati Ranginui recalls a case when, as a 14-year-old boy in the late 1940s, he was asked to act as recorder in an attempted rape hearing. The attempt had got to a point where the assailant had allegedly removed the young woman's underwear before the assault ceased. The chief called a hui of the rangatira of each of the local marae. After whaikorero, the process began.

First the victim came in accompanied by her parents, her aunts and uncles, sisters and brothers and the whanau of the grandparents. Then the whanau of the assailant arrived. They sat on opposite sides of the meeting house.

The boy, who admitted to the offence, was about 17 years old, the girl a year younger. As soon as the boy pleaded guilty, a session of lectures started from the kuia, the old women present. They berated him for his behaviour, for the sacred tapu he had broken by attacking a young woman, for the shame he had brought on himself, his whanau, his people. In next to no time he and his family were reduced to tears.

Following that, the penalty was pronounced. It was decided that for the first 12 months, whenever there was a wedding or a tangi, the family of the boy had to supply all the meat and vegetables. In addition, he had to paint the meeting house. When they examined the meeting house they found that the weatherboards and roofing iron were decayed, so the family had to replace these.

After some time, because the meeting house belonged to them all, the girl and her whanau went along to help prepare the meals for the boy's family while they were working. The two sides came together in a gesture of reconciliation. Eventually they all settled down and together repaired the dining-room and the surrounding fences. The whole process took about two years.

This was modern Maori justice in action – restorative, healing, reconciling. There were no names on the criminal pages of the media, no police record to haunt the boy in his future life, and the victim received due recognition in the process and was healed of her trauma.

But marae justice is not just something from the past. In an *Inside New Zealand* television documentary, *Marae Justice*, shown in Aotearoa in August 1994, actual marae hearings were filmed and shown nationwide. These were examples employing a traditional Maori justice setting where the whanau acted as prosecutor and sentencing court.

We were taken to the Korapatu Marae where a 24-year-old local woman alleged she had been raped and sexually abused repeatedly between the ages of eight and 16 years. Three brothers were among her abusers. She described how she had been treated as a slave and raped repeatedly.

> It would happen once a day. Sometimes once a week. We thought it was normal. I can remember being dragged under the house. If I didn't go I got a hiding. I just let them do what they wanted. I was so terrified – I was really scared. I don't know why they hated me so much. I was just a little kid, trying to live, trying to survive.[2]

The three offending brothers had been summoned by the whanau to the hearing. Such is the power of the whanau that there is no escaping from them if they wish to remain a part of it. The family sit in judgment on the allegations; there were no lawyers, no judge, no police.

Aroha Terry, as advocate, read out the charges of multiple rape, sexual violation and abuse. All listened in silence. Each of the three men pleaded guilty. One added he was glad it had come out into the open. Another said he took full responsibility for what he had done. They all then listened to the woman speak of her pain, her abject suffering over many years, her feelings of rejection, distrust, hatred, anger. She finished by saying that after many months of counselling prior to the hearing, she now felt ready to forgive them. What had moved her finally to that point was hearing them acknowledge what they had done was wrong, that they took full personal responsibility for their actions, and that they deeply regretted the hurt and pain she had suffered.

The aroha present enabled healing and reconciliation to occur. The openness of the accused and their acceptance of responsibility coupled with a desire to change their behaviour and make some amends meant progress could be made towards healing for all.

The sentence for the three men as decided by the whanau was severe but positive. The whakama that each had experienced by appearing before other family members and their acceptance of responsibility and pleas of guilty were taken into consideration and given considerable weight.

Each was to undergo extensive counselling and commissioned to go to work on behalf of the whanau and tell others of the need to end sexual abuse. They had to speak to groups and families of their own experiences and offences, and encourage others to treat their children and their whanau with respect. This process was to be carefully monitored to make sure that there was full compliance.

The victim expressed delight at the progress made. She said she 'felt good' that the balance had been partially redressed and the men had acknowledged their offending. She was glad there were no more skeletons in the cupboard. Maori women generally found it hard to speak out, but she was glad that she had.[3]

Another woman featured in the same programme alleged abuse by her stepfather.

> I figured that if he abused me as the eldest, he might leave my sisters alone. I felt like I wanted to kill him. He used to hold me down over the wash-house sink with the broom handle. He told me he would kill me if I told Mum. I used to get into the shower and bath-tub and try and scrub myself clean.[4]

The stepfather pleaded guilty at a marae hearing. The whanau stripped him of his mana and matuatanga and kaumatua status and banned him from the marae. But eight months later when filming took place he was in denial. He claimed he was drunk all the time, and had never abused anyone.

There was a time when belonging to a gang almost certainly meant having to be involved with rape in order to be seen to be 'staunch'. Such was the case with Black Power, probably New Zealand's best-known gang. For years women were treated as objects to be enjoyed at gang members' behest, and no amount of imprisonment for rape and other charges of violence made any difference. Prison was seen as a place to recruit new members. The traditional retributive justice process could not stem the violence towards women. In effect it increased it.

Then came a dramatic shift in attitude. At their 1978 national convention, Black Power, led by their president, Rei Harris, banned rape. Rediscovery of traditional Maori justice and values had a significant part to play in this conversion. So too did the strength and integrity of the president and some of his chief supporters.

But for some old habits die hard. There were subsequent cases that Black Power dealt with themselves. Bill Maung, former judge and legal adviser to Black Power, has talked about how the gang dealt with such violations of their moral code.

He tells of one incident when a young woman came to the Wellington chapter and reported that she had been raped by three of their members. She preferred not to go to the police, so it was agreed they would be dealt with on a marae. Amster Reedy of Ngati Porou, at that time a lecturer at teachers' college and a kaumatua, was one of about 50 who gathered to hear the case: Maori wardens, social workers, whanau, Black Power members.

After hearing the young woman's story, the hui reflected on what should happen to the three young men. One of them came from Taranaki and his kuia berated him tearfully, saying that their tribe had always walked with pride, and now he had made them all crawl seeking forgiveness. One suggestion was that they should all be exiled from Aotearoa forever, banished and forced to leave the country and the people they had so betrayed.

The offenders then took the floor and admitted the rapes. Their remorse was overwhelming, their desire to change and do reparation genuine. Pills and alcohol had obviously been contributing factors, though they claimed no mitigation from that source. They experienced tremendous shame in front of their whanau, their peers, their tribes. They vowed never to re-offend.

Then the young woman spoke, saying that she forgave them. Later, in explaining why, she said that for once in her life she had felt in control of a major situation, so she felt she could afford to be generous to them given the sorrow they had expressed.

Finally the penalty was spelt out. Quoting an old Maori proverb, Reedy noted that shame would be their principal punishment. There was, he said, no more powerful punishment in Maori society than whakama. People had been known to will themselves to death because the finger of shame had been pointed at them. The young men were also placed under close supervision and ordered to pay $20 a week each from their meagre incomes to the woman for six months. This constituted about a quarter of their incomes.

None of the men involved re-offended. One later committed suicide, though no definite connection was made with his rape offence. Another became a strong family man and a leader in the development of his whanau and people. Under Pakeha law, says Maung, they would still be sitting on all their anger in prison, while the woman, after a degrading court experience, would have become a marked woman and would have had to leave town.[5]

In the Whanau Awhina programme at the Hoani Waititi Marae in West Auckland, marae justice using traditional and modern insights seems to be working well. John Perkis, the justice programme chairman, says that 'the purpose of the process is the restoration of a person's mana. To restore him or her to society with mana intact, on the marae we don't discriminate. Raggy-arsed guys are treated the same as the prime minister.'[6]

An evaluation of the marae process by the Crime Prevention Unit concluded that Whanau Awhina is working. The rate of recidivism for clients who completed the pilot period was 22 per cent, compared with 10 per cent at nearby Waitakere's police diversion scheme. If the comparison seems unflattering, the report also shows 80 per cent of Whanau Awhina's clients had considerable criminal histories, whereas the police diversion scheme usually deals with first offenders.

Marae chairman Pita Sharples says that 'Maori being dealt with by Maori is a key factor in achieving results. It's a process of healing. We deal with the circumstances of the case rather than just with the offence. For two to three hours we look at the charge and circumstances and make an action plan. Families are welcomed with a karakia (prayer), with kuia and kaumatua present. Then the real dynamics, the impact of the marae, takes over. That's been our methodology. We're quite proud of the results achieved.'[7]

Whanau Awhina's achievements depend on the passion and commitment of a volunteer panel well-skilled at responding to mute shrugs, one-word answers and long silences. Questioning can be torrid, panel members stern. Family group conferences become emotional as more information is elicited. Inevitably, panel members know the offender's extended family. The panel formulates a plan to break the offending cycle. Idleness, lack of motivation, poor education, low self-esteem, unemployment and financial hardship emerge as the main contributing factors. An offender's community service is often based around marae projects.[8]

Judge Coral Shaw of Henderson is a great admirer of the programme and insists that programmes like Whanau Awhina should be properly funded and included within the legal framework of New Zealand.[9]

[. . .]

This extract is taken from Restorative Justice: Healing the Effects of Crime *(revised edition) (Lyttelton, New Zealand: Ploughshares Publications, 1999), chapter 6.*

Notes

1 *Inside New Zealand* documentary 'Marae Justice', TV3, August 1994.
2 Ibid.
3 Ibid.
4 Ibid.
5 Pamela Stirling, *NZ Listener*, 14 May 1990.
6 Liz Mahoney, *NZ Listener*, 18 April 1998.
7 Ibid.
8 Ibid.
9 Ibid.

11. Christianity: the rediscovery of restorative justice

Pierre Allard and Wayne Northey

> It is not as though Christianity has been tried and found wanting. It has been found hard and left untried.
>
> Ravi Zacharias, 'Diagnosing the Modern Mind' (1983)

During the Vancouver symposium 'Satisfying Justice' held in March 1997, Pierre Allard was to address the topic 'Faith and Crime'. His address was preceded by an Aboriginal speaker recounting the abuses suffered in the residential schools and the healing journey begun by his people. Allard became uneasy. Reflecting further on this uneasiness, he became jealous and angry – until he solved the enigma. His feelings had been triggered by the fact that the Aboriginal community is conscious of having lost a treasure and has engaged on a return journey. The Christian community, on the other hand, seems not even conscious of having lost a great treasure and for the most part is not engaging on a journey of rediscovery. In the area of criminal justice, he concluded, Christianity has been found hard indeed and left untried for so long that it hardly remembers the time when justice could only be thought of in terms of a *restoring justice*. It is the thesis of this chapter that a Christian reading of the Hebrew Scriptures, the life and ministry of Jesus, and the overall witness of the New Testament, point to what we would describe as a restorative justice model and practice in response to crime. For as St John's Gospel proclaims (3: 16), 'God loved the world so much that he gave his only Son, so that everyone who believes in him may not be lost but may have eternal life.' The demonstration of that contention is to what we now turn.

The essence of Christinaity is that God loved humankind so much that God became human. God became human in the person of Jesus. In opening his public ministry, Jesus, the Christ, made clear his option for justice when, according to St Luke's Gospel (4: 18–19), he stood up and read: 'The Spirit of the Lord is on me, because he has anointed me to preach good news to the poor. He has sent me to proclaim freedom for the prisoners and recovery of sight for the blind, to release the oppressed, to proclaim the year of the Lord's favor.' The record is clear that Jesus healed and preached the Good News. He also moved freely among the people, the despised and rejected. In the Sermon on the Mount, as recorded in the Gospel according to St Matthew (5: 38–48), Jesus introduced the revolutionary ethic of forgiveness. As one theologian has explained: 'The proportional ethic of "eye for eye, tooth for tooth" was to be supplanted by turning the other cheek, giving your cloak, and going the second mile. Not only are you to love your neighbor but, especially, are you to love your enemy and those who are unjust.'[1] In Christ, the sinner is given hope, the prodigal is welcomed home. Jesus is the great 'Restorer'. At the same time, as Bishop Harris explained in his study 'The Criminology of Christ', so many things seem unfair (parable of the labourers in the vineyard, the brother of the prodigal son), unbalanced, irrational, as far as I can see. But there is the rub – as far as I can see. Christ came to take our vision beyond the horizon. He came to reveal something his followers felt they had never before experienced: a God who is completely loving – no strings attached – with no ulterior motive. And because His love is total, it is given not because we have earned it, but because we need it. Herein lies the criminology of Christ.[2]

Jesus' option for forgiveness, for merciful restoration, is sealed forever in the mystery of his death and resurrection. The resurrection, says Brian Wren, 'meant that God himself had raised Jesus from death into a new and transformed life, thereby saying "yes" to all that Jesus has said and done in his name'.[3] Jesus' love, as the faithful insist, is boundless, amazing, extravagant. It reaches out to all without distinction, offering hope, fellowship and new beginnings. As Wayne Northey has argued elsewhere, love – as 'forgiveness' in Christian circles, and in wider society – is too often the 'forbidden' word.[4] Yet, as he summarized at that time, forgiveness as technique and tool is also perhaps the most significant process for overcoming the devastation of crime. As Donald Shriver expressed it: 'Forgiveness in political context, then, is an act that joins moral truth, forbearance, empathy, and commitment to repair a fractured human relation.'[5] Seen in that light, forgiveness promises to deliver on learning from the past to actually transcend endlessly recycled violence in response to victimization. Forgiveness liberates us from the very core of our violent impulses.[6]

The early Christian church's attitude of compassion toward offenders is well expressed in the Apostolic Constitutions: 'It therefore behooves you . . . to encourage those who have offended, and lead them to repentance, and afford them hope . . . Receive the penitent with alacrity, and rejoice over them, and with mercy and bowels [sic] of compassion judge the sinners.'[7] Significantly, the death of Christ among criminals, on a cross, was to link Christianity to criminal justice forever. This remained so, no matter how much the first and subsequent generations of Christians would have to struggle to understand the full meaning of Christ's incarnation, followed by his death, his resurrection, and ascension.

No Christian discussion of restorative justice can begin without acknowledging the significance of the Hebrew Scriptures. Here we might highlight three Old Testament features as they connect to New Testament themes pertinent to restorative justice: shalom, the Prophets, and vengeance. *Shalom*, as Perry B. Yoder's seminal study of the concept explains, is the Bible's word for salvation, justice, and peace. Howard Zehr's influential book on restorative justice draws heavily on Yoder's work to make the same point.[8] Yoder concludes in part: 'God's justice is a response to the lack of shalom in order to create the conditions of shalom.'[9] In Hebrew Scripture, therefore, restorative justice is a *peacemaking response* to crime for all those persons affected by it.

The Prophets, Christians claim, all pointed to Jesus the Christ (Messiah), who shatters for all time the legitimacy of scapegoating. From his time on, no enemy may ever be put outside the circle of God's love – or indeed ours. Hebrew prophetic insight, Christians argue, anticipates the advent of a

'Suffering Servant' whom Christians and New Testament witnesses appropriate as their Saviour, Jesus the Christ. So James G. Williams concludes: 'In
understanding his suffering, in standing with him and not with the persecutors,
those who are taught by him begin to transform the structures of sacred
violence.'[10] Against wider cultural trends towards violence and vengeance, for
example, the prophet Amos pointed to the priority of doing justice over
engaging in worship; Hosea's genius was to set the question of deserved
punishment within the family context, where mercy and justice are finally
balanced properly; and Jonah had to learn the hard lesson that God never
ceases to care even for the 'stranger/enemy'. The Hebrew Prophets pulsated
with dynamic pointers to the nonviolent work and words of Jesus, and
proleptically to the nonviolent way of the Cross. New Testament writings in
fact build on an antisacrificial momentum begun in the Old Testament and
point in John 1 and Hebrews 1 to Jesus as the Christians' 'hermeneutic lens'.

Still, there are 'six hundred passages of explicit violence in the Hebrew Bible,
one thousand verses where God's own violent actions of punishment are
described, a hundred passages where Yahweh expressly commands others to
kill for no apparent reason ... Violence ... is easily the most mentioned
activity and central theme of the Hebrew Bible.'[11] And there are portions of
the book of Revelation and other texts scattered about the New Testament
with a violent tinge or avowal. Christian traditions, for reasons which we will
explain later, have regrettably tended to endorse these sources in embracing
retributive justice. As will be seen, part of the problem lies in what René Girard
called a 'scapegoat mechanism' found in early Old Testament traditions. In
the surrogate sacrifice of a ram in place of Isaac, for example, the scapegoat
was an animal instead of a human being.[12] Animal sacrifice in the Old
Testament is never far from human sacrifice. There is, however, a move away
from this scapegoat mechanism, especially during the time of the later
prophets.[13] Thus Micah (6: 8) identifies animal sacrifice as child sacrifice
disguised; importantly, Jesus draws on this very passage in Matthew 23: 23.
Some call Micah 6 the 'high water' mark of Old Testament spirituality. Hosea
rejects all sacrifice except sincere conversion of the heart. The requirement for
sacrifice is countered in Jesus' teaching and is rejected through the Cross. 'It
is mercy I desire and not sacrifice (Matt. 9: 13),' Jesus says straightforwardly,
quoting from Hosea 6: 6.

In his book *The Vengeance of God*, a work thematically close to Timothy
Gorringe's magisterial critique *God's Just Vengeance*, H.G.L. Peels raises a
cautionary note: '... it is clear that the prayer for vengeance in the Old
Testament and the command for love in the New Testament operate on a
different level, and a contrast drawn between such different texts can only
produce a false picture.'[14] Further, Peels discerns that 'Between the vengeance
and the love of God there is no contradiction, but sometimes there is a tension
...'[15] He does note, however, that 'Wrath and vengeance are variables, while
love is a constant in God's relationship with mankind'. He concludes, finally:
'The fact that God's vengeance stands in the service of salvation is the most
evident from the longing for and joy concerning this vengeance, in which there
is, incidentally, no trace of malice ... The God of vengeance and the God of
love are one and the same God. He is the Lord who brings his kingdom in

justice and grace.'[16] Significantly, vengeance is self-consciously omitted from Jesus' agenda – even when he quotes Scripture with such themes in it.[17] Rightly understood, the words 'punishment' and 'retribution' have no place in Christian vocabulary.[18]

James Alison discerns a dynamic of *subversion* at work in Christian theology in light of the resurrection of Jesus; it is a dynamic that reconceptualizes the categories of wrath and vengeance such that they (and God) are completely shorn of violence. He explains:

> So we have a gradual ironic subversion of the language of wrath, whereby that which is initially seen as something active (God being angry) is recast to show God being righteous in the midst of human anger, but without losing the word 'wrath'. Something of the same process can be seen (but more obviously) in the Johannine reworking of the theme of God's judgment whereby God's judgment of humanity consists not in any judgment actively exercised by God, but in the judgment undergone by Jesus at the hands of human beings. We are judged by our relationship to that judgment. We see then how God 'handing over' Jesus to us can be described as God's wrath, when the content of that wrath is the human violence exercised against Jesus, or the simultaneous handing over of ourselves to idolatry typified in the killing of Jesus . . . The true understanding of wrath came about exactly at the same moment as there emerged the possibility of being freed from it: it is the forgiveness of the resurrection which defines the nature of sin.[19]

In light of the Resurrection, God's wrath is, christologically speaking, nothing less than forgiveness. In Jürgen Moltmann's words: 'God's wrath is nothing less than his wounded love and a pain which cuts to the heart. His wrath is therefore an expression of enduring interest in man.'[20] God's wrath is in fact in complete solidarity with our suffering such that the very pain of existence is endured by God, taken up into God's very life. In fact, a trinitarian understanding of God arises from Jesus' death on the cross: God experiences wrath and death in his Son. Thus, 'the material principle of the doctrine of the Trinity is the cross. The formal principle of the theology of the cross is the doctrine of the Trinity.'[21] Seen in this light, God's wrath experienced as abandonment, as 'Godforsakenness',[22] becomes one's hope and joy in the power of the Resurrection.[23] God's exercise of vengeance is forgiveness and liberation; this is, to borrow a book title from James Alison, 'the joy of being wrong' in Jesus. Jesus determines to disarm every state executioner and to set every prisoner free.[24]

Many forces were to combine through the centuries to bury the richness of biblical restorative justice and make it virtually disappear. [. . .]

The historical record is certainly clear that the *persecuted* church quickly became the *persecutor* in its response to pagans, Jews, other outsiders, and eventually criminals.

Kee says [. . .]: 'It is not that the perspective of the early church provides the norm for critically assessing the life of the church today. To the contrary, after Constantine, it is the church under the sway of imperial values which now provides the perspective for reading the Bible.'[25] Certainly hermeneutics of the founding biblical texts themselves becomes an issue before the texts are even read. This does not make the issue of Jesus' teaching in this matter any easier!

A large body of twentieth-century biblical scholarship[26] based upon a rereading of the founding texts has discovered the truth of Gandhi's statement that 'the message of Jesus, as I understand it, is contained in the Sermon on the Mount . . . Much of what passes as Christianity is a negation of the Sermon on the Mount.'[27] Or again, he observed: 'the only people on earth who do not see Christ and his teachings as nonviolent are Christians.'[28] While not agreeing fully with Gandhi, both Walter Wink and Glen H. Stassen offer in their books a sustained rereading of Jesus that points up 'a great irony of history that the cross, symbol of the ultimate triumph of peaceful means to peaceful ends, has been used as a standard in battle'.[29] This includes the 'war' against crime.

To measure properly the consequences of such a move – from the biblical, restorative concept to a Roman punitive concept – one turns to the distinguished Dutch historian of law, Herman Bianchi. His special expertise lies in biblical justice, especially as it relates to the legal system and, more specifically, to the penal law system. From the very beginning, he points out, Christianity claimed to be a leaven for the entire culture, including the legal system. Yet, 'nowhere else did the Christian religion have less chance to accomplish this claim than exactly in the legal system . . . And no legal system was ever more fit for resistance than the Roman legal system, as it was continued in continental Europe after the fall of the Roman empire and even officially adopted later in the Middle Ages. The glamour of this legal system was so strong that it radiated also to Britain.'[30] Perhaps this would not have been so significant were it not for one striking fact: the legal system had little or nothing whatever to do with the teachings of Christian doctrine. But because the Middle Ages pretended to be a totally Christian culture, the Roman system was accepted as consistent with Christian doctrine. Thomas Aquinas went even further and proclaimed the Greco-Roman idea of justice to be *the* ideal of justice. Hence, Bianchi explains, 'it came to be that the Western legal system continued to be Greco-Roman in nature and was nevermore endangered by any biblical thought. The Reformation attacked many ideas of medieval doctrine, [but] it never ever pronounced any doubts concerning the legitimacy of Greco-Roman justice for a Christian culture.'

Bianchi's [. . .] English publication, *Justice as Sanctuary*, nuances the understanding of 'Greco-Roman' legal traditions to explain that Roman slave law was indeed brutal, and that it was precisely this retributive law that was taken over into highly punitive Western ways of criminal justice. From a biblical, Christian concept of justice, however, where the victim's voice is the primary voice, we move progressively to a concept of justice where the emerging State is central; this constitutes a shift from a dynamic concept of attempting to place centre stage genuine reconciliation, restoration, and shalom between offender–victim, to a situation where the victim's voice becomes increasingly silenced.[31] In short, the victim has been displaced by the King (or Emperor) as the supreme authority responsible for 'keeping the peace' within the kingdom.

The battle lines between the 'secular' and the 'spiritual' were drawn by Pope Gregory VII when publishing his twenty-seven terse propositions in *Dictatus Papae* in 1075. The implications were far-reaching, as Harold J. Berman contends:

The Papal Revolution gave birth to a new conception of kingship in Western Christendom. The king was no longer the supreme head of the church. The era of 'sacral kinship' gradually came to an end. In matters denominated as 'spiritual', the bishop of Rome was supreme – not only over kings but also over the most important sovereign of all, the emperor. For the first time emperor and kings were conceived to be 'secular' rulers, whose principal tasks were, first, to keep the peace within their respective kingdoms, that is, to control violence, and second, to do justice, that is, to govern in the political and economic spheres. Even in these matters, moreover, the church played an important role. The reduction of royal authority in ecclesiastical matters was compensated, however, by a very large increase in royal authority in relation to other secular polities – tribal, local, feudal, and urban. In Joseph Strayer's words, 'The Gregorian concept of the Church almost demanded the invention of the concept of the State.'[32] [And] as the Papal Revolution gave birth to the modern Western State, so it gave birth also to modern Western legal systems, the first of which was the modern system of canon law.[33]

When one combines with the Gregorian Reform, or 'Revolution', the emergence of the theology of satisfaction under the influence of Anselm of Canterbury's eleventh-century *Cur Deus Homo*, one has great difficulty recognizing the good news of the Gospel. As Berman explains:

> However broadly Anselm conceived justice, reason required that he stop at the boundary of grace. God is bound by his own justice. If it is divinely just for a man to pay the price for his sins, it would be unjust, and therefore impossible, for God to remit the price. In *Cur Deus Homo* Anselm's theology is a theology of law.
>
> Before the time of Anselm (and in the Eastern Church still) it would have been considered wrong to analyze God's justice in this way. It would have been said, first, that these ultimate mysteries cannot be fitted into the concepts and constructs of the human intellect; that reason is inseparable from faith – one is not the servant of the other, but rather the two are indivisible; and the whole exercise of a theology of law is a contradiction in terms. And second, it would have been said that it is not only, and not primarily, divine justice that establishes our relationship with God but also, and primarily, his grace and his mercy; that is his grace and mercy, and not only his justice, which explains the crucifixion, since by it mankind was ransomed from the power of the devil and the demons of death – the very power which had procured the slaying of Jesus in the first place but which then itself was finally conquered through the resurrection.[34]

Anselm's theory profoundly influenced what Gorringe has called the 'structure of affect' of subsequent centuries. By that he was referring to cultural sensibilities that responded retributively to crime. Although Anselm's theology of Satisfaction, of Atonement was never proclaimed as the 'official' doctrine of the Christian church, it was widely accepted both in Catholicism and Protestantism;[35] it was to have a number of negative impacts, especially when applied to the criminal justice system. Over the differing voices of Lombard, Abelard, Blake, Campbell and Moberly, and others, Anselm's voice remained the strongest. In his *God's Just Vengeance*, Timothy Gorringe explains it thus:

> For the Church Fathers, it is the devil who – illegitimately – insists on the payment of the debt incurred by humankind. Anselm inverts this. Now it is God

who, legitimately, exacts the payment of debt ... In both Old and New Testaments an indebted person could be 'redeemed' by the payment of his or her debt. Jesus, following Deuteronomy, insists on the cancelling of debt as a fundamental aspect of Christian practice. Anselm, however, makes God the one who *insists* on debt. The debt humanity has incurred must be paid with human blood. The penal consequences of this doctrine were grim indeed. As it entered the cultural bloodstream, was imaged in crucifixions, painted over church chancels, recited at each celebration of the Eucharist, or hymned, so it created its own structure of affect, one in which earthly punishment was demanded because God himself had demanded the death of his Son. When the social reformer Joseph Gerald was tried in March 1794, he pointed out that Jesus Christ had himself been a reformer. Lord Braxfield, the presiding judge, turned to his fellow judges and remarked: 'Muckle he made o' that; *he* was hanget.' And many generations of the poor, like Gerrald, paid the price of maintaining the 'justice' of a confessedly hierarchical system.[36]

So instead of a merciful, compassionate God as revealed in Jesus the Christ, the Christian God became a severe judge bent on punishment and almost literally 'blood-thirsty'. The Christians who used the cross to scapegoat the Jews, to lead Crusades, and persecute others totally reversed what the cross stood for in Jesus' death and resurrection. ' "Quick, head off, away with it, in order that the earth does not become full of the ungodly." The voice is distinctly Martin Luther's. Rulers are the ministers of God's wrath, Luther insisted; it is their duty to use the sword against offenders. They are "God's hangmen".'[37] Luther is merely one of many representatives of dominant Protestant and Catholic church theory and practice since the eleventh century.

Charles Wesley's Journal of 1738 bears graphic witness to the tensions between 'secular' and 'spiritual' priorities. Here he recorded his ministry in Newgate prison on the night before the execution of nine prisoners: 'We wrestled in mighty prayer ... Joy was visible in all their faces. We sang "Behold the saviour of Mankind: nailed to the shameful tree. How vast the love that him inclined, To bleed and die for thee." It was one of the most triumphant hours I have known.' The next morning he accompanied them to the gallows: 'They were all cheerful, full of comfort, peace and triumph, assuredly persuaded that Christ had died for them and waited to receive them into paradise ... I never saw such calm triumph, such incredible indifference to dying.' He returned home and wrote: 'Full of peace and confidence in our friends' happiness. That hour under the gallows was the most blessed hour of my life.'[38]

Such ministers as the Wesley brothers, Father John Fletcher (called the Anglican St Francis), and their followers were genuinely concerned for the poor. But where the editors of the *Spectator* readily recognized that 'law grinds the poor' simply because 'such men make the law', Wesley saw no injustice in hanging thieves. But as Gorringe plaintively asks:

What was it, then, which prevented them from seeing what the editors of the *Spectator* so clearly perceived? How was it that they could see people like Wilkes, whose hopeless background they perfectly understood, go to the gallows for offences which were trivial and which involved no violence against the person, without exerting themselves to have the sentence commuted? . . . How is it that the question whether the law might be wrong, or even wicked, does not arise for these good Christian people? How could they come away from scenes of judicial murder feeling that this was 'the most blessed day of their lives'?[39]

[. . .]

Throughout the centuries, the restorative voice of the Gospel did not die completely, but found deep echoes in such movements as the Anabaptist tradition. But, in the words of the Most Rev. E.W. Scott, 'all too often the State has claimed divine authority for legal actions for which no such authority exists. In this process the church, which should have been challenging or critiquing the civil authority from a Biblical perspective, has too often allowed itself to be "domesticated" and has blessed and sanctioned when it ought to have challenged.'[40] In the first centuries CE, as the Church and the State were defining their own identity, they had engaged in a duet of cooperation. In the twelfth century, the duet became an outright duel, where the dividing lines of power were clearly drawn. Not until the modern period did it lead to full disengagement. In the area of criminal justice, the Christian church has moved over the centuries from a theology of grace and servanthood, to a theology of law and punishment.

Over the last twenty-five years, there have been a number of initiatives in many countries challenging us to go beyond a retributive justice to a restorative justice. These initiatives have been emerging signs of hope calling for a radical reengagement of the Christian faith in criminal justice issues from a restorative justice perspective. One can recapture the heartbeat of God for restoration, reconciliation, and peaceful communities in a great number of Scriptural passages: in Matthew (5–7) and Luke 6, in Romans (5: 6–11 and 12: 1–21); from 2 Corinthians (5: 11–21) to Ephesians (2: 11–22 and 5: 1, 2) and in many other passages of the New Testament. Other passages, however, were often read politically and used to justify wars, crusades, and vengeful attitudes towards offenders. These include St Paul's letter to the Romans (chapter 13), the first Epistle to Peter (chapter 2), and the Epistle to Titus (chapter 3). We can nonetheless reconcile these texts, and make them work restoratively. As Gorringe writes:

> Our fundamental hermeneutic principle must be derived from the overall *direction* of the New Testament documents. The central story they tell speaks of God's movement 'downwards and to the periphery, his unconditional solidarity with those who have nothing, those who suffer, the humiliated and injured'. This represents a diametrically opposite perception to the Roman view which assumed that, as Caesar once said to his rebellious soldiers, 'as the great ordain, so the affairs of this world are directed'. The crucifixion of Jesus, on the other hand, constitutes 'a permanent and effective protest against those structures which continually bring about separation at the centre and the margin'. It is this protest rather than an endorsement of expiatory sacrifice, which is the heart of the New Testament witness. Turning Christianity into a cult centred on an expiatory death achieved long ago, and honoured in the present by other – or inworldly – asceticism, represented an easy option, a refusal of the costliness of the gospel ethic, of a realization of the Jubilee prescriptions. The recovery of a text of protest

and critique would serve to create quite different mentalities and structures of affect from those avowed by Christendom.[41]

The new paradigm of healing, reconciliation and forgiveness has led many practitioners in the justice field – both professional and lay – to undertake restorative justice initiatives. What follows are but a few initiatives now engaging the Christian churches in a reexamination of their attitudes toward the criminal justice system. Over twenty-five years ago, Canadians pioneered the Victim Offender Reconciliation Programs (VORP) which, as its title suggests, focuses on reconciliation. Used at first in property crimes, the Victim Offender Mediation Program (VOMP)[42] in British Columbia, Canada, has provided ample proof over the last several years that, properly done, victim offender mediation can be successfully applied even in the most serious cases.

Relentlessly through the years, the *Church Council for Justice and Corrections (CCJC)* has engaged the churches of Canada on a journey of rediscovery of the theological and biblical foundations of a more satisfying, transformative, justice. CCJC played a significant role in the abolition of capital punishment in Canada and has provided the churches with many valuable hands-on tools in the area of criminal justice.[43] Indeed, the missions of both the Correctional Service of Canada and the National Parole Board are a commitment to enlightened corrections where offenders, victims, and the communities must be treated with respect and professionalism of the highest order. As was evident in the 1997 Vancouver Symposium on 'Satisfying Justice', new partnerships are being formed between various government departments and the private sectors in order to move forward a restorative justice agenda. Initiatives such as Circle Sentencing, family conferencing, restorative parole, and so forth, are now the subject of daily conversation in many quarters. Community Chaplaincies and Circles of Support constitute growing initiatives which seek to involve the faith communities in playing a more significant role with offenders and victims, and for ensuring that crime is returned to the communities for creative solutions.[44] Annually in November, 'Restorative Justice Week' takes place in Canada, and is proving to be one of the most effective educational tools to sensitize people of faith to the challenges of doing justice in a biblical way. Then too, 'A Call to Justice' was a 1997 proclamation by the Interfaith Committee on Chaplaincy in the Correctional Service of Canada; it aims at calling for restorative justice by rediscovering our spiritual roots.

In *An Ethic for Christians* William Stringfellow wrote that 'There comes a moment when words must either become incarnate or the words, even if literally true, are rendered false'.[45] As we have seen, Christianity is beginning to unearth and revivify the spiritual roots of restorative justice inherent in the original Gospel. The signs are encouraging. Theological reflection on criminal justice evokes a call to creativity, a call to repentance and conversion, and a call to community. As Christians return to the spiritual roots of restorative justice, they will be challenged to discover new ways of doing justice. Repentance, or 'changing one's course in life', should lead to a commitment to influence through servanthood and not through power; to change one's perspectives on crime in the knowledge that the line dividing good and evil cuts through every human being. Restorative justice is a call to build new communities where acceptance and reconciliation are realities. Restoration and reconciliation are lived in the community of the covenant of love between God and humankind, and between individual persons. It is becoming part of a community committed to justice in a world of injustices, a community committed to listening to all sides when crime happens, and a community committed to truth beyond the 'guilty/not guilty' dichotomy. It is becoming a community committed to offering opportunities for reparation and peacemaking so that offenders and victims find healing in a community of hope.

This extract is taken from 'Christianity: the Rediscovery of Restorative Justice', Pierre Allard and Wayne Northey, in M. Hadley (ed.), The Spiritual Roots of Restorative Justice *(Albany, NY: SUNY Press, 2001), pp. 119–41.*

Notes

1 Mackey, *Punishment*, p. 15.
2 Harris, 'The Criminology of Christ', p. 9.
3 Wren, *Education for Justice*, p. 50.
4 Northey, 'Rediscovering Spiritual Roots: The Judeo-Christian Tradition and Criminal Justice', pp. 60ff.
5 Shriver, *An Ethic for Enemies*, p. 9.
6 The best biblical story told by Jesus illustrating forgiveness is Luke 15: 11–32.
7 Roberts and Donaldson, *Apostolic Constitutions*, p. 402.
8 Zehr, *Changing Lenses*, pp. 126–57.
9 Yoder, *Shalom*, p. 34.
10 Williams, *The Bible, Violence, and the Sacred*, p. 162.
11 Wink, *Engaging the Powers*, p. 146.
12 See the poignant story in Genesis 22: 1–18.
13 Barbé, *A Theology of Conflict*, pp. 24ff.
14 Peels, *The Vengeance of God*, p. 244.
15 Ibid.: p. 294.
16 Ibid.: p. 295.
17 See Jeremias, *New Testament Theology*, pp. 204ff.
18 For a discussion of the concepts see Moule, *Punishment and Retribution*.
19 Alison, *The Joy of Being Wrong*, p. 128.
20 Moltmann, *The Experiment of Hope*, p. 76.
21 Ibid.: p. 81.
22 Moltmann's term in ibid.: p. 79.
23 The best biblical illustration of the transformation or subversion of wrath is John 8: 1–11.
24 See Luke 4: 16ff. Early Church Father Tertullian said that when Jesus disarmed Peter (Matt. 26: 51ff), he thereby disarmed the Church forever.
25 Kee, *Constantine versus Christ*, p. 168.
26 See 'Notes' in both books cited below for examples.
27 Cited in Stassen, *Just Peacemaking*, p. 33.
28 Cited in Wink, *Engaging the Powers*, p. 216.
29 Anderson, 'Jesus and Peace', p. 104.
30 For this and the following see 'Tsedeka Justice', p. 308. These issues, particularly the concept of Tsedeka justice, are thoroughly discussed in Bianchi, *Justice as Sanctuary*, pp. 1–48.

31 This process is well described by Van Ness and Strong in *Restoring Justice*.
32 Berman, *Law and Revolution*, p. 404.
33 Ibid.: p. 115.
34 Ibid.: p. 180.
35 There have been three discernible views of the atonement in the history of the church, of which the second, the 'satisfaction theory', has been the most dominant in Western history since the eleventh century. 'The second group of theories may be said to have originated with Anselm, who saw sin as dishonour to the majesty of God. Thus on the cross the God-man rendered satisfaction for this dishonour. Along similar lines the Reformers thought that Christ paid the penalty sinners incurred when they broke God's law' (Morris, 'Atonement', p. 83).
36 Gorringe, *God's Just Vengeance*, p. 102.
37 Ibid.: p. 131.
38 Linebaugh, *The London Hanged*, pp. 214–15; cited in Gorringe, *God's Just Vengeance*, pp. 3–4.
39 Ibid.: pp. 4–5.
40 Scott, 'Is Canadian Justice Just?', p. 107.
41 Gorringe, *God's Just Vengeance*, p. 82.
42 Copies of two evaluations of this program and more on the program itself, may be obtained from FRCJIA, 101-0678 Eastleigh Cres., Langley, BC, V3A 4C4, Canada.
43 One of its most helpful resources for this discussion is CCJC, *Satisfying Justice*.
44 These documents may be obtained from CSC Chaplaincy, 340 Laurier Ave W, Ottawa, Ontario, K1A 0P9, Canada.
45 Stringfellow, *An Ethic for Christians*, p. 21.

References

Alison, J. (1997) *The Joy of Being Wrong: Original Sin through Easter Eyes* (New York, NY: Crossroad).

Anderson, P. (1992) 'Jesus and Peace', in Miller, M. and Gingerich, B. (eds) *The Church's Peace Witness* (Grand Rapids, Mich: Eerdmans), pp. 104–30).

Barbé, D. (1989) *A Theology of Conflict and other Writings on Nonviolence* (Maryknoll, NY: Orbis Press).

Berman, H.J. (1997) *Law and Revolution: The Formation of the Western Legal Tradition* (1983, reprint) (Cambridge: Cambridge University Press).

Bianchi, H. (1973) 'Tsedeka-Justice', in *Review for Philosophy and Theology* (London: Blackwell), pp. 308–20.

Bianchi, H. (1994) *Justice as Sanctuary: Toward a New System of Crime Control* (Bloomington, IN: Indiana University Press).

CCJC (Church Council on Justice and Corrections) (1996) *Satisfying Justice: A Compendium of Initiatives, Programs and Legislative Measures* (Ottawa: Correctional Services Canada).

Gorringe, T. (1996) *God's Just Vengeance: Crime, Violence and the Rhetoric of Salvation* (Cambridge: Cambridge University Press).

Harris, Bishop A. (1978) 'The Criminology of Christ' *New Life*, August, pp. 6–9.

Jeremias, J. (1971) *New Testament Theology. Part one, The Proclamation of Jesus*. Trans. John Bowden (London: S.C.M.).

Kee, A. (1982) *Constantine versus Christ: The Triumph of Ideology* (London: SCM Press).

Linebaugh, P. (1991) *The London Hanged: Crime and Civil Society in the Eighteenth Century* (Harmondsworth: Penguin).

Mackey, V. (1981) *Punishment in the Scripture and Tradition of Judaism, Christianity and Islam* (New York, NY: National Interreligious Task Force on Criminal Justice).

Moltmann, J. (1975) *The Experiment of Hope.* (ed. and trans. D. Meeks) (Philadelphia, PA: Fortress Press).

Morris, L. (1974) 'Atonement', in Douglas, J.D. (ed.) *The New International Dictionary of the Christian Church* (Grand Rapids, MI: Zondervan Publishing House), pp. 83–4.

Moule, C.F.D. (1990) *Punishment and Retribution: An Attempt to Delimit their Scope in New Testament Thought* (Akron, OH: Mennonite Central Committee).

Northey, W. (1998) 'Rediscovering Spiritual Roots: The Judeo-Christian Tradition and Criminal Justice', *The Justice Professional*, II, pp. 47–70.

Peels, H.G.L. (1995) *The Vengeance of God: The Meaning of the Root NQM and the Function of the NQM-Texts in the Context of Divine Revelation in the Old Testament* (Leiden, NY: E.J. Brill).

Roberts, Rev. A. and Donaldson, J. (eds) (1886) *Apostolic Constitutions: The Ante-nicene Fathers. Vol. VII* (Buffalo, NY: The Christian Literature Co.).

Scott, Most Rev. E.W. (1981) 'Is Canadian Justice Just'. A Biblical Perspective (Winnipeg: Canadian Congress for the Prevention of Crime).

Shriver, D.W. (1995) *An Ethic for Enemies: Forgiveness in Politics* (New York, NY: Oxford University Press).

Stringfellow, W. (1973) *An Ethic for Christians and other Aliens in a Strange Land* (Waco, TX: Word Books).

Van Ness, D. and Heetderks Strong, K. (1997) *Restoring Justice* (Cincinnati, OH: Anderson Publishing).

Williams, J.G. (1991) *The Bible, Violence, and the Sacred: Liberation from the Myth of Sanctioned Violence* (San Francisco, CA: Harper).

Wink, W. (1992) *Engaging the Powers: Discernment and Resistance in a World of Domination* (Philadelphia:, PA: Fortress Press).

Wren, B. (1977) *Education for Justice: Pedagogical Principles* (Maryknoll, NY: Orbis Books).

Yoder, P.B. (1987) *Shalom: The Bible's Word for Salvation, Justice and Peace* (Newton, KN: Faith & Life Press).

Zacharias, R. (1983) 'Diagnosing the Modern Mind.' Paper from Canadian Consultation on Evangelism, Toronto, 6–9 June.

Zehr, H. (1996) *Changing Lenses: A New Focus for Crime and Punishment* (1990, reprint) (Scottsdale, PA: Herald Press).

Part C

Restorative justice practice: variations, development and rationales

Introduction

Part C contains a number of readings describing the core forms of restorative justice practice, indicating how they developed, explaining the ideas and principles embodied in these practices, and exploring issues that arise when attempts are made to implement these practices within criminal justice systems. Some of the readings also present results of evaluations of these practices and raise method-ological questions which must be confronted in any attempt to evaluate restorative justice. This section does not attempt to present an up-to-date account of the practical development and empirical evaluation of restorative justice. Many of the examples are from the early years of restorative justice, and the purpose of reproducing them here is simply to introduce and discuss the fundamental types of restorative justice practice. Useful reports on current developments can be found in Morris and Maxwell (2001), Walgrave (2002) and Weitekamp and Kerner (2002).

The section starts with Dean E. Peachey's account of the now famous 'Kitchener Experiment' which began in 1974 and is regarded by many as the start of restorative justice. This account illustrates the way restorative justice developed, not as the practical implementation of ideas first conceived in theory, but out of small-scale practical initiatives which were shaped by a range of theoretical ideas as they developed, and eventually crystallised, into more coherent reform programmes.

Peachey shows how a Mennonite probation officer, applying the pacifist ideas of that faith to responses to crime, initiated an experiment in which offenders met their victims and offered them restitution. In the early part of the experiment, the goal of reconciling victims and offenders emerged as the central purpose of this process. Later, however, other goals emerged: encouraging offenders to take responsibility for their behaviour; challenging the victims' stereotypes of offenders; empowering lay people (victims, offenders and community volunteers) in the criminal justice process. All these goals have since become core features of restorative justice discourse and practice.

This account also illustrates how the restorative justice campaign developed from being a probation service initiative to becoming a much broader amalgam of interventions into the lives of victims, offenders and communities. At first, the victim/offender reconciliation project functioned as a sentencing alternative. As it developed, however, attempts were made to bypass the courts – and in some cases the entire criminal justice system – by using community-based mediation services to resolve interpersonal disputes which gave rise to specific criminal acts. Accordingly, the scope of the restorative justice critique of conventional criminal justice broadened. Previously, the target was conventional forms of punishment and therapy. Now, the entire legal system was criticised on the ground that its adversarial nature was unsuitable for dealing with many criminal incidents, which arose from disputes between citizens. VORPs became not just a restitutive alternative to punishment but, in the form of victim–offender mediation, a community mediation alternative to court-based adversarial justice. Subsequently, in the early 1980s, a further development occurred as the initiators of the Kitchener Experiment began to divert their attention to the creation of a victim services programme.

Peachey's chapter can serve as a useful corrective to those who seek a definition of restorative justice which will identify its essence and those who criticise restorative justice as incoherent because it seems impossible to produce such a definition. It illustrates how a range of quite divergent practical initiatives and projects could be linked, not by reference to some overarching goal or underlying philosophy but as the products of an experimental/reformative impulse which produces a constantly mutating mixture of alternative approaches to the conventional way of viewing and handling criminal incidents.

For many, the core distinctive idea of restorative justice is that offenders should repair the harm they caused, rather than being punished for causing it. However, as we have seen in a number of articles, for many advocates an equally important idea is that many potential criminal cases can and should be 'diverted' to community mediation instead of being processed through the criminal courts. This idea is discussed in the next reading, from the second edition of Martin Wright's very influential book *Justice for Victims and Offenders* (1996, first edition 1991).

Wright traces the origins of contemporary mediation schemes to the convergence, in the 1960s and 1970s, of a legal theoretical interest in the way other cultures – without Western law courts – resolve their disputes, and to the concerns of community activists to broaden access to justice and to empower ordinary people and communities. Legal theorists argued that many conflicts that in Western society would end up in court are dealt with, in more simple societies, by processes such as the Kpelle Moot. In these processes, achieving desirable outcomes – such as justice, abatement of conflict and social harmony – is more important than strict application of formal rules and attachment of blame and fault. Among the things emphasised in this literature is that, in such traditional processes of dispute resolution, ordinary people retain control over their own relationships and have greater access to some form of justice than they might have in the West with its expensive, time-consuming, inhospitable law courts (cf. Pavlich 1996). Such messages had appeal to a range of community activists – including political radicals and members of the Society of Friends (Quakers) – who initiated a wide array of community dispute settlement programmes, neighbourhood justice centres, etc. What emerged from all this was a 'Western model' of mediation.

This mediation model has been subjected to a range of criticisms, some of which are discussed by Wright (see also Pavlich, 1996: chs 4–5; Matthews, 1988). Critics have suggested that enthusiasts of mediation have romanticised the practices of simple societies and underestimated the complexity of importing such models into complex modern societies, where the 'community' base for such practices does not exist. Others argue that that mediation serves the interests of the justice system rather than that of parties locked in conflict and that it tends to weaken, rather than empower, already weak parties in disputes. Wright's response to these criticisms tends to be to treat them as warnings of what mediation schemes could become (and in some cases have become) but to insist that they are based on inaccurate characterisations of most existing community mediation projects. Wright also addresses the complex question of the relation of mediation schemes to the courts. Most usefully, towards the end of the chapter, he discusses the crucially important issues of what the principal goals of mediation should be and how we should assess their success or failure. Here, he points to important tensions between different goals of mediation, such as delivering a *superior* form of justice versus increasing *access* to justice, or expert mediation versus lay mediation.

Since the early 1990s, the format which has lent itself most to the application of restorative justice principles to criminal cases has been the family group conference (FGC). The next extract (Chapter 8), from Allison Morris and Gabrielle Maxwell, describes the introduction of FGCs into the New Zealand youth justice system in 1989.[1] They suggest that, although the debates surrounding the introduction of FGCs made no specific mention of restorative justice, the underlying philosophy of FGCs is that of restorative justice. FGCs are designed to heal the damage caused by youth crime, involve those most affected by a youth crime in the process by which it is decided what is to be done about it, and make things better for both offenders and their victims.

Morris and Maxwell describe how FGCs fit into a youth justice system based on the principle that the vast majority of youth crimes will be dealt with outside the courts. In such a system, FGCs are used for cases which are considered too serious for a lower-key response (such as an immediate warning), where a young person admits committing the offence. Morris and Maxwell then describe the process in detail. One feature of FGCs worth mentioning is that part of their aim is to increase the family's sense of responsibility for the behaviour of their youthful members. Such an aim has been pursued in the UK but usually takes the form of blaming and punishing parents for the wayward behaviour of their offspring. In FGCs, however, the idea is that families will be encouraged in constructive ways to take responsibility for devising and implementing more effective strategies for supervision of children and that they will be supported in their efforts to do so.

Morris and Maxwell go on to introduce and discuss some of the results of research which they conducted on FGCs in the years following their introduction. Compared with some advocates of restorative justice their claims tend to be modest and carefully qualified. They do suggest that well implemented FGCs can significantly improve the satisfaction of various groups with the criminal justice process, hold young people accountable for their criminal behaviour more effectively than traditional criminal justice processes, and significantly reduce the chances of the young person reoffending. However, they seem equally if not more concerned to identify the aspects of the process which account for such success and the factors which reduce the chance of a successful outcome. Their research seems more designed to find out how FGCs can be made more successful in achieving their goals than to come up with meaningful comparisons of the success of restorative justice compared with conventional forms of criminal justice. Those seeking emphatic evidence that 'restorative justice works' may not find it in the cautious claims presented by Morris and Maxwell. However, their research seems useful for those wishing to implement successful restorative justice interventions.

The next reading (Chapter 15), from David Moore and Terry O'Connell, describes how FGCs were introduced, in a rather different form, in Wagga Wagga, a small city in New South Wales, Australia. The 'Wagga model', as it subsequently became known, has been extremely influential. In the UK, it was the model adopted by the Thames Valley Police for their restorative cautioning initiative, launched in 1998 (see *Young*). This initiative played an enormous role in making 'restorative justice' a familiar term in UK criminal justice circles.

The most distinctive feature of the 'Wagga model' is that FGCs are co-ordinated not, as is the case in New Zealand, by welfare professionals but by the police. It operates not with statutory authority but through the powers of the police to administer cautions to people who admit offences and meet other conditions for a caution. Instead of administering a simple police caution, the police organise an FGC as part of an 'effective cautioning scheme'.

One of the remarkable achievements of the initiators of the Wagga Wagga scheme was getting the police interested in something like restorative justice. Even though the police tended to be dissatisfied with the existing system, in which the vast majority of arrestees were sent straight to court, they perceived that system as safe in that it achieved a balance between the competing demands made on the police. Moore and O'Connell describe how they, and a number of other pioneers, eventually convinced the police that restorative justice was not a soft option and that it was an effective use of their time and other resources.

A seemingly crucial development in this process was the adoption of John Braithwaite's theory of reintegrative shaming as a point of reference. As Moore and O'Connell put it, Braithwaite, in trying to explain why people obey the law, argued that informal controls were far more significant than formal punishment. People are pressurised to conform by the fear of social disapproval (external control/shame avoidance) and by pangs of conscience (internal control/shame experience). It is only when these informal controls are too weak that the state steps in with formal criminal punishment. However, when the state punishes it degrades offenders and separates them from the rest of the community. When people are controlled informally, the concern is to reintegrate them into the community of law-abiding citizens.

Moore and O'Connell depicted (and persuaded Braithwaite to depict) FGCs as examples of informal reintegrative shaming. Hence, FGCs were to be contrasted with conventional criminal punishment, which was a ceremony of degradation. FGCs were to be understood as ceremonies of reintegration. The role of the police would now be, not to channel offenders towards the degradation ceremonies of conventional criminal justice, but to organise reintegration ceremonies in which members of the community could express their disapproval of the offender's behaviour, while remaining centrally concerned with bringing the offender back into the fold. The police, then, were to become organisers and co-ordinators of informal community control rather than the mere gatekeepers of a system of formal stigmatic punishment.

As might be expected, many liberal-minded people are highly suspicious when confronted with this idea of the police performing such a role (see *Young*, *Ashworth*). One particular concern has been that, in such a scheme, important rights of alleged offenders may be infringed. Moore and O'Connell respond to this criticism by stating that FGCs are used only in cases where there is no denial of guilt and that 'offenders' are reminded at the outset of an FGC that they have a right to 'walk out' and to have their case heard in a court.[2] They then go on to raise the broader question about the proper balance of rights and responsibilities. In the process, they link the 'Wagga model' of FGCs to a communitarian political theory. According to this theory, what we need is not a totalitarian society (strong on responsibilities/weak on rights) or a libertarian society (strong on rights/weak on responsibilities), but a vibrant democratic community which is strong on both and achieves a proper balance.

The final reading in this section (Chapter 16) is by Gordon Bazemore and Mark Umbreit, leading initiators of and researchers into restorative justice in the USA. Their paper describes four different types of restorative justice process, explaining their procedures and goals, how they are administered, issues which arise in implementation and the key findings of studies of each model in practice. Two of these models have been discussed in previous chapters: victim–offender mediation (*Wright*) and family group conferencing (*Morris and Maxwell*; *Moore and O'Connell*). However, Bazemore and Umbreit's account is worth reading as it provides more concrete descriptions of these approaches as they work in practice. The other two approaches are community reparative boards and circle sentencing.

Although some proponents would not include community reparative boards among the core forms of restorative justice practice, they do – as Bazemore and Umbreit show – exemplify many restorative justice principles. For example, community reparative boards 'provide opportunities for victims and community members to confront offenders in a constructive manner about their behavior'. The inclusion of community reparative boards as a conferencing model is useful in that it works against the tendency to overidentify restorative justice with a particular practice, such as mediation or FGCs. It also makes us realise that, although the specific concept of restorative justice has emerged relatively recently, some of its principles and practices have been around for a lot longer, even in Western criminal justice systems. Community reparative boards are a contemporary version of a form of sanctioning juvenile crime that has existed since the 1920s. The example of circle sentencing shows, in fact, that restorative justice practices have been around much, much longer. As David Cayley (1998: 182) states: 'Thrashing out problems in a circle must be as old as human society.'

Notes

1 FGCs were introduced (via the Children, Young Persons and their Families Act 1989) partly in response to Maori concerns about the impact of conventional criminal justice practices – see *Consedine*.
2 In my view, what is otherwise an excellent chapter is marred somewhat by Moore and O'Connell's tendency to pour scorn on their critics rather than respond constructively to the criticisms made by these critics.

References

Cayley, D. (1998) *The Expanding Prison: The Crisis in Crime and Punishment and the Search for Alternatives* (Cleveland, OH: Pilgrim Press).

Matthews, R. (ed.) (1988) *Informal Justice?* (London: Sage).

Morris, A. and Maxwell, G. (eds) (2001) *Restorative Justice for Juveniles: Conferencing, Mediation and Circles* (Oxford: Hart Publishing).

Pavlich, G. (1996) *Justice Fragmented: Mediating Community Disputes under Postmodern Conditions* (London: Routledge).

Walgrave, L. (ed.) (2002) *Restorative Justice and the Law* (Cullompton: Willan).

Weitekamp, E. and Kerner, H. (eds) (2002) *Restorative Justice in Context: International Practices and Directions* (Cullompton: Willan).

Wright, M. (1996) *Justice for Victims and Offenders: A Restorative Response to Crime* (2nd edn) (1st edn published by Open University Press, 1991) (Winchester: Waterside Press).

12. The Kitchener experiment

Dean E. Peachey

The Victim/Offender Reconciliation Program in Kitchener, Ontario, is frequently recognized as the forerunner of programmes that bring convicted offenders into face-to-face meetings with their victims to explore interpersonal reconciliation and build a plan for reparation (Alper and Nichols, 1981: 69–70; Umbreit [1989]).

Ideas and innovations sometimes have humble, and even unplanned beginnings. A Saturday night vandalism spree by a couple of intoxicated teenagers resentful of the local police in a small town called Elmira was hardly the making of headlines or criminal justice history. And when the two young men were subsequently apprehended and pleaded guilty on 28 May 1974 to twenty-two counts of wilful damage, they had no idea that their experiences would be told and retold as the 'Elmira Case' in countless articles, speeches, and conference presentations. They were simply instructed to return to court in July to receive their sentences, and they spent the next couple of months in their homes in Elmira, a few miles north of Kitchener, Ontario.

The probation officer who was assigned to prepare their pre-sentence reports was hardly a crusading reformer. But he was prone to dreaming about new ways of doing things. Mark Yantzi had worked in the probation office in Kitchener for five years, after being a full-time volunteer under a programme sponsored by the Mennonite Central Committee (MCC). To be so directly tied to a part of the criminal justice system was itself an experiment for him as a Mennonite: the church had traditionally maintained a separation from government affairs, and particularly from the legal system with its reliance on coercive power.

At a meeting of a committee that MCC had just convened to explore other forms of involvement with the criminal justice system, the recent vandalism case from Elmira was discussed. 'Wouldn't it be neat for these offenders to meet the victims?', Yantzi said to the group (Bender, 1985). As a member of the Mennonite church, which has maintained a strong pacifist tradition since its beginnings in the Protestant Reformation in the sixteenth century, Yantzi liked the practical peace-making implications of offenders and victims meeting each other. He then dismissed the idea, assuming that the judge would not even entertain such a notion.

Dave Worth, another participant in the meeting who worked for MCC, challenged Yantzi to give it a try. After struggling over whether to risk his reputation as a probation officer by suggesting something that had no basis in law, Yantzi accepted Worth's challenge. When he submitted his pre-sentence report to the judge, Yantzi enclosed a letter suggesting that 'there could be some therapeutic value in these two young men having to personally face up to the victims of their numerous offences'.

On the day the case was scheduled for sentencing, Worth and Yantzi met in chambers with Judge Gordon McConnell of Provincial Court to present their plan to him. The judge replied that he did not think it was possible for him to ask the offenders to meet the victims. Worth and Yantzi resigned themselves to the inevitable, and went into the courtroom to await the case. When the case was called, the judge ordered a one-month remand to allow time for the convicted pair to meet the victims and assess their losses, 'with the assistance of Dave Worth and Mark Yantzi'. As Worth recounts the scene:

> I don't know who was more surprised. I remember that Bill Morrison, the Crown Attorney, turned to look at us with a quizzical expression on his face (as if to say, what is this all about?). The two offenders certainly looked confused. The judge had a smile on his face. Mark and I looked at each other. Now what were we going to do? (Worth, 1986)

Accompanied by Worth and Yantzi, the two offenders (aged 18 and 19) retraced their steps from the night of vandalism. They visited each of the places where they had damaged property, slashed tyres, or broken windows. The circuit took them to private homes, two churches, and a beer store. The probation officer and the MCC representative simply stood by with their notepads while the two youths knocked on doors, explained who they were, and why they were there. In all they spoke to twenty-one victims (an additional victim had moved and could not be contacted) whose damages totalled $2189.04. Approximately half of that amount had already been covered by the victims' insurance policies, leaving $1065.12 in actual losses to the victims.

On 26 August the youths appeared in court and Yantzi reported to the judge what had happened. The judge ordered a $200 fine for each, and placed them on probation for eighteen months. Drawing on the information that was presented to him, the judge included as a term of the probation order that each youth should make restitution in an amount up to $550 to be paid to the victims as the probation officer arranged. Both the fine and the restitution were to be paid within three months.

Three months later the youths had visited all the victims and handed each a certified cheque for the amount of his or her loss. The experience of personally confronting the victims had been a difficult one for the two teenagers, but one that also had its rewards. One of them commented afterwards, 'I didn't quit because of my self-respect, and I didn't want to have to look over my shoulder all the time' (Yantzi and Worth, 1977).

On receiving the restitution payments, the victims expressed a wide variety of reactions, as reflected by the following comments:

> Thanks, I never expected to see that money. I think I'll spend it in a very special way to help somebody else.

> Thanks a lot. I was young, too, only some of us didn't get caught.

> Aren't you ashamed of yourself? You know this really isn't going to cover it all. Who is going to pay for all those trips to Guelph for parts? Who is going to pay when they raise my insurance premiums? I don't want anybody to go to jail, but you know I hope we don't ever have this problem with you again, or anybody else. (Yantzi and Worth, 1977)

This first experimental case identified issues that were to continue to haunt the concept throughout succeeding years: multiple victims with a range of personal responses, the involvement of insurance companies in restitution,[1] and the considerable time lapse between the occurrence of an offence and the completion of the restitution process. But the experiment was also successful beyond everyone's expectations.

Buoyed by their results, Worth, Yantzi, and the MCC committee continued to brainstorm ideas and refine the process upon which they had stumbled. Although they were unaware of anyone else who was conducting victim/offender meetings of this type, they were operating in a milieu that encouraged experimentation. The Elmira case occurred at a time when the Canadian Law Reform Commission was issuing a series of working papers on alternative ways of dealing with offenders, and the Ontario probation service was just beginning to promote community involvement in corrections.[2] Elsewhere a few groups were starting to promote restitution as a primary response to crime (e.g. Hudson and Galaway, 1977). Only a few years earlier the Columbus (Ohio) Night Prosecutor Program began operating as the widely publicized forerunner of numerous programmes in the United States to mediate minor disputes out of court.

The intuitive and experiential orientation of the Kitchener group distinguished them from some of these other initiatives. Yantzi and his colleagues did not work toward a defined set of objectives. Instead, they continued to experiment with a handful of cases, while they tried to understand what it was that they were attempting to do. When they eventually formulated a programme proposal in the summer of 1975, they used the name Victim/Offender Reconciliation Project. The name was awkward, but it deliberately reflected their emerging perspective on the work. *Reconciliation* between victims and offenders was becoming an important goal. The use of the term 'project' as compared to 'programme' also indicated a deliberate effort to remain fluid and avoid becoming settled into any particular mode of operation:

> We see ourselves as being continually involved in a process of refining our purpose and function. The project was not begun with a definitive plan, and it is still exploring new avenues of application. We are learning by our mistakes and successes and are moving slowly but steadily, making every effort to consult with and keep informed those persons affected directly or indirectly by our project. (Yantzi and Worth, 1977: 1)

The evolutionary nature of the project complicates the current task of chronicling its development. The Kitchener VORP has operated under three distinctly different organizational structures. Office forms and statistics kept by the project have moved through successive transformations, and the earliest information categories do not necessarily match current ones. For example, the probation base of the initiative in its early years meant that despite the avowed emphasis on meeting the needs of both victims and offenders, early records pertained almost entirely to offenders. Aside from some short-term research efforts, little is known about the victims in the first few years of the programme.

In late 1975 two people were hired as 'researchers' for seven months through a government employment programme. They worked under Yantzi's supervision, their principal methodology being participant observation, as they conducted and reflected on victim/offender meetings. During this phase VORP dealt with 61 offenders and 128 victims, mostly involving property-related offences. Forty-eight offenders met their victims and 46 of these reached an agreement and followed through on it.

Eventually some structures developed for the project. By 1977 one-half of Yantzi's workload as a probation officer was devoted to VORP. He was supervised in this work by a steering committee composed of representatives from probation, the MCC, and community volunteers. Although the project name highlighted reconciliation, the organizers increasingly saw VORP as a testing ground for several ideas. Meeting the victim face to face and repaying the losses were viewed as ways of encouraging offenders to take greater responsibility for their actions. Although victims received the concrete benefits of restitution, the VORP process was also a way of challenging victims' stereotypes about 'offenders' through personal contact.

Beyond these readily apparent notions, however, the organizers developed a distinctive emphasis on empowering lay participation in the justice-making process. The goals of restitution and personal encounter could have been met through court-ordered restitution or apologies. But as it evolved, the programme developed a stronger view that the victim and the offender should be the ones to decide how much would be paid, and according to what timetable. Influenced by Christie (1977), Yantzi and Worth began to talk about how the state had 'stolen' conflicts away from individuals and developed a monopoly on the criminal justice process. The innovators became reformers as they began to envision a fundamentally different approach to justice – one that placed the disputing parties at centre stage and defined justice primarily as psychological and material restoration rather than as retribution.

This concern for deprofessionalizing the criminal justice process and enhancing citizen participation was extended to the project's staffing. Volunteers played an increasingly important role as case workers who visited victims, explained the project, and then set up and facilitated the victim/offender meetings. Yantzi's role became one of coordinating and supervising the volunteers. Initially volunteers received only a half-day of orientation to VORP. By 1980 this had grown to a twenty-hour curriculum including information about the criminal justice process and training in mediation skills.

Undoubtedly because of its probation base, the project functioned as a post-conviction sentencing alternative. The usual procedure was for a judge to place the offender on probation, with participation in VORP being a term of the probation order. Judges began to exercise this option in an increasing variety of cases, sometimes with less than satisfactory results. In November 1975, a memorandum to judges and prosecutors indicated that VORP had been most successful when the victims were individuals or small businesses. The same report attempted to suggest some uniform wording for the probation order that would instruct the person being sentenced to 'come to mutual agreement with the victim regarding restitution, with the assistance of the Probation Officer or a person designated by the Probation Officer. If no agreement can be reached, the matter will be referred back to court.' The brief report concluded on a visionary note: 'It is our hope that the process of bringing victims and offenders together to reach a mutual agreement regarding restitution will become the norm.'

Yantzi interviewed each offender referred by the judge to explain the reconciliation process. Although VORP was prescribed in the probation order, Yantzi stressed to offenders that they could choose not to meet the victim and allow the court to determine the amount of restitution. Not surprisingly, about 90 per cent of the offenders opted to deal with the victim rather than take their chances with the judge.

No longer did the mediator simply follow an offender to the victim's door and observe as the anxious individual explained the purpose of the visit. After the offender agreed to participate in the project, a volunteer visited the victim to explain VORP and respond to the victim's questions about the process. Approximately 80 per cent of the victims opted to participate subsequently in victim/offender meetings that were arranged at the convenience of both parties.

The most common place for the reconciliation meeting was the home or business where the crime had occurred. Sometimes, however, the probation office was used, and the mediators even experimented with a park bench and a hamburger restaurant as meeting places.

The project dealt primarily with breaking and entering, theft, vandalism, and other property offences. Although most situations involved fairly small amounts of money, it was not uncommon to handle cases involving several thousands of dollars. If an offender failed to live up to the terms of the agreement, the project would attempt to renegotiate a more workable payment schedule, or otherwise salvage the case. Rarely did offenders default entirely on the agreement. When this happened, however, they were charged with a breach of probation, and returned to court.

The project's novel, yet common-sense approach of 'making right the wrong', soon began to attract considerable attention beyond Kitchener. Presentations by Yantzi and Worth at criminal justice conferences led to requests for training and consultation in a number of Ontario communities. VORP was cited in books and articles on criminal justice innovations (e.g. PREAP, 1976). The interest spilled over into the popular media as well, and the project received coverage in periodicals such as *Reader's Digest* as well as news and feature programmes on national television.

Despite its widespread publicity, the Kitchener programme was never subjected to a formal evaluation. Although numerous undergraduate and graduate students at local universities have studied the programme as a part of course projects,[3] a more rigorous evaluation has not been attempted. In part, the programme's sponsors have discouraged an evaluation, fearing that attempts to measure programme outcomes would focus too heavily on restitution or monetary results. 'How do you measure reconciliation?' has been an oft-repeated question whenever the possibility of an evaluation has been discussed. The difficulty and expense of developing measures that would assess the reconciliation process were generally deemed prohibitive for so small a programme. The lack of a readily available control group also contributed to the low interest in rigorous research.

Despite this lack of empirical documentation, the Ontario probation service actively promoted the development of similar programmes throughout the province. Although approximately twenty VORPs were initiated in Ontario by the early 1980s, the province never undertook a comprehensive research programme on VORP.[4]

Through all this activity, the Kitchener VORP remained relatively small. By 1980, the annual case-load had grown to 144 offenders and 149 victims, and Yantzi was relieved of his remaining probation case-load to work full time for VORP and other innovations.

The Kitchener group remained true to their innovative intentions. They began to think that in some cases – most notably those where the victim and offender already knew each other – it would be best if mediation could take place *before* the case went to court or even entered the criminal justice system. The adversary nature of the legal system with its emphasis on determining guilt or innocence seemed particularly unsuited for handling cases between acquaintances, where both may have contributed to a disagreement leading to an assault or property damage. By handling such conflicts through mediation it might be possible to resolve the dispute to the satisfaction of both parties, and prevent it from escalating to the point where a more serious offence might take place.

Thus, in 1980, they created the Community Mediation Service to deal with neighbourhood and interpersonal disputes outside the legal system.[5] Since it worked with cases before they went to court, or even before charges were laid, it was deemed to be outside the mandate of probation. Community Mediation Service came to be sponsored by the MCC, and within a few months VORP moved from being a joint Probation–MCC project to exclusive MCC sponsorship. However, Probation continued to fund VORP through a contract with MCC, as a part of their increasing emphasis on privatizing services in the community.

Within a year, Yantzi and others involved in VORP also began formulating ideas for providing additional services to victims of crime. For a while the programme became known as Victim/Offender Services, as they conducted a victims' needs assessment. This led to the creation of a separate Victim Services programme under MCC in 1982.[6] After seven years of involvement with VORP, Yantzi left the project to work full-time with the new victims' programme.

Victim Services gradually developed an extensive programme of self-help groups for victims of rape and incest. Once again, concern for dealing with both parties to a crime and a readiness to experiment took the victims' programme in new directions. In December 1982, Yantzi and his associates also began to work with sexual offenders, and especially with families where incest had occurred. Self-help groups were set up not only for victims, but also for offenders, and the mothers and siblings in the families.

The quest for new understandings of reconciliation has also been applied to this area. Although in some cases incest spells the dissolution of the family unit, there are other times when the family decided to stay together or to re-integrate upon the offender's release from prison. In such situations the programme has provided an on-going peer support group for couples who are dealing with similar situations. The programme has also sponsored weekend retreats on sexuality that bring together sexual offenders and victims of sexual abuse.

A further organizational metamorphosis occurred in 1982 as the growing cluster of programmes formed their own structure independent of MCC. This move was in accord with an MCC objective of establishing new programmes, and then allowing them to develop an independent status in the community. The new 'umbrella' organization was called 'Community Justice Initiatives', to demonstrate a concern for working toward the goal of justice in the community, through an evolving pattern of methods.

VORP continued to operate as a distinct service, but around this time the letterhead was changed to read 'Victim Offender Reconciliation *Program*'. Perhaps some forms of institutionalization were inevitable. In any event, the individuals operating VORP were responding to concerns that VORP should be seen as an enduring operation rather than of a limited duration, as implied by the term 'project'.

[. . .]

If measured by the current case volume, the Kitchener VORP appears to be in a frustrated decline. If, however, the experiment that began in 1974 is viewed not as an attempt to build a fixed programme model, but rather as a continuing effort to apply principles of reconciliation and interpersonal healing to the criminal justice system through a growing number of ways, then indeed the innovations have borne fruit. The principles underlying victim/offender meetings have been applied in the Kitchener community to situations ranging from minor neighbourhood disputes to more serious cases of sexual abuse. The concern for helping victims deal with the psychological consequences of crime has given rise to a broadened range of services to victims. Efforts to deprofessionalize some of the process have given rise to volunteer involvement in a variety of programmes and a continuing emphasis on self-help responses to problems.

In a larger context, the Kitchener experiment provided the inspiration that led to further innovation in dozens of communities in Canada, the United States, and Europe [. . .].

Finally, it must be recognized that unlike a 'demonstration project', which attempts to demonstrate a known process, a true experiment is a risky venture into uncharted waters. Demonstrations may fail, but experiments in themselves do not succeed or fail. They only yield information that can be used to revise or further refine the process under investigation. To quote again from Yantzi and Worth: 'We are learning by our mistakes and successes and moving slowly but steadily, making every effort to consult with and keep informed those persons affected directly and indirectly by our project' (1977: 1). So the factors identified in this chapter that may have contributed to the reduced VORP case-load may also present suggestions for addressing some of the problems encountered in Kitchener and elsewhere. By comparison, they also highlight the significant successes that victim/offender reconciliation programmes have achieved in numerous other communities.

This extract is taken from 'The Kitchener Experiment', by Dean E. Peachey, in M. Wright and B. Galaway (eds), Mediation and Criminal Justice *(London: Sage Publications, 1989), pp. 14–26.*

Notes

1 The Crown Prosecutor suggested in this case that restitution should be paid to the insurance companies that had reimbursed some of the victims for a portion of the losses. The judge rejected this proposal, but in subsequent cases the judges did at times require restitution to be paid to insurance companies.

2 The Kitchener programme would likely never have developed were it not for the receptive attitude of the area probation manager, John Gaskell. A native of England who was familiar with contemporary British probation innovations, he had already championed Yantzi's efforts to develop a volunteer probation programme. Although he was initially dubious about the legality of victim/offender meetings, he released an increasing portion of Yantzi's time for the VORP, and became a staunch proponent of the project who encouraged experimentation while requiring minimal demonstrations of immediate benefits.

3 One of these studies (Dittenhoffer and Ericson, 1983) was published and raised some critical questions about the programme, but its appearance in a law journal did not attract much attention from individuals working in corrections.

4 A small evaluation was conducted of the Ajax–Pickering programme in 1982–3 by the Ministry of Correctional Services, but because of methodological problems, it has not been released to the public.

5 Community Mediation Service was a pioneer project in Ontario, and is [at the time of writing] the longest continuously operated programme of its type in Canada. It has been instrumental in facilitating the development of similar programmes through publications, training courses, and convening two national workshops on mediation.

6 The Victim Services programme has two components. For the first part MCC persuaded the local police to operate a service to victims, using civilian employees of the police department to provide information and emotional support to victims. MCC sponsored a second 'community' component, housed in the same office with VORP and the Community Mediation Service. The purpose of the community component was initially open-ended. It was intended to serve victims who might not fall within the mandate of the police programme, as well as to fulfil an advocacy function for victims. Its primary work gradually developed in self-help responses to sexual abuse. The programme now sponsors over fifteen self-help groups for victims and offenders in sexual abuse.

References

Alper, B.S. and Nichols, L.T. (1981) *Beyond the Courtroom: Programs in Community Justice and Conflict Resolution* (Lexington, MA: Lexington Books).

Bender, J. (1985) 'Reconciliation Begins in Canada', *Christian Living*, 32:12, pp. 6–8.

Christie, N. (1977) 'Conflict as Property', *British Journal of Criminology*, 17:4, pp. 1–15.

Dittenhoffer, T. and Ericson, R. (1983) 'The Victim Offender Reconciliation Program: A Message to Correctional Reformers', *University of Toronto Law Journal*, 33, pp. 315–47.

Hudson, J. and Galaway, B. (1977) *Restitution in Criminal Justice* (Lexington, MA: D.C. Heath).

Peachey, D. and Skeen, C. (1986) *Directory of Canadian Dispute Resolution Programs* (Kitchener, Ontario: Network for Community Justice and Conflict Resolution).

PREAP (1976) *Instead of Prisons: A Handbook for Abolitionists* (Syracuse, NY: Prison Research Education and Action Project).

Umbreit, M. (1989) 'Violent Offenders and their Victims', in Wright, M. and Galaway, B. (eds) *Mediation and Criminal Justice: Victims, Offenders and Community* (London: Sage).

Worth, D. (1986) 'VORP: A Look at the Past and Future', *Community Justice Report*, 5:1, Supplement.

Yantzi, M. and Worth, D. (1977) 'The Developmental Steps of the Victim/Offender Reconciliation Project.' Unpublished paper.

13. Justice without lawyers: enabling people to resolve their conflicts

Martin Wright

Ideas from other cultures

In the 1960s and 1970s, as dissatisfaction with the conventional justice system grew, a number of legal theorists in the United States were becoming aware of descriptions of the traditional practices in other cultures. These, instead of trying to make the rambling edifice of the law more serviceable by demolishing parts of it and adding new extensions, seemed to offer a fundamentally new approach.

The Harvard jurist Lon L. Fuller, studying the principles of dispute resolution, found that some conflicts arising from relationships are too complex to be justiciable: a judge applies some principle to the decision of a case, and cannot adjudicate where there are no principles (Fuller, 1963, quoted by McGillis and Mullen, 1977: 24–5). In mediation Fuller discerned some features of a different kind. Law is a structure, in which a set of norms is defined; mediation is a process, 'commonly directed, not toward achieving conformity to norms, but toward the creation of the relevant norms themselves' (Fuller, 1971: 308). Fuller shows how, since mediators claim no authority, they can empower people to regain control over their own relationships, rather than 'assume that all social order must be imposed by some kind of "authority"' (1971: 315); mediation's central quality is 'its capacity to reorient the parties toward each other, not by imposing rules on them, but by helping them to achieve a new and shared perception of their relationship, a perception that will redirect their attitudes and dispositions toward one another' (1971: 325). He warns, however, that mediation is not suitable where questions of fact have to be decided, such as whether *A* drove through a red light, nor where the underlying relationship is such that 'it is best organized by impersonal act-oriented rules' (1971: 328, 330).

One of the articles most often cited in literature on mediation is James Gibbs's on the traditional moot of the Kpelle people of Liberia. Despite cultural differences, this example shows aspects which are and are not incorporated into some present-day western theory and practice.

The first parallel is that among the Kpelle the moots exist alongside courts which are used for cases of assault and theft 'where the litigants are not linked in a relationship after the trial'. According to Gibbs (1963/1967: 278–9) the courts' authoritarian style restricts the opportunity to air grievances surrounding the case: the 'harsh tone tends to drive the spouses farther apart rather than reconcile them. The moot, in contrast, is more effective in handling such cases.' The moot is thus comparable to projects that offer an alternative to courts, but not to those, like the Victim/Offender Reconciliation Programs [. . .] operating after conviction. [. . .]

The airing of grievances is more complete than in court, and the range of relevance is extremely broad. The hearing in the moot takes place promptly, unlike that of the court, and in informal surroundings. All of these features are commonly found in US mediation projects. Gibbs considers that the moot's procedure is not only conciliatory but also therapeutic (1963/1967: 277, 284). He states that the Kpelle also make no unilateral ascription of blame, although elsewhere he speaks of the 'winning' and 'losing' parties (1963/1967: 282) and of mediation foundering because no one will be the first to admit fault – whereas US projects often make a virtue of not requiring such an admission. The aim is to reach an acceptable consensus. The 'losing' party apologizes and brings token gifts, and rum or beer for those who heard the case (rather as, in some circles in British society, an offender against the norms can atone and secure reacceptance by buying a round of drinks). But in addition, the 'winning' party gives a smaller token in return, to show good will; this is analogous to mediated agreements described in western literature as incorporating concessions or undertakings by both sides. In the Kpelle procedure, a group of those present may take either party on one side for discussion; if this happens in a US project, it is done by the mediators, and they generally see both parties.

Finally, both methods work on the basis of rewarding socially approved behaviour, or in psychological terms 'positive reinforcement'. Gibbs speaks of praise, concern and affection; in one US project, when juveniles have made reparation by completing community service, they are invited to receive certificates at a ceremony. The longest applause is given to those who have worked the most hours – who are those whose original offence was the most serious (Swann, personal communication).

A common technique is to allow participants to talk about anything they consider relevant, and to vent their spleen and aim for the 'minimax' goal – give a little, get a little, as in the Mexican Zapotec court, which has some features of a moot. The judge combines the roles of mediator, adjudicator and therapist (Nader, 1969: 85–8; Nader and Todd, 1978).

How are mediated agreements enforced? In the moot in Tanzania, where cases from petty offences to homicide were resolved by mediation, 'although compensation of twelve shillings was agreed to, only six shillings and twenty cents were actually handed over. People did not expect the rest to be paid' (Gulliver, 1969: 48). Once injuries had healed satisfactorily 'the matter was now ended: it should not be raised again, or the whole dispute might be renewed.' Thus what mattered was first the amount agreed publicly, which symbolized the seriousness of the offence, and second the closure of the incident; the amount actually handed over was less important. (This may be compared to the practice in some western countries of imposing prison sentences intended to express the seriousness of the crime, then releasing some classes of prisoners earlier.) In these small, cohesive societies, the participatory process of justice helps people, and particularly the victim, to clarify and affirm the norms of behaviour (Christie, 1977). Gulliver criticizes the 'fruitless concern with what "law" is, instead of concentrating on what "law" does' (in Nader, 1969: 17).

[. . .]

Law and process

One basic comparison between traditional and 'new wave' mediation is that in simple societies the underlying principle of resolving conflict is often not the *law* as the basis for a decision imposed by a learned judge, but a *process* to enable the parties themselves or their supporters to reach an agreement, which is expressed by an experienced conciliator. Importance is not attached to precedent (Nader, 1969: 84); 'law' is a western concept (Gulliver, 1969: 12). The Koreans believe that 'to tell the truth and nothing but the truth' is meaningless because no one can tell objective truth (Nader, 1969: 84); as an American jurist and judge remarked, 'facts are guesses' (Frank 1949: ch. 3). Village tribunals are 'less anxious to find "truth" and give "justice" than to abate conflict and promote harmony' (Rudolph and Rudolph 1967: 258). In a significant article Abel (1973: 222) quotes the anthropologist Evans-Pritchard as saying that 'In a strict sense the Nuer [of the Sudan] have no law. There are conventional compensations for damage, adultery, loss of limb and so forth, but there is no authority with power to adjudicate on such matters or to enforce a verdict.' Later, however, Evans-Pritchard appears to have conceded that the definition of law could be extended to cover this process, and Malinowski criticized the 'error' of defining the forces of law in terms of central authority, courts and constables (Abel, 1973: 223). In one approach disputes are seen as deviations from a trouble-free norm, with an authority that decides individual cases according to an established body of rules and precedents, while in the other, disputes are regarded as a normal feature of the human condition, requiring a process in which the parties themselves are helped to reach an agreement acceptable to them, with a procedure that is not merely a means to an end but an essential part of attaining reconciliation.

Other anthropologists, like Gluckman and Bohannan, in their studies of the Barotse and the Tiv respectively, concentrated on the judicial *processes*, rather than the institutions or rules: it is a question of compromise, bargaining, not a zero-sum, win-or-lose decision (Roberts, 1979: 199–201). Gluckman (1968) makes the comparison: 'In developed systems of law, written pleadings by the parties, usually presented by their counsels, have to be stated according to particular formulas which strip away what is believed to be irrelevant'; by contrast, in tribal societies 'Litigants are allowed to state their respective claims in apparently full, and often seemingly irrelevant, detail.' Indeed were they to be confined to directly relevant issues, 'they would be robbed of their main method of arriving at the truth' (Gluckman, 1955: 95). Here Gluckman seems to suggest that 'truth' is the goal, rather than the other goals identified by Nader and Christie such as norm-setting, having everything 'out in the open' and thus reducing tensions. Elsewhere, however, Gluckman sees the judges in tribal courts as 'attempting to reconcile the parties and enable them to resume living and working together'; he notes that 'The Lozi disapprove of any irremediable breaking of relationships ... Therefore the court tends to be conciliating, it strives to effect a compromise acceptable to, and accepted by, all the parties' (Gluckman, 1955: 20–1). Another example is the Kuta (council or court) of the Barotse; it may quote precedents, but 'More often, the judges cite not past court decisions, but actual instances of upright behaviour, to show how people ought to behave ... Law in this sense is constantly exhibited in the conformity of upright people to norms' (Gluckman, 1955: 93).

Towards a western model of mediation

The interest in other models was born of disillusion with current western justice and the desire to do something about it, although there may also have been some attraction to the ideal of the simple community. One strand in the development of mediation was a meeting of minds between community activists and anthropologists. Among the former was Paul Wahrhaftig, a civil rights lawyer, who in 1969 was leading a bail reform project of the American Friends' Service Committee. Being interested in the spread of ideas, he produced a newsletter, the *Pre-Trial Justice Quarterly*, and organized conferences. On his project's advisory committee was a young anthropologist, Michael Lowy, who had written a thesis on the use of moots in villages in Ghana, and put forward the idea that bail reform and pre-trial diversion from the criminal justice system had the effect of extending the net of State control to people who otherwise would not have been convicted. Instead, he proposed that the concept of the moot should be transformed into urban neighbourhoods in the United States. This aroused the interest of activists like Wahrhaftig, who soon changed the title of his newsletter to *The Mooter*, and later to *Conflict Resolution Notes*. (This account is based on a personal communication from Wahrhaftig in 1988.)

Another strand in the development of mediation in the US, and its introduction into Britain, was the work of the Society of Friends (Quakers). In the 1960s they gave training in non-violent techniques to marshals of civil rights marches. Two Quakers who had been working with juvenile delinquents, Eileen Stief and Betsey Leonard, felt that court procedure was unsuited to many of their cases. They trained as mediators, and in 1976 the Friends' Suburban Project in Philadelphia started the Community Dispute Settlement Program with Eileen Stief as director. In 1982 the first National Conference on Peacemaking and Conflict Resolution brought together mediators from different backgrounds, including four British representatives – two Quakers and two from the Newham (London) Conflict and Change Project.

[...]

The case for reform based on decentralization, rather than for replication of existing institutions, was put forward by, among others, Richard Danzig, then a professor at Stanford Law School. At a conference in late 1972 he described the 'liberal's dilemma' in the reform of justice: we are excellent at diagnosing problems, such as discrimination against the poor and ethnic minorities, but we tend to come up with solutions that require those in power, such as judges, to agree with our analysis. Danzig legitimized these ideas, notably in an influential article in the *Stanford Law Review* (1973). Concerned with what he saw as the overcentralization of city government in New York, he advocated a package of measures to give self-determination and cohesion to local communities, such as the right to determine whether certain activities should be treated as crimes, and the organization at neighbourhood level of police units, analogous perhaps to Britain's special constables or traffic wardens, to deal with minor matters of order maintenance. Of Danzig's suggestions, the 'community moot' was the one which attracted support: for local disputes and minor delinquency, he proposed, we could 'stop thinking of courts as adjudicators, and view them instead as parts of a therapeutic process aimed at conciliation of disputants or reintegration of deviants into society' (Danzig, 1973: 42). There would be no compulsion, no records suggesting guilt, and the complainant would have nothing to lose by turning first to the moot (1973: 47–8). He drew examples from, among others, some of the anthropological studies mentioned above (notably James Gibbs, 1963 and Laura Nader, 1969; Lowy, incidentally, had studied under Nader).

[. . .]

Mediation in the United Kingdom

In Britain the first community mediation service was the Newham Conflict and Change Project, started in 1982. About 50 local services were members of the national body Mediation UK by 1994/95, the year in which it received government funding for the first time. In 1994 the Department of the Environment sent a circular to the chief officers responsible for all local authority noise control and housing, advocating the use of mediation in neighbour disputes (DoE, 1994). Meanwhile the government had asked Lord Woolf, a senior Lord of Appeal, to review the civil court system. His interim report in 1995, *Access to Justice*, recommended the use – and funding – of mediation and other alternatives to litigation. The Lord Chancellor's Department issued a booklet on resolving disputes without going to court (1995), and in the following year the introduction of a pilot mediation service in the London county court was announced. The growing interest of the legal profession was shown by the formation of a British Association of Lawyers in Mediation.

Meanwhile mediation has been developing in many other fields of conflict. In England and Wales the most publicized has been in the field of divorce, because of the controversy over the Family Law Bill of 1995, which proposes that all divorcing couples will have an explanation of what mediation can offer. Two organizations provide mediation in this field, using different models: the Family Mediators Association and National Family Mediation. Commercial mediation is being developed, particularly by the ADR Group and the (non-profit making) Centre for Dispute Resolution.

Of particular interest, because of its potential for the future, is work in schools. Children are being taught not only to handle their own disputes instead of resorting to force, but also to use ground rules such as respecting feelings, affirming people and not putting them down, and working together for a common solution. As in other mediation, the no-blame approach is used. Work is also in progress on mediation in voluntary organizations, in churches, in the Health Service, in environmental disputes, and other fields of human activity and conflict, as well as victim/offender mediation. [. . .]

Critiques of mediation

The ideal of mediation has not won universal approval. Critics have argued that its advocates are trying to build too many ideals on a base that cannot sustain them, and that in certain circumstances it serves the interests of the powerful or the authorities rather than of those citizens who most need protection. There has also been criticism of some of its techniques, but that is a matter of practice rather than theory, and will not be dealt with in detail here.

Attemping the impossible?

The model of mediation used as an example by Danzig, Christie and others is that of small, relatively simple African societies. Can this nostalgia for the moot be a basis for dispute resolution schemes in complex western societies?

In looking to other cultures for inspiration, it is important not to idealize them: some primitive societies resolve disputes simply by fighting or retaliation. It is true that talking ('jaw-jaw') can reduce tension, but shouting can increase it; in one society, the Jale of the New Guinea Highlands, the language does not contain a word for settlement-directed talk, apart from one translated as 'shouting match' (Roberts, 1979: 15, 116–20). Some simple communities, in addition to mediation, use coercive and even violent enforcement; the people's courts in socialist countries, which some have taken as a model, were often committed to implanting a new ideology, and some were empowered to impose penalties (Merry, 1982: 173A). It has also been suggested, for example by Felstiner (1974), the methods suitable for technologically simple, poor societies, with strong informal social control and little mobility, are not appropriate to technologically complex, rich societies where, among other things, it is much more feasible to deal with disputes by avoidance – 'lumping it'. But these reservations about mediation, expressed when the movement for neighbourhood dispute resolution had not been under way for very long, were questioned by Danzig and Lowy (1975); they conceded that mediation is not useful in all settings in a country like the United States, but considered that Felstiner underestimated both the demand for mediation and the personal costs of avoidance.

Others have criticized the over-optimistic reliance on 'community' initiatives, when all that can really be said of them is that they are local (Marshall, 1986). If the legal system needs reform, we should not look for solutions to the 'mythical "community" ' (Hofrichter, 1977/1982: 246); 'community' can be an 'aerosol word' sprayed over deteriorating institutions (Basten, 1982: 29). The concept of community is analysed by Wahrhaftig (1982: 95–7), who concludes that it should be seen as a network of relationships. This definition, however, tends to limit the size of the community, which in turn limits the potential caseload of community-based projects, and creates pressure to increase it either by obtaining referrals from the justice system or by extending the catchment area beyond the community. Without this, the project will, in order to remain solvent, have to obtain funding outside its municipality or rely on voluntary staffing.

One critic, Jerold Auerbach, considered that community dispute resolution worked where it was indigenous to an immigrant community – Jewish or Chinese for example – but became an instrument of extended social control when it was an adjunct of the traditional justice system, used mainly by the disadvantaged for whom the courts are often inaccessible (Auerbach, 1983: 114, 120–5). This view assumes that traditional justice is the preferable method of resolving disputes, which is precisely what advocates of mediation were challenging. But some of them would agree with Auerbach, first, in being suspicious of 'top-down' introduction of what they wanted to be a grass-roots movement; Wahrhaftig, Shonholtz and others argued that the Neighborhood Justice Centers should be community based, and in the case of Venice/Mar Vista succeeded to some extent (Wahrhaftig, personal communication, 1988). The Community Boards of San Francisco, initiated by Shonholtz in 1976, refused to accept cases over which the official justice system still had any control. Second, many accepted that in some cases, for example where there was great disparity of power between the disputants and no genuine commitment to compromise on the part of the more powerful, for example a landlord, legal redress could be more appropriate.

But it is possible that mediation, besides resolving individual disputes, can contribute to the rehabilitation of communities. Sally Engle Merry, by no means an uncritical advocate of mediation, suggests that neighbourhood justice centres can limit the power of the State over the lives of individual citizens, and provide them with a greater ability to cope with their problems (Merry, 1982: 188); but Tomasic, in the same volume, is not optimistic (1982: 230). A British observer, Roger Matthews, after a review of the critical literature, has concluded that what he calls 'informal courts' (a term mediators would reject) can not only resolve conflicts which would mostly not have reached the courts, but also prevent them and transform them (1988: 23). And in objecting to planning 'from the top down' one has to be clear what is meant. Without it, will anything happen? When a community is in decline, and potential leaders within it have either left or become dispirited, any move to rehabilitate it is likely to require a stimulus from outside. There does not seem to be anything inherently wrong with this, provided that the initiators from outside act only as catalysts, enablers, and involve indigenous people fully from the outset. Raymond Shonholtz emerged from the university, not the community, to found the grassroots Community Boards Program, and Gloria Patterson, originator of the 'homespun' Community Association for Mediation in Pittsburgh, had been 'thoroughly indoctrinated in mediation' by working for the American Friends' Service Committee (Wahrhaftig, 1982: 89, 94). Perhaps there are advantages in initiatives at least from the 'middle' down.

Whose interests are served?

Two criticisms of mediation are that it serves the interests of one of the parties at the expense of the other, and that it benefits the justice system more than either. Can true mediation take place where one party has much more administrative or economic power, or personal dominance, than the other, or is physically violent? This could happen where an individual had a dispute with a large company (as customer or employee), a local authority (perhaps as a tenant), or an aggressive member of the family. The answer will depend on circumstances. The essential prerequisite is that both sides are willing to negotiate in good faith, and not use mediation to legitimize an unfair solution. To some extent it is possible for the mediators to redress the balance, for example by allowing each side roughly equal speaking time, by discreetly helping less articulate people to express their point of view, and by not calling some 'Mr' or 'Mrs' and others by their first name (unless they are children, of course). Mediators can also use information elicited from the weaker party during a private session to stiffen his resolve, or they can discourage him from concluding an agreement that does not give him his due. Some mediation services have a policy of excluding such disputes: for example rather than let landlords (municipal or private) 'divide and rule' their tenants by negotiating with some individuals while continuing to exploit the less assertive ones, it might be better to encourage all the tenants to take collective action or go to law. Mediation initiatives, if they are alive to this, can act as centres for the collection of such information, so that individual grievances can be transformed into effective political action (Merry, 1982: 188–9); thus they can help a demoralized community to rehabilitate itself. Mediation between even quite large groups is possible, however, provided each can agree on a small number of spokespeople. In cases where a child is at odds with a school, there is certainly disparity of power; but where deadlock has been reached over some breach of school rules, or simply non-attendance, mediation can let both sides off the hook, provided always that both are genuinely willing to negotiate. This can be helpful to the school, in finding out the real cause of the child's resistance; the child can ask the school to agree to make some change, which shows that it cares about the child, and may benefit other pupils as well. Sometimes power is only apparent. Fisher and Ury, in their best-selling guide to the use of mediation *Getting to Yes*, give the example of a wealthy tourist who wants to buy a brass pot from a vendor at Bombay railway station: the vendor, though poor, knows the market, but the tourist is in a hurry and may not know whether it would be difficult, or more costly, to buy a similar pot elsewhere (Fisher and Ury, 1987: 106–7).

A substantial strand of criticism is based not so much on mediation in itself as on the relationship of some projects with the established judicial system. Critics like Harrington see Neighborhood Justice Centers as not so much a non-adversarial, problem-solving approach to disputes, offering welcome relief from the delays and protocol of the official system, as an informal 'shadow justice' which 'expands the capacity of the justice system to manage minor conflicts' and attempts to persuade people to seek consensus at the expense of their legally enforceable rights (Harrington, 1985: 170, 173). In the same vein Abel takes informal justice apart. It is coercive, and adds to social control of the economically, socially and politically oppressed (Abel, 1982: 2714). Neighbourhood justice is a myth, because there are few neighbourhoods (1982: 277). Abel does not see mediation offering a way of resolving disputes which people find hard to handle, but 'state informal control' undermining time-honoured informal social controls such as gossip, boycott and self-help (does he mean taking the law into their own hands?), and perpetuating the 'theft of the conflict' identified by Christie (1977). In relation to disputes between customers and merchants, employees and employers, informal procedures 'neutralize conflict that could threaten state or capital,' for example by increasing the proportion of claims paid so that almost every claimant gets something, but reducing the amount paid to each (Abel, 1982: 280–1). 'The proponents of informalism seek to reduce conflict by curtailing demands, never acknowledging that just as much conflict would be eliminated if those to whom the demands are addressed would accede – cease discriminating, polluting, exploiting, oppressing' (Abel, 1982: 285).

These criticisms cannot be ignored, but they cannot be accepted without question. Some mediators might wonder if they are working in the same movement as Harrington and Abel describe, with their references to coercion, penalties and judgment (Abel, 1982: 270–1, 274). Mediation can operate in different ways. Some projects are court-based, the agreements reached are court-enforceable, and disputants cannot get access to the courts without attempting to reach agreement first. Others are independent, agreements are not court-enforceable, and they provide an alternative for those who prefer not to litigate. Mediators recognize that there are some disputes which are not suitable for mediation; it might be more appropriate, for example, for tenants to combine and take legal action against a negligent landlord. Abel himself asks rhetorically whether informal methods equalize or aggravate inequalities, increase or curtail popular participation, accelerate or delay the process, and so on, and concludes that 'The answer to virtually every question will be – both' (Abel, 1982: 270). Many users like informal procedures (1982: 283), and Abel concludes that informalism is not an 'evil to be resisted'; it expresses values such as the preference for harmony over conflict, mechanisms that offer access to the many, quickly and cheaply, and achieve substantive justice rather than frustrating it in the name of form. Abel's views can be taken as a salutary warning of how mediation projects could be, and in some cases have been, absorbed into the existing system's values and power structure (though not as universally as he implies). That leaves two other possibilities: that the formal system should adopt the best values of mediation, as Abel would prefer, and/or that independently based mediation offers a method that is preferable because it is nearer to the people it serves, spreads knowledge of a different approach to handling conflict, and may help a little to re-create local communities.

[. . .]

Second-class justice for the poor?

Some critics fear that mediation is a way of providing second-class, low-cost justice for people with low incomes, particularly in the United States where the State provides little financial support for litigation (e.g. Marks et al., 1984: 51–2). Some projects, which have not arisen from a secure base within the community, appear to be operating largely as a safety-valve easing the pressure on the courts. Provided the cases referred are the most suitable, this creates no problem for a mediation project. Another suggestion, however, is that cases referred by police or courts may be those which no one else wants: the mediation project becomes a 'dumping ground'. This could also 'widen the net', if the agreement is court-enforceable; when it is broken, and a sanction is imposed, the offender is worse off than if mediation had not existed. This danger could be avoided either by making mediated agreements not enforceable in court, and relying on persuasion; or by defining types of offences, such as assaults, harassment, and theft and property damage among parties known to each other, where mediation would normally be available in preference to courts (Weigend, 1981: 45–8), or where an attempt at mediation would be required before the case could proceed to the criminal court, as in the *Schiedsmann* (official mediator) system in Germany. This is a form of coercion into mediation, but Professor Sander considers that 'modest pressure' of this kind can be regarded as acceptable: it is coercion *within* mediation that must be avoided (Sander, 1984: 106–7). [. . .]

Mediation has to co-exist, for the time being at least, with the courts. The nature of this relationship is a further subject of debate. For some, the courts are there as a safeguard, to deal with cases not suitable for mediation or to enforce mediation agreements that have not been kept. Others see this as an example of the courts' reluctance to let go; Merry, for example, thinks that 'mediation programs could be more creative in developing non-court forms of pressure' to observe agreements, and finds it ironic that the mediation movement, which was set up to offer a more appropriate mechanism for resolving conflicts, relies heavily on the courts to generate referrals and to enforce agreements (Merry, 1982: 180).

In Australia the charge of 'second-class justice' to which low-income groups are 'shunted' (Tomasic, 1982: 246) has been robustly answered by Kevin Anderson, Deputy Chief Stipendiary Magistrate of New South Wales: 'In 35 years in magistrates' courts administration, I have not seen many examples of first class justice' (Anderson, 1982: 246). In the United States, people who can afford to choose are using professional mediation; indeed there is a counter-assertion that privately financed dispute resolution systems could become a 'luxury class justice' accessible only to large corporations and other major litigants (Marks *et al.*, 1984: 52–3). The answer seems to be that mediation has great potential for resolving at least some kinds of disputes; the fairness or otherwise depends on whether it is available to anyone who could benefit by it.

Is mediation succeeding?

Advocates of mediation maintain that it offers a way of resolving disputes for people who would otherwise have to choose between passive endurance, private retaliation or the vagaries of the courts; and that in so doing it can empower not only those individuals but also whole communities. Critics question whether the agreements reached are always more satisfactory to the weaker party than would have been achieved in court; they also suggest that mediation projects have often been co-opted by the courts, first into easing pressure on the official system by accepting its overload, and second into allowing courts to retain the final say in the disposition of cases.

As always in evaluating initiatives of this kind [. . .], it is necessary to agree not only on the principal aims but also on their order of priority if there should be competing interests. Then ways have to be found of assessing the attainment of these, and not merely of subsidiary ones which happen to be easier to measure, unless that is the only feasible approximation. The primary aim could be regarded as the 'product', the subsidiary ones as aspects of 'quality control'. For example if a project aims primarily at satisfying its participants, some extra expense may be tolerable, but exorbitant costs would invalidate it, even though the primary aim was achieved. Conversely if a project set saving costs or relieving the traditional system as its primary aim, it could be invalidated if individuals were highly dissatisfied or their rights infringed.

There is a lack of agreement on the primary aim of mediation. Is it to divert part of the caseload of the criminal justice system, or to provide a service to ordinary citizens (Marshall, 1985: 76)? Is the project aiming to be a mediation programme or a community programme?

If the basic concern is particular participants and the failure of the criminal justice system to meet their needs, the mediation services ought to be provided by a small number of experienced, highly motivated and closely supervised mediators. If on the other hand mediation is seen as an aspect of a community's struggle to settle its own quarrels, to take responsibility for its own social control and its own fate, then the base of mediators must be broad, even at the cost of less effective individual mediations (Felstiner and Williams, 1980: 122–3): These aims were balanced in one project in a Hispanic area of New York by recruiting community leaders and opinion-formers for the first intake of mediators, so that they would spread the word about mediation; for later intakes, selection was primarily on criteria of suitability as mediators (interview with Dana Vermilye, Washington Heights, NY, October 1983). Advocates of community mediation would argue that trained lay mediators are in some ways better than professionals at individual mediation. They are more readily available out of working hours. They tend not to become 'case-hardened' because they undertake fewer cases; with their community contacts, they spread knowledge of mediation among friends and colleagues. They need supervision and support; but in a good project, with regular feedback and monitoring, they probably receive more than, for example, lay magistrates.

Other possible benefits are listed by McGillis (1982: 62, 74):

1. *Benefits for individuals in dispute:* a better way of handling conflict because disputants can explore underlying problems, without lawyers and the restrictions of legal procedure; and improved access to this service.
2. *Benefits to the community:* enhancement of community power *vis-à-vis* the authorities, by teaching citizens a new technique for solving problems collectively; improving the quality of life through increased citizen partici-pation in major life decisions; reducing community tensions through effective conflict resolution.
3. *Benefits to the justice system:* diverting cases from the courts, freeing them to attend to more serious cases.

Many projects would claim to work towards all three of these, but there are bound to be circumstances where one aim can be achieved only at the expense of another. Projects could be evaluated more clearly if each would define its priority: indeed this would help the mediation movement itself to work towards a consensus.

In practice, the needs of the judicial system, as a criterion for 'success', have taken precedence over those of individuals and the community, and many projects have acquiesced in this because they depend on the justice system for an adequate supply of referrals, according to Professor Sally Merry. She found (1982: 181–90) that evaluations tend to focus on caseload data such as numbers, speed and costs.

As regards access to justice, clearly this is not much improved if a project obtains most of its referrals from the court: the participants will by definition already have found their way there. But if the primary claim for mediation is that it is superior to traditional adjudication, at least for certain types of case, then a transfer of such cases from the latter to the former can be counted as success. The quality of the process itself is harder to assess, which may be why Merry found no study that had investigated it (1982: 187). It is impossible for researchers to determine what would be a just result in each of the cases examined, and then measure the proportion in which the actual outcome coincided with it; they are therefore thrown back on assessing users' satisfaction. Some disputants may be satisfied with something less than justice, either because they are unaware of their rights or because the process of mediation is more congenial and makes a less-than-ideal outcome acceptable. There is of course no guarantee that they would have fared better under the traditional system. Also some criteria can be monitored by day-to-day record-keeping in the project, while others require special research.

The criterion of empowering the community appears to be regarded, for example by Wahrhaftig (1982), as much the same as empowering individuals: the latter leads to the former. If anything, he seems to put the interests of the community first, implying that a project is failing in its task if it does not collect and collate information about community problems, in addition to helping individuals with disputes. Wahrhaftig suggests as criteria: Has the project acted as a mechanism for community fact-finding? Is it run by the community served or by a more educated elite? Has the community changed since the project started, and would any difference be noticed if it stopped? [. . .] (Wahrhaftig, 1982: 80–1, 85, 87). There are various indicators of community involvement in a project, such as whether the community's social, ethnic and linguistic composition is reflected among the members of the management committee and the volunteer mediators; actual influence would have to be inferred from events which demonstrate whether members of the community had acquired, or regained, the capacity to negotiate with the local authority, large landlords, local firms, and the like, about matters of communal concern.

The direct impact of the justice system, if any, could ultimately be mainly in the form of a numerical reduction of caseload, although only the large US projects closely integrated with the traditional system have achieved this so far. It is also possible that mediation projects may have an indirect effect on its procedures. As Tony Marshall, then director of FIRM (now Mediation UK), commented (1988: 50), the idea of 'co-operative problem solving', in the eyes of many of its advocates, 'could, if it attracts widespread adherence, constitute a reform of fundamental proportions in the nature of society'. The effect of the number of cases, whether civil or criminal, transferred from the courts to mediation, is limited by the basic premiss that all involve some form of relationship between the parties. The impact on the system, as well as on individuals, is considerably widened if mediation is introduced in criminal cases where there was no prior relationship [. . .].

This extract is taken from 'Justice without Lawyers: Enabling People to Resolve their Conflicts', chapter 4 in Justice for Victims and Offenders: a Restorative Response to Crime, *by Martin Wright, second edition (Winchester: Waterside Press, 1996).*

References

Abel, R.L. (1973) 'A Comparative Theory of Dispute Institutions in Society', *Law and Society Review*, 8:1, pp. 217–347.

Abel, R.L. (ed.) (1982) *The Politics of Informal Justice. Vol. 1.1. The American Experience* (New York, NY: Academic Press).

Anderson, K. (1982) 'Community Justice Centres in NSW', in Sydney University Law School, Institute of Criminology, *Proceedings of a Seminar in Community Justice Centres, 10 March 1982* (Sydney: Institute of Criminology).

Auerbach, J.S. (1983) *Justice without Law? Resolving Disputes without Lawyers* (New York, NY: Oxford University Press).

Basten, J. (1982) 'CJCs – a Comment', in Sydney University Law School, Institute of Criminology, *Proceedings of a Seminar in Community Justice Centres, 10 March 1982* (Sydney: Institute of Criminology).

Christie, N. (1977) 'Conflicts as Property', *British Journal of Criminology*, 17:1, pp. 1–15, reprinted in Galaway, B. and Hudson, J. (eds) (1981) *Perspectives on Crime Victims* (St Louis, MO: C.V. Mosby).

Danzig, R. (1973) 'Towards the Creation of a Complementary, Decentralized System of Criminal Justice', *Stanford Law Review*, 26:1, pp. 1–54.

Danzig, R. and Lowy, M.J. (1975) 'Everyday Disputes and Mediation in the US: A Reply to Professor Felstiner', *Law and Society Review*, 9:4, pp. 675–94.

Department of the Environment (1994) *Mediation: Benefits and Practice* (London: DoE).

Felstiner, W.L.F. (1974) 'Influences of Social Organization on Dispute Processing', *Law and Society Review*, 9, pp. 63–93.

Felstiner, W.L.F. and Williams, L.A. (1980) *Community Mediation in Dorchester, Mass* (Washington, DC: US Department of Justice, National Institute of Justice).

Fisher, R. and Ury, W. (1987) *Getting to Yes: Negotiating Agreement without Giving In* (London: Arrow Books).

Frank, J. (1949) *Courts on Trial: Myth and Reality in American Justice* (Princeton, NJ: Princeton University Press).

Fuller, L.L. (1963) 'Collective Bargaining and the Arbitrator', *Wisconsin Law Review*, 23, pp. 3–46.

Fuller, L.L. (1971) 'Mediation: Its Forms and Functions', *South California Law Review*, 44, pp. 305–39.

Gibbs, J.L., jr (1963) 'The Kpelle Moot', *Africa*, 33:1, pp. 1–10, reprinted in Bohannan P. (ed.) (1967) *Law and Warfare: Studies in the Anthropology of Conflict* (Garden City, NY: Natural History Press).

Gluckman, M. (1955) *The Judicial Process among the Barotse of Northern Rhodesia* (Manchester: Manchester University Press).

Gluckman, M. (1968) 'Judicial Process: Comparative Aspects', in *International Encyclopedia of the Social Sciences* (New York, NY: Macmillan; Glencoe, IL: Free Press).

Gulliver, P.H. (1969) 'Dispute Settlement Without Courts: The Ndendenli of Southern Tanzania', in Nader, L. (ed.) *Law in Culture and Society* (Chicago, IL: Aldine).

Harrington, C.B. (1985) *The Ideology and Institutionalization of Alternatives to Court* (Westport, CT: Greenwood Press).

Hofrichter, R. (1977) 'Justice Centers Raise Basic Questions', *New Directions*, 2:6, pp. 168–72, reprinted in Tomasic, R. and Feeley, M. (eds) (1982) *Neighborhood Justice: Assessment of an Emerging Idea* (New York, NY: Longman).

Lord Chancellor's Department (1995) *Resolving Disputes without Going to Court* (London: LCD).

McGillis, D. (1982) 'Minor Dispute Processing: A Review of Recent Developments', in Tomasic, R. and Feeley, M. (eds) *Neighborhood Justice: Assessment of an Emerging Idea* (New York, NY: Longman).

McGillis, D. and Mullen, J. (1977) *Neighborhood Justice Centers: An Analysis of Potential Models* (Washington, DC: National Institute of Law Enforcement and Criminal Justice).

Marks, J.B., Johnson, E. and Szanton, P.L. (1984) *Dispute Resolution in America: Processes in Evolution* (National Institute for Dispute Resolution, 1901 L Street NW, Washington, DC 20036).

Marshall, T. and Merry, S. (1985) *Alternatives to Criminal Courts: The Potential for Non-Judicial Dispute Resolution* (Aldershot: Gower).

Marshall, T. and Merry, S. (1986) 'Keeping the Alternative in Alternative Dispute Resolution.' Paper to 3rd National Conference on Peacemaking and Conflict Resolution, Denver, Co.

Marshall, T. and Merry, S. (1988) 'Out of Court: More or Less Justice?' in Matthews, R. (ed.) *Informal Justice?* (London: Sage).

Matthews, R. (1988) 'Reassessing Informal Justice', in Matthews, R. (ed.) *Informal Justice?* (London: Sage).

Merry, S.E. (1982) 'Defining "Success" in the Neighborhood Justice Movement', in Tomasic, R. and Feeley, M. (eds) *Neighborhood Justice: Assessment of an Emerging Idea* (New York, NY: Longman).

Nader, L. (ed.) (1969) *Law in Culture and Society* (Chicago, IL: Aldine).

Nader, L. and Todd, H. (eds) (1978) *The Disputing Process: Law in Ten Societies* (New York, NY: Columbia University Press).

Roberts, S. (1979) *Order and Dispute: An Introduction to Legal Anthropology* (Harmondsworth: Penguin).

Sander, F.E.A. (1984) 'Observations Regarding the Symposium Discussion and Thoughts about the Future of Dispute Resolution', in Vermont Law School, *A Study of Barriers to the Use of Alternative Methods of Dispute Resolution* (South Royalton, VT: Vermont Law School Dispute Resolution Project).

Tomasic, R. (1982) 'Mediation as an Alternative to Adjudication: Rhetoric and Reality in the Neighborhood Justice Movement', in Tomasic, R. and Feeley, M. (eds) *Neighborhood Justice: Assessment of an Emerging Idea* (New York, NY: Longman).

Wahrhaftig, P. (1982) 'An Overview of Community-oriented Citizen Dispute Resolution Programs in the United States', in Abel, R.L. (ed.) *The Politics of Informal Justice.* Vol. 1. The American Experience (New York, NY: Academic Press).

Weigend, T. (1981) *Assessing the Victim: A Report on Efforts to Strengthen the Position of the Victim in the American System of Criminal Justice* (Freiburg in Breisgau: Max Planck Institute for Foreign and International Criminal Law).

14. Restorative justice in New Zealand: family group conferences as a case study

Allison Morris and Gabrielle Maxwell

[. . .]

Despite the absence of specific reference to restorative justice in the debates introducing family group conferences in New Zealand in 1989, their underlying philosophy incorporates key features of restorative justice. In particular, they aim to heal the damage that has been caused by youthful offending, to involve those most affected by the offending in determining appropriate responses to it and to 'make things better' both for young people who have committed offences and for their victims. This paper outlines the principles underlying the introduction of family group conferences and describes the role they play in New Zealand's youth justice system.[1] It draws from research we conducted in 1990 and 1991 (Maxwell and Morris, 1993, 1996) and in 1996 (Morris and Maxwell, 1997). But first we describe briefly the youth justice system introduced in New Zealand by the Children, Young Persons and their Families Act 1989 ('the 1989 Act').

The practice of youth justice in New Zealand

The intention underlying New Zealand's youth justice system is to encourage the police to adopt low-key responses to juvenile offending whenever possible. Thus, as in most jurisdictions now, minor and first offenders are diverted from prosecution by means of an immediate (street) warning. Where further action is thought necessary, the police refer the young person to the police Youth Aid Section (a specialist unit) for follow-up. The Youth Aid Section may issue a warning in the presence of the young person's parents, require an apology to the victim, impose an additional sanction (for example, community work) or, when such sanctions have not been successful in the past or when the offending is more serious, refer the young person to a family group conference. During 1996, 22 per cent of young offenders known to the police were given warnings by them, a further 59 per cent were diverted by Youth Aid, and another 9 per cent were referred by Youth Aid for a family group conference. Thus, the police cannot refer a young person directly to court unless he or she has been arrested (we deal with this below). They must seek a family group conference if they wish the young person to be dealt with in court and, if the family group conference can arrive at a satisfactory outcome acceptable to all the parties, that is the end of the matter.

Juvenile offenders can only be arrested if certain tightly drawn conditions are met and, in 1996, only 11 per cent of young people who offended were arrested. It is usually only this arrested group who will subsequently appear in the Youth Court: a branch of the District Court dealing exclusively with youth justice issues. The Youth Court is closed to the public to preserve the confidentiality of its proceedings. The Youth Court routinely appoints a youth advocate (a lawyer) to represent the young person, if the young person does not already have a legal representative. The intention of the 1989 Act was to allow young persons, their families, and victims to be involved in the judicial process and to influence outcomes. Thus, the Youth Court cannot make a disposition unless a family group conference has been held, and it must take into account in its decisions any plan or recommendations put forward by the family group conference.[2] In all, therefore, around 20 per cent of all young offenders known to the police are dealt with through family group conferences: that is, approximately 5,000 family group conferences are held each year. [. . .]

Describing family group conferences[3]

Family group conferences are made up of the young person who has committed the offence, members of his or her family and whoever the family invites, the victim(s) or their representative, a support person for the victim(s), a representative of the police, and the mediator or manager of the process (the manager of the process is called a youth justice coordinator and is an employee of the Department of Social Welfare). Sometimes, a social worker and/or a lawyer is present. The main goal of a conference is to formulate a plan about how best to deal with the offending. There are three principal components to this process:

- ascertaining whether or not the young person admits the offence – conferences only proceed if the young person does so or if the offence has been proved in the Youth Court;

- sharing information among all the parties at the conference about the nature of the offence, the effects of the offence on the victims, the reasons for the offending, any prior offending by the young person, and so on;

- deciding the outcome or recommendation.

The family group conference is a meeting between those entitled to attend, in a relatively informal setting. The room is usually arranged with comfortable chairs in a circle. When all are present, the meeting may open with a prayer or a blessing, depending on the customs of those involved. The youth justice coordinator then welcomes the participants, introduces each of them, and describes the purposes of the meeting. What happens next can vary, but usually the police representative then reads out the summary of the offence. The young person is asked if he or she agrees that this is what happened and any variation is noted. If he or she does not agree, the meeting progresses no further and the police may consider referring the case to the Youth Court for a hearing. Assuming the young person agrees, the victim, or a spokesperson for the victim, is then usually asked to describe what the events meant for them. Next, a general discussion of the offence and the circumstances underlying it occurs.

There can be a lot of emotion expressed at this point. It is at this point, too, that the young person and his or her family may express their remorse for what has happened and make an apology to the victim, although more often this occurs later on (and sometimes it does not happen at all). Once everybody has discussed what the offending has meant and options for making good the damage, the professionals and the victim leave the family and the young person to meet privately to discuss what plans and recommendation they wish to make to repair the damage and to prevent reoffending. The private family time can take as little as half an hour or much longer. When the family are ready, the others return and the meeting is reconvened. Sometimes this is the point at which the young person and the family apologise to the victim. A spokesperson for the family outlines what they propose and all discuss the proposal. Once there is agreement among all present, the details are formally recorded and the conference concludes, sometimes with the sharing of food.

Professionals are expected to play a low key role in the family group conference. The youth justice coordinator ensures that everyone understands the tasks that need to be done, that all relevant issues are discussed and that the venting of emotion is managed as constructively as possible. The role of the police is usually limited to describing the offence, and possibly the impact of it on the victim. The police may also voice their concerns if the proposals of the family seem inadequate or excessive. The youth advocate's main role is to advise on legal issues and to protect the young person's rights; they may also express an opinion about the proposed penalties if these seem excessive. The social worker, if present, will normally only provide background information on the young person and participate in supporting the plans of the family and the young person for the future. Practice can, however, vary considerably. Conferences are intended to be flexible and responsive to young people, families and victims. All these values can be breached at times, especially when professionals do not understand or accept their roles.[4]

Provided that the plans and decisions have been agreed to by all those attending the family group conference and, for court-referred cases, are accepted by the Youth Court judge, they are binding on all those involved. The plans are meant to take into account the views of the victims, the need to make the young person accountable for his or her offending, and any measures that may prevent future re-offending by enhancing the well-being of the offender or strengthening the family. The range of possible sanctions here is extensive and can include an apology, community work, reparation, or involvement in a program. Conferences take much longer than courts to reach resolutions. Just under a third of the conferences in our research (Maxwell and Morris, 1993) took less than an hour, almost a third took between an hour and an hour and a half, and more than a quarter took between one and a half and two hours. Around 10 per cent took more than two hours. Family group conferences can take place wherever the family wish, provided that the victim agrees. Most commonly they are held in rooms at the Department of Social Welfare or in community rooms; occasionally they are held on *marae* (meeting houses) or in the family's home.

[. . .]

Family group conferences and restorative justice

As we noted earlier, restorative justice per se did not feature in the debates surrounding the introduction of family group conferences. But, the combination of ideas flowing from Maori critics of conventional justice processes and from victims' advocates, together with a deep dissatisfaction of current youth justice processes, produced a new system that clearly shared the ideas underlying restorative justice. The rest of this article evaluates what this has meant in practice. One important point needs to be made here, however, which is that family group conferences are essentially restorative *processes* which may or may not result in restorative *outcomes*. This distinction is crucial and we will comment on it further below.

Family group conferences and young people

The participation of young people in family group conferences goes beyond simply being there. They are, of course, present in any court proceedings involving them; but there, they usually remain passive participants throughout, primarily because the principal players in court are the professionals. This is not so in family group conferences, where youthful offenders, at least in principle, are expected to actively participate in discussions about how best to deal with their offending.

Young people (and families) participating in our research (Maxwell and Morris, 1993) on family group conferences were asked a number of key questions: 'Did you feel that you made the decision?' 'How involved were you in reaching the decisions?' and 'In your view, who really decided?' About a third of the young people said that they had felt involved in the process. If responses indicating that the young person felt 'partly' involved are added to this, then we can conclude that nearly half of the young people felt involved in some way. They were able to say what they wanted to and to speak openly without pressure. However, almost half felt that they had not been actively involved in the family group conferences and that decisions had been made about them, not with them.[5] Technically, outcomes have to be agreed to by all the parties at the conference, but the young person's voice often seems to become subsumed within the family's. It should be noted, however, that even these relatively low rates of involvement in conferences are still considerably higher than young people's involvement in conventional courts (see, for example, Asquith's (1983) discussion of young people's involvement in juvenile courts in England and children's hearings in Scotland).

Family group conferences and families

In the most direct sense, families are involved in family group conferences by being present. But it goes further than this: for example, families should be invited to determine the process and procedures to be followed, who should be invited to participate in the conference, and the venue for the conference. They should also be expected to devise a plan to deal with the offending. There is no doubt that families do actively participate in conferences. In our research (Maxwell and Morris, 1993), almost all conferences had family members present and two fifths had members of the young person's extended family also present (the figure for Maori was much higher: almost 60 per cent). More than two thirds of the families interviewed felt that they had been involved in the process of the family group conference and about the same proportion of families identified themselves as the decision-makers, at least in part.[6] Less than a fifth said that they had not felt involved in what happened.

Bringing victims and offenders together for a family group conference was a constructive process for most families. Few families found the presence of the victim to be at all unusual or inappropriate. Moreover, many commented that they viewed the victim's presence positively, because of the possibility of reconciling the victim and the offender, and because the victim's contribution could help teach the young person to accept responsibility and to be accountable for what he or she had done.

Overall, there was little doubt that families preferred the process of family group conferences to the process of courts. Their comments highlighted the participatory nature of the family group conference process and the greater degree of support available to them at the family group conference in contrast to the stress that accompanied a court appearance. As well as feeling more comfortable at the family group conference, families also understood more of what had happened and believed that it provided a more realistic forum for decision-making.

Thus, through conferencing, families are not only expected but *enabled* to participate in the decisions that are made when their children offend. In this way, 'making parents responsible' can be given a constructive meaning. Conferencing offers a participatory option that empowers families and allows them, without increasing the stigma or blame, to play a pivotal role in arriving at decisions about their children.

Family group conferences and victims

Victims can also feel involved in conferences by being present at the conference. Though our research (Maxwell and Morris, 1993) indicated that victims attended only about half of the family group conferences, the reasons for this were related primarily to poor practice: they were not invited, the time was unsuitable for them, or they were given inadequate notice of the family group conference. Good practice suggests that victims should be consulted about the time and venue of conferences and informed of them in good time. There will always be a minority of victims who choose not to participate in conferencing, but our (Maxwell and Morris, 1993) research found that only 6 per cent of victims, when asked, said that they did not wish to meet the offender. This is a clear indicator of victims' willingness, indeed desire, to be involved in these processes.

Our research also showed, that when victims were involved in conferencing, many found it a positive process. About 60 per cent of the victims interviewed described the family group conference they attended as helpful, positive, and rewarding. Generally, they said that they were effectively involved in the process and felt better as a result of participating. Victims also commented on two other specific benefits for them. First, it provided them with a voice in determining appropriate outcomes. Second, they were able to meet the offender and the offender's family face-to-face, so that they could assess their attitude, understand better why the offence had occurred, and assess the likelihood of its recurring.

About a quarter of the victims said that they felt worse as a result of attending the family group conference. There were a variety of reasons for this. The most frequent and perhaps the most important was that the victim did not feel that the young person and/or his or her family were truly sorry. Other less common reasons included the inability of the family and young person to make reparation, the victims' inability to express themselves adequately, the difficulty of communicating cross-culturally, a lack of support for them in contrast to the support given to offenders, feeling that their concerns had not been adequately listened to and feeling that other participants were disinterested in or unsympathetic to them. These findings point again to the need for good practice guidelines. Most of the concerns expressed by victims can be addressed through briefing the participants about what to expect at a conference and training the managers of the process to be effective mediators. The concerns raised were not fundamental objections to conferencing *per se*.

Satisfaction with outcomes

We asked participants about their satisfaction with the outcomes of the family group conference. Understanding what people actually mean when they answer such questions has proved problematic for researchers but this is, by definition, the most important measure of how participants view the processes in which they participate. The failure to deconstruct the concept of 'satisfaction' almost certainly reflects the fact that people vary in both their level of expectation and the type of outcomes they view as appropriate; hence, their 'satisfaction' cannot be predicted from examining outcomes alone. In reporting the results of answers to these questions we have, therefore, attempted to tease out the various factors that affected the satisfaction of young people, families, and victims. But first, we set out in Table [8.]1 the responses of the young people, families, and victims in our sample on their satisfaction with outcomes from the family group conference.

Eighty-four per cent of the young people and 85 per cent of the parents said that they were satisfied with the outcomes of the family group conference. The levels of satisfaction were high regardless of whether or not the case was referred by the Youth Court or directly by the police. Only a few young people (nine per cent) and parents (11 per cent) actually expressed dissatisfaction with the outcome. For parents, the issues seem to have been either that the young person 'got off too lightly' or, more commonly, that some kind of help or

Table [14.]1   Young people's families, and victims' satisfaction with outcomes from the family group conference

Satisfaction	Young people Per cent	Parents Per cent	Victims Per cent
Yes	84	85	49
Partly satisfied	2	3	2
No	9	11	31
Don't know	4	2	18
N of cases	152	169	141

treatment they thought necessary was not offered. For the young people, the issue was almost invariably how their outcome compared with that of co-offenders or, more generally, with their notion of appropriate penalties.

It is possible also that young people's and parents' high level of satisfaction meant nothing more than relief that nothing worse happened to the young person. There is some support for this suggestion. Young people who received the most severe penalties were almost three times as likely to express dissatisfaction as those receiving less severe penalties, and the parents of those receiving the most severe penalties were twice as likely to express dissatisfaction as the parents of young people who received less severe penalties.

About half of the victims we interviewed[7] said that they were satisfied with the outcomes from conferences. About a third, however, were dissatisfied. For some, this was because they saw the decision of the family group conference as too soft or too harsh. But, more frequently, victims were dissatisfied because the promised arrangements fell down afterwards or they were simply never informed about the eventual outcome of the family group conference. The responsibility for this lay more often with professional staff than with the young person and his or her family. Victims were less satisfied with outcomes than the professionals and families, but even this lower figure is probably higher than the levels of satisfaction victims would express after court hearings and sentences by judges.

Family group conferences and accountability

About 85 per cent of the young people in our sample who took part in family group conferences agreed to carry out what we have called 'active penalties', that is to say community work, reparation and the like. If we add 'apologies' to this, the figure comes closer to 95 per cent. Before the 1989 Act, a similar proportion of young people appeared before the court as appear now at family group conferences, but only 60 per cent of them received an 'active' penalty, and apologies to victims were uncommon. On the other hand, custodial or residential penalties are rarely recommended by today's family group conferences. Thus, more young people are made accountable than in the past, but in ways that emphasise restoration.

Family group conferences and reconviction

We analysed data on the reconviction of the original 1990–91 family group conference sample (Morris and Maxwell, 1997) up to December 1994. A matching sample against which to compare these data is not available. However, our general conclusion after reviewing other local and overseas reconviction studies is that the proportion reconvicted in the first year following a family group conference (26 per cent) is certainly no worse and is possibly better than samples dealt with in the criminal justice system.

Furthermore, there is some evidence from this study that the probability of reconviction was *reduced* when certain of the potentially restorative aspects of family group conferences were achieved. The factor 'victim satisfaction' was least often reported for persistent recidivists; this group was also least likely to have completed the tasks agreed to at the family group conference.

Regression analysis also suggested that those offenders who failed to apologise to victims were more likely to be reconvicted than those who had apologised. The initial modeling of whether or not reconviction occurred identified the following as independent significant predictors: offending prior to the family group conference; being Maori; having extended family or *whanau* present at the family group conference; the failure to apologise; and the greater seriousness and number of family group conference offences. Odds ratios were calculated. The results of this regression analysis are set out in Table [8.]2.

Table [8.]2 shows that most of the significant factors[8] that emerged in the regression analysis were between two and four and a half times more likely to be found among those reconvicted than among those who were not. Thus, for example, those who failed to apologise were three times more likely to be reconvicted than those who had apologised.

The offence-related variables identified here are comparable to those identified in previous studies of reconviction; the relevance of ethnicity has also been previously identified. In addition, two factors related to the family group conference also emerged: having extended family or *whanau* present and making an apology. 'Having extended family or *whanau* present' can be interpreted as reflecting the gravity with which the offence was regarded by the family and statutory agencies. But the emergence of failing to apologise as a predictor of reconviction is a new and important finding, which provides

Table [14.]2   Stepwise logistic regression to predict reconviction (n = 154)

	Probability of chi-square	Odds ratio
Offending prior to FGC	0.001	4.5
Maori	0.003	4.1
Extended family present	0.017	3.2
No apology	0.039	3.1
Greater seriousness of FGC offence	0.066	2.1
More FGC offenses	0.058	1.2

Table [14.]3   Stepwise logistic regression to predict 'persistence' (n = 101)[9]

Variable	Probability of chi square	Odds ratio
Welfare services provided	0.015	4.1
Maori	0.021	4.1
Victims not present at the FGC	0.026	4.5
Offending prior to FGC	0.037	13.7
More FGC offences	0.047	1.3

support for theories of restorative justice. However, it is not a secure finding as it did not emerge as a significant variable in the original analysis and its importance may be linked to other factors in the regression.

A second regression was calculated to model the variables that might predict the difference between the two most distinctive groups: the 'persistent' and the 'non-reconvicted' groups. The first point to note is that a stronger prediction is possible for the persistent versus the non-reconvicted group because the difference between these two groups is much sharper than the difference between reconvicted and non-reconvicted. The solution identified a slightly different pattern of variables from the earlier analysis. Table [8.]3 sets out the results of this regression.

The significant independent predictors were in order of significance and direction of association with persistent reconviction: having welfare services provided; being Maori; victims not being present at the family group conference; offending prior to the family group conference; and the greater number of family group conference offences. The seriousness of the offending was rather less important with a probability of only .09. Odds ratios show that most of these factors were between four and four and a half times more probable among those who were in the persistent group compared to those who were not reconvicted. But offending prior to the family group conference was nearly 14 times more probable among the persistently reconvicted.

These variables, although slightly different, are consistent in meaning with those identified in Table [8.]2. 'Welfare services', which was correlated with 'extended family or *whanau* present', has emerged in its place and 'victim present' has replaced the correlated variable 'apology'. This analysis increases confidence in the earlier interpretation of what predicts reconviction and indicates that prediction is more successful when the groups are more highly contrasted with respect to their reconviction patterns.

Family group conferences as restorative processes not restorative outcomes

The family group conference is a mechanism for making decisions about how best to deal with a young person's criminal behavior. To the extent that it involves the young person, the victim, and their respective communities of interest in this decision, then that process can be described as restorative. Outcomes may, and often do, include putting things right for victims. For example, the young person or his or her family may make reparation to the victim, or the young person may perform some community work either for the victim or for an organisation or person nominated by the victim. To this extent, outcomes may also be restorative. But outcomes might also involve counseling or some other program for the young person, while the victims' needs remain unmet. And, too often in our experience, promised outcomes have not been delivered (usually as a result of some failure on the part of professionals rather than on the part of the young persons and/or their families). Moreover, it was not uncommon for victims to express satisfaction at the end of the family group conference or immediately afterwards, only to express dissatisfaction some time down the track. Such outcomes cannot be described as restorative. These need not, however, detract from the power and potential of the process as a restorative one.

Conclusion

[. . .]

In practice, our research on family group conferences showed that:

- victims were willing and able to participate in restorative justice processes;
- a significant proportion of victims felt positively toward the process and were satisfied with the outcomes;
- offenders were held accountable;
- reconviction rates were no worse and may be better than for court-based samples; and
- factors in restorative justice processes may be linked to a lower probability of reconviction.

These encouraging findings and the fact that restorative justice processes are already being used in New Zealand in a variety of shapes and forms, both within and outside the criminal justice system, provides a sufficient basis for New Zealand to move further forward in the implementation of restorative justice processes for adult offenders. They also enable other countries wishing to move towards more restorative approaches to consider family group conferences as a useful strategy.

This extract is taken from 'Restorative Justice in New Zealand: Family Group Conferences as a Case Study', by Allison Morris and Gabrielle Maxwell in Western Criminolgy Review *1(1), 1998.*

Notes

1 The youth justice system in New Zealand deals primarily with 14 to 17 year olds who offend, but can, in certain situations, deal with offending by those aged 10 to 14.

2 People in other jurisdictions often ask about whether or not there are certain cases for which family group conferences are not appropriate, for instance very serious offences. In New Zealand all cases involving young offenders will have a family group conference so that the views of families and victims can be heard. However, the Youth Court has the right to review the cases and to make a different disposition from that recommended if there are grounds for this and, for the most serious offences, the Youth Court can refer the matter to the adult courts for sentence. The Youth Court will also decide when participants at the conference fail to agree. Cases of murder and manslaughter are dealt with in the High Court.

3 Family group conferences also take place in the 'care and protection' system which deals with children who have been abused or neglected. These are managed differently from youth justice family group conferences. For information, see Hudson *et al.* (1996).

4 One example of the confusion that can exist about professional roles is provided in a recent analysis of the role of youth advocates (Morris *et al.*, 1997).

5 Although about a quarter of the young people said they did not know who had decided the outcome, the group most frequently identified by them as the decision-makers was their family. This was stated by about a third.

6 The professionals alone were identified as the decision-makers by 15 per cent of the families. These professionals seemed not to have accepted a redefined role for themselves: as information providers and support givers rather than decision-makers. This could be resolved by better briefing of professionals about their roles and better training of them in the objectives of conferencing.

7 These interviews sometimes took place soon after the family group conference but most of them occurred about two to three months later.

8 The significant factors in this context are those that were entered in the logistic stepwise regression at the cut-off point of 5 per cent probability.

9 The probabilities are not as low as in the previous example because the numbers are smaller (only the persistent and the no conviction group are being compared). There is also less of a close relationship between the size of the odds ratios and the probabilities, in part because of the smaller numbers but also because of differences in the relative probabilities of being scored as 'yes' or 'no' on the variable.

References

Asquith, S. (1983) *Children and Justice: Decision-making in Children's Hearings and Juvenile Courts* (Edinburgh: Edinburgh University Press).

Hudson, J., Morris, A., Maxwell, G. and Galaway, B. (eds) (1996) *Family Group Conferences: Perspectives on Policy and Practice* (Annandale, NSW: Federation Press).

Maxwell, G.M. and Morris, A. (1993) *Families, Victims and Culture: Youth Justice in New Zealand* (Wellington: Department of Social Welfare and Institute of Criminology).

Maxwell, G.M. and Morris, A. (1996) 'Research on Family Group Conferences with Young Offenders in New Zealand' in Hudson, J. *et al.* (eds) *Family Group Conferences: Perspectives in Policy and Practice* (Annandale, NSW: Federation Press).

Morris, A. and Maxwell, G.M. (1997) *Family Group Conferences and Convictions. Occasional Papers in Criminology, New Series* (Wellington: Institute of Criminology).

Morris, A., Maxwell, G. and Shepherd, P. (1997) *Being a Youth Advocate: An Analysis of their Role and Responsibilities* (Wellington: Institute of Criminology).

15. Family conferencing in Wagga Wagga: a communitarian model of justice

D.B. Moore and T.A. O'Connell

[...]

Origins

Members of the New South Wales Police Service introduced a version of family conferencing in Wagga as part of an 'effective cautioning scheme' in August 1991. Before being introduced, the scheme was given consideration by the local Community Consultative Committee and was subject to wide public debate. Although the proposed scheme was greeted largely with support and even enthusiasm from many members of the Wagga community, it was initially viewed with suspicion by a number of police. Two years later, however, it was hard to find a critic of the scheme either among police or among the several thousand people in the Wagga district who had attended a family conference as a victim, an offender or a supporter. This alone would not constitute sufficient reason to proselytise for the scheme's implementation elsewhere; nor would the positive conclusions of various evaluations of the scheme that have been conducted to date. The numbers involved in these evaluations have been too small to produce statistically powerful results. Science proceeds, however, by proposing hypotheses and attempting to disprove them. The working hypothesis of those who have designed and implemented the 'effective cautioning scheme' in Wagga is that, in response to juvenile offending, the scheme provides a more just and more meaningful outcome for victims, offenders and their supporters. That hypothesis has yet to be disproved.

Rather than attempting to disprove this hypothesis, some of the scheme's critics have attempted to close the debate by conceding that, although the scheme may indeed achieve its modest aims in Wagga, it is unlikely to work in other areas. Wagga, they argue, is an unusual place. But the debate is not so easily closed. We should certainly ask whether there is some clear reason why the scheme was started in Wagga rather than elsewhere in New South Wales or elsewhere in Australia? There are three quite distinct questions here. The first question concerns the social, economic and institutional arrangements in the city and district of Wagga Wagga. The second question concerns the current legislative and administrative arrangements of the New South Wales Police Service, since it was ultimately members of that organisation who took the initiative to import family conferencing from across the Tasman and use it as the basis of their 'effective cautioning scheme'. The third question concerns the interests of those individuals who have championed the scheme.

The social and economic arrangements of Wagga Wagga might readily be compared to those of half-a-dozen cities in Australia. With an urban population of 55,000 – closer to 75,000 if outlying areas are included – Wagga is the largest city in inland New South Wales. [. . . It is] a relatively prosperous city that caters to farmers, returns conservatives to state and federal parliaments and produces accomplished cricketers.

The suggestion that police can experiment with popular schemes here since they do not have to deal with the crime problem faced by their urban counterparts is, however, simply incorrect. Wagga has its share of social problems, including a significant number of property offences and offences against the person committed by young people. [. . .]

An explanation for the [. . .] development of the effective cautioning scheme in Wagga is to be found [. . .] in the interests of those individuals championing the scheme. Both the district commander and the patrol commander had shown a willingness to consult, to experiment with new programs, and to further devolve responsibility to sectors within patrols. This was true of the various community based policing programs in Wagga, and particularly true of the Beat Policing program introduced in November 1990. Here the choice of officer to establish the program was significant. Senior Sergeant Terry O'Connell had several portfolios at this time. In addition to his local responsibilities, he was Deputy President of the New South Wales Police Association, a position that made him responsible for the welfare of fellow officers across the State. At the same time, he was completing a degree in Social Sciences at Charles Sturt University. This made him one of a growing number of officers in town who were actively bridging the gap between academics and police, a gap long marked by a degree of suspicion and prejudice on both sides. A similar rapprochement can now be observed around the country but it is of particular significance in a city the size of Wagga, where professional networks tend to overlap with social networks rather more than they do in the larger metropolitan centres. The resulting dialogue has encouraged police more readily to evaluate the efficacy of their programs while encouraging academics to make constructive suggestions rather than chant the smug mantra of purported police insensitivity to issues of class, gender and ethnicity.

The Beat Police program, established towards the end of 1990 and prompted by Patrol Commander Kevin Wales, placed a high priority on dealing with the consequences of juvenile crime. The Beat Police took a conscious decision to apply the 'problem-solving policing' approach to all areas of concern, rather than endlessly dealing with symptoms (Goldstein, 1990). Identification of a clear link between school truancy and juvenile crime, for instance, led to the proposal of an 'Alternative Program for Adolescent School Refusers'. In the process, a closer working relationship was developed with the Department of Education's local Home School Liaison Officer. Better links with other community and state welfare agencies were also established. As a result of these initiatives, many of the support networks that would make possible a more effective and more just response to juvenile offending in Wagga were in place when the new approach was proposed.

A key player in the next stage of the development was based not in Wagga but in Sydney. John McDonald, adviser to the Police Commissioner on Youth and Juvenile Justice, had spent part of his career – some nine years – as a school teacher. Much of that time was spent in Cabramatta and Chester Hill, areas where victimisation of and by young people is not unknown. Later, as a member of the steering committee of the *Kids in Justice* Report, McDonald had put his name to proposals for reform in the juvenile justice system (Youth Justice Coalition, 1990). He was not confident, however, that these proposals were adequate. In 1990, he travelled to New Zealand with a colleague from the Policy and Planning Branch of the Police Service. They spoke in New Zealand with police officers, welfare workers, judges and community leaders, all of whom had had some experience with the new justice system provided for by the 1989 Act. One statistic that provided a stark contrast between the arrangements on either side of the Tasman was the comparison of case disposition in New Zealand and New South Wales. In the former jurisdiction, 90 per cent of cases were dealt with by way of negotiated reparation. Only 10 per cent went to court. In New South Wales, however, over 80 per cent of alleged young offenders went straight to court (McDonald and Ireland, 1990). This seemed neither just nor efficient.

On their return to Sydney, McDonald and his colleague, Steve Ireland, produced a report proposing that a version of the New Zealand juvenile justice model be implemented in New South Wales. The key difference between the New Zealand model and that now being proposed was the choice of coordinating department. The main player in New Zealand is the welfare department. In McDonald's alternative version, the scheme would be more truly diversionary, more truly community-based, if it operated at the first point of contact with the justice system for victim and offender. The best outcome for all concerned would be achieved if the problems arising from the offence could be addressed effectively with recourse to a minimum of government departments. Logically then, the harm caused by the offence might be minimised most effectively if conferences were to be coordinated by the department responsible for that first contact – the police department.

The basic proposals in McDonald and Ireland's report received considerable support from the Police Service State Executive Group and, indeed, from other State government departments and agencies. Judge Mick Brown, who had played a key role in overhauling the New Zealand juvenile justice system, spoke about the new system in an address to members of the New South Wales parliament. McDonald subsequently canvassed the proposal among a long list of patrol commanders, without evincing great enthusiasm. The proposals were also put to Terry O'Connell in his role of Police Association Deputy President. O'Connell argued that if the philosophy of community policing were to be taken seriously, the proposals were best put not to the Police Association executive, but to members of a community in which the new model of juvenile justice might be trialed. Equally importantly, the local police who would have ultimate responsibility for implementing the new model would have to be fully consulted, and would have to be allowed and encouraged to contribute to its design. Considerable politicking would be required even to have the proposal seriously considered, let alone to have it implemented. That process of politicking began in Wagga early in 1991.

Now formally equipped with the methodology of the social sciences, O'Connell set about randomly surveying some fifty police in the Wagga Patrol.

The results revealed a not surprising scepticism about the proposals for a changed approach to juvenile justice. Certainly, officers expressed unanimous dissatisfaction with the current system in which, according to all respondents:

- young offenders were treated too leniently;
- current responses to juvenile offending largely ignored victims;
- families of young offenders often showed little interest in their child(ren);
- the whole community suffered from the effects of juvenile offending.

Despite this dissatisfaction, proposals for change were greeted warily. In the current system, at least, police knew where they stood. They viewed cautions as a soft and therefore inadequate option; they presumed that the victims of juvenile crime felt the same way. Compensation for damage was a matter for the courts alone, since arrangements for compensation could not be enforced legally if they were agreed to in the process of a police caution. Police understood the dissatisfaction with the current system felt by victims of crime but police would bear no responsibility for that dissatisfaction. If the courts were seen to be too lenient with young offenders, victims should direct their anger at the courts. Police would continue to deliver the same recidivists to court until the judges lost patience with those recidivists and had them locked away in the local detention centre. Police would later have to deal with some of them as adult offenders but the problem was solved in the short term.

O'Connell's survey confirmed that most of his colleagues were guided by three concerns when dealing with issues of juvenile justice:

- a concern with the perceived attitude of the young alleged offender – respect for police and remorse for victims were expected but often not forthcoming;
- a concern for public accountability – complaints were a constant threat, and scrutiny from internal affairs or external watchdogs was feared;
- the perception that policing was essentially about law enforcement.

Police acceptance of the current system was, like so much else in policing, a strategy of minimising risk while maintaining a modicum of discretion. It was a way of striking some sort of balance between the conflicting demands of various groups. On the one hand, police would be criticised by most academic criminologists, many welfare workers, and some journalists for being too tough on young offenders. They would be criticised by many of the same, and by legal formalists, for exercising too much discretion. On the other hand, police would be criticised by a growing victims' rights movement, by chambers of commerce and by tabloid newspaper editors for being lenient with young offenders. As long as they adhered to the growing list of disciplinary rules, however, police would be safe. As long as they retained the option of cautioning young offenders, they retained their apparent ability to influence the attitudes of these young people. And as long as they struck some sort of balance between those pundits calling for leniency and those calling for toughness –

with a slight bias in favour of the latter – the existing juvenile justice system would remain in equilibrium. People would be cynical but they would know their place. The system would be stable.

The challenge of changing this stable system appeared daunting. Change was unlikely to come from any single agency. It would require cooperation between people who could transcend a loyalty to the immediate, short-term requirements of their particular bureaucracy and who could work, instead, towards a broader, long-term goal. More importantly, it would require a new way of understanding the causes and consequences of juvenile offending. The solution to this latter problem came not from Wagga or Sydney, but from Canberra. John Braithwaite, a Professor at the Australian National University, had published his book *Crime, Shame and Reintegration* in 1989, the same year in which New Zealand's juvenile justice Act was passed. After travelling to New Zealand the following year and after reading Braithwaite's book, John McDonald contacted Braithwaite and pointed out the obvious parallels between the latter's theories and the new practices being implemented in New Zealand's justice system. The family group conference, both agreed, came very close to the sort of arrangements advocated by Braithwaite.

The connection between Braithwaite's theories and the practice of family conferencing was made again at a meeting of police, academics and justice and welfare professionals held in Wagga in mid-1991. Several of the Charles Sturt University academics in attendance were familiar with Braithwaite's work and saw the potential of McDonald's proposed scheme to translate the theories of *Crime, Shame and Reintegration* into practice. David Moore suggested that Braithwaite's terminology be used in the debate from that point on; that people be encouraged to debate the merits of 'reintegrative shaming'.

The point of the proposal to debate the relevance of Braithwaite's theories in Wagga was not so much to augment the status of the proposed program – although it had that effect. Rather, the link with Braithwaite's theories would give whatever practices emerged in Wagga a clear point of reference – a link with some carefully articulated and defensible values. New practices could be checked for conformity with the key values of the theoretical model. Indeed, Braithwaite's co-authored work *Not Just Deserts*, published in 1990, provided a comprehensive list of values that should inform what he and his co-author call 'a republican system of justice'. According to Braithwaite and Pettit (1990), agencies within such a system would share the principles of: parsimony or frugality; checking the power of officials and agencies; reprobation of inappropriate behaviour; and social reintegration of those who have offended against the ethical principles underlying official laws. If the proposed new model of justice violated any of these four principles, it would be unacceptable.

The cautious approval of the proposed model by a group of academics and justice and welfare professionals was matched by the willingness of Wagga's Community Consultative Committee to support a pilot scheme of family conferencing in their city. Members of the committee had already considered the option of experimenting with Community Aid Panels as an alternative approach to the cautioning of young offenders. But they were aware that the South Australian Parliament was about to phase Children's Aid Panels out of the juvenile justice system after a decade-and-a-half of exceedingly modest success (Wundersitz, 1992; Juvenile Justice Advisory Council, 1993). Family conferences looked like a more meaningful option.

The next obstacle to implementation was the difficulty of convincing a group of understandably cautious and collectively cynical police to agree to a trial of the proposed scheme. The way forward was to get those involved in beat policing and general duties to consider the following assertions:

- police are the gatekeepers of the criminal justice system, key players in the initial intervention for a transgression of the law;

- the nature of the initial intervention has a significant influence on whatever process follows;

- the decision whether to caution or send a young alleged offender to court is generally taken as a result of this initial intervention;

- victims and police are generally unimpressed with the outcome of court cases for young alleged offenders.

Consequently, any means of increasing the impact of a police caution without violating the rights of the young person concerned, and any means of involving the victim in the process, should prove more acceptable to police and to victims. It may also produce a better outcome for the young offender and the young offender's family. It might also, therefore, represent a better overall outcome for police.

The surveyed officers found these suggestions uncontroversial. It was proposed then, that a new method of juvenile cautioning should be introduced, and that the new method would make use of the family conferencing model from New Zealand. Its aim would be to 'maximise the impact of juvenile cautioning'. However, the police working party established to consider this approach quickly decided that the stated aim implied an exclusive focus on the young offender. Such a focus would, they argued, lead police to create a scheme with the same flaws as the existing system. An exclusive focus on the young offender would ignore the interests and concerns of the victim. It would ignore the interests of parents and friends of the victim, and parents and friends of the offender. It would do little to accommodate the concerns of the police who were seeking to address not only the consequences but also the causes of offending behaviour. Accordingly, the single, ill-defined aim of 'maximising the impact of juvenile cautioning' was replaced with a set of seven objectives:

- to ensure that the young offender understands the seriousness of his/her offending behaviour;

- to minimise the likelihood of the young person reoffending;

- to provide the juvenile offender with an opportunity to accept responsibility for his/her offending behaviour;

- to address the issue of family and community accountability;

- to provide the victim(s) with an opportunity to contribute to the cautioning process;

- to increase the likelihood of achieving reparation compensation for the victim;

- to enable police to offer a more meaningful response to the harm caused by young offenders.

The conference process was then developed to meet these objectives. The sergeant convening a conference would contact the victim of an offence and explain the rationale of the process. If the victim was willing to attend a conference, contact would then be made with the offender and the offender's family. Since the focus of the conference was the offence rather than the character of the young offender or the psychological state of the victim, more than one victim or offender might be involved. Indeed, all of the victims and all of the offenders involved in a given incident could attend the conference. The supporters of both parties would contribute during the conference process but would also act as subsequent guarantors of any agreement reached at that conference. Unless unreasonable demands were made, the nature of the agreements would be left largely to the discretion of the key parties involved in the dispute and to their supporters. And this was a leap of faith on the part of the officers establishing the scheme. If unreasonable demands were made the scheme would quickly lose both credibility and legitimacy.

The task of reviewing cases and convening all cautions involving family conferences was initially given to two sergeants. Terry O'Connell dealt with the first few cases, which involved vandalism, stolen motorbikes and other property offences. Full material restitution was achieved in all cases, but O'Connell was more impressed by the change of attitude on the part of victims and offenders. A degree of mutual respect was restored. Victims and offenders who had entered the conference room as enemies dramatically changed their opinion of each other during the course of the conference. Victims wanted to have their say; they wanted any stolen goods returned; they wanted an apology. But they appeared to have no interest in retributive punishment as such [. . .].

Positive reports about these early conferences arrived unsolicited at the police station. Intelligent media coverage was given to an agreement reached between a group of high school students and the owner of a carwash that had been damaged by the students during a 'treasure hunt'.

The apparent success of some of these first conferences convinced many of O'Connell's sceptical colleagues that there might be more scope for diversion as an alternative to court. Reports suggested that the family conference was not just another 'soft option' as the sceptics had feared it would be. Satisfactory agreements for compensation had been reached; longstanding disputes had been resolved; victims felt relieved of much of their anger, and satisfied that they had 'got through' to the young offender. Enthusiastic support for the new scheme by many who had attended a family conference prompted the search for a stronger institutional framework, and that search led, in turn, to the formation of a sergeants' review panel. This group began to meet weekly, in order to decide whether a young person who had been charged and had admitted an offence should be given the option of attending a family conference or should be sent to court, as would hitherto have been the case. Since guilt is readily acknowledged by most young offenders, the sergeants were faced with the option of diverting most cases to a family conference rather than to court. The extent to which they exercised that diversionary option was a measure of their growing confidence in the new cautioning scheme.

An additional effect of the new arrangement is illustrated dramatically in the Wagga Police charge books for this period. The number of charges for minor public order offences (many of which amount to 'lack of respect for police officer') began to decline rapidly. There appear to be two reasons for this. One is that general duties police officers had to take account of the fact that a panel of sergeants would review any charge they might make and would not take kindly to trivialities that involved the wounded pride of an officer on the beat or on patrol. A second and perhaps more significant reason seems to be that the rationale for charging young people is shifting. Increasingly, the real issue is not whether there has been some minor technical infringement of the law, but whether anybody had been a victim of the offending behaviour. Anticipating the sergeants' review process, and having the option to involve victims, seems to be causing police to reassess the purpose of their intervention when young people offend.

Here we have a system, then, with much to recommend it. Early assessments [. . .] suggest that the conference process offers an outcome that victims, offenders and the supporters of both consider to be more just, more constructive and more meaningful than that offered by other juvenile processes. Furthermore, the family conference allows policy to play a much more constructive role in the juvenile justice system. It also encourages them to think more carefully about the purpose of their work. [. . .]

Theory

[. . .]

Braithwaite does not ask why some people break the law some of the time, but why most people obey the law most of the time. His answer is not that people are generally deterred by the threat of official punishment. Rather, they are deterred from offending against their fellow citizens by two 'informal' controls; firstly the potential of social disapproval that would greet an offending act; and secondly, by pangs of conscience. The pressure to conform with collective values is thus applied both externally in the form of disapproval – and internally – through conscience. Only when these two informal controls fail is the state obliged to respond with the formal control of punishment. This is one of those insights that seems so obvious that it is hard to understand why few have managed to state it so clearly. But the really profound aspect of Braithwaite's theory is his recognition that the underlying aims of formal state control and informal social control can be diametrically opposed. Formal, official punishment seeks to stigmatise those who have transgressed the law; it aims to separate them from the law-abiding majority. It does this in varying degrees, all of which are degrading. [. . .]

In contrast to formal, official punishment, which generally seeks to stigmatise offenders, informal, unofficial punishment generally seeks their social reintegration. And according to Braithwaite, the key to understanding social reintegration is the phenomenon of shame. When people seek to avoid social disapproval and when they feel pangs of conscience, they are avoiding one form of shame and experiencing another. They are avoiding what Carl Schneider has called 'disgrace shame'. They are experiencing a milder form of shame which Schneider calls 'discretion shame' (Schneider, 1977, ch. 3). The exercise of this discretion shame prevents people from transgressing against their fellow citizens. It provides a psychological means to distinguish that which is socially appropriate from that which is not.

If this analysis is correct, then shame is not the destructive phenomenon from which twentieth-century psychoanalysis has sought to liberate us. On the contrary, shame is essential to the regulation of social life. It is a vital emotion of self-assessment. Simultaneously cognitive and emotive, it helps to determine an appropriate balance between excessive closeness to one's fellow citizens, on one hand, and excessive distance from them on the other. It is certainly true that, in a world of social inequality, shame has been put to unjust uses. Whole classes of people have been socialised to feel shame where it suits the purposes of the more politically and economically powerful. Totalitarian leaders, themselves afflicted with exotic shame-based pathologies, have generally understood the phenomenon with an unusual degree of perception. The libertarian conclusion that the social consequences of shame are inherently negative is nevertheless a profound error. Shame can be used for negative or destructive purposes – as can hydrogen or oxygen. On balance, however, the social function of shame is positive: social life is regulated by shame, and by other emotions of self-assessment such as shame's counterpart – pride.

The claim that most people are deterred from offending against their fellow citizens by the feeling of discretion shame and the fear of disgrace shame has profound consequences for our understanding of contemporary criminal justice systems. The processes of criminal justice systems, such as court trials, are designed to make use of shame in order to stigmatise people who have transgressed the law. Shame is used destructively, to set offenders apart from the law-abiding majority. One of the more concise and best-known justifications for the use of shame as a means of stigmatising offenders is Garfinkel's short piece, 'Conditions of Successful Degradation Ceremonies' (1956). As people familiar with this classic of the literature will know, Garfinkel calls the central processes of the criminal justice system 'ceremonies of degradation'. Such ceremonies aim to convey to the offender the moral indignation felt by the wider community. Garfinkel's justification for ceremonies of degradation is strongly utilitarian. In an argument taken directly from Durkheim, degradation ceremonies are said to promote social solidarity. Shared moral indignation draws a community closer together and this is deemed to be a fine thing. It is also claimed that degradation ceremonies serve to remake the offender. Behind this claim is a belief in the hierarchical ordering of society. Having offended against the moral order enshrined in the law, offenders are literally degraded. They are moved to a lower and more appropriate position on the league ladder of human worth, a position deemed commensurate with their illegal and immoral behaviour.

At the heart of Garfinkel's argument is his understanding of the role of shame in the ceremony of degradation. Garfinkel argues that shame serves to protect a person's ego from further attack; it sets the individual apart from the morally indignant collective. Indeed, it is by evoking shame that the degradation process successfully stigmatises and degrades an offender. But two questions spring to mind immediately: is Garfinkel's understanding of the role of shame in degradation processes correct? Secondly, regardless of the accuracy of his explanation of *how* shame operates in the justice system, is Garfinkel's defence of the aim of these processes adequate? Does he provide a convincing answer to the question of *why* the system should aim for degradation rather than persuasion and social reintegration? A generation after Garfinkel penned his well-known piece, Braithwaite answers all of these questions in the negative. The question of how shame operates within justice system ceremonies requires complex answers, some of which have been provided elsewhere (Braithwaite, 1989; Moore, 1993b). However, these answers need not be included in a response to the question of why the justice system should or should not seek to degrade offenders.

Consciously evoking Garfinkel's original formula, Braithwaite and Mugford (1993) rebut his arguments and argue the case against ceremonies of degradation. Instead, they advocate ceremonies of reintegration. The criminal justice system, as they see it, should aim not to degrade those who have committed a criminal offence. Rather, it should seek to integrate such people back into the society against which they have offended. Unless one is prepared to suggest that mistakes can neither be forgiven nor learned from – unless, that is, one wishes to side with the world's backward-looking fundamentalists – one has to recognise that offenders must be reintegrated into society at some point after the official recognition of their offence. Stigmatising offenders, and then weakening their links with family, friends and colleagues by removing them from society, must work directly against the long-term aim of social reintegration. The system should also seek the social reintegration of victims by helping them to deal with their anger and resentment, by teaching them the superficially paradoxical lesson that they need not be ashamed of feeling shame.

[. . .]

A ceremony of reintegration should not seek to equate the ongoing moral status of the offender with the permanent unacceptability of the offence. Rather, a ceremony of reintegration should draw a distinction between the offence and the person who committed it. The behaviour cannot be condoned. The offender, however, should be offered an opportunity to rejoin the moral community which has rejected the offending behaviour. In a truly democratic society, the people most entitled to make a judgment about an instance of offending behaviour would be those most affected by that behaviour: the victim(s), the family, friends and colleagues of the victim(s), and the family and friends of the offender(s). With their fourteen conditions for a successful reintegration ceremony, Braithwaite and Mugford are suggesting one way to achieve this and thus to promote a justice system that is really more just.

The effective cautioning scheme in Wagga, utilising the family conference as its successful reintegration ceremony, has been modified to take account of some of Braithwaite and Mugford's fourteen conditions. But it has met most of these conditions since its inception in 1991, just as it has met the basic institutional conditions for a republican or communitarian system of justice. Admittedly, the scheme deals only with the legal transgressions of one section of the population, as provided for in the Police Commissioner's standing orders on juvenile cautioning. The scheme is also limited to certain categories of offences; police are not legally entitled to convene cautions to deal with serious indictable offences. The apparent success of the scheme nevertheless suggests ways in which the justice system might gradually be transformed in order to provide a more acceptable outcome for all concerned.

Responding to the critics

[. . .]

[A] criticism of the scheme, as articulated by John Seymour in his major study of juvenile justice in Australia, is that 'informal' responses to criminal offences may deprive alleged offenders of important rights (Seymour, 1988, ch. 6). This concern raises a host of questions about our entire common law system, questions with which we cannot deal here. It seems a little glib to say simply, as we will have to, that only in cases where there is no denial of guilt will the sergeant's panel consider giving offender(s) and victim(s) the option of a family conference rather than court. Nevertheless, since there is no denial of guilt in around 90 per cent of juvenile justice cases under existing arrangements, that leaves perhaps 10 per cent of young offenders who may feel coerced by the existence of an alternative to court. It should be noted that, for this minority, an escape clause remains. At the start of each conference a formal statement is made to the young offender(s) and to their family. They are advised that they may call a halt to the proceedings at any stage and, without prejudice, exercise their right to have the matter referred to a court hearing. Since nobody has exercised that right to date, we are unable to report further on what might trigger a decision to opt for court rather than conference.

The family conference addresses a lack of conformity to the ethical standards of a community, rather than to the technical rules of common or statutory law. It is simply unethical to steal someone else's motorbike or the clothes from their washing-line, break into their house, burn their possessions or clobber them with a piece of two-by-four. It should be the ethical unacceptability of such actions, rather than their illegality, that is emphasised in any response to actions of this sort. The family conference emphasises the ethical unacceptability of any sort of victimisation, while simultaneously offering the person responsible for the behaviour the chance to rejoin the moral community. There is, of course, a close match between ethical standards and laws. The philosophy informing the cautioning scheme, however, holds that a collective confirmation of the ethical standards of a community should serve to strengthen social bonds within that community. Conversely, a response that recruits legal officials to deal with conflict within a community may have a debilitating effect on that community.

Interestingly, young offenders who have had the pleasure of a court appearance at some stage prior to their appearance at a family conference have regularly made the comment that the court appearance was 'useless' or a 'joke', and that the real impact of their offending behaviour only became clear to them when they were confronted by the victim(s) of their behaviour in the context of their own community of family and friends. Many victims have also described the court process to us as a 'joke' – but a joke they find exceedingly unfunny. One victim of a crime who recently struggled to attend a family conference with a leg in plaster said after the experience that she would have made it there even with both legs in plaster, knowing as she now did how much more satisfying the experience was in contrast to an earlier court case in which she had been involved. As is the case with most victims once they are actually involved in the process, she did not want the young offenders punished. She did, however, want them to understand the impact of their behaviour and she felt confident afterwards that they had indeed understood. She certainly did not want the young offenders to laugh mockingly at her, as had happened after she had sat in silence through an earlier court case. Shame felt for a breach of an ethical code is something very different to the admission of technical guilt (Moore, 1993b). Victims understand this; some legal formalists appear not to.

The contrast drawn here between the ethical standards upheld in a family conference and the legal rules enforced by courts has made use of strong communitarian language. The implication throughout has been that calls for the full exercise of individual rights should be balanced by calls for a full recognition of individual and collective responsibilities. Again, this raises complex philosophical issues, few of which can be addressed here (*see* ibid). In practice, those who attend family conferences seem to have no problem offering a collective exercise in reparation and harm minimisation in response to individual acts of offending. A common misunderstanding of the critics, however, has been to assume some sort of inverse proportionality between rights and responsibilities: as one increases responsibilities, so one diminishes rights. But this is fatuous. Totalitarian regimes are strong on responsibilities to the collective and weak on individual rights. Libertarians are strong on rights and weak on responsibilities. Vibrant, democratic communities, however, are strong on both rights and responsibilities. They guarantee rights while also requiring their members not to neglect their responsibilities – and not to infringe the rights of others. [. . .]

Conclusion

In Wagga, only two years after the alternative cautioning scheme began operation, staff at local and district schools began debating whether the approach taken by police should not, in turn, force schools to review their approach to matters of discipline, education, and social support. The consensus was that a review would be appropriate. Police certainly agreed with this assessment. They are as aware as anyone that police cannot work in isolation, nor can they provide the additional support required by many young people – although the Police and Citizens' Youth Club do their bit. However, when explaining the principle behind their cautioning scheme to school staff, O'Connell and colleagues began with a warning and disclaimer: don't see this simply as a cautioning scheme. Conferences are convened legitimately under the provisions for cautioning young offenders. But as we have learned, conferences are not just about young offenders, nor are they simply concerned with redress for victims. They are an effective way of reaching collective agreement that we need to respect the rights of fellow citizens and fulfil our responsibilities to them. These are conferences about community accountability.

To emphasise the point, and to mark the end of its first two years, the scheme's standard terminology was changed in August 1993. Rather than talking about an effective cautioning scheme using family conferences, police and other members of the community are now talking about 'community accountability conferences'. Those who have experienced such a conference know that the phrase 'community accountability' comes close to capturing the complexity of the processes that occur in a conference. The critics may still need persuading. Few of the participants do. They have experienced an alternative response to the problems caused by the offending behaviour of young people. That alternative response is neither a hard option nor a soft option. It is an effective option, and one that treats people with respect. It provides a practical demonstration that 'mobilising the resources of the community' really can produce a more constructive and more just response to incivility and crime.

This extract is taken from 'Family Conferencing in Wagga Wagga: a Communitarian Model of Justice', by D.B. Moore and T.A. O'Connell, in J. Alder and J. Wundersitz (eds), Family Conferencing and Juvenile Justice *(Canberra: Australian Institute of Criminology), pp. 45–86.*

References

Braithwaite, J. (1989) *Crime, Shame and Reintegration* (Cambridge: Cambridge Univ. Press).

Braithwaite, J. and Pettit, P. (1990) *Not Just Deserts* (Oxford: Oxford University Press).

Braithwaite, J. and Mugford, S. (1994) 'Conditions of Successful Reintegration Ceremonies', *British Journal of Criminology*, 32:2.

Garfinkel, H. (1956) 'Conditions of Successful Degradation Ceremonies', *American Journal of Sociology*, 61, pp. 420–4.

Goldstein, H. (1990) *Problem-oriented Policing* (New York, NY: McGraw-Hill).

Juvenile Justice Advisory Council of New South Wales (1993) *Green Paper: Future Directions in Juvenile Justice* (Sydney).

McDonald, J. and Ireland, S. (1990) 'Can it be Done Another Way?' Internal Report to the New South Wales Police Service, Sydney.

Moore, D.B. (1993a) 'Facing the Consequences', in Atkinson, L. and Gerull, S.A. (eds) *National Conference on Juvenile Justice. Conference Proceedings* 22 (Canberra: Australian Institute of Criminology).

Moore, D.B. (1993b) 'Shame, Forgiveness and Juvenile Justice,' *Criminal Justice Ethics*, 12:1, pp. 3–25.

Schneider, C.D. (1977) *Shame, Exposure and Privacy* (Boston, MA: Beacon).

Seymour, J. (1988) *Dealing with Young Offenders* (Sydney: The Law Book Company).

Wundersitz, J. (1992) 'The Netwidening Effect of Aid Panels and Screening Panels in the South Australian Juvenile Justice System', *Australian and New Zealand Journal of Criminology*, 25, pp. 115–34.

Youth Justice Coalition (NSW) (1990) *Kids in Justice: A Blueprint for the 90s* (Sydney).

16. A comparison of four restorative conferencing models

Gordon Bazemore and Mark Umbreit

[. . .]

Victim–offender mediation

Background and concept

Although still unfamiliar to many mainstream juvenile and criminal justice audiences and marginal to the court process in some jurisdictions where they do operate, victim–offender mediation programs – referred to in some communities as 'victim–offender reconciliation programs' and, increasingly as 'victim–offender dialog programs' – have a respectable 20-year track record in the United States, Canada, and Europe. Currently, there are approximately 320 victim–offender mediation programs in the United States and Canada and more than 700 in Europe. Several programs in North America currently receive nearly 1,000 case referrals annually from local courts. Although the greatest proportion of cases involve less serious property crimes committed by young people, the process is used increasingly in response to serious and violent crimes committed by both juveniles and adults (Umbreit, 1997).

The victim–offender mediation process offers victims an opportunity to meet offenders in a safe, structured setting and engage in a mediated discussion of the crime.[1] With the assistance of a trained mediator, the victim is able to tell the offender about the crime's physical, emotional, and financial impact; receive answers to lingering questions about the crime and the offender; and be directly involved in developing a restitution plan for the offender to pay back any financial debt to the victim. The process is different from mediation as practiced in civil or commercial disputes, because the involved parties are in agreement about their respective roles in the crime. Also, the process should not be primarily focused on reaching a settlement, although most sessions do, in fact, result in a signed restitution agreement.[2] Because of these fundamental differences, the terms 'victim–offender meeting', 'conferencing', and 'dialog' are becoming increasingly popular to describe variations from standard mediation practices (Umbreit, 1997).

Procedures and goals

Cases may be referred to victim–offender mediation programs by judges, probation officers, victim advocates, prosecutors, defense attorneys, and law enforcement. In some programs, cases are primarily referred as a diversion

---

An example of a victim–offender mediation session

The victim was a middle-aged woman. The offender, a 14-year-old neighbor of the victim, had broken into the victim's home and stolen a VCR. The mediation session took place in the basement of the victim's church.

In the presence of a mediator, the victim and offender talked for 2 hours. At times, their conversation was heated and emotional. When they finished, the mediator felt that they had heard each other's stories and learned something important about the impact of the crime and about each other.

The participants agreed that the offender would pay $200 in restitution to cover the cost of damages to the victim's home resulting from the break-in and would also reimburse the victim for the cost of the stolen VCR (estimated at $150). They also worked out a payment schedule.

During the session, the offender made several apologies to the victim and agreed to complete community service hours working in a food bank sponsored by the victim's church. The victim said that she felt less angry and fearful after learning more about the offender and the details of the crime. She also thanked the mediator for allowing the session to be held at her church.

---

from prosecution (assuming that any agreement reached during the mediation session is successfully completed). In other programs, cases are usually referred after a formal admission of guilt has been accepted by the court, with mediation being a condition of probation or other disposition (if the victim has volunteered to participate). Some programs receive case referrals at both stages.

During mediation sessions, victims explain how the crime affected them and are given the opportunity to ask questions about the incident and help develop a plan for restoring losses. Offenders are given the opportunity to tell their stories and take direct responsibility through making amends in some form (Umbreit, 1994).

The goals of victim–offender mediation include the following:

- Supporting the healing process of victims by providing a safe, controlled setting for them to meet and speak with offenders on a strictly voluntary basis.

- Allowing offenders to learn about the impact of their crimes on the victims and take direct responsibility for their behavior.

- Providing an opportunity for the victim and offender to develop a mutually acceptable plan that addresses the harm caused by the crime.

Considerations in implementation

In implementing any victim–offender mediation program, it is critically important to maintain sensitivity to the needs of the victim. First and foremost, the mediator must do everything possible to ensure that the victim will not be harmed in any way. Additionally, the victim's participation must be completely voluntary. The offender's participation should also be voluntary. Offenders are typically given the option of participating in mediation or dialogue as one of several dispositional choices. Although offenders almost never have absolute choice (e.g. the option of no juvenile justice intervention), they should never be coerced into meetings with victims. The victim should also be given choices, whenever possible, about procedures, such as when and where the mediation session will take place, who will be present, and who will speak first. Cases should be carefully screened regarding the readiness of both victim and offender to participate. The mediator should conduct in-person premediation sessions with both parties to clarify the issues to be resolved. The mediator should also make followup contacts and monitor any agreement reached.

Lessons learned

A large multisite study of victim–offender mediation programs with juvenile offenders (Umbreit, 1994) found the following:

- In cases referred to the four study-site programs during a 2-year period, 95 per cent of mediation sessions resulted in a successfully negotiated restitution agreement to restore the victim's financial losses.

- Victims who met with offenders in the presence of a trained mediator were more likely to be satisfied with the justice system than were similar victims who went through the standard court process (79 per cent versus 57 per cent).

- After meeting offenders, victims were significantly less fearful of being revictimized.

- Offenders who met with victims were far more likely to successfully complete their restitution obligation than were similar offenders who did not participate in mediation (81 per cent versus 58 per cent).

- Recidivism rates were lower among offenders who participated in mediation than among offenders who did not participate (18 per cent versus 27 per cent); furthermore, participating offenders' subsequent crimes tended to be less serious.[3]

Multisite studies (Coates and Gehm, 1989; Umbreit, 1994) also found that although restitution was an important motivator for victim participation in mediation sessions, victims consistently viewed actual receipt of restitution as secondary to the opportunity to talk about the impact of the crime, meet the offender, and learn the offender's circumstances. The studies also found that offenders appreciated the opportunity to talk to the victim and felt better after doing so.

A recent statewide survey of victim service providers in Minnesota found that 91 per cent believed that victim–offender mediation should be available in every judicial district because it represents an important victim service. The American Bar Association recently endorsed victim–offender mediation and recommends its use throughout the United States. As of 1997, victim–offender mediation programs have been identified in nearly every State (Umbreit and Schug, 1997).

[. . .]

Community reparative boards

Background and concept

The community reparative board is a recent version of a much older and more widespread community sanctioning response to youth crime, generally known by such terms as youth panels, neighborhood boards, or community diversion boards. These panels or boards have been in use in the United States since the 1920s, and their contemporary counterparts, reparative boards, have been in use since the mid-1990s, principally in Vermont. There, the boards are primarily used with adult offenders convicted of nonviolent and minor offences; more recently, the boards have also been used with juvenile offenders.[4] Reparative boards typically are composed of a small group of citizens, prepared for their function by intensive training, who conduct public, face-to-face meetings with offenders ordered by the court to participate in the process. The boards develop sanction agreement with offenders, monitor compliance, and submit compliance reports to the court.

Procedures and goals

During reparative board meetings, board members discuss with the offender the nature of the offence and its negative consequences. Then board members develop a set of proposed sanctions, which they discuss with the offender until an agreement is reached on the specific actions the offender will take within a given time period to make reparation for the crime. Subsequently, the offender must document his or her progress in fulfilling the terms of the agreement. After the stipulated period of time has passed, the board submits a report to the court on the offender's compliance with the agreed-upon sanctions. At this point, the board's involvement with the offender ends.

The goals of community reparative boards include the following:

- Promoting citizens' ownership of the criminal and juvenile justice systems by involving them directly in the justice process.

- Providing an opportunity for victims and community members to confront offenders in a constructive manner about their behavior.

- Providing opportunities for offenders to take personal responsibility and be held directly accountable for the harm they caused to victims and communities.

- Generating meaningful community-driven consequences for criminal and delinquent actions, thereby reducing costly reliance on formal justice system processing.

Considerations in implementation

The Vermont Department of Corrections implemented its Reparative Probation Program in 1995, in response to a 1994 public opinion survey (conducted
by John Doble and Associates) in which citizens indicated broad support for
programs with a reparative emphasis and active community involvement. The
program's reparative boards are part of a mandated separation of probation
into community corrections service units (designed to provide supervision for
more serious cases) and court and reparative service units (which coordinate
and provide administrative support to reparative boards).

   Based on Vermont's experience, the following factors have been identified
by the Vermont Department of Corrections as important in implementing
community-driven reparative board programs.

- Marketing the program effectively to the justice system (to judges, prosecutors, and defense attorneys).

- Having a committed, well-trained staff.

- Working with victim organizations and ensuring that victims are represented
  and provided adequate opportunity to participate.[5]

- Processing cases expeditiously and in a manner that is easy for community
  members to understand.

- Facilitating a positive experience for the board members.

- Providing quality training for the boards.

- Supporting the program with adequate resources (e.g. space, time, and staff).

- Striving for successful outcomes for offenders, victims, and community
  participants in the board's initial cases.

- Getting support from judges in limiting the time the offender is in the
  program and on probation.

Lessons learned

Only limited quantitative data have been collected on the effectiveness of
community reparative boards. There is growing concern that evaluations of
reparative board programs should consider measures beyond the standard
offender-focused measure of recidivism. Additional measures should include
responsiveness to victim and community needs, victim and community
satisfaction, and impact on the community (including physical improvements
resulting from board-imposed community work sanctions and indicators of
healthy relationships among citizens). At this point, experiential and anecdotal
information indicates that reparative boards show much promise as an effective
response to nonviolent crime.

   [. . .]

An example of a community reparative board session

The reparative board convened to consider the case of a 17-year-old who had been caught driving with an open can of beer in his father's pickup truck. The youth had been sentenced by a judge to reparative probation, and it was the board's responsibility to decide what form the probation should take. For about 30 minutes, the citizen members of the board asked the youth several simple, straightforward questions. The board members then went to another room to deliberate on an appropriate sanction for the youth. The youth awaited the board's decision nervously, because he did not know whether to expect something tougher or much easier than regular probation.

When the board returned, the chairperson explained the four conditions of the offender's probation contract: (1) begin work to pay off his traffic tickets, (2) complete a State police defensive driving course, (3) undergo an alcohol assessment, and (4) write a three-page paper on how alcohol had negatively affected his life. The youth signed the contract, and the chairperson adjourned the meeting.

Family group conferencing

Background and concept

Family group conferencing is based on centuries-old sanctioning and dispute resolution traditions of the Maori of New Zealand. In its modern form, the model was adopted into national legislation in New Zealand in 1989, making it the most systemically institutionalized of any of the four models. In South Australia, family conferencing is now widely used in modified form as a police-initiated diversion approach known as the Wagga Wagga model. (Developed by the Wagga Wagga Police Department, this model uses police

---

An example of a family group conferencing session

A family conferencing group convened in a local school to consider a case in which a student had injured a teacher and broken the teacher's glasses in an altercation. Group members included the offender, his mother and grandfather, the victim, the police officer who made the arrest, and about 10 other interested parties (including 2 of the offender's teachers and 2 friends of the victim).

The conferencing process began with comments by the offender, his mother and grandfather, the victim, and the arresting officer. Each spoke about the offense and its impact. The youth justice coordinator next asked for input from the other group members and then asked all participants what they thought the offender should do to pay back the victim and the community for the damage caused by his crime. In the remaining 30 minutes of the hour-long conference, the group suggested that the offender should make restitution to the victim for his medical expenses and the cost of new glasses and that the offender should also perform community service work on the school grounds.

officers or school officials to set up and facilitate family conferencing meetings.) Conferencing is also being used in US cities in Minnesota, Montana, Pennsylvania, Vermont, and several other States and in parts of Canada. (The Wagga Wagga model is the primary approach that has taken hold in North America.) A variety of offences have been resolved through family group conferencing, including theft, arson, minor assaults, drug offences, vandalism, and, in a number of States, child maltreatment cases. In New Zealand, conferencing is used in the disposition of all but the most violent and serious delinquency cases (Alder and Wundersitz, 1994; Maxwell and Morris, 1993; McElrea, 1993).

Family group conferencing involves the community of people most affected by the crime – the victim, the offender, and the family, friends, and key supporters of both – in deciding the resolution of a criminal or delinquent incident. The affected parties are brought together by a trained facilitator to discuss how they and others have been harmed by the offence and how that harm might be repaired.

Procedures and goals

The conference facilitator contacts the victim and offender to explain the process and invite them to the conference. The facilitator also asks the victim and offender to identify key members of their support systems, who also will be invited to participate. The conference typically begins with the offender describing the incident. The other participants then describe the impact of the incident on their lives. Some argue that it is preferable to allow the victim to start the discussion, if he or she wishes to do so (Umbreit and Stacy, 1996). Through these narrations, the offender is faced with the impact of his or her behavior on the victim, on those close to the victim, and on the offender's own family and friends, and the victim has the opportunity to express feelings and ask questions about the incident. After a thorough discussion of impacts, the victim is asked to identify desired outcomes from the conference; in this way, the victim can help to shape the obligations that will be placed on the offender. All participants contribute to the problem-solving process of determining how the offender might best repair the harm he or she has caused. The session ends with participants signing an agreement that outlines their expectations and commitments.

Goals of family group conferencing include the following:

- Providing an opportunity for the victim to be directly involved in the discussion of the offence and in decisions regarding appropriate sanctions to be placed on the offender.

- Increasing the offender's awareness of the human impact of his or her behavior and providing the offender an opportunity to take full responsibility for it.

- Engaging the collective responsibility of the offender's support system for making amends and shaping the offender's future behavior.

- Allowing both offender and victim to reconnect to key community support systems.

Considerations in implementation

The family group conferencing process has been implemented in schools, police departments, probation offices, residential programs, community mediation programs, and neighborhood groups. Conferencing is most often used as diversion from the court process for juveniles but can also be used after adjudication and disposition to address unresolved issues or determine specific terms of restitution. Conferencing programs have been implemented within single agencies and developed collaboratively among several agencies. After completing a training course, either volunteers or paid employees can serve as conference facilitators.

Participation by all involved in conferences is voluntary. In addition to the victim and offender and their family members, a conference might involve teachers, other relatives, peers, special adult friends, and community resource people.

Lessons learned

To date, two studies have been conducted to assess the impact of family group conferencing with young offenders. One study (Maxwell and Morris, 1993) assessed the impact of New Zealand's mandating the widespread use of conferencing. It found that families of offenders in conferencing programs are more frequently and actively involved in the justice process than are families of offenders whose cases are handled by standard procedures. It also found that offenders, victims, and their families described the conference process as helpful. Preliminary evaluations of conferencing programs in the United States also indicate high levels of victim satisfaction with the conference process and high rates of offender compliance with agreements reached during conferences (Fercello and Umbreit, 1999; McCold and Wachtel, 1998).

Practitioners involved in family group conferencing programs observe a reduction in fear for many victims. When used as a diversion from court, conferencing can provide a much speedier and more satisfying resolution of incidents than would otherwise be the case. Family group conferencing also builds community skills in conflict resolution and participatory decisionmaking.

[. . .]

Circle sentencing

Background and concept

Circle sentencing is an updated version of the traditional sanctioning and healing practices of aboriginal peoples in Canada and American Indians in the United States (Stuart, 1995; Melton, 1995). Sentencing circles – sometimes called peacemaking circles – were resurrected in 1991 by judges and community justice committees in the Yukon Territory and other northern Canadian communities. Circle sentencing has been developed most extensively in Saskatchewan, Manitoba, and the Yukon and has been used occasionally in several other communities. Its use spread to the United States in 1996, when a pilot project was initiated in Minnesota. Circle sentencing has been used for adult and juvenile offenders, for a variety of offences, and in both rural and urban settings.

Circle sentencing is a holistic reintegrative strategy designed not only to address the criminal and delinquent behavior of offenders but also to consider the needs of victims, families, and communities. Within the 'circle', crime victims, offenders, family and friends of both, justice and social service personnel, and interested community residents speak from the heart in a shared search for an understanding of the event. Together they identify the steps necessary to assist in healing all affected parties and prevent future crimes. The significance of the circle is more than symbolic: all circle members – police officers, lawyers, judges, victims, offenders, and community residents – participate in deliberations to arrive at a consensus for a sentencing plan that addresses the concerns of all interested parties.

Procedures and goals

Circle sentencing typically involves a multi-step procedure that includes (1) application by the offender to participate in the circle process, (2) a healing circle for the victim, (3) a healing circle for the offender, (4) a sentencing circle to develop consensus on the elements of a sentencing plan, and (5) followup circles to monitor the progress of the offender. In addition to commitments by the offender, the sentencing plan may incorporate commitments by the justice system, community, and family members. Specifics of the circle process vary from community to community and are designed locally to fit community needs and culture.

Goals of circle sentencing include the following:

- Promoting healing for all affected parties.
- Providing an opportunity for the offender to make amends.
- Empowering victims, community members, families, and offenders by giving them a voice and a shared responsibility in finding constructive resolutions.
- Addressing the underlying causes of criminal behavior.
- Building a sense of community and its capacity for resolving conflict.
- Promoting and sharing community values.

Considerations in implementation

The success of the circle sentencing process depends to a large extent on a healthy partnership between the formal juvenile justice system and the

An example of a circle sentencing session

The victim was a middle-aged man whose parked car had been badly damaged when the offender, a 16-year-old, crashed into it while joyriding in another vehicle. The offender had also damaged a police vehicle.

In the circle, the victim talked about the emotional shock of seeing what had happened to his car and his costs to repair it (he was uninsured). Then, an elder leader of the First Nations community where the circle sentencing session was being held (and an uncle of the offender) expressed his disappointment and anger with the boy. The elder observed that this incident, along with several prior offenses by the boy, had brought shame to his family. The elder also noted that in the old days, the boy would have been required to pay the victim's family substantial compensation as a result of such behavior. After the elder finished, a feather (the 'talking piece') was passed to the next person in the circle, a young man who spoke about the contributions the offender had made to the community, the kindness he had shown towards elders, and his willingness to help others with home repairs.

Having heard all this, the judge asked the Crown Council (Canadian prosecutor) and the public defender, who were also sitting in the circle, to make statements and then asked if anyone else in the circle wanted to speak. The Royal Canadian Mounted Police officer, whose vehicle had also been damaged, then took the feather and spoke on the offender's behalf. The officer proposed to the judge that in lieu of statutorily required jail time for the offense, the offender be allowed to meet with him on a regular basis for counseling and community service. After asking the victim and the prosecutor if either had any objections, the judge accepted this proposal. The judge also ordered restitution to the victim and asked the young adult who had spoken on the offender's behalf to serve as a mentor for the offender.

After a prayer in which the entire group held hands, the circle disbanded and everyone retreated to the kitchen area of the community center for refreshments.

community. Participants from both need training and skill building in the circle process and in peacemaking and consensus building. It is critically important that the community's planning process allow sufficient time for strong relationships to develop between justice professionals and community members. Implementation procedures should be highly flexible, because the circle process will evolve over time based on the community's knowledge and experience. As it gains experience, the community can customize the circle process to fit local resources and culture.

In many communities that have implemented the circle sentencing concept, direction and leadership have come from a community justice committee that decides which cases to accept, develops support groups for the victim and offender, and helps to conduct the circles. In most communities, circles are facilitated by a trained community member, who is often called a keeper.

Although circles have been used as a response to serious and violent crimes, circle sentencing is not an appropriate response to all offences. Key factors in determining whether a case is appropriate for the circle process include the offender's character and personality, sincerity, and connection to the community; the victim's input; and the dedication of the offender's and victim's support groups. Moreover, circles are often labor intensive and require a substantial investment of citizen time and effort; circles should not, therefore, be used extensively as a response to first offenders and minor crime.

The capacity of the circle to advance solutions capable of improving the lives of participants and the overall well-being of the community depends on the effectiveness of the participating volunteers. To ensure a cadre of capable volunteers, the program should support a paid community-based volunteer coordinator to supply logistical support, establish linkages with other agencies and community representatives, and provide appropriate training for all staff.

Lessons learned

Very little research has been conducted to date on the effectiveness of circle sentencing. One study conducted by Judge Barry Stuart in Canada in 1996 indicated that recidivism was less likely among offenders who had participated in circles than among offenders who were processed traditionally (Stuart, 1996). Those who have been involved with circles report that circles empower participants to resolve conflict in a manner that promotes sharing of responsibility for outcomes, generates constructive relationships, enhances respect and understanding among all involved, and fosters enduring, innovative solutions.

[. . . See Tables 10.1 and 10.2.]

Comparing and contrasting the four models: summary

In comparing these four models, it must be remembered that [. . .] the philosophy and practice of any given restorative conferencing program may deviate substantially from the prototypes presented here. Indeed, the evolution of the restorative justice movement is producing significant changes as practitioners think more carefully about the implications of restorative principles for their practice. For example, reparative boards and victim–offender mediation have been influenced by family group conferencing models, and some family group conferencing programs have recently adopted components of circle sentencing.

The most important conclusion to be drawn from this comparison of the four models is that there is no one best approach for every community or for every case within a community. For example, circle sentencing is perhaps the most holistic of the models. Yet circles also demand the greatest time commitment from participants and thus are not wisely used on minor or less complex cases.

Some have suggested that the future may bring a single hybrid model. More practically, however, jurisdictions can consider developing a 'menu' of

Table [16.]1   *Restorative conferencing models: administration and process*

	Victim–offender mediation	Reparative boards	Family group conferencing	Circle sentencing
Origin	Since mid-1970s	Since 1995 (similar youth panels: since 1920)	New Zealand, 1989; Australia, 1991	Since approximately 1992
Current applications	Throughout North America and Europe	Vermont; selected jurisdictions and neighborhoods in other States	Australia; New Zealand; United States (since 1990s), in cities and towns in Montana, Minnesota, Pennsylvania, and other States	Primarily the Yukon, sporadically in other parts of Canada. Minnesota, Colorado, and Massachusetts
Referral point in system	Mostly diversion and probation option. Some use in residential facilities for more serious cases	One of several probation options (youth panels: almost exclusively diversion)	New Zealand: throughout juvenile justice system. Australian Wagga Wagga model: police diversion. United States: mostly diversion, some use in schools and post-adjudication	Various stages. May be diversion or alternative to formal court hearings and corrections process for indictable offences
Eligibility and target group	Varies. Primarily diversion cases and property offenders. In some locations, used with serious and violent	Target group is nonviolent offenders; eligibility limited to offenders given probation and assigned to the boards	New Zealand: all juvenile offenders eligible except those charged with murder and manslaughter. Australian Wagga Wagga	Offenders who admit guilt and express willingness to change. Entire range of offences and offenders eligible; chronic offenders

	offenders (at victim's request)		model: determined by police discretion or diversion criteria	targeted
Staffing	Mediator. Other positions vary	Reparative coordinator (probation staff)	Community justice coordinator	Community justice coordinator
Setting	Neutral setting (meeting room in library, church, community center; victim's home (occasionally, if all parties approve)	Public building or community center	Social welfare office, school, community building, police facility (occasionally)	Community center, school, other public building, church
Process and protocols	Victim speaks first. Mediator facilitates but encourages victim and offender to speak, does not adhere to script	Mostly private deliberation by board after questioning offender and hearing statements. Some variation emerging in local boards (youth panel members generally deliberate)	Australian Wagga Wagga model: coordinator follows script in which offender speaks first, then victim and others. New Zealand: model not scripted, allows consensus decisionmaking after private meeting of family members	Keeper opens session and allows for comments from judge. Prosecutors and defense present legal facts of case (for more serious crimes). All participants allowed to speak when 'talking piece' (feather or stick) is passed to them. Consensus decisionmaking
Managing dialog	Mediator manages	Board chairperson manages. Participants speak when asked	Coordinator manages	After keeper initiates, dialog managed by process of passing talking piece

Table [16.]2　Restorative conferencing models: community involvement and other dimensions

	Victim–offender mediation	Reparative boards	Family group conferencing	Circle sentencing
Who participates? (the community)	Mediator, victim, offender are standard participants. Parents often involved. Others occasionally involved	Reparative coordinator (probation employee), community reparative board, offender and supporters, victim (on a limited basis). Youth panels (a related approach) use diversion staff	Coordinator identifies key participants. Close kin of victim and offender invited. Police, social services, or other support persons also invited. Broader community not encouraged to participate	Judge, prosecutor, defense counsel participate in serious cases. Victim(s), offender(s), service providers, support group present. Open to entire community. Justice committee ensures participation of key residents
Victim role	Expresses feelings regarding crime and impact. Has major role in decision regarding offender obligation and content of reparative plan. Has ultimate right of refusal; consent is essential	Input into plan sought by some boards. Inclusion of victims rare but currently encouraged; more active role being considered	Expresses feelings about crime, gives input into reparative plan	Participates in circle and decisionmaking; gives input into eligibility of offender, chooses support group, and may participate in a healing conference
Gatekeepers	Courts and other entities make referrals	Judge	New Zealand: court and community justice coordinator. Australia and United States: police and school officials	Community justice committee

Relationship to formal system	Varies on continuum from core process in diversion and disposition to marginal programs with minimal impact on court caseloads	One of several probation options for eligible low-risk offenders with minimal service needs. Plans to expand. Some impact on caseloads anticipated	New Zealand: primary process of hearing juvenile cases, required ceding of disposition power, major impact on court caseloads. Australia (Wagga Wagga) and United States: police-driven process, variable impact on caseloads, concern regarding net-widening; in United States, used for very minor cases (most commonly shoplifting)	Judge, prosecution, court officials share power with community, i.e. selection, sanctioning, followup. Presently minimal impact on court caseloads
Preparation	Typically, face-to-face preparation with victim and offender to explain process. Some programs use phone contact	Preservice training provided to board members. No advance preparation for individual hearings	Phone contact with all parties to encourage participation and explain process. New Zealand model requires face-to-face visits with offender, offender's family, and victim	Extensive work with offender and victim prior to circle. Explain process and rules of circle
Followup (enforcement and monitoring)	Varies. Mediator may follow up. Probation and/or other program staff may be responsible	Condition of probation. Coordinator monitors and brings petition of revocation to board, if necessary	Unclear. Australia (Wagga Wagga): police. New Zealand: coordinator. United States and Canada: others	Community justice committee. Judge may hold jail sentence as incentive for offender to comply with plan

Table [16.]2 Continued

Primary outcome(s) sought	Allow victim to relay impact of crime to offender, express feelings and needs; victim satisfied with process; offender has increased awareness of harm, gains empathy with victim; agreement on reparative plan	Engage and involve citizens in decisionmaking process; decide appropriate reparative plan for offender; require victim awareness, education, and other activities that address ways to avoid reoffending in future	Clarify facts of case. Denounce crime while affirming and supporting offender; restore victim loss; encourage offender reintegration. Focus on 'deed not need' (i.e. on offence and harm done, not offender's needs). Some emphasis on collective accountability	Increase community strength and capacity to resolve disputes and prevent crime; develop reparative and rehabilitative plan; address victim concerns and public safety issues; assign victim and offender support group responsibilities and identify resources

Table [16.]3 Restorative community justice: least- to most-restorative impact

Least-restorative impact	**Most-restorative impact**
Entire focus is on determining the amount of financial restitution to be paid, with no opportunity to talk directly about the full impact of the crime on the victim and the community, and also on the offender	Primary focus is on providing an opportunity for victims and offenders to talk directly to each other, to allow victims to describe the impact of the crime on their lives and receive answers to questions, and to allow offenders to appreciate the human impact of their behavior and take responsibility for making things right
No separate preparation meetings with the victim and offender prior to bringing the parties together	Separate preparation meetings with the victim and offender, with emphasis on listening to how the crime has affected them, identifying needs, and answering questions about the mediation process

Table [16.]3   Continued

Victims not given choice of meeting place (where they would feel most comfortable) or participants; given only written notice to appear for mediation session at preset time, with no preparation	Victims continually given choices throughout the process: where to meet, whom they would like to be present, etc.
Mediator or facilitator describes offence and offender then speaks, with the victim simply asking a few questions or responding to questions from the mediator	Victims given choice to speak first and encouraged to describe offence and participate actively
Highly directive styles of mediation or facilitation, with the mediator talking most of the time, little if any direct dialog between the involved parties	Nondirective style of mediation or facilitation with minimal mediator interference, and use of a humanistic or transformative mediation model
Low tolerance for moments of silence or expression of feelings	High tolerance for silence, expression of feelings, and discussion of the full impact of the crime
Voluntary for victim but required of offender regardless of whether he or she takes responsibility	Voluntary for victim and offender
Settlement-driven and very brief (10–15 minutes)	Dialog-driven and typically lasts about an hour (or longer)
Paid attorneys or other professionals serve as mediators	Trained community volunteers serve as mediators or facilitators, along with agency staff

conferencing alternatives to respond to diverse case needs and to make the most efficient use of scarce resources. For example, a brief encounter with a reparative board may be the most appropriate and cost-effective response to a property offender with few prior incidents and no other complications requiring more intensive intervention, whereas circle sentencing may be more appropriate for serious and chronic offenders involved in dysfunctional relationships.

Each of the four models has its strengths and weaknesses in a variety of dimensions in addition to those considered here. Although much remains to be learned, and there is much room for improvement, each model has demonstrated its unique value to juvenile justice systems and communities that are trying to develop more meaningful sanctioning responses to youth crime.
[. . . See Table 10.3.]

This extract is taken from 'A Comparison of Four Restorative Conferencing Models', by Gordon Bazemore and Mark Umbreit, in OJJDP *Juvenile Justice Bulletin (February 2001).*

Notes

1 In some programs, parents of the offender are also often part of the mediation session.
2 Not all mediation sessions lead to financial restitution.
3 In the absence of pure control groups, selection bias cannot be ruled out for the comparison drawn in this study.
4 Reparative boards are highly localized models, and information on them is sketchy. This [article] uses the Vermont reparative boards as a prototype and case study. As noted above, Vermont has used the boards primarily with adult offenders but more recently has begun to use them with juvenile offenders too. Substantial information is available on the operating procedures of the Vermont boards, and the Vermont model can serve as a new prototype for the board/panel-based approach to youth crime.
5 As noted earlier, reparative boards are intended to provide an opportunity for victims and community members to confront offenders in a constructive manner. In practice thus far, however, these opportunities have proved better suited to community input than victim involvement. Because of this relatively weak involvement of victims, some suggest that reparative boards are not pure examples of restorative justice. [. . .]

References

Alder, C. and Wundersitz, J. (eds) (1994) *Family Group Conferencing and Juvenile Justice: The Way Forward or Misplaced Optimism?* (Canberra: Australian Institute of Criminology).
Coates, R. and Gehm, J. (1989) 'An Empirical Assessment', in *Mediation and Criminal Justice* (London: Sage).
Fercello, C. and Umbreit, M. (1999) *Client Evaluation of Family Group Conferencing* (St Paul, MN: Center for Restorative Justice and Mediation, University of Minnesota).

Maxwell, G. and Morris, A. (1993) *Family Participation, Cultural Diversity and Victim Involvement in Youth Justice: A New Zealand Experiment* (Wellington: Victoria University).

McCold, P. and Wachtel, B. (1998) *Restorative Policing Experiment: The Bethlehem, Pennsylvania, Police Family Group Conferencing Project* (Pipersville, PA: Community Service Foundation).

McElrea, F.W.M. (1993) 'A New Model of Justice', in Brown, B.J. (ed.) *The Youth Court in New Zealand: A New Model of Justice* (Auckland: Legal Research Foundation).

Melton, A. (1995) 'Indigenous Justice Systems and Tribal Society', *Judicature*, 70:3, pp. 126–33.

Stuart, B. (1995) 'Sentencing Circles – Making "Real" Differences.' Unpublished paper, Whitehorse, Canada, Territorial Court of the Yukon.

Stuart, B. (1996) 'Circle Sentencing – Turning Swords into Ploughshares', in Galaway, B. and Hudson, J. (eds) *Restorative Justice: International Perspectives* (Monsey, NY: Criminal Justice Press), pp. 193–206.

Umbreit, M. (1994) *Victim Meets Offender: The Impact of Restorative Justice and Mediation* (Monsey, NY: Criminal Justice Press).

Umbreit, M. (1997) 'Humanistic Mediation: A Transformation Journey of Peacemaking', *Mediation Quarterly*, 14:3, pp. 201–13.

Umbreit, M. and Schug, B.A. (1997) *Directory of Victim Offender Mediation Programs in the US* (St Paul, MN: Center for Restorative Justice and Mediation, University of Minnesota).

Umbreit, M. and Stacy, S. (1996) 'Family Group Conferencing Comes to the US: A Comparison with Victim Offender Mediation', *Juvenile and Family Court Journal*, 47:2, pp. 29–39.

Part D

Doing restorative justice in modern society

Introduction

It is one thing to argue that restorative justice was the routine response to crime centuries ago in Europe and that it is still used today by aboriginal peoples in North America, Australasia and elsewhere. It is quite another to suggest that it can become the routine response to crime in modern societies. This requires some explanation of how restorative justice processes and values will be applied to the handling of crime in modern societies, where huge and elaborate criminal justice systems already exist and are unlikely to be dismantled. The problem then tends to become one of showing how restorative justice will be developed within (or alongside) these systems, as an alternative to their conventional modes of operation, thereby radically transforming them. Showing that restorative justice is applicable in modern societies also requires an account of the sorts of social relations found in those societies, and of how they might support restorative interventions or be reformed so that they are capable of supporting them.

The readings in Part D address such issues in various ways. In the process, they develop the idea of restorative justice and help clarify what it is that its proponents are after. In particular, the readings in this section tend to stress, in different ways, that restorative justice is not really about replacing punishment with *financial* reparation. Rather, it is more about repairing the emotional harm, the sense of injustice and the ruptured social bonds which result from criminal behaviour. Promoting restorative justice within the criminal justice system and in the wider society is about providing arenas where these previously neglected symbolic, psychological and relational issues can be addressed constructively in various ways.

The first reading, by Lode Walgrave, was published in 1995, and Walgrave's thinking about restorative justice has developed considerably since then. Nevertheless, the paper is still worth reading because of the influence it had upon thinking about restorative criminal justice and because many of the issues it raises and addresses are still of the utmost interest and importance.

A frequently heard criticism of restorative justice is that it reduces criminality to a mere private wrong which can be redressed by the perpetrator compensating the person harmed. Such a 'privatised' conception of crime would have some value in that it brings into focus the direct victim of the crime whose plight and interest in the way the wrong is defined and dealt with were once notoriously ignored and denied by the criminal justice system. However, many feel that restorative justice goes too far the other way and forgets that crime is also a public wrong – in the sense that it is a violation of fundamental societal values – and that the public also has a legitimate interest in the way it is defined and handled (see von Hirsch and Ashworth, 1998: 300–11).[1]

Walgrave seeks to correct such a misconception (if it is that) of restorative justice. He suggests that restorative justice is not restricted to mediation programmes designed to enable victims and offenders to reach agreement on the amount and form of financial reparation due. Rather, he claims, restorative justice acknowledges that crime is detrimental to community life and requires a response which repairs the harm done to the community. However, conventional criminal law penalties do not repair such harm, no more than they repair the harm done to the direct victims of crime. What is required is that the offender does community service. But this should be understood not as a punishment but as a positive act of practical and/or symbolic compensation or reparation. Hence, for Walgrave, restorative justice is composed of *mediation and community service*.

For Walgrave, one of the biggest problems facing the restorative justice movement is to prevent it being understood and employed as a mere *technique*, which can enable the criminal justice system to achieve more effectively its traditional retributive and rehabilitative goals. The most serious threat to its development comes not from its overt detractors, but from those police officers, judges, etc., who are attracted to it because of its 'effectiveness' but who do not grasp its underlying socio-ethical principles. Hence, it is important to develop and promote restorative justice, not only as a new technique which is effective in satisfying victims and preventing reoffending, but as an alternative way of conceptualising and practising justice and as an alternative set of values.

Those concerned to promote restorative justice as 'a fully fledged alternative' need to address questions about the limits of the approach. Many sceptics do not object to restorative justice per se; rather they regard it as of limited applicability. They assume that serious offenders must incur a really punitive response. They doubt the willingness of victims and offenders to co-operate with a restorative process, especially in serious cases. And, they assume that security considerations make mediation plus community service too risky a response for serious or repeat offenders. In my view, this particular article by Walgrave is more important for raising these questions than for the brief and rather inadequate answers it offers.[2] For all that the debate has moved on significantly since the publication of this paper, the questions raised by Walgrave remain among the most pressing for the campaign for restorative justice.

The reading from Daniel Van Ness is a more recent attempt to spell out what a fully elaborated system of restorative justice might look like. Along with many others, Van Ness assumes there are degrees of restorativeness, i.e. we should think of restorative values and attributes as lying at one end of a continuum, with values and attributes that characterize conventional criminal justice at the other end. The appropriate questions then become 'how restorative is a particular system?' and 'in which aspects is it restorative?'.

Van Ness then turns to the question of how we might go about constructing a model of a restorative system. In doing so, he raises the important question of whether and how we could create a restorative system capable of handling the numerous situations regularly encountered in administration of criminal justice, such as serious crimes, contested cases and 'offenders' and victims who are unwilling or unable to participate in the process. It is worth emphasising here that Van Ness is interested in exploring the possibility of creating a restorative system that could deal with all kinds of crimes and be applied at all stages of the criminal justice process. Many commentators – both supporters and critics – now take it for granted that restorative justice is an alternative only to the conventional process of sentencing and sanctioning, i.e. it comes into play only when an offence has been admitted or legal guilt has been determined (Van Ness's hybrid model, cf. *Duff, Ashworth*). Van Ness seems to retain the ambitious belief, prevalent at earlier stages of the campaign for restorative justice, that restorative justice is feasible as an alternative to the entire conventional criminal justice system, i.e. that it might replace the adversarial trial and all the terminology and procedures associated with it, as well as taking over at the 'sentencing' stage.

One of the most intriguing questions raised by the campaign for restorative justice is whether forgiveness can and should play a part in criminal justice. This issue is addressed in Chapter 19 by John R. Gehm, where he defines forgiveness as 'a process of ceasing to feel resentment'. Hence, forgiveness seems the antithesis of our 'natural' emotional response to being wronged, which is the impulse to feel anger and resentment towards the wrongdoer and to want to strike back at him or her, meeting hurt with hurt. Forgiveness, if it deflects us away from such an impulse, seems clearly to benefit offenders and also might contribute to peace in the community.[3] Drawing upon psychological theories, Gehm suggests – less obviously – that forgiveness can also benefit the forgiver. The anger we feel towards those who subject us to injustices may be useful as a psychological defensive mechanism but, according to many psychotherapists, unless that anger is eventually released it can be extremely damaging to our health.

One way by which people try to release anger is, of course, by taking revenge on those who wronged them. The criminal justice system might therefore be understood as functioning to provide a safe and regulated outlet for the anger and resentment people feel towards criminal wrongdoers. According to Gehm, however, the expression of anger is of limited value for releasing people from its grip. To overcome anger – to overcome the power which an offence and the offender have over them – people must make a conscious decision to forgive. Forgiveness, in short, is crucial to the victim's recovery from the trauma of crime victimisation.

From this perspective, modern criminal justice systems, which do not provide any encouragement of or space for forgiveness, are lacking and contribute to the health problems – as well as relationship problems – which stem from anger. Modern criminal justice systems provide some outlet for vengeful emotions and increasingly pay some attention to the need for economic reparation. But these do not dissipate anger. For Gehm, the criminal justice system needs to encourage and provide space for the process of forgiveness. It can do this by incorporating victim–offender reconciliation programmes. In these, offenders can apologise to those they have harmed and make efforts to repair the harm they caused, thereby placing them in a position to seek forgiveness from those they wronged and making it easier for victims to relinquish their right to resentment. Victims would not thereby have a moral obligation towards the offender to forgive him or her. But they might have an 'obligation' towards themselves to do so.

This focus on emotional and symbolic reparation – as more important than financial or material reparation – is taken up in the next reading. Heather Strang (in Chapter 20) starts by describing the traditional neglect of the victim in criminal justice, pointing in particular to the system's failure to validate the victim's status as the person harmed. Since the 1970s, various groups promoting victims' rights have emerged to change this situation. An early result of victim agitation was the creation of state-run reparation schemes in many jurisdictions. According to Strang, however, such schemes failed to meet the needs of victims. Partly, this was because they were poorly funded and so on. But also, and more importantly, financial compensation is not the top priority for most victims. Victims have a greater need, Strang contends, for statements legitimating their status and for acknowledgement of the emotional harm they have experienced. Emotional and symbolic reparation is more important, for most victims, than financial reparation. And to the extent that financial reparation is wanted, it is usually less for its financial worth, more for its value as a gesture of responsibility. Hence, it is important for victims that financial reparation comes from the offender rather than the state, even if this means the victim receives less money.

Strang points to research indicating that what many victims would like from a justice process is an apology from the offender. Hence, the absence in Western criminal justice systems of any role for apology is a serious shortcoming. This has not always been corrected by victim–offender mediation programmes which have tended to be based on the notion that financial reparation is the most important outcome. Hence, for Strang, restorative justice practices should be incorporated into the criminal justice system as these can provide the opportunity for offenders to apologise to their victims. But for these practices to achieve restorative justice, they must themselves be adjusted so that the emphasis is more on apology and emotional reparation than on financial reparation.

Researchers, too, must adjust their designs. It may be easy to find out: whether restorative conferences result in agreements for financial reparation; how much is agreed; and whether the amount is paid. It is less easy to identify whether and to what extent emotional reparation has taken place. Yet, that is the truer measure of whether victims' needs have been meet. Researchers need to examine whether processes of apology and forgiveness have taken place and whether these have succeeded in resolving the feelings of animosity and distress resulting from the crime.

The next extract in this section (Chapter 21), from a paper by Paul McCold and Benjamin Wachtel, addresses one of the most important and difficult questions facing the movement for restorative justice. As we have seen, something like restorative justice might work in historical and contemporary aboriginal societies in which a strong sense of community exists (*Yazzie and Zion*). The community can then exercise informal moralising control over its members, obviating any need for formal punitive control. However, according to many sceptics, modern societies lack such a vibrant sense of community, and therefore cannot exercise such control over their members. Our societies tend to be characterised, rather, by excessive individualism, and this itself is a cause of much of our crime problem.

The response of many proponents of restorative justice, including McCold and Wachtel, is to insist that although the feeling of connectedness that we call community may not often be found amongst individuals who live closely to each other in modern towns and cities, this does not mean that community does not exist in modern society. Communities do exist, but they tend to consist of networks of interpersonal relationships between geographically dispersed individuals – e.g. members of the same bowling league (see Johnstone, 2002: chs 3 and 7; cf. Putnam, 1995).

However, many proponents of restorative justice themselves are still unclear about how to define community and make the mistake of thinking of it as a place. This has deleterious consequences. For instance, as we have seen (*Walgrave*), one concern of restorative justice is to repair the harm which crime causes *to the community*. In the absence of a clear definition of 'community', the term comes to be understood as synonymous with society. As a result, the restorative justice goal can become difficult to distinguish from the traditional retributive idea of offenders paying their debt to society. Also, those organising restorative justice schemes may tend to achieve community involvement by inviting 'community leaders' to partici-pate in the process, and neglect to invite members of the offender's and the victim's 'communities of care'.

One of the crucial practical problems addressed indirectly in this reading is, in fact, that of how one decides who should participate in a restorative justice process such as a 'community conference'. For McCold and Wachtel, the people there should be the offender's and the victim's 'microcommunities'. These are not necessarily members of the offender's and victim's neighbourhoods. Rather, they are people who have a strong emotional or personal connection to the victims or offender. One question about this solution is whether it is definite enough for use by practitioners. However, another problem is that it assumes that it is a simple matter to determine who the victim of a crime is. But, if – as McCold and Wachtel suggest – the community is harmed by crime (and the community here is something more specific than the 'society' of traditional criminal justice theory), then it is not so clear that the victim is simply the person who owned private property that was stolen or damaged or who was punched, etc. Nevertheless, McCold and Wachtel seem to define out of the process 'vicarious victims' (i.e. people harmed indirectly by the commission of a crime in their neighbourhood). For McCold and Wachtel, vicarious victims need reassurance that something is being done, but they are not themselves 'stakeholders' in the process.

Even if we accept this, there are still awkward questions about our identification of the victim to which McCold and Wachtel do not avert. In cases of damage to public property, there are obviously victims (those whose lives are affected detrimentally by the damage), but they may constitute a large and indefinite group. In cases of street robbery, the perpetrator who may have robbed dozens or more people may only be charged with a handful of offences. Similar difficulties often emerge in cases of shoplifting where the manager of a huge department store may be invited to a conference as – often implausibly to offenders – 'the victim'.

McCold and Wachtel's paper raises questions about the social structures and values which underpin conventional criminal justice and restorative justice, respect-ively. These issues are addressed explicitly in the next reading (Chapter 22), from Michael Schluter, Chairman of the Relationships Foundation in Cambridge.[4] Accord-ing to Schluter, long-term stable relationships with other people are essential to our well-being. It is only through such relationships that we obtain a sense of purpose, fulfilment and happiness and can realise our potential as human beings. Also, he suggests, it is through human relationships that individuals acquire a sense of obligation to others. However, Schluter argues, we are currently witnessing a breakup of such relations. As a result, our sense of responsibility towards, and our ability to empathise with, other people is declining. Consequently, crime increases and our ability to deal with it declines. People are increasingly victimised before our eyes, yet increasingly we do absolutely nothing about it.

Schluter's chapter contains two different explanations for this breakup of relational bonding. One is the rise of a political philosophy in which maximum individual freedom and responsibility are supreme values and economic growth is assumed to be the key to their achievement. The other points to longer-term developments in technology and related structural trends in British society, which in some ways facilitate human relationships but overall tend to undermine them.

For Schluter, if we are to find a solution to the imminent 'breakdown' of criminal justice, we need somehow to work against this trend. We need to think relationally about criminal justice. Such a perspective is called 'relational justice' by Schluter, but it is very close to at least some versions of restorative justice. In this perspective crime is understood as a result and cause of weak human relationships; crime prevention is best achieved by strengthening relationships; and effective interventions into the lives of individual offenders require a relationship between 'us and them'.

Schluter's chapter is of immense value for helping us understand the link between the campaign for restorative justice and broader thinking about the sorts of values which should guide our personal and public lives. However, what is left unanswered in this particular account is the question of how it might be possible to develop restorative or relational justice in an environment that seems so hostile to it and which presumably is not going to be easy to change.

As the previous two readings suggest, the campaign for restorative justice has strong links with a broader movement emphasising the need for and benefits of greater public participation in crime control and criminal justice. This broader movement is in tension with an increasing concern about the growth of 'populist punitiveness' (Bottoms, 1995: 39; cf. Ryan, 1999; Garland, 2001). Whereas many see the existence of 'populist punitiveness' as a reason for restraining public influence in the arena of criminal justice, others see an increase in *meaningful* public participation in the handling of crime as a possible means of checking and reversing public demands for tough punishment (Johnstone, 2000).

Such issues, which are of crucial importance to our thinking about the possibility and desirability of restorative justice, are addressed in the short essay by Adam Crawford (Chapter 23; this essay briefly summarises a much more detailed essay – see the list of sources for details – as well as drawing upon Crawford's considerable experience in researching issues of lay and community involvement in crime prevention activities). As Crawford points out, once we start thinking about the role of public participation within criminal justice, we are (or should be) inevitably drawn into fundamental questions about the nature and purpose of criminal justice itself. Crawford points to problems in two conflicting tendencies in thinking about the role and value of public participation in justice: managerialism and communitarianism. Crucially, he suggests an alternative framework: deliberative justice. As well as providing an appealing way of thinking about what restorative justice should be like, this concept can usefully connect the debate about restorative justice to broader notions of deliberative democracy. This allows Crawford to address – if not resolve – crucial questions about how to set limits to public participation in justice and how to justify those limits, without slipping back into managerialist assumptions.

The question which most people ask when they hear about restorative justice is 'does it work?' The final chapter of this section (Chapter 24) is arguably among the most thorough and sophisticated attempts to answer his question, through a review of the available empirical (mostly statistical) evidence. Based on his analysis of a staggering number of research reports, from all over the world, John Braithwaite presents a careful defence of the thesis that restorative justice restores and satisfies victims, offenders and communities better than existing justice practices. Whilst, unlike some restorative justice enthusiasts, Braithwaite avoids making grandiose claims based on limited evidence or defective studies, Braithwaite nevertheless declares that there is sufficient evidence to suggest that restorative justice has enough potential to reduce reoffending and to achieve other positive outcomes to warrant a huge investment in research and development.

Braithwaite points out that, in thinking of whether restorative justice works, we should not think solely in terms of crime reduction. Restorative justice works, he claims, by delivering a sense of justice and healing to crime victims, a sense of fairness to offenders, and by building microcommunities. Given the evidence that it achieves these positive effects, we may be warranted in investing in restorative justice, provided that diverting cases away from conventional criminal justice to restorative justice does not lead to an increase in reoffending. None of the studies Braithwaite reviews has found such an increase. The only really disappointing results he reports are in relation to drink-driving offences, which are explained by the fact that conferences have no power to deprive drink-drivers of their licences. And many studies suggest, albeit almost always on limited data, that restorative justice is promising as a strategy for reducing crime. Interestingly, Braithwaite draws upon his previous research into corporate wrongdoing to demonstrate this point.

However, there is an important and controversial element to Braithwaite's argument that needs to be flagged up. For Braithwaite, restorative justice works best *when it is backed up by punitive justice*. Here, Braithwaite parts company with some proponents of restorative justice for whom punitive justice is completely unjustifiable (e.g. Sullivan and Tifft, 2001). What Braithwaite advocates is certainly not abolition of punishment and its replacement by restorative justice. For him, this would probably render restorative justice ineffective. The most effective way of regulating crime is weak law enforcement and strong 'conversational regulation'. But the effectiveness of the latter depends upon it taking place within a larger system in which there is always the possibility of resorting to punitive justice. For Braithwaite, then, punishment is to be marginalised, placed in the background and used only as a last resort. But, it is essential to have it there as a last resort if restorative justice is going to work.

A careful explanation of this position may well allay the fears of those who think that social control without the power to punish is an unrealistic and dangerous ideal. Braithwaite does not attack the power to punish but simply insists that it should be reserved for those cases where restorative justice has repeatedly failed. However, this does raise questions of how such a last resort system of punishment could be justified (cf. *Ashworth*). Braithwaite's 'defence' is based on wholly consequentialist grounds: without such a system to fall back on, restorative justice cannot achieve its good effects (or at least cannot achieve them to the extent that it does). Some proponents of restorative justice, who are attracted to it as a viable alternative to an ethically unacceptable practice of state punishment, may be troubled by this.[5]

Notes

1 The conventional view is still confidently reiterated – as unchallengeable truth – in criminal law texts. For instance:

> A crime is a public wrong in the sense that the public at large is affected by it. The community is threatened or offended by the crime. For example, the crime of rape does more than harm the victim. Society is threatened and made less

secure by the rape: the rapist could strike again. Accordingly, society is not
prepared to leave the matter to the victim to seek compensation. Rape is made a
crime and society attempts to apprehend the rapist and secure his punishment
(Clarkson, 2001: 2).

2 In subsequent writing, however, Walgrave has returned to such issues in a more
   sustained way (see, in particular, Walgrave, 2002).
3 Many deterrence theorists would, of course, insist that forgiveness, to the extent that
   it softens society's response to crime, would encourage the commission of crime.
4 See their website (www.relationshipsfoundation.org). The Relationships Foundation
   also publishes a quarterly bulletin: the *Relational Justice Bulletin*.
5 As indeed will those who agree that a system of criminal punishment is justifiable,
   but do not think such a system can be justified in Braithwaite's consequentialist
   terms (see Duff, 2001).

References

Bottoms, A. (1995) 'The Philosophy and Politics of Punishment and Sentencing', in
    Clarkson, C. and Morgan, R. (eds) *The Politics of Sentencing Reform* (Oxford: Clarendon
    Press), pp. 17–49.
Clarkson, C. (2001) *Understanding Criminal Law* (3rd edn) (London: Sweet & Maxwell).
Duff, R. (2001) *Punishment, Communication, and Community* (Oxford: Oxford University
    Press).
Garland, D. (2001) *The Culture of Control: Crime and Social Order in Contemporary Society*
    (Oxford: Oxford University Press).
Johnstone, G. (2000) 'Penal Policy Making: Elitist, Populist or Participatory?' *Punishment
    and Society*, 2:2, pp. 161–80.
Johnstone, G. (2002) *Restorative Justice: Ideas, Values, Debates* (Cullompton: Willan).
Putnam, R. (1995) 'Bowling Alone: America's Declining Social Capital', *Journal of
    Democracy*, 6, pp. 65–78.
Ryan, M. (1999) 'Penal Policy Making towards the Millennium: Elites and Populists;
    New Labour and the New Criminology', *International Journal of the Sociology of Law*,
    27:1, pp. 1–22.
Sullivan, D. and Tifft, L. (2001) *Restorative Justice: Healing the Foundations of our Everyday
    Lives* (Monsey, NY: Willow Tree Press).
von Hirsch, A. and Ashworth, A. (1998) *Principled Sentencing: Readings on Theory and Policy*
    (2nd edn) (Oxford: Hart Publishing).
Walgrave, L. (ed) (2002) *Restorative Justice and the Law* (Cullompton: Willan).

17. Restorative justice for juveniles: just a technique or a fully fledged alternative?

Lode Walgrave

[...]

In search for principles of restorative justice

1. Two complementary basic schemes

The origins of the concept of restorative justice are to be found in experiments with mediation. It is easy to see why. The harm caused by the offence to the individual victim is often visible and there are yardsticks to measure it. The restorative action aims at repairing material damage, or at compensating physical and/or psychological injury. Mediation is about setting up and guiding negotiations between victim and offender, in order to reach agreement on the type and the extent of reparation or compensation, and about monitoring implementation of that agreement. All these steps can be observed and controlled.

This type of societal reaction to an offence will not suffice, however. The pragmatic reason for this is that pure reparation of injuries as the sole reaction would reduce criminality to a mere gamble. 'I steal a car. If I am not caught, I have a car. If I am caught, I'll give back the car. Next time, I'll be luckier.'

From the standpoint of principles, pure mediation would reduce the official response to offending to civil settlement for damages between two (groups of) citizens. This is a civil law matter. Penal law regulates the reaction of community towards an offence. That is different. Civil law is reactive, that is, it acts only in response to a complaint. If no complaint is made about an alleged wrong suffered, civil justice will not be activated. In principle, penal law is proactive. That means that it can itself initiate the proceedings. Even when, in practice, penal justice acts proactively only to a small degree, the difference in basic intervention rules shows that other principles are at stake here. It would seem that not just the victim and offender, but also society itself is concerned by the wrongdoing. There are, therefore, three parties involved. It is not just a matter of loss caused to an identifiable victim. Penal law holds itself out as the defender of fundamental values of society. The wrongdoing throws into question much more general, fundamental societal norms than would be the case in a civil law dispute, even when one can discuss the pertinence of the supposed consensus over norms and norm enforcement in society. By criminalising certain acts, organised society as such shows itself to be a concerned party (Van Ness, 1990; Queloz, 1991).

If 'public order and legality' being 'the safeguards of fundamental values' are 'harmed' by a crime, questions arise as to the restorative approach.

What 'public loss' is caused by an offence? With no precedent on the matter, it is as yet difficult to say and quantify. It may be direct, as where public goods are damaged or stolen. Very often, it is indirect. Van Ness (1990) speaks of 'loss of public safety, damage to community values and the disruption, caused by crime' (p. 9). A crime is detrimental to the solidarity and mutual respect essential to community life. It creates feelings of insecurity which diminish the quality of life. Crime requires costly preventive and intervention arrangements to be established. It is clear that community as such is wronged by criminal behaviour and crime.

How is it to be made good? Conventional criminal law penalties have no restorative effect. As Wright (1992) puts it: 'Balancing the harm done by the offender with further harm inflicted on the offender, only adds to the total amount of harm in the world' (p. 525). This is where types of community service come into play. Community has been 'victimised' by the disruption of public order and can demand compensation for it in the form of a (compensatory) service to community. From one who jeopardised community life by a lack of respect for others and social order, community can demand a (symbolic) effort in favour of community to compensate for the harm done (Tulkens, 1993; Van Ness, 1990; Dünkel, 1990; Walgrave, 1992).

Mediation and community service are both parts of an ethico-juridical tendency which can be described as *restorative justice*. They have in common (i) a definition of crime as an injury to victims (concrete and societal); (ii) the orientation towards restoration, which may be in symbolic terms; (iii) the active and direct implication of the offender in restoration, and (iv) the judicial framework making possible use of coercive power and legal moderation at the same time.

Community service is the necessary complement which translates the involvement of the community as such in the problem of crime. If the restorative approach were to be confined to offender–victim mediation, then it would not be 'restorative justice' but merely a restorative technique used by a retributive or rehabilitative justice system.[1]

2. From 'crime' to 'social conflict'

Decriminalisation of wrongdoing by a restorative justice reaction does not belittle transgression of norm, but partly redefines it. The offence, defined by concepts of guilt and amends is reconsidered primarily as a (possibly serious) 'conflict', a (grave) 'problem' requiring the most advantageous social solution possible (Zehr, 1985; Steinert, 1988). The conflict between the parties, 'appropriated' by the state in the retributive system and denied in the rehabilitative system, is given back to the parties concerned (Christie, 1978; Hackler, 1988), whose responsibility it is to work out a fitting solution. It is an approach which gives scope for capitalising on 'the conception of rights (of children and young people) from a global perspective which emphasises responsibility and social solidarity' propounded by Queloz (1991, p. 41).

The state has a dual role here. In mediation, it ensures that the conflict is effectively settled without abuse of power by either the victim or offender. The function of the government law officers (public prosecutors, government attorney) is to put the case for the community's demands for compensation.

3. Constructive social ethics

Recently, renewed attention has been paid to morality and ethics in criminology and penal justice. Often, however, it merely accentuates emphasis on traditional values, such as personal security and the right to property, which are injured by crime and should be defended more rigorously by penal reactions (Novak, 1989; Hirsch Ballin, 1993). Neither these values, nor the punitive machinery of penal justice, are in question. The ethical basis of this view of penal justice lies in the Kantian premise that it is necessary to punish a wrong in order to maintain rules and restore the socio-moral balance. Punishment must fit the crime and he who causes suffering to another must be compelled to undergo equivalent suffering. In fact, the retributive function of penal law can be equated with channelling revenge through the systems of the constitutional state. Punishment in the form of rejection and exclusion does not, to me, seem the most fortuitous ethical principle by which to govern community life.

Restorative justice operates according to different ethical principles, whose approach is more emancipatory. An emancipatory society develops in accordance with two fundamental principles – autonomy and solidarity between individuals and community.

Autonomy also engenders responsibility, which means 'being answerable for the consequences of one's own actions' (Van de Kerchove, cited in Tulkens, 1993, p. 483). The person who causes loss by his own independent act must bear the consequences of it. This is a responsibility incumbent not only on individual members of society, but also on societal institutions themselves. A responsible society is concerned about the consequences of its penal justice, therefore.

The quality of those consequences is measured by the other principle – solidarity. If it is fair not to tolerate violence by one person towards others by reason of the lack of respect and solidarity it demonstrates, it is no less necessary to avoid a reaction by society which would demonstrate an equal lack of solidarity and understanding for victim and offender alike. Society's reaction must first and foremost be to restore the quality of relations between the individuals who incurred loss from crime, the community as a whole, and the one who caused that loss. It must reassert solidarity while preserving the utmost autonomy. To put it in Braithwaite's (1989) terms: social reaction to crime must contribute to a 'communitarianist' society by producing 'reintegrative shaming'.

From the ethical standpoint, then, the primary aim must be to seek to repair harm by an obligation to do good: the one who caused loss must repair it or compensate it (Del Vecchio, 1975; Wright, 1992). Mediation, reparation, reonciliation and forgiveness are far more socially constructive forms of inter-personal relations than the use of force, hatred and revenge. They contribute more greatly to harmonious community life and collective emancipation (Mackay, 1992).

Here, we are close to the autonomous morality described by Piaget as the adult moral level in which the system of norms or rules is considered as the product of agreements between people, and sanctions for transgressing them must focus chiefly on repairing the disrupted relations.

4. From theory to practice: questions and uncertainties

These are a series of arguments to be found in favour of a judicial reaction to offences which places more emphasis on restoration than on punishment, or even treatment. The question, however, is whether and to what extent those principles can be applied in practice. Experiments of the past two decades have already provided much food for thought, though the initiators have not always referred expressly to this trend in justice. Most of their results have been published [. . .] (Galaway and Hudson, 1990; Dünkel and Zermatten, 1990; Messmer and Otto, 1992).

What stands out from these experiences is the difficulty of putting the theories into practice. Very often, good ideas lose their credibility by bad implementations. Good ideas and good will are not enough to make a mediation programme effective. It also requires co-operation from the judiciary, a structured setting, appropriately chosen cases, a coherent team of mediators, a suitable mediation technique, and so forth (Mair, 1990). An exercise in mediation or community service may sometimes be thwarted by insurmountable practical obstacles or failings in strategies which say nothing about the quality of the principles or practices of the ideas to which they relate.

Broadly speaking, the problems encountered can be classified as either legal or practical.

Restorative justice and democracy: in search of a legal framework

At present, experiments in restorative orientation must take place within a retributive or rehabilitative justice system; this makes it hard to preserve the integrity of its legal concepts and statuses. Mediation and community service take place within or outside the system, at varying stages in the judicial process, with a wide variety of objectives and techniques. It is a miscellaneous profusion, an odd assortment of good intentions, opportunism and clear visions. It is an uncontrolled growth which may at times conflict with fundamental principles which govern the function of justice in a democratic state (Dézalay, 1988). It also threatens the replacement value of the restorative approach before it has truly developed.

1. Diversion or sanction

Offender/victim mediation may be used as a diversion strategy (Feest, 1990). The possibility that a victim may obtain satisfaction without setting the entire penal machinery in motion reduces the need to have recourse to the penal system; the victim may be less inclined to lay a complaint, therefore, the prosecutor may make successful mediation a condition of entering a *nolle prosequi*, the court may make compensation a condition of probation. Indeed, in several countries, this is fairly current practice.

The position as regards community service is less clear, however. In practice, community service is imposed (or 'proposed') by court, prosecuting authority, and even on occasion by police. This 'experimental flux' poses problems with respect to legal principles. Community service must expressly be seen as a sanction. The idea of direct restoration is foregone [*sic*] here, which blurs the link between the offence and the action taken in respect of it. Defining the link becomes more difficult and delicate, therefore. The idea of settlement of loss by negotiated agreement is also absent here. Community service expressly embodies a restriction on liberty imposed as a result of crime. The degree of guilt for the offence and the extent of restriction on liberty must be fixed, which in our legal system can be done only by the court.[2] Consequently, it must be reserved for judgment after the procedure has run its full course.

2. Negotiation and the rights of the parties

The negotiating element of the restorative justice intervention may jeopardise the rights of the parties concerned. It is essential that they be preserved. Mediation requires co-operation from the victim, who may not always be willing to give it. It is important to ensure that undue pressure does not result in a sort of secondary victimisation. The rights of the victim not to engage in a mediation exercise must be respected (Wright, 1991).

Less formal procedures may also mean that less attention is paid to legal rights of the offender, such as presumption of innocence, right to a defence, and right to a proportionate sanction (Feest, 1990). This is one reason for the requirement that community service should be ordered only by a court. But in mediation, it is not impossible that young offenders, through ignorance or lack of a defender, might be pressured into accepting a mediation outcome which has weightier consequences for them than if they had submitted to the due process of ordinary law (Orlando, 1992). Unequal power relations and/or social prestige of the victim and the socially vulnerable young offender may also lead to similar results. For that reason, mediation must always be conducted under court supervision (indirect if needs be).

3. 'Alternative sanctions': a catch-all

The most significant threat to the status of restorative justice within the judicial framework is the enormous confusion which surrounds the idea of 'alternative sanctions' – an expression which embraces a miscellany of practices, innovative rehabilitation programmes, novel educative and therapeutic programmes, pure compensation, community service and much more besides (Verhellen *et al.*, 1987). All these programmes differ markedly in their objectives, basic philosophies, legal status and scope. The confusion has led to these so-called alternative sanctions being lumped together as a variegated collection with all the existing sanctions and measures, thus depriving them of their truly innovative aspect. Some light needs to be shed on them, therefore.

Learning of social skills, sports/outward bound activities, and other transformational programmes may be worthwhile alternatives in the (re)education process, but have nothing to do with restorative justice. They are no more than alternative forms of treatment whose aim, like others, is to rehabilitate the juvenile offender. As such, they are part of rehabilitative justice.

Mediation and community service have been incorporated as techniques in the rehabilitative approach. Rather than 'alternative sanctions', they have in fact become 'alternative treatments'. The purpose of intervention has switched from restoration of loss to their educative effect on the young offender (Scieur, 1990; Dongier and Van Doosselaere, 1992). The nature and extent of sanction depend not on the crime, but on the offender as an individual. The victim and his loss are no longer taken into account as elements in their own right, but rather as 'demonstrative elements' in the treatment of the offender. This is not to deny the educative importance of the content of mediation or community service, but it must remain a secondary objective. The restorative intervention must remain first and foremost a sanction linked to the losses by a crime, otherwise the drawbacks mentioned earlier connected with the pure rehabilitation will remain: legal guarantees for the offender will be minimal, the victim's position is secondary, and risks of netwidening are considerable (Houchon, 1984; Van de Kerchove, 1986; Orlando, 1992).

Restorative obligation is also often misused in a punitive 'just deserts' approach. Compensation for the victim, or even community service, are imposed in addition to a penal sanction (Houchon, 1984; Dünkel, 1990), or are ordered against juveniles who would have incurred no penalty at all had restorative interventions not existed. In both cases, therefore, one can legitimately speak of net-widening and of 'additional' rather than 'alternative' sanctions.

Restorative justice approach is not a variant of penal justice nor yet of the educative approach. It is a third avenue in its own right. But there is a real risk of its being incorporated into conventional intervention approaches, as is shown by the existing day-to-day practice. Paradoxically, one could even say that the most serious threat to restorative justice is the enthusiasm with which police officers, magistrates and social workers insert mediation and community service as simple techniques into their traditional punitive or rehabilitative approaches. That is why further research on restorative principles and conscious implementation strategies are badly needed. Reflection on socio-ethical, philosophical and legal theory must be further developed in order to construct a coherent paradigm of reparation (restoration)-oriented justice which can serve as a frame of reference to ensure correct application in practice and to guide experimentation with fitting methods and techniques.

Empirical evidence: issues of instrumentalism

From the instrumentalist standpoint, the essential question pertains to the effects of restorative interventions. We are now better informed about the way in which those concerned, that is, the victims, offenders and 'the public' perceive the actions of restorative justice.

1. Victims

The experience acquired with victims through mediation is clearly central. Not all victims are disposed to accept mediation. Figures on voluntary participation vary. In various reports published in Messmer and Otto (1992), figures are varying between 50% and 80%. In addition to a series of personal characteristics, more 'objective' factors such as nature and circumstances of the crime, and the way in which mediation is proposed, also play a very significant role. In general, there is considerable willingness to participate. Even victims of severe physical violence can be favourably inclined towards mediation (Marshall, 1992; Weitekamp, 1992; Umbreit, 1992). From a series of evaluation researches, presented in Messmer and Otto (1992), it seems that, when there is an agreement on reparation or compensation, between 64% and 100% of them is effectively performed, with the majority of positive outcomes falling around 80%.

Umbreit has conducted a large-scale survey of victims' perceptions of mediation in the United States (Umbreit and Coates, 1992).[3] Victims who co-operated pronounced themselves satisfied in 79% of cases, compared to only 57% of those who had not engaged in mediation. Reasons cited included the ability to take an active part in 'their' case, the correct conduct of proceedings, the perceived fairness of final agreements, and especially, the emotional satisfaction. Eighty-three per cent of mediation participants considered the outcome fair, while only 53% and 62% of those who went through the normal court procedure felt the same.

Other more qualitative-oriented research describes the emotional relief felt by victims after the procedure. Gehm (1992) for example, emphasises the importance of forgiveness, in which the victim deliberately forgoes his 'right' to 'pay the offender back in kind'. The stress-producing tension which accompanies the right is reduced and victims receive a psychological boost from their feelings of 'magnanimity'.

It would appear, then, that the fierce punitive reaction often felt by victims immediately after having suffered an offence can be generally attributed to immediate emotions and lack of information about other possibilities. On each occasion, it subsequently appears that victims were chiefly concerned to secure respect and recognition for their position as victim, reparation of (emotional as much as material) harm, and certainty that the offender would not offend again (against themselves or others) (Steinert, 1988; Coates and Gehm, 1985; Davis, 1992).

2. The offender

Literature suggests various reasons why the effect on offenders may be more beneficial. The offender is confronted more directly with the consequences of his act and an active effort is demanded of him to repair or compensate the harm; he will therefore presumably develop a better understanding of the rule, experience an appeal to responsible citizenship and may partially escape the negative effects of penal justice. The clarity of the rule and the conferring of responsibility – both important educative elements – represent considerable advances over the rehabilitative model (Walgrave, 1985; Van der Laan, 1991).

This is not easily determined from empirical evidence. Scientific assessment of the effects on offenders is extremely difficult (Cornejo, 1981; Mair, 1990; Walgrave, 1992). The characteristics of the offenders, and hence the possible effects, differ greatly. It is hard to determine with precision the objectives of penal intervention or court-ordered reparation. It is not the sole purpose of penal proceedings to prevent reoffending, and the reoffending rate is harder to measure than is generally thought. Control groups need to be formed to make reliable comparisons. The outcomes may be influenced by practical problems, which give no precise indications about the model applied itself. Data and intepretations may be skewed by the interests of and pressure from practitioners and politicians.

As yet, little in-depth research has been conducted on the effects of court-ordered reparation on offenders. Two seemingly prominent aspects are common to mediation and community service, however.

(i) Offenders who have taken part in mediation and performed the agreements generally feel their treatment to have been fairer and more reasonable than do those to whom a conventional penalty has been applied. Umbreit (1992) reports feelings of satisfaction in 87% and fairness in 89% of offenders who participated in mediation, compared to 78% in those who did not. Similar figures are reported for community service (Junger-Tas, 1981).

(ii) Some writers report a tangible decline in recidivism rates amongst mediation programme particpants (Hayley and Neugebauer, 1992; Marshall, 1992), although this is qualified by others (Umbreit, 1992). Nor does community service always lead to a fall in the recidivism figures (Junger-Tas, 1981; Van der Laan, 1991). It is likely that differences in the findings stem, *inter alia*, from differences in the methods of selection, proposal and support for these approaches. What is clear is that judicially-ordered reparation may sometimes lower, sometimes not affect, but never increases reoffending rates.

3. The public

Replacing a judicial punitive reaction with a non-punitive response which often takes place outside the judicial systems (but always under court control, however), raises questions of 'public opinion'. Very often, 'public opinion' is used to justify the punitive approach to crime. Repeated surveys provide no evidence in support of this claim. If the possibility of restitution is presented in a realistic way, the majority of those surveyed choose that type of reaction over others. The seriousness and type of offence carry less weight than had been thought (Galaway, 1984; Wright, 1989).[4]

Restorative justice: new technique or fully fledged judicial alternative?

Mediation and community service have developed within the existing judicial systems. They were principally designed to unburden on [*sic*] and/or refine judicial retribution or rehabilitation. With this in mind, restoraion was applied 'prudently', that is, to less serious offences, and especially to young (adult) offenders. Growing confidence, however, has resulted in an extension of the restorative approach to more serious situations and offences (Umbreit, 1989; Dünkel, 1990; Weitekamp, 1992; De Martelaere and Peeters, 1985). Restitutive philosophy is also developing, such that restorative justice is now being mooted as an alternative in its own right to retributive and rehabilitative approaches. It is a hypothesis which raises pointed questions about the limits of restorative justice.

1. The seriousness of the offence

Seriousness of the offence is very often treated as making decisive difference. We accept that a simple victim/offender mediation cannot be sufficient as the only societal response to serious offences. The gravity of the disruption of community life is embodied in the seriousness of the offence, such as to make it quite understandable that the community should demand more than mere compensation for the victim. But the restorative approach does not end there. It is hard to find good grounds for excluding serious offenders from community service.

(i) The idea that serious offenders have to incur a really punitive sanction goes back to a purely retributive interpretation of the societal response to crime. I do not believe that revenge, even when canalised within a legal framework, is a good basis for a civilised governance of society. Other considerations must apply too.

(ii) The contention that 'the public' would not accept serious offenders being made to do community service rests on a stereotype. As has been shown, the punitive reaction is not nearly so widespread as is suggested by some authorities.

(iii) The assumption that serious offenders would be less receptive to the influence of community service rests upon a naive aetiological supposition that the seriousness of an offence reflects the severity and influenceability of a psychosocial disorder. This is not confirmed by empirical research. Serious offenders are just as capable of complying with court orders to make restitution and drawing the rehabilitative benefits of it with no greater risk of reoffending (Umbreit, 1989; Dünkel, 1990; Weitekamp, 1992; De Martelaere and Peeters, 1985).

2. The motives of the parties

Theoretically, the propensity to co-operate should be easy to determine. A finding that either the offender, or the victim, or both, are unwilling to co-operate in a mediation programme should be enough to lead to the abandonment of the idea. However, the way in which the proposal is made influences that willingness, and it may be that time is required for a party to come round to the idea (Marshall, 1992). Even so, a proportion of victims remain unwilling to take part in a restorative procedure. Their decision must be respected. But even in such cases, the possibilities for restorative justice may not be exhausted. The offender may, for example, be made to perform community service, the revenue from which would be paid into a victim support fund.

Greater difficulty arises where the offender himself refuses to co-operate in direct mediation with the victim and/or fails to see the point of community service. Refusal is relative. Conventional penalties also entail custodial sanctions and imposed conditions which take no account of the offender's preferences. The obligation to perform community service and even participate in mediation could be introduced by analogy with the existing conditions for probation as already happens in certain countries, for example (Junger and Van Hecke, 1989; Galaway, 1992). Even if non-custodial community service were to be excluded, service to the community or for a victim support fund could be imposed in a residential environment.

3. Security

Security considerations may mean that mediation or non-custodial (even supervised) community service entails too great a risk of serious recidivism. The limits are hard to set. Two observations must be made.

- Imprisonment is not absolutely secure either. So diverse are arrangements and regimes of imprisonment that periods of unsupervised contact with society are often included. The fact that relatively few 'incidents' occur show that security considerations should not be overstated. Many offenders currently serving terms of imprisonment could perfectly well undertake non-institutional reparation at no risk.

- Imprisonment should not necessarily be devoid of restorative purpose. Various authors have suggested that the length of custodial sentence could be made dependent on performing prison work to contribute to a victim support fund, or even direct compensation of the victim (Spencer, 1975 and Smith, 1975, both cited in Weitekamp, 1992).

The challenge: extending the limits of restorative justice

It must be confessed that the boundaries of restorative justice have not been drawn. Experiments have been overly-cautious, focussed on 'no-risk' cases.

Once off the beaten path, however, horizons widen and the need to resort to the conventional penal system diminishes. Thus far, comparison of principles and empirical data has supported the hypothesis that a system of restorative justice can be a fully-fledged alternative to a retributive justice system.

Many problems remain, such as, for example, how 'material, psychological and/or social harm' will be defined and measured, and how it will be repaired or compensated; the myriad problems of legal and procedural security; relations with insurers; the development of suitable techniques of mediation, control and supporting models for restorative sanctions, etc. But problems still persist with the other systems too. Rehabilitative justice for juveniles was introduced at the [beginning of the twentieth] century with great hopes, and a considerable investment in resources and scientific expertise. It cannot lay claim to startling success. Furthermore the so-called 'rights without penalties' very often appeared to be penalties without rights. Penal justice has centuries of experimentation behind it and massive state resources and support. But consider the results: 'a series of harms' (Bentham, cited in Tulkens, 1993) with no demonstrably positive results.

Socio-ethical and empirical arguments militate in favour of continuing the effort to extend the bounds of restorative justice to their very outermost limits – for beyond them lies retribution. Resorting to penal justice is 'a sign of failure and powerlessness' (Tulkens, 1993, p. 489). It would appear to be needed only because society has failed to offer certain of its members rewards which would induce them to conform, and because it has failed to regulate the problem of crime in a constructive fashion. They must be pushed back as far as possible. 'The best reform of penal law would be to replace it not with a better penal law, but rather with something better' (Radbruch, cited in Tulkens, 1993). That 'something' is to be sought in the restorative approach.

Nor does restorative justice exclude rehabilitation. Rehabilitation of an offender (if it is truly necessary, which is far from obvious in the majority of cases) is a noble, humane aim, but does not fit within a judicial framework. The function of justice in a society is not to treat its citizens, nor to make them happy. It is simply to place clearly defined limits on what society will tolerate while trying not to place new obstacles in the way of successful integration of its 'clients'. Rehabilitation must take place outside the justice system. Restorative justice must (and can) ensure that extra-judicial rehabilitative approaches are not precluded by its actions.

In such a situation moreover, there is no reason to maintain a separate system of juvenile justice distinct from that for adults. Both groups are entitled to a constructive, minimally-excluding reaction, ordered in accordance with clearly defined, controllable rules of law. The restorative approach combines the best of both criteria for both groups.

The idea of restorative justice is far more than a hypothesis, however. It is also an ideal of justice in an ideal of society. Giving priority to reparation rather than retribution calls for a change in social ethics and a different ideology of society. That means a society governed with the aims of individual and collective emancipation, in which autonomy and solidarity are not seen as diametrically opposed, but as mutually reinforcing principles. A society doing its utmost to avoid exclusion of its members, because it is a society which draws its strength not from fear but from the high social ethics by which it is governed.

Is this utopianism? Yes, but we need a utopia to motivate us and provide guidance for our actions in society. Consider the Ancient Greek myth of Sisyphus. He never succeeded in pushing his stone to the very top of his hill, but he had to continue trying to do [so], otherwise the stone would crush him. We know full well that we shall never achieve an ideal society, but we must go on trying, otherwise the one we have will disintegrate rapidly. There is nothing more practical than a good utopia.

This extract is taken from 'Restorative Justice for Juveniles: Just a Technique or a Fully Fledged Alternative', by Lode Walgrave, in The Howard Journal of Criminal Justice, *34:3 (1995), pp. 228–49.*

Notes

1 Restorative approach to normbreaking is not new. It is an old-established principle which predates public penal systems (see for example, Schafer, 1977). Moreover, restoration continues to play a central role in non-western societies, like in Japan (Sanders and Hamilton, 1992; Haley and Neugebauer, 1992) or in Africa (Shaidi, 1992; Ntanda Nsereko, 1992).
2 In the Netherlands, community service may be ordered either by the court or the public prosecutor's department. In practice, the public prosecutor's department rarely does so (Van der Laan, 1991).
3 The study largely deals with victims of young criminals, chiefly burglaries and to a lesser extent muggings. In all, 948 victims and offenders were interviewed in four States of the USA and instances of mediation analysed. 532 interviews were conducted with participants in mediation; 198 with individuals who were offered mediation and refused, and 218 with individuals to whom mediation was not offered (the type and the gravity of the offences were similar in all three groups). Agreement was achieved in 95% of all mediations undertaken.
4 General prevention is one of the priority aims of retributive justice. According to several studies, the eventual preventive effects of retribution would not relate to the severity of the punishment, but rather to the likelihood of getting caught. Restorative justice would not alter that probability.

References

Braithwaite, J. (1990) *Crime, Shame and Reintegration* (Cambridge: Cambridge University Press).
Christie, N. (1978) 'Conflicts as Property', *British Journal of Criminology*,17, pp. 1–15.
Coates, R. and Gehm, J. (1985) *Victim Meets Offenders: An Evaluation of Victim-Offender Reconciliation Programs* (Valparaiso: PACT).
Cornejo, J. (1981) *Le Problème de l'Efficacité et de l'Evaluation des Interventions de Prévention de la Délinquance. Cahiers de Criminologie et de Pathologie sociale* 18 (Louvain la Neuve: UCL).
Davis, G. (1992) 'Reparation in the UK: Dominant Themes and Neglected Themes', in Messmer, H. and Otto, H.U. (eds) *Restorative Justice on Trial* (Dordrecht/Boston, MA: Kluwer Academic).

Del Vecchio, G. (1975) 'The Problem of Penal Justice', in Hudson, J. and Galaway, B. (eds) *Considering the Victim* (Springfield, IL: Thomas).

De Martelaere, G. and Peeters, J. (1985) 'Een experiment van alternatieve sancties aan de jeugdrechtbank te Mechelen', *Panopticon*, 1, pp. 34–44.

Dézalay, Y. (1988) 'Présentation', *Annales de Vaucresson*, 2 (special issue on 'Les paradoxes de la médiation'), pp. 7–18.

Dünkel, F. (1990) 'Médiation délinquant-victime et Réparation des Dommages. Nouvelle Évolution du Droit Pénal et de la Pratique Judiciaire dans une Comparaison Internationale', in Dünkel, F. and Zermatten, J. (eds) *Nouvelles Tendances dans le Droit Pénal des Mineurs. Médiation, Travail au Profit de la Communauté et Traitement Intermédiaire* (Freiburg: Kriminologische Forschungsberichte aus dem Max-Planck-Institut).

Dünkel, F. and Zermatten, J. (eds) (1990) *Nouvelles Tendances dans le Droit Pénal des Mineurs. Médiation, Travail au Profit de la Communauté et Traitement Intermédiaire* (Freiburg: Kriminologische Forschungsberichte aus deu Max-Planck-Institut).

Feest, J. (1990) 'Courses of Action Designed to Avoid Entry in the Criminal Justice Process or to Interrupt the Process,' in Council of Europe (ed.) *New Social Strategies and the Criminal Justice System* (Nineteenth Criminological Research Conference) (Strassbourg: Council of Europe).

Galaway, B. (1984) 'A Survey of Public Acceptance of Restitution as an Alternative to Imprisonment for Property Offenders', *Australian and New Zealand Journal of Criminology*, 2, pp. 108–17.

Galaway, B. (1992) 'The New Zealand Experience of Implementing Reparation as a Restorative Sentence', in Messmer, H. and Otto, H.U. (eds) *Restorative Justice on Trial* (Dordrecht/Boston, MA: Kluwer Academic).

Galaway, B. and Hudson, J. (1990) 'Towards Resorative Justice', in Galaway, B. and Hudson, J. (eds) *Criminal Justice, Restitution and Reconciliation* (Monsey, NY: Willow Tree Press).

Gehm, J. (1992) 'The Function of Forgiveness in the Criminal Justice System', in Messmer, H. and Otto, H.U. (eds) *Restorative Justice on Trial* (Dordrecht/Boston, MA: Kluwer Academic).

Hackler, J. (1988) 'Increasing Confrontation in Criminal Justice: Contrasting Changes in North America with Trends in Europe', in Walgrave, L. (ed.) *Changes in Society and Juvenile Delinquency. vol. 2 (Sixth International Workshop on Juvenile Criminology)* (Leuven: Acco).

Haley, J. and Neugebauer, A. (1992) 'Victim-Offender Mediation: Japanese and American Comparisons', in Messmer, H. and Otto, H.U. (eds) *Restorative Justice on Trial* (Dordrecht/Boston, MA: Kluwer Academic).

Hirsch Ballin, T. (1993) 'Publieke Moraal en Justitie', *Justitiële Verkenningen*, 2, pp. 9–27.

Houchon, G. (1984) 'A la Recherche du Temps Perdu', *Déviance et Société*, 2, pp. 199–206.

Junger, M. and Van Hecke, T. (1989) 'Schadevergoeding als Straf', *Panopticon*, 4, pp. 350–68.

Junger-Tas, J. (1981) 'Community Service en Dienstverlening: Een Kritische Beschouwing', *Delikt en Delinkwent*, 1, pp. 5–23.

Mackay, R. (1992) 'Restitution and Ethics: An Aristotelian Approach', in Messmer, H. and Otto, H.U. (eds) *Restorative Justice on Trial* (Dordrecht/Boston, MA: Kluwer Academic).

Mair, G. (1990) 'Evaluating the Effects of Diversion Strategies in the Attitudes and Practices of Agents of the Criminal Justice System', in Council of Europe (ed.) *New Social Strategies and the Criminal Justice System (Nineteenth Criminological Research Conference)* (Strassbourg: Council of Europe).

Marshall, T. (1992) 'Restorative Justice on Trial in Britain', in Messmer, H. and Otto, H.U. (eds) *Restorative Justice on Trial* (Dordrecht/Boston, MA: Kluwer Academic).

Messmer, H. and Otto, H.U. (eds) (1992) *Restorative Justice on Trial* (Dordrecht/Boston, MA: Kluwer Academic).

Novak, M. (1989) *Force de Caractère et Crime* (Paris: VRIN).

Ntanda Nsereko (1992) 'Victims of Crime and their Rights', in Unicri (ed.) *Criminology in Africa* (Roma: Unicri).

Orlando, F. (1992) 'Mediation Involving Children in the United States. Legal and Ethical Conflicts', in Messmer, H. and Otto, H.U. (eds) *Restorative Justice on Trial* (Dordrecht/Boston, MA: Kluwer Academic).

Queloz, N. (1991) 'Protection, Intervention and the Rights of Children and Young People', in Booth, T. (ed.) *Juvenile Justice in Europe* (Sheffield: Social Service Monographs).

Sanders, J. and Hamilton, V. (1992) 'Legal Cultures and Punishment Repertoires in Japan, Russia and the United States', *Law and Society Review*, 26, pp. 117–38.

Schafer, S. (1977) *Victimology. The Victim and his Criminal* (Reston: Prentice Hall).

Scieur, Y. (1990) 'La Prestation Communautaire: Une Logique Pour le Magistrat de la Jeunesse', in Dünkel, F. and Zermatten, J. (eds) *Nouvelles Tendances dans le Droit Pénal des Mineurs. Médiation, Travail au Profit de la Communauté et Traitement Intermédiaire* (Freiburg: Kriminologische Forschungsberichte aus dem Max-Planck-Institut).

Shaidi, L. (1992) 'Traditional, Colonial and Present Day Administration of Criminal Justice', in Unicri (ed.) *Criminology in Africa* (Roma: Unicri).

Steinert, H. (1988) 'Kriminalität als Konflikt', *Kriminalsoziologische Bibliografie* (Spezialheft), 58/59, pp. 11–20.

Tulkens, F. (1993) 'Les Transformations du Droit Pénal aux Etats-Unis. Pour un Autre Modèle de Justice', in *Nouveaux Itinéraires en Droit. Hommage à François Rigaux* (Bruxelles: Bruylant, Bibliothèque de la Faculté de droit de l'UCL).

Umbreit, M. (1989) 'Crime Victims Seeking Fairness, not Revenge: Toward Restorative Justice', *Federal Probation*, 3, pp. 52–7.

Umbreit, M. (1992) 'Mediating Victim-Offender Conflict: From Single-site to Multi-site Analysis in the US', in Messmer, H. and Otto, H.U. (eds) *Restorative Justice on Trial* (Dordrecht/Boston, MA: Kluwer Academic).

Umbreit, M. and Coates, R. (1992) *Victim/Offender Mediation: An Analysis of Programs in Four States of the US* (Minneapolis, MN: Minnesota Citizens Council on Crime and Justice).

Van de Kerchove, M. (1986) 'Signification Juridique de la Sanction en Matière de Délinquance Juvénile', in De Troy, C. *et al.* (eds) *Délinquance des Jeunes. Politiques et Interventions* (Bruxelles: Story).

Van der Laan, P. (1991) *Experimenteren met Alternatieve Sancties voor Minderjarigen* (Arnhem/den Haag: Gouda Quint/WODC).

Van Doosselaere, D. (1988) 'Du Stimulus Aversif à la Cognition Sociale. L'Efficacité de la Sanction Selon un Modèle de Psychologie Expérimentale', *Deviance et Société*, 3, pp. 269–87.

Van Ness, D. (1990) 'Restorative Justice', in Galaway, B. and Hudson, J. (eds) *Criminal Justice, Restitution and Reconciliation* (Monsey, NY: Willow Tree Press).

Verhellen, E., Eliaerts, C. and Cappelaere, G. (1987) *Alternatieve Sanctionering van Jongeren* (Gent: Studie- en Documentatiecentrum voor Rechten van Kinderen, R.U. Gent, Cahier 5).

Walgrave, L. (1985) 'La Repénalisation de la Délinquance Juvénile: Une Fuite en Avant', *Revue de Droit Pénal et de Criminologie*, 4, pp. 603–23.

Walgrave, L. (1992) 'Mediation and Community Service as Models of a Restorative Approach: Why would it be Better?', in Messmer, H. and Otto, H.U. (eds) *Restorative Justice on Trial* (Dordrecht/Boston, MA: Kluwer Academic).

Weitekamp, E. (1992) 'Can Restitution Serve as a Reasonable Alternative to Imprisonment?' in Messmer, H. and Otto, H.U. (eds) *Restorative Justice on Trial* (Dordrecht/Boston, MA: Kluwer Academic).

Wright, M. (1989) 'What the Public Wants', in Wright, M. and Galaway, B. (eds) *Mediation in Criminal Justice: Victims, Offenders and Community* (London: Sage).

Wright, M. (1991) *Justice for Victims and Offenders: A Restorative Approach to Crime* (Milton Keynes: Open University Press).

Wright, M. (1992) 'Victim-Offender Mediation as a Step towards a Restorative System of Justice', in Messmer, H. and Otto, H.U. (eds) *Restorative Justice on Trial* (Dordrecht/Boston, MA: Kluwer Academic).

Zehr, H. (1985) *Retributive Justice. Restorative Justice* (Akron, PA: Mennonite Central Committee).

18. Creating restorative systems

Daniel W. Van Ness

[...]

There is no fully elaborated system of restorative/community justice, not only in the sense that no jurisdiction has fully embraced restorative/community values and practices but also in the sense that no one has clearly articulated how such a system might work. It is time to begin that work, for reasons I will go into in some detail later. To do so, we must consider several issues.

First, are there degrees of restorativeness, or is a system either restorative or not? Karen Strong and I have assumed the former (Van Ness and Strong, 2002), as have others,[1] although we have approached the problem differently. This assumption seems merited for several reasons. First, change is usually incremental, which means that restorative approaches that work as designed will begin to have some effect even before all the restorative reforms are implemented. Second, restorative justice reflects values, and is not limited to particular programme elements, which means that it is possible to reflect those values fully or partially. When they are partially expressed, there will be some restorative impact, but not a fully restorative outcome.

What I would like to do in this chapter is further develop how we might assess whether a system is minimally, moderately or fully restorative. Finally, I would like to propose the broad outlines of a restorative system.

Plotting the 'restorativeness' of a system

A variety of values or attributes have been used from time to time to describe restorative processes and outcomes. Sometimes these are treated as though they were discrete elements that are either completely present or else completely absent. Experience shows, however, that these may be partially present and absent. For example, amends – making things right – is certainly a value of restorative justice. But one offender might make amends by paying restitution, offering an apology and agreeing to acts of rehabilitation and generosity that the offender and victim have agreed to. Another offender may only pay restitution. Both have taken steps to make amends, but one has done more than the other has.

Similarly, processes may reflect restorative values in degree or fully. Non-coercion or voluntariness is affirmed as a restorative value, but in fact many – perhaps most – offenders participate in restorative programmes not because that is what they desire, but because it is the least onerous of the options given them. Surely we would acknowledge that programmes that use such limited options have a less stringent definition of 'non-coercive' than do others that would use no coercion at all.

For these reasons, it is best to think of restorative values or attributes as lying on the end of a continuum on the other end of which is a value or attribute

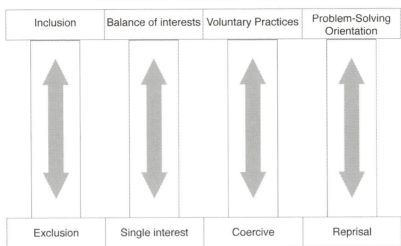

Figure *[18.]1: Continuum of attributes of the restorative process.*

that characterizes contemporary criminal justice. Furthermore, it would be helpful for us to include values or attributes regardless of whether they seem to concern restorative processes or restorative outcomes. During the recent exchanges between Paul McCold, Lode Walgrave, Gordon Bazemore and others on the Purist and Maximalist models of restorative justice,[2] several observers and the participants themselves noted that this discussion hinged in part on whether restorative values relate to process or outcome. It may be my own inclination to look for harmony when two notes are struck, but it seems apparent to me that both process and outcome are important in a restorative perspective.[3]

Let me propose four values or attributes that might be described as restorative processes and four that are more in the nature of restorative outcomes. I suggest that we think of each of these as lying on a continuum, the other end of which represents its antithesis. The four values related to restorative processes are inclusion, balance of interests, voluntary practice, and problem-solving orientation.[4] They and their antitheses are summarized in Figure 18.1.

Inclusion means that all stakeholders are invited to participate. Traditional stakeholders are the government and the offender. Restorative justice adds the victim and community to those two. It is understood that the victim and community have their own interests to pursue; they are not involved only to help the government or defence with their cases. This means that the process will need to be adapted when necessary to allow the parties to participate and to look after their interests. At the other end of the continuum is the exclusion of all parties except to the extent required to determine whether the offender broke the law (see Van Ness and Strong, 2002).

Balance of interests means that restorative programmes avoid focusing on one task alone, and instead attempt to accommodate the interests of all the parties. For example, while restorative programmes respect the importance of the

Attributes of Restorative Outcomes

Encounter	Amends	Reintegration	Whole Truth

Separation	Harm	Ostracism	Legal Truth

Figure [18.]2: Continuum of attributes of restorative outcomes.

public interest in resolving crimes, they do not address that to the exclusion of the interests of others. The objective is to maintain an appropriate balance between all the interests at stake. At the other end of the continuum is the situation in which the only interest pursued is that of determining guilt.

Voluntary practice means that parties participate and assume responsibilities because they have chosen to, and not because they were required to. In practice, the choice to participate is made in the context of other alternatives, so the 'voluntariness' of a party's decision may be limited to the lesser of available evils. For example, an offender may summon the courage to meet with the victim in order to avoid going to prison. At the other end lies a process that routinely relies on coercion to gain the participation of the accused and of witnesses.

The *problem-solving* orientation of restorative justice causes it to look to the future even as it addresses the past. Among other things, this means that it is more likely to view crime in its social context than as an isolated event. Contemporary criminal justice focuses instead on whether and how to impose some sort of reprisal on the guilty offender (Dignan and Lowey, 2000: 6).

Figure 18.2 depicts the values or attributes of restorative outcomes. The first continuum addresses the extent to which the parties have come together in arriving at the restorative resolution. At one end is the situation in which all interested parties were able to encounter each other. This will have given them an opportunity to work together to achieve the other restorative outcomes. At the other end is the situation in which the parties have been separated by the criminal justice process.

The second continuum represents differing understandings of how to respond to the offender's criminal behaviour. At one end is amends, in which the offender has made restitution, offering an apology, undertaken specific behaviours that will lead to change and acts of generosity. At the other end is the situation in which the offender has been required to 'pay' for committing the crime by suffering harm.

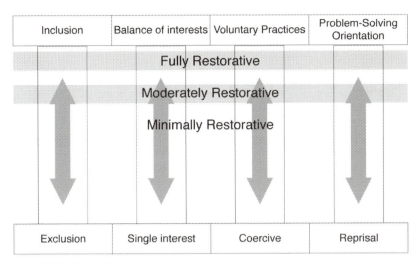

Figure [18.]3: Attributes of restorative processes.

The third continuum depicts the relationship between the parties and their communities at the end of the process. At one end is the full integration of both into their communities as productive and contributing members. At the other end is ostracism either through enforced separation of the offender (perhaps through a sentence to prison) or through continuing stigmatization of both in their roles as victim and offender. In contemporary criminal justice, the separation of the offender is a desired outcome, and stigmatization of victims and offenders is a consequential outcome.

The final continuum concerns the nature and extent of the truth that is discovered in the course of the process. At one end, the parties discover the whole truth about the offence, including matters of culpability, harm, the perspectives of the parties, community impact and the shared values of the parties. They are able to explore any matter that concerns them. At the other end lies the more limited legal truth around which contemporary criminal justice focuses its efforts. It is concerned with what law was broken and whether the defendant is the one who broke it. Other matters are considered irrelevant and perhaps prejudicial.

Assume for a moment that these eight continuums capture the key values of restorative processes and outcomes. Assume as well that we are able to calibrate where a programme or system lies along each of these eight continuums. Under those circumstances, we could identify degrees of 'restora-tiveness' for both processes and outcomes.

I will give examples to illustrate why we might think in terms of degrees of restorativeness, although I do not want to suggest that particular restorative programmes are necessarily more or less restorative than others. What makes any process restorative is the extent to which it reflects restorative values and attributes, not the name it goes by. An example of a fully restorative process might be the circles of Hollow Water, a First Nations community in Canada. In instances of sexual violence, for example, there will be separate healing circles for the victim and the offender, together with their families, supporters

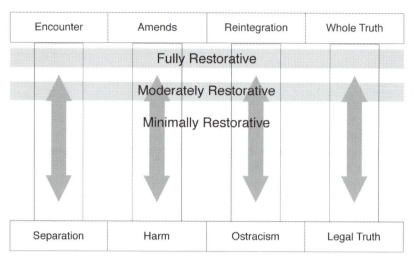

Figure [18.]4: Attributes of restorative outcomes.

and members of their community. After a time, these give way to new circles in which all parties may participate, with the objective being to develop a plan for the future. An example of a moderately restorative process could be a conference in which the victim, offender and their supporters meet to discuss the crime and work toward a resolution. The offender chooses to participate rather than go to court. Because of the relative brevity of the meeting, there is little time to probe underlying issues. An example of a minimally restorative process might be a conference that involves only the offender and his supporters. The victim has chosen not to participate, and a police officer or community volunteer attempts to provide the kind of perspective that the victim would have offered.

In the same way we might construct a range of restorative outcomes. An example of a fully restorative outcome might be one in which the victim, offender and community members were able to meet and talk, all came to a more complete understanding of what took place and of the harm that resulted, the offender offered an apology as well as restitution, and the community members helped organize necessary support for each of them. An example of a moderately restorative outcome might be one in which the victim and offender met and talked about what took place and the fear the victim experienced, the offender answered all questions the victim had and then apologized, and the offender agreed to return to school and participate in a substance abuse treatment programme. An example of a minimally restorative outcome might be one in which the offender met with community members and the victim of a similar crime (the actual victim chose not to participate), the offender agreed to pay restitution and perform community service rather than face a potential prison sentence, and the offender agreed to return to school.

When we design our restorative system, we want one that includes restorative processes and outcomes. This forces us to consider a constellation of options more complex than two sets of four continuums, because we will

System of Processes and Outcomes

Figure [18.]5: System of processes and outcomes.

need to explore how the two interrelate. A moderately restorative process will not necessarily yield a moderately restorative outcome. Figure 18.5 shows a grid with one axis representing processes and another representing outcomes. Many processes and outcomes are not restorative at all (these portions are represented in white). Others are minimally, moderately or fully restorative (dark grey, medium grey and light grey, respectively). If we require a restorative programme or system to exhibit both restorative processes and outcomes, we narrow the possibilities significantly. Further, if we assume that a lower degree of restorativeness on one axis is only marginally improved by a higher degree on the other, we see that there are a number of ways that systems can be at least minimally restorative but only one way to make them fully restorative.

[. . .]

Constructing a unified restorative model

How we might go about constructing a model of a restorative system. For a number of reasons, it is important to begin designing such a system now, even as restorative applications continue to spread rapidly and as we consider issues such as relative restorativeness and community–government cooperation.

First, if changes continue to be made incrementally, restorative justice runs the risk of becoming marginalized. Rather than letting the values and principles of restorative justice transform our entire approach to crime, particular restorative programmes will be annexed to existing structures in such a way that their influence is contained.

Second, many proponents have made the claim that restorative justice represents a paradigm shift, a change in patterns of thinking, a new lens through which we look at crime. If so, one would expect a wholesale change in how we approach crime and justice. A shift of the magnitude we claim would surely produce an entirely new system with very different programmes, institutions, processes and outcomes.

Third, some policymakers are asking for a system model. The not unreasonable expectation is that after a decade of experimentation, development, evaluation and experience, restorative justice practitioners and advocates would have reasonably clear ideas about what a restorative system might look like. We run two risks in responding to that expectation. The first is to offer incomplete and ill-considered proposals that if implemented would short-change the transformational potential of restorative justice. The second is to lose credibility when it becomes clear that we have done only a limited amount of thinking about what such a system might look like.

Finally, there are hard questions about the feasibility and comprehensiveness of restorative justice that may never be answered until serious attempts are made to construct a restorative system. Comprehensiveness is an issue because some conditions have traditionally been viewed as prerequisites for a restorative response (admission of guilt, willingness to participate, ability to make reparation, etc.). What happens when those conditions are not present? How could a system respond restoratively with all serious crimes as well as all minor ones? With offenders and victims who are unwilling or unable to participate, as well as those who are willing and able? With cases in which the accused denies guilt? A fully restorative justice system of the sort anticipated by this project must be capable of effectively and restoratively addressing the myriad conditions and issues that are normal and routine in the administration of justice.

The second issue has to do with the feasibility of such a system. The 'criminal justice system' is not a system at all, but a collection of responses by public and private agencies, often in the context of conflicting goals and interests. Is it reasonable to suggest that a system with restorative values and norms could be implemented when so many different players must be involved? Furthermore, political concerns are (and should be) of great importance to policymakers. How might a policymaker consider alternative strategies for introducing and implementing a restorative system? Finally, can a restorative system handle high volumes of cases efficiently yet restoratively? Not simply the current high volume of criminal cases (which represent only a fraction of all crimes because they are only those in which accused offenders have been identified and caught) but also all those other crimes in which there are victims, but no identified offenders.

I have elsewhere suggested that a restorative system might take one of four forms in the way it would relate to conventional criminal justice systems (see

Four Models

Stage	Unified model	Dual track model	Safety-net model	Hybrid model

Figure [18.]6: Four models of the relationship between conventional and restorative justice systems.

Figure 18.6) (Van Ness, 2002). The first is a unitary model in which the restorative system is the only one available. The second is a dual-track model in which both systems stand side by side, with designated passages between them for parties to move back and forth. The third is a safety-net model in which the restorative system is the basic response to crime, but conventional processes are available when needed (for example, for determining guilt when that issue is contested). The final model is a hybrid, in which both approaches are linked into a single system. The example showed in Figure 18.6 is one that uses conventional processes until guilt is ascertained, at which point it shifts to restorative processes.

Models one and two assume that restorative justice is capable of dealing with all kinds of crimes and at all stages of the justice system. Models three and four assume that for either conceptual or practical reasons, it will not do so. Consequently, the more challenging models to examine are the first two, since they must be able to address the issues of comprehensiveness and feasibility. Perhaps a way to begin is to construct the second model, the dual track system, and then explore how that could be transformed into a unitary model.

I think that there are several likely elements to either of the two models. The first is a significant governmental role in organizing the restorative system and making it available to all. This is how the New Zealand Family Group Conferencing programme is organized. The government arm responsible for this (we might call it the Office of Restorative Interventions) will require sufficient staff to provide a stable programme, but built into its operations would be a large number of volunteer participants recruited from communities. These volunteers would play critical, not cosmetic or supportive roles, which means that both they and the Office of Restorative Interventions would understand their critical nature.

The Office would need to organize responses from the moment that a crime occurs until the final restorative elements have been completed. This means that victim services and support would need to be made available regardless of whether the accused offender is apprehended. These services and support would continue to be available at the request of the victim regardless of the pace of the processes determining offender accountability and response. The Office would also need to organize an investigatory service that would seek to minimize harm even as it explored what happened, who participated and what steps are needed to insure that this person is available for determining accountability.

I anticipate the development of a restorative method of dealing with situations in which the defendant denies having caused harm or violated laws to prevent harm.[5] The defendant and the victim should have the opportunity to get a full and complete explanation of the available processes so that they could make informed decisions. This briefing would probably be given by carefully trained volunteer supporters who would be available to both parties. Furthermore, to the extent that the community had been adversely affected by the crime, a representative of the community might be invited to participate in all future proceedings as a representative of the community. This would ensure that a general invitation to the community is neither ignored or unheard.

A full range of restorative processes should be available during the adjudication and sentencing or responsibility phases.[6] It may be that these processes will be used multiple times in the same matter. For example, there may be a need to proceed with an encounter programme without the victim because the victim is unable or unwilling to participate within the time in which it is reasonable to seek to determine the defendant's responsibility. Conferences may take place without the direct victim, and instead community members or surrogate victims may participate. At a later date, if the victim decides that it would be useful to meet with the defendant, then a conference, circle or mediation/dialogue might be conducted for those purposes.

The restorative processes used to facilitate the adjudication and responsibility phases would be modified to ensure that the agreement is carried out. If some sort of incapacitation were needed, a form of prison would be available, characterized by two features. First, the goal would be to work with the prisoner so that the need for prison was eliminated. Second, the prison should have meaningful work opportunities within it so that the prisoner could work, earn money and pay restitution.

Conclusion

Much has changed in fifteen years in the restorative justice movement. The question we must ask is whether in another fifteen years restorative justice will play a marginal role in a criminal justice system dominated by other values, or whether it will become the principal response to crime in at least some jurisdictions. The answer to that question will depend on our abilities to measure the restorativeness of systems and programmes, to understand and take full advantage of the community–government relationship, and to construct conceptual models.

This extract is taken from 'Creating Restorative Systems', by Daniel W. Van Ness, in L. Walgrave (ed.), Restorative Justice and the Law *(Cullompton, Devon: Willan, 2002) pp. 130–49.*

Notes

1 Paul McCold, for example, in describing his Purist model of restorative justice has proposed that programmes could be classified based on the extent to which they meet the needs of victims, offenders and their communities. He assigns the name holistic to programmes that meet the needs of all three parties. Mostly restorative programmes are those that address the interests of only two. Partly restorative programmes meet the needs of only one. Pseudo-restorative programmes are those that call themselves restorative but in fact fail to address the interests of any of the parties (McCold, 2000). In other words, the degree of restorativeness of programmes (and presumably of systems) is based on the extent to which they meet the needs of all, as opposed to some, of the parties.

2 A thorough discussion of the Purist and Maximalist models, featuring articles by McCold, Walgrave, Bazemore and others, may be found in *Contemporary Justice Review*, Dec. 2000, 3(4).

3 Part of the difficulty here may be that the distinction between processes and outcomes, while seeming clear, becomes cloudier on close inspection. Can a process really be examined independently of the outcome that results? Can an outcome be considered restorative regardless of how it was achieved? The answers to both questions seems to be 'no', which is why I suggest that we address both processes and outcomes as each relates to the other.

4 These are adapted from Dignan and Lowey, 2000.

5 I use the name given to the accused under contemporary criminal justice processes only so that it is clear to whom I am referring. Presumably different names would be assigned that better reflect the person's true position in what should be a less adversarial process.

6 See the disclaimer concerning names in the previous note.

References

Dignan, J. and Lowey, K. (2000) *Restorative Justice Options for Northern Ireland.* Report commissioned for the Review of the Criminal Justice System in Northern Ireland. Research Report No. 10. Belfast: Criminal Justice Review Commission/Northern Ireland Office.

McCold, P. (2000) 'Toward a Holistic Vision of Restorative Juvenile Justice: A Reply to the Maximalist Model', *Contemporary Justice Review*, 3(4): 357–72.

Van Ness, D. (2002) 'The Shape of Things to Come: A Framework for Thinking about A Restorative Justice System', in Weitekamp, G. and Kerrer, H. (eds) *Restorative Justice: Theoretical Foundations* (Cullompton, Devon: Willan).

Van Ness, D. and Strong, K.H. (2002) *Restoring Justice* (2nd edn). Cincinatti, OH: Anderson.

19. The function of forgiveness in the criminal justice system

John R. Gehm

Introduction

Forgiveness, defined as a process of ceasing to feel resentment, has both long standing religious connotations as well as more recent secular ones. 'Forgiveness' is a central tenet of most major religious traditions (Pingleton, 1989; Newman, 1987). Forgiveness, as a religious teaching, leads not only to the restoration of right relationships between and among communities but also because God commands it. Whether forgiveness is used as the basis for a doctrine of undeserved mercy shown by an all-powerful sovereign to his servants or as the key for turning away anger with love, the central component of forgiveness appears to be best understood as 'comprising the antithesis of an individual's natural and predictable response to violation and victimization' (Pingleton, 1989, p. 27).

In psychotherapy, forgiveness as a *technique* for releasing anger and resentment is beginning to receive increasing attention from researchers and theoreticians (Fitzgibbons, 1986; Pingleton, 1989). Forgiveness, however, remains a relatively understudied phenomenon (Pattison, 1965; Wapnick, 1985; Shontz and Rosenak, 1988). Such inattention may be due, in part, to the traditional associations of forgiveness with religion or spirituality, areas believed by some to fall outside the domain of legitimate empirical investigation for the social sciences. Forgiveness remains a difficult construct to operationalize.

What both the religious as well as the psychological conceptualizations have in common, however, is the role forgiveness plays in releasing anger engendered by real or perceived inequity. In the former, the outcome is 'right relationships'; in the latter, it is improved emotional and mental health.

Forgiveness defined

It is no less accurate to say that 'the rose is red' as to say that 'the rose is beautiful'. Both statements can be true simultaneously. So, too, forgiveness may be discussed from what at first might seem like incongruous perspectives. Clearly, forgiveness has multiple dimensions that touch on religion, psychology, and even justice (Murphy, 1988; Murphy and Hampton, 1988).

According to Webster's dictionary, forgiveness is defined as a process of ceasing to feel resentment against someone. It has been characterized as 'giving up one's right to hurt back' (Pingleton, 1989). In general, it would seem to appear that forgiveness implies a kind of a setting aside or a 'giving away' of one's natural impulse to strike back or exact revenge. 'Don't get mad – get even', the bumper sticker philosophy of our era, echoes through history. Indeed, to turn away from the anticipated pleasures of retribution, very much at the center of that complex emotion of anger, is viewed by most as weak. In short, there is little cultural reinforcement for the notion of letting the perpetrator of injustice 'off the hook' or in 'giving in' or turning the other cheek.

However, neither religious nor psychological conceptualizations of forgiveness are seen as synonymous with either excusing or condoning the act or the actor. Forgiveness does not diminish the seriousness of what happened, nor its significance to the individual or to the community. Forgiveness is letting go of the *power* that the offence and the offender have over a person while not condoning or excusing the actor (Zehr, 1990, p. 47). Newman (1987), in his explication of the Mishnah, a 2nd century primary rabbinic text, suggests that in the Judaic tradition, forgiveness, rather than relieving the offender of the accountability for his acts, actually draws attention to and underscores the seriousness of what has occurred. He notes that the ancient authorities both locate forgiveness in the context of other social responsibilities and recognize its essential paradox: that while forgiveness calls attention to the act, at the same time, it facilitates a bridging of the gap.

For Newman, forgiveness contains two essential aspects: 'Just as one restores a situation of material equity through the payment of damages, one must likewise restore that state of moral equilibrium which has been disturbed by the offence in question' (p. 159).

This need for forgiveness arises when there has been a breach in relationships. Lauritzen (1987) proposes the following 'ethical model'.

1. A injures B, thus creating a moral debt between A and B and breach in the relationship between A and B.
2. This debt is characterized, on the one hand, by A's obligation to B to apologize, make restitution, etc., and, on the other hand, by B's justified retributive response of resentment.
3. A discharges his obligations to B and seeks forgiveness from B.
4. B relinquishes his right to resentment (thus cancelling the debt) and readjusts his attitudes towards A in line with a relationship of moral equality (thus repairing the breach in the relationship between himself and A). (p. 144)

The question of what to do in the case of the unrepentant sinner, the unremorseful offender, remains an open one. There is some evidence to suggest, according to the ancient texts, that the offender bears the responsibility for initiating the process of forgiveness (Newman, 1987, p. 160). Failing that, one may argue that there is no 'moral obligation' to forgive at least with respect to moral obligations that relate to the offender; there may, however, be moral obligations that relate to the self.

Discussion

The psychology of forgiveness: anger and release

While acknowledging the value of healthy relationships within communities, McGary (1989) states that:

> [t]he nature of forgiveness need not be a desire to relieve the suffering of the repentant wrongdoer. It could simply be to rid one's self of the destructive emotion of resentment that has gone beyond its appropriate limits. (p. 346)

The psychological model focuses on the process by which the injury threatens the self. Inequity is viewed as constituting an injury to the self in terms of esteem, pride, and omnipotence. An injury of this sort typically results in a deeper awareness of the self's vulnerability, helplessness, dependency, and inadequacy. To ward off the pain of this 'narcissistic wound', the ego adapts by projecting the self's internal fear, guilt, and outrage on to the violator via anger and resentment (Pingleton, 1989, p. 30).

Anger, then, becomes an empowering, defensive externalization of blame. It can, however, become maladaptive when excessive mental energy is channelled into destructive fantasies that produce unexpressed rage, bitterness, and resentment. Often, this can damage other healthy relationships and can ultimately produce psychosomatic illness and other health problems (Diamond, 1982; Shekelle *et al.*, 1983).

A second adaptive response to this sort of injury to the ego is the development of 'punitive guilt' by the victim. Blame for the act is turned inward. Such self-hatred, for example, may lead to reparative attempts to punish oneself for this intrinsic sense of vulnerability (Pingleton, 1989, p. 30). Such self-blame, he notes, can lead to a downward spiral of continuing self-recrimination, frustration, and resentment.

While the majority of work on the psychological aspects of forgiveness is based on intrafamilial victimization and childhood experiences concerning real or imagined inequities, similar dynamics apply to victims' reactions to the trauma of crime. Victims' experiences with respect to self-blaming, denial, and the nursing of various revenge fantasies are reported by Bard and Sangrey (1986) and elsewhere (Van Ness, 1986). These various reactions or coping mechanisms are linked by the way in which they focus on releasing anger. Anger is the natural product of both mental and physical injury. Crime victims are angry and have a moral justification for that anger. Anger arouses a desire for revenge that does not diminish until it is recognized and released. Psychologists suggest that without this recognition and release, anger may be displaced on to self or others – years, or even decades, later. However, for some individuals the benefits of anger outweigh the advantages of giving up their anger because as Fitzgibbons (1986) points out:

> this emotion is used as an unconscious defence . . . As long as the individual is angry, he or she is able to ward off the underlying sadness which gave rise to the anger. Some patients are able to do this for many years. (p. 632)

Eventually, however, anger must be discharged. There are three primary mechanisms for dealing with anger: denial, expression, and forgiveness (Fitzgibbon, 1986, p. 629). While the expression of anger is to be encouraged, it has only limited value with respect to lessening the desire for revenge and release from its power (Horowitz, 1981; Lerner, 1985). Fitzgibbons concludes that '[a]nger is not fully resolved until a conscious decision is made to let go of the desire for revenge or to forgive' (1986, p. 629). Smedes (1984) describes the process as 'hurt – hate – heal'.

Forgiveness (a) helps individuals forget the painful experiences of their past and frees them from the subtle control of individuals and events of the past; (b) facilitates the reconciliation of relationships more than the expression of anger; (c) decreases the likelihood that anger will be misdirected in later loving relationships; and (d) lessens the subconscious fear of being punished because of unconscious violent impulses (Fitzgibbons, 1986, p. 630).

The research on forgiveness then, though limited, focuses primarily on anger, its healthy resolution, and the role that it plays in allowing individuals to get on with their lives less encumbered by the pain and power of the past. The research also acknowledges, however, that some victims who have been deeply hurt are unable to use the word forgiveness. Rather, they may be more comfortable stating that they are willing to let go of their desire for revenge (Fitzgibbons, 1986, p. 630).

Kenel (1988) observes how anger and its expression are sources of difficulty in the lives of many women involved in religious conflicts at both the institutional and interpersonal levels. Forgiveness represents an important and powerful technique for transcending anger in this context. Lerner (1977) explores the process of psychogenesis, an approach to therapy that attempts to re-empower those individuals who feel powerless. Here there are clear analogies with criminal victimization. While this technique focuses typically on the childhood roots of powerlessness, a key component in the successful resolution of many traumas related to powerlessness is the linkage between anger and forgiveness.

Sharma and Cheatham (1986) discuss sexual assault counseling models for serving victims of rape and incest. Their research identifies a range of emotions experienced by victims during the recovery process that includes anger and forgiveness. Fitzgibbons (1986) and Pingleton (1989) suggest that forgiveness may have a much larger role in the recovery process than is presently understood. Much of the work focuses on anger. But because anger is so central to the dynamics of the victimization process, extension of this general work holds promise in the area of criminal justice.

[...]

To talk of forgiveness, however, in the same breath as retribution, incapacitation, deterrence, and other more traditional functions of the criminal justice process seems somewhat incongruous. Yet forgiveness lies at the very heart and center of processes for overcoming the deleterious effects of crime and other social inequity. There is increasing evidence to suggest that victim–offender reconciliation programs may have the potential for far broader applications than was previously thought possible or desirable. Umbreit (1988), for example, urges states to consider adopting policies that provide all crime victims with the basic right to confront their offender through a structured mediation process.

Citizens and communities victimized by physical, emotional, or economic harm are justifiably angry and require a means to address the injustice that that anger represents. Whether drawing from traditions stemming from equity theory, restorative justice, or more recent work on victims' perceptions of fairness, balance needs to be restored to compensate for the inequity that has been experienced. While the civil justice system meets that need through a calculus of costs and claims, the criminal justice system does so primarily by enabling a 'just measure' of revenge – constraining liberty and inflicting pain.

However, research in psychotherapy suggests that anger often remains even after economic reparations and expressions of revenge have been made. Forgiveness – defined here as a conscious release of the desire for revenge – is gaining recognition as a powerful therapeutic tool on the individual level, releasing persons from the control of others or of unpleasant past events. Victim–offender reconciliation and other programs that empower the victim to become involved in sanctions that repair rather than revenge would seem to hold out considerable promise for releasing victim and community (and offender) from the destructive effects of unresolved or ineffectively released anger.

Yet despite the fact that VORP has been demonstrated to have potentially therapeutic benefits, judges in the US still appear reluctant to utilize it for serious cases or in cases in which no material restitution is at stake.

Providing structured opportunities for forgiveness continue to be met with skepticism. While this may be due in part to the religious implications of the terminology, more likely, forgiveness implies a release of the traditional confrontational ethic.

In a culture trained to think in dichotomies and categories of knowledge: good and bad, black and white, recidivism/rehabilitation, there exists a world of the heart and a world of the head. There is secular knowledge and spiritual matters, reason and emotion. In such a fragmented, individualistic culture, we pit advocates for the victims against advocates for the defendants, pitted against those representing the interests of the State. To attempt to describe a holistic conceptualization of justice that spans these boundaries, as discussions of forgiveness will continue to put forward, simply does not compute.

Two paths seem to be developing: the 'hard', 'traditional' justice based on a retributive model and a 'soft', 'alternative' one based on a restorative model. 'Forgiveness' may be the link that spans the softer and the harder paths of justice. There is a need for research that investigates the process and dynamics of forgiveness with specific application to the psychology of recovery from crime at both the individual as well as the community level. Research is also necessary that would begin to investigate the degree to which need for rituals of forgiveness and release from anger are desired by the public.

Without the conscious development of a bridge between the hard and soft, between the retributive and the restorative paths, we may be left with the two-track system of justice Haley (1989) describes in Japan – but without the positive reinforcement. 'Forgiveness rituals', rather than, as Haley describes, moderating the hard path in a less retributive direction may serve only as quaint signposts while the highway heads in another direction entirely.

This extract is taken from 'The Function of Forgiveness in the Criminal Justice System', by John R. Gehm, in H. Messmer and H. Otto (eds), Restorative Justice on Trial (Netherlands: Kluwer, 1992), pp. 541–50.

References

Bard, M. and Sangrey, D. (1986) *The Crime Victim's Book* (2nd edn) (New York, NY: Brunner/Mazel Publishers).

Diamond, E.L. (1982) The role of anger in essential hypertension and coronary heart disease. *Psychological Bulletin*, 92, pp. 410–33.

Fitzgibbons, R.P. (1986) 'The Cognitive and Emotive Uses of Forgiveness in the Treatment of Anger', *Psychotherapy*, 23, pp. 629–33.

Haley, J. (1989) 'Confession, Repentance and Absolution', in Wright, M. and Galaway, P. (eds) *Mediation and Criminal Justice: Victims, Offenders and Communities* (London: Sage), pp. 195–211.

Horowitz, M.J. (1981) 'Self-righteous Rage and the Attribution of Blame', *Archives of General Psychiatry*, 38, pp. 1233–8.

Kenel, M.E. (1988) 'Religious Women and the Problem of Anger', *Journal of Religion and Health*, 27, pp. 236–44.

Lauritzen, P. (1987) 'Forgiveness: Moral Prerogative or Religious Duty?', *Journal of Religious Ethics*, 15, pp. 141–54.

Lerner, H.G. (1985) *The Danger of Anger* (New York, NY: Harper & Row).

McGary, H. (1989) 'Forgiveness', *American Philosophical Quarterly*, 26, pp. 343–51.

Murphy, J. (1988) 'Forgiveness, Mercy, and the Retributive Emotions', *Criminal Justice Ethics*, 7, pp. 3–15.

Murphy, J.G. and Hampton, J. (1988) *Forgiveness and Mercy* (Cambridge: Cambridge University Press).

Newman, L.F. (1987) 'The Quality of Mercy: On the Duty to Forgive in the Judaic Tradition', *Journal of Religious Ethics*, 15, pp. 155–77.

Pattison, M. (1965) 'On the Failure to Forgive or to be Forgiven', *American Journal of Psychotherapy*, 31, pp. 106–15.

Pingleton, J.P. (1989) 'The Role and Function of Forgiveness in the Psychotherapeutic Process', *Journal of Psychology and Theology*, 17, pp. 27–35.

Sharma, A. and Cheatham, H.E. (1986) 'A Women's Center Support Group for Sexual Assault Victims', *Journal of Counseling and Development*, 64, pp. 525–7.

Shekelle, A.B., Gale, M., Ostfeld, A.M. and Oglesby, P. (1983) 'Hostility, Risk of Coronary Heart Disease, and Mortality', *Psychosomatic Medicine*, 45, pp. 109–14.

Shontz, E.C. and Rosenak, C. (1988) 'Psychological Theories and the Need for Forgiveness: Assessment and Critique', *Journal of Psychology and Christianity*, 7, pp. 57–66.

Smedes, L.B. (1984) *Forgive and Forget: Healing the Hurts We Don't Deserve* (San Francisco, CA: Harper & Row).

Umbreit, M. (1988) *Victim Understanding of Fairness: Burglary Victims in Victim Offender Mediation* (Minneapolis, MN: Minnesota Citizens Council on Crime and Justice).

Wapnick, K. (1985) 'Forgiveness: A Spiritual Psychotherapy', in Stern, E.M. (ed.) *Psychotherapy and the Religiously Committed Patient* (New York, NY: Haworth Press), pp. 47–54.

20. Justice for victims of young offenders: the centrality of emotional harm and restoration

Heather Strang

Introduction

The story of the decline in the role that victims can play in Western criminal justice system is now a familiar one. A thousand years ago, victims' rights to compensation for wrongdoing was codified in written laws (Jeffrey, 1957), though the implementation of these rights often depended on the threat of the kinship feud (Walklate, 1989; Weitekamp, 1999). Only with the rise of the modern state has the responsibility for the investigation, prosecution, and disposition of personal crime ceased to be the victim's responsibility, and become a matter for the Crown or state. The philosophical justification for this was that:

> The wrong done to an individual extends beyond his own family: it is a wrong done to the community of which he is a member, and thus the wrongdoer may be regarded as a public enemy.
>
> (Pollock and Maitland, 1898, quoted by Wright, 1991: 5)

The erosion of victims' rights over the centuries led eventually to their removal from any meaningful role in the justice system in common law countries (Hudson and Galaway, 1975). The victim had become just another witness.

Victims were so comprehensively forgotten that it was not until the middle of the twentieth century that any academic or practical interest in them was revived. Indeed, it was the mid-seventies before researchers, justice policy makers and the broader community began to express concern about their predicament and before victims themselves began agitating about their own role, or rather its absence, in the criminal justice system. For example, Wolfgang (1972: 18) observed: 'The whole criminal justice system – from police to parole – ignores the victim except as he contributes to the evidence against the offender.' Even seventeen years later, when the role and status of victims were finally receiving some attention, Gottfredson (1989: 210) summarised their circumstances as consisting of 'inconvenience, inattention, anxiety-provoking arrangements . . . a failure to validate the victim's status as the person harmed and a lack of information about what is happening in the prosecution of the case'.

Restoring victims: material and emotional dimensions

The swell of activism around the plight of crime victims became, by the late 1970s, a fully fledged social movement with lobbies working towards the alleviation of the negative consequences for victims of both the crime and the criminal justice process, and towards legislative reform focused on victims' rights. Many early activities were directed towards the establishment of state-run victim reparation schemes, which, following the early precedent set by New Zealand in 1963, gradually became the norm in North America, Europe and Australasia. However, these schemes were rarely generously funded and were not usually associated in any way with the judicial processing of the offence which resulted in the injury (Barton, 1996). But Shapland (1986) found that victims saw compensation as a proper objective of the court process and as integral to the criminal justice system: they did not see it as a kind of charity to be given by the state. More than that, compensation was seen as a means of making a symbolic statement about the offence. Indeed, victims revealed their concern with issues beyond the relatively simple question of material compensation with their strong preference for restitution directly by the offender rather than by the state. Shapland *et al.* (1985) found that the amounts that victims suggested as appropriate restitution were often very small so as to make it feasible for the offender to pay. One victim was very plain about this: 'It should be £50 from the court or £200 from the CICB [Criminal Injuries Compensation Board]' (Shapland *et al.*, 1985: 123).

This need for a symbolic statement about the legitimacy of the victims' status and an acknowledgment of the emotional harm experienced is an aspect of victimisation which has only recently been given attention. Beyond the calculable material loss the victim may suffer, these emotional dimensions to the loss have routinely been ignored by the criminal justice system and, I suggest, need to be redressed if the experience is to be satisfactorily resolved. Murphy and Hampton (1988: 25) explained the emotional impact of victimisation this way:

> Intentional wrongdoing insults us and attempts (sometimes successfully) to degrade us ... It is moral injury, and we care about such injuries ... and it is simply part of the human condition that we are weak and vulnerable in these ways. And thus when we are treated with contempt by others it attacks us in profound and deeply threatening ways.

Indeed, there is evidence to suggest that victims may often see emotional restoration as far more important than material or financial reparation. For example, Umbreit *et al.* (1994) found that a quarter of the victims who had experienced mediation spontaneously mentioned the importance of the process for resolving feelings of distress resulting from the crime; this is a higher proportion than mentioned material restitution as a primary benefit. They also found that, for many victims, restitution from the offender was important to them only as a gesture of responsibility for the harm. Marshall and Merry's (1990) review of British victim offender mediation programmes found that often what victims wanted most was not substantial reparation but rather symbolic reparation, primarily an apology.

The Canberra Reintegrative Shaming Experiments (RISE) have also found that victims did not always regard material restoration as of primary importance: when they were asked why they decided to attend a conference, less than a third said that wanting to ensure repayment for the harm they had suffered was an important reason. This tendency to see material restitution as no more than secondary was well expressed by a victim whose babysitter had stolen from her family. In the conference, she said:

> It's not just money, that's nothing, it's the way it's affected all of us. We aren't here because money's an issue at all. We aren't here for our pound of flesh.

Another victim had been assaulted while riding his bicycle by an angry motorist. He said that he felt he probably should have received some money from the offender but made a decision in the conference not to ask for it. This was not because he felt powerless to do so, but because the emotions in the conference had been so raw that he felt it was inappropriate to ask for it and also because he discovered that he and his assailant were in the same kind of employment so he felt a sense of solidarity with him. These cases support Braithwaite's (1999) argument that a real problem exists in evaluating how well restorative justice restores, even on the apparently straightforward dimension of material restoration, because the dynamics of a conference may result in some victims preferring to act generously rather than insisting on getting their financial just deserts.

In fact, RISE data indicated that victims were not often awarded money in either the conference setting or in court,[1] though more than a quarter of the conference group received other forms of material restitution from their offenders, usually voluntary work either for themelves or for a charitable organisation they nominated. But given that conferences appeared to be no more effective than court at delivering financial restitution to victims, it is interesting to discover that there was considerable difference between the two groups in terms of how much they wanted money awarded. More of the court victims than the conference victims said they wanted money as an outcome (46 per cent compared with 37 per cent). It appeared that the conference experience affected victims' opinions of whether financial restitution was an appropriate outcome.

In general, the victimology literature makes little mention of victims' desire for apologies from their offenders. This is a surprise for anyone who has observed the interactions between victims and offenders in restorative justice processes, where the offer and acceptance of a sincere apology seems natural and essential in resolving the offence. This absence is a consequence of operating within the dominant retributive paradigm – what is the point in asking victims whether they want an apology when no opportunity exists for a direct exchange between the principals? The absence of a role for apology in Western justice systems may be related to the tendency for our legal system to reduce all harms to a monetary metric, even when no economic loss is entailed. This tendency can also be found in victim offender mediation programmes, with their emphasis on material restitution as the primary outcome. The opportunity to come face to face with one's offender presented by restorative justice programmes of all kinds enhances the likelihood of victims gaining emotional restoration too, as we shall see, though we must always be conscious of the attendant risks of this confrontation.

Apology and forgiveness are so familiar and so much a part of everyday interaction in our society, for offences trivial and serious, that it is worth looking more closely at the transaction to appreciate what Tavuchis (1991: 6) called 'the almost miraculous qualities of a satisfying apology'. It is also worth considering whether what victims really want even more than an apology is the opportunity to forgive and so to be relieved of the burden of anger and bitterness which may result from the sense that their emotional hurt is unacknowledged. Arendt (1958) made the point that forgiveness releases the victim from feelings of punishment and revenge and also works to limit the possibility of escalating dispute.

Tavuchis (1991: 3) suggested that apology must minimally entail 'acknowledgment of the legitimacy of the violated rule, admission of fault and responsibility for its violation, and the expression of genuine regret and remorse for the harm done'. However, the magic of apology is that, while it cannot undo the past, somehow this is precisely what is achieved. The goal of apology is the granting of forgiveness and, when both occur, the parties join in a ritual of reconciliation, with the apology as a gift accepted through an expression of forgiveness. Each party needs a response from the other before social harmony can be restored.

In writings on restorative justice generally, apology is usually seen as a goal to be sought and as a sign of victims' satisfaction when it is given. But more recently, in discussions of conferencing, the apology has come to be seen as central to the process of restoration. Retzinger and Scheff (1996: 316) place the phenomenon of apology and forgiveness within a theoretical framework that they refer to as 'symbolic reparation', where these two steps are the 'core sequence'. They suggested that within conferences:

> Without the core sequence [apology and forgiveness], the path towards settlement is strewn with impediments, whatever settlement is reached does not decrease the tension level in the room, and leaves the participants with a feeling of arbitrariness and dissatisfaction. Thus, it is crucially important to give symbolic reparation at least parity with material settlement . . . Symbolic reparation is the vital element that differentiates conferences from all other forms of crime control (1996: 317).

In empirical studies, such as Stewart's (1996) detailed description of the process of New Zealand family group conferencing, apology was the centre-piece. McCold and Wachtel (1998) also found high levels of apology in their Bethlehem study, along with high levels of victims' satisfaction. As well, the significance of apology as an indication of a genuine desire for reconciliation was suggested by Morris and Maxwell's findings (1997) that offenders who failed to apologise were three times more likely to reoffend than those who did so. However, apology (and forgiveness), when it occurs, is most often the end result of a series of interactions between victims and offenders signalling various stages of emotional restoration that the parties experience. As Daly (2000: 42) said 'one cannot begin a restorative justice process by announcing "let's reconcile", "let's negotiate", or "let's reintegrate" '. The RISE study provided an opportunity to examine what the elements of emotional harm and restoration were for the victims of the offences included in the experiments and how successful the conferencing programme was at giving them the emotional recovery they sought.

Victims in the reintegrative shaming experiments (RISE)

RISE involved the random assignment of middle-range property and violence offences to either court processing or to the restorative justice alternative of conferencing. All the offences were committed by young offenders who had made full admissions of responsibility, and all of them would normally have been dealt with in court. [. . .]

Apology and forgiveness

I have suggested that acknowledgment of emotional harm and of the need for emotional restoration are central to the dynamics of a successful conference, and that the apology–forgiveness transaction is of great significance in restorative justice as it is in everyday life. It comes as no surprise, therefore, to find that, when RISE victims were asked whether or not they believed that they should have received an apology from their offender, around 90 per cent of both the court group and the conference group said that they should have. However, when they were asked whether in fact their offenders had apologised, almost three-quarters (82 per cent) of the conference victims said that they had done so, compared with only 11 per cent of the court victims. And, of those who had received an apology, none of the court victims said that it was part of the court outcome, while 90 per cent of the conference victims said that it was part of the conference outcome.

Interestingly, there was also a significant difference between the court and conference victims when they were asked how they rated the sincerity of the apology: over three quarters (77 per cent) of the conference victims believed it was sincere compared with only 36 per cent of the court victims. Conference victims, it seems, not only got more apologies but also better quality apologies. This may be due to the circumstances in which they were offered: most of the apologies received by victims whose cases went to court seem to have been coerced by the offender's family, while apologies forthcoming at a conference usually emerged spontaneously as the discussion evolved. A shopkeeper victim of theft, who said he was not interested in conferences and who had, in any case, forgotten to attend, said that he had plenty of experience of the court system with shoptheft; he was, however, impressed with conferencing because this was the first occasion on which an offender had come into the shop and apologised sincerely (as was agreed as part of the outcome). The victim told the offender's mother that it took 'real guts' to do this and that he appreciated it.

It is worth noting that possibly many offenders who go before the court experience genuine remorse for their behaviour, but there is no means available through the court system for victims ever to know of their offenders' feelings. For example, in a case involving a house break-in, the police incident report stated: '[The offender] stated that he did not know why he committed the burglaries and took the property . . . *He wanted to apologise to the people for what had been done*' (my emphasis). One of the victims in this case told me:

> I got most of my stuff back – all except the roller blades. I really wanted the roller blades back as I'll never be able to afford another pair. But mostly I wanted an apology for all the mess.

But neither the police nor the court had conveyed to her that the offender wanted to apologise; nor was any compensation ordered for the loss of the blades.

Concern has sometimes been expressed that the restorative setting, with its focus on reconciliation, could inhibit victims and 'harm victims who are not ready and willing to forgive' (Brown, 1994: 1263). This does not seem to have been the case for most conference victims in RISE: almost half said that since the conference they had felt indifferent towards their offender, but a further 40 per cent said that they felt forgiving. The more emotional nature of the cases involving violent offences is reflected in the more emotional reaction by victims of violent offenders to this question: more of them remained unforgiving (20 per cent compared with 5 per cent of the property victims) and more of them felt forgiving (48 per cent compared with 35 per cent of the property victims).

A sense of forgiveness often accompanied the feeling that, after the conference, offenders had a proper understanding of the harm caused and a belief that their offender had learnt their lesson and deserved a second chance. Indeed, 40 per cent of all conference victims indicated that 'wanting to help the offender' was an important reason for their attending the conference at all. For example, the victim of a small-store shoplift said:

> When everyone let their feelings out by talking I felt better. She [the offender] apparently learned by the conference which made me feel better about what happened . . . Next day she came past the shop and saw me and waved hello. To me that meant she had learned from what happened. It was reassuring – she showed a bit of respect.

Finally, those who had *not* received an apology were asked whether or not they thought an apology would have helped them to forgive their offenders. Fifty-six per cent of the court victims and 61 per cent of the conference victims said that it would have helped them to do so.

[. . .]

This extract is taken from 'Justice for Victims of Young Offenders: the Centrality of Emotional Harm and Restoration', by Heather Strang, in A. Morris and G. Maxwell (eds) Restorative Justice for Juveniles: Conferencing, Mediation and Circles *(Oxford: Hart Publishing, 2001), pp. 183–93.*

Note

1 Only about 15 per cent of both groups were awarded money.

References

Arendt, H. (1958) *The Human Condition* (Chicago, IL: University of Chicago Press).

Barton, C. (1996) 'Revenge and Victim Justice: A Philosophical Analysis and Evaluation.' Unpublished doctoral dissertation, Australian National University, Canberra.

Braithwaite, J. (1999) 'Restorative Justice: Assessing Optimistic and Pessimistic Accounts', in Tonry, M. (ed.) *Crime and Justice: A Review of Research. Vol. 25* (Chicago, IL: University of Chicago Press).

Brown, J. (1994) 'The Uses of Mediation to Resolve Criminal Cases: A Procedural Critique', *Emory Law Journal*, 43, pp. 1247–309.

Daly, K. (2000) 'Revisiting the Relationship between Retributive and Restorative Justice', in Strang, H. and Braithwaite, J. (eds) *Restorative Justice: Philosophy to Practice* (Aldershot: Ashgate).

Gottfredson, G. (1989) 'The Experience of Violent and Serious Victimization', in Weiner, N. and Wolfgang, M. (eds) *Pathways to Criminal Violence* (Newbury Park, CA: Sage).

Hudson, J. and Galaway, B. (1975) 'Conclusions', in *Considering the Victim: Readings in Restitution and Victim Compensation* (Springfield, IL: Charles C. Thomas).

Jeffrey, C. (1957) 'The Development of Crime in Early English Society', *Journal of Criminal Law, Criminology and Police Science*, 47, pp. 647–66.

McCold, P. and Wachtel, B. (1998) *Restorative Policing Experiment: The Bethlehem Pennsylvania Police Family Group Conferencing Project* (Pipersville, PA: Community Service Foundation).

Marshall, T. and Merry, S. (1990) *Crime and Accountability: Victim/Offender Mediation in Practice* (London: HMSO).

Morris, A. and Maxwell, G. (1997) *Family Group Conferences and Convictions. Occasional Papers in Criminology, New Series 5* (Wellington: Victoria University).

Morris, A., Maxwell, G., Hudson, J. and Galaway, B. (1996) 'Concluding Thoughts', in Hudson, J. *et al.* (eds) *Family Group Conferences: Perspectives on Policy and Practice* (Sydney: Federation Press).

Murphy, J. and Hampton, J. (1988) *Forgiveness and Mercy* (Cambridge: Cambridge University Press).

Pollock, Sir F. and Maitland, F. (1988) *The History of the English Criminal Law before the Time of Edward I* (Cambridge: Cambridge University Press, 1898, reprinted 1988).

Retzinger, S. and Scheff, T. (1996) 'Strategy for Community Conferences: Emotions and Social Bonds', in Galaway, B. and Hudson, J. (eds) *Restorative Justice: International Perspectives* (Amsterdam: Kugler Publications and Monsey, NY: Criminal Justice Press).

Shapland, J. (1986) 'Victims and the Criminal Justice System', in Fattah, F. (ed.) *From Crime Policy to Victim Policy: Reorienting the Justice System* (London: Macmillan).

Shapland, J., Willmore, J. and Duff, P. (1985) *Victims in the Criminal Justice System* (Aldershot: Gower).

Stewart, T. (1996) 'Family Group Conferences with Young Offenders in New Zealand', in Hudson, J. *et al.* (eds) *Family Group Conferences* (Leichhardt: The Federation Press).

Tavuchis, N. (1991) *Mea Culpa: A Sociology of Apology and Reconciliation* (Stanford, CA: Stanford University Press).

Umbreit, M., Coates, R. and Kalanj, B. (1994) *Victim Meets Offender: The Impact of Restorative Justice and Mediation* (Monsey, NY: Criminal Justice Press).

Walklate, S. (1989) *Victimology: The Victim and the Criminal Justice Process* (London: Unwin Hyman).

Weitekamp, E. (1999) 'History of Restorative Justice', in Bazemore, G. and Walgrave, I. (eds) *Restorative Juvenile Justice: Repairing the Harm by Youth Crime* (Monsey, NY: Criminal Justice Press).

Wolfgang, M. (1972) 'Making the Criminal Justice System Accountable', *Crime and Delinquency*, pp. 15–22.

Wright, M. (1991) *Justice for Victims and Offenders: A Restorative Response to Crime* (Milton Keynes: Open University Press).

21. Community is not a place: a new look at community justice initiatives

Paul McCold and Benjamin Wachtel

Community justice initiatives, such as community policing and restorative justice, have tended to define community rather loosely, if at all. This has led to confusion about the variation in what exactly constitutes a community justice program. In community policing, community has often been equated with neighborhood. In restorative justice literature, community is often indistinguishable from society. These ways of defining community have significant consequences for these new justice initiatives. Not only do they affect the way in which these approaches are designed and implemented, but they may cause confusion about underlying values and may undermine the goals of community justice.

Critics and evaluators of community policing initiatives have noted the variety of forms and goals that these efforts assume (Rosenbaum, 1994). There is some consensus that a primary goal is to mobilize communities to be active partners in responding to crime; however, community policing initiatives have largely failed to reach this goal. One of the obstacles seems to be that, in many areas, 'genuine' community does not in fact exist.

Advocates for the new justice paradigm known variously as restorative justice, transformative justice, and relational justice, have also differed greatly in their conceptualization of community. There is general agreement, in theory, that community is as central to restorative justice as are the victim and the offender (McCold, 1997). However, the actual involvement of those other than the facilitator, victim and offender varies widely in restorative justice practice.

If community justice is going to have any success, then, it is necessary to take a deeper look at the meaning of community. This article will discuss the importance of defining exactly what is meant by the term 'community' in community justice initiatives, especially community policing and restorative justice. We propose a non-geographic perspective on community which can be used to focus and define what community justice initiatives should look like and what they should be trying to achieve. This perspective is based on recent developments in restorative justice and community policing, especially the Wagga/Real Justice model of family group conferences which, when used by police, exemplifies an integration of restorative justice and community policing. The implications of this perspective for community justice initiatives in general will be explored.

Defining community

What is community? Community is a feeling, a perception of connectedness – personal connectedness both to other individual human beings and to a group.

Building community, then, involves building bonds between human beings. Where there is no perception of connectedness among a group of people, there is no community. Although we may live in the same neighborhood, municipality, county, state or nation, be governed and served by the same institutions, we may have no sense of connection with each other, no sense that we are part of a unified group. As such, we are not of one community.

On the other hand, we may belong to the same bowling league, go to the same place of worship, work in the same office, or go to the same school. We may be relatives or friends. As such, if we perceive a connection between each other and a common interest in the activities and well-being of the group – the sports league, the religious group, the workplace, the school, the family, the circle of friends – then we are, by definition, part of a community.

When we speak about the 'sense of community' that is missing from modern society, we are speaking about the absence of meaningful interrelationships between human beings and the absence of a sense of belonging to and common interest in something greater than ourselves. At a societal level, this manifests itself as individualism. Excessive individualism tends to breed selfishness and a lack of empathy, which lays the groundwork for crime (Braithwaite, 1989; Moore, 1997).

We can, of course, simultaneously value both ideals of the individual and of the group. In terms of political philosophy we might equate this with valuing elements of both libertarianism and communitarianism. In modern society we have a problem in that we seem to undervalue collective responsibility and overvalue individual rights, thus losing a sense of balance between the two (if such a balance ever actually existed). As such, we have diminished respect for others and have only a limited sense of responsibility to the collective.

Thus, the promise of community justice initiatives to empower and build community has strong popular appeal. Against a tide of individualism and a perceived decline of community life, we long for a sense of connectedness in our lives and a sense of safety in our neighborhoods. Our sense of safety is obstructed when neighbors are strangers. As Kay Pranis, restorative justice planner for the Minnesota Department of Corrections, has suggested, neighborhoods are caught up 'in a downward spiral where crime leads to greater fear and increased isolation and distrust among community members, which in turn leads to even more crime. As community bonds are weakened by fear and isolation, the power of community disapproval is reduced and crime increases' (Pranis, 1996a, p. 10).

Place, therefore, can play a role in creating a community of interest around a crime in a specific location, but only coincidentally. In and of itself, community is not a place, other than as a mythical reflection of a romanticized past. Geographical units rarely constitute or correspond to communities. The resident population may lack a sense of shared interests and there may be relatively few interpersonal connections between neighbors. Even where genuine community does seem to coincide with place, 'the socio-political constructions of that community may differ greatly from one culture to another' (Tyler, 1995). There is most likely not one unified community, but a number of fairly distinct communities, perhaps at odds with one another.

The consequences of crime extend beyond neighborhoods, towns and cities, because our networks of relationships are not confined by geographical boundaries. A theft committed against a family member in another state would probably affect someone more personally than a burglary committed in his or her own neighborhood. The problem with many community justice initiatives is that they have defined community primarily in terms of geography, ignoring the very vibrant sense of community that exists in personal networks of relationships. In doing so they may, in reality, be indistinguishable from existing justice practices, failing to address collateral harm and the weakening of community caused by crime, and failing to establish meaningful roles for community members in justice interventions.

Retributive justice approaches can actually make matters worse by alienating both offenders and victims. John Braithwaite explains how offenders who have been stigmatized by the justice system often are drawn together to form their own subcultures. These become communities in themselves, unsympathetic to the norms of conduct and morality of the larger society (Braithwaite, 1989). Ironically, members of these 'criminal subcultures' may have a greater sense of belonging and connection than members of mainstream society. The influence that any community has on individuals belonging to that community – community as a perception of connectedness to an individual or a group – is an important source of informal social control (Weiss, 1987). It is a powerful motivator in maintaining group norms, whether these norms are positive or negative.

For community justice initiatives to be effective they must capitalize on the fact that people act in a certain way because they want to avoid experiencing the external shame of disapproval by people they care about and because of the internal shame experienced through conscience. Conscience is largely developed through a maturation process in which the behavioral values of interdependence become internalized. Where conscience is not fully developed, approval of others is the primary motivator, not punishment or fear of punishment (Braithwaite, 1989).

It follows, then, that a primary goal for community justice should be mobilizing informal social control mechanisms by strengthening, creating or restoring healthy interdependencies and by encouraging the development of mature internalized control, or conscience. In this process, harm can be repaired, offenders and victims can be reintegrated and supported, empathy can be fostered and relationships can be healed and formed. Fundamentally, community justice is about building and utilizing perceptions of connectedness to individuals and groups as a way to respond to and prevent crime and wrongdoing.

[. . .]

Community in restorative justice

Central in understanding the new restorative justice paradigm is an under-standing of the roles of stakeholders in crime and the response to crime. The stakeholders in restorative justice include the victim, the offender and the community (Zehr, 1990). Yet, for the most part, community remains a concept vaguely defined. While restorative justice advocates are less likely to fall prey to the fallacy of community as place, there is a tendency, by some restorative justice advocates, to confuse the role of community with the role of society. The problem begins with an ill-defined concept of the victim. To whom does the offender owe reparation: (1) the victim, (2) the victim and the community, or (3) the victim, the community and society? All three perspectives are represented in the descriptions of programs calling themselves 'restorative'.

Since it seems to be a basic principle of restorative justice that crime harms communities and that some sort of action needs to be taken to repair that harm, how we define community becomes crucial to the development of restorative justice practice. The community 'wants reassurance that what happened was wrong, that something is being done about it, and that steps are being taken to discourage its recurrence' (Zehr, 1990, p. 195). These are needs shared by all three categories of crime victims – primary, secondary and vicarious victims (the public or society; in other words, those who become aware of the crime). A geographic definition of community brings this assertion dangerously close to the traditional justice system view that offenders must pay their debt to society. Restorative justice initiatives may, in reality, be no different than existing practices and continue to weaken community by stigmatizing offenders and neglecting victims.

A fundamental principle of restorative justice is that society is not the victim, government is not the victim, the victim is the victim (McCold, 1996). Christie's (1977) principle of ownership reminds us of the danger that the conflict is easily 'stolen' from the victim by defining the society as the victim. The question for restorative justice is 'Can the principle of private ownership coexist with public ownership of crime?' The current solution to this dilemma has been to order the two principles. For example, here is Ron Claassen's (1995) first principle of restorative justice: 'Crime is primarily an offence against human relationships and secondarily a violation of a law.'

Van Ness and Strong (1997) attempt to deal with the community/society dilemma by distinguishing between the role of the community and the role of government. 'In promoting justice, the government is responsible for preserving order, and the community is responsible for establishing peace' (Van Ness, 1989, p. 20). Thus, there are actually four parties in restorative justice: victim, offender, community and government. Van Ness and Strong suggest that it is in the balancing of the order function of government with the conflict resolution and peacemaking functions of community that 'balanced and restorative' justice is produced. While they distinguish the local geographical community from the community of interests (microcommunities), they fail to distinguish the injuries, needs and responsibilities of the local community from those of the personal microcommunities.

With the advent of family group conferencing and sentencing circles, the restorative justice movement has recognized the importance of including the personal communities of care of both offenders and victims in resolution of criminal conflict (Umbreit and Zehr, 1996). Restorative justice practice is moving from excluding the microcommunity under early victim–offender mediation models to including them as a central part of the restorative process (Van Ness and Strong, 1997; Wright, 1996).

Tony Marshall (1994) suggests that restorative justice seeks to reduce crime by strengthening bonds of interdependency while holding offenders accountable. Marshall defines restorative justice as a process whereby all the parties with a stake in a particular offence come together to resolve collectively how to deal with the aftermath of the offence and its implications for the future. Parties with a stake in an offence include, of course, the victim and the offender, but they also include the families of each, and any other members of their respective communities who may be affected, or who may be able to contribute to prevention of a recurrence[1] (Marshall, 1996).

Thus, restorative justice, like problem-oriented policing, is moving toward a more practical microcommunities perspective. If done correctly, restorative justice programs empower the victim and offender with control over the nature of the reparation, and empower the personal communities to exercise informal social support and control of the process. Not only are the microcommunities important in the restoration process, but they are the means through which healing and reintegration is possible (Wundersitz and Hetzel, 1996).

Restorative policing

The collaborative processes developed from restorative justice practitioners are a natural tool for police interested in engaging communities for crime control and prevention and might be called 'restorative policing'. While those experienced at mediation tend to be distrustful of the police and stereotype them as authoritarian, the police have tended to distrust 'social workers' and stereotype them as naive and permissive. There is some truth in both perceptions, but both are largely incorrect. Conscientious police officers have always used soothing and smoothing techniques in the vast majority of encounters with citizens (Walter and Wagner, 1996).

> Against the background of major work in the development of mediation and other dispute-resolution techniques in both the public and private sectors, relatively little systematic attention has been given to perfecting the methods of responding to disputes by the governmental agency that probably handles the greatest number of them (Goldstein, 1990, p. 113).

Research on police-based family group conferencing projects has demonstrated that police officers are quite capable of assuming the non-directive, empowering role of facilitator (McCold and Stahr, 1996; Sherman and Strang, 1997). Restorative justice and community policing come together in the Wagga/Real Justice model of family group conferencing, which operationalizes the microcommunity perspective. A powerful way of demonstrating the community-empowerment and community-building potential of conferences is through a conference story:

> In an upper-middle-class suburb a group of youths vandalized a number of ice fishing houses on a local lake. The public prosecutor, because of the difficulty of matching specific damage to specific offenders, decided not to pursue the case. The traditional justice system failed to deal with the crime.
> The police, however, had implemented a family group conference program for juvenile offences and offered the victims an alternative response to the

wrongdoing they had suffered. One particular victim, whose elaborate two-storey ice fishing house had suffered considerable damage, was particularly irate, agreed only begrudgingly to attend the conference and threatened to display his rage at the conference.

The perpetrators, ice fishing house owners, and their respective family and friends gathered for the family group conference. First, the offenders admitted their wrongdoing and described the damage that they had done. Then each of the victims expressed how they had been affected by the destruction of the ice fishing houses that they had built themselves, over many years, with their families and friends.

The son of the owner of the two-story fishing house spoke for his father and expressed, in rather poignant terms, how he had spent much of his childhood working with his father and the rest of his family building their house for each winter fishing season. He suddenly realized, when faced with the destruction the youths had caused, how much that experience meant to him. His father, instead of expressing his rage as he had threatened, saved his comments for the close of the conference, after the whole group had worked out the terms of reparation.

Then he spoke with great emotion and thanked the youths for having vandalized his ice fishing house. He explained that until the conference he had never heard his son express how much all those years of shared experience meant to him.

The conference participants developed a reparation agreement. When the damage was finally repaired, the father had all the boys and their fathers over to spend a weekend with his family fishing on the lake.

All of the people who participated in this conference lived in geographic proximity, but until they were grouped into a 'microcommunity' through this powerful restorative justice process, they hardly knew each other. After the conference, bonds had been established that did not exist before the conference. Community, for purposes of a family group conference, can be defined identically to Goldstein's description of community that is used by good problem-oriented police officers. 'They use "community" rather deftly to describe those affected in any way by the specific problem they are attempting to address.'

Community and government

There is still a minor problem with this concept of microcommunity and its implications for community justice processes. It could be argued that anyone 'affected in any way', as Goldstein puts it, is anyone who becomes aware of the crime; it follows then that they should be included in the intervention, whether they are members of the same neighborhood, the same state or the same world. Thus all government agencies are affected because they have the responsibility to enforce the laws of society within specified geographic boundaries. In practical terms, membership in the microcommunity should be limited to those with a strong personal or emotional connection to the victim or offender.

There is a great danger in confusing the needs and responsibilities of personal communities of victims and offenders with more abstract notions of community. The natural informal social control mechanisms that operate in everyday life all involve the personal communities of care of each of us. When we include organizational relationships such as workplace, recreation and worship relationships as part of these personal microcommunities, the social control structures become more apparent.

It is the deeply interpersonal nature of such interrelations that give the collective community its character and strength. The greater the abstraction in defining community, the further it is removed from interdependency and the locus of existing informal social control. That is why it is important for community justice to encourage and create community, as a perception of connectedness to an individual or group, in its efforts to respond to and prevent crime. The microcommunities created by incidents of crime are a useful framework for action.

Place is relevant only where proximity to a crime has generated fear and concern, thereby creating a host of vicarious victims. The most constructive response to these vicarious victims is to provide reassurance that what happened was wrong, that something constructive is being done about it, and that steps are being taken to discourage its recurrence. In this way, microcommunity empowerment meets the main needs of the 'broader' community – to know that something constructive is being done about crime locally (McCold, 1997).

Because some microcommunities may be punitive and stigmatizing, care must be taken in all community justice programs that reparative or reintegrative principles are structured into the process, for example, by providing positive examples of reparative solutions when only punitive ones are suggested. In this way, government ensures that outcomes are fair and legal. As Kay Pranis advises, 'Formal government is the source of legal authority, as contrasted with the moral authority of the community. The government is in a position of broader oversight than the community and the government is the guardian of individual concerns, in contrast to the community responsibility to collective concerns' (1996b, p. 3).

There is a danger in involving 'official' community representatives in conferences, because their role as direct stakeholders in the crime may not be legitimate. Such 'community' volunteers may represent interests that are anything but restorative or reintegrative. They may display an attitude of moral superiority which could disrupt the resolution process. These official community representatives may be little more than geographic or government-al representatives, with no real emotional connection to the crime or to those affected by the crime. Ultimately, the best solution to the problems of crime come not from government or society, but from the individuals directly affected by crime, the microcommunity (McCold, 1997).

The role of government officials, such as police, should be limited to that of facilitators and information providers, not key contributors to the decision-making process. The responsibility of government is to recognize patterns of dysfunction in society and help provide solutions. Since individuals and communities cannot be expected to have the capacity to address these larger concerns, that responsibility falls to the municipal, county, state and national government. The responsibility of the microcommunity involved in each specific criminal incident is to intervene constructively in repairing the harm.

For this, they need effective informal social control mechanisms. Where these are not available, government has the responsibility to provide them.

Government, however, cannot effectively address crime without the moral authority and informal social control provided by community. By continuing to define community in official geographic and governmental terms, our so-called community justice initiatives can only fail. But by recognizing that community defines itself through individual perceptions of common interest, such as those created by a criminal incident, we can successfully engage a wide range of individuals in the resolution of their own problems.

This extract is taken from 'Community is not a Place: a New Look at Community Justice Initiatives', by Paul McCold and Benjamin Watchel, in Contemporary Justice Review, *1:1 (1998), pp. 71–85.*

Note

1 The Alliance of Non-Governmental Organizations Committee on Crime Prevention and Criminal Justice's Working Party on Restorative Justice adopted Marshall's definition as its working definition for drafting resolution language to the Tenth United Nations Crime Congress in 2000. The remainder of that definition is as follows:

> Coming together may occur as one event, as in Family (or Community) Group Conferencing, or it may occur through a series of less all embracing meetings (e.g. victim–offender mediation and a separate conference between the offender and his/her family), depending on the complexity of the case and other practicalities. The coming together may also occur just once, or may happen repeatedly over a more or less extended period of time.
>
> In order to effect the coming together and a collective resolution, there is a crucial role for the neutral facilitator (mediator) with the skills to prepare people for the process, ensure that it progresses in a safe and civilised manner, guide parties through difficult phases, and encourage them to enter fully and creatively into the process.
>
> The aftermath of the offence includes ensuring the material well-being or satisfaction of the victim, the re-affirmation that they are not to blame, attention to the victim's emotional needs, resolution of any conflict between the victim and the offender (whether because of the offence or existing beforehand), the resolution of similar conflicts between their families or communities, resolving any difficulties between the offender and his/her family and other friends as a result of the offence (e.g. being ashamed to know him/her), and giving the offender a chance to absolve his/her own feelings of guilt through apology and reparation.
>
> The implications for the future include tackling the reasons for the offending, producing a plan for rehabilitation, and agreement among the family and community members present on a system of support for the offender to ensure that he/she is able to adhere to the plan. (Marshall, 1997)

References

Braithwaite, J. (1989) *Crime, Shame and Reintegration* (New York, NY: Cambridge University Press).

Christie, N. (1977) 'Conflict as Property', *British Journal of Criminology*, 17:1, pp. 1–14.

Claassen, R. (1995) 'Restorative Justice Principles and Evaluation Continuums.' Paper presented at National Center for Peacemaking and Conflict Resolution, Fresno Pacific College, May.

Goldstein, H. (1990) *Problem-oriented Policing* (Philadelphia, PA: Temple University Press).

Marshall, T. (1996) 'The Evolution of Restorative Justice in Britain', *European Journal of Criminal Policy and Research*, 4(4): 21–43.

McCold, P. (1996) 'The Role of Community in Restorative Justice', in Galaway, B. and Hudson, J. (eds) *Restorative Justice: International Perspectives* (Monsey, NY: Criminal Justice Press), pp. 85–102.

McCold, P. (1997) 'Restorative Justice: Variations on a Theme.' Paper presented at the Restorative Justice for Juveniles–Potentialities, Risks and Problems for Research, International Conference in Leuven, Belgium, May.

McCold, P. and Stahr, J. (1996) 'Bethlehem Police Family Group Conferencing Project.' Paper presented at the American Society of Criminology Conference, annual meeting, Chicago, November.

Moore, D.B. (1997) 'Pride, Shame, and Empathy in Peer Relations: New Theory and Practice in Education and Juvenile Justice', in Rigby, K. and Slee, P. (eds) *Children's Peer Relations* (London: Routledge), pp. 212–35.

Pranis, K. (1996a) 'Building Community Support for Restorative Justice: Principles and Strategies' (from http://www.quaker.org/fcadp/Community.html).

Pranis, K. (1996b) 'Communities and the Justice System: Turning the Relationship Upside Down.' Address given to Communities, Crime and Justice: Making Community Partnerships Work, sponsored by Office of Justice Programs, US Department of Justice.

Rosenbaum, D.P. (ed.) (1994) *The Challenge of Community Policing: Testing the Promises* (Thousand Oaks, CA: Sage).

Sherman, L. and Strang, H. (1997) *The Right Kind of Shame from Crime Prevention. RISE Working Paper 1*, April (Australia National University, and University of Maryland).

Tyler, W. (1995) 'Community-based Strategies in Aboriginal Criminal Justice: The Northern Territory Experience', *Australian and New Zealand Journal of Criminology*, 28:2, pp. 127–42.

Umbreit, M. and Zehr, H. (1996) 'Family Group Conferences: A Challenge to Victim Offender Mediation?', *Victim Offenders Mediation Association Quarterly*, 7:1, pp. 4–8.

Van Ness, D. (1989) 'Pursuing a Restorative Vision of Justice', in Arthur, P. (ed.) *Justice: The Restorative Vision. New Perspectives on Crime and Justice* (Akron, PA: Mennonite Central Committee Office of Criminal Justice), pp. 17–30.

Van Ness, D. and Strong, K. (1997) *Restoring Justice* (Cincinnati, OH: Anderson Publishing).

Walter, M. and Wagner, A. (1996) 'How Police Officers Manage Difficult Situations: The Predominance of Soothing and Smoothing Strategies', in Galaway, B. and Hudson, J. (eds) *Restorative Justice: International Perspectives* (Monsey, NY: Criminal Justice Press), pp. 271–82.

Weiss, R.P. (1987) 'The Community and Prevention', in Johnson, E.H. (ed.) *Handbook on Crime and Delinquency Prevention* (Westport, CT: Greenwood Press), pp. 113–35.

Wright, M. (1996) *Justice for Victims and Offenders: A Restorative Response to Crime* (2nd edn) (Winchester: Waterside Press).

Wundersitz, J. and Hetzel, S. (1996) 'Family Conferencing for Young Offenders: The South Australian Experience', in Maxwell, G. and Morris, A. (eds) *Family Group Conferences: Perspectives on Policy and Practice* (Monsey, NY: Criminal Justice Press).

Zehr, H. (1990) *Changing Lenses: A New Focus for Crime and Justice* (Scottsdale, PA: Herald Press).

22. What is relational justice?

Michael Schluter

The classic cause of nervous breakdown is mounting pressure over a period of time coupled with a simultaneous decline in the ability of the person to handle the problems. Eventually, the psyche reaches breaking-point, often with tragic results. Are we approaching a 'nervous breakdown' in our criminal justice system?

The gathering storm

The signs are ominous. No-one will dispute the evidence of growing levels of crime in British society as a long-term trend. For one year alone, 1991, the *rise* in recorded crime was greater than the total level of crime in 1950.[1] Even this does not tell the whole story. Certain categories of crime are consistently under-reported. For example, shoplifting is now so prevalent that whereas in 1950 the police would generally be called so that a crime could be recorded, today retailers no longer bother as cases are so commonplace. The proportion of crimes which reach court and result in a conviction is about two per cent.[2] So the prison system represents no more than the tip of the iceberg in terms of the numbers involved in crime.

The effects of crime are far-reaching. Not least is the fear of violence which affects many more people than simply past victims. When Rachel Nickell was murdered on Wimbledon Common in 1992, many women thought again about walking their dogs in London, even in broad daylight. Motorists are generally unwilling to give hitchhikers lifts owing to a relatively small number of incidents where drivers have been attacked. What mother now feels that it is safe to leave her child in the pram outside the corner shop while she drops in for a loaf of bread?

At the same time our ability to deal with crime is declining. Once described as 'a practice without a policy',[3] credence has been afforded by criminal justice policy-makers to imprisonment as a solution. Prison appears to be ineffective either as a deterrent or as a means of reform. Home Office research shows a reconviction rate of nearly 70 per cent within four years for male offenders and of 82 per cent for those under 21.[4] We need to escape the paradox of imprisonment being increasingly condemned and yet increasingly used. Yet if prison is not the solution to growing rates of crime, it seems that other court dispositions such as community sentences have yet to become sufficiently acceptable to the public for it to be said that these can provide the answer.

So is the criminal justice system nearing a crisis similar in character to nervous breakdown? Or is there a way to narrow the gap between the scale of the problem and the efficacy of the response? Such a means must touch not just responses but causes, not the procedures of justice but its purpose, not institutions but individuals, not only the mind but also the heart.

The prevailing social ethos

In the decade to 1994 the prevailing political *zeitgeist* [. . .] sought the welfare of society through an emphasis on personal freedom and responsibility. The assumption [had] been that economic growth is the key. Not only does it make everyone better off financially but it establishes a framework within which all people may achieve personal fulfilment provided that they – and everyone else – abide by the rules. In commerce and finance, the goal [was] to deregulate markets so as to increase freedom and opportunity for the enterprising and to increase choice for the consumer. Professor Elliot Currie has drawn attention to the way in which the United Kingdom has evolved from a market economy into a market society,[5] defined as one in which the pursuit of private gain has become the guiding principle for all areas of social life, not merely economic organization.

In the public services, the new ethos is epitomized by performance-related pay, new procedures for contracting out services, and tough financial performance indicators. Success is defined largely in financial terms even for the so-called 'service sectors' delivering education, health and welfare. For the Department of Social Security, beneficiaries have become 'customers', benefits have become 'products' and local offices have been tuned to provide 'one-step shopping' for those on welfare. While few would question the need to make public services thoroughly cost-effective, it is always disturbing when means are transmuted into ends.

The values of materialism and individualism in contemporary Britain have even started to influence the way in which prisons are run. The 'market' becomes the invisible but controlling hand behind the way that new institutions are designed and offenders are treated. To take an example, if it is cheaper to have prisoners collect their food and eat in their cells rather than in a communal dining hall – because less guards are required – the market will dictate that food is to be eaten alone. It helps to ensure minimum cost per day per prisoner. There is no room in this conceptual framework for considerations of long-term mental health, communication skills, or the likely impact on a prisoner's relational well-being. There is a real danger that privatized prisons could become, in effect, down-market, fenced-in hotels or perhaps, in the future, zoos.

Crime and criminal justice are inevitably a product of the society we choose to create. What kind of society do we want? One option is undoubtedly to continue to place the emphasis on unfettered individual freedom. However, this absence of community creates conditions in which crime spreads like an epidemic. Ironically, then, the result of such a pursuit of freedom will be 'fortress Britain', where individuals who are excluded from, or who opt out of, the material bonanza are kept under control by surveillance cameras, electronic tagging and prison walls. [. . .]

Why think relationally?

An antidote to this largely materialist perspective on the world would be a political philosophy which has as its starting point the centrality of human relationships, for it is in relationships that we define our identity and recognize our well-being. A good illustration is found in the film *Dances with Wolves*, where the hero – a cavalry officer in the American Civil War – finds himself caught up with a group of native Indians. Twice he comments that the experience of living in the close community of Indian tribal society has enabled him to 'find himself'. It is a truism to say it is only in and through relationships that our characters can express themselves. To live entirely alone is to lose one's humanity.

Not only self-understanding but also a sense of purpose, fulfilment and happiness come from our relationships. Multi-disciplinary research has established the wide range of areas in which stable and committed relationships contribute to the well-being of adults and children alike. Close, long-term relationships, whether with family or friends, play a crucial role in enabling individuals to enjoy good health, to achieve career goals and to cope with the difficulties encountered in old age.[6] For children, long-term stable relationships are the key to learning to communicate, in having the confidence to explore the world when young and to develop relationships with peers. The most socially competent children are generally those with secure attachments to their parents.[7]

Moral development also appears to be linked to the quality of relationships formed in childhood. Sympathy for strangers is a by-product of sympathy for one's kin. Family relationships comprise the natural forum within which each individual learns to balance his or her interests against those of the group. They enable the individual to learn to hold in balance choice (my freedom to do as I wish) and obligation (my responsibility towards others). Such individual self-understanding is the bedrock on which public order is built, and is the foundation of the criminal justice system, and it depends almost entirely on the stability of relationships and individual experiences in childhood.

At the opposite extreme, research shows that inadequate or absent parent–child relationships are associated with juvenile delinquency, violence and a range of psychological disorders including schizophrenia, eating disorders, adolescent depression and difficulty in developing social relationships. Children brought up in care, or in some adoption situations, more often have difficulty in developing relationships in later years except where the adoption was early in the child's life or where the surrogate parents have had a long-term, committed, stable relationship with the child. The effect of divorce is often insecure relationships at home with feelings of rejection in the child, or feelings of deprivation; this can then result in consequential lower self-esteem, lower social competence and, in boys especially, non-compliant behaviour.[8]

What many people have failed to appreciate is that the attitudes held in domestic relationships, and the importance that we attach to them, is determined not just by what happens in our private lives, but by the pattern of relationships in places of work, in national politics and in a host of other public institutions. The business world, for example, can be understood in terms of relationships – between employer and employee, buyer and supplier, salesperson and customer. These relationships are governed in part by the ethos of the institution, which is in turn influenced by the wider pattern of social values, as well as the personality and background, of the individuals involved. The business schools in recent years have attributed business growth and success increasingly to relational factors.[9]

What is true in business is also true in other areas of public life. The key to understanding changes within and between organizations often lies in the relational dimension. An institution like a hospital can be analysed in terms of patterns of internal relationships among patients and various categories of staff, and external relationships with government departments, commercial suppliers, and a host of other bodies. In each case there are interactions between individuals and these are governed by both formal procedures and unwritten rules.

The shift towards 'the market' in the ethos of public institutions – with the strong priority given to material considerations – is likely to have had an influence in the private lives of those who work in them or are touched by them. If consistently driven at work to give priority to cost factors over human welfare considerations, it would be easy to adopt the same attitude in the domestic environment. The pressure to achieve material success in business can lead to little time for relationships at home, just as a breakdown of relationships at home will affect performance at work. Relationships at work and at home are bound to overlap and to influence one another.

Relationships and duty

It is the relationships that we experience in both public and private life which replenish social resources of commitment and constraint and make us willing to fulfil our obligations. Where relationships within a society or community are becoming less 'close', one would expect a weakened sense of duty towards other people. The relational thesis is that a break up of relational bonding in society has weakened our sense of duty, or obligation.[10]

A person's sense of obligation to a neighbour is generally in direct proportion to how well they know that person. In the Netherlands in the summer of 1993, a girl aged nine drowned in a lake with several hundred people watching, yet no-one dived in to help her. It was all recorded by a man with a video camera, and his film was then used in a television news programme. Why did no-one take action to help the girl? The reason seems to lie in a lack of relational 'proximity' or 'closeness' in society generally. When people do not know a person in trouble, they do not feel an obligation to get involved.

The impact of this lack of a sense of 'relational proximity', which causes an absence of community involvement and responsibility can be seen over and again in reports in the press or by the media of criminal acts. A woman is dragged screaming from a bus queue to be raped and murdered, and nobody intervenes. A woman is murdered over a half hour period at the bottom of two tower blocks, repeatedly calling for help, with over a hundred people watching from their windows. Nobody goes to help; nobody even calls the police.

To understand this absence of 'relational proximity', it is helpful to explore its component parts. What is it that results in people being 'close' to each other, in having empathy with their neighbours' needs and situations? In *The R-factor*, five dimensions are set out which provide a basis or framework for good relationships.[11] These are:

(a) Directness – the ideal that people should meet as far as possible *face-to-face* rather than having contact through a third party, or through impersonal media.
(b) Continuity – that people should meet frequently, regularly and over a sustained period of time.
(c) Multiplexity – that people should have contact in more than one role or context, so that they can see how people respond in different situations.
(d) Parity – that people should meet as equals, not in terms of role or status but in terms of their sense of personal worth or value.
(e) Commonality – that people should have as far as possible common purpose, and common experience, as these help to cement relationships.

Each of these aspects of relationship, when present, contribute towards getting to know a person better, having a common bonding, developing a sense of mutual obligation. They contribute to mutual empathy, although not necessarily to intimacy. Each of them has been affected by major social trends since 1945. This is considered below.

There is one main argument commonly deployed against the relational thesis that closeness of relationship benefits all parties, and in particular children. This is the case of marriage. Here is an arrangement where two people live in the closest proximity to one another, with every advantage of intimacy in their relationship, and yet we see so many of these relationships break down irretrievably. Why?

In many cases it is a matter of personality, incompatibility, misunderstanding or just plain bad-temper or pig-headedness. However, the reason may also be found in the social environment. For example, the reason for high divorce rates may lie in part in financial pressures emanating from debt and unemployment. A couple may find themselves relationally isolated, with few close friends, neighbours and relatives to provide a framework of supportive relationships. Sociologists use the term 'implosion' to describe what happens when a violent argument can find no outlet or mediation outside the home. More expectation has been placed on the marriage or home situation than the parties are able to bear. This may help to explain the extraordinarily high incidence of violence which occurs in a domestic context.

Social trends since 1945

A number of major trends in economic and political life have a bearing on how British society has changed since 1945. Four of these trends are considered briefly below:

Technology

What effect has technology had upon the way we conduct our relationships? Modern telephone technology and motor transport allow closer contact between geographically separated family and friends than was the case with previous generations. On the other hand, such developments can result in less face-to-face contact. When we collect money from the bank e.g. we now use a cashpoint instead of speaking to a cashier. The government plans to distribute pensions by cheque through the post rather than through the local post office. Television inevitably results in fewer conversation-based family meals in the home, whereas the phenomenon of households equipped with several television sets reduces the opportunity for shared experiences yet further. Computer games involve less face-to-face encounters between friends than the street games of old such as 'tag' and 'hopscotch'. The impact of technology is complex: much depends on how it is used at both institutional and individual levels.

Mobility

Increasing mobility has been a feature of Western societies since 1945. These are not the great waves of long-term migration, where whole villages or even larger communities moved *en masse*. Rather, it is the mobility of nuclear families or single people, where movement resembles an electron dance. There is a Russian proverb which states: 'To know a man intimately, one must eat several bushels of salt with him.' As salt is consumed in very small amounts at each meal, this points to the length of time people need to spend with each other in order to establish intimacy. Mobility is one factor inhibiting such prolonged acquaintance. Nonetheless, in its defence, it may, perhaps, be said to have helped to open up relationships in British society by contributing to a breakdown of class barriers.

Size of institutions

Another change since 1945 has been the growth in the size of public institutions, whether hospitals, schools, companies or prisons. This has helped to keep down unit costs and has allowed the introduction of technology which would have been uneconomic in smaller organizations. However, the relational consequences of greater size are often negative. Generally, the larger the organization the less face-to-face contact a person will have with a specific colleague and the more hierarchical the entire structure will be. A greater number of contacts takes the place of fewer, deeper relationships. While this can offer a *greater sense* of personal freedom, it can also lead to a decreased sense of obligation and loyalty.

The role of government

Another characteristic of the modern day is the way in which life is touched or even controlled by government. The state has increased its role in the provision of health, education and welfare, with benefits in terms of fairness and universal coverage. In 1910 the entire government share of total spending in the economy was still around ten per cent; today it is close to 50 per cent. At the same time, there has been a shift from local to central government. As recently as 1979 the proportion of a local authority budget which was set and raised locally amounted to 57 per cent: today the figure is 18 per cent.[12] How have these changes affected the way people relate to each other? Arguably, one consequence has been to remove responsibility for decision-making from families and local councils, thereby removing an important source of common interest and bonding. Could the reduced *role* of the family and locality be connected with the evident lack of commitment people feel towards other family members and neighbours? Could this be connected, indirectly, with the growth of crime?

This brief survey of social trends since 1945 is intended to do no more than illustrate the way in which a number of factors in the external environment and in public life are having a major impact on relationships in the home and neighbourhood. Since [. . .] the relational context provides helpful insights into understanding and responding to crime, these changes have great significance for the criminal justice system. At the same time, the changing social environment should provide an additional impetus for a re-examination of the criminal justice system itself to assess its impact on relationships in both public and private life.

Thinking relationally about justice

The implications of relational thinking are far reaching. Bringing a relational perspective to bear upon the problems raised by the criminal justice system may represent a radical departure. This perspective we have termed 'Relational Justice'.

One of the foundations of this new approach is to regard crime primarily as a breakdown in relationships; even in those cases where the offender does not personally know the victim, a relationship can be said to exist by virtue of their being citizens together, bound together by rules governing social behaviour. Crime is only secondarily to be regarded as an offence against the state and its laws.

The relational damage of a crime occurs first and foremost at the level of the individuals immediately concerned – the offender and the victim. However, other relationships are also affected, including the offender's relationship with his or her family, that of the victim with his or her family, and that of the offender's family and the local community. In addition, where a crime induces fear in a neighbourhood, the knock-on effects in terms of relationships may be widespread. It is like a stone going through a spider's web and which breaches a whole nexus of interwoven relationships. It is a breach that demands attention. How might it be repaired?

Empirical research highlights how weak relationships in the family and in the locality are a significant factor in seeking to understand the causes of crime. David Farrington has traced statistically significant links between 'cold' family relationships and anti-social behaviour, a rather wider term than crime.[13] This is because poor parenting results in an absence of internalized norms and a lack of understanding as to how other people feel and react. He also argues that an absence of family and community bonding increases the likelihood that anti-social feelings in an individual will be translated into offending behaviour. This is because where concern by people for one another is weak, there are good opportunities to commit crimes, and because factors like drug addiction, unemployment and drinking which lead to crime are more likely to be present.

John Braithwaite, an Australian criminologist, has argued that weak relationships in the family and the community also inhibit our ability to punish effectively.[14] He argues that punishment should shame the wrongdoer concerned and bring home to him the reality of his or her wrong-doing. But punishment is not an end in itself: it normally has in view the restoration of the individual who is punished. Braithwaite contends that shaming, at its most effective, helps to reintegrate the offender into the community and it is counter-productive when it results in stigmatization. Reintegrative shaming is disapproval dispensed within an ongoing relationship with the offender that is based on respect. It is shaming which focuses on the evil of the deed rather than on the offender as irredeemably evil. Stigmatization, by contrast, is shaming where bonds of respect with the offender are not sustained. The result is to create outcasts for whom criminality has become a master-status trait that drives out all other identities.

This analysis is helpful in understanding the response to a 14-year-old delinquent who took to hiding in a housing estate ventilation shaft when the police were looking for him. He was quickly dubbed 'Ratboy' by the national press. Only his mother, it seemed, could hang onto who he really was, 'He's not a rat. He's my son.'[15]

However, it is hard to be shamed unless there are people whose opinions the person being shamed cares about. Strong relationships are essential to effective shaming. So it is hard to achieve 'reintegrative shaming' today when, so often, we know people in only one social role. The prison system exacerbates the isolation of the offender from both his family and the locality, further reducing any prospect of reintegrative shaming for the future.
[. . .]

This extract is taken from 'What is Relational Justice?', by Michael Schluter, in J. Burnside and N. Baker (eds), Relational Justice: Repairing the Breach *(Winchester: Waterside Press, 1994), pp. 17–27.*

Notes

1 *Home Office Prison Statistics, England and Wales* (London: HMSO, 1994).
2 Information on the criminal justice system in England and Wales from *Digest* 2 (London: Home Office Research and Statistics Department, 1993).
3 Speller, A. (1986) *Breaking Out* (London: Hodder & Stoughton).
4 Quoted in the *Guardian*, 24 June 1994.
5 Cited in Kelly, R. (1993) 'The Invisible Hand behind the Inexorable Increase in the Rate of Crime', *Guardian*, 1 September.

6 For a summary of the evidence, from psychology and the social sciences, see Watt, E. (1994) *For Better or for Worse: The Case for Long-term Commitment in Family Relationships* (Cambridge: Jubilee Centre).

7 Ibid.

8 Ibid.

9 For evidence of this, see Schluter, M. and Lee, D. (1993) *The R-factor* (London: Hodder & Stoughton) pp. 219–33.

10 Ibid.

11 Ibid.: ch. 3.

12 CIPFA (1978) *Finance, General and Rating Statistics, 1978–9* (London: CIPFA) and CIPFA (1992) *Councillor's Guide to Local Government Finance* (London: CIPFA).

13 Farrington, D.P. (1993) 'The Challenge of Teenage Antisocial Behaviour.' Unpublished paper prepared for Marbach Castle conference on Youth in the Year 2000, p. 33.

14 Braithwaite, J. (1989) *Crime, Shame and Reintegration* (Cambridge: Cambridge University Press).

15 'Profile: A 14 year-old Becomes a Byword for Trouble', *The Independent*, 9 October 1993.

23. In the hands of the public?

Adam Crawford

The last twenty years in the UK have witnessed a radical transformation in relations between the public and the state with regard to criminal justice policy and practice. There has been an increasing acknowledgement and recognition of the state's own limitations in its capacity to guarantee and maintain public order. In part, this stems from a series of recent crises in the apparatus of criminal justice established over the preceding 200 years or so, in which the role and involvement of the public have been pivotal sources of concern. It is a relevant issue for Relational Justice, which has as its motif a chain of persons holding the sword and the scales of justice at either end. This article explores the scope for public involvement and participation in an age of increasing 'punitive populism' and, crucially, the form that this might take.

The current limitations of the state stem from a fourfold crisis of effectiveness, efficiency, cost and confidence in the criminal justice process. Firstly, increased recorded crime rates have placed growing pressure upon criminal justice institutions. This has left them unable to respond in a traditional manner, continually looking for novel ways of managing the mass of cases through efficiency gains (e.g. 'fast-track' prosecution). Secondly, there has been a pervasive sense of failure as to the capacity of formal criminal justice systems to meet their own objectives of crime reduction, leading to what Garland has called, a 'crisis of penal modernism'.[1] Thirdly, traditional modes of crime control place an increasing financial burden upon the public purse. Fourthly, there has been a simultaneous crisis of confidence, with public attitudes towards the criminal justice system (including the police) becoming apparently more critical and less deferential. Given the crucial role that the public plays within criminal justice, as witnesses and victims particularly, a loss of confidence can adversely affect the flow of information between public and criminal justice institutions.

'Leave it to the professionals'

Part of the problem has been that, over the last two centuries, the criminal justice apparatus has placed increasing emphasis on bureaucratisation, rationalisation and professional specialism as the pillars of legitimacy and public confidence. During the same period, public involvement has declined. Recent managerialist and modernising agendas have implied a reduction in lay participation in court processes and an increased reliance on paid and legally qualified professionals. In one way and another, the public was left behind. The result is that the state has assumed a monopolistic and paternalistic approach to the public with regard to crime control and prevention. The underlying message was 'leave it to the professionals'.

Victims, in particular, have been marginalised to the point of constituting the 'forgotten party' in criminal justice, whose own conflicts, according to Nils Christie have been 'stolen' by professionals and experts.[2] The result is 'an outsourcing approach to crime',[3] in which the public have come to expect specialist institutions to solve most problems for them. The same trend, of increasing professionalism at the expense of lay involvement, can still be recognised today. The central practices of participatory democracy at the heart of traditional criminal justice have been the institutions of the jury system and the lay magistracy, both of which share the notion of 'judgement by one's peers'. Yet both are currently under threat.

Partners against crime

Of course, the public is involved in different forms of public participation and involvement at the different stages of criminal justice. They are involved, in different capacities and to varying degrees of satisfaction, as victims, as witnesses, as offenders, as active private citizens (in community safety initiatives), as lay volunteers and as a wide variety of community representatives. There are all sorts of practical barriers to voluntary participation (including not having enough time, conflicts with domestic commitments, difficulties getting employers to grant time off from work commitments, and so on) but perhaps the greatest deterrent is that participation itself is perceived to be tokenistic, pointless or a waste of time.[4] Volunteers need to feel, not only supported and valued, but also that their time commitments are meaningful: that they are affecting change. Instead of seeing participation as an add-on to what the criminal justice system already does, we must ask: what is it that lay people can bring to the workings of criminal justice that is of intrinsic social value and in what way can volunteers themselves benefit?

Policy-makers have recently come to realise the fundamental role that the public plays in crime control and prevention, in the provison of information as witnesses or victims, through informal social control – as parents, peers, friends and family, kinship and community members – and in giving legitimacy to the system. As a result, citizens are being reconfigured as 'partners against crime' as governments seek to mitigate and reverse the decline of social capital in civil society.[5] Successive governments have sought to increase the level and commitment to 'voluntary activity' on the part of the public. For example, currently one of the Home Office's performance targets is of 'substantial progress by 2004 towards one million more people being actively involved in their communities'.

A mixed message

Yet the rhetoric remains ambiguous. Certainly, it has not filtered down to the level of practice, where public participation in criminal justice remains minimal. It is a 'mixed message' that is undermined in practice by contrary messages.

There are a number of important reasons why public involvement matters and why facilitating public participation is an essential government responsibility. Firstly, public involvement can increase public confidence and assuage public fears. This can be achieved through greater information and by moderating public expectations of what criminal justice can deliver. In particular, it can be a means of addressing misperceptions by explaining sentencing policy through information and education. In this way, greater public involvement in criminal justice could be a check against more punitive Government responses and the growing use of imprisonment. Secondly, public participation may help encourage greater synergy and increase the flow of information from the public. However, a genuine 'partnership' of this kind is a two-way relationship which imposes responsibilities upon the criminal justice system. This includes facilitating (and in some cases protecting) people in exercising and maximising their involvement with the criminal justice process.

A relational dynamic

Thirdly, public participation may strengthen and reaffirm communal bonds and encourage a civic responsibility. Fourthly, it allows those involved to develop a keener understanding of the workings, principles and values of the system. This is important because criminal justice is a highly 'public' process in the sense that it occurs in the name of the public, but in practice it is something about which the public remains considerably uninformed. Fifthly, it can help to break down inward-looking cultures and ensures a degree of transparency and accountability. Finally, it assures a relational dynamic. It can help ensure that proceedings which may otherwise be dominated by technical, bureaucratic or managerial demands also accord to the emotional and expressive needs of responses to crime and in a similar vein, ensures fairness.

Contrary to popular belief, public involvement does not necessarily reduce costs. Lay volunteers tend to work at a slower pace than do professional counterparts. Just because a system is based on unpaid volunteers (such as the lay magistracy and youth offender panels), this, of itself, does not mean that it is necessarily cheap. There are significant costs associated with providing training, advice and information for volunteers, which are required simply because volunteers are involved. In any case, to couch public participation in terms of 'value for money' maintains a paternalistic relationship between the public and criminal justice institutions and professionals.

'Citizen action' versus 'vigilantism'

Public involvement can take a number of diverse, and sometimes competing, forms. Clearly, the capacity for public participation is greater at the 'front-end' of the system with regard to policing and community safety than it is in relation to forms of punishment, such as imprisonment.

Public participation is not a self-evident good (recall the stocks and public executions). Strategies aimed at empowering the public with regard to crime have injected ambiguity into the power to define the legitimate use of force. Most notably, this is apparent in struggles over the distinction between appropriate 'citizen action' and 'vigilantism'. There is a need for government and criminal justice authorities to synchronise private and public provision of security services and active citizenry. The question is whether the state (either local or national) can adapt to this new role as 'power container' without slipping back into pretensions of monopolistic authority.

In addition, there are a number of limits to the potential scope of public participation. Public participation is limited by practical difficulties as well as by the potential unintended consequences of participation. For one thing, it is becoming harder to attract lay volunteers. Given the time demands of training, the travel demands (which may require lay people travelling across a county – particularly with the closure of local police stations, courthouses etc) and the difficulties for those in employment of matching voluntary work with their careers, whilst those unemployed may jeopardise their chances of obtaining a job.

Limits to participation

There is not always an unambiguous correspondence between volunteering and representativeness. As a consequence, representatives may poorly represent the diverse publics from which they are drawn, and may be perceived by others to be unrepresentative and, therefore, less legitimate. In addition, lay people drawn into criminal justice may become 'professionalised' and lose the very qualities which made them valuable in the first place.

Also, there tends to be an inverse relationship between activity and need. Participation in local crime prevention activities is highest (and success most likely) among people who are moderately concerned about crime but where crime levels are low. High levels of fear of crime can become incapacitating.

Moreover, there are limits to what citizens can accomplish through institutions of civil society alone as well as knock-on consequences (through crime displacement) of private or collective activity for others. One person's (or community's) security may adversely impact upon that of others. Furthermore, we need to be as aware of dangers of 'unsocial capital' as the advantages of 'social capital'. Also, criminal justice, by its nature, is coercive, hence, absolutist notions of voluntariness are unhelpful. In addition, there will be situations – given the nature of the offence or the relationship between the parties – in which participation is undesirable and safety issues may be a particular consideration. Finally, the involvement of lay people within the processes of justice necessitates that due concern is given to any conflict of interests that lay people may bring to their participation, particularly where they are cast in a decision-making role.

Rethinking public participation

Rethinking public participation means moving the debate on from seeing public participation in criminal justice as merely a question of how lay people can act as (cheap) adjuncts to the current justice system. Instead, we need to move on to the point where we begin to rethink the nature and purpose of criminal justice itself and the role of public participation therein.

We need to develop a language which speaks of active citizenship, community participation in public life, and the stimulation of ethical values as necessary ingredients in a more socially just public polity. But such a language would not see these as the antithesis, or instead, of 'public' provision. Rather, the state has a fundamental role in seeking to empower and enable individuals, groups and communities to realise their potential and to integrate them within a wider social frame. But in rethinking the role and value of public participation in criminal justice and the precise terms upon which such participation should be organised, we must tread a careful path between two recently fashionable tendencies: the managerialisation of public services and the communitarian appeals to local justice.

Limits of community

On the one hand, there is the managerialist obsession with speed, cost reductions, performance measurement and efficiency gains, which in the field of criminal justice has often led to a move away from 'local justice' – understood as local people contributing to the handling of cases in their own local area – and a professionalisation in which lay members of the public have less involvement. On the other hand, there is the communitarian lobby which calls for communities to take control of their own policing, crime control and dispute processing: the 'policing by communities rather than the policing of communities',[6] such that 'the more viable communities are, the less the need for policing.'[7] Despite decades of research to the contrary, this implies, rather simplistically, that more 'community' equals less crime.

The problem with the managerialist impulse is that it allows little space for the human, expressive and emotive aspects of criminal justice. As a consequence, it rides rough-shod over questions of party involvement, fairness, legitimacy and public confidence. It prioritises organisationally defined outputs over social outcomes. By contrast, the communitarian urge over-exaggerates the role that communities can play in responses to, and preventing, crime. It over-idealises as unproblematic the nature of communities' moral orders. 'An assertion of "community" identity at a local level can be beautifully conciliatory, socially nuanced, and constructive but it can also be parochial, intolerant, oppressive, and unjust.'[8] Appeals to 'community justice' often fail to address the relations that connect local institutions to the wider civil society of which the locality is a part or the manner in which local justice may impact upon neighbouring areas. The role of community as a force for social cohesion is limited by the current reality of geographic inequality, the spatial concentration of wealth and poverty and increased social polarisation.

Deliberative justice

An alternative to both the technocratic and managerialist notions of bureaucratic justice, on the one hand, and communitarian inspired notions of community justice as parochial and local forms of control, on the other hand, might be a version of deliberative justice. 'Deliberative' justice occurs where people 'deliberate' over the consequences of crimes and how to deal with them and try to prevent their recurrence.[9] The form of deliberative justice I have in mind is one in which public participation is contained within a framework which accords to standards of procedural fairness and human rights.

Deliberate justice encourages public discussion and emphasises reasoning, debate, communication and normative appeals, offering proposals for how best to solve problems or meet legitimate needs. Deliberation opens up opportunities for changing conditions of injustice and promoting justice. Within this should be embodied elements of both procedural and substantive justice. We need to maximise the opportunities for participation while constructing minimal, yet critical, limitations on the nature and form of participation.

As an element of democratic renewal, public participation in criminal justice implies representation. All of the public cannot (nor will they necessarily want to) participate all of the time. Certain members of the public – through their participation in criminal justice – will need to act as representatives of public interests. As such, they need to be authorised and held to account. This suggests further anticipatory and retrospective discussion as to public participation and representation. Participation should not stand as an opposite to representation but one should require and imply the other. Without citizen participation, the connection between representative and constituents is most liable to break down – potentially turning the representative into a detached élite. Certainly, there is a need for professionals and procedures to contain and regulate aspects of public participation by mitigating power differentials between the parties, challenging arbitrary outcomes, rendering procedures open, accountable and contestable under the rule of law. However, it is not clear that this cannot occur in interest-based and party-centred negotiations as distinct from rights-based and lawyer-centred proceedings.

Untamed justice

Formal legal rights and due process should act as bounding mechanisms that empower and constitutionalise informal processes. For example, the notion of proportionality – with regard to the relationship between the harm done and the agreed outcome – has a role to play as a principle in deliberative justice. This does not suggest that all outcomes will be the same for the same offence, but that there are accepted boundaries as to both minimum and excessive outcomes. What is not being argued for is the replacement of criminal justice by an untamed form of community justice – as some commentators advocate[10] – but that the two be held in a complementary, dynamic tension such as to enhance a form of deliberative justice: reducing but not eradicating the specialist professional management of crime.

'Relational' and 'restorative' justice can be described as forms of 'deliberative' justice.[11] 'Deliberative' justice is facilitated where there are existing relations of care and trust and where a commitment to collective problem-solving is apparent. However, there will be circumstances in which deliberation cannot even begin and individuals who refuse to engage in deliberative processes for a variety of reasons. In these instances, a greater emphasis upon the professional management of cases and problem-solving will be required. Moreover, the role of criminal justice in solving problems remains severely limited. Hence, synergy with other policy arenas – education, health, employment, housing and so on – more able to deliver solutions is paramount.

Communal morality

To sum up, much more can be done to encourage greater public participation in criminal justice and this has the potential to reverse the vicious circle of punitiveness in recent policy-making. As well as considering public participation as an add-on to existing criminal justice institutions, in which the public supplements organisational practices, we need to re-examine the role of the public at the heart of criminal justice. There is considerable scope for criminal justice to be a more deliberative process which, in drawing upon public participation, strengthens active responsibility and fosters a more civic public polity.

However, at the same time as maximising the opportunities for public participation, we also need to set minimal, yet critical, limitations on the form of that participation. We need a socially inclusive process – particularly with regard to traditionally neglected and suppressed groups – to protect against majoritarian rule and safeguard vulnerable minorities from the coercive and oppressive power of communal morality. We also need procedural mechanisms – particularly with regard to conflict negotiation and communication – to check power differentials and guarantee a minimum respect for the different parties involved. In this way, we can envision a form of public participation that is fair and just, which acts as a check upon state power, but which also maximises its democratic and civic potential.

This extract is taken from 'In the Hands of the Public?', by Adam Crawford, in Relational Justice Bulletin, *issue 13, January 2002, pp. 6–8.*

Notes

1 Garland, D. (2001) *The Culture of Control* (Oxford: Oxford University Press).
2 Christie, N. (1977) 'Conflicts as Property', *British Journal of Criminology*, 17: 1, pp. 1–15.
3 Leadbeater, C. (1996) *The Self-Policing Society* (London: Demos), p. 1.
4 This is also supported by the findings of the IPPR focus groups (see Edwards, L. (2001) *What Role for the Public in Tackling Crime?* (London: IPPR)).

5 Putnam, R. (1995) 'Bowling Alone: America's Declining Social Capital', *Journal of Democracy*, 6, pp. 64–78.

6 Leadbeater, C. (1996) *The Self-Policing Society* (London: Demos).

7 Etzioni, A. (1995) *The Spirit of Community* (London: Fontana), pp. ix–x. Recent policy initiatives such as 'zero tolerance' policing, anti-social behaviour orders and child curfews have all been justified in this vein (Straw, 1998).

8 Crawford, A. (1997) *The Local Governance of Crime: Appeals to Community and Partnerships* (Oxford: Clarendon Press), p. 294.

9 Braithwaite, J. (1998) 'Restorative Justice', in Tonry, M. (ed.) *Handbook of Crime and Punishment* (New York, NY: Oxford University Press), pp. 323–44.

10 Clear, T.R. and Karp, D.R. (1999) *The Community Justice Ideal* (Boulder, CO: Westview Press), Nellis, M. (2000) 'Creating Community Justice', in Ballintyne, S. *et al.* (eds) *Secure Foundations: Key Issues in Crime Prevention, Crime Reduction and Community Safety* (London: IPPR), pp. 67–86.

11 Braithwaite, J. (1998) 'Restorative Justice', in Tonry, M. (ed.) *Handbook of Crime and Punishment* (New York, NY: Oxford University Press), pp. 323–44.

24. Does restorative justice work?

John Braithwaite

This chapter summarizes the now considerable empirical evidence about the effectiveness of restorative justice. The literature review is organized around three broad and simple hypotheses:

1. Restorative justice restores and satisfies victims better than existing criminal justice practices
2. Restorative justice restores and satisfies offenders better than existing criminal justice practices
3. Restorative justice restores and satisfies communities better than existing criminal justice practices

[. . .]

Restorative justice practices restore and satisfy victims better than existing criminal justice practices

A consistent picture emerges from the welter of data reviewed in this section: it is one of comparatively high victim approval of their restorative justice experiences, though often lower levels of approval than one finds among other participants in the process. So long as the arrangements are convenient, it is only a small minority of victims who do not *want* to participate in restorative justice processes. Consistent with this picture, preliminary data from Lawrence Sherman and Heather Strang's Canberra experiments show only 3 per cent of offenders and 2 per cent of community representatives at conferences compared with 12 per cent of victims disagreeing with the statements: 'The government should use conferences as an alternative to court more often' (Strang, 2000). Most of the data to date are limited to a small range of outcomes; we are still awaiting the first systematic data on some of the dimensions of restoration [. . .]. On the limited range of outcomes explored to date, victims do seem to get more restoration out of restorative justice agreements than court orders, and restorative justice agreements seem to be more likely to be delivered than court orders even when the former are not legally enforceable.

Operationalizing victim restoration

There is a deep problem in evaluating how well restorative justice restores. Empowerment of victims to define the restoration that matters to them is a keystone of a restorative justice philosophy. Three paths can be taken. One is to posit a list of types of restoration that are important to most victims [. . .].

The problem with this is that even with as uncontroversial a dimension of restoration as restoring property loss, some victims will prefer mercy to insisting on getting their money back; indeed, it may be that act of grace which gives them a spiritual restoration that is critical for them.[1] The second path sidesteps a debate on what dimensions of restoration are universal enough to evaluate. Instead, it measures overall satisfaction of victims with restorative justice processes and outcomes, assuming (without evidence) that satisfaction is a proxy for victims getting restoration on the things that are most important for them. This is the path followed in the review of the next section, largely because this was the kind of information available when the earlier version of the review was published in 1999. The third path is the best one but also the most unmanageable in large quantitative evaluations. It is to ask victims to define the kinds of restoration they were seeking and then to report how much restoration they attained in these terms that matter most to them.

As this book goes to press, Heather Strang (forthcoming) has completed a manuscript that pulls off something close to this third approach. Strang reviewed the empirical literature on what victims said they wanted out of the criminal justice process and then confirmed the accuracy of that list of aspirations on Canberra crime victims whose cases were randomly assigned to court versus restorative justice conferences. The set of victim preferences she identified were:

- A less formal process where their views count

- More information about both the processing and the outcome of their case

- To participate in their case

- To be treated respectfully and fairly

- Material restoration

- Emotional restoration, including an apology

Strang then went on to show that indeed these victim aspirations were more consistently realized in cases randomly assigned to conferences as opposed to court:

> Feelings of anger, fear and anxiety towards their offenders fell markedly after their conference while feelings of security for themselves and sympathy for their offender increased. The conference usually had a beneficial effect on victims' feelings of dignity, self-respect and self-confidence and led to reduced levels of embarrassment and shame about the offence. Overall, victims most often said their conferences had been a helpful experience in allowing them to feel more settled about the offence, to feel forgiving towards their offender and to experience a sense of closure. (Strang, 2000, pp. iv–v).

Strang's most striking result concerns the capacity of conferences to deal with the feeling of revenge that so often eat away at victims. More than half of court-assigned violence victims said they would harm their offender if they had the chance, compared with only 7 per cent of those assigned to restorative justice.

Notwithstanding the strong affirmation overall that victims were more likely to have their needs, especially their emotional needs, met in conference than in court, Strang found a subset of victims who were worse off as a result of their case being assigned to conference. She concluded that these were not so much cases that refuted principles of restorative justice as cases that revealed bungled administration of justice (see Box [22.]1). One group of victims who were more dissatisfied than victims whose case was sent straight to court were those whose case was assigned to a conference, but the conference fell through and actually ended up going to court. The lesson here is that badly administered programs that do not deliver on their restorative promises to victims can actually make things a lot worse for them. Overall, Strang's results are extremely encouraging, especially since no one today would suggest that the Canberra program is the best one in Australia. Canberra is a first-generation program, and the evidence reviewed here suggests higher levels of satisfaction of victims and others in the later Australian programs that learned from some of its mistakes.[2]

Victim participation and satisfaction

While traditional criminal justice practices are notoriously unsatisfying to victims, it is also true that victims emerge from many restorative justice programs less satisfied than other participants. Clairmont (1994, pp. 16–17) found little victim involvement in four restorative justice programs for First Nations offenders in Canada. There seems to be a wider pattern of greater satisfaction among First Nations leaders and offenders than among victims for restorative projects on Canadian Aboriginal communities (Obonsawin-Irwin Consulting Inc., 1992a, 1992b; Clairmont, 1994; LaPrairie, 1995).

Early British victim–offender mediation programs reported what Dignan (1992) called sham reparation, for example, Davis's (1992) reporting of offers rather than actual repair, tokenism, and even dictated letters of apology. In some of these programs victims were little more than a new kind of prop in welfare programs: the 'new deal for victims' came in Britain to be seen as a 'new deal for offenders' (Crawford, 1996, p. 7). However, Crawford's (1996) conclusion that the British restorative justice programs that survived into the 1990s after weathering this storm 'have done much to answer their critics' (p. 7) seems consistent with the evidence. Dignan (1992) reports 71 per cent satisfaction among English corporate victims and 61 per cent among individual victims in one of the early adult offender reparation programs.

In New Zealand, victims attended only half the conferences conducted during the early years of the program[3] and when they did attend were less in agreement (51 per cent satisfaction) with family group conference outcomes than were offenders (84 per cent), police (91 per cent), and other participants (85 per cent; Maxwell and Morris, 1993, pp. 115, 120). About a quarter of victims reported that they felt worse as a result of attending the family group conference. Australian studies by Daly (1996) and Strang and Sherman (1997) also found a significant minority of victims who felt worse after the conference, upset over something said, or victimized by disrespect, though they were

---

Box [24.]1: Scapegoating: procedural injustice and the forgotten victim

Matthew, the 24-year-old victim in this assault matter, was drinking on licensed premises when a fight broke out involving one of his friends. He said that in the general melee he tried to pull his friend out of the fight, when a 'bouncer' hit him over the head and ejected him into the car park, where the fighting continued involving both patrons and security staff. Subsequently Charlie, aged 18 and employed on security at the pub, attended the police station and made full admissions about having punched Matthew in the face. In the view of the apprehending officer, other staff were directing blame at Charlie and it appeared that he had been offered as the sole offender because he was young with no prior convictions and likely not to be prosecuted.

The conference was attended by a large number of supporters of both Matthew and Charlie. As soon as it began, Matthew said that Charlie could not have been the person who assaulted him because he did not look anything like that person. Charlie's employer and workmates insisted that it was Charlie who was the assailant (though his family did not appear to believe that he had been involved). There were many claims and counter-claims in the course of the conference flowing from poor police investigation into the incident, including allegations that the victim and his friends had provoked the brawl. It was complicated by poor and untrusting relations between the licensee and the police, who frequently attended incidents at his premises. After about an hour of acrimonious discussion, the conference was abandoned as it was apparent that there was no agreement on what had happened and no likelihood of reaching an outcome acceptable to all the parties.

After further enquiries the police decided to take no further action with the case. Matthew was very angry and disappointed: his rage at the injustice of having effectively nothing happen following the assault led to his carrying a knife for several months, and in fact to pull it out when the same friend again got into a fight. He spontaneously said at interview that if he 'ran into' his assailants from the original incident he would probably attack them in revenge for what happened to him. He had been very upset at the way the conference unfolded, although he believed that the police had been fair and that he had had an opportunity to express his views. He wished the case had gone to court because he believed that way all the co-offenders would have been prosecuted and punished (in fact this could not have happened as only Charlie had been identified as being involved). Two years after the incident he remained extremely angry because he saw the licensee and his security staff as having 'got away' with assaulting him.

Source: From Strang, 2000, p. 168

---

greatly outnumbered by victims who felt healing as a result of the conference. Similarly, Birchall *et al.* (1992) report 27 per cent of victims feeling worse after meeting their offender and 70 per cent feeling better in Western Australia's Midland Pilot Reparation Scheme. The Ministry of Justice, Western Australia (1994), reports 95 per cent victim satisfaction with their restorative justice conference program (Juvenile Justice Teams). Chatterjee (2000, p. 3) reports that 94 per cent of victims in Royal Canadian Mounted Police convened family group conferences were satisfied with the fairness of the agreement. McCold and Wachtel (1998) found 96 per cent victim satisfaction with cases randomly assigned to conferences in Bethlehem, Pennsylvania, compared with 79 per cent satisfaction when cases were assigned to court and 73 per cent satisfaction when the case went to court after being assigned to conference and the conference was declined. Conferenced victims were also somewhat more likely to believe that they experienced fairness (96 per cent), that the offender was adequately held accountable for the offence (93 per cent), and that their opinion regarding the offence and circumstances was adequately considered in the case (94 per cent). Ninety-three per cent of victims found the conference helpful, 98 per cent found that it 'allowed me to express my feelings without being victimized', 96 per cent believed that the offender had apologized, and 75 per cent believed that the offender was sincere. Ninety-four per cent said they would choose a conference if they had to do it over again. The Bethlehem results are complicated by a 'decline' group as large as the control group, where either offenders or victims could cause the case to be declined. In the Canberra RISE experiment, victim participation is currently 80 per cent (Strang, 2000). Reports on the Wagga Wagga conferencing model in Australia are also more optimistic about victim participation and satisfaction, reporting 90 per cent victim satisfaction and victim participation exceeding 90 per cent (Moore and O'Connell, 1994). Trimboli's (2000, p. 28) evaluation of the NSW Youth Justice Conferencing Scheme finds even higher levels of victim satisfaction than with the Wagga Wagga model conferencing programs, though lower levels of victim participation of 74 per cent than in Wagga and Canberra.

Trimboli's NSW victims were much more satisfied than the Canberra victims over being kept informed about what was happening, and were more likely to feel that they were treated with respect, that they had the opportunity to express their views in the conference, and that these views actually affected the decision on what should be done about the case. The highest published satisfaction and fairness ratings (both 98 per cent) have been reported by the Queensland Department of Justice conferencing program (Palk *et al.*, 1998). Seventy-eight per cent of victims felt the conference and the agreement helped 'make up for the offence', and only 6 per cent said they would be 'concerned if you met the young person in the street today' (Hayes *et al.*, 1998, pp. 26, 27). A high 90 per cent of offenders made verbal apologies, and a further 12 per cent made written apologies in this program. One reason for the program's exceptionally positive results is that it excludes conferencing from cases where victims do not wish to participate, meaning that no data are collected from the least cooperative victims who just want to walk away.

McGarrell *et al.* (2000, p. 45) not only found markedly higher levels of satisfaction among victims in cases randomly assigned to a restorative justice conference but also found that 97 per cent of conference victims 'felt involved', compared with 38 per cent of control group victims, and that 95 per cent of conference victims felt they had the opportunity to express their views, compared with 56 per cent of control group victims.

Umbreit and Coates's (1992) survey found that 79 per cent of victims who cooperated in four US mediation programs were satisfied, compared with only

57 per cent of those who did not have mediation (for earlier similar findings, see Umbreit, 1990). In a subsequent study Umbreit (1998) found victim *procedural* satisfaction at 78 per cent at four combined Canadian sites and 62 per cent at two combined English mediation sites. Victim satisfaction with *outcomes* was higher still: 90 per cent (four US sites), 89 per cent (four Canadian sites), and 84 per cent (two English sites). However, victim satisfaction was still generally lower across the sites than offender satisfaction. Eighty-three per cent of US mediation victims perceived the outcome as 'fair' (as opposed to being 'satisfied'), compared with 62 per cent of those who went through the normal court process. Umbreit and Coates (1992) also report reduced fear and anxiety among victims following mediation, a finding Strang (2000) has replicated on Canberra conferences. Victims afraid of being victimized again dropped from 25 per cent prior to mediation to 10 per cent afterward in a study by Umbreit and Coates (1992), again results comparable to those obtained by Strang on conferences. A survey of German institutions involved in model mediation projects found that the rate of voluntary victim participation generally ranged from 81 to 92 per cent and never dropped below 70 per cent (Kerner *et al.*, 1992).

McCold and Wachtel (2000) compared systematically thirty-nine program samples (including most of those discussed here) according to whether they were 'fully restorative', 'mostly restorative', or 'not restorative', where restorativeness was operationalized in terms of stakeholder participation. On average, victim perception of both fairness and satisfaction was highest for fully restorative programs and lowest for nonrestorative programs.

In summary, while many programs accomplish very high levels of victim participation, programs vary considerably on this dimension. Consistently, however, across disparate programs victims are highly satisfied with the fairness of procedures and outcomes – more satisfied than victims whose cases go to court, though not as satisfied as offenders and other participants in restorative justice processes. In a meta-analysis of 13 evaluations with a control group, Latimer, Dowden and Muise (2001) found victim satisfaction to be significantly higher in the restorative justice group. Victims also experienced reduced fear and increased emotional restoration after the restorative justice process. Heather Strang's (2000) data suggest, however, that one group whose satisfaction and emotional well-being are adversely affected by the offer of a restorative justice conference is victims whose conference falls through. This points up a methodological deficiency in most of the studies reviewed here (that does not apply to Strang's work): they measure satisfaction levels among victims whose conferences actually come to pass, failing to correct for the reduced levels of satisfaction that would apply if cases were included where conferences were offered but not delivered. Trimboli (2000) actually compares NSW results from completed conferences with RISE results of cases randomly assigned to conference (many of which actually ended up in court).

Honoring of obligations to victims

Haley and Neugebauer's (1992) analysis of restorative justice programs in the United States, Canada, and Great Britain revealed between 64 and 100 per cent completion of reparation and compensation agreements. I assume here, of course, that completion of undertakings that victims have agreed to is important for victim restoration. Marshall's (1992) study of cases referred to mediation programs in Britain found that over 80 per cent of agreements were completed. Galaway (1992) reports that 58 per cent of agreements reached through mediation in New Zealand were fully complied with within one year. In a Finnish study, 85 per cent of agreements reached through mediation were fully completed (Iivari, 1987, 1992). From England, Dignan (1992) reports 86 per cent participant agreement with mediation outcomes, with 91 per cent of agreements honored in full. Trenczek (1990), in a study of pilot victim–offender reconciliation projects in Braunschweig, Cologne, and Reutlingen, West Germany (see also Kuhn, 1987), reports a full completion rate of 76 per cent and a partial completion rate of 5 per cent. Pate's (1990) study of victim–offender reconciliation projects found a rate of noncompletion of agreements of between 5 and 10 per cent in Alberta, Canada, and less than 1 per cent in the case of a Calgary program. Wundersitz and Hetzel (1996, p. 133) found 86 per cent full compliance with conference agreements in South Australia, with another 3 per cent waived for near compliance. Fry (1997, p. 5) reported 100 per cent completion of agreements in a pilot of twenty-six Northern Territory police-coordinated juvenile conferences, and Waters (1993, p. 9) reported 91 per cent payment of compensation agreed in Wagga Wagga conferences. In another Wagga-style program, McCold and Wachtel (1998, p. 4) report 94 per cent compliance with the terms of conference agreements. McGarrell *et al.* (2000, p. 47) found 83 per cent completion of conference agreements in Indianapolis, compared with 58 per cent completion of diversion programs in the control group.

Umbreit and Coates (1992) compared 81 per cent completion of restitution obligations settled through mediation to 58 per cent completion of court-ordered restitution in their multisite study. Ervin and Schneider (1990), in a random assignment evaluation of six US restitution programs, found 89 per cent completion of restitution, compared with 75 per cent completion of traditional programs. Most of Ervin and Schneider's restitution programs, however, were not restorative in the sense of involving meetings of victims and offenders. Latimer, Dowden and Muise (2001, p. 17) found in a meta-analysis of 8 studies with a control group that restitution compliance was 33 per cent higher in the restorative justice cases than among controls. In summary, the research suggests high levels of compliance with restorative justice agreements, substantially higher than with court orders.

Symbolic reparation

One reason that the level of satisfaction of victims is surprisingly high in processes that so often give them so little material reparation is that they get symbolic reparation, which is more important to them (Retzinger and Scheff, 1996). Apology is at the heart of this: preliminary results from the RISE experiment in Canberra show that 71 per cent of victims whose cases were randomly assigned to a conference got an apology, compared with 17 per cent in cases randomly assigned to court; while 77 per cent of the conference apologies were regarded as 'sincere' or 'somewhat sincere', this was true of only 36 per cent of apologies to victims whose cases went to court (Strang, 2000). Sixty-five per cent of victims felt 'quite' or 'very' angry before the Canberra conferences, and 27 per cent felt so afterward. Obversely, the proportion of victims feeling sympathetic to the offender almost tripled (from 18 to 50 per cent) by the end of the conference (Strang, 2000). We will see that there is a large body of research evidence showing that victims are not as punitive as the rather atypical victims whose bitter calls for brutal punishment get most media coverage. Studies by both Strang and Sherman (1997) and Umbreit (1992, p. 443) report victim fear of revictimization and victim upset about the crime as having declined following the restorative justice process.

In Goodes's (1995) study of juvenile family group conferences in South Australia, where victim attendance ranges from 75 to 80 per cent (Wundersitz and Hetzel, 1996), the most common reason victims gave for attending their conference was to try to help the offender, followed by the desire to express feelings, make statements to the offender, or ask questions like 'why me' (what Retzinger and Scheff [1996] call symbolic reparation), followed by 'curiosity and a desire to "have a look" ', followed by 'responsibility as citizens to attend'. The desire to ensure that the penalty was appropriate and the desire for material reparation rated behind all of these motivations to attend. The response rate in the Goodes (1995) study was poor, and there may be a strong social desirability bias in these victim reports; yet that may be precisely because the context of conference attendance is one that nurtures responsible citizenship cognitions by victims. Eighty-eight per cent of Goodes's (1995) victims agreed with the conference outcome, 90 per cent found it helpful to them, and 90 per cent said they would attend again if they were a victim again (Goodes, 1995).

With all these quantitative findings, one can lose sight of what most moves restorative justice advocates who have seen restorative processes work well. I am not a spiritual enough person to capture it in words: it is about grace, shalom. Van Ness (1986, p. 125) characterizes shalom as 'peace as the result of doing justice'. Trish Stewart (1993, p. 49) gets near its evocation when she reports one victim who said in the closing round of a conference: 'Today I have observed and taken part in justice administered with love.' Psychologists are developing improved ways of measuring spirituality – self-transcendence, meaning in life beyond one's self. So in the future it will be possible to undertake systematic research on self-reported spirituality and conferences to see whether results are obtained analogous to Reed's (1986, 1987, 1992) findings that greater healing occurred among terminally ill individuals whose psychosocial response was imbued with a spiritual dimension.

For the moment, we must accept an East–West divide in the way participants think about spiritual leadership in conferences. Maori, North American, and Australian Aboriginal peoples tend to think it important to have elders with special gifts of spirituality, what Maori call *mana*, attend restorative justice processes (Tauri and Morris, 1997, pp. 149–50). This is the Confucian view as well. These traditions are critical of the ethos Western advocates such as myself have brought to conferences, which has not seen it as important to have elders with *mana* at conferences. Several years ago in Indonesia I was told of restorative justice rituals in western Sumatra that were jointly conducted by a religious leader and a scholar – the person in the community seen as having the greatest spiritual riches and the person seen as having the greatest riches of learning. My inclination then was to recoil from the elitism of this and insist that many (if not most) citizens have the resources (given a little help with training) to facilitate processes of healing. While I still believe this, I now think it might be a mistake to seek to persuade Asians to democratize their restorative justice practices. There may be merit in special efforts to recruit exemplars of virtue, grace, *mana*, to participate. Increasingly, I am tempted to so interpret our experience with RISE in recruiting community representatives with grace to participate in drunk driving conferences where there is no victim. However, as Power (2000) and Miller and Blackler (2000) correctly point out, the Canberra experience with community representatives has been far from universally positive. Many have been decidedly short of *mana* and long on punitive speech. Nevertheless, a research and development program for restorative justice that still appeals to me is how to do well at locating elders with grace to act as community representatives in restorative justice programs in Western cities.

Restorative justice practices restore and satisfy offenders better than existing criminal justice practices

This section concludes that offender satisfaction with both corporate and traditional individual restorative justice programs has been extremely high. The evidence of offenders being restored in the sense of desisting from criminal conduct is extremely encouraging with victim–offender mediation, conferencing, restorative business regulatory programs, and whole-school antibullying programs, though not with peer mediation programs for bullying.[4] However, only some of these studies adequately control for important variables, and only five randomly assigned cases to restorative versus punitive justice. The business regulatory studies are instructive in suggesting that (1) restorative justice works best when it is backed up by punitive justice in those (quite common) individual cases where restorative justice fails and (2) trying restorative justice first increases perceived justice.

Fairness and satisfaction for offenders

[... Offenders] are more likely to respond positively to criminal justice processing when they perceive it as just. Moore with Forsythe's (1995, p. 248) ethnographic work concludes that most offenders, like victims, experienced quite profound 'procedural, material and psychological justice' in restorative justice conferences. Umbreit (1992) reports from his cross-site study in the United States an 89 per cent perception of fairness on the part of offenders with victim–offender mediation programs, compared with 78 per cent perceived fairness in unmediated cases. Umbreit (1998) reports 80 per cent offender perception of fairness of victim–offender mediation across four Canadian studies and 89 per cent at two combined English sites. The Ministry of Justice, Western Australia (1994), reports 95 per cent offender satisfaction with its restorative justice conference program (Juvenile Justice Teams). McCold and Wachtel (1998, pp. 59–61) report 97 per cent satisfaction with 'the way your case was handled' and 97 per cent fairness in the Bethlehem police conferencing program, a better result than in the four comparisons with Bethlehem cases that went to court. McGarrell et al. (2000, p. 45) report that conference offenders in Indianapolis were more likely than control group offenders to have 'felt involved' (84 per cent versus 47 per cent) and to feel they have had an opportunity to express their views (86 per cent versus 55 per cent). Coates and Gehm (1985, 1989) found 83 per cent offender satisfaction with the victim–offender reconciliation experience based on a study of programs in Indiana and Ohio. Smith, Blagg and Derricourt (1985), in a limited survey of the initial years of a South Yorkshire mediation project, found that 10 out of 13 offenders were satisfied with the mediation experience and felt that the scheme had helped alter their behavior. Dignan (1990), on the basis of a random sample of offenders (N = 50) involved in victim–offender mediations in Kettering, Northamptonshire, found 96 per cent were either satisfied or very satisfied with the process. [...] Barnes (1999) found higher perceptions of a number of facets of procedural and outcome fairness in RISE conferences compared with Canberra courts. However, Trimboli (2000, pp. 34–54) has reported even higher levels of offender perceptions of fairness and outcome satisfaction in NSW compared with RISE conferences. The strongest published result was again on 113 juvenile offenders in the Queensland Department of Justice conferencing program, where 98 per cent thought their conference fair and 99 per cent were satisfied with the agreement (Palk et al., 1998). Ninety-six per cent of young offenders reported that they 'would be more likely to go to your family now if you were in trouble or needed help' and that they had 'been able to put the whole experience behind you'.

McCold and Wachtel (2000) compared systematically thirty-four program samples (including most of those discussed here) according to whether they were 'fully restorative', 'mostly restorative', or 'not restorative', where restorativeness was operationalized in terms of stakeholder participation. As with victim perceptions, offender perception of both fairness and satisfaction was highest for fully restorative programs and lowest for nonrestorative programs. For 13 studies with a control group, Latimer, Dowden and Muise's (2001, p. 14) meta-analysis found restorative justice offenders to be more satisfied about how their case was handled compared with controls.

Reduced reoffending as offender restoration

Meta-analysis of restitution programs suggests that these have some (modest) effect in reducing reoffending (e.g. Gendreau et al., 1996; Cullen and Gendreau, 2000; see also Butts and Snyder, 1991; Schneider, 1986; Geudens and Walgrave, 1998; Schiff, 1998; Bazemore, 1999). I do not consider this literature here because most of these programs do not involve a restorative *process* (i.e. the restitution is usually imposed by a traditional court, often as punishment rather than in pursuit of any restorative *values*).

Pate (1990), Nugent and Paddock (1995), and Wynne (1996) all report a decline in recidivism among mediation cases. Umbreit, with Coates and Kalanj (1994) found 18 per cent recidivism across four victim–offender mediation sites (N = 160) and 27 per cent (N = 160) for comparable nonmediation cases at those sites, a difference that was encouraging but fell short of statistical significance. However, a follow-up in 2000 on these and several other programs on a much expanded sample of 1,298 again found mediation recidivism to be one-third lower than court recidivism (19 per cent versus 28 per cent), this time a statistically significant result after entering appropriate controls (Nugent *et al.* forthcoming). Similarly, Marshall and Merry (1990, p. 196) report for an even smaller sample than Umbreit, with Coates and Kalanj (1994) that offending declined for victim–offender mediation cases, especially when there was an actual meeting (as opposed to indirect shuttle diplomacy by a mediation), while offending went up for controls. However, the differences were not statistically significant. A German study by Dolling and Hartman (2000) found reoffending to be one-third lower in cases where victim–offender mediation was completed compared with a control group. The effect was significant after entering controls. However, including cases where mediation was not successfully completed reduced the p value to .08, which would not normally be accepted as significant.

In an experimental evaluation of six US restitution programs, Schneider (1986, 1990) found a significant reduction in recidivism across the six programs. This result is widely cited by restorative justice advocates as evidence for the efficacy of restorative justice. However, all but one of these programs seem to involve mandated restitution to victims without any mediation or restorative justice deliberation by victims and offenders. The one program that seems to meet the process definition of restorative justice, the one in Washington, DC, did produce significantly lower rates of reoffending for cases randomly assigned to victim–offender mediation and restitution compared with cases assigned to regular probation.[5]

There is no satisfactory evidence on the impact of the New Zealand juvenile family group conferences on recidivism. The story is similar with Wagga Wagga. Forsythe (1995) shows a 20 per cent reoffending rate for cases going to conference, compared with a 48 per cent rate for juvenile court cases. This is a big effect; most of it is likely a social selection effect of tougher cases going to court, as there is no matching, no controls, though it is hard to account for the entire association in these terms given the pattern of the data (see Forsythe, 1995, pp. 245–46).

Another big effect with the same social selection worry was obtained with only the first sixty-three cases to go through family group conferences in Singapore. The conference reoffending rate was 2 per cent, compared with 30 per cent over the same period for offenders who went to court (Chan, 1996; Hsien, 1996).

McCold and Wachtel's (1998) experimental evaluation of Bethlehem, Pennsylvania's, Wagga-style police conferencing program involved a more determined attempt to tackle social selection problems through randomization.

Unfortunately, however, this study fell victim to another kind of selection effect as a result of unacceptably high crossover rates on the treatments assigned in the experiment. For property cases, there was a tendency for conferenced cases to have higher recidivism than court cases, but the difference was not statistically significant. For violence cases, conferenced offenders had a significantly lower reoffending rate than offenders who went to court. However, this result was not statistically valid because the violent offenders with the highest reoffending rate were those who were randomly assigned to conference but who actually ended up going to court because either the offender or the victim refused to cooperate in the conference. In other words, the experiment failed to achieve an adequate test of the effect of conferences on recidivism both on grounds of statistical power and because of unsatisfactory assurance that the assigned treatment was delivered.

Clearer results were obtained from McGarrell *et al.*'s (2000) Indianapolis Restorative Justice Experiment, which involved random assignment of young first offenders to a Wagga-style conference convened by the police versus assignment to the normal range of diversion programs. Rearrest was 40 per cent lower in the conference group than in the control group after six months, an effect that decayed to a 25 per cent reduction after twelve months. At the Winchester conference in 2001 McGarrell reported that the analysis of further cases revealed a decay to higher than this 25 per cent reduction, but these results are not yet published.

Preliminary reoffending results have been put up on the Web (aic.gov.au) by Sherman, Strang and Woods (2000) from the RISE restorative justice experiment in Canberra. In this experiment 1,300 cases were randomly assigned either to court or to a restorative justice conference on the Wagga model. While the experiment showed a sharp decline in officially recorded repeat criminal offending for violent juvenile and young adult offenders randomly assigned to conference in comparison to those assigned to court, the results were not encouraging on adult drunk drivers and juvenile property offenders (though not all the latter results were discouraging). Sherman, Strang and Woods (2000, p. 20) conclude that compared with court, the effect of diversionary conferences is to cause the following:

- Big drop in offending rates by violent offenders (by 38 crimes per 100 per year)
- Very small increase in offending by drink drivers (by 6 crimes per 100 offenders per year)
- Lack of any difference in repeat offending by juvenile property offenders or shoplifters (though after-only analysis shows a drop in reoffending by shoplifters)

The drunk driving results are particularly disappointing. These are conferences without a victim, as all cases involve nonaccidents detected by random breath testing. Sherman, Strang and Woods (2000, p. 11) interpret the pattern of the results as suggesting that courts reduce reoffending through their power to suspend drivers' licenses, a power not available to conferences in the experiment. However, more detailed decomposition of results is yet to be done on this question.

One conferencing program that has dealt convincingly with the social selection problem without randomization is a Royal Canadian Mounted Police program in the Canadian coal mining town of Sparwood, British Columbia. For almost three years from the commencement of the program in 1995 until late 1997, *no* young offender from Sparwood went to court.[6] All were cautioned or conferenced. Three youths who had been conferenced on at least two previous occasions went to court in late 1997. No cases have been to court during 1998 up until the time the data could be checked (20 October 1998). In the year prior to the program (1994), sixty-four youths went to court. Over the ensuing three years and nine months, this net was narrowed to eighty-eight conferences and three court cases. This was probably not just a net-narrowing effect, however. It looks like a real reduction in offending. According to police records, compared with the 1994 youth offending rate, the 1995 rate was down 26 per cent, and the 1996 rate was down 67 per cent. Reoffending rates for conference cases were 8 per cent in 1995, 3 per cent in 1996, 10 per cent in 1997, and 0 per cent for the first nine months of 1998, compared with a national rate of 40 per cent per annum for court cases (which is similar to that in towns surrounding Sparwood). Reoffending rates for Sparwood court cases prior to 1995 have not been collected. While social selection bias is convincingly dealt with here by the universality of the switch to restorative justice for the first three years, eighty-eight conferences are only a modest basis for inference.

Burford and Pennell's (1998) study of a restorative conference-based approach to family violence in Newfoundland found a marked reduction in both child abuse/neglect and abuse of mothers/wives after the intervention. A halving of abuse/neglect incidents was found for thirty-two families in the year after the conference compared with the year before, while incidents increased markedly for thirty-one control families. Pennell and Burford's (1997) research is also a model of sophisticated process development and process evaluation and of methodological triangulation. While sixty-three families might seem modest for quantitative purposes, this is actually a statistically persuasive study in demonstrating that this intervention reduced family violence. There were actually 472 participants in the conferences for the thirty-two families, and 115 of these were interviewed to estimate levels of violence affecting different participants (Pennell and Burford, 2000). Moreover, within each case a before and after pattern was tested against thirty-one types of events (e.g. abuse of child, child abuses mother, attempted suicide, father keeps income from mother) where events can be relevant to more than one member of the family. Given this pattern matching of families by events by individual family members, it understates the statistical power of the design to say it is based on only sixty-three cases. Burford and Pennell (1998, p. 253) also report reduced drinking problems after conferences. The Newfoundland conferences were less successful in cases where young people were abusing their mothers, a matter worthy of further investigation.

While the universality of the New Zealand juvenile conferencing program has made it difficult to evaluate the impact on recidivism compared with a control group, Maxwell, Morris and Anderson (1999) have now published an important evaluation of two adult programs, which they describe as sharing enough of the core principles of restorative justice to serve as case studies of restorative justice. Te Whanau Awhina (a program only for Maori offenders) and Project Turnaround refer adult offenders to a panel (rather akin to the Vermont Reparation Boards). However, family and social service providers for the family, victims and victim supporters, and the police also frequently attend. For 100 offenders referred to each of these schemes, both reoffending and the seriousness of reoffending were significantly reduced under both schemes compared with 100 controls matched for criminal history, demographic factors, and offence characteristics who went to court. Twelve-month reconviction rates were 16 per cent for Project Turnaround compared with 30 per cent for controls. For Te Whanau Awhina, reconviction was 33 per cent, compared with 47 per cent for controls.

Another important recent adult evaluation is of the John Howard Society's Restorative Resolutions program in Winnipeg (Bonta et al., 1998). The seriousness of the offending gives special importance to this evaluation: there was 90 per cent success in reserving entry to the program to serious adult offenders who were facing a prosecutorial recommendation of at least six months prison time (and preferably having histories of incarceration and probation violation). Like the New Zealand programs discussed in the previous paragraph, Restorative Resolutions secured enough of the principles of restorative justice to be accepted as a test of the approach without securing all of them: notwithstanding good-faith consultation with victims, most offenders did not actually meet their victim, and eighteen offenders had their restorative resolution accepted by the court but then with a judicially imposed sentence on top of it. Since this initial report was published, there has been follow-up over three years of a control group of seventy-two offenders, carefully matched on a variety of risk factors; the seventy-two Restorative Resolutions serious offenders had half the criminal reoffending of the control group.

[A] recent study by Michael Little (2001), is of particular importance in that it applies restorative justice to the most persistent offenders. Little's study was conducted in Kent, England. It applied to juvenile offenders who either had been previously sentenced to custody or had failed to complete a community sentence. A second condition for entry was being charged or cautioned on three or more occasions for offences that would permit a court to sentence to custody. Basically they were the most persistent young offenders in Kent. Twenty-four offenders were randomly assigned to a multisystemic approach that involved a family group conference, joint and heightened supervision by police and social services staff, and improved assessment combined with an individual treatment plan and mentoring by a young volunteer. This was called the Intensive Supervision and Support Program. Fifty-five young offenders were assigned to two control groups. The reduction in rearrest during two years of follow-up was substantial and statistically significant. Because the treatment was multisystematic, however, there was no way of assessing whether it was restorative justice, some other component of the program, or a general placebo effect that produced the success. [Elsewhere] we consider the theoretical reasons why a combination of restorative justice and intensive rehabilitation in hard cases may be more effective than restorative justice and intensive rehabilitation alone. The results of this randomized trial are

Box [24.]2: Pig, pig, pig!

The incident began during the morning roll call when the boy in charge called a girl by her (unappreciated) nickname of 'pig'. The girl was offended and refused to answer, so the boy raised his voice and yelled the word several times . . . Later that morning during the break several children gathered around the girl and chanted, 'Pig, pig, pig'. Deeply hurt . . . she ran away from the group. For the remainder of the school day she did not speak a word; that afternoon she went home and would refuse to return for a week. The teacher in charge of the class had not been present during the periods when the girl was insulted, so she did not appreciate what had happened.

   Later that day the girl's mother called to ask what had gone on. Immediately the principal began a quiet investigation in co-operation with the teacher. By that evening, parts of the story were known, and the principal visited the child's home to apologise to her parents. The next day, and on each successive day until the problem was solved, special teachers' meetings were held with all present to seek a solution. On three occasions the principal or the girl's homeroom teacher went to the girl's home and talked with her. The final resolution involved a visit by the entire class to the girl's home, where apologies were offered along with a request that the insulted girl forgive her friends. Two days later she returned to school, and two weeks later the teacher read a final report to the regular teachers' meeting and then apologised for having caused the school so much trouble.

Source: Cummings, 1980, pp. 118–19, cited in Masters, 1997

compelling because part of the intervention was more intensive police surveillance. This should have produced an increase in the number of offences detected by the police in the restorative justice group.

Restorative antibullying programs in schools, generally referred to as *whole-school* approaches (Rigby, 1996), which combine community deliberation among students, teachers and parents about how to prevent bullying with mediation of specific cases, have been systematically evaluated with positive results (Farrington, 1993; Pitts and Smith, 1995; Pepler *et al.*, 1993; Rigby, 1996) the most impressive being a program in Norway where a 50 per cent reduction in bullying has been reported (Olweus, 1993). Gentry and Benenson's (1993) data further suggest that skills for mediating playground disputes learned and practiced by children in school may transfer to the home setting, resulting in reduced conflict, particularly with siblings. The restorative approaches to bullying in Japanese schools, which Master's (1997) qualitative work found to be a success, can also be read as even more radically 'whole-school' than the Norwegian innovations (see Box [22.]2).

However, Gottfredson's (1997) and Brewer *et al.*'s (1995) reviews of school peer mediation programs that simply train children to resolve disputes when conflicts arise among students showed nonsignificant or weak effects on observable behavior such as fighting. Only one of four studies with quasi-experimental or true experimental designs found peer mediation to be associated with a decrease in aggressive behavior. Lam's (1989) review of fourteen evaluations of peer mediation programs with mostly weak methods found no programs that made violence worse. It appears a whole-school approach is needed that not just tackles individual incidents but also links incidents to a change program for the culture of the school, in particular to how seriously members of the school community take rules about bullying. Put another way, the school not only must resolve the bullying incident; but also must use it as a resource to affirm the disapproval of bullying in the culture of the school.

Statistical power, randomization, and control have been weak in much of the research reported here. Fairly consistently encouraging results from these weak designs, however, should be combined with the reduced reoffending evident under stronger designs in the studies by Schneider (1986), Olweus (1993) and the other antibullying researchers, Burford and Pennell (1998), the Sparwood police, Maxwell, Morris and Anderson (1999), Bonta Rooney and Wallace-Capretta (1998), McGarrell *et al.* (2000), and Little (2001). However, the research with the strongest design, by Sherman, Strang and Woods (2000), is encouraging only with respect to violent offenders. My own reading of the three dozen studies of reoffending reviewed is that while restorative justice programs do not involve a consistent guarantee of reducing offending, even badly managed restorative justice programs are most unlikely to make reoffending worse. After all, restorative justice is based on principles of socializing children that have demonstrably reduced delinquency when parents have applied them in raising their children (in comparison to punitive/ stigmatizing socialization) (Braithwaite, 1989; Sampson and Laub, 1993). If we invest in working out how to improve the quality of the delivery of restorative justice programs, they are likely to show us how to substantially reduce reoffending. That investment means looking below the surface to understand the theoretical conditions of success and failure [. . .].

Restorative justice advocates are frequently admonished not to make 'exaggerated claims' for the likely effects on recidivism of a one- or two-hour intervention. Yet when it is modest benefits on the order of 10 to 20 per cent lower levels of reoffending that are predicted, it can be equally irresponsible to cite a study with a sample size of 100 (which lacks the statistical power to detect an effect of this order as statistically significant) as demonstrating no effect. If we are modest in our expectations, we should expect reviewers like Braithwaite (1999) to report a study by Umbreit (1994) on a small sample finding a nonsignificant reduction in offending and then in this review to have Braithwaite report an expanded sample by Umbreit and his colleagues to now be strongly significant. [Recently] there has been a surge of positive recidivism results from the United States, Canada, Germany, the United Kingdom, Australia, and New Zealand. [Most] of these very recent positive results are not incorporated into the meta analysis of thirty-two studies with control groups conducted for the Canadian Department of Justice by Latimer, Dowden and Muise (2001). Equally, Latimer, Dowden and Muise have uncovered unpublished evaluations of a dozen recent restorative justice programs not covered by the review in this chapter. Across their thirty-two studies Latimer, Dowden and Muise found a modest but statistically significant effect of restorative justice in reducing recidivism (effect size 0.07). This means approximately seven per cent lower recidivism on average in the restorative justice programs compared to controls or comparison groups. This is indeed a modest accomplishment compared to effect sizes for the best rehabilitation programs. During R and D on first and second generation programs, however, our interest should not be on comparing average restorative justice effect sizes with those of the best rehabilitation programs. It should be on the effect sizes we might accomplish by integration of best restorative justice practice with best rehabilitative practice [. . .]. One important difference in the conclusion reached from the set of studies reviewed in this chapter is that Latimer, Dowden and Muise found a bigger tendency for victim satisfaction to be higher in cases that went to restorative justice (effect size 0.19) than the tendency for offender satisfaction to be higher in restorative justice cases (effect size 0.10).

So now we must remember that it is possible to make Type II as well as Type I errors; we can make the error of wrongly believing that 'nothing makes much difference'. In recent criminological history we have seen this Type II error institutionalized in the doctrine that 'nothing works' with respect to offender rehabilitation. Restorative justice clearly has the promise to justify a huge R and D effort now. Certainly there are some notable research failures. Here we might remember the often-quoted retrospective of medical texts that it was not until the advances in medicine during World War I that the average patient left an encounter with the average doctor better off. The question at the beginning of the twentieth century was whether there was enough promise in medicine to justify a huge research investment in it. Clearly there was, notwithstanding a lot of mediocre results from mediocre practice. The results in this section show that there are very strong reasons to think that funding restorative justice R and D will be a good investment for the twenty-first century, especially when [. . .] restorative justice is conceived as a superior vehicle for delivering other crime prevention strategies that work, and conceived holistically as a way of living rather than just an eighty-minute intervention.

It may be that the key to explaining why the Indianapolis Juvenile Restorative Justice Experiment had a major effect on reoffending while the RISE adult drunk driving experiment did not can be understood in terms of the potential for restorative justice to be a superior vehicle for prevention to be realized in the former case but not the latter. Eighty-three per cent of those randomly assigned to conferences in Indianapolis completed their diversion program, whereas completion occurred for only 58 per cent of the control group assigned to the standard suite of diversion options (McGarrell *et al.*, 2000, p. 47). [Restorative] justice is potentially a superior vehicle for getting offenders and their families to commit to rehabilitative and other preventive measures. The RISE drunk driving conferences generally did not confront underlying drinking problems, with police encouraging the view that drunk driving, not drinking, is the offence. Court did not do any better in this regard, but at least the Canberra courts took away driver's licenses, a preventive measure that was not available to conferences and that probably worked.

Reduced reoffending in corporate restorative justice programs

[Elsewhere] I recounted how corporate crime researchers like myself began to wonder if the more restorative approach to corporate criminal law might actually be more effective than the punitive approach to street crime. What made us wonder this? When we observed inspectors moving around factories (as in Hawkins's [1984] study of British pollution inspectors), we noticed how talk often got the job done. The occupational health and safety inspector could talk with the workers and managers responsible for a safety problem, and they would fix it – with no punishment, not even threats of punishment. A restorative justice reading of regulatory inspection was also consistent with the quantitative picture. The probability that any given occupational health and safety violation will be detected has always been slight and the average penalty for Occupational Safety and Health Administration (OSHA) violations in the post-Watergate United States was $37 (Kelman, 1984). So the economically rational firm did not have to worry about OSHA enforcement: when interviewed, its representatives would say it was a trivial cost of doing business. Yet there was quantitative evidence that workplace injuries fell after OSHA inspections or when inspection levels increased (Scholz and Gray, 1990).

There was even stronger evidence that Mine Safety and Health Administration inspections in the United States saved lives and prevented injuries (Braithwaite, 1985, pp. 77–84; Lewis-Beck and Alford, 1980; Perry, 1981a, 1981b; Boden, 1983). Boden's data showed that a 25 per cent increase in inspections was associated with a 7 to 20 per cent reduction in fatalities on a pooled cross-sectional analysis of 535 mines with controls for geological, technological, and managerial factors; these inspections took place at a time when the average penalty for a successful citation was $173 (Braithwaite, 1985, p. 3). They were inspections ending with an 'exit conference' that I observed to be often quite restorative. Boden (1983) and the Mine Enforcement and Safety Administration (1977) found no association between the level of penalties and safety improvement, however.

This was just the opposite of the picture we were getting from the literature on law enforcement and street crime. On the streets, the picture was of tough enforcement, more police, and more jails failing to make a difference. In coal mines we saw weak enforcement (no imprisonment) but convincing evidence that what Julia Black later came to call 'conventional regulation' (Black, 1997, 1998) can work – more inspectors reduced offending and saved lives (Braithwaite, 1985).

My book was called *To Punish or Persuade: Enforcement of Coal Mine Safety*, and it concluded that while persuasion works better than punishment, credible punishment is needed as well to back up persuasion when it fails. Writing the book was a somewhat emotional conversion to restorative justice for me, as I came to it as a kind of victims' supporter, a boy from a coal mining town who wanted to write an angry book for friends killed in the mines. My research also found strong empirical evidence that persuasion works better when workers and unions (representing the victims of the crime) are involved in deliberative regulatory processes.[7] Nearly all serious mine safety accidents can be prevented if only the law is obeyed (Braithwaite, 1985, pp. 20–4, 75–7); the great historical lesson of the coal industry is that the way to accomplish this is through a rich dialogue among victims and offenders on why the law is important, a dialogue given a deeper meaning after each fatality is investigated. The shift from punitive to restorative justice in that industry and the results of that shift have been considerable. During the first fifty years of mine safety enforcement in Britain (until World War I), in a number of years a thousand miners lost their lives in the pits. Fatalities decreased from 1,484 in 1866 to 44 in 1982–83, after which the British industry collapsed. In the years immediately prior to World War I, the average annual number of criminal prosecutions for coal mine safety offences in the United Kingdom was 1,309. In both 1980 and 1981 there were none (Braithwaite, 1985, p. 4).

The qualitative research doing ride-alongs with mine safety inspectors in several countries resolved the puzzle for me. Persuasion worked much of the time; workers' participation in a dialogue about their own security worked. However, the data also suggested that persuasion worked best in the contexts where it was backed by the possibility of punishment.

In the United Kingdom during the 1970s, fifty pits were selected each year for a special safety campaign; these pits showed a consistently greater improvement in accident rates than other British pits (Collinson, 1978, p. 77). I found the safety leaders in the industry were companies that not only thoroughly involved everyone concerned after a serious accident to reach consensual agreement on what must be done to prevent recurrence but also did this after 'near accidents' (Braithwaite, 1985, p. 67), as well as discussing safety audit results with workers even when there was no near accident. In a remarkable foreshadowing of what we now believe to be reasons for the effectiveness of whole-school approaches to bullying and family group conferences, Davis and Stahl's (1967, p. 26) study of twelve companies that had been winners of the industry's two safety awards found one recurring initiative was 'safety letter to families of workers enlisting family support in promoting safe work habits'. That is, safety leaders engaged a community of care beyond the workplace in building a safety culture. In *To Punish or Persuade* I shocked myself by concluding that after mine disasters, including the terrible one in my hometown that had motivated me to write the book, so long as there had been an open public dialogue among all those affected, the families of the miners cared for, and a credible plan to prevent recurrence put in place, criminal punishment served little purpose. The process of the public inquiry and helping the families of the miners for whom they were responsible seemed such a potent general deterrent that a criminal trial could be gratuitous and might corrupt the restorative justice process that I found in so many of the thirty-nine disaster investigations I studied.

Joseph Rees (1988, 1994) is the scholar who has done most to work through the promise of what he calls *communitarian regulation*, which we might read as restorative regulatory justice. First Rees (1988) studied the Cooperative Compliance Program of OSHA between 1979 and 1984. OSHA essentially empowered labor-management safety committees at seven Californian sites to take over the law enforcement role, to solve the underlying problems revealed by breaches of the law. Satisfaction of workers, management and government participants was high because they believed the program 'worked'. It seemed to. Accident rates ranged from one-third lower to five times as low as the Californian rate for comparable projects of the same companies, as the rate in the same project before the cooperative compliance program compared with after (Rees, 1988, pp. 2–3).

Rees' next study of communitarian regulation was of US nuclear regulation after the incident at Three Mile Island. The industry realized that it had to transform the nature of its regulation and self-regulation from a rule book, hardware orientation to one oriented to people, corporate cultures, and software. The industry's CEOs set up the Institute of Nuclear Power Operations (INPO) to achieve these ends. Peers from other nuclear power plants would take three weeks off from their own jobs to join an INPO review team that engaged representatives of the inspected facility in a dialogue about how they could improve. Safety performance ratings were also issued by the review team; comparative ratings of all the firms in the industry were displayed and discussed at meetings of all the CEOs in the industry and at separate meetings of safety officers. Rees (1994) sees these as reintegrative shaming sessions. The following is an excerpt from a videotape of a meeting of the safety officers:

> It's not particularly easy to come up here and talk about an event at a plant in which you have a lot of pride, a lot of pride in the performance, in the operators . . . It's also tough going through the agonizing thinking of what it is you want to say. How do you want to confess? How do you want to couch it in a way that, even though you did something wrong, you're still okay? You get a chance to talk to Ken Strahm and Terry Sullivan [INPO vice presidents] and you go over what your plans are, and they tell you, 'No, Fred, you've got to really bare your soul' . . . It's a painful thing to do. (Rees, 1994, p. 107)

What was the effect of the shift in the center of gravity of the regulatory regime from a Nuclear Regulatory Commission driven by political sensitivities to be tough and prescriptive to INPO's communitarian regulation (focused on a dialogue about how to achieve outcomes rather than rule book enforcement)? Rees (1994, pp. 183–6) shows considerable improvement across a range of indicators of the safety performance of the US nuclear power industry since INPO was established. Improvement has continued since the completion of Rees' study. For example, more recent World Association of Nuclear Operators data show scrams (automatic emergency shutdowns) declined in the United States from over 7 per unit in 1980 to 0.1 by the late 1990s.

[Elsewhere] we saw that shifting nursing home regulation from rule book enforcement to restorative justice was associated with improved regulatory outcomes and that the inspectors who shifted most toward restorative justice improved compliance most (those who used praise and trust more than threat, those who used reintegrative shaming rather than tolerance or stimatization, those who restored self-efficacy). [While these results are discussed elsewhere, for] the moment, I simply report that communitarian regulation has had considerable documented success in restoring coal mining firms, nuclear power plants, and nursing homes in a more responsible approach to compliance with the law. Equally, writers such as Gunningham (1995) and Haines (1997) have shown that there are serious limits to communitarian regulation – rapacious big firms and incompetent little ones that will not or cannot respond responsibly. Deterrence and incapacitation are needed, and needed in larger measure than these regimes currently provide, when restorative justice fails (see also Ayres and Braithwaite, 1992; Gunningham and Grabosky, 1998).

Carol Heimer pointed out in comments on a draft of this chapter, 'If high-level white collar workers are more likely to get restorative justice, it may be because their corporate colleagues and other members of the society believe that their contributions are not easily replaced, so that offenders must be salvaged' (see Heimer and Staffen, 1995). This is right, I suspect, and a reason that justice is most likely to be restorative in the hands of communities of care that can see the value of salvaging the offender and the victim.

Restorative justice practices restore and satisfy communities better than existing criminal justice practices

In every place where a reform debate has occurred about the introduction of family group conferences, two community concerns have been paramount: (1) while victims might be forgiving in New Zealand, giving free rein to victim anger 'here' will tear at our community; (2) while families may be strong elsewhere, 'here' our worst offenders are alienated and alone, their families are so dysfunctional and uncaring that they will not participate meaningfully. But as Morris *et al.* (1996, p. 223) conclude from perspectives on this question summarized from a number of jurisdictions: 'Concerns about not being able to locate extended family or family supporters, to engage families or to effectively involve so-called "dysfunctional" families, about families forming a coalition to conceal abuse and about families' failing to honour agreements do not prove to have been well-founded in any of the jurisdictions reported in this book.'

In his discussion of the Hollow Water experience of using healing circles to deal with rampant sexual abuse of children in a Canadian First Nations community, Ross (1996, p. 150) emphasizes the centrality of restoring communities for restoring individuals: 'If you are dealing with people whose relationships have been built on power and abuse, you must actually *show* them, then give them the experience of, relationships based on respect . . . [so] . . . the healing process must involve a healthy *group* of people, as opposed to single therapists. A single therapist cannot, by definition, do more than *talk* about healthy relationships.'

The most sophisticated implementation of this ideal that has been well evaluated is Burford and Pennell's (1998) Family Group Decision Making Project to confront violence and child neglect in families. Beyond the positive effects on the direct objective of reducing violence, the evaluation found a posttest increase in family support, concrete (e.g. baby-sitting) and emotional, and enhanced family unity, even in circumstances where some conference plans involved separation of parents from their children. The philosophy of this program was to look for strengths in families that were in very deep trouble and build on them. [Elsewhere,] building on the work of Mary Kaldor (1999), I argue that this is the restorative justice prescription to the nature of contemporary armed conflict – find the islands of civility in the war-torn nation and build out from the strength in those islands of civil society.

Members of the community beyond the offender and the victim who attend restorative justice processes tend, like offenders, victims, and the police, to come away with high levels of satisfaction. In Pennell and Burford's (1995) family group conferences for family violence, 94 per cent of family members were 'satisfied with the way it was run'; 92 per cent felt they were 'able to say what was important'; and 92 per cent 'agreed with the plan decided on'. Clairmont (1994, p. 28) also reports that among native peoples in Canada the restorative justice initiatives he reviewed have 'proven to be popular with offenders . . . and to have broad, general support within communities'. The Ministry of Justice, Western Australia (1994) reports 93 per cent parental satisfaction, 84 per cent police satisfaction, and 67 per cent judicial satisfaction, plus (and crucially) satisfaction of Aboriginal organizations with its restorative justice conference program (Juvenile Justice Teams). In Singapore, 95 per cent of family members who attended family group conferences said that they benefited personally from the experience (Hsien, 1996). For the Bethlehem police conferencing experiment, parents of offenders were more satisfied (97 per cent) and more likely to believe that justice had been fair (97 per cent) than in cases that went to court (McCold and Wachtel, 1998, pp. 65–72). Parental satisfaction and perceptions of justice were similarly high in the Indianapolis experiment (McGarrell et al., 2000). Eighty per cent of the conference parents 'felt involved', compared with 40 per cent for the children who were randomly assigned to other diversion programs. Ninety per cent of the conference parents felt they had the opportunity to express their views, compared with 68 per cent in the control group.

A study by Schneider (1990) found that *completing* restitution and community service was associated with enhanced commitment to community and feelings of citizenship (and reduced recidivism). While the evidence is overwhelming that where communities show strong social support, criminality is less (Cullen, 1994; Chamlin and Cochran, 1997), it might be optimistic to expect that restorative justice could ever have sufficient impacts in restoring microcommunities to cause a shift in the macro impact of community on the crime rate (cf. Brown and Polk, 1996). On the other hand, Tom Tyler's most recent book with Yuen Huo (Tyler and Huo, 2001) finds that procedural fairness by authorities quite strongly increases trust in authorities, and trust in authorities in turn has considerable effects in increasing identification with one's community and society and ultimately participation in the community. [In Tyler's work we] see there is consistent evidence that restorative justice is perceived as more procedurally fair in a number of ways compared with courtroom justice. Tyler's work opens up exciting new lines of research on why restorative justice might contribute to community building.

Building the microcommunity of a school or restoring social bonds in a family can have important implications for crime in that school or that family. Moreover, the restoring of microcommunity has a value of its own, independent of the size of the impact on crime. The previous section described how whole-school approaches can halve bullying in schools. There is a more important point of deliberative programs to give all the citizens of the school community an opportunity to be involved in deciding how to make their school safer and more caring. It is that they make their schools more decent places to live while one is being educated. Evidence from Australia suggests that restorative sexual harassment programs in workplaces may reduce sexual harassment (Parker, 1998). Again, more important than the improved compliance with the law may be the more general improvements in the respect with which women are treated in workplaces as a result of the deliberation and social support integral to such programs when they are effective.

We have seen restorative justice conferences where supporters of a boy offender and a girl victim of a sexual assault agreed to work together to confront a culture of exploitative masculinity in an Australian school that unjustly characterized the girl as 'getting what she asked for' (Braithwaite and Daly, 1994). Conversely, we have seen conferences that have missed the opportunity to confront homophobic cultures in schools revealed by graffiti humiliating allegedly gay men and boys (Retzinger and Scheff, 1996). After one early New Zealand conference concerning breaking into and damaging the restaurant of a refugee Cambodian, the offender agreed to watch a video of *The Killing Fields* and 'pass the word on the street' that the Cambodian restaurateur was struggling to survive and should not be harassed. A small victory for civil community life, perhaps, but a large one for that Cambodian man.

One of the most stirring conferences I know of occurred in an outback town after four Aboriginal children manifested their antagonism toward the middle-class matriarchs of the town by ransacking the Country Women's Association Hall. The conference was so moving because it brought the Aboriginal and the white women together, shocked and upset by what the children had done, to talk to each other about why the women no longer spoke to one another across the racial divide in the way they had in earlier times. Did there have to be such an incivility as this to discover the loss of their shared communal life? Those black and white women and children rebuilt that communal life as they restored the devastated Country Women's Association Hall, working together, respectfully once more (for more details on this case, see the Real Justice Web site at http://www.realjustice.org/).

One might summarize that the evidence of restorative justice restoring communities points to very small accomplishments of microcommunity-building and of modest numbers of community members going away overwhelmingly satisfied with the justice in which they feel they have had a meaningful opportunity to participate. Maori critics of Pakeha restorative justice such as Moana Jackson (1987) and Juan Tauri (1998) point out that it falls far short of restoring Maori community control over justice. Neocolonial controls from Pakeha courts remain on top of restorative justice in Maori communities. This critique seems undeniable; nowhere in the world has restorative justice enabled major steps toward restoring precolonial forms of community among colonized peoples; nowhere have the courts of the colonial power given up their power to trump the decisions of the Indigenous justice forums.

At the same time, there is a feminist critique of this Indigenous critique of community restoration. [. . .]

With all the attention we have given to the microcommunity-building of routine restorative justice conferences, we must not lose sight of historically rare moments of restorative justice that reframe macrocommunity. I refer, for example, to the release of IRA terrorists from prison so that they could participate in the IRA meetings of 1998 that voted for the renunciation of violent struggle. I refer to much more partially successful examples, such as the Camp David mediations of President Carter with the leaders of Egypt and Israel (more partially successful because they excluded the Palestinians themselves) and to more totally successful local peacemaking such as that of the Kulka Women's Club in the highlands of New Guinea (see Box [22.]3).

Conclusion

There do seem to be empirical grounds for optimism that restorative justice can 'work' in restoring victims, offenders, and communities. When the restorative practice helps bring a war-torn nation to peace, as in the civil wars

---

Box [24.]3: Kulka Women's Club peacemaking

Alan Rumsey (2000) has documented the extraordinary intervention of the Kulka Women's Club to end a New Guinea highlands tribal war. The context is that, after an initial period of colonial pacification, in many parts of the New Guinea highlands tribal fighting has become worse, and more deadly, in recent decades, with guns replacing spears and arrows. What the Kulka Women's Club did on 13 September 1982 was to march between two opposing armies under the national flag, exhorting both sides with gifts to put down their arms, which they did. Note that as in so many of the important non-Western forms of restorative justice, the victims move the offenders by giving them gifts rather than asking for compensation (see the Javanese case at note 1, and the Crow practice of buying the ways (Austin, 1984, p. 36)).[8] The distinctive peacemaking intervention of the Kulka Women's Club seems to have been unique, rather than a recurrent Melanesian cultural pattern. Its importance is that it had a long-lasting effect, the peace having held until the present, during two decades when hostilities among surrounding tribes escalated. Though the intervention seems unique, Maev O'Collins (2000) links it to peace and reconciliation meetings organized by women in war-torn Bougainville and women marching in Port Moresby to protest against male violence. In June 2000 a group of seventy women wearing scarfs in the colors of the national flag approached the two warring groups in the Solomon Islands civil war, asking them to talk peace, which they did (*The Dominion*, 17 June 2000). Rumsay's (2000, p. 9) work is important because it shows the need for highly contextualized analysis of the macrotransformative moments of restorative justice: 'The very factors that make one area relatively conducive to peacemaking are the same ones that make it more difficult in the neighbouring region.'

of the Solomons and Bougainville (see Box [22.]3: Kulka Women's Club, Peacemaking [. . .]), we might say restorative justice works with dramatic effect. As the endeavors of the Truth and Reconciliation Commission in South Africa and those of a number of other nations now demonstrate, 'working' in terms of healing a nation is more important than working simply conceived as reducing crime. At a more micro level, 'working' as healing a workplace after sexual harassment (Parker, 1998), a school after bullying (Rigby, 1996), and a family after violence (Burford and Pennell, 1998) are exceptionally important outcomes that have been considered in this chapter. [. . .] Finally, to conceive 'working' in the traditional criminological way of reducing crime forgets victims. We conclude, following Strang (2000), that restorative justice mostly works well in granting justice, closure, restoration of dignity, transcendence of shame, and healing for victims.

All that said, we have found that restorative justice shows great promise as a strategy of crime reduction. A mistake criminologists could make now is to do more and more research to compare the efficacy of restorative justice, statically conceived, with traditional Western justice. Rather, we must think more dynamically about developing the restorative justice process and the values that guide it. In my view, this chapter demonstrates that we already know that restorative justice has much promise. The research and development agenda now is to enlarge our understanding of the conditions under which that promise is realized. It will become clear that my own theoretical position inclines me to believe that restorative justice can work better if it is designed to enhance the efficacy of deterrence, incapacitation, and particularly rehabilitation and community prevention. Obversely, these strategies of crime reduction can work better if they are embedded in a responsive regulatory pyramid that enhances the efficacy of restorative justice. It follows that comparing the efficacy of a pure restorative justice strategy with that of a pure punishment strategy is not the best research path for the future.

[. . .]

This extract is taken from 'Does Restorative Justice Work?', chapter 3 of Restorative Justice and Responsive Regulation *(Oxford University Press, 2002), by John Braithwaite.*

Notes

1 I am reminded of a village in Java where I was told of a boy caught stealing. The outcome of a restorative village meeting was that the offender was given a bag of rice: 'We should be ashamed because one from our village should be so poor as to steal. We should be ashamed as a village.'
2 The evidence reviewed below also in fact suggests lower levels of victim satisfaction and participation than in its predecessor the Wagga Wagga program, a difference I attribute to the extraordinary gifts Terry O'Connell brought to that program and the extraordinary way the Wagga community got behind the program.
3 The evidence seems to be that this was due mainly to limitations in the program administration that made it difficult for victims to attend, not to the fact that most

victims did not want to attend; only 6 per cent did not want to meet their offender (Maxwell and Morris, 1996).

4 The word *extremely* has been added to this sentence since my 1999 review of the evidence, indicating an accumulation of encouraging results.

5 This test is reported in Schneider, 1986, but for mysterious reasons Schneider, 1990 reports only the nonsignificant differences between before and after offending rates for the control and experimental groups separately, rather than the significant difference between the experimental and control group (which is the relevant comparison).

6 I am indebted to Glen Purdy, a Sparwood lawyer in private practice, for these data. The data until early 1997 are also available at www.titanlink.com.

7 For example, DeMichiei *et al.*'s (1982, p. i) comparison of mines with exceptionally high injury rates with matched mines with exceptionally low injury rates found that at the low injury mines: 'Open lines of communication permit management and labor to jointly reconcile problems affecting safety and health; Representatives of labor become actively involved in issues concerning safety, health and production; and Management and labor identify and accept their joint responsibility for correcting unsafe conditions and practices.'

8 Cree elder Roland Duneuette tells the story of the father and mother of a homicide victim taking in the offender as a son to teach him the Cree ways. Alan Rumsay tells me that in the highlands of New Guinea more widely, when one tribe is owed substantial compensation by another that has wronged them, the process that leads to the paying of that compensation starts with the wronged tribe offering a gift to the wrongdoer. In New Guinea, even when the offender acts first by offering compensation to a victim, the preserving of relationships will often also involve the expectation of a smaller but significant reciprocal gift back to the offender by the victim. Such a way of thinking is not unknown in the West. We see it in *Les Misérables*, part of the Western literary canon, and in Pope John Paul visiting and presenting a gift to the man who shot him.

References

Austin, W.T. (1984) 'Crow Indian Justice: Strategies of Informal Social Control', *Deviant Behavior*, 5, pp. 31–46.

Ayres, I. and Braithwaite, J. (1992) *Response Regulation: Transcending the Deregulation Debate* (New York, NY: Oxford University Press).

Barnes, G. (1999) 'Procedural Justice in Two Contexts: Testing the Fairness of Diversionary Conferencing for Intoxicated Drivers.' PhD dissertation, Institute of Criminal Justice and Criminology, University of Maryland.

Bazemore, G. (1999) 'Communities, Victims, and Offender Rehabilitation: Restorative Justice and Earned Redemption', in Etzioni, A. (ed.) *Civic Repentance* (Lanham, MD: Rowman & Littlefield).

Birchall, P., Namour, S. and Syme, H. (1992) 'Report on the Midland Pilot Reparation Scheme.' Unpublished paper, Western Australia.

Black, J. (1998) 'Talking about Regulation', *Public Law*, spring, pp. 77–105.

Boden, L.I. (1983) 'Government Regulation of Occupational Safety: Underground Coal Mine Accidents 1973–1975.' Unpublished manuscript, Harvard School of Public Health.

Bonta, J., Rooney, J. and Wallace-Capretta, S. (1998) *Restorative Justice: An Evaluation of the Restorative Resolution Project* (Ottawa: Solicitor General Canada).

Braithwaite, J. (1985) *To Punish or Persuade: Enforcement of Coal Mine Safety* (Albany, NY: State University of New York Press).

Braithwaite, J. (1989) *Crime, Shame and Reintegration* (Cambridge: Cambridge University Press).

Braithwaite, J. (1999) 'Restorative Justice: Assessing Optimistic and Pessimistic Accounts', in Tonry, M. (ed.) *Crime and Justice: A Review of Research Vol. 25* (Chicago, IL: University of Chicago Press).

Braithwaite, J. and Daly, K. (1994) 'Masculinities, Violence and Communitarian Control', in Newbury, T. and Stanka, E. (eds) *Just Boys Doing Business* (London: Routledge).

Brewer, D.D., Hawkins, J.D., Catalano, R.F. and Neckerman, H.J. (1995) 'Preventing Serious, Violent, and Chronic Juvenile Offending: A Review of Evaluations of Selected Strategies in Childhood, Adolescence, and the Community', in Howell, J.C. *et al.* (eds) *A Sourcebook: Serious, Violent, and Chronic Juvenile Offenders* (Thousand Oaks, CA: Sage).

Brown, M. and Polk, K. (1996) 'Taking Fear of Crime Seriously: The Tasmanian Approach to Community Crime Prevention', *Crime and Delinquency*, 42, pp. 398–420.

Burford, G. and Pennell, J. (1998) *Family Group Decision Making Project: Outcome Report Volume I* (St John's: Memorial University, Newfoundland).

Butts, J. and Snyder, H. (1991) *Restitution and Juvenile Recidivism* (Pittsburgh, PA: National Center for Juvenile Justice).

Chamlin, M.B. and Cochran, J.K. (1997) 'Social Altruism and Crime', *Criminology*, 35, pp. 203–28.

Chan, W.Y. (1996) 'Family Conferences in the Juvenile Justice Process: Survey on the Impact of Family Conferencing on Juvenile Offenders and their Families', in *Subordinate Courts Statistics and Planning Unit Research Bulletin* (Singapore).

Chatterjee, J. (2000) *RCMP's Restorative Justice Initiative* (Ottawa: Research and Evaluation Branch, Community Contract and Aboriginal Policing Services, Royal Canadian Mounted Police).

Clairmont, D. (1994) 'Alternative Justice Issues for Aboriginal Justice.' Paper prepared for the Aboriginal Justice Directorate, Department of Justice, Ottawa.

Coates, R. and Gehm, J. (1985) *Victim Meets Offender: An Evaluation of Victim Offender Reconciliation Programs* (Valparaiso, IN: PACT Institute of Justice).

Coates, R. and Gehm, J. (1989) 'An Empirical Assessment', in Wright, M. and Galaway, B. (eds) *Mediation and Criminal Justice* (London: Sage).

Collinson, J.L. (1978) 'Safety: Pleas and Prophylactics', *Mining Engineer*, July: pp. 73–83.

Crawford, A. (1996) 'Victim/Offender Mediation and Reparation in Comparative European Cultures: France, England and Wales.' Paper presented at the Australian and New Zealand Society of Criminology Conference, Wellington, January–February.

Cullen, F.T. (1994) 'Social Support as an Organizing Concept for Criminology: Presidential Address to the Academy of Criminal Justice Sciences', *Justice Quarterly*, 11, pp. 527–59.

Cullen, P.T. and Gendreau, P. (2000) 'Assessing Correctional Rehabilitation: Policy, Practice, and Prospects', in Horney, J. (ed.) *Policies, Processes, and Decisions of the Criminal Justice System Vol. 3* (Washington, DC: US Department of Justice).

Cummings, W.I. (1980) *Education and Equality in Japan* (Princeton: Princeton University Press).

Daly, K. (1996) 'Diversionary Conference in Australia: A Reply to the Optimists and Skeptics.' Paper presented at the annual meeting of the American Society of Criminology, 20–23 November.

Davis, G. (1992) *Making Amends: Mediation and Reparation in Criminal Justice* (London: Routledge).

Davis, R.T. and Stahl, R.W. (1967) 'Safety Organization and Activities of Award-winning Companies in the Coal Mining Industry', in *Bureau of Mines Information Circular 8224* (Washington, DC: Bureau of Mines).

DeMichiei, J.M., Langton, J.F., Bullock, K.A. and Wiles, T.C. (1982) *Factors Associated with Disabling Injuries in Underground Coal Mines* (Washington, DC: Mine Safety and Health Administration).

Dignan, J. (1990) *An Evaluation of an Experimental Adult Reparation Scheme in Kettering, Northamptonshire* (Sheffield: Centre for Criminological and Legal Research, University of Sheffield).

Dignan, J. (1992) 'Repairing the Damage: Can Reparation Work in the Service of Diversion?', *British Journal of Criminology*, 32, pp. 453–72.

Dolling, D. and Harman, A. (2000) 'Reoffending after Victim–Offender Mediation in Juvenile Court Proceedings.' Paper to Fourth International Conference on Restorative Justice for Juveniles, Tübingen, Germany.

Ervin, L. and Schneider, A. (1990) 'Explaining the Effects of Restitution on Offenders: Results from a National Experiment in Juvenile Courts', in Galaway, B. and Hudson, J. (eds) *Criminal Justice, Restitution and Reconciliation* (New York, NY: Willow Tree Press).

Farrington, D.P. (1993) 'Understanding and Preventing Bullying', in Tonry, M. (ed.) *Crime and Justice Annual Review of Research. Vol. 17* (Chicago, IL: University of Chicago Press).

Forsythe, L. (1995) 'An Analysis of Juvenile Apprehension Characteristics and Reapprehension Rates', in Moore, D. *et al.* (eds) *New Approach to Juvenile Justice: An Evaluation of Family Conferencing in Wagga Wagga. A Report to the Criminology Research Council* (Wagga Wagga, Australia: Charles Sturt University).

Fry, D. (1997) *A Report on Diversionary Conferencing* (Alice Springs, Australia: Northern Territory Police).

Galaway, B. (1992) 'The New Zealand Experience Implementing the Reparation Sentence', in Messmer, H. and Otto, H.U. (eds) *Restorative Justice on Trial: Pitfalls and Potentials of Victim–Offender Mediation – International Research Perspectives* (Dordrecht and Boston, MA: Kluwer Academic).

Gendreau, P., Clark, K. and Gray, G.A. (1996) 'Intensive Surveillance Programs: They Don't Work', *Community Corrections Report*, 3:3, pp. 1–15.

Gentry, D.B. and Benenson, W.A. (1993) 'School-to-Home Transfer of Conflict Management Skills among School-age Children', *Families in Society*, February, pp. 67–73.

Geudens, H. (1998) 'The Recidivism Rate of Community Service as a Restitutive Judicial Sanction in Comparison with the Traditional Juvenile Justice Measure', in Walgrave, L. (ed.) *Restorative Justice for Juveniles: Potentialities, Risks and Problems for Research* (Leuven: Leuven University Press).

Goodes, T. (1995) *Victims and Family Conferences: Juvenile Justice in South Australia* (Adelaide: Family Conferencing Team).

Gottfredson, D. (1997) 'School-based Crime Prevention', in Sherman, L. *et al.* (eds) *Preventing Crime: What Works, What Doesn't, What's Promising. A Report to the United States Congress* (Washington, DC: National Institute of Justice).

Gunningham, N. (1995) 'Environment, Self-regulation and the Chemical Industry: Assessing Responsible Care', *Law and Policy*, 17, pp. 57–109.

Gunningham, N. and Grabosky, P. (1998) *Smart Regulation: Designing Environmental Policy* (Oxford: Clarendon Press).

Haines, F. (1997) *Corporate Regulation: Beyond 'Punish or Persuade'* (Oxford: Clarendon Press).

Haley, J. assisted by Neugebauer, A.M. (1992) 'Victim–Offender Mediations: Japanese and American Comparisons', in Messmer, H. and Otto, H.U. (eds) *Restorative Justice on Trial: Pitfalls and Potentials of Victim–Offender Mediation – International Research Perspective* (Dordrecht and Boston, MA: Kluwer Academic).

Hawkins, K. (1984) *Environment and Enforcement: Regulation and the Social Definition of Pollution* (Oxford: Clarendon Press).

Hayes, H., Prenzler, T. with Wortley, R. (1998) *Making Amends: Final Evaluation of the Queensland Community Conferencing Pilot* (School of Criminology and Criminal Justice, Griffith University).

Heimer, C.A. and Staffen, L.R. (1995) 'Interdependence and Reintegrative Social Control: Labelling and Reforming "Inappropriate" Parents in Neonatal Intensive Care Units', *American Sociological Review*, 60, pp. 635–54.

Hsien, L.I. (1996) 'Family Conferencing Good for Young Delinquents: Report' *Straits Times*, 6 March.

Iivari, J. (1987) 'Mediation as a Conflict Resolution: Some Topical Issues in Mediation Project in Vantaa.' Paper presented to the International Seminar on Mediation, Finland, September.

Iivari, J. (1992) 'The Process of Mediation in Finland: A Special Reference to the Question "How to Get Cases for Mediation" ', in Messmer, H. and Otto, H.U. (eds) *Restorative Justice on Trial: Pitfalls and Potentials of Victim–Offender Mediation – International Research Perspectives* (Dordrecht and Boston, MA: Kluwer Academic).

Jackson, M. (1987) *The Maori and the Criminal Justice System: A New Perspective – He Whaipaanga Hou. Report for New Zealand Department of Justice* (Wellington: Policy and Research Division, Department of Justice).

Kaldor, M. (1999) *New and Old Wars: Organised Violence in a Global Era* (Cambridge: Polity Press).

Kelman, S. (1984) 'Enforcement of Occupational Safety and Health Regulations: A Comparison of Swedish and American Practices', in Hawkins, K. and Thomas, J.M. (eds) *Enforcing Regulations* (Boston, MA: Kluwer-Nijhoff).

Kerner, H., Marks, E. and Schreckling, J. (1992) 'Implementation and Acceptance of Victim–Offender Mediation Programs in the Federal Republic of Germany: A Survey of Criminal Justice Institutions', in Messmer, H. and Otto, H.U. (eds) *Restorative Justice on Trial: Pitfalls and Potentials of Victim–Offender Mediation – International Research Perspectives* (Dordrecht and Boston, MA: Kluwer Academic).

Kuhn, A. (1987) 'Koperverletzung als Konflikt, Zwischenbericht 1987 zum Project Handschlag.' Unpublished paper cited in T. Trenczak, 'A Review and Assessment of Victim–Offender Reconciliation Programming in West Germany', in Galaway, B. and Hudson, J. (eds) *Criminal Justice, Restitution and Reconciliation* (Monsey, NY: Willow Press).

Lam, J.A. (1989) *The Impact of Conflict Resolution Programs on Schools: A Review and Synthesis of the Evidence* (Amherst, MA: National Association for Mediation in Education).

Lam, J.A. (1995) 'Altering Course: New Directions in Criminal Justice and Correc-tions. Sentencing Circles and Family Group Conferences', *Australian and New Zealand Journal of Criminology*, December, pp. 78–99.

La, Prairie, C. (1995) 'Altering Course: New Directions in Criminal Justice and Corrections, Sentencing-Circles and Family Group Conferences'. *Australian and New Zealand Journal of Criminology*, December: 78–99.

Latimer, J., Dowden, C. and Muise, D. (2001) *The Effectiveness of Restorative Justice Practices: A Meta-analysis* (Ottawa: Department of Justice, Canada).

Lewis-Beck, M.S. and Alford, J.R. (1980) 'Can Government Regulate Safety: The Coal Mine Example', *American Political Science Review*, 74, pp. 745–56.

Little, M. (2001) 'ISSP: An Experience in Multi-Systemic Responses to Persistent Young Offenders Known to Children's Services.' Unpublished paper, University of Chicago.

Marshall, T.F. (1992) 'Restorative Justice on Trial in Britain', in Messmer, H. and Otto, H.U. (eds) *Restorative Justice on Trial: Pitfalls and Potentials of Victim–Offender Mediation – International Research Perspectives* (Dordrecht and Boston, MA: Kluwer Academic).

Marshall, T.F. and Merry, S. (1990) *Crime and Accountability: Victim Offender Mediation in Practice* (London: Home Office).

Masters, G. (1997) 'Reintegrative Shaming in Theory and Practice.' PhD dissertation, Lancaster University.

Maxwell, G.M. and Morris, A. (1993) *Family, Victims and Culture: Youth Justice in New Zealand* (Wellington: Special Policy Agency and Institute of Criminology, Victoria University of Wellington).

Maxwell, G.M. and Morris, A. (1996) 'Research on Family Group Conferences with Young Offenders in New Zealand', in Hudson, J. *et al.* (eds) *Family Group Conferences: Perspectives on Policy and Practice* (Sydney: Federation Press and Criminal Justice Press).

Maxwell, G.M., Morris, A. and Anderson, T. (1999) *Community Panel Adult Pretrial Diversion: Supplementary Evaluation. Research Report* (Wellington: Crime Prevention Unit, Department of Prime Minister and Cabinet and Institute of Criminology, Victoria University of Wellington).

McCold, P. and Wachtel, B. (1998) 'Restorative Policing Experiment: The Bethlehem Pennsylvania Police Family Group Conferencing Project' (Pipersville, PA: Community Service Foundation).

McCold, I. and Wachtel, T. (2000) 'Restorative Justice Theory Validation.' Paper presented to the Fourth International Conference on Restorative Justice for Juveniles, Tübingen, Germany (www.restorativepractices.org).

McGarrell, E.F., Olivares, K., Crawford, K. and Kroovand, N. (2000) *Returning Justice to the Community: The Indianapolis Juvenile Restorative Justice Experiment* (Indianapolis, IN: Hudson Institute).

Miller, S. and Blackler, J. (2000) 'Restorative Justice Retribution, Confession and Shame', in Strang, H. and Braithwaite, J. (eds) *Restorative Justice: Philosophy to Practice* (Aldershot: Ashgate Dartmouth).

Mine Enforcement and Safety Administration (1977) *A Report on Civil Penalty Effectiveness* (Washington, DC: Mine Enforcement and Safety Administration).

Ministry of Justice, Western Australia (1994) *Juvenile Justice Teams: A Six-Month Evaluation* (Perth: Ministry of Justice).

Moore, D.B. with Forsythe, L. (1995) *A New Approach to Juvenile Justice: An Evaluation of Family Conferencing in Wagga Wagga* (Wagga Wagga: Charles Sturt University).

Moore, D.B. and O'Connell, T. (1994) 'Family Conferencing in Wagga Wagga: A Communitarian Model of Justice', in Alder, C. and Wundersitz, J. (eds) *Family Conferencing and Juvenile Justice* (Canberra: Australian Studies in Law, Crime and Justice, Australian Institute of Criminology).

Morris, A., Maxwell, G., Hudson, J. and Galaway, B. (1996) 'Concluding Thoughts', in Hudson, J. *et al.* (eds) *Family Group Conferences: Perspectives on Policy and Practice* (Sydney: Federation Press and Criminal Justice Press).

Nugent, W.R. and Paddock, J.B. (1995) 'The Effect of Victim–Offender Mediation on Severity of Reoffense', *Mediation Quarterly*, 12, pp. 353–67.

Nugent, W.R., Umbreit, M.S., Wiinamaki, L. and Paddock, G. (forthcoming) 'Participation in Victim–Offender Mediation and Re-offense: Successful Replication?', *Journal of Research on Social Work Practice*.

Obonsawin-Irwin Consulting Inc. (1992a) *An Evaluation of the Attawapiskat First Nation Justice Project* (Ontario: Ministry of the Attorney General).

Obonsawin-Irwin Consulting Inc. (1992b) *An Evaluation of the Sandy Lake First Nation Justice Project* (Ontario: Ministry of the Attorney General).

O'Collins, M. (2000) 'Images of Violence in Papua New Guinea: Whose Images? Whose Reality?', in Dinnen, S. and Ley, A. (eds) *Reflection on Violence in Melanesia* (Annandale, NSW, and Canberra: Hawkins Press/Asia Pacific Press).

Olweus, I. (1993) 'Annotation: Bullying at School – Basic Facts and Effects of a School-based Intervention Program', *Journal of Child Psychology and Psychiatry*, 35, pp. 1171–90.

Palk, G., Hayes, H. and Prenzler, T. (1998) 'Restorative Justice and Community Conferencing: Summary of Findings from a Pilot Study', *Current Issues in Criminal Justice*, 10, pp. 138–55.

Parker, C. (1998) 'Public Rights in Private Government: Corporate Compliance with Sexual Harassment Legislation', *Australian Journal of Human Rights*, 5, pp. 159–93.

Pate, K. (1990) 'Victim–Offender Restitution Programs in Canada', in Galaway, B. and Hudson, J. (eds) *Criminal Justice, Restitution and Reconciliation* (New York, NY: Willow Tree Press).

Pennell, J. and Burford, G. (1995) *Family Group Decision Making: New Rules for 'Old' Partners in Resolving Family Violence. Implementation Report. Vol. 1* (St John's: Family Group Decision Making Project, School of Social Work, University of Newfoundland).

Pennell, J. and Burford, G. (1997) *Family Group Decision Making: After the Conference – Progress in Resolving Violence and Promoting Well-Being* (St John's: Family Group Decision Making Project, School of Social Work, University of Newfoundland).

Pennell, J. and Burford, G. (2000) 'Family Group Decision Making: Protecting Children and Women', *Child Welfare*, 79, pp. 131–58.

Pepler, D.J., Craig, W., Ziegler, S. and Charach, A. (1993) 'A School-based Antibullying Intervention', in Tatum, D. (ed.) *Understanding and Managing Bullying* (London: Heinemann).

Perry, C.S. (1981a) 'Dying to Dig Coal: Fatalities in Deep and Surface Coal Mining in Appalachian States, 1930–1978.' Unpublished manuscript. Department of Sociology, University of Kentucky.

Perry, C.S. (1981b) 'Safety Laws and Spending Saves Lives: An Analysis of Coal Mine Fatality Rates 1930–1979.' Unpublished manuscript, Department of Sociology, University of Kentucky.

Pitts, J. and Smith, P. (1995) *Preventing School Bullying. Police Research Group Crime Detection and Prevention Series Paper 63* (London: Home Office).

Power, P. (2000) 'Restorative Conferences in Australia and New Zealand.' PhD dissertation, Law School, University of Sydney.

Reed, P. (1986) 'Developmental Resources and Depression in the Elderly', *Nursing Research*, 36, pp. 368–74.

Reed, P. (1987) 'Spirituality and Well Being in Terminally Ill Hospitalized Adults', *Research in Nursing and Health*, 10, pp. 335–44.

Reed, P. (1992) 'An Emerging Paradigm for the Study of Spirituality in Nursing', *Research in Nursing and Health* 15, pp. 349–57.

Rees, J.V. (1988) *Reforming the Workplace* (Philadelphia, PA: University of Pennsylvania Press).

Rees, J.V. (1994) *Hostages of Each Other: The Transformation of Nuclear Safety since Three Mile Island* (Chicago: University of Chicago Press).

Retzinger, S. and Scheff, T.J. (1996) 'Strategy for Community Conferences: Emotions and Social Bonds', in Galaway, B. and Hudson, J. (eds) *Restorative Justice: International Perspectives* (Monsey, NY: Criminal Justice Press).

Rigby, K. (1996) *Bullying in Schools and What to Do about It* (Melbourne: Australian Council for Educational Research).

Ross, R. (1996) *Returning to the Teachings: Exploring Aboriginal Justice* (London: Penguin).

Rumsey, A. (2000) 'Women as Peacemakers in the New Guinea Highlands: A Case from the Nebilyer Valley, Western Highlands Province', in Dinnen, S. and Ley, A. (eds) *Reflection on Violence in Melanesia* (Leichhardt, NSW: Hawkins Press).

Sampson, R. and Laub, J.H. (1993) *Crime in the Making: Pathways and Turning Points through Life* (Cambridge, MA: Harvard University Press).

Schiff, M.F. (1998) 'The Impact of Restorative Interventions on Juvenile Offenders', in Walgrave, L. and Brazemore, G. (eds) *Restoring Juvenile Justice* (Monsey, NY: Criminal Justice Press).

Schneider, A. (1986) 'Restitution and Recidivism Rates of Juvenile Offenders: Results from Four Experimental Studies', *Criminology*, 24, pp. 533–52.

Schneider, A. (1990) *Deterrence and Juvenile Crime: Results from a National Policy Experiment* (New York, NY: Springer-Verlag).

Scholz, J.T. and Gray, W.B. (1990) 'OSHA Enforcement and Workplace Injuries: A Behavioral Approach to Risk Assessment', *Journal of Risk and Uncertainty*, 3, pp. 283–305.

Sherman, L.W., Strang, H. and Woods, D. (2000) *Recidivism Patterns in the Canberra Reintegrative Sharing Experiments (RISE)* (Canberra: Centre for Restorative Justice, Australian National University).

Smith, D., Blagg, H. and Derricourt, N. (1985) 'Victim–Offender Mediation Project. Report to the Chief Officers' Group, South Yorkshire Probation Service', cited in Marshall, T. and Merry, S. (eds) *Crime and Accountability: Victim–Offender Mediation in Practice* (London: Home Office, 1990).

Stewart, T. (1993) 'The Youth Justice Co-ordinator's Role: A Personal Perspective of the New Legislation in Action', in Brown, B.J. and McElrea, F.W.M. (eds) *The Youth Court in New Zealand: A New Model of Justice* (Auckland: Legal Research Foundation).

Strang, H. (2000) 'Victim Participation in a Restorative Justice Process: The Canberra Reintegrative Shaming Experiments.' PhD dissertation, Australian National University.

Strang, H. (2001) *Victim Participation in a Restorative Justice Process* (Oxford: Oxford University Press).

Strang, H. and Sherman, L.W. (1997) *The Victim's Perspective. RISE Working Paper* (Canberra: Law Program, RSSS, Australian National University).

Tauri, J. (1998) 'Family Group Conferencing: A Case Study of the Indigenisation of New Zealand's Justice System', *Current Issues in Criminal Justice*, 10, pp. 168–82.

Tauri, J. and Morris, A. (1997) 'Re-forming Justice: The Potential of Maori Processes', *Australian and New Zealand Journal of Criminology*, 30, pp. 149–67.

Trenczek, T. (1990) 'A Review and Assessment of Victim–Offender Reconciliation Programming in West Germany', in Galaway, B. and Hudson, J. (eds) *Criminal Justice, Restitution and Reconciliation* (Monsey, NY: Willow Press).

Trimboli, L. (2000) *An Evaluation of the NSW Youth Justice Conferencing Scheme* (Sydney: NSW Bureau of Crime Statistics and Research).

Tyler, T. and Huo, Y.J. (2001) *Trust and the Rule of Law: A Law-abidingness Model of Social Control* (New York: Russel Sage).

Umbreit, M. (1990) 'Mediation in the Nineties: Pushing Back the Boundaries', *Mediation*, 6, pp. 27–9.

Umbreit, M. (1992) 'Mediating Victim–Offender Conflict: From Single-site to Multi-site Analysis in the US', in Messmer, H. and Otto, H.U. (eds) *Restorative Justice on Trial: Pitfalls and Potentials of Victim–Offender Mediation – International Research Perspectives* (Dordrecht and Boston, MA: Kluwer Academic).

Umbreit, M. (1998) 'Restorative Justice through Juvenile Victim–Offender Mediation', in Walgrave, L. and Bazemore, G. (eds) *Restoring Juvenile Justice* (Monsey, NY: Criminal Justice Press).

Umbreit, M. and Coates, R. (1992) *Victim–Offender Mediation: An Analysis of Programs in Four States of the US* (Minneapolis, MN: Citizens Council Mediation Services).

Umbreit, M. with Coates, R. and Kalanj, B. (1994) *Victim Meets Offender: The Impact of Restorative Justice and Mediation* (Monsey, NY: Criminal Justice Press).

Van Ness, D. (1986) *Crime and its Victims: What We Can Do?* (Downers Grove, IL: Intervarsity Press).

Waters, A. (1993) 'The Wagga Wagga Effective Cautioning Program: Reintegrative or Degrading?' BA honors thesis, University of Melbourne.

Wundersitz, J. and Hetzel, S. (1996) 'Family Conferencing for Young Offenders: The South Australian Experience', in Hudson, J. *et al.* (eds) *Family Group Conferences: Perspectives on Policy and Practice* (Sydney: Federation Press and Criminal Justice Press).

Wynne, J. (1996) 'Leeds Mediation and Reparation Service: Ten Years Experience with Victim–Offender Mediation', in Galaway, B. and Hudson, J. (eds) *Restorative Justice: International Perspectives* (Monsey, NY: Criminal Justice Press).

Part E

Some critical issues

Introduction

Restorative justice has been met in some quarters with considerable scepticism and disparagement.[1] However, whilst the readings in Part E present serious challenges to its proponents, they by no means dismiss restorative justice as worthless or completely unacceptable. They raise profound questions about how we should understand and represent restorative interventions. And they suggest that there are considerable limitations and dangers in certain versions of the ideal. But, for the most part, they accept that there is considerable value in a revised and more careful development of the concept and practice of restorative justice. These readings are crucial, not only for identifying and explaining certain potential pitfalls of restorative justice, but for their implicit or explicit suggestions about how the idea and practice might be better developed in the future. Proponents of restorative justice may not want to accept all these criticisms and suggestions; but it is of the utmost importance that they engage with them.

Part E opens with an extract from a recent essay by Kathleen Daly, in which she criticises the way restorative justice has been characterised and promoted by its advocates. She presents her critique as a 'debunking' of four misleading 'myths' – i.e. partial and distorted characterisations – about restorative justice.[2] She is highly critical of the use which proponents of restorative justice make of simplistic oppositional contrasts to describe and promote restorative justice. The most fundamental of these dichotomies is that between retributive and restorative justice (see *Zehr*). Daly rejects this contrast as based upon a caricature of 'old' criminal justice and because it obscures the extent to which restorative justice practices incorporate (quite properly for Daly) retributive as well as restorative principles and goals. Daly also criticises the claim that contemporary restorative justice practices can be understood as a revival of ancient and indigenous justice practices (see Part B of this volume). For Daly, this 'extraordinary claim' romanticises olden and aboriginal practices and disguises the fact that contemporary restorative justice practices incorporate elements which are quite alien to indigenous justice models. Perhaps more seriously, in making such claims, restorative justice proponents leave themselves open to charges of the very ethnocentricism they want to avoid. Daly is equally critical of the claim that restorative justice can be understood as a feminine (or feminist) response to crime, to be contrasted with a conventional criminal justice founded upon masculine moral reasoning.

All these dichotomies, for Daly, are attempts to set up a simple bad/good opposition between the established response to crime and the response favoured by proponents of restorative justice. Whatever their rhetorical value, they have little to do with the reality of practices, such as youth conferencing, which proponents of restorative justice are seeking to promote.

In her analysis of 'myth 4', Daly takes on a quite different type of claim about the potential of restorative justice practices. Advocates of the approach are wont to presenting dramatic tales of people's lives being transformed positively as a result of a restorative conference (compare *Braithwaite*'s discussion of Sam and Uncle George in Chapter 5 of this volume with Daly's discussion of the same example).

Daly argues, drawing upon empirical research, that such spectacular changes are likely to occur at most in 10 per cent of cases. Yet, she claims, they are presented as the normal expected outcome of a restorative intervention. This creates all the problems we might expect when grossly exaggerated claims are made about some new process. It also, according to Daly, detracts attention away from a much more modest positive effect of restorative justice: that many perceive it as procedurally fair and therefore more legitimate than 'old justice' practices.

Daly leaves those who accept her analysis, yet remain enthusiastic about restorative justice, with a dilemma. The simplistic myths about restorative justice, for all that they are misleading, seem useful in getting a fledgling idea going. The real story of restorative justice, for all its value for those interested in a sophisticated understanding of the nature and potential of restorative justice practices, has less political appeal. There is no straightforward choice between myth and scientific truth (although Daly's own inclinations are clear). Perhaps what is most important is that advocates and practitioners of restorative justice do not confuse the two.

The next extract in Part E (Chapter 26) is from a recent essay by R.A. Duff, which is of immense value in its own right but should also prompt those serious about restorative justice to read his recent book *Punishment, Communication, and Community* (2001). Duff, like Daly, argues that the frequently posited dichotomy between punishment and restorative justice (or between retributive and restorative justice) is a false one. Proponents of restorative justice are mistaken to suppose that restorative justice is an alternative to retributive punishment. To the contrary, he suggests, restoration is not only compatible with punishment, it requires punishment. However, proponents of 'just deserts' retributivism are equally wrong to the extent that they assume that commitment to the 'punishment paradigm' entails rejection of the paradigm of restorative justice. To the contrary, for Duff, restorative justice is a paradigm of what punishment ought to be.[3]

My guess is that many resolute proponents of restorative justice will strongly resist any suggestion that what they should be promoting is an alternative *form of* punishment rather than an alternative *to* punishment. For them, the notions of 'retribution' and 'punishment' are too imbued with negative meaning to make any such switch palatable. Nevertheless, they can still learn much from Duff's essay. His clarification of the concept of restoration, his analysis of the meaning of apology for criminal wrongdoing and his insistence on a normative rather than empirical understanding of the damage caused by crime are all of great interest. Also of value is his insistence that crimes be understood as public wrongs, not in the conventional sense that the public at large is affected by them, but in the sense that certain types of wrong done to people are so serious as to be matters of public concern. This provides a fruitful way out of the tangle in which many restorative justice proponents get caught when, in their efforts to draw attention to the plight of the direct victim, they define crime almost as a private or civil wrong.

Richard Young (in Chapter 27) is concerned to examine claims about restorative justice in the light of empirical research. His focus is on police-led restorative conferencing schemes, especially the UK Thames Valley Police initiative which is the subject of an action-research study directed by Young. However, whereas *Daly* is concerned to debunk certain claims made by supporters of restorative justice, Young's main concern is to assess whether certain common criticisms of police-led restorative conferencing programmes are warranted.

These schemes have raised important concerns, mostly to do with the fact that they appear to concentrate too much (punitive) power in one agency: the police. A typical response to such concerns is to point out that conferences are not intended or designed to empower the police or to be punitive. Rather, conferences are merely *facilitated* by the police; power is placed in the hands of ordinary people whose lives are affected by a criminal incident. Facilitators are trained, moreover, to guide participants towards a *reintegrative* shaming process rather than towards a stigmatising or punitive process.

These counterclaims appear to be borne out by studies of police-led restorative conferencing in Canberra, Australia, and Bethlehem, USA. Young, however, is critical of the methods of these studies, particularly what he sees as their over-reliance upon tick-box questionnaires. He suggest that more sophisticated studies, based upon a more complex understanding of how power is exercised (drawn from Foucault 1977) and upon indepth qualitative interviews and observations, yield a very different and less sanguine picture. The very setting in which police-led restorative conferences take place colours what happens, producing disciplinary effects. The police facilitators frequently overstep the limited role of facilitator, slipping (back) into the role of professional police officers, and so on. Moreover, evidence from other studies indicating that offenders experience the process as fair is put in perspective by evidence showing that they have such low expectations of the criminal justice system that any process which gives them a chance to speak and to be heard and which shows any respect for them is likely to be welcomed, even though it may fall well short of respecting rights which many offenders possess but of which they are unaware.

Such findings put in question the rather idealised picture of police-led restorative conferencing painted by other restorative justice proponents and researchers. However, they should not be read as completely damning criticisms. The Thames Valley Police have co-operated fully with Young's research and are committed to adjusting their practice – in what is still a very unusual and progressive venture for a police force – in the light of such criticisms.

The existence of police support for restorative justice helps draw attention to one of the most interesting things about it: the way it has attracted strong support from otherwise opposed interests and sides in the debate about how we should respond to offenders. In particular, both 'liberals' and 'conservatives' (using these terms in the USA sense) have proclaimed restorative justice as a significant part of the solution to the contemporary crime problem. However, whilst this 'cross-party' support helps ensure that restorative justice programmes are launched, resourced and survive political changes, it also raises questions about how restorative justice is likely to be developed. If 'conservatives' and 'liberals' both support restorative justice, they are not necessarily attracted to the same aspects of it. What interests 'conservatives' is perhaps its emphasis upon the needs of crime victims and its potential for providing a tougher response to offenders who currently tend to escape accountability and meaningful sanctions for their behaviour. 'Liberals' also stress the fact that restorative justice meets the needs of victims and provides meaningful accountability for offenders. However, unlike 'conservatives', they tend to support restorative justice on the ground that it provides a less hostile and more 'reconstructive' approach to offenders than other approaches (see *Daly* on the retributive–restorative dichotomy).

In 'Reconsidering Restorative Justice', Levrant *et al*. (in Chapter 28) highlight what they see as the risk that restorative justice will be developed in a 'conservative' direction, to serve non-progressive goals. Whilst 'liberals' may promote it as a benevolent response to crime, 'conservatives' are likely to exploit the approach's informality and lack of procedural safeguards to extend the net of social control and increase the toughness of our system for controlling offenders. Hence, as 'liberals' put restorative justice into practice, it is likely to have consequences far different and quite opposed to those they intend.

In a somewhat different type of argument, Levrant *et al*. also question proponents' claims that restorative justice can make a significant contribution to the reduction of crime or recidivism. As it is currently implemented, they contend, restorative justice fails to adhere to principles of effective intervention which have been identified by researchers interested in 'what works' in correctional treatment. Hence, the claims of restorative justice proponents are dismissed by Levrant *et al*. as 'wishful thinking'. This, however, may be too damning. As Levrant *et al*. realise, their critique is directed at restorative justice as they see it currently being implemented. Restorative justice programmes could be developed in such a way that they incorporate principles of effective intervention. This would require a significant change in direction and a merging of restorative justice with other correctional programmes. Arguably, however, doing this is neither impossible nor inconsistent with the fundamental principles of restorative justice.

In 'Responsibilities, Rights and Restorative Justice' (Chapter 29), Andrew Ashworth assesses the values and procedures of restorative justice from the perspective of the rights and responsibilities of various parties: the state, communities, victims and offenders. In the extract reproduced here he takes on the assertion, found regularly in the discourse of restorative justice, that victims should be enabled and encouraged to participate in the disposition of 'their' criminal cases. Ashworth argues against this claim on a number of grounds: the victim's legitimate interest is in compensation or reparation, and not in the form or amount of punishment inflicted upon an offender; suspects have a right to an impartial tribunal and that the victim's involvement detracts from impartiality; and the principle of proportionality of punishment to the offence is threatened by victim involvement in sentencing decisions. The thrust of these arguments is not that restorative justice is inevitably inconsistent with fundamental principles of justice, but that *many* of its values clash with these principles and therefore should be abandoned or modified. Ashworth accepts that versions of restorative justice *could* be developed which would not fall foul of what he and many others regard as basic principles of justice.

Interestingly, Ashworth also criticises the thinking of some restorative justice proponents on the design of a default system for those cases which for some reason cannot be handled through a restorative process. His particular target here is Braithwaite's 'enforcement pyramid', in which restorative justice forms the base of a larger social control system in which strategies of deterrence and incapacitation also exist (and, for Braithwaite, are useful for the successful functioning of restorative justice – see Chapter 24).

An important challenge facing the restorative justice movement – and the closely related movement for abolition of imprisonment and other repressive responses to crime – is demonstrating how restorative justice could provide satisfactory remedies for racial, sexual and domestic violence. As the extract from

Barbara Hudson shows, conventional criminal justice *could* contribute to the remedying of these unacceptable behaviours by symbolizing the state's authoritative disapproval of them. One of the notorious failings of actual criminal justice is that, through its relatively light treatment of perpetrators of racial, sexual and domestic violence, it sends out the message that such behaviour is not as bad as ordinary burglary, car theft, street robbery and the like. Hence, many critics have called for more repressive responses to racial, sexual and domestic violence – higher rates of arrest and prosecution, tougher penalties, etc. – to demonstrate that the state *does* regard these as serious wrongs.

This creates a dilemma for certain progressives who, on the one hand, want much more to be done about racial, sexual and domestic violence, yet, on the other hand, are concerned to reduce or even abolish the use of penal repression and who lament the punitive turn taken by many modern western societies in recent decades. One possible way out of this dilemma is to devise ways of redressing racial, sexual and domestic violence, which are less repressive than conventional criminal justice interventions, but more effective than them in protecting the victims of such violence and communicating how objectionable it is. Some promote restorative justice as fulfilling these conditions. Hudson asks whether it can. In particular, even if restorative justice can outperform punishment in the instrumental tasks of criminal justice, can it perform effectively the expressive functions of penal intervention, especially the function of conveying authoritative disapproval of sexual and racial violence?

Proponents of restorative justice claim various advantages for its processes when it comes to crimes involving racial, sexual and domestic violence. Restorative processes can enable the victim's definitions and understandings of the wrongs to be voiced, explained and indeed made central. As a process, Hudson points out, restorative justice can perform a norm-creation role, resulting in a more progressive moral consensus (here she draws upon Jürgen Habermas's notion of discourse ethics). However, problems remain, especially when proponents of restorative justice advocate the continued existence of non-restorative penal interventions, such as imprisonment, for cases when restorative justice repeatedly fails (see *Braithwaite*, part D). Then, the very existence of custodial sanctions, which are widely perceived as more severe than restorative interventions, can result in people concluding that wrongs dealt with by restorative justice must be among the 'less serious'.

Hudson, then, poses no easy solutions to the dilemma. However, she does suggest that the core principles of abolitionism and restorative justice hold true, and that creative consideration of the relationship of restorative justice to formal criminal law may result in a better solution to the problem of sexual and racial violence either than that which we have now or that which is proposed by those who seek enhanced penalties.

One of the central tensions within the restorative justice movement is over its relationship to the conventional criminal justice system (cf. *Walgrave*). Proponents of restorative justice frequently espouse the ambitious goal of creating a radical alternative to state criminal justice: a new paradigm of justice which will be community based, treat offenders with respect and meet the needs of victims. In practice, however, many are developing restorative justice as a set of programmes within criminal justice systems that are predominantly shaped by and reflect more conventional (non-restorative) concepts, assumptions and commitments.

This tension is explored in George Pavlich's essay 'Deconstructing Restoration' (Chapter 31). Deploying concepts and techniques derived from Jacques Derrida's strategy of deconstruction, Pavlich suggests that, for all its talk of alternative visions and practices of justice, the restorative justice movement remains trapped within a pretty conventional framework of regarding and responding to crime. Restorative interventions are triggered by what the state criminal law defines as wrongful acts. It regards conflict as a pathology to be contained and stopped, rather than recognising its potential to instigate progressive social change. It remains committed to the conventional offender/victim dyad. The discourse of restorative justice, in short, repeats the very assumptions it would need to contest in order to live up to its rhetorical claims of providing a genuine alternative. In practice, it runs the risk of being used as a supplement to state criminal justice, providing a cheaper, less formal alternative to its mainstream practices, thereby increasing the overall efficiency and reach of the criminal justice system.[4]

Pavlich also questions the assumption he detects in restorative justice discourse that crimes can be handled without coercive state control within homogeneous, consensual and unified communities. As we have seen in a number of readings, many doubt whether such communities can be found in modern society. But Pavlich's main point is that the very attempt to develop communities is fraught with danger. For Pavlich, imposing images of community over relations between people is not as positive or innocuous as it seems (see also Pavlich 2001). Communities always exclude and fortify themselves against the outsider, as well as including and assimilating the insider. There is always a strong hint of totalitarianism in images of community, and invocations of the term can encourage obsessions with member purity.

The question, of course, is whether there are alternative images of modes of association between people which do the positive work of the image of community (holding up some image of solidarity to oppose to the classic liberal picture of isolated autonomous individuals), but which prompt recognition of ethical responsibility to 'the unalike' and hence avoid the totalitarian possibilities of appeals to community. What Pavlich offers is an image he derives from the works of Derrida: 'hospitality.' This idea clearly needs more development (see Pavlich, 2001). However, regardless of how convincing we find this positive suggestion, Pavlich's highlighting of potential dangers in uncritical evocations of 'community' poses proponents of restorative justice with one of their most interesting and important challenges.[5]

In the final extract in this section, a leading proponent of restorative justice responds to some 'typical' criticisms of it. Allison Morris acknowledges that the restorative justice literature is plagued with confusion and that restorative justice proponents frequently make exaggerated claims on its behalf. She also makes it clear that she does not seek to defend all practices that claim to be examples of restorative justice. However, she does argue that criticism of restorative justice is often based upon some fundamental misunderstandings of its nature and goals, as well as upon misinterpretations of research findings. In addition, Morris dismisses certain 'philosophical' critiques, such as those emanating from champions of 'just deserts' in sentencing, on the ground that they inappropriately judge restorative justice by reference to precisely those values which the restorative justice movement seeks to put in question. Morris's position – to which many other restorative justice theorists subscribe – appears to be that we should evaluate restorative justice in its own terms and not judge it using criteria derived from a punitive paradigm which it rejects and seeks to replace (for a view to the contrary, see *Ashworth*; on the idea of restorative justice as an alternative paradigm, see *Barnett* and *Zehr*).

Morris goes on to identify and criticise a number of standard criticisms of restorative justice. In doing so, she provides an excellent baseline for further debate:

- Does Morris identify the most important criticisms of restorative justice?

- Does her account of these criticisms capture their full force?

- How adequate and persuasive is her response to these criticisms?

- What further empirical information and theoretical development is required to resolve some of these issues?

Those participating in such debates would do well to heed two important points made by Morris. First, critics of restorative justice should have an good understanding of the object of their critique. Second, in discussing the pros and cons of restorative justice, it is useful to ask, not does it meet our highest ideals, but rather is it (potentially) better than what we currently have or than any other feasible alternative to what we currently have.

Notes

1 See, for example, Edis (2002). For an attempt to list and respond to the main criticisms, see *Morris*.
2 For the most part, Daly uses the concept of 'myth' to describe stories about restorative justice which she argues are inaccurate and misleading. Her main concern is to debunk these myths (although she herself does not use the term 'debunk') and to present in outline a more correct and adequate account. However, in part of the essay not reproduced here, she does suggest that these 'myths' may require another form of analysis: an examination of how they function to sell the idea of restorative justice to a wide audience.
3 To grasp this latter point fully, one would need to read Duff (2001). See Norrie (2000: ch. 6) for a critique of Duff's justification of (a certain conception of) punishment.
4 For versions of restorative justice which seek to avoid such a predicament, see Shearing (2001) and Sullivan and Tifft (2001). For some of the problems with the latter, see Johnstone (2002).
5 Duff (1999, 2001) proposes a sophisticated conception of community which arguably goes some way towards addressing the sorts of problem identified by Pavlich. Those restorative justice proponents who are concerned by what Pavlich has to say should engage with Duff's account as well as Pavlich's own notion of hospitality.

References

Duff, R.A. (1999) 'Penal Communities', *Punishment and Society*, 1:1, pp. 27–43.
Duff, R. (2001) *Punishment, Communication, and Community* (Oxford University Press).

Edis, A. (2002) 'Book Review (Johnstone)', *The Times Higher Education Supplement*, 15 February.

Foucault, M. (1977) *Discipline and Punish: The Birth of the Prison* (trans. A. Sheridan) (London: Allen Lane).

Johnstone, G. (2002) 'Book Review (Sullivan and Tifft)', *Howard Journal of Criminal Justice*, pp. 302–3.

Norrie, A. (2000) *Punishment, Responsibility and Justice: A Relational Critique* (Oxford: Oxford University Press).

Pavlich, G. (2001) 'The Force of Community', in Strang, H. and Braithwaite, J. (eds) *Restorative Justice and Civil Society* (Cambridge: Cambridge University Press), pp. 56–68.

Shearing, C. (2001) 'Transforming Security: A South African Experiment', in Strang, H. and Braithwaite, J. (eds) *Restorative Justice and Civil Society* (Cambridge: Cambridge University Press), pp. 14–34.

Sullivan, D. and Tifft, L. (2001) *Restorative Justice: Healing the Foundations of our Everyday Lives* (Monsey, NY: Willow Tree Press).

25. Restorative justice: the real story

Kathleen Daly

[. . .]

Myths about restorative justice

Myth 1. Restorative justice is the opposite of retributive justice

When one first dips into the restorative justice literature, the first thing one 'learns' is that restorative justice differs sharply from retributive justice. It is said that:

1. restorative justice focuses on *repairing the harm* caused by crime, whereas retributive justice focuses on *punishing an offence*;
2. restorative justice is characterized by *dialogue* and *negotiation* among the parties; where retributive justice is characterized by *adversarial relations* among the parties;
3. restorative justice assumes that community members or organizations take a more active role, whereas for retributive justice, 'the community' is represented by the state.

Most striking is that all the elements associated with restorative justice are *good*, whereas all those associated with retributive justice are *bad*. The retributive– restorative oppositional contrast is not only made by restorative justice advocates, but increasingly one finds it canonized in criminology and juvenile justice textbooks. The question arises, is it right?

On empirical and normative grounds, I suggest that in characterizing justice aims and practices, it is neither accurate nor defensible. While I am not alone in taking this position (see Barton, 2000; Miller and Blackler, 2000; Duff, 2001), it is currently held by a small number of us in the field. Despite advocates' well-meaning intentions, the contrast is a highly misleading simplification, which is used to sell the superiority of restorative justice and its set of justice products. To make the sales pitch simple, definite boundaries need to be marked between the *good* (restorative) and the *bad* (retributive) justice, to which one might add the *ugly* (rehabilitative) justice. Advocates seem to assume that an ideal justice system should be of one type only, that it should be pure and not contaminated by or mixed with others.[1] Before demonstrating the problems with this position, I give a sympathetic reading of what I think advocates are trying to say.

Mead's (1917–18) 'The Psychology of Punitive Justice' (as reprinted in Melossi, 1998; 33–60) contrasts two methods of responding to crime. One he termed 'the attitude of hostility toward the lawbreaker' (p. 48), which 'brings with it the attitudes of retribution, repression, and exclusion' (pp. 47–28) and

363

which sees a lawbreaker as 'enemy'. The other, exemplified in the (then) emerging juvenile court, is the 'reconstructive attitude' (p. 55), which tries to 'understand the causes of social and individual breakdown, to mend . . . the defective situation', to determine responsibility 'not to place punishment but to obtain future results' (p. 52). Most restorative justice advocates see the justice world through this Meadian lens; they reject the 'attitude of hostility toward the lawbreaker', do not wish to view him or her as 'enemy', and desire an alternative kind of justice. On that score, I concur, as no doubt many other researchers and observers of justice system practices would. However, the 'attitude of hostility' is a caricature of criminal justice, which over the last century and a half has wavered between desires to 'treat' some and 'punish' others, and which surely cannot be encapsulated in the one term, 'retributive justice'. By framing justice aims (or principles) and practices in oppositional terms, restorative justice advocates not only do a disservice to history, they also give a restricted view of the present. They assume that restorative justice *practices* should exclude elements of retribution; and in rejecting an 'attitude of hostility', they assume that retribution as a justice *principle* must also be rejected.

When observing conferences, I discovered that participants engaged in a flexible incorporation of *multiple* justice aims, which included:

1. some elements of retributive justice (that is, censure for past offences);
2. some elements of rehabilitative justice (for example, by asking, what shall we do to encourage future law-abiding behaviour?); and
3. some elements of restorative justice (for example, by asking, how can the offender make up for what he or she did to the victim?).

When reporting these findings, one colleague said, 'yes, this is a problem' (Walgrave, personal communication). This speaker's concern was that as restorative justice was being incorporated into the regular justice system, it would turn out to be a set of 'simple techniques', rather than an 'ideal of justice . . . in an ideal of society' (Walgrave, 1995: 240, 245) and that its core values would be lost. Another said (paraphrasing), 'retribution may well be present now in conferences, but you wouldn't want to make the argument that it *should* be present' (Braithwaite, personal communication).

These comments provoked me to consider the relationship between restorative and retributive justice, and the role of punishment in restorative justice, in normative terms. Distilling from other articles (e.g. Daly and Immarigeon, 1998: 32–5; Daly, 2000a, 2000b) and arguments by Duff (1992, 1996, 2001), Hampton (1992, 1998), Zedner (1994) and Barton (2000), I have come to see that apparently contrary principles of retribution and reparation should be viewed as dependent on one another. Retributive censure should ideally occur before reparative gestures (or a victim's interest or movement to negotiate these) are possible in an ethical or psychological sense. Both censure and reparation may be experienced as 'punishment' by offenders (even if this is not the intent of decision-makers), and both censure and reparation need to occur before a victim or community can 'reintegrate' an offender into the community. These complex and contingent interactions are expressed in varied ways and should not be viewed as having to follow any one fixed sequence.

Moreover, one cannot assume that subsequent actions, such as the victim's forgiving the offender or a reconciliation of a victim and offender (or others), should occur. This may take a long time or never occur. In the advocacy literature, however, I find that there is too quick a move to 'repair the harm', 'heal those injured by crime' or to 'reintegrate offenders', passing over a crucial phase of 'holding offenders accountable', which is the retributive part of the process.

A major block in communicating ideas about the relationship of retributive to restorative justice is that there is great variability in how people understand and use key terms such as punishment, retribution and punitiveness. Some argue that incarceration and fines are punishments because they are *intended deprivations*, whereas probation or a reparative measure such as doing work for a crime victim are not punishment because they are *intended to be constructive* (Wright, 1991). Others define punishment more broadly to include anything that is unpleasant, a burden or an imposition of some sort; the intentions of the decision-maker are less significant (Davis, 1992; Duff, 1992, 2001). Some use retribution to describe a *justification* for punishment (i.e. intended to be in proportion to the harm caused), whereas others use it to describe a *form* of punishment (i.e. intended to be of a type that is harsh or painful).[2] On proportionality, restorative justice advocates take different positions: some (e.g. Braithwaite and Pettit, 1990) eschew retributivism, favouring instead a free-ranging consequentialist justification and highly individualized responses, while others wish to limit restorative justice responses to desert-based, proportionate criteria (Van Ness, 1993; Walgrave and Aertsen, 1996). For the form of punishment, some use retribution in a neutral way to refer to a censuring of harms (e.g. Duff, 1996), whereas most use the term to connote a punitive response, which is associated with emotions of revenge or intentions to inflict pain on wrong-doers (Wright, 1991). The term *punitive* is rarely defined, no doubt because everyone seems to know what it means. Precisely because this term is used in a commonsensical way by everyone in the field (not just restorative justice scholars), there is confusion over its meaning. Would we say, for example, that any criminal justice sanction is by definition 'punitive', but sanctions can vary across a continuum of greater to lesser punitiveness? Or, would we say that some sanctions are non-punitive and that restorative justice processes aim to maximize the application of non-punitive sanctions? I will not attempt to adjudicate the many competing claims about punishment, retribution and punitiveness. The sources of antagonism lie not only in varied *definitions*, but also the different *images* these definitions conjure in people's heads about justice relations and practices. However, one way to gain some clarity is to conceptualize punishment, retribution and punitive (and their 'non' counterparts) as separate dimensions, each having its own continuum of meaning, rather than to conflate them, as now typically occurs in the literature.

Because the terms 'retributive justice' and 'restorative justice' have such strong meanings and referents, and are used largely by advocates (and others) as metaphors for the bad and the good justice, perhaps they should be jettisoned in analysing current and future justice practices. Instead, we might refer to 'older' and 'newer' modern justice forms. These terms do not provide a content to justice principles or practices, but they do offer a way to depict developments in the justice field with an eye to recent history and with an appreciation that any 'new' justice practices will have many bits of the 'old' in them.[3] The terms also permit description and explanation of a larger phenomenon, that is, of a profound transformation of justice forms and practices now occurring in most developed societies in the West, and certainly the English-speaking ones of which I am aware. Restorative justice is only a part of that transformation.

By the *old justice*, I refer to modern practices of courthouse justice, which permit no interaction between victim and offender, where legal actors and other experts do the talking and make decisions and whose (stated) aim is to punish, or at times, reform an offender. By the *new justice*,[4] I refer to a variety of recent practices, which normally bring victims and offenders (and others) together in a process in which both lay and legal actors make decisions, and whose (stated) aim is to repair the harm for victims, offenders and perhaps other members of 'the community' in ways that matter to them. (While the stated aim of either justice form may be to 'punish the crime' or to 'repair the harm', we should expect to see mixed justice aims in participants' justice talk and practices.[5]) New justice practices are one of several developments in a larger justice field, which also includes the 'new penology' (Feeley and Simon, 1992) and 'unthinkable punishment policies' (Tonry, 1999). The field is fragmented and moving in contradictory directions (Garland, 1996; Crawford, 1997; O'Malley, 1999; Pratt, 2000).

Myth 2. Restorative justice uses indigenous justice practices and was the dominant form of pre-modern justice

A common theme in the restorative justice literature is that this reputedly new justice form is 'really not new' (Consedine, 1995: 12). As Consedine puts it:

> Biblical justice was restorative. So too was justice in most indigenous cultures. In pre-colonial New Zealand, Maori had a fully integrated system of restorative justice ... It was the traditional philosophy of Pacific nations such as Tonga, Fiji and Samoa ... In pre-Norman Ireland, restorative justice was interwoven ... with the fabric of daily life ... (1995: 12)

Braithwaite argues that restorative justice is 'ground[ed] in traditions of justice from the ancient Arab, Greek, and Roman civilisations that accepted a restorative approach even to homicide' (1999: 1), He continues with a large sweep of human history, citing the 'public assemblies ... of the Germanic peoples', 'Indian Hindu [traditions in] 6000–2000 BC' and 'ancient Buddhist, Taoist, and Confucian traditions ...'; and he concludes that '*restorative justice has been the dominant model of criminal justice throughout most of human history for all the world's peoples*' (1999: 1, my emphasis). What an extraordinary claim!

Linked with the claim that restorative justice has been the dominant form of criminal justice throughout human history is the claim that present-day indigenous justice practices fall within the restorative justice rubric. Thus, for example, Consedine says:

A new paradigm of justice is operating [in New Zealand], which is very traditional in its philosophy, yet revolutionary in its effects. A restorative philosophy of justice has replaced a retributive one. Ironically, 150 years after the traditional Maori restorative praxis was abolished in Aotearoa, youth justice policy is once again operating from the same philosophy. (1995: 99)

Reverence for and romanticization of an indigenous past slide over practices that the modern 'civilized' western mind would object to, such as a variety of harsh physical (bodily) punishments and banishment. At the same time, the modern western mind may not be able to grasp how certain 'harsh punishments' have been sensible within the terms of a particular culture.

Weitekamp combines 'ancient forms' of justice practice (as restorative) and indigenous groups' current practices (as restorative) when he says that:

Some of the new ... programs are in fact very old ... [A]ncient forms of restorative justice have been used in [non-state] societies and by early forms of humankind. [F]amily group conferences [and] ... circle hearings [have been used] by indigenous people such as the Aboriginals, the Inuit, and the native Indians of North and South America ... It is kind of ironic that we have at [the turn of this century] to go back to methods and forms of conflict resolution which were practiced some millennia ago by our ancestors ... (1999: 93)

I confess to a limited knowledge of justice practices and systems throughout the history of humankind. What I know is confined mainly to the past three centuries and to developments in the United States and several other countries. Thus, in addressing this myth, I do so from a position of ignorance in knowing only a small portion of history. Upon reflection, however, my lack of historical knowledge may not matter. All that is required is the realization that advocates do not intend to write *authoritative histories* of justice. Rather, they are constructing origin myths about restorative justice. If the first form of human justice was restorative justice, then advocates can claim a need to recover it from a history of 'takeover' by state-sponsored retributive justice. *And*, by identifying current indigenous practices as restorative justice, advocates can claim a need to recover these practices from a history of 'takeover' by white colonial powers that instituted retributive justice. Thus, the history of justice practices is rewritten by advocates not only to authorize restorative justice as the *first* human form of justice, but also to argue that it is congenial with modern-day indigenous and, as we shall see in Myth 3, feminist social movements for justice.

In the restorative justice field, most commentators focus specifically (and narrowly) on changes that occurred over a 400-year period (8th to 11th centuries) in England (and some European countries), where a system of largely kin-based dispute settlement gave way to a court system, in which feudal lords retained a portion of property forfeited by an offender. In England, this loose system was centralized and consolidated during the century following the Normal Invasion in 1066, as the development of state (crown) law depended on the collection of revenues collected by judges for the king. For restorative justice advocates, the transformation of disputes as offences between individuals to offences against the state is one element that marked the end of pre-modern forms of restorative justice. A second element is the decline in compensation to the victim for the losses from a crime (Weitekamp, 1999).

Advocates' constructions of the history of restorative justice, that is, the origin myth that a superior justice form prevailed before the imposition of retributive justice, is linked to their desire to maintain a strong oppositional contrast between retributive and restorative justice. That is to say, the origin myth and oppositional contrast are both required in telling the true story of restorative justice. I do not see bad faith at work here. Rather, advocates are trying to move an idea into the political and policy arena, and this may necessitate having to utilize a simple contrast of the good and the bad justice, along with an origin myth of how it all came to be.

What does concern me is that the specific histories and practices of justice in pre-modern societies are smoothed over and are lumped together as one justice form. Is it appropriate to refer to all of these justice practices as 'restorative'? No, I think not. What do these justice practices in fact have in common? What is gained, and more importantly, what is lost by this homogenizing move? Efforts to write histories of restorative justice, where a pre-modern past is romantically (and selectively) invoked to justify a current justice practice, are not only in error, but also unwittingly reinscribe an ethnocentrism their authors wish to avoid. As Blagg (1997) and Cain (2000) point out, there has been an orientalist appropriation of indigenous justice practices, largely in the service of strenthening advocates' positions.

A common, albeit erroneous, claim is that the modern idea of conferencing 'has its direct roots in Maori culture' (Shearing, 2001: 218, note 5; see also Consedine, 1995). The real story is that conferencing emerged in the 1980s, in the context of Maori political challenges to white New Zealanders and to their welfare and criminal justice systems. Investing decision-making practices with Maori cultural values meant that family groups (whanau) should have a greater say in what happens, that venues should be culturally appropriate, and that processes should accommodate a mix of culturally appropriate practices. New Zealand's minority group population includes not only the Maori but also Pacific Island Polynesians. Therefore, with the introduction of conferencing, came awareness of the need to incorporate different elements of 'cultural appropriateness' into the conference process. But the devising of a (white, bureaucratic) justice practice that is *flexible and accommodating* towards cultural differences does not mean that conferencing *is* an indigenous justice practice. Maxwell and Morris, who know the New Zealand situation well, are clear on this point:

> A distinction must be drawn between a system, which attempts to re-establish the indigenous model of pre-European times, and a system of justice, which is culturally appropriate. The New Zealand system is an attempt to establish the latter, not to replicate the former. As such, it seeks to incorporate many of the features apparent in whanau decision-making processes and seen in meetings on marae today, but it also contains elements quite alien to indigenous models. (1993: 4)

Conferencing is better understood as a fragmented justice form: it splices white, bureaucratic forms of justice with elements of informal justice that may include non-white (or non-western) values or methods of judgement, with all the attendant dangers of such 'spliced justice' (Pavlich, 1996; Blagg, 1997, 1998; Daly, 1998; Findlay, 2000). With the flexibility of informal justice, practitioners, advocates and members of minority groups may see the potential for introducing culturally sensible and responsive forms of justice. But to say that conferencing *is* an indigenous justice practice (or 'has its roots in indigenous justice') is to re-engage a white-centred view of the world. As Blagg asks rhetorically, 'Are we once again creaming off the cultural value of people simply to suit our own nostalgia in this age of pessimism and melancholia?' (1998: 12). A good deal of the advocacy literature is of this ilk: white-centred, creaming off and homogenizing of cultural difference and specificity.

Myth 3. Restorative justice is a 'care' (or feminine) response to crime in comparison to a 'justice' (or masculine) response

Myths 2 and 3 have a similar oppositional logic, but play with different dichotomies. Figure [23.]1 shows the terms that are often linked to restorative and retributive justice. Note the power inversion, essential to the origin myth of restorative justice, where the subordinated or marginalized groups (pre-modern, indigenous, eastern and feminine) are aligned with the more superior justice form.

Many readers will be familiar with the 'care' and 'justice' dichotomy. It was put forward by Gilligan in her popular book, *In a Different Voice* (1982). For about a decade, it seemed that most feminist legal theory articles were organized around the 'different voice' versus 'male dominance' perspectives of Gilligan (1987) and MacKinnon (1987), respectively. In criminology, Heidensohn (1986) and Harris (1987) attempted to apply the care/justice dichotomy to the criminal justice system. Care responses to crime are depicted as personalized and as based on a concrete and active morality, whereas justice responses are depicted as depersonalized, based on rights and rules and a universalizing and abstract morality. Care responses are associated with the different (female) voice, and these are distinguished from justice responses, which are associated with the general (if male) voice. In her early work, Gilligan argued that both voices should have equal importance in moral reasoning, but women's voices were misheard or judged as morally inferior to

Restorative justice	Retributive justice
Pre-modern	Modern
Indigenous (informal)	State (formal)
Feminine (care)	Masculine (justice)
Eastern (Japan)	Western (US)
Superior justice	Inferior justice

Figure [25.]1: Terms linked to restorative and retributive justice.

men's. A critical literature developed rapidly, and Gilligan began to reformu-
late and clarify her argument. She recognized that 'care' responses in a 'justice'
framework left 'the basic assumptions of a justice framework intact . . . and that
as a moral perspective, care [was] less well elaborated' (Gilligan, 1987: 24). At
the time, the elements that Gilligan associated with a care response to crime
were contextual and relational reasoning, and individualized responses made
by decision-makers who were not detached from the conflict (or crime). In
1989, I came into the debate, arguing that we should challenge the association
of justice and care reasoning with male/masculine and female/feminine voices,
respectively (Daly, 1989). I suggested that this gender-linked association was
not accurate empirically, and I argued that it would be misleading to think
that an alternative to men's forms of criminal law and justice practices could
be found by adding women's voice or reconstituting the system along the lines
of an ethic of care. I viewed the care/justice dichotomy as recapitulating
centuries long debates in modern western criminology and legal philosophy
over the aims and purposes of punishment, e.g. deterrence and retribution or
rehabilitation, and uniform or individualized responses. Further, I noted that
although the dichotomy depicted different ideological emphases in the response
to crime since the 19th century, the relational and concrete reasoning that
Gilligan associated with the female voice was how in fact the criminal law is
interpreted and applied. It *is* the voice of criminal justice practices. The
problem, then, was not that the female voice was absent in criminal court
practices, but rather that certain relations were presupposed, maintained and
reproduced. Feminist analyses of law and criminal justice centre on the
androcentric (some would argue, phallocentric) character of these relations
for what comes to be understood as 'crime', for the meanings of 'consent',
and for punishment (for cogent reviews, see Smart, 1989, 1992; Coombs,
1995). While feminist scholars continue to emphasize the need to bring
women's experiences and 'voices' into the criminological and legal frame,
this is not the same thing as arguing that there is a universal 'female voice'
in moral reasoning. During the late 1980s and 1990s, feminist arguments
moved decisively beyond dichotomous and essentialist readings of sex/
gender in analysing relations of power and 'difference' in law and justice.
Gilligan's different voice construct, though novel and important at the time,
has been superseded by more complex and contingent analyses of ethics and
morality.

But the different voice is back, and unfortunately, the authors who are using it
seem totally unaware of key shifts in feminist thinking. We see now that the
'ethic of care' (Persephone) is pitched as the alternative to retributive justice
(Portia). One example is a recent article by Masters and Smith (1998), who
attempt to demonstrate the Persephone, the voice of caring, is evident in a
variety of restorative responses to crime. Their arguments confuse, however,
because they argue that Persephone is 'informed by an ethic of care as well as
an ethic of justice' (1998: 11). And towards the end of the article, they say 'we
cannot do without Portia (ethic of justice), but neither can we do without
Persephone' (1998: 21). Thus, it is not clear whether, within the terms of their
argument, Persephone stands for the feminine or includes both the masculine
and feminine, or whether we need both Portia and Persephone. They

apparently agree with all three positions. They also see little difference between a 'feminine' and a 'feminist approach', terms that they use interchangeably. In general, they normally credit 'relational justice as a distinctly feminine approach to crime and conflict' (1998: 13). They say that 'reintegrative shaming can be considered a feminine (or Persephone) theory' and that there is a 'fit between reintegrative shaming practice and the *feminist* ethic of care' (1998: 13, my italics since the authors have shifted from a feminine ethic to a feminist ethic). Towards the end of the article, they make the astonishing claim, one that I suspect my colleague John Braithwaite would find difficult to accept, that 'reintegrative shaming is perhaps the first feminist criminological theory'. They argue this is so because the 'practice of reintegrative shaming can be interpreted as being grounded in a feminine, rather than a masculine understanding of the social world' (1998: 20).

There is a lot to unpick here, and I shall not go point by point. Nor do I wish to undermine the spirit of the article since the authors' intentions are laudable, in particular, their desire to define a more progressive way to respond to crime. My concern is that using simple gender dichotomies, or any dichotomies for that matter, to describe principles and practices of justice will always fail us, will always lead to great disappointment.[6] Traditional court-house justice works with the abstraction of criminal law, but must deal with the messy world of people's lives, and hence, must deal with context and relations. 'Care' responses to some offenders can re-victimize some victims; they may be helpful in *some cases* or for *some offenders* or for *some victims* or they may also be oppressive and unjust for other offenders and victims. Likewise, with so-called 'justice' responses. The set of terms lined up along the 'male/masculine' and 'female/feminine' poles is long and varied: some terms are about process, others with modes of response (e.g. repair the harm) and still others, with ways of thinking about culpability for the harm.

I am struck by the frequency with which people use dichotomies such as the male and female voice, retributive and restorative justice or West and East, to depict justice principles and practices. Such dichotomies are also used to construct normative positions about justice, where it is assumed (I think wrongly) that the sensibility of one side of the dualism necessarily excludes (or is antithetical to) the sensibility of the other. Increasingly, scholars are coming to see the value of theorizing justice in hybrid terms, of seeing connections and contingent relations between apparent oppositions (see, for example, Zedner, 1994; Bottoms, 1998; Hudson, 1998; Daly, 2000a; Duff, 2001).

Like the advocates promoting Myth 2, those promoting Myth 3 want to emphasize the importance of identifying a different response to crime than the one currently in use. I am certainly on the side of that aspiration. However, I cannot agree with the terms in which the position has been argued and sold to academic audiences and wider publics. There is a loss of credibility when analyses do not move beyond oppositional justice metaphors, when claims are imprecise and when extraordinary tales of repair and goodwill are assumed to be typical of the restorative justice experience.

Myth 4. Restorative justice can be expected to produce major changes in people

I have said that attention needs to be given to the reality on the ground, to what is actually happening in, and resulting from, practices that fall within the rubric of restorative justice. There are several levels to describe and analyse what is going on: first, what occurs in the justice practice itself; second, the relationship between this and broader system effects; and third, how restorative justice is located in the broader politics of crime control. I focus on the first level and present two forms of evidence: (1) stories of dramatic transformations or moving accounts of reconciliation; and (2) aggregated information across a larger number of cases, drawing from research on conference observations and interviews with participants.

Several reviewers of this article took issue with Myth 4, saying that 'advocates are less likely to claim changes in people' or that 'there is no real evidence that restorative justice of itself can be expected to produce major changes in people'. Although I am open to empirical inquiry, my reading of the advocacy literature from the United States, Canada, Australia and New Zealand suggests that Myth 4 is prevalent. It is exemplified by advocates' stories of how people are transformed or by their general assertions of the benefits of restorative justice. For example, McCold reports that 'facilitators of restorative processes regularly observe a personal and social transformation occur during the course of the process' (2000: 359) and 'we now have a growing body of research on programs that everyone agrees are truly restorative, clearly demonstrating their remarkable success at healing and conciliation' (2000: 363). McCold gives no citations to the research literature. While 'personal and social transformation' undoubtedly occurs some of the time, and is likely to be rare in a courtroom proceeding, advocates lead us to think that it is typical in a restorative justice process. This is accomplished by telling a moving story, which is then used to stand as a generalization.

Stories of restorative justice

Consedine opens his book by excerpting from a 1993 New Zealand news story:

> The families of two South Auckland boys killed by a car welcomed the accused driver yesterday with open arms and forgiveness. The young man, who gave himself up to the police yesterday morning, apologised to the families and was ceremonially reunited with the Tongan and Samoan communities at a special service last night.
> ... The 20-year-old Samoan visited the Tongan families after his court appearance to apologise for the deaths of the two children in Mangere. The Tongan and Samoan communities of Mangere later gathered at the Tongan Methodist Church in a service of reconciliation. The young man sat at the feast table flanked by the mothers of the dead boys. (Consedine, 1995: 9)

Consedine says that this case provides:

ample evidence of the power that healing and forgiveness can play in our daily lives ... The grieving Tongan and Samoan communities simply embraced the young driver ... and forgave him. His deep shame, his fear, his sorrow, his alienation from the community was resolved. (1995: 162)

Another example comes from Umbreit (1994: 1). His book opens with the story of Linda and Bob Jackson, whose house was broken into; they subsequently met with the offender as part of the offender's sentence disposition. The offender, Allan, 'felt better after the mediation ... he was able to make amends to the Jacksons'. Moreover, 'Linda and Bob felt less vulnerable, were able to sleep better and received payment for their losses. All parties were able to put this event behind them.' Later in the book, Umbreit (1994: 197–202) offers another case study of a second couple, Bob and Anne, after their house was burglarized a second time. He summarized the outcome this way:

Bob, Anne, and Jim [the offender] felt the mediation process and outcome was fair. All were very satisfied with participation in the program. Rather than playing passive roles ... [they] actively participated in 'making things right'. During a subsequent conversation with Bob, he commented that 'this was the first time (after several victimizations) that I ever felt any sense of fairness. The courts always ignored me before. They didn't care about my concerns. And Jim isn't such a bad kid after all, was he?' Jim also indicated that he felt better after the mediation and more aware of the impact the burglary had on Bob and Anne. (Umbreit, 1994: 202)

Lastly, there is the fable of Sam, an adolescent offender who attended a diversionary conference, which was first related by Braithwaite (1996) and retold by Shearing (2001: 214–15). Braithwaite says that his story is a 'composite of several Sams I have seen' (1996: 9); thus, while he admits that it is not a real story of Sam, it is said to show the 'essential features ... of restorative justice' (Shearing, 2001: 214). This is something like a building contractor saying to a potential home buyer, 'this is a composite of the house I can build for you; it's not the real house, but it's like many houses I have sold to happy buyers over the years'. What the composite gives and what the building contractor offers us is a *vision of the possible*, of the perfect house. Whether the house can ever be built is less important than imagining its possibility and its perfection. This is the cornerstone of the true story of restorative justice, like many proposed justice innovations of the past.

Sam's story, as told by Braithwaite, is longer than I give here, and thus I leave out emotional details that make any story compelling. Sam, who is homeless and says his parents abused him, has no one who really cares about him except his older sister, his former hockey coach at school and his Uncle George. These people attend the conference, along with the elderly female victim and her daughter. Sam says he knocked over the victim and took her purse because he needed the money. His significant others rebuke him for doing this, but also remember that he had a good side before he started getting into trouble. The victim and daughter describe the effects of the robbery, but Sam does not seem to be affected. After his apparent callous response to the victim, Sam's sister cries, and during a break, she reveals that she too had been abused by their parents. When the conference reconvenes, Sam's sister speaks directly to Sam, and without mentioning details, says she understands what Sam went through. The victim appreciates what is being said and begins to cry. Sam's callous exterior begins to crumble. He says he wants to do something for the victim, but does not know what he can do without a home or job. His sister offers her place for him to stay, and the coach says he can offer him some work. At the end of the conference, the victim hugs Sam and tearfully says good luck. Sam apologizes again and Uncle George says he will continue to help Sam and his sister when needed.

Many questions arise in reading stories like these. *How often* do expressions of kindness and understanding, of movement towards repair and goodwill, actually occur? What are the typical 'effects' on participants? Is the perfect house of restorative justice ever built? Another kind of evidence, aggregated data across a large number of cases, can provide some answers.

Statistical aggregates of restorative justice

Here are some highlights of what has been learned from research on youth justice conferences in Australia and New Zealand.[7] Official data show that about 85 to 90 per cent of conferences resulted in agreed outcomes, and 80 per cent of young people completed their agreements. From New Zealand research in the early 1990s (Maxwell and Morris, 1993), conferences appeared to be largely offender-centred events. In 51 per cent of the 146 cases where a victim was identified, the victim attended the conference (1993: 118). Of all the victims interviewed who attended a conference (sometimes there were multiple victims), 25 per cent said they felt worse as a result of the conference (1993: 119). Negative feelings were linked to being dissatisfied with the conference outcome, which was judged to be too lenient towards the offender. Of all those interviewed (offenders, their supporters and victims) victims were the least satisfied with the outcome of the family conference: 40 per cent said they were satisfied (1993: 120) compared with 84 per cent of young people and 85 per cent of parents (1993: 115). Maxwell and Morris report that 'monitoring of [conference] outcomes was generally poor' (1993: 123), and while they could not give precise percentages, it appeared that 'few [victims] had been informed of the eventual success or otherwise of the outcome' and that this 'was a source of considerable anger for them' (1993: 123). Elsewhere, Maxwell and Morris report that 'the new system remains largely unresponsive to cultural differences' (1996: 95–6) in handling Maori cases, which they argue is a consequence, in part, of too few resources.

The most robust finding across all the studies in the region (see review in Daly, 2001) is that conferences receive very high marks along dimensions of procedural justice, that is, victims and offenders view the process and the outcomes as fair. In the Re-Integrative Shaming Experiments (RISE) in Canberra, admitted offenders were randomly assigned to court and conference. Strang *et al.* (1999) have reported results from the RISE project on their website by showing many pages of percentages for each variable for each of the four offences in the experiment (violent, property, shoplifting and drink-driving). They have summarized this mass of numbers in a set of comparative statements without attaching their claims to percentages. Here is what they report. Compared to those offenders who went to court, those going to conferences have higher levels of procedural justice, higher levels of restorative justice and an increased respect for the police and law. Compared to victims whose cases went to court, conference victims have higher levels of recovery from the offence. Conference victims also had high levels of procedural justice, but they could not be compared to court victims, who rarely attended court proceedings. These summary statements are the tip of the RISE iceberg. In a detailed analysis of the RISE website results, Kurki (2001) finds offence-based differences in the court and conference experiences of RISE participants, and she notes that RISE researchers' reports of claimed court and conference differences are not uniform across offence types.

Like other studies, the South Australia Juvenile Justice (SAJJ) Research on Conferencing Project finds very high levels of procedural justice registered by offenders and victims at conferences. To items such as, were you treated fairly, were you treated with respect, did you have a say in the agreement, among others, 80 to 95 per cent of victims and offenders said that they were treated fairly and had a say. In light of the procedural justice literature (Tyler, 1990; Tyler *et al.*, 1997), these findings are important. Procedural justice scholars argue that when citizens perceive a legal process as fair, when they are listened to and treated with respect, there is an affirmation of the legitimacy of the legal order.

Compared to the high levels of perceived procedural justice, the SAJJ project finds relatively less evidence of restorativeness. The measures of restorativeness tapped the degree to which offenders and victims recognized the other and were affected by the other; they focused on the degree to which there was positive movement between the offender and victim and their supporters during the conference (the SAJJ measures are more concrete and relational measures of restorativeness than those used in RISE). Whereas very high proportions of victims and offenders (80 to 95 per cent) said that the process was fair (among other variables tapping procedural justice), 'restorativeness' was evident in 30 to 50 per cent of conferences (depending on the item), and solidly in no more than about one-third. Thus, in this jurisdiction where conferences are used *routinely*,[8] fairness can more easily be achieved than restorativeness. As but one example, from the interviews we learned that from the victims' perspectives, less than 30 per cent of offenders were perceived as making genuine apologies, but from the offenders' perspectives, close to 60 per cent said their apology was genuine.

The SAJJ results lead me to think that young people (offenders) and victims orient themselves to a conference and what they hope to achieve in it in ways different than the advocacy literature imagines. The stance of empathy and openness to 'the other', the expectation of being able to speak and reflect on one's actions and the presence of new justice norms (or language) emphasizing repair – all of these are novel cultural elements for most participants. Young people appear to be as, if not more, interested in *repairing their own reputations* than in repairing the harm to victims. Among the most important things that the victims hoped would occur at the conference was for the offender to hear how the offence affected them, but half the offenders told us that the victim's story had no effect or only a little effect on them.

How often, then, does the exceptional or 'nirvana' story of repair and goodwill occur? I devised a measure that combined the SAJJ observer's judgement of the degree to which a conference 'ended on a high, a positive note of repair and good will' with one that rated the conference on a five-point scale from poor to exceptional. While the first tapped the degree to which there was movement between victims, offenders and their supporters towards each other, the second tapped a more general feeling about the conference dynamics and how well the conference was managed by the co-ordinator. With this combined measure, 10 per cent of conferences were rated very highly, another 40 per cent, good; and the rest, a mixed, fair or poor rating. If conferencing is used routinely (not just in a select set of cases), I suspect that the story of Sam and Uncle George will be infrequent; it may happen 10 per cent of the time, if that.

Assessing the 'effects' of conferences on participants is complex because such effects change over time and, for victims, they are contingent on whether offenders come through on promises made, as we learned from research in New Zealand. I present findings on victims' sense of having recovered from the offence and on young people's reoffending in the post-conference period. In the Year 2 (1999) interviews with victims, over 60 per cent said they had 'fully recovered' from the offence, that it was 'all behind' them. Their recovery was more likely when offenders completed the agreement than when they did not, but recovery was influenced by a mixture of elements: the conference process, support from family and friends, the passage of time and personal resources such as their own resilience. The SAJJ project finds that conferences *can* have positive effects on reducing victims' anger towards and fear of offenders. Drawing from the victim interviews in 1998 and 1999, over 75 per cent of victims felt angry towards the offender before the conference, but this dropped to 44 per cent after the conference and was 39 per cent a year later. Close to 40 per cent of victims were frightened of the offender before the conference, but this dropped to 25 per cent after the conference and was 18 per cent a year later. Therefore, for victims, meeting offenders in the conference setting can have beneficial results.

The conference effect everyone asks about is, does it reduce reoffending? Proof (or disproof) of reductions in reoffending from conferences (compared *not only to court*, but to other interventions such as formal caution, other diversion approaches or no legal action at all) will not be available for a long time, if ever. The honest answer to the reoffending question is 'we'll probably never know' because the amounts of money would be exorbitant and research methods using experimental designs judged too risky in an ethical and political sense.

To date, there have been three studies of conferencing and reoffending in Australia and New Zealand, one of which compares reoffending for a sample of offenders randomly assigned to conference and court and two that explore whether reoffending can be linked to things that occur in conferences.[9] The RISE project finds that for one of four major offence categories studied (violent offences compared to drink-driving, property offences, shoplifting), those offenders who were assigned to a conference had a significantly reduced rate of reoffending than those who were assigned to court (Sherman *et al.*, 2000).

As others have said (Abel, 1982: 278; Levrant *et al.*, 1999: 17–22), there is a great faith placed on the conference process to change young offenders, when the conditions of their day-to-day lives, which may be conducive to getting into trouble, may not change at all. The SAJJ project asked if there were things that occurred in conferences that could predict reoffending, over and above those variables known to be conducive to lawbreaking (and its detection): past offending and social marginality (Hayes and Daly, 2001). In a regression analysis with a simultaneous inclusion of variables, we found that over and above the young person's race-ethnicity (Aboriginal or non-Aboriginal), sex, whether s/he offended prior to the offence that led to the SAJJ conference and a measure of the young person's mobility and marginality, there were two conference elements associated with reoffending. When young people were observed to be mostly or fully remorseful and when outcomes were achieved by genuine consensus, they were less likely to reoffend during an 8- to 12-month period after the conference. These results are remarkably similar to those of Maxwell and Morris (2000) in their study of reoffending in New Zealand. They found that what happens in conferences (e.g. a young person's expressions of remorse and agreeing [or not] with the outcome, among other variables) could distinguish those young people who were and were not 'persistently reconvicted' during a six-and-a-half-year follow-up period.

[...]

In the political arena, telling the mythical true story of restorative justice may be an effective means of reforming parts of the justice system. It may inspire legislatures to pass new laws and it may provide openings to experiment with alternative justice forms. All of this can be a good thing. Perhaps, in fact, the politics of selling justice ideas may *require* people to tell mythical true stories. The real story attends to the murk and constraints of justice organizations, of people's experiences as offenders and victims and their capacities and desires to 'repair the harm'. It reveals a picture that is less sharp-edged and more equivocal. My reading of the evidence is that face-to-face encounters between victims and offenders and their supporters *is* a practice worth maintaining, and perhaps enlarging, although we should not expect it to deliver strong stories of repair and goodwill most of the time. If we want to avoid the cycle of optimism and pessimism (Matthews, 1988) that so often attaches to any justice innovation, then we should be courageous and tell the real story of restorative justice. But, in telling the real story, there is some risk that a promising, fledgling idea will meet a premature death.

This extract is taken from 'Restorative Justice: the Real Story', by Kathleen Daly, in Punishment and Society, *4:1 (2002), pp. 5–79.*

Notes

1 Even when calling for the need to 'blend restorative, reparative, and transformative justice . . . with the prosecution of paradigmatic violations of human rights', Drumbl

(2000: 296) is unable to avoid using the term 'retributive' to refer to responses that should be reserved for the few.

2 Drawing from Cottingham's (1979) analysis of retribution's many meanings, restorative justice advocates tend to use retributivism to mean 'repayment' (to which they add a punitive kick) whereas desert theorists, such as von Hirsch (1993), use retributivism to mean 'deserved' and would argue for decoupling retribution from punitiveness.

3 It is important to emphasize that new justice practices have not been applied to the fact-finding stage of the criminal process; they are used almost exclusively for the penalty phase. Some comparative claims about restorative justice practices (e.g. they are not adversarial when retributive justice is) are misleading in that restorative justice attends only to the penalty phase when negotiation is possible. No one has yet sketched a restorative justice process for those who do not admit to an offence.

4 I became aware of the term *new justice* from La Prairie's (1999) analysis of developments in Canada. She defines new justice initiatives as representing a 'shift away from a justice discourse of punitiveness and punishment toward one of reconciliation, healing, repair, atonement, and reintegration' (1999: 147), and she sees such developments as part of a new emphasis on 'community' and 'partnership' as analysed by Crawford (1997). There may be better terms than the 'old' and 'new' justice' (e.g. Hudson, 2001, suggests 'established criminal justice' for the old justice), but my general point is that the retributive/restorative couplet has produced, and continues to produce, significant conceptual confusion in the field.

5 Restorative justice advocates speak of the *harm* not of the *crime*, and in doing so, they elide a crucial distinction between a civil and criminal harm, the latter involving both a *harm* and a *wrong* (Duff, 2001).

6 In response to this point, one reader said there had to be some way to theorize varied justice forms (both in an empirical and normative sense), and thus, the disappointment I speak of reflects a disenchantment with the theoretical enterprise adequately to reflect particularity and variation in the empirical social world. This is a long-standing problem in the sociological field. What troubles me, however, is the construction of theoretical terms in the justice field, which use dualisms in adversarial and oppositional relation to one another.

7 The major research studies in the region are Maxwell and Morris (1993) for New Zealand, Strang *et al.* (1999) for the ACT and the RISE project and the results reported here for the SAJJ project in South Australia. See Daly (2001) for a review of these and other studies. Space limitations preclude a detailed review of the methods and results of each study.

8 It is important to distinguish jurisdictions like South Australia, New South Wales and New Zealand, where conferences are routinely used, from other jurisdictions (like Victoria and Queensland), where conferences are used selectively and in a relatively few number of cases (although Queensland practices are undergoing change as of April 2001). When conferences are used routinely, we should not expect to see 'restorativeness' emerging most of the time.

9 Space limitations preclude a review of the definitions and methods used in the reoffending studies; rather general findings are summarized.

References

Abel, R.L. (1982) 'The Contradictions of Informal Justice', in Abel, R.L. (ed.) *The Politics of Informal Justice. Vol. 1* (New York, NY: Academic Press), pp. 267–320.

Barton, C. (2000) 'Empowerment and Retribution in Criminal Justice', in Strang, H. and Braithwaite, J. (eds) *Restorative Justice: Philosophy to Practice* (Aldershot: Ashgate/Dartmouth), pp. 55–76.

Blagg, H. (1997) 'A Just Measure of Shame? Aboriginal Youth and Conferencing in Australia', *British Journal of Criminology*, 37:4, pp. 481–501.

Blagg, H. (1998) 'Restorative Visions and Restorative Justice Practices: Conferencing, Ceremony and Reconciliation in Australia', *Current Issues in Criminal Justice*, 10:1, pp. 5–14.

Bottoms, A.E. (1998) 'Five Puzzles in von Hirsch's Theory of Punishment', in Ashworth, A. and Wasik, M. (eds) *Fundamentals of Sentencing Theory: Essays in Honour of Andrew von Hirsch* (Oxford: Clarendon Press), pp. 53–100.

Braithwaite, J. (1996) 'Restorative Justice and a Better Future', Dorothy J. Killam Memorial Lecture, reprinted in *Dalhousie Review*, 76:1, pp. 9–32.

Braithwaite, J. (1999) 'Restorative Justice: Assessing Optimistic and Pessimistic Accounts', in Tonry, M. (ed.) *Crime and Justice: A Review of Research. Vol. 25* (Chicago, IL: University of Chicago Press), pp. 1–127.

Braithwaite, J. and Pettit, P. (1990) *Not Just Deserts: A Republican Theory of Criminal Justice* (New York, NY: Oxford University Press).

Cain, M. (2000) 'Orientalism, Occidentalism and the Sociology of Crime', *British Journal of Criminology*, 40:2, pp. 239–60.

Consedine, J. (1995) *Restorative Justice: Healing the Effects of Crime* (Lyttelton, New Zealand: Ploughshares Publications).

Coombs, M. (1995) 'Putting Women First', *Michigan Law Review*, 93:6, pp. 1686–712.

Cottingham, J. (1979) 'Varieties of Retribution', *Philosophical Quarterly*, 29, pp. 238–46.

Crawford, A. (1997) *The Local Governance of Crime: Appeals to Community and Partnerships* (Oxford: Clarendon Press).

Daly, K. (1989) 'Criminal Justice Ideologies and Practices in Different Voices: Some Feminist Questions about Justice', *International Journal of the Sociology of Law*, 17:1, pp. 1–18.

Daly, K. (1998) 'Restorative Justice: Moving past the caricatures', paper presented to Seminar on Restorative Justice, Institute of Criminology, University of Sydney Law School, Sydney, April. Available at: http://www.gv.edu.au/school/ccj/kdaly.html.

Daly, K. (2000a) 'Revisiting the Relationship Between Retributive and Restorative Justice', in Strang, H. and Braithwaite, J. (eds) *Restorative Justice: Philosophy to Practice* (Aldershot: Ashgate/Dartmouth), pp. 33–54.

Daly, K. (2000b) 'Sexual Assault and Restorative Justice.' Paper presented to Restorative Justice and Family Violence Conference, Australian National University, Canberra, July (available at: http://www.gu.edu.au/school/ccj/kdaly.html).

Daly, K. (2001) 'Conferencing in Australia and New Zealand: Variations, Research Findings and Prospects', in Morris, A. and Maxwell, G. (eds) *Restorative Justice for Juveniles: Conferencing, Mediation and Circles* (Oxford: Hart Publishing), pp. 59–84 (available at: http://www.gu.edu.au/school/ccj/kdaly.html).

Daly, K. and Immarigeon, R. (1998) 'The Past, Present, and Future of Restorative Justice: Some Critical Reflections', *Contemporary Justice Review*, 1:1, pp. 21–45.

Davis, G. (1992) *Making Amends: Mediation and Reparation in Criminal Justice* (London: Routledge).

Drumbl, M.A. (2000) 'Retributive Justice and the Rwandan Genocide', *Punishment and Society*, 2:3, pp. 287–308.

Duff, R.A. (1992) 'Alternatives to Punishment – or Alternative Punishments?' in Cragg, W. (ed.) *Retributivism and its Critics* (Stuttgart: Franz Steiner), pp. 44–68.

Duff, R.A. (1996) 'Penal Communications: Recent Work in the Philosophy of Punishment', in Tonry, M. (ed.) *Crime and Justice: A Review of Research. Vol. 20* (Chicago, IL: University of Chicago Press), pp. 1–97.

Duff, R.A. (2001) 'Restoration and Retribution.' Paper presented to the Cambridge Seminar on Restorative Justice, Toronto, May.

Feeley, M. and Simon, J. (1992) 'The New Penology: Notes on the Emerging Strategy of Corrections and its Implications', *Criminology*, 30:4, pp. 449–74.

Findlay, M. (2000) 'Decolonising Restoration and Justice in Transitional Cultures', in Strang, H. and Braithwaite, J. (eds) *Restorative Justice: Philosophy to Practice* (Aldershot: Ashgate/Dartmouth), pp. 185–201.

Garland, D. (1996) 'The Limits of the Sovereign State', *British Journal of Criminology*, 36:4, pp. 445–71.

Gilligan, C. (1982) *In a Different Voice* (Cambridge, MA: Harvard University Press).

Gilligan, C. (1987) 'Moral Orientation and Moral Development', in Kittay, E. and Meyers, D. (eds) *Women and Moral Theory* (Totowa, NJ: Rowman & Littlefield), pp. 19–33.

Hampton, J. (1992) 'Correcting Harms versus Righting Wrongs: The Goal of Retribution', *UCLA Law Review*, 39, pp. 1659–702.

Hampton, J. (1998) 'Punishment, Feminism, and Political Identity: A Case Study in the Expressive Meaning of the Law', *Canadian Journal of Law and Jurisprudence*, 11:1, pp. 23–45.

Harris, M.K. (1987) 'Moving into the New Millennium: Toward a Feminist Vision of Justice', *The Prison Journal*, 67:2, pp. 27–38.

Hayes, H. and Daly, K. (2001) 'Family Conferencing in South Australia and Re-offending: Preliminary Results from the SAJJ Project.' Paper presented to the Australian and New Zealand Society of Criminology Conference, Melbourne, February (available at: http://www.gu.edu.au/school/ccj/kdaly.html).

Heidensohn, F. (1986) 'Models of Justice: Portia or Persephone? Some Thoughts on Equality, Fairness and Gender in the Field of Criminal Justice', *International Journal of the Sociology of Law*, 14:3–4, pp. 287–98.

Hudson, B. (2001) 'Victims and Offenders.' Paper presented to the Cambridge Seminar on Restorative Justice, Toronto, May.

Kurki, L. (2001) 'Evaluation of Restorative Justice Practices.' Paper presented to the Cambridge Seminar on Restorative Justice, Toronto, May.

La Prairie, C. (1999) 'Some Reflections on New Criminal Justice Policies in Canada: Restorative Justice, Alternative Measures and Conditional Sentences', *Australian and New Zealand Journal of Criminology*, 32:2, pp. 139–52.

Levrant, S., Cullen, F.T., Fulton, B. and Wozniak, J.F. (1999) 'Reconsidering Restorative Justice: The Corruption of Benevolence Revisited?', *Crime and Delinquency*, 45:1, pp. 3–27.

McCold, P. (2000) 'Toward a Holistic Vision of Restorative Juvenile Justice: A Reply to the Maximalist Model', *Contemporary Justice Review*, 3:4, pp. 357–414.

MacKinnon, C. (1987) *Feminism Unmodified* (Cambridge, MA: Harvard University Press).

Masters, G. and Smith, D. (1998) 'Portia and Persephone Revisited: Thinking about Feeling in Criminal Justice', *Theoretical Criminology*, 2:1, pp. 5–27.

Matthews, R. (1988) 'Reassessing Informal Justice', in Matthews, R. (ed.) *Informal Justice?* (Newbury Park, CA: Sage), pp. 1–24.

Maxwell, G. and Morris, A. (1993) *Family Victims and Culture: Youth Justice in New Zealand* (Wellington: Social Policy Agency and the Institute of Criminology, Victoria University of Wellington).

Maxwell, G. and Morris, A. (1996) 'Research on Family Group Conferences with Young Offenders in New Zealand', in Hudson, J. et al. (eds) *Family Group Conferences: Perspectives on Policy and Practice* (Monsey, NY: Willow Tree Press), pp. 88–110.

Maxwell, G. and Morris, A. (2000) 'Restorative Justice and Reoffending', in Strang,

H. and Braithwaite, J. (eds) *Restorative Justice: Philosophy to Practice* (Aldershot: Ashgate/Dartmouth), pp. 93–103.

Mead, G.H. (1917–18) 'The Psychology of Punitive Justice', *American Journal of Sociology*, 23, pp. 577–602.

Melossi, D. (ed.) (1998) *The Sociology of Punishment: Socio-structural Perspectives* (Aldershot: Ashgate/Dartmouth).

Miller, S. and Blackler, J. (2000) 'Restorative Justice: Retribution, Confession and Shame', in Strang, H. and Braithwaite, J. (eds) *Restorative Justice: Philosophy to Practice* (Aldershot: Ashgate/Dartmouth), pp. 77–91.

O'Malley, P. (1999) 'Volatile and Contradictory Punishment', *Theoretical Criminology*, 3:2, pp. 175–96.

Pavlich, G.C. (1996) *Justice Fragmented: Mediating Community Disputes under Postmodern Conditions* (New York, NY: Routledge).

Pratt, J. (2000) 'The Return of the Wheelbarrow Men or, The Arrival of Postmodern Penality?', *British Journal of Criminology*, 40:1, pp. 127–45.

Shearing, C. (2001) 'Punishment and the Changing Face of the Governance', *Punishment and Society*, 3:2, pp. 203–20.

Sherman, L.W., Strang, H. and Woods, D.J. (2000) *Recidivism Patterns in the Canberra Reintegrative Shaming Experiments (RISE)* (Canberra: Centre for Restorative Justice, Australian National University) (available at: http://www.aic.gov.au/rjustice/rise/recidivism/index.html).

Smart, C. (1989) *Feminism and the Power of Law* (London: Routledge).

Smart, C. (1992) 'The Women of Legal Discourse', *Social and Legal Studies*, 1:1, pp. 29–44.

Strang, H., Sherman, L.W., Barnes, G.C. and Braithwaite, J. (1999) *Experiments in Restorative Policing: A Progress Report to the National Police Research Unit on the Canberra Reintegrative Shaming Experiments (RISE)* (Canberra: Centre for Restorative Justice, Australian National University) (available at: http://www.aic.gov.au/rjustice/rise/index.html).

Tonry, M. (1999) 'Rethinking Unthinkable Punishment Policies in America', *UCLA Law Review*, 46:4, pp. 1751–91.

Tyler, T.R. (1990) *Why People Obey the Law* (New Haven, CT: Yale University Press).

Tyler, T.R., Boeckmann, R.J., Smith, H.J. and Huo, Y.J. (1997) *Social Justice in a Diverse Society* (Boulder, CO: Westview Press).

Umbreit, M. (1994) *Victim Meets Offender: The Impact of Restorative Justice and Mediation* (Monsey, NY: Criminal Justice Press).

Van Ness, D. (1993) 'New Wine and Old Wineskins: Four Challenges of Restorative Justice', *Criminal Law Forum*, 4:2, pp. 251–76.

Von Hirsch, A. (1993) *Censure and Sanctions* (New York, NY: Oxford University Press).

Walgrave, L. (1995) 'Restorative Justice for Juveniles: Just a Technique or a Fully Fledged Alternative?', *The Howard Journal*, 34:3, pp. 228–49.

Walgrave, L. and Aertsen, I. (1996) 'Reintegrative Shaming and Restorative Justice: Interchangeable, Complementary or Different?' *European Journal on Criminal Policy and Research*, 4:4, pp. 67–85.

Weitekamp, E. (1999) 'The History of Restorative Justice', in Bazemore, G. and Walgrave, L. (eds) *Restorative Juvenile Justice: Repairing the Harm of Youth Crime* (Monsey, NY: Criminal Justice Press), pp. 75–102.

Wright, M. (1991) *Justice for Victims and Offenders* (Philadelphia, PA: Open University Press).

Zedner, L. (1994) 'Reparation and Retribution: Are they Reconcilable?', *Modern Law Review*, 57:March, pp. 228–50.

26. Restorative punishment and punitive restoration

R. A. Duff

1. Introduction

My thesis can be stated quite simply. Our responses to crime should aim for 'restoration', for 'restorative justice': but the kind of restoration that criminal wrongdoing makes necessary is properly achieved through a process of retributive punishment. To put it the other way round, offenders should suffer retribution, punishment, for their crimes: but the essential purpose of such punishment should be to achieve restoration. To put it yet more simply, my slogan is 'Restoration through retribution'. That thesis sets me in opposition to advocates of restorative justice, and to those critics of restorative justice who argue for a 'just deserts' retributivism.

Both sides to this controversy are right in important respects. Advocates of restorative justice are right to insist that in our responses to, and understanding of, crime we should seek restoration, and such related aims as reparation and reconciliation; that we should not punish offenders just for the sake of making them suffer, or to deter them and others; and that our existing criminal procedures – our criminal trials, the kinds of punishment typically imposed on offenders – are ill-suited to the restorative ends that we should be pursuing. Proponents of just deserts are right to insist that punishment is the proper response to criminal wrongdoing, and that what justifies punishment is that it is *deserved* for that wrongdoing: it is the state's proper responsibility, and our responsibility as citizens, to bring criminal wrongdoers to suffer the punishments that they deserve.

However, both 'restorative' and 'retributive' theorists are wrong insofar as they suppose, as they often do, that we must choose *between* restoration and retribution as our primary aim. Thus critics of the restorative justice movement often assume that we have to choose between the 'punishment paradigm' and the 'restorative paradigm' (Ashworth, 1993) – and argue that we should choose the former, since the pursuit of restorative aims is incompatible with the demands of penal justice. Advocates of restorative justice often assume that we must choose between restorative and retributive justice – and argue that we must choose the former, since punitive retribution cannot serve the aim of restoration.[1] This shared assumption is, as I will argue, mistaken. Once we understand what restoration must involve in the context of criminal wrongdoing, and what retribution can mean in the context of criminal punishment, we will see that restoration is not only compatible with retribution and punishment, but *requires* it.

Restorative theorists will therefore accuse me of undermining the eirenic, reconciliatory aims of restorative justice by a desire to punish, to 'deliver pain' (see Christie, 1981), which is utterly at odds with those aims; proponents of punishment as 'just deserts' will accuse me of abandoning the principles of penal justice in favour of ill-defined aspirations to 'restoration' which are utterly at odds with the central demands of proportionality and penal restraint. My argument will be, however, that restorative and retributive justice are not thus opposed.

My claim is not that existing 'restorative justice' programmes are punitive (though many do have a punitive dimension); nor that our existing penal practices are generally restorative (which would be absurd). There is an obvious incompatibility between existing restorative practices and existing penal practices, and between the conceptions of 'restoration' favoured by many restorative theorists and the conceptions of punishment held by many advocates of punitive or retributive justice. I will argue, however, that once we gain a better understanding of the *concepts* of restoration and of punishment, we will be able to dissolve the apparent conflict between them, and to see that criminal punishment should aim at restoration, whilst restorative justice programmes should aim to impose appropriate kinds of punishment.

To make out this argument, I begin, in s. 2, with the question of what 'restoration' should mean in the context of wrongdoing – of what needs to be restored and how it can be restored; apology and moral reparation will be crucial here. In s. 3 I apply the results of s. 2 to the case of crime, and offer an account of the proper aims of victim–offender mediation programmes – which are often portrayed as paradigms of restorative justice: such programmes, I will argue, should be understood not as alternatives to punishment, but as paradigms of punishment, and thus as models for the criminal justice system.

2. Restoration and wrongdoing

Standard definitions of 'restorative justice' are, inevitably, rather vague. To say, for instance, that it is 'a process whereby parties with a stake in a specific offence collectively resolve how to deal with the aftermath of the offence and its implications for the future' (Marshall, 1999: 5); or that its purpose 'is the restoration into safe communities of victims and offenders who have resolved their conflicts' (Van Ness, 1993: 258) leaves open crucial questions about the significance of the 'offence' or 'conflict', and about what can count as successfully 'dealing with' the 'aftermath' or 'implications' of the offence, or 'resolving' the conflict. My main concern in this section is with the question of what kind of 'restoration' is made necessary by criminal wrongdoing: but it is worth pausing briefly to think about the implications of the basic idea of 'restoration'.

Many different kinds of thing can be 'restored'. Property which was lost or stolen can be restored, i.e. given back, to its owner; paintings which have been damaged can be restored to their pristine glory. Health which was undermined through illness can be restored – the sick can become well again. Reputations which were damaged by accusation or by slander can be restored, if the truth is established and published, which can also restore the person's standing in the community. Security – both the fact of being safe from danger and the awareness that one is thus safe[2] – can be restored after it has been undermined; the danger which threatened, or seemed to threaten, is removed, and we are re-assured of our safety. Trust which has been undermined can be restored; so too can relationships – of friendship, of love, of collegiality, of fellow citizenship – which have been damaged or weakened. What is common to all these cases is the retrieval of an original favourable condition. That original condition – of health, of security or trust, of good reputation, of friendship, for instance – is lost or removed, so that the good internal to it is lost. But that good is then regained: the condition is reinstated, the *status quo ante* is restored.

Restoration strictly speaking must thus be distinguished from such concepts as reparation and compensation. Restoration requires the re-instatement of the *status quo ante*. A harm was caused, a wrong was done, and its memory might remain: but when restoration is achieved, it is now (apart from the memory) as if the harm or wrong had never occurred. Reparation and compensation, by contrast, seek to make up for the loss of what cannot thus be restored. Thus when property is lost or stolen, it might be restored – the owner might get back the very thing she lost. But it might not be restorable: it might have been destroyed or sold on beyond recall, in which case all that is possible is reparation or compensation rather than restoration. If the silver I inherited from my mother is stolen and melted down, my property cannot be restored; the most I can gain is a replacement, or compensation that will to some degree 'make up for' my loss.[3] Similarly, when health is lost, it might be restorable: the patient might return to as healthy a condition as she was in before illness struck. But it might not be thus restorable: she might be left permanently disabled or weakened; and the pain that she might have undergone during the illness cannot be 'restored', even if the illness is cured. This point raises a serious question about what we could even hope to restore in the context of crime or wrongdoing: we must ask what harm is done, what goods are lost or damaged, that we could even aspire to restore.

We might at first think of the material, physical or psychological effects that wrongdoing typically causes: property is lost or damaged; physical injuries are suffered; fear, anxiety and distress are caused, as may be other, more lasting kinds of psychological damage. But, first, even if some such harms do permit of genuine restoration (if the victim's property or physical or psychological health can be restored), others do not: we cannot make it for the victim as if the wrong had never been done, since we cannot wipe out her suffering; we cannot make it as if she never suffered that fear, anxiety or distress. If we focus on these kinds of non-restorable harm, we must therefore think of reparation or compensation, not of restoration. (This is not to deny that reparation and compensation have an important role to play in an enterprise of restorative justice: it is simply to insist that they cannot in themselves *constitute* restoration – that their role should rather be seen as means to restoration.) Second, to focus on such harms as these is to ignore the fact that the victim was *wronged*. He did not simply lose his property, or suffer accidental damage to it – it was stolen, or maliciously destroyed or damaged; he did not simply suffer injury through natural causes or in an accident – he was *attacked*. Surely the harm he has suffered, what needs to be restored, must be understood in a way that includes its wrongful character.[4]

We might meet both these points by talking not (just) about the material or psychological effects of the wrongdoing on the victim, but about the relationships it damaged – between the wrongdoer and his direct victim (when there is one), between the wrongdoer and the wider communities to which he and the victim belong – communities which might be intimate and close, such as a family or a group of friends; or less intimate but still relatively local, such as a village or residential neighbourhood; or impersonally large, such as a political community whose bounds are co-extensive with those of a particular legal system.[5] Those relationships were damaged by the wrongdoer's deed, and need now to be restored. However, if we are to understand what could restore such relationships, what could even count as their restoration, we must get clear about the kind of damage they have suffered.

It might be tempting to try to describe that damage in purely factual or empirical terms: the victim, and others, are angry with the wrongdoer, or fearful or mistrustful of him, or are unwilling still to engage in their former common activities with him; the wrongdoer himself might feel ill at ease with or estranged from them. Now if we see the damage in such terms, we will naturally see 'restoration' in similarly empirical terms, as a matter of securing such changes in the attitudes and feelings of those concerned that they are no longer angry, fearful, untrusting, or hostile; and we will look for techniques that might help to secure such changes. But such a perspective is quite inadequate, since it leaves out the crucial fact that the victim was *wronged* by the wrongdoer. We are not just dealing with an empirical breakdown in the relationship – a breakdown which, as thus described, leaves it open whether it was anyone's fault; we are dealing with a breach created in the relationship, or damage done to it, by one party's wrongdoing.[6] The wrongdoer denied or flouted the values – of mutual trust, concern and respect – by which their relationship as friends, neighbours, colleagues or fellow citizens was supposedly defined; in doing so, he damaged that relationship as a normative relationship part constituted by those values.

The damage to the relationship must therefore be understood in *normative*, not merely in empirical, terms. There are three crucial features of this normative perspective.

First, we must understand, and appraise, the responses of those involved as responses to a wrong that was done – and as being reasonable or unreasonable, justified or unjustified, as responses to that wrong. The victim is not just angry, but indignant at the wrong he suffered; and we cannot then avoid asking whether his anger is justified. Perhaps it is excessive – the wrong was not *that* serious, the wrongdoer was not *that* culpable. Or perhaps it is too weak – he should be more indignant, more angry, than he is: for not to be angered by a wrong done to me can display a lack of self-respect (see Murphy, 1988: 16–18), or a blindness to the moral quality of others' conduct. The reactions of others, and of the wrongdoer, are likewise subject to normative appraisal: we must ask not just what they in fact feel, but what they should feel; and our understanding of the damage done to their relationships is determined in crucial part by our understanding of their responses as reasonable or as unreasonable. If someone is so angry with me that he will have no more to do with me unless and until I offer him a profuse apology, our relationship has broken down: but our understanding of the character and the implications of that breach will depend on whether his anger is a justified response to some serious wrong that I did him, or an unjustified response to an imagined slight.

Second, we might sometimes want to say – and be justified in saying – that a relationship has been thus damaged even if those directly involved do not react as if it has been damaged, or do not even realise that it has been damaged. Suppose that a friend – or someone I thought was a friend – seriously betrays my trust for his own profit. Perhaps, because I don't want to have to face up to the implications of this, I try to persuade myself that the breach of trust was not that serious; or perhaps I don't even know what he has done, and so sincerely believe that our friendship is intact.[7] Others might still properly say that the friendship *has* been seriously damaged by his betrayal, since that betrayal was utterly inconsistent with, a complete denial of, the bonds of mutual trust and concern by which friendship is defined. If the betrayal was serious enough, others might indeed think that the friendship has been *destroyed*, unless the friend and I together face up to its implications and try to deal with it: whatever relationship we might maintain, that is, can no longer count as a friendship.

Third, when we ask what can restore the relationship, or repair the damage done to it, we must ask not just what will in fact make the parties feel better, or quell their anger, mistrust or fear, but what would be *normatively* adequate to restore it – what would make it *appropriate* to desist from anger, to renew trust, to restore community? Since it was the wrongdoing that damaged the relationship, it is that that must be repaired: but how can that be done? Material damage that was caused might be repaired; property that was stolen might be given back or replaced; physical injuries might be healed: but what can repair the *wrong* that was done?

Different relationships admit of different kinds of repair: but the obvious, paradigm way of repairing the normative harm wrought by wrongdoing is apology; and whilst apology can take various different forms in different relationships and contexts, and can be implicit rather than explicit, we can make some general points about the character or meaning of apologies for wrongdoing.[8] These points can be summarised as the three 'R's of apology: recognition, repentance and reconciliation. Apology expresses the wrongdoer's recognition of the wrong he has done, his repentance, and his desire for reconciliation with those whom he wronged – for the restoration of the relationships he damaged. (I am speaking here of sincere apologies; I will comment later on the problem of insincerity.)

Recognition of the wrong as a wrong is clearly an indispensable first step. It is something that is owed to the victim by others in general (whose sympathetic response to him should be structured by the recognition that he has been not just harmed, but wronged), but especially by the wrongdoer; in recognising the wrong done to him, we recognise his moral standing as a fellow human being who demands our concern and respect (see Gaita, 1991: chs. 1–4). Such recognition on the part of the wrongdoer might of course be spontaneous: she comes, perhaps at once, to see for herself the wrong she has done, and to understand its implications. But it is a painfully familiar fact about human beings that we are for a host of reasons often very slow to recognise our own wrongdoings: we often need others to persuade us to face up to what we have done. This is an important role that such responses as blame, criticism and censure play, as well as the often forcible expression of such emotions as anger and indignation: to bring a wrongdoer to recognise what she has done – a recognition that her apology then expresses.

Recognition includes understanding: to recognise the wrong I have done involves not just realising *that* I did wrong, but coming to grasp the character, seriousness and implications of that wrong. It also includes or leads to repentance: for sincerely to recognise what I did as a wrong is to recognise it as something that I should not have done – which is also to repent my having done it. One who says 'Yes, I recognise that I did wrong, but so what? I'd do it again tomorrow' has not, we should say, truly recognised the wrong as a wrong; at most, he sees it as something that others call 'wrong'.[9] To repent my past wrongdoing is both to own and to disown it: I own it as mine, as something for which I must accept responsibility (and blame); but I disown it as something that I now wish I had not done, and that I repudiate (and, since repentance also involves a commitment to self-reform, as something that I will try to avoid in future). What I owe to those I have wronged, and what others may try to persuade me to if I need persuasion, is such a repentant recognition of the wrong I have done – a repentance that apology can also express. We should note too that such repentance is of its nature painful: the repentant wrongdoer cares, or has come to care, for those whom she wronged, for the values she violated; she must therefore be pained by that wrong and that violation.

An apology which expresses my repentant recognition of the wrong I have done thereby also expresses my desire, my hope, for reconciliation with those whom I wronged. At least in the case of serious wrongs, I realise that I have by my wrongdoing damaged or threatened (if not destroyed) my relationship with them – our friendship, our marriage, our relationship as neighbours or as colleagues; if that relationship is to be restored, I must seek their forgiveness through my apology.[10] For reconciliation to be complete, the other must accept my apology: it might not be possible, psychologically or morally, literally to 'forgive and forget', but the forgiving acceptance of my apology does suffice, normatively, to restore the relationship and to heal the breach.

Now apologies are supposed to be sincere, and in many contexts they have value only if they are, and are known to be, sincere. It is worth noting, however, that there can sometimes be value even in apologies that are not or might not be sincere, in formal apologies that might be to some degree a matter of ritual. Just as – or so it is said – hypocrisy is a homage that vice pays to virtue, so insincere apology can be a homage that an unrepentant wrongdoer pays to social morality: if it is not merely offered out of short-term prudence, it can express a concern to preserve the bonds of community. Furthermore, the demand that the wrongdoer apologise, even if we suspect that his apology will not be sincere, can communicate both to him and to the victim our recognition of the wrong that he did; and we can hope that the experience of apologising might help to bring him to recognise for himself the wrong that he did.[11]

Sometimes, however, merely verbal apology might not be enough, at least for a relatively serious wrong: even a sincere verbal apology might not be adequate to the seriousness of the wrong done. It is a general, deep feature of our lives that we need to give more than merely verbal form and expression to things that matter to us, especially when that expression has a public significance. We express our gratitude for a great service done to us by a gift or, in the public realm, by a public reward or honour; we express our grief at a death through the rituals of a funeral. Such more-than-merely-verbal modes of expression have two related purposes: they make the expression more forceful to others than a merely verbal expression would have been, and they can help to focus the expresser's own attention on what needs to be expressed.

An apology can thus be strengthened, made more forceful, if it is given more than merely verbal form; and this can also help to focus the wrongdoer's attention (an attention which, as we all know from painful personal experience, is all too easily distracted) on the wrong that he did and the need to seek forgiveness and reconciliation for it. Mere words, and especially between strangers, can be too cheap – too easy to say, without any real depth of meaning; too easy to forget, without thinking about their meaning;[12] by giving apology some more material expression, we can both strengthen and express its sincerity.

If we then ask what this more than merely verbal form could be, the obvious answer is that it could consist in some kind of reparation. If the wrongdoing caused a material harm or loss that it is within the wrongdoer's power to make good, he can make reparation by making it good. If it caused no such harm, or if the wrongdoer cannot make the harm good, he must find some other way of 'making up' for what he did: some other way of making his repentant recognition of what he did forcefully clear both to the victim and to others. Depending on the context, on the nature of the wrong, and on the relationship it threatened, this might involve, for instance, undertaking some service for the victim, or for the wider community; or buying the victim a thoughtful gift; or contributing time or money to a suitable charity; or agreeing to seek appropriate help to avoid repeating the wrong (someone whose addiction has led him to steal from his friends might agree to embark on a treatment programme).

We must be clear about the meaning and point of these kinds of reparation, and how they differ from reparation or compensation that aims only to repair or make up for some material harm that I have caused. If I damage or destroy your property through carelessness, it is only just that I should, if I can (and if you are not insured) pay for it to be repaired or replaced: the loss should fall on the person who culpably caused it. In this context, all that matters is that the material loss is made good, as far as that is possible. In particular, whilst I might find the reparations burdensome, it is no part of their purpose or meaning that they be burdensome: if I am so rich that the necessary payment does not impinge even briefly on my financial well-being, the payment still makes adequate reparation – as adequate as it would if I was so poor that it was really burdensome to me. By contrast, the kind of moral reparation that is needed to give an apology for wrongdoing a suitably forceful expression *must* be burdensome to the wrongdoer. Undertaking a task that is in no way burdensome to me (because it is something that I would have done anyway or anyway enjoy doing); or making a payment that is so small relative to my means that it constitutes no financial burden: these cannot constitute the kind of moral reparation that gives force to an apology. If, as I have suggested, mere words might not be enough to constitute a sufficiently serious apology for wrongdoing, a reparation that imposes no real burden on the wrongdoer cannot suffice either – it costs too little to add force to a verbal apology. If I am to show you (and myself) that I really do repent my wrongdoing, by offering a more than merely verbal apology, the reparation I undertake must be something burdensome – something that symbolises the burden of moral injury that I laid on my victims and would now like (if only I could) to take on myself; the burden of wrongdoing that I laid on myself; and the burden of remorse that I now feel.[13]

I have talked so far about our informal responses to moral wrongdoing, and about what 'restoration' can amount to in that context. I have argued so far that what needs 'restoring', and what could conceivably be restored, is not so much any material harm that was caused, as the relationships that were damaged by the wrongdoing; that that damage must be understood in normative terms, as involving a flouting or denial of the normative bonds by which the relationship was defined; that it can be made good only by an apology which expresses the wrongdoer's repentant recognition of his wrongdoing and his desire for reconciliation; and that, at least in the case of serious wrongs, the apology might need to be given more forceful expression by some kind of moral reparation which must be burdensome to the wrongdoer.

I have talked in rather crude, general and abstract terms – terms which might seem quite inadequate to the subtle complexities and variations to be found in the wide range of human relationships within which wrongs may be done and repaired. If we think of the very different ways in which different kinds of wrongdoing can be understood and dealt with between, for instance, lovers; or between friends; or between colleagues; or in local neighbourhoods; or in any of the other kinds of community by which our lives are structured: it might seem simply foolish to hope to give any *general* account of wrongdoing and restoration that would apply to all these different kinds of case. However, first, I do not need to claim that what I have said so far applies to every kind of relationship; all I need, and do, claim is that it applies to many relationships. Second, at least some of these variations in ways of responding to wrongdoing can be seen as variations in ways of expressing or articulating the normative damage done by the wrongdoing, or in the forms that apology and reparation can take: that is to say, the basic structure that I have sketched in this section is still there, but is fleshed out in different ways.

My main concern, however, is to show how these comments about the kind of restoration that wrongdoing requires in informal, extra-legal contexts can clarify the idea of restoration in the context of crime – and make good my claim that restoration is to be achieved through retributive punishment.

3. Crime, mediation and punishment

The criminal law defines a wide range of 'public' wrongs. It specifies types of conduct from which citizens should refrain because they are wrongful, in terms of the (supposedly) shared values of the political community whose law it is; it claims the authority thus to declare what, as citizens, we may or may not do. The wrongs that it defines are 'public', not in the sense that they must cause some harm to the 'public' as distinct from an individual victim, but in the sense that they are matters of proper public concern.[14] In terms of its empirical effects, the violent attack perpetrated by a drunken man on his wife might cause harm only to her; and such attacks have, notoriously, sometimes been seen as 'private' affairs in which the criminal law has no proper interest – 'domestics', as they used to be called by English police who would be very reluctant to intervene in them. To claim that they constitute public wrongs which should be taken seriously by the criminal law is to claim not that they cause further, as yet unnoticed, harm to 'the public' or the community, but that they are a kind of wrong which should concern the community as a whole: we should collectively share in the wrong done to the wife as her fellow citizens, since it is a wrong that flouts the defining values of our polity; it is for us, collectively, to respond to that wrong – rather than leaving it for her to deal with it as a private matter. Similarly, to say that burglary and robbery should be crimes is to say that such wrongs should not be left as private matters between the victim and the wrongdoer, or as matters of civil law, which leaves it to the victim to sue the wrongdoer for private reparation: they are wrongs that should concern us all, as the victim's fellow citizens, and that require a collective response.

But what kind of response is appropriate? Those who think that we must choose between 'restorative' and 'retributive' justice might think that we must choose between a response – for instance, some kind of mediation process – which aims at restoration, and a response – the normal criminal process, for instance – which aims simply to punish the offender. However, my comments in the previous section on informal responses to wrongdoing should have laid the foundations for the argument, to be sketched in this section, that this is a false dichotomy.

Suppose that some kind of mediation programme is available, and that both offender and victim (violent husband and battered wife; burglar and victim) agree to take part in it.[15] What should be the aims of the mediation?

It is important, I suggest, that the mediation focus not just on the harm that was caused, but on the wrong that was done. What matters is not just that the victim has suffered certain kinds of physical injury, or loss of property, or distressing psychological states; nor just that, since it was the offender who culpably caused those harms, the cost of repairing them or of providing compensation for them should fall on him: but that he committed a serious *wrong* against her. It is that wrong on which the criminal law focuses (by contrast, the civil law is concerned with harms or losses, and with who should pay for them); it is on that wrong that any adequate response to the offender's crime, and to the victim, must focus; and we must therefore ask what kind of 'restoration' that wrong makes necessary.

The answer that I suggest should be obvious from the previous section. What needs to be restored, and what can in principle be restored, is the offender's normative relationship with his victim as a fellow citizen, and with his fellow citizens more generally. For the criminal law is concerned not with our more local, intimate and optional relationships as friends, as lovers, as neighbours, as colleagues, but simply with our (somewhat more abstract, detached and non-optional) relationships as fellow citizens: it defines the values and constraints which make our common life as citizens possible. What matters to the criminal law is therefore the wrongs done by one citizen to other citizens, and the damage done by those wrongs to their relationships as citizens. The offender's crime damaged his relationships both with his victim, as a fellow citizen, and with his fellow citizens more generally, by denying those values – of mutual respect and concern – that are supposed to define their civic relations, and that make civic life possible; it is that damage that must be repaired, to restore those relationships.

When such a wrong has been committed, it should be recognised: this is something that is owed to the victim, and is anyway a simple implication of taking seriously the values that the offender has violated. It should be recognised by the victim's fellow citizens, who can manifest that recognition both in their direct responses to the victim (responses of sympathy, of assistance), and in their responses to the offender: in, most obviously, the way in which they condemn or criticise him for what he has done – a kind of condemnation and criticism that is given formal expression by a criminal trial and conviction.[16] It should be recognised by the offender: he owes it to his victim to recognise the wrong he has done to her, and to his fellow citizens to recognise the way in which he has violated the public values of the polity. It is then quite appropriate that one of the initial aims of the mediation process should be, as it is often said to be, to get the offender to recognise, to understand, what he has done (and to give him a chance to explain himself to the victim).

What he should recognise is that he has culpably committed this wrong. Thus the tones in which he is addressed by others in the process (by the victim, by the mediator, by his or the victim's supporters) should be not the neutral tones of bare description, but the normative tones of censure and criticism – of blame.[17] This is not to say that those tones must be hostile, or such as to humiliate him or exclude him: although it is all too easy for censure and blame to become exercises in oppression, humiliation or exclusion, we must try to censure in a way that displays our recognition of, and concern for, the offender as a fellow citizen. But since what we must try to persuade him to recognise, or join with him in recognising, is the wrong that he committed, we cannot but be engaged in censuring him. And, if he comes to recognise for himself the wrong he has committed, he must censure himself: which is to say that, if he comes to recognise it as a wrong that he culpably committed and for which he is responsible, he must thereby come to a remorseful, repentant recognition of his guilt. A mediation process which is to take the wrongdoing seriously, and which aims to get the offender to recognise, to face up to, what he has done, must thus aim to induce remorse and repentance; it must aim to bring the offender to suffer the painful burden both of repentance, and of being censured by his fellow citizens.

What the offender also owes is, minimally, an apology: this is owed both to the victim and to his fellow citizens. If he has come to recognise and repent his wrong, he will want to offer such an apology: to find some way of expressing his repentant recognition and his new or renewed concern both for the victim and for his relationships with his fellow citizens. If he has not yet come to such a recognition, others can properly try to persuade him that he ought to apologise; they might indeed *demand* that he apologise, or – if that is within their power – *require* him to apologise. In making such a demand or requirement, they must of course hope that it will be, or will become, sincere: but the demand or requirement can be justified even if it is likely that the apology will not be sincere. For there can be, as I noted above, value even in ritual or formal apology; and we can hope that the experience of making even a demanded, non-voluntary apology might help bring the offender to a clearer grasp of the character and implications of what he has done. A mediation process that takes the wrongdoing seriously will thus properly aim to bring the offender to apologise to his victim, and to his fellows.

But a mere verbal apology might not, as we have seen, be enough: something more may be necessary to give manifest weight to the apology – and to help to focus the offender's own repentant attention on what he has done. That 'more' might take the form of direct reparation or compensation to the victim; or undertaking – in, as it were, the victim's name – some task or service for the wider community or for a charity; or just making a suitable donation to a charity; or perhaps agreeing to enter a programme that will address the motives and factors that led the offender to commit the wrong.[18] What is at stake here is not material reparation for material harm that was caused, but moral reparation for the wrong that was done (though the moral reparation might of course take the form of making material reparation). It must, therefore, be something that is burdensome for the offender – even if it is a burden that he welcomes, as enabling him to make reparation: for only if it is burdensome can it serve the role of giving more forceful expression to the apology that is owed.

Some restorative theorists, whilst agreeing that the making of reparations as a result of a mediation process might well in fact be burdensome, deny that they *have* to be burdensome: any pain or hardship that they cause is a side-effect, not part of their purpose (see Walgrave, 2001). Suppose, Lode Walgrave once asked me, that the victim would be content with the gift of a box of chocolates: should not that then suffice? Or suppose, John Braithwaite suggested, that victim and offender could be reconciled by a hug: why then insist that the offender must undertake or suffer some further burden?[19] There are two replies to such questions.

First, what matters is not simply whether the victim would be satisfied by, for instance, a box of chocolates: we must ask whether he *should* be so easily satisfied; and we might think that he should not – indeed, that to regard a box of chocolates as adequate moral reparation, as an adequate expression of the wrongdoer's apologetic repentance, would be to close one's eyes to the seriousness of the offence, or to denigrate oneself by implying that that is all one is worth. After all, the gift of a box of chocolates carries a familiar kind of meaning: it is the kind of thing one gives a hostess, or someone one doesn't know that well, or when one can't make the effort to think of something more imaginative. It is a rather trivial gift, and to treat it as sufficient to make up for a serious wrong implies that the wrong is trivial. If we ask why that should matter, part of the answer is that we should try to dissuade the victim from thus denigrating himself; but the more forceful the answer is that the offender owes an apology to his fellow citizens in general, and thus owes it to them to make a kind of reparation that will be proportionate to the seriousness of his offence.

Of course, boxes of chocolates can carry different meanings in different contexts, as can hugs; and I don't wish to claim a priori that neither a box of chocolates nor a hug could ever, in any context or any relationship, be an adequate expression of apology for a serious wrong. But, and this is my second reply, we are dealing here with public, not private, wrongs, and so with public, not private, reparation: we must therefore ask what could count as an adequately forceful expression of apology between citizens, and what public meaning different possible modes of reparation could have – how they could be understood by the rest of the polity. A box of chocolates or a hug, whatever private meanings they might have in particular contexts, do not, I suggest, have the right kind of public meaning.

The kind of mediation that is an appropriate response to crime (at least to serious crime) should therefore aim to bring the offender to recognise and repent the wrong she has done – which involves censuring her; and to make some suitable moral reparation for that wrong. Furthermore, whilst existing mediation programmes typically seek a reparation which is voluntary in the sense that the offender and victim both agree to it, I would argue that it is fully consistent with the aims sketched above to *require* the offender to make reparation if he does not agree to something suitable – in the same way as we could appropriately require a wrongdoer to apologise.[20]

What we have, then, is a process which the offender undertakes or undergoes – a process of being confronted with his wrongdoing, of being censured, of making reparation – because he has committed a crime. That process is focused on, and justified by, his wrongdoing: he is censured for that wrongdoing, he is asked to recognise and repent it, and he must apologise and make reparation for it. The process is also intended to be painful or burdensome, as we have seen. The wrongdoer should be pained by the censure of his fellow citizens: if he is not pained, their censure has failed to achieve its intended result. He should be pained by the recognition of his wrongdoing, since that should be a repentant recognition, and repentance is necessarily painful. He should be burdened, and in that sense pained, by the reparation that he has to make, since it can have the appropriate apologetic meaning only if it is burdensome. These related kinds of pain or burden are not mere side-effects of the process which – if he is lucky – might not ensue; they are integral to the aims of the process as a process of seeking restoration after a crime.

That is to say, however, that the process of what we could call criminal mediation – the kind of mediation appropriate to crime – is a *punitive* process; it constitutes a *punishment* for the offender. For it is something that is imposed on or required of her, for the crime that she committed, and it is intended to be burdensome or painful – to make her suffer for that crime. It is indeed a *retributive* process: for if we ask why it is appropriate that she should be thus burdened, why she should be brought to suffer, the answer is, in effect, that this is what she deserves for her crime. She deserves to suffer the censure of others, and her own remorse: for that censure and that remorse are appropriate responses to her crime. She deserves to suffer the burden of making moral reparation for what she has done: since it was her wrong, as one that she culpably committed, it is just and proper that she should bear that burden. The central retributivist slogan is that the guilty should be punished as they deserve and because that is what they deserve – that punishment should bring them to suffer what they deserve to suffer; and criminal mediation, as I have described it, is precisely a way of trying to bring them thus to suffer what they deserve.[21]

[. . .]

This extract is taken from 'Restorative Punishment and Punitive Restoration', by R.A. Duff, in L. Walgrave (ed.), Restorative Justice and the Law *(Cullompton, Devon: Willan, 2002).*

Notes

1 For just a few examples see Christie, 1981: 11 on 'alternatives to punishment' as opposed to 'alternative punishments'; Marshall, 1988: 47–8 on 'reparative' as against '*retributive*' justice; Zehr, 1990:178–81 on the alternative 'lenses' of retributive and restorative justice; Walgrave, 1994: 57 on 'restorative justice' as against the 'retributive and rehabilitative justice systems'; Dignan, 1999: 54, 60, on the 'restorative justice approach' as against the 'retributive approach'; Braithwaite, 1999: 60 on the need to strive for 'restorative justice' rather than 'retributive justice'. For further references and apt criticism, see Daly and Immarigeon, 1998: 32–34.

2 Compare Braithwaite and Pettit, 1990: 60–65, on 'dominion' as involving both an assured liberty and the knowledge of that assurance. The value of assured liberty and of security depends in crucial part on our knowing that we have such liberty or security.

3 The position with property is complicated by the way in which property is often fully fungible – as far as the owner is concerned, what she owns is not so much a distinctive individual item, but a token of a type, and any token of that type would do. This is most obviously true of money: it would be absurd to deny that the money which I lost had been restored simply on the grounds that I did not get back the individual coins or notes that I lost; what matters is that I lost £100 and got £100 back. It is also to some extent true of other kinds of property, especially purely functional kinds; and to the extent that it is true, property that has been irretrievably destroyed or lost qua individual token can still be fully restored, qua type.

4 I am not suggesting that the wrong done to the victim is separate from the harm caused to him: whilst not all wrongdoings cause any identifiable harm, those that properly concern the criminal law do typically cause or threaten harm, and their character as wrongs is in part determined by that harm. My point is, rather, that we must understand the harm done by wrongdoing as *wrongful* harm, which gives it a normative character crucially distinct from that of naturally or accidentally caused harms: see further Duff, 1996: 366–9.

5 Much more needs to be said about the idea of community as it figures here, especially about the idea of a political community (and about the extent to which

we now have or live in such communities). I cannot pursue this point here, but see Duff, 2001: chs. 2, 5.

6 Some restorative theorists are unhappy with such a focus on wrongdoing; they prefer to talk of 'conflicts' or 'troubles' rather than of 'crimes' or 'wrongdoings' (see e.g. Christie, 1977, Hulsman, 1986 – on which see Duff, 2001: 60–64). Others, however, recognise the importance of the category of wrongdoing, and of the criminal law as defining the kinds of wrongdoing that properly concern the whole political community.

7 My claim that a friendship can be damaged even by wrongdoing that has no empirical or felt impact on its victim, is related to the familiar – if controversial – claim that one can be harmed by wrongdoing even if it has no empirical impact on one's consciousness or material well-being: someone for whom well-being and happiness depend crucially on a faithful and loving marriage is harmed, and their marriage is destroyed, by their spouse's infidelity, even if that infidelity remains concealed and unknown.

8 Apologies are not, of course, always for wrongdoing: I can apologise for some harm or inconvenience that I caused you through non-culpable inadvertence or accident; or for harm that I caused you intentionally but justifiably. But my focus here is on apologies for culpable wrongdoing.

9 If I know myself to be weak-willed, and prone to give in to temptation, I might predict that I will repeat the wrong in future, as I have so often in the past: but that prediction, if it is not to give the lie to my claim to have recognised the wrong, must be infused with pain and remorse.

10 It might of course be questionable whether the relationship can be restored; or whether I can ask that it be restored. This is not an issue that I can pursue here, nor one that can be dealt with in the same way for all kinds of relationship. On the version of it which arises in the case of crime, see Duff, 2001: ch. 4.4.2.

11 I say only 'might', since it is obvious that undertaking such a required apology can have quite different effects, including a resentful anger at those who require the apology and at those to whom it is made. Much depends on the context, the tone and the spirit in which the apology is demanded.

12 Though we should not forget how hard it can be for individuals, for governments, and for other corporate bodies to apologise even when a verbal apology is all that is sought: not just because apologies might open the door to claims for compensation, but because to apologise is to admit wrongdoing.

13 To say that the reparation must be burdensome is not to say that it must be something that the wrongdoer undertakes unwillingly: I can welcome a burden, and undertake it gladly, without its thereby ceasing to be a burden.

14 For fuller explanation of these points, see Marshall and Duff, 1998; Duff, 2001: ch. 2.4.

15 There are important differences between different kinds of mediation programme, which I skate over here (see Marshall and Merry, 1990; Daly and Immarigeon, 1998; Braithwaite, 1999; Kurki, 2000): but I hope that my general claims about the proper nature of criminal mediation can still stand.

16 On the trial, as a procedure which calls a citizen to answer a charge of wrongdoing and condemns her if the charge is proved against her, see Duff, 1986: ch. 4.

17 Compare Christie, 1977: 9, on giving the offender an 'opportunity to receive a type of blame that it would be very difficult to neutralize'.

18 The CHANGE programme for domestically violent men is a good example: it focuses on getting them to accept responsibility both for their own violent behaviour and for finding ways to deal with it: see Scourfield and Dobash, 1999.

19 They raised these questions in discussion: but see also Braithwaite, 1999: p. 20, fn. 6.

20 Compare Walgrave, 2002 on 'coerced restorative sanctions'.
21 It might seem that, in my enthusiasm to portray criminal mediation as punishment, I have skated over two defining features of punishment (see e.g. Hart, 1968: 4–6; Scheid, 1980) – that it is *imposed* on the offender (whereas in mediation programmes the offender must agree to enter mediation and to undertake reparation) *by an authority* (whereas mediation and reparation are matters of negotiation and agreement between the parties involved). I cannot deal with these points here, but would argue that mediation and reparation could properly be required of, and in that sense imposed on, the offender; and that the process should be conducted under the aegis and supervision of the criminal courts. See further Duff, 2001: 96–7, 111, 158–63.

References

Ashworth, A. (1993) 'Some Doubts about Restorative Justice', *Criminal Law Forum*, 4, pp. 277–99.
Braithwaite, J. (1999) 'Restorative Justice: Assessing Optimistic and Pessimistic Accounts', in Tonry, M. (ed.) *Crime and Justice: An Annual Review of Research*. Vol. 25 (Chicago, IL: University of Chicago Press), pp. 1–127.
Braithwaite, J. and Pettit, P. (1990) *Not Just Deserts* (Oxford: Oxford University Press).
Christie, N. (1977) 'Conflicts as Property', *British Journal of Criminology*, 17, pp. 1–15.
Christie, N. (1981) *Limits to Pain* (London: Martin Robertson).
Daly, K. and Immarigeon, R. (1998) 'The Past, Present, and Future of Restorative Justice', *Contemporary Justice Review*, 1, pp. 21–45.
Dignan, J. (1999) 'The Crime and Disorder Act and the Prospects for Restorative Justice', *Criminal Law Review*, pp. 48–60.
Duff, R.A. (1986) *Trials and Punishments* (Cambridge: Cambridge University Press).
Duff, R.A. (1996) *Criminal Attempts* (Oxford: Oxford University Press).
Duff, R.A. (2001) *Punishment, Communication, and Community* (New York: Oxford University Press).
Gaita, R. (1991) *Good and Evil: An Absolute Conception* (London: Macmillan).
Hart, H.L.A. (1968) 'Prolegomenon to the Principles of Punishment', in his *Punishment and Responsibility* (Oxford: Oxford University Press), pp. 1–27.
Hulsman, L. (1986) 'Critical Criminology and the Concept of Crime', *Contemporary Crises*, 10, pp. 63–80.
Kurki, l. (2000) 'Restorative and Community Justice in the United States', in Tonry, M. (ed.) *Crime and Justice: An Annual Review of Research*. Vol. 26 (Chicago, IL: University of Chicago Press).
Marshall, S.E. and Duff, R.A. (1998) 'Criminalization and Sharing Wrongs', *Canadian Journal of Law and Jurisprudence*, 11, pp. 7–22.
Marshall, T.F. (1988) 'Out of Court: More or Less Justice?' in Matthews, R. (ed.) *Informal Justice* (London: Sage), pp. 25–50.
Marshall, T.F. (1999) *Restorative Justice: An Overview* (London: Home Office).
Marshall, T.F. and Merry, S. (1990) *Crime and Accountability: Victim/Offender Mediation in Practice* (London: HMSO).
Murphy, J.G. (1988) 'Forgiveness and Resentment', in Murphy, J.G. and Hampton, J. (eds) *Forgiveness and Mercy* (Cambridge: Cambridge University Press), pp. 14–34.
Scheid, D.E. (1980) 'Note on Defining "Punishment"', *Canadian Journal of Philosophy*, 10, pp. 453–62.
Scourfield, J. and Dobash, R.P. (1999) 'Programmes for Violent Men: Recent Developments in the UK', *Howard Journal of Criminal Justice*, 38, pp. 128–43.

Van Ness, D.W. (1993) 'New Wine and Old Wineskins: Four Challenges of Restorative Justice', *Criminal Law Forum*, 4, pp. 251–76.

Walgrave, L. (1994) 'Beyond Rehabilitation: in Search of a Constructive Alternative in the Judicial Response to Juvenile Crime', *European Journal on Criminal Policy and Research*, 2, pp. 57–75.

Walgrave, L. (2001) 'Restoration and Punishment. On Favourable Similarities and Fortunate Differences', in Maxwell, G. and Morris, A. (eds) *Restoring Justice for Juveniles* (Oxford: Hart Publishing), pp. 17–37.

Walgrave, L. (2002) 'Not Punishing Children but Committing them to Restore', in Weijers, I. and Duff, R.A. (eds) *Punishing Juveniles: Principle and Critique* (Oxford: Hart Publishing).

Zehr, H. (1990) *Changing Lenses: A New Focus for Crime and Justice* (Scottsdale, PA: Herald Press).

27. Just cops doing 'shameful' business? Police-led restorative justice and the lessons of research

Richard Young

[. . .]

Police power and punishment

Perhaps the core concern expressed by critics of police-led conferencing is that it is allowing the police to become 'judge and jury in their own cases'.[1] The police already control the processes of arrest, detention and investigation. Some argue (for example, Ashworth, 2001) that to give them the right to oversee the outcome of their investigations through a restorative conference is to concentrate too much power in one agency and is wrong in principle. Underlying this concern is often the fear that the police are deliberately seeking to expand their punitive power (Sandor, 1994).

What this latter concern assumes, however, is that conferencing *empowers the police* and that it produces *punitive* outcomes. This is the exact reverse of what many restorative justice adherents argue should be the case.[2] Conferences are designed to bring together those with a direct stake in the resolution of the offence, including the victim, offender and their respective supporters, so that the harm caused by the offence can be collectively addressed with a view to reaching a *restorative or compensatory* resolution. Conferences are meant to empower these participants. They are emphatically not meant to empower the persons facilitating the process, whether these be police officers, mediators, social workers or anyone else.

To an important degree, this depiction of conferencing is based on a narrow conception of punishment as something that is destructive, stigmatic, harsh or overly intrusive. A better definition of punishment is any practice which is unpleasant, burdensome, or imposed on the offender *and* which is engaged in because of the wrongfulness of the offending behaviour. [. . .]

If one applies a broad definition of punishment then it is clear that the first Australian model of conferencing provided for in legislation increased police punitive power. The Young Offenders Act 1993 introduced to South Australia a New Zealand style of conferencing (Morris and Maxwell, 2000) for moderately serious cases. Although not police-led, a police officer is legally required to be present at a conference and has the right of veto over any agreement reached. The Act also provides the police with the power in less serious cases to administer a formal caution coupled with a direction that the offender concerned should pay compensation to the victim, carry out up to 75 hours of community service, make an apology, or other 'appropriate' measures.[3] Seen in this light, it is not surprising that police involvement in restorative justice became so controversial in Australia. However, the Wagga Wagga model, far from providing the police with an explicit power to punish, requires that facilitators do not even recommend or suggest particular conference outcomes. As it is this model that appears to be meeting with most success in the international market-place of criminal justice, it might appear that the concern that the police are becoming 'judge and jury' is overstated.

There are, however, more sophisticated claims that need to be considered when thinking about police power. One is that police-facilitation results in offenders (or others) experiencing the process as so intrusive as to amount to *state* inflicted punishment. Another is that police facilitators will be unable to resist the temptation to use the undoubtedly powerful role of the facilitator to exert too great a control over the outcomes reached in conferences. One obvious danger is that the norms of the traditional culture of front-line street-cops will come into play in this setting. At the core of this traditional cop culture is a commitment to the upholding of authority, not least through police or court-imposed control and punishment on individuals drawn from marginalised groups defined as disrespectful, threatening or criminogenic.[4] In assessing the possible influence of cop culture on restorative justice it will be helpful to analyse process and outcome issues in turn.

Is the process the punishment?

An argument that the process of conferencing might be intrusive to the point of being experienced as punishment can be enriched by drawing on Foucault's perspective on power.[5] Power is not seen by Foucault as the property of particular institutions or individuals but rather as inhering in the 'asymmetrical balance of forces which operate whenever and wherever social relations exist' (Garland, 1990: 138). Foucault distinguished between sovereign and juridical forms of power (which would encompass formal state-imposed punishment) and the much less tangible notion of disciplinary power. Discipline is here conceived of in corrective terms (aiming to induce conformity) rather than as punitive in the sense of revengeful retribution. Lacey (1999: 144–5) usefully elucidates disciplinary power in the following manner:

> Disciplinary power inheres in particular discourses and practices, and operates (rather than being exercised) in a subtle and diffused way throughout the social body ... this discipline which is at the core of the modern power to punish inheres as much in the micro-details of prison regimes, uniform, staff attitudes and so on as in the formal sentence of the court and the other more obvious indices of state power.[6]

She further notes (1999: 160) that the development of a range of community justice initiatives over the last twenty years, including those based on reintegrative shaming, has brought this distinction to the fore:

Because many of the relevant institutions operate not primarily in terms of instrumental penalties or by means of sovereignty or juridical power but rather by mobilising pre-existing norms and discourses within which it is sought to reintegrate or rehabilitate offenders or 'at-risk' groups.

As we are examining police-led initiatives in conferencing (rather than conferencing per se), the relevant question is whether police involvement has produced a particular kind of disciplining within restorative conferences. This needs to be analysed at the level of the design of the Wagga Wagga model (since the design may influence the discourses typically mobilised within a conference), as well as at the operational level (since it is not safe to assume that a design will be implemented as intended).

The punitive designs of the police?

There is no doubt that the three police-led initiatives considered here are heavily influenced (to varying degrees) by Braithwaite's (1989) theory of reintegrative shaming. This argues that crime is best controlled through shaming criminal behaviour whilst simultaneously seeking to avoid the long-term stigmatisation of those who offend (with its consequential pushing of offenders into criminal sub-cultures or deviant identities and commitments). Shaming should ideally terminate with forgiveness and reintegration. The Wagga Wagga model posits that shaming is best done by people whose opinion the offender is most likely to care about (such as their family or friends or the victim) and who are best placed to effect reintegration into the 'law-abiding community' (such as their family, friends and, perhaps, a forgiving or understanding victim). It further posits that forgiveness and reintegration are most likely to take place if the offender accepts responsibility for the harm caused by the offence and makes restorative gestures, such as a commitment to desist from further offending, apology, victim-compensation or community service.[7]

An important discourse likely to be mobilised within the reintegrative shaming model of conferencing is that of individual responsibility for crime. Polk (1994) argues that it is assumed in this model that delinquency represents a symptom of individual or family malfunction rather than reflecting powerlessness, institutional racism and sexism, or attenuated access to recreational and educational facilities, public space, health care, and decent jobs and housing. In short, reintegrative shaming 'could easily become a complex form of "victim blaming", where the most vulnerable are identified as the cause, rather than the effect, of social inequalities' (1994: 131). Polk further notes (1994: 132–3) that because the model is operated by the criminal justice system exclusively for offenders it cannot help but confer institutional stigma. In his view, the psychological processes facilitated in a conference can do no more than alleviate the negative effects of a fundamentally coercive and stigmatic institutional experience.[8]

For my purpose, what is notable is that Polk makes these observations in relation to both the (non police-led) New Zealand model and the Wagga

Wagga model. This implies that *police*-led conferencing models are not inherently more stigmatic than those conducted by youth justice co-ordinators in New Zealand. By contrast, Morris and Maxwell (2000: 216–7) argue that the New Zealand model is not based on reintegrative shaming, a theory which they contend could be at odds with restorative ideals. They note that, in Canberra, community participants are invited to conferences where there is no direct victim, thus indicating, in their view, that the primary role of victims generally within that model is to deliver shame. They write:

> It seems unlikely that young offenders see shaming by the police (who were the facilitators in many of these conferences) or by members of a community to which they may have no connection as reintegrative and hence as restorative. It also seems unlikely that the potential power of meetings between offenders and victims to move towards a reconciliation is realized where the primary role of the victim is scripted as 'shamer' (2000: 216).

The point here is not that shaming is inappropriate in a restorative justice conference, but rather that it should neither be inflicted by authority figures nor be seen as an end in itself. Whether police facilitators, community participants or victims actually do place too much emphasis on individualistic shaming is, of course, an empirical question. But the design of the Wagga Wagga model certainly appears to prompt the explicit shaming of behaviour in a way that the New Zealand model does not. Moreover, there is a danger that such encouragement will lead to a shaming of the offender as a person or 'shaming as intimidation' (White, 1994: 189). This might occur if the participants (other than the offender) fail to maintain the distinction between the doer and the deed called for by Braithwaite's theory. Even if they do remain faithful to this distinction, offenders, through having their behaviour shamed to a disproportionate degree, may come to feel that they are shameful people. It is thus arguable that the theoretical commitment to shaming within police-led models is likely to reduce the extent to which the institutional stigma conferred by a criminal justice conference can be alleviated by the reintegrative psychological processes taking place within it. In addition, the attribution of responsibility for crime at the level of the individual may be somewhat sharper, and thus have greater punitive bite, in a model committed to a notion of criminal behaviour as shameful. As Sherman and Strang (1997: 3) put it, in discussing the Canberra model, 'conferences put the offender under the spotlight of critical examination far longer than court proceedings'.

The practice of shaming and disciplining

To what extent are these theoretical concerns about punishment and discipline borne out by empirical observations? The research studies of the Canberra and Bethlehem initiatives will be examined first. The reason for considering them together is that both adopt an experimental design in which the key concern is to compare court processes and outcomes with those of a conference.[9]

Canberra and Bethlehem

Sherman and Strang (1997a: 2) report that in Canberra:

> Observations of hundreds of conferences show that police officers who lead them have generally succeeded in preventing any participants from condemning offenders as bad people. While the conferences have been far more emotionally intense than court, most of the anger and shame have been aimed at offenders' acts and not their character. Canberra police are succeeding in making offenders *feel* ashamed of what they have done without making them into shameful people [emphasis in the original].

The negative way of expressing the same findings would be to say that police officers have sometimes not succeeded in preventing participants from condemning offenders as bad people, and that some of the anger and shame generated by conferences has been directed at offenders' characters.[10] There is nothing, however, in the results so far released by the Canberra team to suggest that the police are *intensifying* the discipline which is inherent to reintegrative shaming. Moreover, it is possible that a non-police facilitator would have been even less successful than were the Canberra facilitators in the task of maintaining the distinction between doer and deed called for by the model. It is difficult to go further than this because the Canberra study was not designed to provide data on these specific questions.

In McCold and Wachtel's (1998) report of the Bethlehem evaluation, based on structured observation of 56 conferences involving juvenile offenders, there is somewhat more discussion of the police facilitator's influence on the process. Soon after the twenty facilitators began running conferences they were brought together to be given critical feedback on their performance by an officer in charge of in-service training. McCold and Wachtel (1998: 27) reveal that:

> In spite of the [initial three day] training the officers had received, some seemed surprised that they were not supposed to lecture the offender or affect the conference agreements ... the officer with the poorest performance evaluation withdrew from the program and a total of five officers never conferenced a second case.

Not surprisingly, police compliance with the programme's protocol showed subsequent improvement. In particular, the 'authoritarian tone of the conferences was dramatically reduced by providing the corrective feedback' (1998: 33). The percentage of facilitators who themselves failed to maintain a stance of censuring the offence whilst avoiding stigmatisation of the offender fell from 21 per cent before the feedback session to 7 per cent afterwards. Nonetheless, some lecturing by the police facilitator was observed to take place in about a third of the conferences observed following the in-service training. The arresting officer took part as a participant in a quarter of all observed conferences. The researchers judged that the facilitator had been the most punitive participant in 4 per cent of all cases, and that it was the arresting officer in a further 4 per cent. There were no doubt other conferences in which the police present were punitive[11] albeit to a lesser degree than other participants. But it would be wrong to conclude that the police are inevitably going to take a harsh stance in conferences: in 35 per cent of the conferences observed 'no participant could be identified as punitive at all' (1998: 35).

Other research findings from Canberra and Bethlehem suggest, however, that offenders do not find the conference oppressive. Nor do they generally appear to perceive police-facilitation as problematic or illegitimate. Thus 96 per cent of offender-respondents in Bethlehem indicated that they found the tone of the conference to be 'generally friendly'.[12] In Canberra, 60 per cent of drink-drivers and 47 per cent of young offenders said that they had gained respect for the police after attending a conference, and the vast majority of all offenders said the police had been fair to them during the proceedings (Sherman and Barnes, 1997: 3–4).[13]

These findings must be treated with care, however, not least for method-ological reasons. In both Canberra and Bethlehem, participants' satisfaction with the conference process is measured by means of a structured question-naire. Thus respondents are typically asked to express their degree of agreement (or disagreement) with statements such as 'the police in Canberra enforce the law fairly', or to tick a yes/no box in response to questions such as 'do you care what the victim thinks about you?' Similarly, the observations carried out by the researchers in both research sites were fairly tightly structured in nature, making use of such devices as checklists and rating scales. This choice of methods reflects the experimental design of both research studies, allowing for robust comparisons to be made between the experiences of those attending conferences and those attending court. These methods are not well suited, however, to exploring the disciplinary nature of conferences in Foucauldian terms.[14] In order to explore the subtle and diffuse nature of discipline, an approach is required which allows both for discourse analysis and an in-depth exploration of how conferences are experienced by participants. The interim study carried out in the Thames Valley employed just such an approach.

Thames Valley

In an important respect, the findings in the Thames Valley mirror those of Canberra and Bethlehem. Our open-ended interviews with participants revealed a high degree of support for the practice of police-led restorative justice. There were few objections to the use of police stations as a venue for cautions and conferences, and most people saw the police as best-placed to run the restorative process for cautionable offences. The most common reason behind this support for the strong policing character of these encounters was a belief that offending should be responded to in an authoritative way.[15] On the other hand, participants were critical of some elements of facilitators' practices which seemed to them over-bearing or misplaced. In addition, the tape-recordings of cautioning sessions illuminated some of the ways in which the police can make a distinctive contribution to the dynamics of conferences and their disciplinary character.[16] To date, the literature on police participation in restorative justice has tended to make rather vague and generalised claims about the issues involved.[17] In what follows the aim is, in part, to bring some specificity to the debate. Given the vast quantity of data collected as part of the Thames Valley research, the discussion is necessarily highly selective.[18]

Echoing the police interview

Police facilitators in the Thames Valley are trained to ask a few open-ended scripted questions designed to help offenders tell their stories, such as 'what were you thinking at the time of the incident?', 'what have you thought about since?' and 'who do you think has been affected by this?'. Some police officer facilitators instead engaged in detailed and judgmental questioning that forced offenders to dwell upon aspects of the offence that the latter clearly found unpalatable. Here is a short example drawn from a conference transcript.[19]

> f: . . . At what point in your own mind then did you decide that you were going to take that and not pay for it. Was it before you went into the shop?
> o: No, it wasn't . . .
> f: No.
> o: . . . pre-planned or anything.
> f: OK, so once you're in there then, so did you have any money on you at the time, did you have enough money to pay for it?
> o: Yeah I did.
> f: You did. [Checks police file and states value of items – under ten pounds.] So you did have enough money on you to pay for that. [Pause – no verbal response] How did you go about concealing it, how did you actually steal it.
> o: I think it was just, putting it in my pocket or sleeve or, I don't [trails off]
> f: You put it in your sleeve in fact.

In total, some 40 questions of similar style were put to the offender by the facilitator at this point in the process. Subsequently we interviewed the offender in this case and asked him one of our standard questions:

> int: At the time you were actually describing the event, how were you feeling then?
> o: The worst bit is telling them what happened, 'how did you take it?', that's the worst part.
> int: How does that feel?
> o: You have to feel like, you feel like a real, you know, convict; well not a convict but like scum of the earth. It's like they make you feel that it's something that you do all the time. It's like 'so how do you do it?' I don't know, it made me feel they thought it was something that I do regularly, because I have a routine to how I steal things. And that's not true.

This questioning style seemed to us to have been adopted partly out of habit (the style was that of a standard police interview) and partly as an attempt to understand or categorise an offender's behaviour. But from the offender's point of view, the police discourse was seen as implying that they were committed to offending and thus shameful in character. In other words, questions of this nature can undermine the conference goal of avoiding stigmatisation.[20]

Police authority and police knowledge

One of the most prominent discourses observed at play within restorative processes facilitated by police officers was that of police authority. The imperative to maintain this authority as a bulwark against disorder is a key feature of street-level cop-culture (Sanders and Young, 2000: 76). Whilst the theory of conferencing is that the participants are empowered, there was no doubt that the institutional background of police facilitators placed the latter in a particularly authoritative position. This authority was intimately linked to police knowledge. From a Foucauldian perspective, knowledge is key to the operation of disciplinary power because the more the characteristics of an individual are known the more controllable they become (Garland, 1990: 138–9).

The police facilitators' knowledge of offenders derived from a number of sources. Most notably, they had often spoken to the officer-in-charge of the case and they invariably had access to the investigative file.[21] In practice, facilitators were frequently observed to invoke the institutional police knowledge of the particular offence or offender. In ten of the twenty-three cases observed, police facilitators referred to the official version of the case at a point when offenders were supposed to be telling their stories without interruption or correction. In several cases, facilitators kept the police file open throughout the cautioning session and occasionally drew on it to verify or add to the offender's story.[22] The police file became the source of a narrative which competed (on uneven terms) with the offender's story. This increased the risk of offenders becoming defensive as a police account was related which might be seen as inaccurate in various ways.[23]

Use of the police file was also seen to be of critical importance when a police facilitator asked offenders about their involvement in offences other than the one for which the restorative justice session had been arranged. This might be done by asking them whether or not they had any prior involvement with the police, by inquiring whether or not they had committed other offences, or by checking whether or not their involvement in the present offence extended further than they had previously admitted. When combined with the tactic of leafing through the police file this put offenders in an awkward situation, as it can seem to them that their veracity is on trial. This sometimes led to the disclosure of information not already known to the police:

f: Had you had any previous involvement with the police before this? [Pause, the facilitator leafs noisily through the police file]
o: Yeah. [Reluctant admission]
f: What was that for?
o: It was for something that this man, another man did. The police came round and straight in; the man came down and accused me of it, because my arms had like tattoos like the bloke he attempted to stop, so he thought it was me.
f: Yeah.
o: Like that, so . . .
f: [Interrupting] Right. But you've never been into a police station, having been arrested or anything like that before.
o: No.

What the above extract illustrates is that facilitators may ask about previous involvement with the police even when they have no objective ground to suspect there has been any. In the following example, the facilitator does know of previous police involvement, but probes the issue anyway:

    f: Right, OK. So you were taken back to the police station?
    o: Yeah.
    f: And, what was the procedure like there, cause, have, have you had any involvement with the police before now?
    o: Yeah.
    f: What was that for?
    o: Um, criminal damage.
    f: And what happened on that occasion?
    o: Basically the same.
    f: So, the, the procedure at the police station, then, wasn't something entirely new to you.
    o: No.
    f: You were twelve then weren't you, according to this. [Looking down at the police file]
    o: Yeah, think so.

It seemed that the facilitator asked these questions in order to gauge how much of an impact the arrest and detention of the offender was likely to have had in the current case. But one effect was to diffuse the restorative justice model's focus on a specific offence and the harm it caused. Indeed, one might argue that it undercut the effort to avoid people making judgments about whether the offender was a 'good or bad person'.

In four of the sixteen conferences observed the officer-in-charge of the case (usually the arresting officer) was present. This brought new forms of power-knowledge into play. The Thames Valley training emphasises that any professionals should be treated by the facilitator as peripheral to the conference. However, in two of these four conferences, the arresting officer played an active role from an early point in the process. In one conference, concerned with aiding and abetting a theft, the offender mentioned that the principal offender had dumped the stolen goods at a particular place. This prompted an indignant intervention by the officer-in-charge:

    o-i-c: Are you actually saying that you know where it went, when the lot was taken?
    o: Yeah, he said that he dropped it near, I think he said that he dropped it near the bus station.
    o-i-c: Mmm, cos you omitted to tell me that at the time I arrested you. [seems annoyed] . . . So did you find this information out, because you were arrested on the day and questioned, so you must have found this out after I originally arrested you, didn't you?
    o: Yeah, cos like I walked home from here [police station] didn't I?
    o-i-c: Right, but why didn't you actually bring that extra information to me, after I'd arrested you, because obviously you was on bail and could have actually brought that to my attention and we'd maybe find [the item] maybe sitting

in the found property office at the bus station. You could have actually made an effort to, maybe, highlighted that to me at a later date, couldn't you?

o: Hmm. [Sounds doubtful]

o-i-c: [pause] Yeah? [pause] Hey?

o: Yeah, I dare say I could have, but I didn't see the point in it, didn't think of it.

o-i-c: Believe it or not people round here if they find abandoned property they don't all go round nicking it again – they actually do bring it in to the police station and possibly say, 'I've found this', and obviously we'll make inquiries to see if it's stolen or lost property.

o: It could have been anyone, couldn't it, not me, don't have to be me [that told you].

o-i-c: Yeah, obviously you might have done.

Amongst other things, the officer's intervention communicated the judgement that the offender was someone who could not be expected to understand the norms of the law-abiding. It also censured the offender for failing to be a model citizen by returning to the police station to report the whereabouts of the stolen goods.

Finally, it is worth making the obvious point that police authoritarianism can intrude into a restorative process in non-verbal ways. One officer-in-charge sat outside the circle of participants and played the role of an observer. But this is not how it seemed to the young offender in this conference, whose mother told us in interview:

> The only thing I didn't agree with, well, he [offender] told me after the meeting, that the copper who'd actually arrested him was giving him dirty looks all through the meeting, and that. And so I don't think he should have been there, and that. But that's like what [my son] said to me. Whether it's true or not I don't know 'cos I wasn't looking at the police officer. That's all he went on about on the way home – the way the copper kept giving him dirty looks.

Whether this allegation is true or not is, in one sense, irrelevant.[24] The danger of placing an observing officer in the offender's line of vision is that the former's presence may be experienced as intrusive or disciplinary, whatever the officer's intentions might be.

On the other hand, it was clear from interviews with participants, including offenders, that many of them wanted the process to include police officers who had a good knowledge of the case. This was because these participants sought an authoritative disposition on the matter and/or because they saw such knowledge as important if the process was not to founder on arguments about factual details, such as who had done what to whom. The issue is not, therefore, whether police knowledge should be deployed in restorative conferences, but rather how it is deployed and to what end. There will be situations in which a restrained injection of *relevant* information will further restorative goals. The trick is to avoid using the police 'version of events' to set the agenda, to dominate the interactions, or to undermine someone's story when this is not being contested by other participants.

[. . .]

Procedural fairness and police accountability

Amongst a cluster of inter-related concerns about procedural fairness, Warner (1994) questions whether or not police malpractice at the investigatory stage will become less visible and whether or not the police will become less accountable in the absence of judicial oversight. Braithwaite (1999) argues to the contrary that police accountability to the community is enhanced by the conference process. This is because conferences allow more time and space for participants to voice opinions and concerns and because the police know that, if relations break down in the conference, the case may go to court. In addressing these issues it is important to take into account relevant empirical findings.

   [. . .]

Thames Valley

Generally speaking, the participants interviewed saw the restorative cautioning process as fair. The open-ended nature of these interviews allowed exploration of the underlying reasons for this perception. The main element of fair process as comprehended by all the key participants was being allowed to have their say on an equal footing with everyone else present. The more a cautioning session adhered to the principles of restorative justice, the more offenders, victims and others were likely to describe the session as fair. Offenders were particularly impressed when other participants listened carefully to what they had to say, an experience they were unfamiliar with in the context of criminal justice.

   This finding of general satisfaction regarding procedural fairness should nonetheless be interpreted in a circumspect manner. Offenders and their supporters, in particular, had low expectations of the cautioning session. Many of them had previously experienced non-restorative old-style cautioning (Young and Goold, 1999) or poor treatment on arrest and detention, and were thus pleasantly surprised by even minor gestures of fairness during the cautioning session. Those treated in accordance with high standards of procedural fairness sometimes reported feelings of amazement. Moreover, behind these general appraisals lay some specific concerns about particular features of some cautions and conferences. In illustrating these concerns, I am not suggesting that such features are inevitable in police-led restorative justice; rather they highlight the need for stronger accountability mechanisms than are inherent in the semi-public nature of the process and its systemic setting in the shadow of the court.

Investigative fairness

In several cases, the offender was asked by the facilitator about their recent and current offending behaviour (as opposed to questioning in relation to behaviour that had led to police involvement in the past – a practice discussed above).

Any evidence obtained in this way might be admissible in court, as exclusion is not necessarily mandated in this type of situation.[25] At the very least, information secured by this means becomes part of the stock of local police knowledge. None of the safeguards which normally apply to a police interview, such as the right to have a legal adviser present, were in operation. It is true that all offenders will have been offered free legal advice when first formally interviewed at the police station, but few of the offenders in our phase three sample had taken up this offer and only two out of the twenty-six we interviewed had received advice on whether to accept a restorative caution.[26]

Here is one example of how restorative justice can become transformed into an investigative tool:

> f: Right. So who found the [stolen goods] then, the store staff?
> o: Yeah.
> f: Yeah. OK, and I think there was a knife found, nearby, wasn't there, do you remember that?
> o: [eight second pause] Yeah there was, yeah, there was, uh, something like that, yeah.
> f: Yeah.
> o: Supposedly put there by me.
> f: Right.
> o: Which it wasn't.
> f: Which it wasn't?
> o: No.

The pursuit of such extraneous matters places the perceived legitimacy of police-facilitation in jeopardy. When interviewed, the offender's mother took objection to the way the cautioning session had taken on this aspect of a re-interview:

> Yeah, I was a little bit miffed with the bit to do with the knife, but I wasn't going to jump in, start kicking it around. I felt that it was slightly unjustified in being brought up because it was a silly situation. I doubt very much if it was [offender]'s and he's turned round to him [original interviewing officer] and said 'no it wasn't mine'. And he wasn't charged with that. I was just a bit miffed about that.

In other cases, participants were asked to provide details on the extent of the involvement of other people in committing offences, or to supply general criminal intelligence, as in the following extract:

> v: Trouble is he's in with the wrong gang.
> f: Is he?
> v: The wrong gang, they're all troublemakers, the gang that he's in with.
> o: It's not a gang, it's just some friends.
> f: Who do you hang around with then Matthew?

This exchange continued until all the relevant names had been provided. In another case, an officer-in-charge intervened to ask the offender whether he had committed the offence recklessly, as he had admitted in interview, or intentionally, as the officer obviously suspected. This under-cut the most recent offender supporter's contributions, which had been to express some pride in the fact that the offender had been honest about the offence and taken full responsibility for what he had done.

It is important to stress that no police facilitators or officers-in-charge we spoke with gave any indication that they purposely set out to use the process to gather criminal intelligence. Moreover, the script used by Thames Valley Police can itself be seen as requiring facilitators to tread a fine line in that they must tease out the offender's story whilst avoiding questions that could be perceived as investigatory in tone or nature. Indeed, forgetting to leave personal and professional baggage outside of the conference room is something that all facilitators need to guard against, not just police officers. Thus, in the four of our twenty-three cases which were facilitated by social workers, there was a distinct tendency for the facilitator to turn the session into an assessment of the offender or to engage in individual or family therapy.

The concern of Warner (1994) that police malpractice at the investigative stage will be swept under the conference carpet is thus revealed as too narrow. Conferences provide a new opportunity for inappropriate or counter-productive professional behaviour. The kinds of problems documented above are to be expected in any new initiative which is grafted on to an existing criminal justice structure (Daly and Immarigeon, 1998). What is important is to recognise and accept that this is so, and then to take remedial action once the anticipated problems have emerged and their precise nature is documented.

Challenging police behaviour

As for Braithwaite's suggestion that inappropriate police behaviour will be challenged in the conference setting, the Thames Valley research found much evidence to the contrary. In one sense this is surprising, given that some police facilitators made a point of asking offenders detailed questions about their treatment when arrested and detained in the police station. But the purpose of such questioning was not to encourage complaints but rather to focus the offender's attention on an unpleasant experience in what seemed to be an attempt to maximise the deterrent aspect of the encounter. When, during these exchanges, criticisms were made by an offender, however faintly or implicitly, the typical reaction of the facilitator was defensive, as in the following example:

> f: Did you spend any time in a cell?
> o: Yeah.
> f: How long were you in there for?
> o: Five hours.
> f: Were you? What was that like?
> o: Boring!
> f: Boring! [half laughs]. Oh right. And that was probably because there was more than just you and it takes time to process all of you and these things do take time don't they?
> o: Yeah.
> f: And then to interview you all as well and decide what's going to happen.

Such defensive comments achieve little other than conveying to offenders that criticisms of the police will not be welcomed. This problem, again, is something to be expected given that a key aspect of traditional cop culture is solidarity with colleagues in the face of external threats (Waddington, 1999: 302).

Another structural disincentive to raise criticisms is the facilitator's use of the police file as an authoritative source of 'the facts'. This is unlikely to document inappropriate police behaviour, while offenders may feel it trumps their own version of events. This possibility was raised most starkly in our data by the cases where the police were the victim (that is to say, offences of drunk and disorderly, public order, or assault on a police officer). In one restorative caution, the facilitator, reading from the police file, gave a graphic account of the offence from the police victim's point of view:

> f: [The police officer] says they've been called, because of this incident inside the disco, so they were there legitimately to try and find out what was going on. Apparently you refused to get off the bus, you were telling him to 'fuck off' and similar language. And then you were seen by several people actually grabbing a police officer around the throat and having to be sort of dragged off and restrained. You then had to be forced really to the ground so that they could try and get handcuffs on you, this [police officer's] there using distraction blows in the form of knee strikes on your legs, I don't know you if you had any bruises after that but, [laughs] . . .
>
> o: Yeah I had a few there.
>
> f: . . . that would explain those maybe. You were quite aggressive, you were telling people to 'fuck off and leave me alone', 'do you fucking want some?' [Pause – turns over a page in the file] At one point one of the police officers actually drew his CS spray, you know the spray that we all carry these days. I think in view of the fact that there was so many people around it wasn't possible to actually use it but I think things were so bad that it obviously went through his mind that, you know, if he felt justified in using it, he could have done. [Pause, flicks through the police file to garner more details] Yeah, continued to struggle on the ground, refused to follow any instructions that were put to you, they had to get the transit van, they had to take you back to the police station and then again you had to be restrained in a cell while they searched you to see what you had on, on your body, so all in all, [sighs] it's a bit of a, a disappointing evening, as, you know, certainly as far as we were concerned.

This statement reminded the offender of a violent and humiliating encounter with the police in a way which discouraged him from challenging the official version of events. There is a total identification here between the interests of the facilitator and the interests of the victimised police – as when the facilitator notes that 'we all carry CS spray these days'. In substance, the facilitator is defending the police actions throughout the entire passage. One offender was asked in interview if there was anything he had not felt able to talk about in the cautioning session. He replied:

> Yeah, there was one thing. When he [facilitator] said about the need to restrain me on arrest. When I got home that morning, all my face was cut and bruised up. I had marks all down my legs and back. I'd certainly taken a bit more of a battering than I should have done – unless I was that much of a handful. But I'll

say again, I can't remember, because I was drunk. But I was certainly covered, head to toe.

One negative side-effect of intimidating offenders in this way is that it makes it less likely that they will speak openly about their feelings more generally. In consequence, it will be hard to encourage them to take a proper degree of responsibility for their actions and the harm they caused.[27] That, in turn, will undermine the chances of victims finding the conference experience a satisfying and reparative one.

One conclusion to be drawn from this sub-section is that cases in which the police feature as victims need to be handled with particular care. Whilst defensive solidarity with colleagues may be a matter of unconscious instinct, it will normally be present and these cases would be better facilitated by someone from another agency. A similar difficulty arose in our sample in a case in which a social worker facilitated a case in which the victim was a care home run by social workers. Here, also, there was too great an identification with the interests of the victim, thus illustrating that professional solidarity is not only a problem for police facilitators.

Finally, there is little sense in the Thames Valley that cases on the restorative caution or conference track may end up in court. It is theoretically possible but extremely unlikely to occur. None of those observed made any attempt to withdraw from the process. Offenders are usually told at the start of a conference that they can leave at any time but 'that the matter might then have to be dealt with differently'. Interviews with offenders, nearly all of whom had yet to experience a court appearance, show that one of their strongest concerns is to avoid prosecution. Thus the notion that the police will behave in more accountable ways because of the fear that a conferenced case may end up in court is not borne out in this setting. On the other hand, it is arguable that accountability has been enhanced in the Thames Valley in a way which is not true of Canberra or Bethlehem. In the latter two sites, cases have been diverted away from the public court into a semi-private setting. In Thames Valley, by contrast, cases that were previously disposed of by the police in an almost wholly private and unsupervised ad hoc manner (old-style cautioning) are now handled in a more open, standardised way.[28]

[. . .]

This extract is taken from 'Just Cops Doing "Shameful" Business? Police-led, Restorative Justice and the Lessons of Research', by Richard Young, in A. Morris and G. Maxwell (eds), Restorative Justice for Juveniles: Conferencing, Mediation and Circles *(Oxford: Hart Publishing, 2001), pp. 195–226.*

Notes

1 This was expressed to me by David Dixon during the British Criminology Conference in 1997. See also the discussion in Braithwaite (1999).

2 See, for example, Walgrave (2000), and the critical reflections of Daly and Immarigeon (1998).

3 A good overview of the South Australian model is provided by Wundersitz and Hetzel (1996); for more critical reflections, see White (1994: 190).

4 For discussion of the enduring features of cop culture, coupled with a recognition that it can vary from place to place, over time, and by police specialism, see Chan (1996), Waddington (1999) and Sanders and Young (2000).

5 The key text is Foucault (1977). Minor and Morrison (1996) contains a useful discussion of how Foucault's ideas can be applied in critiquing restorative justice. As Garland (1990: 163) notes, Foucault's perspective is best used not as a general explanatory theory but as a heuristic device, 'producing questions and interpretations which can later be balanced against the weight of evidence and alternative explanations'. The adoption of a Foucauldian perspective suits my particular objective in this chapter, which is to expose the forms of power-knowledge at play in police-led conferencing so that the potential dangers can be more successfully guarded against.

6 Lacey draws here on the study by Carlen (1983) of the nature of women's imprisonment.

7 The case for employing the theory of reintegrative shaming within conferences is best put by Braithwaite and Mugford (1994).

8 See also White (1994). For a response to Polk, see Braithwaite (1999).

9 Canberra adopts the classic experimental design in that random allocation to courts or conferences occurs only after offenders have expressed their willingness to attend a conference. In Bethlehem, random allocation occurred before offenders were asked if they would be prepared to attend a conference, and this method resulted in not just control and treatment groups (court and conference respectively) but also a conference declined group.

10 See also the acknowledgement by Sherman and Strang (1997a: 3–4) that drink-drivers sent to conferences were more likely than those sent to court to feel ashamed of themselves 'as distinct from what they had done'.

11 This term is not defined at this point in McCold and Wachtel (1998) although a reasonable inference is that they mean 'stigmatic', or 'seeking a harsh outcome' rather than meaning disciplinary in a Foucauldian (corrective) sense.

12 Although McCold and Wachtel (1998: 61) report that 96 per cent 'said the tone was friendly', the instrument they used (1998: 118) shows that offenders were asked a tick-box question of a less clear-cut nature: 'Would you say the tone of the conference was *generally*: friendly, hostile, or other (specify)' [my emphasis].

13 Similar findings have been reported in more recent progress reports from Canberra. See Strang *et al.* (1999: Tables 5–9 to 5–12).

14 See, for example, footnote 20 and accompanying text. There are other obvious difficulties with these findings, which include that participants may have low expectations of the police and thus be easy to please; or that their evaluations may be critically affected by the fact that they have avoided court, and so on. See the related discussion under the sub-heading Procedural Fairness and [Police] Accountability.

15 In addition, some victims saw the police station as a safe place to hold a restorative encounter.

16 From a Foucauldian perspective, all restorative practices discipline, by teaching offenders victim-empathy, how to repair wrongs, and so forth (Minor and Morrison, 1996: 126–7). The police-led sessions we observed were no different in this. In this chapter, however, my main concern is with the particular forms of discipline that are attributable to the involvement of the police.

17 There is a more developed, and empirically-based, critical literature on police involvement in the handling of disputes. See, for example, Kemp *et al.* (1992), Leng (1993), Walter and Wagner (1996) and Hoyle (1998).

18 Some of the more praiseworthy aspects of the Thames Valley initiative are discussed in Young and Goold (1999) and Young (2000). This chapter contains more critical observations than my earlier writing because its aim is to highlight some potential pitfalls of police-led restorative justice in order that these may be anticipated and guarded against by those working in this field.

19 In quoted extracts from restorative cautions and conferences, and from interviews, the following key is used: o=offender; os=offender supporter; v=victim; f=facilitator; oic=officer in charge of the case; int=interviewer. Names and minor factual details have been changed in order to preserve anonymity.

20 It is unlikely that a tick-box questionnaire would have uncovered these perceptions adequately. Thus, for example, the offender who said the process made him feel like 'scum' answered our specific questions on procedural fairness by saying that he had been treated fairly in the meeting 'because I was allowed to talk'; that the facilitator's way of running the meeting had been 'fine'; and that since his arrest the police had been 'really nice and helpful'.

21 The facilitators we observed were never directly concerned in the investigation of the case that had resulted in a restorative justice process.

22 For one example see the extract from the transcript quoted above under the sub-heading: *Echoing the police interview.*

23 Studies such as McConville, Sanders and Leng (1991) have shown that these files do not contain the unvarnished truth but rather are constructed so as to further police goals.

24 Our observational data are inconclusive on this point. One of the difficulties of observing conferences (typically organised in circles) is that it is impossible to see everyone's face. In addition, so as not to be obtrusive, we usually placed ourselves so that we were not observing the participants face-on.

25 Restorative cautioning in England and Wales has developed without any specific legislative or judicial authority or intervention. The position is thus governed by the Police and Criminal Evidence Act 1984 under which a court would have to exclude such evidence if it thought it had been obtained in conditions which made it unreliable (s. 76) and would have the discretion to exclude if it took the view that to admit the evidence would have an adverse effect on the fairness of the proceedings (s. 78).

26 One often encounters in the literature the suggestion that offers of legal advice amount to a safeguard against unfairness (see, for example, Morris and Young, 2000: 23). But offers in themselves may do little to safeguard the rights of either offenders or victims, as the extensive literature on the provision of legal advice to persons arrested shows (Sanders and Young, 2000: chapter 4). Most notably, offers are turned down more often than they are accepted.

27 That police victim cases can be handled by police facilitators in a way which is much more consistent with the tenets of restorative justice is illustrated in Young (2000: 240–2).

28 For a discussion of the practices that made up old-style cautioning, and of the degree to which these were transformed by the introduction of restorative justice in one Thames Valley Police area, see Young and Goold (1999).

References

Ashworth, A. (forthcoming) 'Is Restorative Justice the Way Forward for Criminal Justice?', *Current Legal Problems.*

Braithwaite, J. (1989) *Crime, Shame and Reintegration* (Cambridge: Cambridge University Press).

Braithwaite, J. (1999) *Restorative Justice: Assessing Optimistic and Pessimistic Accounts, Crime and Justice – A Review of Research. Vol. 25* (Chicago, IL: University of Chicago Press).

Braithwaite, J. and Mugford, S. (1994) 'Conditions of Successful Reintegration Ceremonies', *British Journal of Criminology*, 34, p. 139.

Carlen, P. (1983) *Women's Imprisonment: A Study in Social Control* (London: Routledge).

Carlen, P. (2000) 'Youth Justice? Arguments for Holism and Democracy in Responses to Crime', in Green, P. and Rutherford, A. (eds) *Criminal Policy in Transition* (Oxford: Hart Publishing 2000).

Chan, J. (1996) 'Changing Police Culture', *British Journal of Criminology*, 36, p. 109.

Daly, K. and Immarigeon, R. (1998) 'The Past, Present, and Future of Restorative Justice: Some Critical Reflections', *Contemporary Justice Review*, 1, p. 21.

Foucault, M. (1977) *Discipline and Punish: The Birth of the Prison* (Harmondsworth: Penguin).

Garland, D. (1990) *Punishment and Modern Society* (Oxford: Clarendon Press).

Hoyle, C. (1998) *Negotiating Domestic Violence* (Oxford: Clarendon Press).

Kemp, C., Norris, C. and Fielding, N. (1992) 'Legal Manoeuvres in Police Handling of Disputes', in Farrington, D. and Walklate, S. (eds) *Offenders and Victims: Theory and Policy* (London: British Society of Criminology).

Lacey, N. (1999) 'Penal Practices and Political Theory: An Agenda for Dialogue', in Matravers, M. (ed.) *Punishment and Political Theory* (Oxford: Hart Publishing).

Leng, R. (1993) 'Police Involvement in Dispute Resolution', in Sampson, C. and McBride, J. (eds) *Alternative Dispute Resolution* (Sainte-Foy: University of Laval Press).

McCold, P. and Wachtel, B. (1998) *Restorative Policing Experiment: The Bethlehem Pennsylvania Police Family Group Conferencing Project* (Pipersville, PA: Community Service Foundation).

McConville, M., Sanders, A. and Leng, R. (1991) *The Case for the Prosecution* (London: Routledge).

Minor, K.I. and Morrison, J.T. (1996) 'A Theoretical Study and Critique of Restorative Justice', in Galaway, B. and Hudson, J. (eds) *Restorative Justice: International Perspectives* (Amsterdam: Kugler).

Morris, A. and Maxwell, G. (2000) 'The Practice of Family Group Conferences in New Zealand: Assessing the Place, Potential and Pitfalls of Restorative Justice', in Crawford, A. and Goodey, J. (eds) *Integrating a Victim Perspective within Criminal Justice* (Aldershot: Ashgate).

Morris, A. and Young, W. (2000) 'Reforming Criminal Justice: The Potential of Restorative Justice', in Strang, H. and Braithwaite, J. (eds) *Restorative Justice: Philosophy to Practice* (Aldershot: Ashgate).

Polk, K. (1994) 'Family Conferencing: Theoretical and Evaluative Concerns', in Alder, C. and Wundersitz, J. (eds) *Family Conferencing and Juvenile Justice: The Way Forward or Misplaced Optimism?* (Canberra: Australian Institute of Criminology).

Sanders, A. and Young, R. (2000) *Criminal Justice* (London: Butterworths).

Sandor, D. (1994) 'The Thickening Blue Wedge in Juvenile Justice', in Alder, C. and Wundersitz, J. (eds) *Family Conferencing and Juvenile Justice: The Way Forward or Misplaced Optimism?* (Canberra: Australian Institute of Criminology).

Sherman, L. and Barnes, G. (1997) *Restorative Justice and Offenders' Respect for the Law. RISE Working Paper.*

Sherman, L. and Strang, H. (1997) *The Right Kind of Shame for Crime Prevention. RISE Working Paper.*

Strang, H., Barnes, G., Braithwaite, J. and Sherman, L. (1999) *Experiments in Restorative Policing: A Progress Report on the Canberra Reintegrative Shaming Experiments (RISE)* (Canberra: Australian National University).

Waddington, P.A.J. (1999) 'Police (Canteen) Sub-culture: An Appreciation', *British Journal of Criminology*, 39, p. 286.

Walgrave, L. (2000) 'Restorative Justice and the Republican Theory of Criminal Justice: An Exercise in Normative Theorising on Restorative Justice', in Strang, H. and Braithwaite, J. (eds) *Restorative Justice: Philosophy to Practice* (Aldershot: Ashgate).

Walter, M. and Wagner, A. (1996) 'How Police Officers Manage Difficult Situations: The Predominance of Soothing and Smoothing Strategies', in Galaway, B. and Hudson, J. (eds) *Restorative Justice: International Perspectives* (Amsterdam: Kugler).

Warner, K. (1994) 'Family Group Conferences and the Rights of the Offender', in Alder, C. and Wundersitz, J. (eds) *Family Conferencing and Juvenile Justice: The Way Forward or Misplaced Optimism?* (Canberra: Australian Institute of Criminology).

White, R. (1994) 'Shame and Reintegration Strategies: Individuals, State Power and Social Interests', in Alder, C. and Wundersitz, J. (eds) *Family Conferencing and Juvenile Justice: The Way Forward or Misplaced Optimism?* (Canberra: Australian Institute of Criminology).

Wundersitz, J. and Hetzel, S. (1996) 'Family Conferencing for Young Offenders: The South Australian Experience', in Hudson, J. *et al.* (eds) *Family Group Conferences* (Annandale: Federation Press).

Young, R. (2000) 'Integrating a Multi-victim Perspective through Restorative Justice Conferences', in Crawford, A. and Goodey, J. (eds) *Integrating a Victim Perspective within Criminal Justice* (Aldershot: Ashgate).

Young, R. and Goold, B. (1999) 'Restorative Police Cautioning in Aylesbury – from Degrading to Reintegrative Shaming Ceremonies?', *Criminal Law Review*, 126.

28. Reconsidering restorative justice: the corruption of benevolence revisited?

Sharon Levrant, Francis T. Cullen, Betsy Fulton and John F. Wozniak

[. . .]

The corruption of benevolence?

In the 1970s, many liberals joined with conservatives in rejecting rehabilitation and in endorsing reforms, especially determinate sentencing, that constrained the discretion exercised by criminal justice officials. Believing that these reforms would result in increased justice (e.g., equity in sentencing decisions), liberals largely overlooked the possibility that their strange bedfellows – conservatives – would use the rejection of the rehabilitative ideal as a means to achieve their goal of getting tough on offenders. In hindsight, it now appears that the liberals' benevolent hopes of doing justice were corrupted by conservatives who succeeded in passing harsh laws that ultimately increased the punishment of and harm done to offenders (Cullen and Gilbert, 1982; Griset, 1991).

In endorsing restorative justice, liberals once again are embracing a reform also being trumpeted by conservatives. In doing so, it seems prudent to consider the lesson of the antirehabilitation movement: Progressive sentiments are no guarantee that reforms will not be corrupted and serve punitive ends. In this context, this section explores four potential unanticipated consequences of restorative justice: (1) it will serve as a means of getting tough on offenders; (2) it will not be restorative for victims, offenders, or communities; (3) it will be more of a symbolic than a substantive reform; and (4) it will reinforce existing race and class biases besetting the criminal justice system.

Getting tough through restorative justice

According to progressive advocates, restorative justice policies offer potential benefits to offenders, including the opportunity to reconcile with their victims, a more lenient sentence, and the chance for reintegration into society. It remains to be seen, however, whether conservatives will endorse these goals and work with liberals to create a balanced reform or whether they will use restorative justice as yet another opportunity to impose more punishment of offenders. Six considerations suggest that the restorative justice movement may not achieve its progressive goals and, in fact, may increase the extent and harshness of criminal sanctions.

First, Brown (1994) notes that restorative justice systems lack the due process protections and procedural safeguards that are awarded to offenders in the more formal adversarial system. Although programs vary, counsel are generally discouraged from attending mediation hearings because they create barriers for a smooth mediation process. Furthermore, the informality of the system contributes to more lenient rules of evidence. Information presented at conferences also can be used in a formal trial if the offender fails to reach an agreement with the victim during mediation. Restorative justice advocates believe that the cost of diminished offender rights is outweighed by the benefits of accountability (Berzins and Prashaw, 1997; Van Ness, 1986). Brown (1994) argues, however, that the loss of rights can result in an offender receiving more severe punishment than he or she would receive through the adversarial process.

Second, despite the progressive rhetoric of restoration, offenders may be coerced into participating in the mediation process because of perceived threats of a harsher punishment if they refuse to do so (Brown, 1994; Van Ness and Strong, 1997). According to Brown (1994), in certain jurisdictions, prosecutors and judges can consider offenders' refusal to participate in VOM conferences in their charging and sentencing decisions. The problem of coercion can be exacerbated if people who normally would not be subjected to state controls through the formal criminal justice process are coerced into participating in restorative justice programming.

Third and relatedly, restorative justice programs can potentially widen the net of social control (Bazemore and Umbreit, 1995; Umbreit and Zehr, 1996; Van Ness and Strong, 1997). The increased influence that the community has in sanctioning can lead restorative justice programs to target offenders who commit minor offences and are at a low risk of reoffending. For example, market research in Vermont revealed that citizens wanted the criminal justice system to take minor offences more seriously (Walther and Perry, 1997). Thus, instead of diverting offenders from intrusive forms of punishment (e.g., electronic monitoring, intensive supervision probation, incarceration), restorative justice may place more control over the lives of nonserious offenders who may have otherwise received no formal supervision.

Fourth, Bazemore and Umbreit (1995) contend that if broad changes do not take place to make the system restorative, then restorative justice sanctions will likely increase the supervisory requirements that offenders must satisfy. A survey of offenders participating in Vermont's Reparative Probation Program revealed that offenders perceived the program to be much more demanding than regular probation (Walther and Perry, 1997). Furthermore, it was discovered that contrary to the program's design, offenders were subjected to both reparative conditions and traditional probation supervision. Until a complete paradigm shift has occurred, restorative justice policies will potentially inflict additional punishment on offenders.

Fifth, as conditions of probation expand through restorative justice programs, the potential that offenders will not meet these conditions also increases. This higher level of noncompliance, combined with heightened public scrutiny and a demand for offender accountability, will likely result in the revocation of more offenders. Other community corrections reforms have experienced a similar phenomenon. For example, the closer surveillance of offenders in intensive supervision programs has led to the increased detection of technical violations (Cullen *et al.*, 1996). Because of an emphasis on stringent responses to noncompliance, detection violations in these programs have often been followed by the revocation of probation and incarceration (Petersilia and Turner, 1993). Thus, restorative justice programs may not only increase social control within the community but may also result in more offenders being sent to prison because they fail to comply with the additional sanctions imposed within the restorative justice framework.

According to Braithwaite and Mugford (1994), one strategy to circumvent this problem is to provide offenders with the opportunity to have multiple conferences when they fail to fulfill the requirements of their mediation agreements. Still, if the victim–offender agreements reached at conferences are to be meaningful, limits will have to be placed on how many repeated conferences there can be before an offender must be held accountable in criminal court and risk incarceration. Even if offenders are not incarcerated for failing to comply with the mediation agreement, they will face an escalating number of conditions. Net-widening and revocation for technical violations are the likely result.

Sixth, restorative justice may increase punishment if reforms fail to develop policies and programs that are able to reintegrate offenders into society. Karp (1998) notes, however, that shaming penalties are gaining popularity because they can fulfill the retributive aims of the public. Lawrence (1991) also sees a danger in advocating shaming activities. He suggests that they may be wrongly interpreted as a revival of support for public shaming practices, such as the ducking stool and the scarlet letter, without an emphasis on the reintegrative element of community acceptance and support.

In summary, although restorative justice policies are being advocated as a benevolent means of addressing the crime problem, they may increase the punitiveness of the social control imposed on offenders in several ways: offenders may lose certain rights and privileges that they are granted through the current adversarial process, offenders may be coerced into participating in restorative justice programs because of formal pressures from practitioners within the criminal justice system, restorative justice may widen the net of social control by targeting low risk offenders, offenders may be subjected to greater levels of supervision, offenders may have a greater likelihood of incarceration for technical violations because of the increased probation conditions and scrutiny they face, and, finally, restorative justice programs may not achieve their goal of offender reintegration and therefore fail to restore fully the harmed relationships that result from the crime. This propensity for getting tough with restorative justice creates doubt about the restorative capacities of current practices.

[. . .]

Changing offender behavior: the utilitarian challenge

Many correctional reforms over the past 20 years have developed in response to correctional crises and political pressures rather than from a careful evaluation of policy options and empirical evidence of effectiveness (Cochran, 1992). In fact, the very argument that contributed to the demise of rehabilitation – that it failed to reduce recidivism and protect public safety – has been all but ignored in recent progressive reforms. Instead, liberals have tried to promote reforms that promised to reduce the use of incarceration and to advance the legal rights granted to offenders. Whatever the value of these reforms, the result has been that correctional policy has largely been forfeited to conservatives who boldly claim that crime can be reduced by locking up more offenders (Cullen, Van Voorhis and Sundt, 1996). By failing to critically evaluate the capacity for restorative justice practices to lower crime, liberal advocates are in danger of experiencing another setback in their quest for a more progressive system of justice.

Restorative justice proponents, either explicitly or implicitly, argue that crime can be lessened through restorative practices. Pranis (1996) asserts that programs rooted in a restorative justice philosophy decrease crime by strengthening community bonds and enhancing informal mechanisms of social control. Braithwaite (1989) argues that the reintegrative aspect of restorative justice policies reduces recidivism by allowing an offender to remain a part of society and to avoid the criminal subcultures and the labeling process that perpetuate delinquency. Still others claim that specific restorative justice programs have the capacity to change offender behavior. For example, it is argued that victim–offender mediation can facilitate changes in offenders' behavior by forcing them to recognize the harm that their criminal behavior causes to victims and communities (Ruddell, 1996; Umbreit, 1994). Bazemore and Maloney (1994) suggest that community service would be more rehabilitative in nature if it was guided by a restorative justice philosophy.

These claims, however, seem more based on wishful thinking than on a systematic understanding of how to change the conduct of offenders. Although programs with a restorative orientation may occasionally reduce recidivism (see, e.g., Umbreit, 1994), the current knowledge base on offender change would suggest that restorative interventions are likely to have effects on recidivism that are modest, if not inconsequential. In the following section, we elaborate this point by assessing the extent to which restorative programs have features that coincide with the principles of effective treatment.

Effective correctional interventions

Since 1975, an abundance of literature reviews and meta-analyses have examined the effectiveness of various correctional interventions (Palmer, 1992). There is an increasing consensus that programs that achieve a reduction in recidivism share common features (Andrews *et al.*, 1990; Gendreau and Andrews, 1990; Izzo and Ross, 1990; Lipsey and Wilson, 1998). These characteristics, often referred to as 'the principles of effective intervention', are summarized briefly below (Andrews *et al.*, 1990; Gendreau, 1996; Gendreau and Andrews, 1990).

Three principles of effective intervention address the importance of matching offenders to services based on their risk, need, and personal characteristics (Andrews and Bonta, 1994; Andrews *et al.*, 1990). The risk principle suggests that levels of service should be matched to the risk level of the offender (Andrews and Bonta, 1994). This principle is based on several studies that have found that intensive services are necessary to achieve a significant reduction in recidivism among high-risk offenders, but that when applied to low-risk offenders, intensive services have a minimal or positive effect on recidivism (Andrews et al., 1990). This latter phenomenon has been called an interaction effect in which additional efforts to intervene with low-risk offenders actually increase recidivism (Clear and Hardyman, 1990; Neithercutt and Gottfredson, 1974).

The need principle suggests that changes in recidivism are dependent on changes in the criminogenic needs of offenders (Andrews and Bonta, 1994). Criminogenic needs are dynamic factors that are potentially changeable and that are associated with recidivism, such as antisocial attitudes, substance abuse, poor family communication, and antisocial peer associations (Andrews and Bonta, 1990). Thus, when these factors are reduced, there is a decreased likelihood of recidivism. The responsivity principle suggests that in addition to matching services with an offender's risks and needs, the learning styles and personality characteristics of offenders can influence treatment effectiveness (Andrews and Bonta, 1990; Van Voorhis, 1997). For example, high anxiety offenders do not generally respond well to confrontation (Warren, 1983), whereas offenders with below-average intellectual abilities do not respond to cognitive skills programs as well as do offenders with above-average intellectual abilities (Fabiano et al., 1991).

In addition to the above-mentioned principles relevant to offender-treatment matching, effective interventions are rooted in behavioral or cognitive-behavioral models of treatment (Clements, 1988; Gendreau, 1996; Izzo and Ross, 1990; Palmer, 1996). According to Gendreau (1996), well-designed behavioral programs combine a system of reinforcement with modeling by the treatment provider to teach and motivate offenders to perform prosocial behaviors. Cognitive-behavioral models are designed to enhance perspective taking, interpersonal problem solving, and self-control techniques so as to improve offenders' responses to their environments and stressful situations (Clements, 1988).

The most effective interventions possess other similar characteristics. First, they occupy 40 per cent to 70 per cent of high-risk offenders' time (Gendreau, 1996). Second, they last at least 23 weeks (Lipsey and Wilson, 1998). Third, they employ service providers who relate to offenders in interpersonally sensitive and constructive ways and who are trained and supervised appropriately. Fourth, they use relapse prevention techniques to monitor and to anticipate problem situations and to train offenders to rehearse alternative behaviors. Last, effective interventions link offenders to other services in the community that are relevant to their needs.

Meta-analyses of correctional interventions have found that programs that meet these principles are achieving, on average, a recidivism reduction of 50 per cent (Andrews et al., 1990). Interventions that depart from these principles have a dismal success rate. For example, a meta-analysis of studies on punishment and deterrence-based programs, such as intensive supervision, boot camp, Scared Straight programs, and electronic monitoring programs, revealed that these strategies produced slight increases in recidivism (Gendreau *et al.*, 2000; Gendreau and Little, 1993; see also Lipsey and Wilson, 1998). Given the increasing knowledge base on what works to change offender behavior, to what extent can we expect restorative justice programs to reduce recidivism? In addressing this question, the next section will examine the degree to which restorative justice programs reflect these principles.

Assessing restorative justice programs

As currently implemented, most restorative justice programs fail to incorporate the principles of effective intervention, particularly as they relate to the risk, need, and responsivity principles. In restorative justice, the primary criterion for matching sanctions to offenders is the nature and extent of the harm caused by the crime. The seriousness of the offence, however, is not consistently related to an offender's risk of recidivism (Correctional Service Canada, 1989; Goldkamp and Gottfredson, 1985). Thus, restorative justice programs run the dual risks of producing an interaction effect in low-risk offenders and of underservicing high-risk offenders.

Traditionally, restorative justice programs have targeted low-risk nonviolent offenders for participation (Dooley, 1996; Ruddell, 1996). These offenders typically are unlikely to recidivate. If subjected to unnecessary sanctions and services, however, their chances for noncompliance, and hence revocation, are increased (Clear and Hardyman, 1990). The opposite problems exist for high-risk offenders who increasingly are being included in restorative justice programs. Given research findings that suggest that intensive services are required to reduce recidivism among high-risk offenders, it is unlikely that, for example, a one-hour victim–offender mediation session will lessen criminal propensities among these offenders. Thus, the restorative approach runs the risk of becoming the progressives' equivalent of conservative Scared Straight programs, which attempt to shock youth into positive behavior by subjecting them to an afternoon in prison (Finckenauer, 1982).

It is also highly unlikely that restorative justice programs will, as currently implemented, produce lasting changes in an offender's criminogenic needs. As discussed previously, restorative justice programs are currently implemented in a piecemeal fashion and are focused primarily on victim restoration. The only criminogenic need that is even remotely targeted by these practices is lack of empathy or sensitivity to others – a part of many offenders' antisocial values system (Gendreau *et al.*, 1992). Victim–offender mediation and victim-impact panels are common approaches to developing an offender's empathy toward victims of crime. However, they lack the behavioral framework and relapse-prevention component needed to reinforce improved attitudes in a manner that leads to internalization and continued improvements. Instead, they provide only short-term confrontations with victims that may result in more punishment for the offender. Furthermore, these victim-oriented programs fail to help offenders make generalizations about how their behavior influences others over the long-term or fail to teach offenders alternative ways of behaving.

Findings from a study of a restitution program demonstrate the limitations of restorative justice programs that do not abide by the responsivity principle.

Van Voorhis (1985) found that low-maturity offenders, as measured by Kohlberg's stages of moral development, were more likely than high-maturity offenders to view restitution as a means of obtaining a lenient sentence and were significantly less likely to provide restitution to their victims. Thus, restitution does not appear to be a viable mechanism for changing the antisocial attitudes of low-maturity offenders and, more important, for reducing the likelihood of their future criminal behavior.

More generally, meta-analyses conclude that restitution programs have modest, if not weak, effects on recidivism. In a meta-analysis of 10 restitution interventions with serious, noninstitutionalized juvenile offenders, Lipsey and Wilson (1998) found that the mean effect of restitution on recidivism across the studies was 0.17. Although not inconsequential, this result is modest when compared with behaviorally oriented and individual counseling programs that had an effect size in Lipsey and Wilson's analysis of 0.43. Even less promising results were found in Gendreau et al.'s (2000) meta-analysis of 16 studies of restitution programs. They found that the mean size of the effect of restitution on recidivism was only 0.04.

Community service programs also have failed to incorporate the principles of effective intervention. Bazemore and Maloney (1994) suggest that to achieve the full potential of community service, the assigned activity should 'bring the offender and conventional adults together' and 'provide for a sense of accomplishment, closure, and community recognition' (p. 30). Programs designed in this manner would provide offenders with the modeling and positive reinforcement that are needed to motivate prosocial behavior. However, because community service has historically been imposed as an additional punishment or condition of probation supervision, little attention has been paid to such treatment goals and related practices. In fact, the image of offenders in bright orange jumpsuits picking up trash on the side of the road suggests that some community service assignments may be stigmatizing. In these instances, the extent to which offenders learn attitudes and skills conducive to prosocial behavior is likely to be limited.

In contrast, victim-impact classes conducted by the California Youth Authority may prove more effective. The primary goal of these classes is to make offenders understand the devastating effects of crime (Seymour, 1996). Youth participate in a six-week course that teaches alternative ways to resolve conflict. According to Seymour (1996), the curriculum is an educational model that is culturally sensitive and appropriate for the offenders' age and cognitive development. Although too brief in duration for high-risk offenders, this curriculum appears to include the behavioral and cognitive components required to change offender behavior.

Until more programs operating within the restorative justice framework incorporate the principles of effective intervention, the likelihood of producing reductions in recidivism is limited. This, in turn, will compromise the extent to which other restorative goals can be achieved because victims and communities will continue to suffer from the criminal behavior of these repeat offenders. A truly restorative program will be rooted in empirical evidence on what works in changing offender behavior.

[. . .]

This extract is taken from 'Reconsidering Restorative Justice: the Corruption of Benevolence Revisited?' by S. Levrant, F.T. Cullen, B. Fulton and J.F. Wozniak in Crime and Deliquency, *Vol. 45, no. 1, Jan. 1999, pp. 3–27.*

References

Andrews, D.A. and Bonta, J. (1994) *The Psychology of Criminal Conduct* (Cincinnati, OH: Anderson).

Andrews, D.A., Bonta, J. and Hoge, R.D.C. (1990) 'Classification for Effective Rehabilitation: Rediscovering Psychology', *Criminal Justice and Behavior*, 17, pp. 19–52.

Andrews, D.A., Zinger, I., Hoge, R.D., Bonta, J., Gendreau, P. and Cullen, F.T. (1990) 'Does Correctional Treatment Work? Clinically Relevant and Psychologically Informed Meta-analysis', *Criminology*, 28, pp. 369–404.

Bazemore, G. and Maloney, D. (1994) 'Rehabilitating Community Service: Toward Restorative Service Sanctions in a Balanced Justice System', *Federal Probation*, 58:1, pp. 24–35.

Bazemore, G. and Umbreit, M. (1995) 'Rethinking the Sanctioning Function in Juvenile Court', *Crime and Delinquency*, 41, pp. 296–316.

Berzins, L. and Prashaw, R. (1997) 'A New Imagination for Justice and Corrections', *The ICCA Journal of Community Corrections*, 8:2, pp. 22–5.

Braithwaite, J. (1989) *Crime, Shame and Reintegration* (New York, NY: Cambridge University Press).

Braithwaite, J. and Mugford, S. (1994) 'Conditions of Successful Reintegration Ceremonies: Dealing with Juvenile Offenders', *British Jnl of Criminology*, pp. 139–71.

Brown, J.G. (1994) 'The Use of Mediation to Resolve Criminal Cases: A Procedural Critique', *Emory Law Journal*, 43, pp. 1247–309.

Clear, T.R. and Hardyman, P. (1990) 'The New Intensive Supervision Movement', *Crime and Delinquency*, 36, pp. 42–60.

Clements, C. (1988) 'Delinquency Prevention and Treatment: A Community-centered Perspective', *Criminal Justice and Behavior*, 15, pp. 286–305.

Cochran, D. (1992) 'The Long Road from Policy Development to Real Change in Sanctioning Practice', in Bryne, J. *et al.* (eds) *Smart Sentencing: The Emergence of Intermediate Sanctions* (Newbury Park, CA: Sage), pp. 307–18.

Correctional Service Canada (1989) 'What Does Type of Offense Tell us about Recidivism?' *Forum on Corrections Research*, 1:2, pp. 3–4.

Cullen, F.T. and Gilbert, K.E. (1982) *Reaffirming Rehabilitation* (Cincinnati, OH: Anderson).

Cullen, F.T., Van Voorhis, P. and Sundt, J.L. (1996) 'Prisons in Crisis: The American Experience', in Matthews, R. and Francis, P. (eds) *Prisons 2000: An International Perspective on the Current State and Future of Imprisonment* (New York, NY: St Martin's Press), pp. 21–52.

Cullen, F.T., Wright, J.P. and Applegate, B.K. (1996) 'Control in the Community: The Limits of Reform?', in Harland, A.T. (ed.) *Choosing Correctional Interventions that Work: Defining the Demand and Evaluating the Supply* (Newbury Park, CA: Sage), pp. 69–116.

Currie, E. (1998) *Crime and Punishment in America* (New York, NY: Metropolitan).

Dooley, M.J. (1996) 'Reparative Probation Boards', in Fulton, B. (ed.) *Restoring Hope through Community Partnerships: The Real Deal in Crime Control* (Lexington, KY: American Probation and Parole Association), pp. 185–92.

Fabiano, E., Porporino, F. and Robinson, D. (1991) 'Canada's Cognitive Skills Program Corrects Offenders' Faulty Thinking', *Corrections Today*, 53: August, pp. 102–8.

Finckenauer, J.O. (1982) *Scared Straight! And the Panacea Phenomenon* (Englewood Cliffs, NJ: Prentice Hall).

Gendreau, P. (1996) 'The Principles of Effective Intervention with Offenders', in Harland, A.T. (ed.) *Choosing Correctional Options that Work* (Thousand Oaks, CA: Sage), pp. 117–30.

Gendreau, P. and Andrews, D.A. (1990) 'Tertiary Prevention: What the Meta-analyses of the Offender Treatment Literature Tell us about what Works', *Canadian Journal of Criminology*, 32, pp. 173–84.

Gendreau, P., Fulton, B. and Goggin, C. (2000) 'Intensive Supervision in Probation and Parole Settings', in Hollin, C.R. (ed.) *Handbook of Offender Assessment and Treatment* (Chichester: Wiley).

Gendreau, P. and Little, T. (1993) 'A Meta-analysis of the Effectiveness of Sanctions on Offender Recidivism.' Department of Psychology, University of New Brunswick, St John. Unpublished manuscript.

Goldkamp, J. and Gottfredson, M. (1985) *Policy Guidelines for Bail: An Experiment in Court Reform* (Philadelphia, PA: Temple University).

Griset, P.L. (1991) *Determinate Sentencing: The Promise and the Reality of Retributive Justice* (Albany, NY: State University of New York Press).

Izzo, R. and Ross, R. (1990) 'Meta-analysis of Rehabilitation Programs for Juvenile Delinquents: A Brief Report', *Criminal Justice and Behavior*, 17, pp. 134–42.

Karp, D.R. (1998) 'The Judicial and Judicious Use of Shame Penalties', *Crime and Delinquency*, 44, pp. 277–94.

Lawrence, R. (1991) 'Reexamining Community Corrections Models', *Crime and Delinquency*, 37, pp. 449–64.

Lipsey, M. and Wilson, D. (1998) 'Effective Intervention for Serious Juvenile Offenders: A Synthesis of Research', in Loebe, R. and Farrington, D.P. (eds) *Serious and Violent Juvenile Offenders* (Thousand Oaks, CA: Sage), pp. 313–45.

Neithercutt, M.G. and Gottfredson, D.M. (1974) *Caseload Size Variation and Differences in Probation/Parole Performance* (Washington, DC: National Center for Juvenile Justice).

Palmer, T. (1992) *The Re-Emergence of Correctional Intervention* (Newbury Park, CA: Sage).

Petersilia, J. and Turner, S. (1993) 'Evaluating Intensive Supervision Probation/Parole: Results of Nationwide Experiment.' Research in Brief, NIJ, Washington, DC.

Pranis, K. (1996) 'A Hometown Approach to Restorative Justice', *State Government News*, 39:9, pp. 14–16.

Ruddell, R. (1996) 'Victim Offender Reconciliation Program', in Fulton, B. (ed.) *Restoring Hope through Community Partnerships: The Real Deal in Crime Control* (Lexington, KY: American Probation and Parole Association), pp. 171–2.

Seymour, A. (1996) 'Putting Victims First', *State Government News*, 39:9, pp. 24–5.

Umbreit, M.S. (1994) 'Victim Empowerment through Mediation: The Impact of Victim Offender Mediation in Four Cities', *Perspectives* (Special Issue), pp. 25–30.

Umbreit, M. and Zehr, H. (1996) 'Restorative Family Group Conferences: Differing Models and Guidelines for Practice', *Federal Probation*, 60:3, pp. 24–9.

Van Ness, D.W. (1986) *Crime and its Victims* (Downers Grove, IL: InterVarsity Press).

Van Ness, D.W. and Strong, K.H. (1997) *Restoring Justice* (Cincinnati, OH: Anderson).

Van Voorhis, P. (1985) 'Restitution Outcome and Probationers' Assessments of Restitution', *Criminal Justice and Behavior*, 12, pp. 249–87.

Walther, L. and Perry, J. (1997) 'The Vermont Reparative Probation Program', *The ICCA Journal on Community Corrections*, 8:2, pp. 26–34.

Warren, M. (1983) 'Application of Interpersonal Maturity Theory to Offender Populations', in Laufer, W. and Day, J. (eds) *Personality Theory, Moral Development, and Criminal Behavior* (Lexington, MA: Lexington Books), pp. 23–49.

29. Responsibilities, rights and restorative justice

Andrew Ashworth

[...]

Rights and responsibilities of the victim

It is common for those writing on restorative justice to insist that all parties 'with a stake in the offence' ought to be able to participate in the disposition of the case, through a circle, conference, etc. (e.g. Llewellyn and Howse, 1998: 19). The victim certainly has 'a stake', and Christie's (1977) assertion that the 'conflict' in some sense 'belongs' to the victim has become a modern orthodoxy among restorative justice supporters (e.g. Morris and Maxwell, 2000: 207, who write of 'returning the offence to those most affected by it and encouraging them to determine appropriate responses to it'). The approach has ancient roots (Braithwaite, 1999: 1–2 for a summary and references), although the growing awareness of the existence of secondary victimization (e.g. Morgan and Zedner, 1992 on child victims) demonstrates the complexity of the issues arising.

The politico-historical argument is that most modern legal systems exclude the victim so as to bolster their own power. Originally the state wanted to take over criminal proceedings from victims as an assertion of power, and what now passes for 'normal' is simply a usurpation that has no claim to be the natural order. My concern is not to dispute this rather romantic interpretation of criminal justice in early history (Daly, 2000 does this splendidly; also Johnstone, 2001: ch. 3) but rather to raise three points of principle which have a bearing on the nature and extent of victims' rights: the principle of compensation for wrongs, the principle of proportionality, and the principle of independence and impartiality.

The first point of principle is the most direct of all in its target. What I want to argue is that the victim's legitimate interest is in compensation and/or reparation from the offender, and not in the form or quantum of the offender's punishment. The distinction between punishment and compensation is not widely appreciated: when a court fines an offender £300 for careless driving in a case where death resulted (but where there was no conviction for the more serious offence of causing death by dangerous driving), newspapers will often report comments such as 'my son's life has been valued at just £300'. However, the size of the fine will usually be related to the offender's culpability (and financial resources), and will not be a 'valuation' of the loss. Compensation for loss, from whatever source, is a separate matter. It may not require a separate civil case: English criminal courts are required to consider ordering the offender to pay compensation to the victim or victim's family, so far as the offender's means allow. However, in many cases the offender will not have the funds to pay realistic compensation. It is now recognized as part of the state's responsibility for criminal justice that it should provide a compensation fund for victims of crimes of violence, at least (see Ashworth, 1986 and, on the current scheme, Miers, 1997). This is not to deny that victims primarily have a right to compensation from the offender: that is clear on legal and moral grounds, if not always practical.

The key question is whether the victim's legitimate interest goes beyond reparation or compensation (and the right to victim services and support, and to proper protection from further harm), and extends to the question of punishment. It would be wrong to suggest that the victim has no legitimate interest in the disposition of the offender in his or her case, but the victim's interest is surely no greater than yours or mine. The victim's interest is as a citizen, as one of many citizens who make up the community or state. In democratic theory all citizens have a right to vote at elections and sometimes on other occasions, and to petition their elected representatives about issues affecting them. If I am an ardent advocate of restorative justice or of indeterminate imprisonment for repeat offenders, I can petition my MP about it, or join a pressure group. Just because a person commits an offence against me, however, that does not privilege my voice above that of the court (acting 'in the general public interest') in the matter of the offender's punishment. A justification for this lies in social contract reasoning, along the lines that the state may be said to undertake the duty of administering justice and protecting citizens in return for citizens giving up their right to self-help (except in cases of urgency) in the cause of better social order. This returns to the earlier argument about the state's responsibility, and to the 'rule of law' values of impartiality, independence and consistency in the administration of criminal justice.

This principle is not opposed by all those who advocate a version of restorative justice. Thus Michael Cavadino and James Dignan (1997) draw a strong distinction between the victim's right to reparation and the public interest in responding to the offence. In their view it is right to empower victims to participate in the process which determines what reparation is to be made by the offender, and reparation to the victim should be the major element of the response. In serious cases some additional response (punishment) may be considered necessary, and they then insist on a form of limiting retributivism in which proportionality sets upper and lower boundaries for the burdens placed on offenders (and also serves as a default setting for cases where a conference or circle proves impossible or inappropriate). It is a matter for regret that few restorative justice theorists refer to Cavadino and Dignan's attempt to preserve as many of the values of restorative justice as possible whilst insisting upon principled limits. They rightly see the distinction between compensation and punishment as crucial, even though their proportionality constraints are looser than many desert theorists would require, and they regard victim involvement as a value to be enhanced where possible. 'Victim personal statements' must now be taken into account by English courts before sentencing: Edna Erez claims that 'providing victims with a voice has therapeutic advantages' (1999: 555; cf. Edwards, 2001), but findings from the

English pilot projects indicated no great psychological benefits to participant victims and some evidence of disillusionment (Sanders *et al.*, 2001: 450).

The second point of principle concerns proportionality. Sentencing is *for* an offence, and respect for the offender as a citizen capable of choice suggests that the sentence should bear a relationship to the seriousness of the offence committed. To desert theorists this is axiomatic: punishment should always be proportionate to the offence, taking account of harm and culpability (von Hirsch, 1993: ch. 2), unless a highly persuasive argument for creating a class of exceptional cases can be sustained. It is a strong criticism of deterrent sentencing and of risk theory that they accord priority to predictions and not to the seriousness of the offence committed: von Hirsch and Ashworth (1998: chs 2, 3). The proportionality principle is not the sole preserve of desert theorists: on the contrary, versions of it are widely accepted as limiting the quantum of punishment that may be imposed on offenders, whether as a major tenet of the Council of Europe's recommendation on sentencing (1993: para. A4) or as an element in Nicola Lacey's communitarian approach to punishment (Lacey, 1988: 194). Other important functions of the proportionality principle are that it should ensure consistency of treatment among offenders, and that it should give protection against discrimination, by attempting to rule out certain factors from sentencing calculations. It is not being suggested that existing sentencing systems always pursue these principles successfully, but it is vital that they be recognized as goals and efforts made to fulfil them.

The principle of proportionality goes against victim involvement in sentencing decisions because the views of victims may vary. Some victims will be forgiving, others will be vindictive; some will be interested in new forms of sentence, others will not; some shops will have one policy in relation to thieves, others may have a different policy. If victim satisfaction is one of the aims of circles and conferences, then proportionate sentencing cannot be assured and may be overtaken in some cases by deterrent or risk-based sentencing. Two replies may be anticipated. First, it may be argued that in fact the involvement of victims assures *greater* proportionality (Erez and Rogers, 1999; Erez, 1999; cf. Sanders *et al.*, 2001: 451): the actual harm to the victim becomes clear, and in general victims do not desire disproportionate sentences. But these are aggregative findings, whereas the point of the principle is to ensure that in no individual case is an offender liable to a disproportionate penalty. A second reply would be to concede that victim involvement should be subject to proportionality limits, so that no agreement reached in a circle or conference should be out of proportion to the seriousness of the offence. The significance of this concession depends on the nature of the proportionality constraint. There is a range of possible proportionality theories: desert theory requires the sentence to be proportionate to the seriousness of the offence, within fairly narrow bands (von Hirsch, 1993: chs 2 and 4), whereas various forms of limiting retributivism recognize looser boundaries. Michael Tonry, for example, argues against the 'strong proportionality' of desert theorists and in favour of 'upper limits' set in accordance with a less precise notion of proportionality (Tonry, 1994). Among restorative justice theorists, Braithwaite refers to 'guaranteeing offenders against punishment beyond a maximum'

(1999: 105), but it is unclear whether his 'guarantee' adopts as much of proportionality theory as Tonry seems prepared to accept, and whether it imposes similar constraints or even less demanding ones. Most restorative justice theorists would insist that one of their objectives is to reduce levels of punitiveness, not to increase them; but some questions will be raised below about the contours of the 'background' penal system which is envisaged for cases where restorative justice processes fail or are rejected.

The third point is that everyone should have the right to a fair hearing 'by an independent and impartial tribunal', as Article 6.1 of the European Convention on Human Rights declares. This right expresses a fundamental principle of justice. Under the European Convention it applies to the sentencing stage as much as to trials. Do conferences and other restorative processes respect the right? Insofar as a victim plays a part in determining the disposition of a criminal case, is a conference 'independent and impartial'? The victim cannot be expected to be impartial, nor can the victim be expected to know about the available range of orders and other principles for the disposition of criminal cases. All of this suggests that conferences may fail to meet the basic standards of a fair hearing, insofar as the victim or victim's family plays a part in determining the outcome.

Most restorative justice supporters will be unimpressed with this, because the argument simply assumes that what has become conventional in modern criminal justice systems is absolutely right. But the issue of principle must be confronted, since it is supported by the European Convention, the International Covenant on Civil and Political Rights and many other human rights documents. One reply from restorative justice supporters might be that the required 'impartiality' and 'objectivity' produce such an impersonal and detached tribunal as to demonstrate exactly what is wrong with conventional systems, and why they fail. But that reply neglects, or certainly undervalues, the link between independence, impartiality and procedural justice. Might it be possible to sidestep the objection by characterizing conferences and other restorative justice processes as alternatives to sentencing rather than as sentencing processes, and therefore not bound by the same principles? This might be thought apposite where any agreement reached in the conference or circle has to be submitted for approval by a court, and where the offender may withdraw from the conference and go to the court at any time.

This is an appropriate point at which to question the reality of the consent that is said to underlie restorative justice processes and outcomes. The general principle is that 'restorative processes should be used only with the free and voluntary consent of the parties. The parties should be able to withdraw that consent at any time during the process' (UN, 2000: para. 7). This suggests that the offender may simply walk out and take his or her chances in the 'conventional' system. However, the result of doing so would usually be to propel the case into a formal criminal justice system that is perceived to be harsher in general, or that the offender may expect to be harsher on someone who has walked away from a restorative justice process. On some occasions, then, as in plea-bargaining (Sanders and Young, 2000: ch. 7; Ashworth, 1998: ch. 9), the 'consent' may proceed from a small amount of free will and a large slice of (perceived) coercion. Where the 'consent' is that of young people, and it is the police who explain matters to them, the danger of perceived coercion may be acute (Daly, 2001). The United Nations draft principles attempt to deal with some of these issues, by providing that failure to reach agreement or failure to implement an agreement 'may not be used as a justification for a more severe sentence in subsequent criminal justice proceedings' (UN, 2000: paras. 15, 16). But it is right to remain sceptical of the reality of consent, from the offender's point of view.

Returning to the right to an independent and impartial tribunal, is it breached if the victim makes a statement about sentencing, written or oral, to the court or other body that is to take the sentencing decision? This refers to statements that go beyond a victim impact statement, and are not limited to the issue of compensation. The ruling of the European Commission on Human Rights in *McCourt* v. *United Kingdom* (1993) 15 EHRR CD110 may be taken to suggest that such a statement on sentence could prejudice the impartiality of the tribunal, but this might be thought to go too far, not least because defendants have the right to make a 'plea in mitigation', in which their lawyers usually argue against certain outcomes and (sometimes) for a certain sentence. A stronger argument here is to return to the principles of compensation and of proportionality, discussed above, and to assert that the victim's view as to sentence should not be received because it is not relevant. Consider the case of *Nunn*, where the defendant had been sentenced to four years' imprisonment for causing the death of a close friend by dangerous driving. When Nunn's appeal against the sentence came before the Court of Appeal, the court had before it some lengthy written statements by the victim's mother and sister, recognizing that some punishment had to follow such a terrible offence, but stating that their own grief was being increased by the thought of the victim's close friend being in prison for so long. They added that the victim's father and other sister took a different view. In the Court of Appeal, Lord Justice Judge said this:

> We mean no disrespect to the mother and sister of the deceased, but the opinions of the victim, or the surviving members of the family, about the appropriate level of sentence do not provide any sound basis for reassessing a sentence. If the victim feels utterly merciful towards the criminal, and some do, the crime has still been committed and must be punished as it deserves. If the victim is obsessed with vengeance, which can in reality only be assuaged by a very long sentence, as also happens, the punishment cannot be made longer by the court than would otherwise be appropriate. Otherwise cases with identical features would be dealt with in widely differing ways, leading to improper and unfair disparity, and even in this particular case . . . the views of the members of the family of the deceased are not absolutely identical. (*Nunn* [1996] 2 Cr. App. R. (S) 136, at p. 140; see also *Roche* [1999] 2 Cr. App. R. (S) 105)

This statement captures the principles well.[1] Neither one victim's forgiveness of an offender, nor another's desire for vengeance against an offender, should be relevant when the community's response to an offence (as distinct from compensation) is being considered. The plea in *Nunn* was for leniency in the outcome, as also in the New Zealand case of *Clotworthy* (see Braithwaite, 1999: 87–8). There are other cases where victims and their families campaign for severity, some with a very high profile (e.g. the case of Thompson and Venables, convicted at the age of 11 of the murder of James Bulger, whose family campaigned, with considerable support from the mass media, in favour of prolonging the imprisonment of the offenders). In dismissing an application by James Bulger's father for judicial review of the tariff set by the Lord Chief Justice, the Queen's Bench Divisional Court noted with approval that Lord Woolf had invited the Bulger family to make representations about the impact of their son's death on them, 'but had not invited them to give their views on what they thought was an appropriate tariff' (*R* v. *Secretary of State for the Home Department, ex parte Bulger, The Times,* 16 February 2001).

The above discussion of the three principles of compensation for wrongs, of independent and impartial tribunals, and of proportionality of sentence, suggests that the substantive and procedural rights of victims at the stage of disposal (sentence) ought to be limited. This should apply whether the rights of victims are being considered in the context of restorative justice or of a 'conventional' sentencing system. The rights of victims should chiefly be to receive support, proper services, and (where the offender is unable to pay) state compensation for violent crimes. There are arguments for going further, so as to achieve some measure of victim participation: this would require the provision of better and fuller information to victims, and the objective would be to enable some genuine participation in the process of disposal 'without giving [victims] the power to influence decisions that are not appropriately theirs' (Sanders *et al.*, 2001: 458). This would be a fine line to tread, as the debate following the decision of the US Supreme Court to allow victim impact statements in capital cases demonstrates: *Payne* v. *Tennessee* (1991) 111 S Ct 2597, discussed by Sarat, 1997.

Exploring the 'default setting': when restorative justice runs out

Although some restorative justice practitioners and writers express themselves as if there are no aspects of criminal justice with which restorative justice could not deal, most are realistic enough to recognize that provision must be made for some cases to be handled outside restorative justice processes. We have noted that Cavadino and Dignan provide for a 'default system' to deal with cases in which a circle or conference does not prove possible, perhaps because the necessary consents are not forthcoming. Certain writers make much stronger claims for the ability of restorative justice to handle a wide range of disputes in criminal justice, schools, industry, and business regulation (e.g. Wachtel and McCold, 2001). But even some of those recognize that there must be some form of 'background system' in place (Braithwaite, 1999). If one adds together the groups of offenders for whom such a system may be needed – those who refuse to participate in restorative justice, or whose victims refuse to participate,[2] or who have failed to comply with previous restorative justice outcomes – the numbers might be considerable. It has been argued above that some restorative justice processes themselves are incompatible with principles

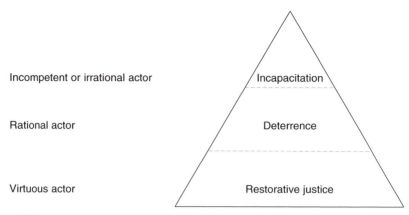

Figure [29.]1

of justice on independence, impartiality, proportionality, and so on. How does thet 'default' or 'background' system measure up to these principles?

Braithwaite explains his background system by reference to this enforcement pyramid, developed in relation to regulatory enforcement (1999: 61) [Figure 29.1]. The idea is that one starts with restorative justice at the base of the pyramid. It may be tried more than once. If it clearly fails, then one would move to an 'active deterrence' strategy, which Braithwaite distinguishes carefully from the 'passive deterrence' described in most of the punishment literature (see Ayres and Braithwaite, 1992: ch. 2). To have this kind of deterrence in the background helps restorative justice to work, in Braithwaite's view. Nonetheless, he warns that:

> The problem is that if deterrent threats cause defiance and reactance, restorative justice may be compromised by what sits above it in a dynamic pyramidal strategy of deterrence and incapacitation . . . The challenge is to have the Sword of Damocles always threatening in the background but never threatened in the foreground. (Braithwaite, 1999: 63–4)

From the point of view of principle, this approach is troubling. It seems that, once we leave the softly, softly world of restorative justice, offenders may be delivered into raging deterrent and incapacitative strategies, with rogue elements like Uncle Harry calling the shots (see the remarkable paragraphs in Braithwaite, 1999: 66–7, on Uncle Harry), and with only the vaguest of gestures towards 'guaranteeing offenders against punishment beyond a maximum' (*ibid.*: 105). When Philip Pettit and John Braithwaite state that, in pursuit of the goal of 'community reassurance', sentencers should take account of 'how common that offence has become in the community' and 'how far the offender is capable of re-offending again' (1993, excerpted in von Hirsch and Ashworth, 1998: 326), the glass becomes very dark, and the excesses of the 'risk society' seem to beckon.

Braithwaite and Pettit (1990: ch. 7) would answer that current maximum penalties should provide the guarantee in the first instance, and that there should then be a 'decremental strategy' of lowering those maxima progressively so as to reduce levels of punitiveness. But statutory maximum sentences are often very high, and certainly much higher than most proportionality theorists (including Tonry's looser approach to limits) would accept. It is also countered that desert-based critics are not paying attention to the difference between the usual run of consequentialist theories based on ('passive') deterrence and incapacitation, and the meaning of those strategies within a 'republican' framework which respects the dominion of each individual (Braithwaite and Pettit, 1990). We should not find these aspects of Braithwaite's restorative justice theory threatening, it is contended, if we looked at the practical meaning of the pyramid of enforcement and took account of the emphasis on penal parsimony in a republican system. But it is not enough to proclaim penal parsimony and yet to give such prominence, even in a 'background system', to deterrent and incapacitative strategies. What types of deterrent strategy are permissible, within what kinds of limits? What forms of incapacitation? To what extent does the background system permit, nay encourage, sentencing on the basis of previous record rather than present offence? The answers to these questions about restorative justice and recalcitrant offenders remain unclear (see von Hirsch and Ashworth, 1998: 317–35), but the need for firm safeguards against undue severity does not disappear if a system is labelled 'restorative'. Penal history yields plenty of examples of apparently benign policies resulting in repressive controls.

Conclusions

It has been argued that, despite the decline of statism and the rise of neo-liberal and 'advanced liberal' programmes for the responsibilization of other agencies of security, it should still be acknowledged to be a fundamental role of the state to maintain a system for the administration of justice and to ensure that proper standards of procedural protection are applied. It is recognized that there have been and are failures of state-led criminal justice, just as there have been and are manifest failures of states to deliver security (Garland, 2001: ch. 5). The growth of restorative justice schemes is encouraged by both these phenomena. However, it should remain the responsibility of the state towards its citizens to ensure that justice is administered by independent and impartial tribunals, and that there are proportionality limits which should not only constrain the measures agreed at restorative justice conferences etc. but also ensure some similarity in the treatment of equally situated offenders. If the state does delegate certain spheres of criminal justice to some form of community-based conference, the importance of insisting on the protection of basic rights for defendants is not diminished.

Many of the innovations urged by restorative justice advocates ought to be tested and evaluated – the effect on victims and on offenders of face-to-face meetings, the value of apologies, the effect on victims and offenders of reparation agreements, the effect on victims and offenders of victim participation in conferences, and so forth. Too often, however, enthusiasm for such processes leads proponents either to overlook the need for safeguards, or to imply that they are not relevant. The steps being taken to develop standards for restorative justice processes are important in this respect (see UN, 2000; Braithwaite [2002]), but they must be accompanied by a re-examination of deeper issues. In order to ensure that there is no deficit of procedural justice or human rights, it was argued above that governments must retain a primary role, that community-based processes and outcomes should be scrutinized closely, and that the proper role of the victim in criminal justice processes should be reappraised. Thus any restorative justice processes for offenders who might otherwise go to court should (a) be led by an independent and impartial person;[3] (b) be required to submit its decisions for court approval; (c) allow the participation of the victim, the offender, and their families or significant others; (d) make provision for access to legal advice before and after any restorative justice processes, at a minimum (Council of Europe, 2000, para. 8; cf. UN, 2000: para. 12); (e) focus on apology and on the appropriate reparation and/or compensation for the offence; and (f) be required to respect relevant principles, such as not imposing on the offender a financial burden that is not means-related. If, contrary to the argument here, a restorative justice conference is permitted to make proposals for community restoration or other responses going beyond reparation to the individual victim(s), there should be clear and circumscribed proportionality limits for those measures. However, the practical implications of 'restoration of the community' call for closer examination than they have hitherto received.

Criticisms of this kind seem to leave many restorative justice practitioners baffled, however. They may protest that restorative justice processes are not about punishment anyway; that all the safeguards are about offenders, not victims; and that in practice restorative justice encounters no problems about undue severity, etc. On the first point, Kathleen Daly (2000) rightly calls for caution among those restorative justice advocates who claim not to be in the punishment business but to be engaged in constructive and non-punitive responses to wrongdoing. Even if one were to adopt a narrow definition (that only measures intended to be punitive count as punishment), many restorative justice outcomes satisfy that definition inasmuch as they are known to impose obligations or deprivations on offenders: Johnstone, 2001: 106–10; cf. Walgrave, 2001. The argument that such obligations or deprivations proceed from full consent is, as we have seen, unconvincing. So far as the bias of rights towards offenders is concerned, it must be conceded that most human rights documents do not incorporate victims' rights into their framework – although there are well-known (separate) declarations of victims' rights. This imbalance ought to be rectified, but only after focusing on the arguments presented above. The third point (the absence of severity) may be generally true, since most of those interested in promoting restorative justice seem to oppose penal severity; but attention was drawn above to Braithwaite's 'background system', and even within restorative justice clear limits are important to prevent violations of rights behind a mask of benevolence. Once it is conceded that restorative justice cannot deal with absolutely all criminal cases, the relationship between the formal system and any restorative justice processes must be carefully crafted so as to avoid inequities. This third point is particularly important where enthusiasm for restorative justice leads a government to 'parachute' elements of restorative justice into a system suffused with rather different principles and practices, as has been done with youth justice in England and Wales (Morris and Gelsthorpe, 2000; Ball, 2000).

This extract is taken from 'Responsibilities, Rights and Restorative Justice', by Andrew Ashworth, in British Journal of Criminology, *43:3, 2002, pp. 578–95.*

Notes

1 The *Nunn* case also points to the practical problem arising where two or more victims have different views on the proper response to the crime. A further complication would be where there is a disagreement between the victim and the community representatives over outcome (cf. Law Commission of Canada, 1999: 38), although this should be resolved on the basis that the victim's interest lies in reparation and compensation whereas the state's (or community's) interest lies in measures going beyond that.
2 Some RJ schemes are prepared to proceed with a conference in the absence of the victim, which expands the role of the facilitator or coordinator: see, e.g. Daly (2001) on South Australia.
3 This raises the question of police-led conferences, used in England in certain types of case (Young, 2001). Braithwaite asks 'whether there is something wrong in principle with the police facilitating a conference. Does it make the police investigator, prosecutor, judge and jury?' (1999: 99). He never answers the question of principle, and instead points out the need to have someone assume the role of facilitator, and suggests that police involvement might have beneficial effects on police culture. But the question of principle must surely be answered by stating that this is wrong. It is not appropriate for the police to take on what is a quasi-judicial role, when they are so heavily involved in investigations. More strongly, it is inappropriate for the police to be involved in any 'shaming' of offenders (cf. Cunneen, 1997 and Blagg, 1997 with Braithwaite, 1997). It is insufficient to reply that offenders who have misgivings can withdraw their consent: as stated above, the 'consent' in these situations may take a severely diluted form. This critique is, of course, no less applicable to the ongoing practice of police cautioning of adults.

References

Ashworth, A. (1986) 'Punishment and Compensation: State, Victim and Offender', *Oxford Journal of Legal Studies*, 6, pp. 86–122.

Ashworth, A. (1998) *The Criminal Process* (2nd edn) (Oxford: Oxford Univesity Press).

Ayres, I. and Braithwaite, J. (1992) *Responsive Regulation: Transcending the Deregulation Debate* (New York, NY: Oxford University Press).

Ball, C. (2000) 'The Youth Justice and Criminal Evidence Act 1999: A Significant Move towards Restorative Justice, or a Recipe for Unintended Consequences?', *Criminal Law Review*, pp. 211–22.

Blagg, H. (1997) 'A Just Measure of Shame? Aboriginal Youth and Conferencing in Australia', *British Journal of Criminology*, 37:4, pp. 481–501.

Braithwaite, J. (1997) 'Conferencing and Plurality: Reply to Blagg', *British Journal of Criminology*, 37:4, pp. 502–6.

Braithwaite, J. (1999) 'Restorative Justice: Assessing Optimistic and Pessimistic Accounts', *Crime and Justice: A Review of Research*, 25, pp. 1–110.

Braithwaite, J. (2002) 'Setting Standards for Restorative Justice', *British Journal of Criminology*, 42, pp. 563–77.

Braithwaite, J. and Pettit, P. (1990) *Not Just Deserts* (Oxford: Oxford University Press).

Cavadino, M. and Dignan, J. (1997) 'Reparation, Retribution and Rights', *International Review of Victimology*, 4, pp. 233–71.

Christie, N. (1977) 'Conflicts as Property', *British Journal of Criminology*, 17:1, pp. 1–15.

Council of Europe (1993) *Consistency in Sentencing* (Recommendation R (92) 18) (Strasbourg: Council of Europe).

Council of Europe (2000) *Mediation in Penal Matters* (Recommendation R (99) 19) (Strasbourg: Council of Europe).

Cunneen, C. (1997) 'Community Conferencing and the Fiction of Indigenous Control', *Australia and New Zealand Journal of Criminology*, 30, pp. 297–320.

Daly, K. (2000) 'Restorative Justice: The Real Story.' Unpublished paper presented to Scottish Criminology Conference (www.gu.edu.au/school/ccj/kdaly.html).

Daly, K. (2001) 'Conferencing in Australia and New Zealand: Variations, Research Findings and Prospects', in Morris, A. and Maxwell, G. (eds) *Restorative Justice for Juveniles: Conferencing, Mediation and Circles* (Oxford: Hart Publishing).

Edwards, I. (2001) 'Victim Participation in Sentencing: The Problems of Incoherence', *Howard Journal of Criminal Justice*, 40, pp. 39–54.

Erez, E. (1999) 'Who's Afraid of the Big Bad Victim? Victim Impact Statements as Empowerment and Enhancement of Justice', *Criminal Law Review*, pp. 545–56.

Erez, E. and Rogers, L. (1999) 'Victim Impact Statements and Sentencing Outcomes and Processes: The Perspectives of Legal Professionals', *British Journal of Criminology*, 39:2, pp. 216–39.

Garland, D. (2001) *The Culture of Control: Crime and Social Order in Contemporary Society* (Oxford: Oxford University Press).

Johnstone, G. (2001) *Restorative Justice* (Cullompton: Willan Publishing).

Lacey, N. (1988) *State Punishment* (London: Routledge).

Law Commission of Canada (1999) *From Restorative Justice to Transformative Justice* (discussion paper) (Ottawa: Law Commission).

Llewellyn, J.J. and Howse, R. (1998) *Restorative Justice: A Conceptual Framework* (Ottawa: Law Commission of Canada).

Miers, D. (1997) *State Compensation for Criminal Injuries* (London: Blackstone).

Morgan, J. and Zedner, L. (1992) *Child Victims* (Oxford: Oxford University Press).

Morris, A. and Gelsthorpe, L. (2000) 'Something Old, Something Borrowed, Something Blue, but Something New? Comment on the Prospects for Restorative Justice under the Crime and Disorder Act', *Criminal Law Review*, pp. 18–30.

Morris, A. and Maxwell, G. (2000) 'The Practice of Family Group Conferences in New Zealand: Assessing the Place, Potential and Pitfalls of Restorative Justice', in Crawford, A. and Goodey, J. (eds) *Integrating a Victim Perspective within Criminal Justice* (Aldershot: Ashgate).

Pettit, P. with Braithwaite, J. (1993) 'Not Just Deserts, Even in Sentencing', *Current Issues in Criminal Justice*, 4, pp. 222–32.

Sanders, A., Hoyle, C., Morgan, R. and Cape, E. (2001) 'Victim Impact Statements: Can't Work, Won't Work', *Criminal Law Review*, pp. 447–58.

Sarat, A. (1997) 'Vengeance, Victims and Identities of Law', *Social and Legal Studies*, 6, pp. 163–84.

Tonry, M. (1994) 'Proportionality, Parsimony and Interchangeability of Punishments', in Duff, A. *et al.* (eds) *Penal Theory and Practice* (Manchester: Manchester University Press).

United Nations (2000) *Basic Principles on the Use of Restorative Justice Programmes in Criminal Matters* (www.restorativejustice.org/.ents/UNDecBasicPrinciplesofRJ.htm).

von Hirsch, A. (1993) *Censure and Sanctions* (Oxford: Oxford University Press).

von Hirsch, A. and Ashworth, A. (eds) (1998) *Principled Sentencing: Readings on Theory and Policy* (Oxford: Hart Publishing).

Wachtel, T. and McCold, P. (2001) 'Restorative Justice in Everyday Life', in Strang, H. and Braithwaite, J. (eds) *Restorative Justice and Civil Society* (Cambridge: Cambridge University Press), pp. 114–29.

Walgrave, L. (2001) 'On Restoration and Punishment', in Morris, A. and Maxwell, G. (eds) *Restorative Justice for Juveniles* (Oxford: Hart Publishing), pp. 17–40.

Young, R. (2001) 'Just Cops Doing "Shameful" Business? Police-Led Restorative Justice and the Lessons of Research', in Morris, A. and Maxwell, G. (eds) *Restorative Justice for Juveniles* (Oxford: Hart Publishing), pp. 195–226.

30. Restorative justice: the challenge of sexual and racial violence

Barbara Hudson

[. . .]

The failure of criminal justice

It is common cause among those advocating women's rights, child protection, and the protection of minority communities that traditional criminal justice has failed to provide remedies for violence against women, children, and minority ethnic victims. The failings of criminal justice are well documented, especially in the case of violence against women.[1] They include social and judicial attitudes which have regarded matters that happen in the private domain, as no concern of criminal law; attitudes among police and prosecutors that victims are unlikely to sustain complaints and that therefore action is generally wasteful of time and effort; humiliating and intrusive interrogation of victims to determine issues of consent or provocation; victims' unwillingness to press charges because of fears of retaliation; difficulties of obtaining corroborating evidence when abuse takes place in private, and so on. These obstacles to obtaining remedy (and getting the behaviour stopped!) are especially formidable in the case of ethnic groups such as Britain's Asians, who risk rejection and hostility by their relatives and neighbours if they turn to the police and the courts.[2]

Racial violence has been difficult to measure.[3] Even when policy suggests that racist elements should be considered as aggravating circumstances leading to enhanced penalties, and when police forces take an inclusive approach to recording cases as racially-linked (including offences on the basis of victim characteristics and/or victim reporting of the offence as racially motivated, rather than excluding cases unless the arresting officer or other official assesses the case as racially motivated), the racial aspect tends to be lost as the case progresses through the various criminal justice processes. In a survey of cases recorded by Northumbria Police as racially linked, my co-researchers and I found that cases of abuse and harassment or other public order offences tended not to be prosecuted usually for lack of evidence; in cases such as theft and robbery from Asian or other minority shops and homes, the racial link 'disappeared' from agency information systems and the cases were prosecuted and sentenced like those with white victims. Again, the usual reason given was lack of evidence for the racial motivation. A recent report by the group Human Rights Watch documents alarming levels of racial violence in England and Wales, and deplores the failure of criminal justice to prosecute and penalize the perpetrators.[4]

The most notorious case recently in Britain has been the murder of Stephen Lawrence, a black youth who was killed by a group of white youths, whilst he was waiting for a bus. Although a number of white young men have been identified as responsible for the killing, they have not been convicted because of lack of evidence. The Lawrence family and their supporters say that evidence was not obtained primarily because police approached their investigations with the view that Stephen Lawrence and his companion must have been engaged in some sort of unlawful activity, and that the death must have been the result of some sort of spontaneous fracas amongst lawless youth, rather than a law-abiding, hard-working student engaged on peaceful, proper activities being attacked by racist thugs. This case demonstrates a further difficulty which black victims have in obtaining remedy through criminal justice: they are more readily seen as 'suitable enemies' than as 'ideal victims'.[5] (This same problem, of having to fit the constructions of 'ideal victim' in order to obtain conviction of one's aggressor, has affected women, for example prostitute women or other independent, sexually-active women, attempting to bring rape charges.)

Criminal justice has failed to deliver on the first demand made by feminist and anti-racist activists calling for increased criminalization or for alternative forms of justice – to make evident the extent of racialized and sexualized violence – because of the obstacles to reporting, prosecution, and conviction that it poses. Criminalization means that most offenders are left free to continue their activities, and most victims are left unprotected.

Those urging that racial and sexual violence should be taken more seriously, including groups such as the Commission for Racial Equality, have complained that even where prosecutions are successful, penalties are insufficient.[6] Fines and community penalties too often induce resentment and the desire for revenge, rather than repentance, in the perpetrator, and provide no protection for the victim or other potential victims. If criminalization and penalization are the ways of demonstrating that society is opposed to certain behaviours and takes them seriously, then the message given by the composition of prison populations in Britain, the United States of America and similar countries is that racial and sexual violence are less serious wrongs than burglary, theft, and many other property offences. Women's groups, and anti-racist campaigners, therefore, have been demanding not only higher rates of arrest and prosecution, but also tougher penalties for those committing offences of racial and sexual violence.

Acknowledging that in Scandinavia, as elsewhere in Europe, women who would support reduced imprisonment for the property crimes of the poor, demand more and longer prison sentences for sexual and domestic violence, Liv Finstad urges abolitionists to take up the challenge of devising more constructive ways of responding to sexualized violence precisely because of its damaging, domineering, harmful nature: if these most serious of crimes could be dealt with without imprisonment, the case for abolition of imprisonment for other less serious crimes would be established.[7] Finstad insists that any non-imprisoning response to sexual violence must satisfy certain demands:

> Guilt and responsibility must be firmly and unequivocally attached to the perpetrator;
> protection and compensation must be effected for the victim;
> the extent and seriousness of sexualized violence must not be made invisible.

These are the demands made of justice processes by other writers who either advocate or are sympathetic to restorative justice, for example, Braithwaite and Daly.[8] I would endorse them, and again, I would insist on parallel demands for any response to racial violence.

Racialized, sexualized, and domestic violence: the potential of restorative justice

Even if more cases could be prosecuted successfully, the dilemma highlighted by Finstad, Meima, Braithwaite and Daly, and others who take up the challenge of abolitionism's response to sexualized and racialized violence, is that of moving away from punitive reactions which – even when enforced – further brutalize perpetrators, without, by leniency of reaction, giving the impression that sexualized or racialized violence is acceptable behaviour.[9] As Sim summarizes the dilemma in relation to rape:

> The lenient sentences for such crimes and the symbolic messages which men take from leniency can be contrasted with the fact that longer prison sentences offer no solution to the problem of rape and indeed may simply exacerbate the problem at an individual level by placing the rapist in a masculine culture which reinforces the misogynist fantasies that were part of his behaviour pattern outside the walls.[10]

This statement points to the fact that there is an important difference between racial and sexual crimes, and the street crimes of the powerless which seem to be the behaviours which most abolitionists have most clearly in view. This difference is that, as shown above, sexual, domestic, and racial violence has not, until very recently, been taken seriously. These crimes have been over-tolerated, whereas burglary, car theft, street robbery, and the like have been over-penalized. In other words, the censuring, moral-boundary-declaring, symbolic purposes of criminal law have already been served in relation to these latter types of offence, whereas with racialized and sexualized violence, the symbolic force of criminal law has only recently, and only partially (especially in the case of racial violence) been deployed to demonstrate that society, at least in its official organization, disapproves of these forms of behaviour.

Sim's words echo Garland's description of the 'tragic quality' of punishment: that it is simultaneously necessary to symbolize the state's authoritative disapproval of certain forms of behaviour and futile in its effects at controlling that behaviour.[11] Certainly, it is desirable for society to demonstrate that it is opposed to racial and sexual violence. On the other hand, could not the response to such behaviour be organized according to a logic that makes for more effective remedies than either doing nothing (or, at most, very little), or punishing offenders by confining them in settings where their racist and sexist attitudes, and their fantasies of violence and sexuality, will be further fuelled? Garland's depiction of the tragic duality of punishment refers to its expressive and instrumental functions, which may often be in conflict. Abolitionism and other critiques have usually concentrated on the instrumental aspects of punishments, and left its expressive tasks unaddressed. If restorative justice is to provide an adequate response to racial and sexual violence, its processes and remedies will have to address both the expressive and instrumental functions of traditional retributive criminal justice.

The argument of abolitionists such as Bianchi and Mathiesen with regard to people who pose a clear danger to the physical safety of others is generally that there are few such offenders; incapacitative institutions where they can be restrained and kept away from potential victims therefore are needed, but there is need for only a small number of such facilities, and imprisonment as the response to crime can become the exceptional rather than the normal practice. Violence against women, children, and minority ethnic citizens is, however, widespread and frequent. Chesney-Lind and Bloom report that an estimated three to four million women are battered in the United States of America every year according to a former Surgeon General; that population surveys estimate that 21 to 30 per cent of United States women will be beaten by a partner at least once in their lifetimes; that almost half of all batterers beat their partners at least three times a year.[12] The 1996 British Crime Survey reports 1 million incidents of domestic violence, with the caveat that this is likely to be an undercount.[13] As revealed by the survey, domestic violence accounted for more incidents than stranger violence of all kinds. From the figures given in the survey, domestic violence certainly appears to be a more serious problem than mugging (street robbery): 990,000 reported incidents of domestic violence compared with 390,000 reported incidents of mugging; victims were also more likely to sustain injury in domestic violence, with only 31 per cent of reported domestic violence incidents resulting in no injury compared to 67 per cent of muggings.[14]

Not only is domestic violence widespread, it is increasing, and whilst some of the apparent increase can perhaps be attributed to increased reporting, there is no doubt that the behaviour is widespread, and that it continues to be under-reported. The same sort of detailed figures are not available for racial violence, but police forces throughout England and Wales have recorded rising levels of racial attacks and harassment throughout the 1990s. Home Office figures show that police recorded 12,222 racial incidents in 1995/96, 3 per cent more than in 1994/95.[15] It is widely accepted that racial violence is significantly under-recorded, partly because of the difficulties of ascertaining racial motivation, and partly because of under-reporting by victims and their communities who lack confidence that the police and other enforcement agencies will take the problem seriously. Sexual offences, including offences against children, though now revealed as more frequent than had long been assumed, remain relatively rare. 30,0436 [sic] sexual offences were recorded in England and Wales in 1995/96, in a toal of more than 5 million offences overall, but of course each and every one needs to be taken seriously.

Violence against women, children and minority ethnic citizens is deplorable, but its incidence is hardly surprising in the light of current criminological theories. New understandings of the components of 'masculinities', and especially the pressures to accomplish an identity which approximates to 'hegemonic' masculinity help explain why in a socially unequal society which pushes so many young men into economic marginality, those who cannot demonstrate the affluence of successful masculinity will be likely to exaggerate – through violence – their claims that they are racially superior, heterosexual, and 'macho'.[16]

As well as challenging the abolitionist assumption that the number of dangerous offenders is small, these offences challenge the argument that criminal justice is targeted against the powerless, on behalf of the powerful. Feminists who advocate imprisonment and 'zero tolerance' for domestic violence, as well as those who urge longer sentences for offences against children, and for racial violence, point out that the crimes are acted out on victims who, within the crime relationship, lack power: the point of such offences is to dominate, for the offender to exercise power over the victim. Whilst it may be true that it is among the poor and the marginalized that such aggression is likely to lead to punishment rather than counselling, it must be acknowledged that the power relationships in domestic, sexual, and racial crime are different from those in property offences and other kinds of 'economic survival' crimes. The logic of restorative justice makes the relationship between victim and offender central, displacing that between offender and state, and it could therefore be argued that restorative processes would reproduce and reinforce the imbalance of power of the crime relationship, rather than confronting the offender with the power of the state acting on behalf of (in the place of) the victim.

Racial and sexual violence thus pose some difficulties for the domain assumptions of abolitionist theories. These behaviours challenge restorative justice to formulate strategies that can deal with large numbers of victims and offenders; that can provide protection and redress for victims; that can change social attitudes from tolerance to disapproval; that can inculcate remorse and a desire for change in perpetrators, and that can bring about a rebalancing of power within the crime relationship.

The process model advocated by most formulations of restorative justice is that of the community forum, or, especially in the writings of John Braithwaite, the community or family conference.[17] This is a rather broader concept than 'mediation' or 'reparation' – sometimes advocated as an addition to present criminal justice processes, either as an alternative to prosecution (caution plus), or as an alternative to fines or community penalties (or to damages and compensation payments in civil cases) – which signifies a remedy of conciliation and compensation worked out between victim and offender. Practices being termed 'restorative justice' by some police forces in England at the present time fit the 'caution plus' model rather than the conception of restorative justice under discussion here. The conference model of Braithwaite and other theorists assumes the involvement of other parties, and would address the 'safe community' objective as well as the relationships between victim and offender.

An implicit assumption in the ideas of meetings and forums put forward by the 1970s and 1980s abolitionists and proponents of various other forms of 'alternative dispute settlement' that is problematic in the case of these types of offences, is that there is some common understanding, some agreed perspective, which can be arrived at between victim and offender. As Finstad argues, the earlier model of informal or civil justice appears to presume that an account of 'what happened' can be negotiated which will be somewhere between the victim's and offender's perspectives, whereas, with sexualized violence, there are two separate, non-negotiable perspectives – his and hers.[18] This is the case, she says, wherever the offence involves huge imbalances of power between victim and perpetrator. It is also, obviously, the case where the offence involves majority and minority race or ethnicity, and even more so, when the case involves child victim and adult perpetrator.

The conference model allows for the victim to have representatives to urge her view of the events, and Braithwaite and Daly argue that one of the benefits of the model as compared with existing criminal justice processes is that a feminist – or racial/ethnic/religious – standpoint can be accommodated. Instead of having a lawyer attuned to legal criteria and world views, women's groups, community leaders, victim support movements, and the like can all be heard. The victim's perspective is made central to proceedings, whereas it is only a source of evidence (as far as rules of admissibility allow) in criminal cases. Hulsman makes a similar claim in relation to the use of civil rather than criminal procedures in cases of rape and sexual assault: the victim's definition of harm and threat is at the centre of proceedings; she is transformed from the humiliated victim of criminal proceedings to an active claimant, identifying her own requirements and drawing her own lines in future contacts with the perpetrator.[19]

The point being made by these writers is that in fact it is the conventions of present criminal law which reproduce the power relations that produce racial and sexual crime: the victim is one person, on the down-side of power, confronting, and having to conform to, the gender and racial ordering of law, which is itself reflective of the society in which that law is embedded.[20] Restorative justice, on the other hand, enables the parties to be equally represented; it enables other narratives to be heard; it empowers standpoints which are otherwise powerless and excluded, or at least circumscribed.

For the proponents of restorative justice, the desired outcome of these conferences would be that the offender acknowledges not just his own responsibility for the act, but also that he appreciates the victim's perspective: he should acknowledge that he performed the act; that it was wrong; and that it was harmful. He should be ashamed, and determined to avoid repetition of the behaviour. The contemporary restorative justice paradigm owes much to Braithwaite's ideas of *reintegrative shaming*.[21] He contrasts the reintegrative shaming of the good parent – who makes clear her disapproval of bad behaviour without rejecting the child – with the stigmatizing shame of modern criminal justice. Stigmatizing shame labels the person rather than the act, and imposes a status change which has generalized, deleterious, and often irreversible consequences.[22] In the stigmatizing processes of retributive justice, the offender is given more incentives to contest the label than to repent the behaviour; the 'sin' which people try to avoid is as likely to be that of being found out as that of behaving badly. With restorative justice, the community is involved in expressing disapproval, and in providing and guaranteeing protection and redress for victims, but it is also involved in supporting the perpetrator in his efforts to change, and in maintaining him as a member of the community.

It has sometimes been asked whether 'the community' is likely to express strong enough disapproval to induce shame; that the pomp and ceremony of the court is necessary for the shaming ritual. Current experience of responses to sexual offending show that the community is somewhat in advance of judicial attitudes: lenient sentencing for rape cases; failure to imprison wife batterers and sexual attackers have been widely criticized by publics through-out Europe, North America, and Australia. Indeed, developments such as Megan's Law in the United States of America, and similar community notification schemes in the United Kingdom and elsewhere show that the community is, if anything, too strong in its disapproval and is certainly willing to provide guarantees of enforcement of remedies.

Racial violence provokes less strong reaction, but few would express dissent from disapproval in a public forum. Another claim made by the restorative justice movement is that progressive views about matters such as the need to express disapproval of racial harassment and abuse, and to protect minority citizens, tend to be strengthened during discussion: dissenters feel discouraged from expressing racist views, and an emergent consensus of attitude can be firmed into a resolve to act. A narrative style of proceedings can therefore not only perform the norm-affirming expressive role of adversarial criminal justice; it can also perform an additional, norm-creating role.

Abolitionists and other advocates of restorative justice here echo or draw upon Habermas's model of 'communicative morality' or 'discourse ethics': that it is in the exposition of views, the listening to accounts of harm, the attempting to justify prejudice, that more progressive moral consensus can be reached. Habermas in his two-volume *Theory of Communicative Action* develops a dialogic view of morality, in which a plurivocal evolved consensus replaces the monologic voice of law.[23] In the dialogic process of defining and legitimating norms, moral judgments are reached not by consideration of the impartial voice of – male – judicial reason, but by the communication between 'concrete others'; between participants expressing their viewpoints and needs. The condition for such debates to generate normative categories and binding decisions is the 'ideal speech situation', the creation of a situation in which all participants can take part without constraint or oppression. Descriptions of conferences and other procedures given by Braithwaite and Daly, and by Hulsman seem very much like strategies to approximate this ideal speech situation, in which women, children, and members of minority ethnic groups will be empowered and protected to an extent that is not approached by present criminal justice processes.

Habermas's theory has been criticized by writers affirming a politics of difference on the grounds that it still presupposes a negotiated outcome (a rational consensus); that at times it appears to submerge the 'concrete others' into a transcendental 'universal other'; and that the situation of the ideal speech situation is as abstract and unrealizable as Rawls's 'veil of ignorance'.[24] Nonetheless, the idea of a communicative or discursive ethics, together with Braithwaite's concept of reintegrative shaming, advance both the theory and strategy of restorative justice a great deal.

[. . .]

The problem of the offender who continues to pose danger, or who refuses to accept the account, wishes, and proposals of the victim is addressed by the various formulations, and this is an issue about which differences arise. Bianchi and some other European abolitionists propose revival of the institution of 'sanctuary', as somewhere where a person who poses danger to others can be safe from vengeance from victims and communities, whilst awaiting processes and remedies.[25] Bianchi's description of sanctuary, however, presupposes some sort of negotiation, and upholds the right of a victim to demand a trial if the perpetrator continually refuses to negotiate. What the last resort of failed negotiations should be is unclear.

For Finstad, the last resort provision is coerced deprivation of liberty, but she invokes a medical model of hospitalization rather than a criminal model of imprisonment.[26] The danger here is that the individual becomes pathologized rather than the behaviour being condemned. Braithwaite and Daly apply the idea of an *enforcement pyramid*, with prison at its apex.[27] Depending on the willingness or otherwise of the perpetrator to accept responsibility, admit the wrongness of the behaviour, and take steps to ensure that it does not recur, an escalating repertoire of responses is provided, ranging from informal disapproval by family and friends, through reparative measures decided upon by neighbourhood conferences, through to penal sanctions and finally, for the most recalcitrant, imprisonment. Like Bianchi and other abolitionists and proponents of restorative justice, Braithwaite and Daly foresee that most offenders will come to accept their behaviour as wrong; that most victims will be content with acknowledgement of guilt, compensation/reparation, and some firm assurance (such as the undertaking of educative or therapeutic measures) that the behaviour is unlikely to recur. Unlike thorough-going abolitionists, however, they see that the 'big stick' of penal sanctions – including imprisonment – is necessary to reinforce the authority of restorative remedies. The big stick of imprisonment, they say, allows justice to 'speak more softly' in most cases.

The difficulty with their position is that the existence of the custodial possibility could perpetuate the present situation, which is that unless (long) prison sentences are imposed, the message of a case is that the behaviour is not really serious. Community disapproval, redress and attempts to change could be seen as 'getting away with it', just as the proponents of get tough sentencing designate non-custodial penalties for a range of offences now. This points to the importance of restorative responses to domestic, sexual, and racial violence being introduced in a general framework of restorative justice. They should not be used – as was the complaint against some earlier initiatives in informal justice – as second-rate justice for offences that don't really matter.[28] Braithwaite has consistently argued for across-the-board reductions in the resort to punitive sanctions and the introduction of conference procedures and restorative measures for most offence types. In such circumstances of general penal deflation, introduction of the enforcement pyramid should not mean that sexual or racial violence was taken less seriously than other offence types, but it could perpetuate one of the elements of current criminal procedures that are objected to by many advocates of tougher responses to domestic violence, which is that violence appears only to be seen as serious if it is repeated.

Existence of the 'big stick' of imprisonment might well mean, in other words, that the pronouncement of a prison sentence is still the expressive yardstick for the condemnation of behaviour. Victims and their relatives might feel that their injury was being taken less seriously than an incident which did result in imprisonment: the lynch mob, after all, exists in relation to awareness of the possibility of execution and perception that this is the mark of stern disapproval. To serve the expressive functions of punishment, restorative processes will have to devise ways of clearly separating condemnation of the act from the negotiation of measures appropriate to the relationships between the particular victim, the offender, and the community.

Restorative justice or enhanced penalties?

Tolerance and/or denial of the extent and seriousness of crimes against women, children, and minority ethnic citizens make the demand for increased penalization understandable, but as well as believing that the infliction of suffering generally makes people worse rather than better, my own abolitionist instincts are strengthened by fear of the punitive inflation that occurs if, whenever a group gains recognition for its harms, such recognition is expressed through increased penalization. Penal measures, as van Swaaningen argues, do not have a simple *ad hoc* validity, but always have a *general* impact.[29] Feminists may successfuly persuade legislators and judges of the serious harms of domestic and sexual violence; environmentalists successfully urge the seriousness of pollution; politicians pontificate about the evils of car crime and drug-taking: if all these claims lead to increased punishment of offenders, the carceral society envisioned by Foucault and Cohen would indeed be a reality! As Chesney-Lind and Bloom put it in relation to domestic violence, zero tolerance activism has supplied the system with 'new men to jail, particularly men of color'.[30]

On the other hand, to forego penalization in a punitive society would look like tolerance of intolerable behaviour. Whilst it is correct to argue that racial and sexual violence will only be diminished by reducing the economic, racial, and sexual inequalities in power that exist in present societies, we cannot ask women, children, and victims of racial violence and abuse to wait for protection and compensation until the achievement of wholesale social transformation. We cannot, furthermore, reasonably expect them to give up such protection, remedy, and condemnation of violence as is afforded by criminal law, in present society with its systems of criminal rather than restorative justice.

What should be taken from feminist, anti-racist and other 'zero tolerance' campaigners is that racial, sexual, and domestic violence should always be taken seriously. Spousal violence should not be dismissed as 'a domestic', of concern to no one outside the household; a victim's claim of racial motivation should be taken seriously; children should be listened to and any violence (sexual or non-sexual) against them should be regarded as reprehensible. From the abolitionists, however, we should learn that punishment is morally problematic in that it involves the state inflicting pain or deprivation on an individual; that it adds the suffering of the offender to the suffering already endured by the victim; that it deflects attention from the victim; that it generally offers little by way of protection and usually makes people worse rather than better. Punishment therefore needs justification, not just in general but in every particular case, and more constructive, less violent responses to the most serious forms of anti-social behaviour need to be developed with some alacrity.

The positives of restorative justice – compensation as of right; hearing the harms endured by the victim as well as weighing the evidence against the offender; considering how best to ensure the restoration of relationships between victims, offenders, and relevant communities – should be pursued as priorities. The negative reforms – abolishing imprisonment as a normal response to injury; finding restorative, rehabilitative alternatives to punishment in most cases – should be part of an overall move to a less retributive, more restorative justice. These reforms will need to be accompanied by vigorous 'policy preparation' along the lines suggested by Braithwaite and Mathiesen: that is, vigorous social education to make sure that domestic, sexual, and racial violence is behaviour which is strongly and generally disapproved, and about which perpetrators feel a strong sense of shame.[31] On the other hand, shaming should be of Braithwaite's reintegrative variety, rather than the rampaging vengeance that is being seen in some 'community' naming-and-shaming responses to sexual offending.

What the abolitionists and other penal reductionists fear is that responsiveness to the legitimate claims for attention by victims, and acknowledgement of the seriousness of racial, sexual, and domestic violence will further fuel the harsh penal politics of these law-and-order times; it is also likely that unchecked punitiveness in relation to offences where corroborative evidence is difficult to obtain will lead to the adoption of civil law standards of proof, but with such cases resulting in criminal law punishments. What we also strongly suspect is that penal toughness towards racial, sexual, and domestic violence would only be inflicted on the poor and marginalized, with the powerful continuing to perpetrate their racist and misogynist behaviour behind closed doors: penal toughness will lead, to paraphrase Reiman, to the rich getting counselling and the poor getting prison.[32]

I am aware that I, like others who have addressed these difficult issues, am not coming to any firm or innovative conclusions. I can merely urge more abolitionist thinking about the problems posed by behaviour that is seriously harmful and widespread; that has not been subject to vigorous condemnation and penalization by the state, and which involves the exercise of power by offenders over victims. In particular, the problems of identifying the relevant 'community' and securing its participation, representation, and co-operation, and the problem of the last-resort sanction for recalcitrant offenders, need to be addressed.

Whatever the difficulties, however, the core principles of abolitionism hold true: the punitive power of the state needs to be curbed not expanded; penal strategies will be directed predominantly at those who are powerless and marginalized in the wider society, even if they are more powerful than their victims in the individual crime relationship; and punishment is more likely to reinforce racism, sexism, and other anti-social attitudes than to produce the chastened anti-racist and anti-sexist good citizen. The work of Braithwaite and Habermas provides a considerable advance in the theoretical resources available to restorative justice, whilst experiments with family conferences, community forums, and other processes being carried out in Australia, New Zealand, the Netherlands and elsewhere provide valuable experience in the viability of extending restorative justice processes to more seriouis forms of crime.

The key to reconciling the problems and possibilities of restorative justice lies in creative consideration of its relationship to formal criminal law. Problems of how to deal with recalcitrant offenders; how to ensure that restorative procedures are not seen as second-class justice; how to balance expressive and instrumental functions of justice; and above all, how to ensure that the voice of any party does not become submerged in an emergent unitary consensus all turn on the relationship between the discursive processes of restorative approaches and the role of formal law in modern societies in relation to defining relationships and allocating rights.

The developing perspective of 'guaranteeism' proposes a role for law as guarantor of rights, both general, in the sense of protecting human rights for all, and specific, for example, women's rights.[33] Formal law could stand behind restorative justice procedures as a guarantor of rights: that each party has certain rights which cannot be overridden by any decisions arrived at by consensus or majority. It could mean, for example, that an offender's rights would be protected against a vengeful community; that a victim's rights would be protected against a community view which did not take the harm seriously; that either party would have rights guaranteed against persuasion of the group by a stronger advocate. Guaranteeism would protect rights enjoyed in a generality of situations and contexts against the outcome of negotiations in a particular situation and context. This is quite different from the role of law in the present criminal justice system, which can adjudicate between competing rights, and which can order the suspension of certain rights (including, in the United States of America, for example, the right to life). If penality in modern societies is, as Foucault has described, a political economy of rights, then a role for law as guarantor of rights would be a progressive and appropriate development.

Further elaboration of Habermas's discursive ethics, especially as informed by feminists and those more generally engaged in developing philosophies of difference, and of perspectives such as legal guaranteeism, may solve many of the dilemmas of restorative justice. In particular, such work could enable restorative justice to maintain an orientation towards the 'others' involved in conflictual situations which is the essence of the problem-solving restorative approach in contrast to the rule-following retributive approach. Less easy to envisage, at least in present-day Britain and the United States of America, is recovery of a culture of social inclusion which would underpin and support the development of processes whose outcome is shaming that was reintegrative rather than eliminative, and where the ultimate goal is the enhancement of social justice. This is the most intractable problem in the path of restorative justice, and it is one that is beyond the ability of proponents of any theory of penal reform to solve.

This extract is taken from 'Restorative Justice: the Challenge of Sexual and Racial Violence', by Barbara Hudson, in Journal of Law and Society *(25:2), 1998, pp. 237–56.*

Notes

1 R.E. Dobash and R.P. Dobash, *Women, Violence and Social Change* (1992).
2 Idid.
3 B. Bowling, 'Racial Harassment and the Process of Victimization: Conceptual and Methodological Implications for the Local Crime Survey' (1993) 33 *Brit. J. of Criminology* 231.
4 *Observer*, 11 May 1997.
5 N. Christie, 'The Ideal Victim' in *From Crime Policy to Victim Policy: Reorienting the Justice System*, ed. E. A. Fattah (1986).
6 Dobash and Dobash, op. cit., n. 1; M.D. Fields, 'Criminal justice responses to violence against women' in *Penal theory and practice: tradition and innovation in criminal justice*, eds. A. Duff *et al.* (1994).
7 L. Finstad, 'Sexual Offenders Out of Prison: Principles for a Realistic Utopia' (1990) 18 *International J. of the Sociology of Law* 157.
8 J. Braithwaite and K. Daly, 'Masculinities and communitarian control' in *Just Boys Doing Business? Men, Masculinities and Crime*, ed. T. Newburn and E.A. Stanko (1994).
9 Finstad, op. cit., n. 27; M. Meima, 'Sexual Violence, Criminal Law and Abolitionism' in *Gender, Sexuality and Social Controls*, eds. B. Rolston and M. Tomlinson (1990); Braithwaite and Daly, id.
10 J. Sim, review of Bianchi and Van Swaaningen (1990) 18 *International J. of the Sociology of Law* 97.
11 D. Garland, *Punishment and Modern Society* (1990) at 80.
12 M. Chesney-Lind and B. Bloom, 'Feminist Criminology: Thinking About Women and Crime' in *Thinking Critically About Crime*, eds. B.D. MacLean and D. Milanovic (1997).
13 Home Office, *The 1996 British Crime Survey, England and Wales* (1996) at 28.
14 id, at p. 65.
15 National Association for the Care and Resettlement of Offenders (NACRO), *Criminal Justice Digest*, no. 91 (1997) at 17.
16 Newburn and Stanko, op. cit., n. 8; R.W. Connell, *Gender, Power and Society: the Person and Sexual Politics* (1987); J. Messerschmidt, *Masculinities and Crime: Critique and reconceptualization of theory* (1993) and *Crime as Structured Action: Gender, Race, Class and Crime in the Making* (1997).
17 Braithwaite, 'Inequality and Republican Criminology' in *Crime and Inequality*, eds J. Hagan and R.D. Peterson (1995); R. Van Swaaningen, *Critical Criminology: Visions from Europe* (1997).
18 Finstad, op. cit., n. 7.
19 L. Hulsman, 'The Abolitionist Case: Alternative Crime Policies' (1991) 25 *Israeli Law Rev.* 681.
20 R. Van Swaaningen, 'Feminism, Criminology and Criminal Law' in *Gender, Sexuality and Social Control*, eds. B. Rolston and M. Tomlinson (1990).
21 J. Braithwaite, *Crime, Shame and Reintegration* (1989).
22 H. Becker, *Outsiders: Studies in the Sociology of Deviance* (1963); A. Cicourel, *The Social Organisation of Juvenile Justice* (1956).
23 J. Habermas, *The Theory of Communicative Action*, vols. 1 and 2 (1984 and 1987); P. Pettit, 'Habermas on Truth and Justice' (1982) *Royal Institution of Philosophy Lecture Series* 207; I.M. Young, *Justice and the Politics of Difference* (1990).

24 S. Benhabib, *Critique, Norm and Utopia* (1986); Young, id.
25 H. Bianchi, 'Abolition, assensus and sanctuary' in *A Reader on Punishment*, eds. A. Duff and D. Garland (1994).
26 Finstad, op. cit., n. 7.
27 Braithwaite and Daly, op. cit., n. 8.
28 M. Cain, 'Beyond Informal Justice' (1985) 9 *Contemporary Crises* 335; C. Harrington, *Shadow Justice? The Ideology and Institutionalization of Alternatives to Court* (1985).
29 Van Swaaningen, op. cit., n. 20, p. 218.
30 Chesney-Lind and Bloom, op. cit., n. 12, p. 46.
31 Braithwaite, op. cit., n. 21; T. Mathiesen, *Prison on Trial: A Critical Assessment* (1990).
32 J.H. Reiman, *The Rich Get Richer and the Poor Get Prison* (1979).
33 T. Pitch, *Limited Responsibilities: Social Movements and Criminal Justice* (1990, English ed. 1995); Van Swaaningen, op. cit., n. 17.

References

Bianchi, H. (1994) 'Abolition assensus and sanctuary' in *A Reader on Punishment*, eds A. Duff and D. Garland.

Braithwaite, J. (1995) 'Inequality and Republican Criminology' in *Crime and Inequality*, eds J. Hagan and R.D. Peterson; R. Van Swaaningen, *Critical Criminology: Visions from Europe* (1997).

31. Deconstructing restoration: the promise of restorative justice

George Pavlich

[...]

[What] precisely are we to understand by restorative justice, and more specifically how might one assess its promise? Responding to the question is no easy task, given the exponential growth of diverse discourses in the area. Even so, in this chapter, I shall offer an overview of some important themes that underscore two of restorative justice's key promises; namely, to (i) initiate a form of justice that discards the state's 'repressive' or 'rehabilitative' responses to crime, and (ii) to nurture harmonious communities that embrace restorative – rather than the state's legal – justice practices. I point to certain paradoxes and dangers in the ways that the promise of justice and community are enunciated by influential restorative justice discourses. This discussion leads me to review both justice and community through deconstructionist lenses, and to consider restorative justice as a way of challenging, continuously, any given calculation of justice and collective solidarity. My endeavour bears traces of Derridean deconstruction in the sense that its overriding approach is one of opening up concepts rather than closing them off as necessary, immutable, or inevitable decrees (see Derrida, 1997, 1976). But deconstruction is not destruction; it is one way of coming to grips with the radical contingency, and paradox, of any discourse that speaks now about what might come.

[...]

Promises of popular justice beyond law

The basic problem is of course whether we consider restorative justice as merely a series of techniques which are to be integrated into the existing systems of penal or re-educative responses to crime or restorative justice has to become a fully fledged alternative which should in the longer term replace maximally the existing systems (Walgrave, 1995: 12).

Walgrave's statement alludes to a paradox surrounding the promise of justice within restorative justice discourses: on the one hand, advocates claim legitimacy by promising 'maximal' transformations of current justice systems; on the other, they defer to closed principles of justice that – by virtue of their homologies with existing criminal justice formulations – do not permit such 'maximal' replacements. The paradox is encompassed by the ambiguity of the term 'restoration'. Restoration can connote ideas of 'replenishment', and even 'refurbishment' (thereby suggesting degrees of change); equally it often refers to 'reinstatement', 'return' (as in returning to the way things were before) when used by conservative programs. The contradictory meanings often curtail restorative justice's promise to create *alternative* processes that revitalise democratic patterns of association. How so?

As noted, much restorative justice discourse centres on social change, and claiming to provide alternatives to professional courtroom justice (i.e. with its costly, time-consuming, inefficient, alienating, etc., processes that frequently escalate conflict). Walgrave's statement notes the prospect of 'maximally' replacing legal institutions with those that adhere to 'restoring' or 'healing' principles.[1] This maximal replacement would extend over philosophies and institutions (e.g. Nicholl, 2000; Umbreit, 1995). Rhetorically, at least, this commits restorative justice protagonists to fairly significant transformations of the legal *status quo*, and demands reforms that empower individuals and communities to assume responsibility for conflict (see Bush and Folger, 1994). There are various conceptions of the changes to be made, including those centred on spiritual fellowship, the redressing of harm, communitarian quests for empowered moral communities, as well as political calls for viable civil societies and democracies (Braithwaite, 1999). Despite their differences, all see restorative justice as an alternative vision and practice of justice – restorative justice, in other words, is concerned with changes to the communities currently associated with professional legal justice.

At the same time, however, many protagonists view restorative justice as a way of redressing wrongs, as defined from within a given *status quo*. For instance, reflecting a common enough theme in the discourse, Cooley argues that restorative justice proceeds from the basic premise that, 'the most effective response to conflict is to repair the harm done by the wrongful act' (1999: 5). Furthermore, he notes,

> Restorative justice approaches turn on the existence of a wrong. Restorative justice begins with the premise that a wrong has occurred. Restorative justice works well within the criminal justice system because the criminal law provides a ready-made list of wrongs and an easily identifiable wrongdoer ... For restorative justice, because the culpability of the wrongdoer is taken for granted, determining what happened is important only to address the wrong (1999: 38).

Although raised to ponder whether restorative justice is suited to civil jurisdictions, Cooley's statement could equally be used for another purpose; namely, to signal just how much restorative justice's promise of alternative frameworks of justice is compromised by a dogged allegiance to (mostly individual) conceptions of wrong, or harming doing. That is, if restorative justice is premised simply on repairing wrongs as enunciated from given contexts, then how can it accommodate calls for significant social change? Viewing restorative justice as a slave to contextual definitions of wrong commits adherents to the assumption that restorative justice's main purpose is to redress wrongful acts. Missing in this logic is, for instance, the possibility that certain kinds of conflict may well be needed to spearhead important social changes (e.g. to totalitarian contexts). What, asks someone like R. Morris (1995), about the harms that produce the sometimes tragic lives of offenders? Can a justice tied to wrong-doing adequately challenge existing criminal justice institutions, or is it merely an extension of criminal law? Many have pointed to the net-widening dangers of restorative justice (see Levrant *et al.*, 1999) and community justice (Cohen, 1985), but there is also the danger of a self-imposed limitation that would mark restorative justice as a mere complement to state justice, as a way to mop up its overt failures. The latter radically reverses the spirit of restorative justice's promise to provide a 'maximal' replacement to law's crime and punishment model.

In sum, responding to individual harms within communities through narrowly conceived restorative justice practices (e.g. FGC, mediation, conciliation, etc.) restricts what sorts of change is possible. For instance, can restorative justice significantly challenge the 'norms' that define 'harm' in a given context, or challenge the idea of harm when enunciated exclusively in individual/community terms? And if it cannot do this, then is restorative justice really all that different from the criminal justice systems it seeks to 'maximally' replace? In what sense does it breathe life into alternatives that promise an actively lived justice? Concentrating effort on local harms leads protagonists to develop political arenas (FGCs) to contain, isolate and thwart the very conflict that might otherwise encourage broader political resistance to oppressive collective domination. Restorative justice may avoid the state's emphasis on legal guilt, but it still assumes that some wrong *has* occurred, that there is a responsible offender and a receiving victim/community. Adjudication is replaced with consensus-seeking restorative devices that seek peaceable agreements to narrowly defined 'problems' (e.g. individual harm – see Bazemore, 1998).

In the process, many legal assumptions and objectives are replicated: placing culpability for harm on individuals (or groups); serving reasonable, law-abiding individuals in communities; seeking communal order by resolving particular conflicts (as opposed to dealing with wider power structures); focussing conflict resolution process on micro cases; etc.. Restorative justice practices may differ (e.g. mediation versus adjudication), but the fundamental continuities between the assumptions of existing criminal justice and restorative justice initiatives are transparent. Very often, restorative justice (even if inadvertently) replicates the very thought systems it was supposed to eschew. That is why, perhaps, its promises do not so much carve out new conceptual horizons of justice but delineate what restorative justice is not (i.e. it is not repressive, not reactive, reparative, distributive, etc.). One might say that the basis for conceiving restorative justice lies in current criminal justice provisions, indicating a mutually constitutive relation between restorative justice and state law (Pavlich, 1996a; Fitzpatrick, 1988).

Adding to this, and following some of Foucault's precepts, various authors have argued that medieval 'law and sovereign' models of power survived in modern societies through the support of disciplinary powers designed to create normal individuals in society.[2] It may be that under postmodern conditions, law and discipline are increasingly subjected to governmental priorities, such as the rise of restorative justice's attempts to restore selves to peaceful, harmonious and secure communities (Pavlich, 2000). In any case, opposing restorative justice with the law is all too often a deceptive ruse. The homologies, mutual constitutions and common assumptions shared by these are far greater than their differences. Advocates who see restorative justice as a logical complement of liberal legal assumptions readily concede the point; but that concession comes at the cost of diluting restorative justice's promise to nurture fundamental alternatives.[3] As such, one could argue that law's justice is not restorative justice's opponent. Instead, both legal and restorative justice fall on the side of liberal and/or communitarian images of justice; in turn, both could be situated against a deconstructive vision of justice as a promise that endlessly invites its own recalculation.

Derrida (1992) and Lyotard and Thébaud (1985) elaborate upon the possibility of such an open-ended notion of justice.[4] One need not agree with their approaches to underscore the basic point: it is possible to conceptualise justice beyond the common assumptions of either legal or restorative justice. Indicating what such a formulation might mean, Derrida insists that justice does not exist as such; it is never present, an absolute entity, a reality or even a definable ideal to which our institutions might strive. Justice instead implies,

> non-gathering, dissociation, heterogeneity, non-identity with itself, endless inad-equation, infinite transcendance. That is why the call to justice is never, never fully answered. That is why no one can say 'I am just'. If someone tells you 'I am just', you can be sure that he or she is wrong, because being just is not a matter of theoretical determination (Derrida, 1997: 17).

If anything, justice is an incalculable, non-definable 'there being', that forever calls us from the mists of the future. Its promise is always on the way, always to come, always beyond what is presently calculated in its name. Justice emerges as an incalculable promise requiring calculations in its name; law and restorative justice are two such calculations, but neither is ever entirely just, for justice always extends beyond any particular reckoning. As such, justice is – if it is anything – but a promise that calls us to calculate in its name, realising that no formulation/practice can ever embrace it entirely.

This suggests the value of approaching restorative justice with a sense of disquiet, with vigilance to the inevitable dangers of any calculations of justice and remaining open to other possible computations. The latter implies a welcoming of otherness, of claims and formulations outside the ambit of given conceptions of the just. Derrida (1992) notes the importance of remaining forever open to the other, to the future, preventing any image of justice declaring itself as a necessary event, as unquestionably better than any other. In the illusory comforts of such decrees reside all the atrocities of totalitarian social formations. So, one may insist upon a primary responsibility to what lies outside, what is other to, a given calculation of the just. This view implies a sense of justice that welcomes alterity, never portraying the present as necessary; any given present is always constituted by its connection with the 'other'. It also views justice as involving a constant reflection and recalculation of present limit formations, opening up to democratic practices that are themselves always open (Derrida, 1995, 1997).

Promises of community versus hospitability

> Central to restorative justice is recognition of the community, rather than criminal justice agencies, as the prime site of control (New Zealand Ministry of Justice, 1995: 1).

> If by community one implies, as is often the case, a harmonious group, consensus, and fundamental agreement beneath phenomena of discord or war, then I don't believe in it very much and I sense in it as much threat as promise (Derrida, 1995: 355)

Restorative justice's promise to develop/restore/replenish harmonious, peaceful, warm community relations is closely tied to the legitimising rationales of the discourse. So too are its calls to return justice to the community. I have elsewhere echoed Derrida's concerns about promises that centre on the concept of 'community' (Pavlich, 2001, 1996b). Appeals to homogeneous, consensual and unified images of community harbour serious dangers marked by identity through exclusion. For instance, the assumption of harm to be restored is always issued from within a given community, and responsibility for that definition is mostly placed upon self-defined members – not to 'others' at the margins of (and so constituting) that identity formation. This argument rests on the view that a universal community, one that includes everybody, cannot be specified – quite literally, it is meaningless (Young, 1990). Communities always have members and outsiders; the ability to identify a community rests on the assumption of insiders who are somehow not the same as its images of the stranger, the other, the offender, etc. (Bauman, 1997).

This basic definitional requirement of community, for all its warm connotations, involves a responsibility to the like, effectively fortifying them from the unalike. The unity (*unum*), being with (*com*), the identity, the common, is made present through successful exclusions that brace limits, specify boundaries.[5] It is perhaps not surprising that community should be related to the Latin *municeps* (from whence we have 'municipal') that referred to those who were citizens of a Roman city (the *municipium*), but not permitted to be magistrates. Restorative justice's community is like the citizen, who serves the state, but not as a sanctioned official. The walled city keeps strangers outside through the coercions of law's empires, but the community operates through limits carved by its own double-edged sword, its fist in the velvet glove. This is community's secret, the secret of its subtle identification through exclusion. The dark side remains so long as a community does not face the continuous threat of a totalitarian refusal; namely, refusing to accept responsibility for the excluded others that enable specific community identities to be limited as a real, instituted present.

But let me be clear on this score. The promise of community is not necessarily totalitarian, nor something to be denounced out of hand. My point is just that a blind quest to develop communities at all costs is not an unequivocal good, devoid of severe dangers. Rather the threat of totalitarian closures around specific community identities can never be guarded against so long as one heralds, as do so many advocates of restorative justice, the (peaceful, secure, harmonious, etc.) community as panacea for the ills of contemporary state law. The quest for a closed identity that defines a given community and its harms involves closures around specific limits. Furthermore, this should not deceive us: such a community identity does not stand in necessary opposition to the state and its legal justice. As Agamben insightfully notes,

> the state can recognise any claim for identity . . . What the state cannot tolerate in any way, however, is that the singularities form a community without affirming identity, that humans co-belong without any representable condition of belonging (1993: 86).

Agamben's point suggests an interesting alternative to the quest for a closed, identifiable community that can serve state justice, perhaps especially because it claims to oppose the state. He notes a way of calculating collective solidarity without resorting to the definitional closures of specific community images, or indeed those suggested by allied conceptions of 'society'. To be blunt, it may be possible to calculate promises of collective solidarity via meaning horizons beyond the ambit of state justice; perhaps by resisting the tendency to close off (unify) limits and to relentlessly open up particular instances of community. One could, furthermore, calculate collective solidarity differently by using the limitations of restorative justice's community promise to indicate new languages of open resistance to governance centred on closed (community, etc.) identifications. Derrida alludes to the possibility in this passage:

> There is doubtless this irrepressible desire for 'community' to form but also for it to know its limit – and for its limit to be its *opening*. Once it thinks it has understood, taken in, interpreted, *kept* the text, then something of this latter, something in it that is altogether *other* escapes or resists the community, it appeals for another community, it does not let itself be totally interiorised in the memory of a present community. The experience of mourning and promise that institutes that community but also forbids it from collecting itself, this experience stores in itself the reserve of another community that will sign, otherwise, completely new contracts (Derrida, 1995: 355).

I interpret this statement in context thus: the very processes of instating a community (such as those advocated through restorative justice) always involves a dual mourning of past limits, and the promise of new ones. Hence, one could read restorative justice's critique of law's failures and the universality of restorative justice as 'mourning' for a timeless 'justice without law' (e.g. Braithwaite, 1998, 1999; Auerbach, 1983). At the same time, promises of an alternative justice, community and democracy herald new patterns of solidarity. In the interstice between the mourning and the promise, through which specific community identities are pursued, lies the impossibility of ever fully closing off a given calculation of community. The very process of identifying the limits of community, of specifying what it is not, its promise, etc., opens the floodgates of doubt, uncertainty – hence the ambiguity, ambivalence and ethereality of the communities to which restorative justice is addressed. The inability to specify 'community' is not a failure on the part of restorative justice advocates; on the contrary, it is the source of their deliverance. Indeed, this supposed failure brings community limits to the fore, presenting an opening from whence new images of solidarity may be countenanced and promised. This relentless opening up of limits disallows the 'community' from collecting itself into a totalitarian unity, a fortified exclusivity; it always calls for an escape to *other* calculations of collective solidarity.

Perhaps restorative justice's promise of community could be seen as succeeding through its failure to define and fortify the limits of community absolutely. But this is more a matter of circumstance than design, because the approach does not actively ward off the totalitarian dangers inherent to all discourses that champion descriptive closure, and try to eliminate indecision. One could attempt calculations of collective solidarity through images of community that endorse uncertainty, and explicitly disallow fixed closures. Corlett (1989), for example, provides a lengthy analysis of the possibilities of seeking, as its title conveys, a *Community without Unity*. Nancy (1991) too explores various ways of calculating community as an open (and therefore inoperative) frontier of possibility, as one always on guard against the totalitarian dangers attendant upon attempts to close off particular limits as necessary, ordered, etc. Without discounting the value of these attempts to calculate collective solidarity through open images of community, I still wonder whether another concept – less tarnished with the brushstrokes of fascist totalities – might better serve such calculations.

And what candidate concept do I have in mind? Perhaps images of collective solidarity could be rephrased through one that is usefully addressed in Derrida (e.g. 1999, 2000); namely, *hospitality*. I suggest this possibility because it invites us to calculate collective solidarity without implying that the host give up an identity, and yet emphasise a responsibility to the other as guest, the terms of which must always be negotiated in specific contexts. Etymologically, the term derives from the Latin *hospitale* that connotes 'place where guests are received' (Ayto, 1993: 287). The host is one who receives guests in such a place. In this place too, unlike community, hospitality calls for an approach to others not centred on closing off identities to include or exclude; instead it intimates a welcoming, an invitation to the other to cross the threshold of place, a *domus* perhaps. This gesture simultaneously opens the limit of that threshold to otherness and accepts an undecided negotiation of the terms of the host relationship. It extends an invitation to the stranger at various levels, from the guest in my home, to the negotiations of host countries for refugees, immigrants, and so on (Barkan, 2000).

Openings . . .

Not wishing to collect the above into the bindings of a fixed summary, and so reverse its dissociated spirit, I shall instead call for restorative justice to echo its early promise to gaze past what is, towards new calculations of how to be just. This opening gesture might be continuously evoked, always seeking unexpressed possibilities beyond a given present – in the process it sends forth the elusive promise of justice, and invites multiple calculations in its name. As well, restorative justice could incorporate notions of hospitality, rather than community, to direct host and other responsibilities, without assuming fixed (necessary) patterns of being. If both promises endorse a sustained uncertainty, they also intimate opening gestures that welcome what is to come, that embrace – rather than annul – other possibilities, inconceivable within present realities. Out of undecidable spaces that release 'the impossible' one might hospitably replenish restorative justice's promise to face up to, and beyond, present calculations of the just.

This extract is taken from 'Deconstructing Restoration: the Promise of Restorative Justice', by George Pavlich, in E. Weitekamp and H.-J. Kerner (eds), Restorative Justice: Theoretical Foundations *(Cullompton, Devon: Willan, 2002), pp. 90–109.*

Notes

1 Relating to this point, some aspects of the discourse claim that restorative justice is not so much a philosophy as a framework for specific practices (Braithwaite, 1999; Cooley, 1999: 19; Zehr, 1990, etc.). In my view, however, it seems somewhat disingenuous to claim that restorative justice offers alternate principles and visions of justice, as well as a series of guides on how to live justly, and then claiming that this is not a philosophy or theory. Restorative justice's formulate expressly arranges signs into a discourse that give meaning to particular practices, advocating one view of the world rather than another – this constitutes, at the very least, the rudiments of a philosophy of justice.
2 See Pavlich (1996a, 1996b), Fitzpatrick (1988), Matthews (1988) and Foucault (1977).
3 Related to this point, Braithwaite (1999: 93) accepts the claim that law and restorative justice are mutually constituted, but fails to then recognise that this acceptance compromises the claims to alternation that he uses to legitimate the concept.
4 See also Pavlich (1996a: chapter 2).
5 Caputo (1997: 108) notes the relevance of the related *communio* and its intimations of defending and fortification – from *munis*, defence, fortification and *com*, common, etc.

References

Agamben, G. (1993) *The Coming Community* (trans. M. Hardt) (Minneapolis, MN: University of Minnesota Press).
Akester, K. (2000) *Restoring Youth Justice: New Directions in Domestic and International Law and Practice* (London: Justice).
Auerbach, J.S. (1983) *Justice without Law?* (New York, NY: Oxford University Press).
Ayto, J. (1993) *Dictionary of Word Origins* (London: Bloomsbury).
Barkan, E. (2000) *The Guilt of Nations: Restitution and Negotiating Historical Injustices* (New York, NY: Norton).
Bauman, Z. (1997) *Postmodernity and its Discontents* (Cambridge: Polity Press).
Bazemore, G. (1998) 'Restorative Justice and Earned Redemption Communities, victims and offender reintergration', *American Behavioral Scientist*, 41, 768–813.

Braithwaite, J. (1989) *Crime, Shame and Reintegration* (Cambridge and Sydney: Cambridge University Press).

Braithwaite, J. (1998) 'Restorative Justice in Tonry, M. (ed.) *The Handbook of Crime and Punishment* (New York: Oxford University Press).

Braithwaite, J. (1999) 'Restorative Justice: Assessing Optimistic and Pessimistic Accounts', *Crime and Justice*, 25, 1–127.

British Columbia Ministry of Attorney General (1998) *A Restorative Justice Framework: British Columbia Justice Reform* (Victoria: British Columbia Ministry of Attorney General).

Brown, B.J. and McElrea, F.W.M. (1993) *The Youth Court in New Zealand : A New Model of Justice: Four Papers* (Wellington: Legal Research Foundation).

Bush, R. and Folger, J. (1994) *The Promise of Mediation: Responding to Conflict through Empowerment* (San Francisco, CA: Jossey-Bass).

Caputo, J.D. (ed.) (1997) *Deconstruction in a Nutshell: A Conversation with Jacques Derrida* (New York, NY: Fordham University Press).

Cohen, S. (1985) *Visions of Social Control: Crime, Punishment, and Classification* (Oxford: Polity Press).

Consedine, J. (1995) *Restorative Justice: Healing the Effects of Crime* (Lyttelton, New Zealand.: Ploughshares Publications).

Cooley, D. (1999) *From Restorative Justice to Transformative Justice: Discussion Paper* (Ottawa: Law Commission of Canada).

Corlett, W. (1989) *Community Without Unity: A Politics of Derridian Extravagance* (Durham, NC: Duke University Press).

Derrida, J. (1992) 'The Force of Law: The "Mystical Foundation" of Authority', in Cornell, D. *et al.* (eds) *Deconstruction and the Possibility of Justice* (New York, NY: Routledge).

Derrida, J. (1995) *Points . . . Interviews, 1974–1994.* (Stanford, CA: Stanford University Press).

Derrida, J. (1997) 'Roundtable' in Caputo, J.D. (ed.) *Deconstruction in a Nutshell: A Conversation with Jacques Derrida* (New York, NY: Fordham University Press).

Derrida, J. (1999) *Adieu to Emmanuel Levinas* (Stanford, CA: Stanford University Press).

Derrida, J. (2000) *Of Hospitality: Anne Dufourmantelle Invites Jacques Derrida to Respond* (Stanford, CA: Stanford University Press).

Fitzpatrick, P. (1988) 'The Rise and Rise of Informal Justice', in Matthews, R. (ed.) *Informal Justice?* (London and Newbury Park, CA: Sage).

Foucault, M. (1977) *Discipline and Punish: the Birth of the Prison* (New York, NY: Pantheon Books).

Galaway, B. and Hudson, J. (1996) *Restorative Justice: International Perspectives* (Monsey, NY: Criminal Justice Press).

Kurki, L. (1999) *Incorporating Restorative and Community Justice into American Sentencing and Corrections* (Washington, DC: US Department of Justice Office of Justice Programs, National Institute of Justice).

Levrant, S., Cullen, F.T., Fulton, B. and Wozniak, J.F. (1999) 'Reconsidering Restorative Justice: The Corruption of Benevolence Revisited?' *Crime and Delinquency*, 45, pp. 3–27.

Lyotard, J.F. and Thébaud, J.-L. (1985) *Just Gaming* (Minneapolis, MN: University of Minnesota Press).

Matthews, R. (1988) 'Informal Justice?' in *Sage Contemporary Criminology* (London and Newbury Park, CA: Sage Publications).

Merry, S.E. and Milner, N.A. (1993) *The Possibility of Popular Justice: A Case Study of Community Mediation in the United States* (Ann Arbor, MI: University of Michigan Press).

Morris, A. and Young, W. (1987) *Juvenile Justice in New Zealand: Policy and Practice* (Wellington: Institute of Criminology, Victoria University of Wellington).

Morris, R. (1995) 'Not Enough!' *Mediation Quarterly*, 12, pp. 285–91.

Nancy, J.-L. (1991) *The Inoperative Community* (Minneapolis, MN: University of Minnesota Press).

New Zealand Ministry of Justice (1995) *Restorative Justice: A Discussion Paper* (Wellington: Ministry of Justice).

Nicholl, C.G. (2000) *Toolbox for Implementing Restorative Justice and Advancing Community Policing: A Guidebook Prepared for the Office of Community Oriented Policing Services, US Department of Justice* (Washington, DC: US Department of Justice. Office of Community Oriented Policing Services and National Victim Center).

Pavlich, G. (1996a) *Justice Fragmented: Mediating Community Disputes under Postmodern Conditions* (London: Routledge).

Pavlich, G. (1996b) 'The Power of Community Mediation: Government and Formation of Self', *Law and Society Review*, 30, pp. 101–27.

Pavlich, G. (2000) *Critique and Radical Discourses on Crime* (Aldershot: Ashgate/ Dartmouth).

Pavlich, G. (2001) 'The Force of Community', in Strang, H. and Braithwaite, J. (eds) *Restorative Justice and Civil Society* (Cambridge: Cambridge University Press).

Roberts, S. (1979) *Order and Dispute: An Introduction to Legal Anthropology* (New York, NY: St Martin's Press).

Shonholtz, R. (1988/89) 'Community as Peacemaker: Making Neighborhood Justice Work', *Current Municipal Problems*, 15, pp. 291–330.

Strang, H. and Braithwaite, J. (eds) (2001) *Restorative Justice and Civil Society* (Cambridge: Cambridge University Press).

Umbreit, M.S. (1995) 'The Development and Impact of Victim–Offender Mediation in the United States', *Mediation Quarterly*, 12, pp. 263–76.

Van Ness, D.W., Crawford, T. and Justice Fellowship (1989) *Restorative Justice* (Washington, DC: Justice Fellowship).

Walgrave, L. (1995) 'Restorative Justice for Juveniles: Just a Technique or a Fully Fledged Alternative?' *Howard Journal of Criminal Justice*, 34, pp. 228–49.

Walgrave, L. (1998) 'Restorative Justice for Juveniles: Potentialities, Risks, and Problems for Research', in *Samenleving, criminaliteit and strafrechtspleging. 12.* (Leuven: Leuven University Press).

Young, I.M. (1990) 'The Ideal of Community and the Politics of Difference', in Nicholson, L. J. (ed.) *Feminism/Postmodernism* (New York, NY: Routledge).

Zehr, H. (1990) *Changing Lenses: A New Focus for Crime and Justice* (Scottdale, PA: Herald Press).

32. Critiquing the critics: a brief response to critics of restorative justice

Allison Morris

[. . .]

It is not unusual in the criminological literature to come across claims that 'reforms' have had unanticipated and negative consequences (see, for example, Platt, 1969; Martinson, 1974; Pease, 1985; Bottoms, 1987) and this claim has been made with respect to restorative justice. Levrant *et al.* (1999: 16), for example, recently described restorative justice as perhaps doing 'more harm than good'. Similarly, Johnstone (2002: 7) cautions that we 'need to be alert to the ways in which it [restorative justice] could make things worse' and details a 'whole range of deleterious consequences' which might result from a shift to restorative justice. Johnstone later argues that the proliferation of restorative justice programmes 'is not the benign development it is often taken to be, but has a much more sinister side to it' (2002: 25).[1] And Delgrado (2000: 759) asserts that restorative justice renders 'a disservice to victims, offenders and society at large'.

In a related vein, some writers have also questioned whether or not the values of restorative justice can be translated into practical reality. Levrant *et al.*, for example, described restorative justice as 'an unproved movement that risks failure' and claimed that its appeal 'lies more in its humanistic sentiments than in any empirical evidence of its effectiveness' (1999: 16). Kurki (2000: 240) argued that 'there is not yet evidence that the experience yields better results'. And Miers (2001: 88) recently wrote of restorative justice that 'sceptics have much to be sceptical about'. This paper takes issue with these various claims.[2]

I acknowledge that the restorative justice literature is plagued with imprecision and confusion and I do not seek to defend all practices that claim to be restorative justice. These are as diverse as conferencing,[3] victim–offender mediation, sentencing circles, community reparation boards, restitution programmes and much more. I acknowledge also that there is a risk that restorative justice advocates may claim too much. Thus I also try in this paper to make clear what, in my view, restorative justice represents. It seems to me that much of the critique that has emerged is based on fundamental misunderstandings[4] of what restorative justice seeks to achieve, on diluted or distorted applications of the principles of restorative justice[5] or on the misinterpretation of empirical research on restorative justice.[6]

In addition, this paper considers more briefly a very different type of critique: philosophical rather than empirical. Just deserts theorists have argued that the sanctions agreed to within a restorative justice framework may not be proportionate to the severity of the offence and are unlikely to be consistent: offenders involved in similar offending may end up with different sanctions. For example, Ashworth and von Hirsch (1998: 303) complain about the 'absence of safeguards against excessive penalties'. As desert theorists, they affirm the

need for proportionality as a limit on sentences and see restorative justice as
having substituted 'the wishes of the individual victim' (Ashworth, 1992: 8,
cited in Cavadino and Dignan, 1996: 237) or 'the victim disposition' (Ashworth
and von Hirsch, 1998: 332–3). This paper takes issue with these claims and
argues that restorative justice has to be evaluated against the values it
represents and not against those it attacks and seeks to replace.
   [. . .]

Claim: restorative justice erodes legal rights

A common criticism made of restorative justice is that it fails to provide
procedural safeguards or to protect offenders' rights. The picture painted is
that this failure is promoted by restorative justice advocates in order to obtain
more readily offenders' acceptance of their responsibility for their offending
and agreements among participants about how to deal with that offending.
But, restorative justice practitioners have to follow certain guidelines or
practice manuals and, in some examples of restorative justice, there are
statutory guidelines or regulations to follow too.

   Overall, there is nothing in the values of restorative justice which would lead
to a denial or erosion of offenders' legal rights (through their broad emphasis on
human rights). However, different examples of restorative justice have translated
the protection of offenders' rights into practice in different ways. For example, in
South Australia, young people participating in conferences can consult with
lawyers prior to admitting the offence and prior to agreeing with the proposed
outcome, though lawyers tend not to be present at the conference itself. In Real
Justice conferences in the United States, lawyers at conferences have a watching
brief and they can interrupt proceedings if they feel that the young person's legal
rights are being breached (Paul McCold, personal communication). And, in
New Zealand, if facilitators at a family group conference have any concerns
about young offenders' legal rights, they may request the appointment of a
lawyer (paid for by the state). In addition, young people referred to a conference
by the Youth Court can have their court appointed lawyers (youth advocates)[7]
with them during the family group conference, as can adult offenders involved
in the court referred restorative justice pilots.[8]

   And so it is difficult to accept, either with respect to the values of restorative
justice or empirically with respect to these examples at least, the claim that
restorative justice erodes offenders' rights.[9] What restorative justice does is
place a different priority on the protection of offenders' rights by not adopting
a procedure whereby offenders' lawyers are the main protagonists or
spokespersons and their primary purpose is to minimize the offender's
responsibility or to get the most lenient sanction possible.

   And, of course, it is quite farcical for critics of restorative justice to imply
that, in contrast, conventional criminal justice systems adequately protect
offenders' legal rights. It is uncommon for young offenders in the United States
to be legally represented in the juvenile court (they tend to waive this right)
and most cases in the adult criminal courts are dealt with through plea-
bargaining. This is not the place to discuss plea-bargaining in any detail.

Suffice to say that its principal objective is not to protect offenders' rights. Concerns have also been raised about the quality of justice provided by lawyers in English courts (McConville *et al.*, 1993; Darbyshire, 2000).[10]

Claim: restorative justice results in net-widening

It is commonly claimed that restorative justice processes widen the net of social control because they tend to focus on minor offenders at low risk of reoffending (presumably offenders who would otherwise be warned by the police or otherwise diverted) and because they tend to result in these minor offenders being given more incursive penalties than they would otherwise receive. This is not a claim made exclusively of restorative justice, of course: it has been made about the introduction of a whole raft of diversionary practices (including with respect to the expansion of police warnings in England and Wales in the 1970s and the introduction of various alternatives to custody). The key issue in testing the validity of this claim, therefore, is the type of offenders a particular restorative justice practice is aimed at.

In New Zealand, restorative justice processes are used not for relatively minor offenders but rather for the most serious and persistent offenders in the youth justice system and for relatively serious offenders in the adult criminal justice system. Family group conferences are held for about 15–20 per cent of youth offenders; the rest are simply warned or diverted by the police. Some examples of the kinds of offenders dealt with in family group conferences there (taken from Maxwell and Morris, 1993) include a boy who broke into a house and raped a young woman; a group of school children who set fire to and destroyed an entire school block; a boy whose victim was beaten over the head during the process of a robbery; and a boy whose victim barely survived the assault and was left with permanent brain damage. As for the restorative justice pilots for adults, Maxwell *et al.* (1999) document that the two schemes in that evaluation dealt with aggravated robbery, threats to kill, driving causing death, driving with excess alcohol as well as the more 'routine' offences of wilful damage, theft and burglary. In the first year of the operation of the court-referred restorative justice pilots, all property offences with maximum penalties of two years' imprisonment or more and other offences with maximum penalties of one to seven years are eligible for referral to a restorative conference by the judge. Some other jurisdictions (for example, South Australia and New South Wales) also aim their restorative justice processes at medium serious juvenile offenders.

However, some examples of conferencing – particularly those which operate as part of police diversion – do focus on more minor offences and it is possible that net-widening occurs here. Young and Goold (1999) certainly raised this concern with respect to restorative conferencing in the Thames Valley Police area at that time (see also Young, 2001). On the other hand, Maxwell and Morris (1993) specifically examined net-widening in their research on family group conferences in New Zealand and found no evidence of it. Also, in the evaluation of the community panels in New Zealand, most offenders in the pilot groups experienced less incursive penalties than their matched controls who were dealt with solely in conventional criminal courts (Maxwell *et al.*, 1999).

To repeat the point made earlier: the validity of this claim depends on the focus of particular examples of restorative justice and it certainly does not apply to all. Also, many advocates of restorative justice believe that restorative justice processes should be aimed at the more serious and persistent offenders given the practicality of limited resources and the potential in such cases for victims, offenders and communities to receive considerable benefits (in terms of having a better understanding of the offences and their consequences and of providing more opportunities for healing and reintegration).

Claim: restorative justice trivializes crime

This claim is more frequently mentioned with respect to violence against women. Critics tend to see restorative justice processes as decriminalizing men's violence against their partners and as returning it to the status of a 'private' matter. Morris and Gelsthorpe (2000b) have already fully discussed this and I repeat here only the gist of their response to this criticism. Their main point is that the use of restorative justice processes does not signify the trivialization of any crime: the criminal law remains as a signifier and denouncer. In addition, however, restorative justice advocates believe that the offender's family and friends are by far the most potent agents to achieve this objective of denunciation. In the context of men's violence against their partners, denouncing the violence in the presence of the abuser's family and friends means that the message is loud and clear for those who matter most to him.

More broadly, restorative justice arguably takes crime more seriously than conventional criminal justice systems because it focuses on the consequences of the offence for victims and attempts to address these and to find meaningful ways of holding offenders accountable. Crime, on the other hand, is trivialized by processes in which victims have no role (apart, in some situations, as witnesses) and in which offenders are not much more than passive observers.

A slightly different but important point for questioning the legitimacy of this claim that restorative justice processes decriminalizes men's violence against their partners is that, for a range of reasons, only a few of the women who experience violence at the hands of their male partners rely on the law, police or courts to deal with it, at least in the first instance (Mirrlees-Black, 1999).[11] The introduction of restorative justice processes in such cases, on the other hand, at the very least would increase women's choices and, through this involvement of friends and families, might well result in increasing women's safety. In this way, arguably, restorative justice could empower women.[12]

Claim: restorative justice fails to 'restore' victims and offenders

By definition, we would expect restorative justice to 'restore' and it has to be accepted that there is some haziness in the restorative justice literature about what precisely this means. But, for victims, I take it to mean restoring the victim's security, self-respect, dignity and sense of control. There is no doubt that research shows that victims who have taken part in restorative justice processes have high levels of satisfaction with reparative agreements, have reduced levels of fear and seem to have an improved understanding of why the offence occurred and its likelihood of recurrence (for empirical detail, see Daly, 2001; Strang, 2001; Umbreit *et al.*, 2001). It is true, as some critics allege, that full monetary restoration is not always achieved as many offenders have limited resources. However, if we as a community take restorative justice seriously, this type of restoration could, and perhaps should, be a community (state) responsibility. But, more importantly, research consistently suggests that monetary restoration is not what victims want: they are much more interested in emotional reparation than material (Marshall and Merry, 1990; Umbreit *et al.*, 1994; Strang, 2001). Now, of course, emotional reparation also does not always happen. But it seems to happen more often in restorative justice processes than it does not. And it certainly happens more often there than in conventional criminal justice processes. Overall, Latimer *et al.* (2001) con-cluded, on the basis of their recent meta-analysis of 22 studies, which examined the effectiveness of 35 restorative justice programmes, that victims who participated in restorative processes were significantly more satisfied than those who participated in the traditional justice system.

For offenders, again as noted earlier, I take restoration to mean restoring responsibility to them for their offending and its consequences, restoring a sense of control to them to make amends for what they have done and restoring a belief in them that the process and outcomes were fair and just. The evidence seems clear that this can occur. Maxwell and Morris (1993), for example, showed that young offenders felt reasonably involved in the decisions being made in family group conferences in New Zealand. More recent data (Maxwell *et al.*, 2001) on just over 300 young people who were involved in family group conferences in New Zealand in 1998 shows, after preliminary analysis, that over half said they felt involved in making decisions; that more than two-thirds said they had had the opportunity to say what they wanted to; that over 80 per cent said that they understood the decisions; and that two-thirds said that they agreed with the decision. Recent Australian research refers to young offenders seeing conferencing as fair and being satisfied with both conference processes and outcomes (Palk *et al.*, 1998; Cant and Downie, 1998; Strang *et al.*, 1999; Trimboli, 2000; Daly, 2001).

However, I also take 'restoring' to mean redressing the harms caused both by and to the offender. This means that action needs to be taken to address both the factors underlying their offending in the first place and the consequences of that offending. A process, no matter how inclusionary, and an outcome, no matter how reparative, is not likely to magically undo the years of social marginalization and exclusion experienced by so many offenders (see also Polk, 2001) or remove the need for victims to receive long-term support or counselling. Restoration requires an acceptance by the community more generally that the offender has tried to make amends and the provision of programmes that address drug and alcohol abuse, the lack of job skills and so on.[13] It also requires effective help and support for victims. And so here the critics of restorative justice may have a valid point to make – restorative justice is not 'restoring' offenders if they cannot access such programmes and is not 'restoring' victims if they cannot access what they need. However, the critics are aiming at the wrong target. Good programmes addressing the reasons underlying offending and effective support for victims need to accompany good restorative justice processes and practices, but providing (or at least funding) them is a state responsibility.

Claim: restorative justice fails to effect real change

Most critics of restorative justice are sceptical about what it has achieved. Of course, most examples of restorative justice have not been in existence for long enough to track the extent to which the kinds of transformations envisaged by advocates have actually occurred. The New Zealand youth justice system – implemented in 1989 – is an exception. The implementation of restorative justice there has resulted in significant and real changes: fewer young offenders now appear in courts,[14] fewer young offenders are now placed in residences[15] and fewer young offenders are now sentenced to custody.[16] This all, of course, had to result in considerable cost savings. The two restorative justice pilot schemes evaluated by Maxwell *et al.* (1999) also showed significant savings over those matched offenders dealt with entirely by the criminal courts: fewer offenders in one pilot were returned to court for sentence and fewer offenders in the other pilot received custodial penalties when compared with their matched controls.

The major claim made by critics here, however, is that restorative justice has failed to reduce reoffending. It could reasonably be argued that reducing reoffending is not really an objective of restorative justice; its focus is holding offenders accountable and making amends to victims. However, it can also be reasonably argued, at least in principle, that if a particular process reflects restorative values and achieves restorative outcomes then we might expect reoffending to be reduced. Thus, if the offender accepts responsibility for the offending, feels involved in the decision about how to deal with that offending, feels treated fairly and with respect, apologizes and makes amends to the victim and takes part in a programme designed to deal with the reasons underlying his or her offending, then we could at least predict that s/he will be less likely to offend again in the future.

Critics of restorative justice feel otherwise, principally, it seems, because the assumed features of restorative justice do not coincide with the principles of effective treatment (as outlined in, for example, Andrews and Bonta, 1994; Gendreau, 1996). I need to make three points in response.

First, it is quite possible for the parties to reach an agreement, after a restorative process, which would involve a rehabilitative outcome based on the principles of effective treatment (as well as or instead of a reparative or, for that matter, a punitive outcome). I referred to this earlier in the discussion about 'restoring' offenders.

Second, critics seem to have confused here restorative justice processes and restorative outcomes and to have ignored the possibility that both may impact on reoffending. There is now some evidence of the importance of process in shaping attitudes and behaviour. Maxwell and Morris (1999), for example, found that a number of restorative justice related factors were predictive of young people who had been involved in family group conferences in New Zealand not being reconvicted some six years later. These were: feeling remorse,[17] not being made to feel a bad person; feeling involved in the decision making; agreeing with the outcome; and meeting the victim and apologizing to him/her[18] (see also Tyler, 1990 and Paternoster *et al.*, 1997 for the importance of process).

Third, and more importantly, there is now a considerable amount of research which suggests that restorative justice processes and outcomes can reduce reconviction.[19] Indeed, Latimer *et al.*'s (2001) meta-analysis concluded that, on average, restorative justice programme had lower reconviction rates than conventional criminal justice approaches. Compared to comparison or control groups, offenders who participated in restorative justice programmes were significantly more successful at remaining crime free during the follow-up periods.[20] And, importantly, there are no studies that I am aware of that found that restorative justice processes actually increased recidivism rates.

[. . .]

Claim: restorative justice leaves power imbalances untouched

A common argument against the use of restorative justice is the imbalance between supposedly powerless offenders and supposedly powerful victims. However, neither the category 'offender' nor the category 'victim' is as clear cut as this: contrast, for example, the case of a middle-class conman and an elderly pensioner who is defrauded of her life savings; the case of a woman abused over many years by her partner; the case of the 14-year-old immigrant boy beaten by the white racist; the female shoplifter who steals some baby-food from a large chain store to feed her hungry baby; and the drug addict who steals money from his mother. The power relationship between the victim and the offender in each of these examples is very different. But that is not the main point that I want to make here.

Within a restorative justice framework, power imbalances can be addressed by ensuring procedural fairness, by supporting the less powerful, and by challenging the more powerful. Thus restorative justice processes can provide a forum in which victims can make clear to offenders and, importantly, to their friends and families the effects of the offence on them, but it can also provide a forum in which offenders can give victims some insight into the reasons for their offending.[21] Facilitators of restorative justice processes have a responsibility to create an environment that ensures that both victims and offenders can freely participate, by whichever way is necessary. In contrast, power imbalances between defendants and professionals are entrenched in conventional criminal justice systems and the image of an adversarial struggle between two lawyers of equal might is a fiction (McConville *et al.*, 1993).

Claim: restorative justice encourages vigilantism

Restorative justice is sometimes equated with community or popular justice, which is, in turn, equated with vigilantism.[22] It is true that some forms of community justice can be repressive, retributive, hierarchical and patriarchal. But these values are fundamentally at odds with the defining values of restorative justice and cannot, therefore, be part of it. That is also why 'community' involvement in restorative justice processes needs to be defined quite narrowly and in such a way as to exclude the attendance of 'representative' members of geographical or social communities (except where it would be culturally appropriate to do so, as in North American sentencing circles). Also, if there are concerns about communities taking over this process for non-restorative purposes, checks could be introduced – for example, courts could provide some oversight of restorative justice outcomes for the purposes of ensuring that the outcomes are in accordance with restorative justice values. Finally, of course, vigilantism does not require the introduction of restorative processes to emerge. Abrahams (1998) provides many examples of vigilantism from modern day Britain (and elsewhere), which seem rather to have been reactions against the failings of conventional criminal justice processes and sanctions. The spectre of vigilantism in debates on restorative justice, therefore, is something of a red herring.

Claim: restorative justice lacks legitimacy

Tyler (1990) found that citizens treated with respect and listened to by the police were likely to see the law as fair; conversely, when they were treated without respect and were not listened to they were likely to see the law as unfair. He distinguished between 'process control' and 'outcome control' and concluded that 'having a say' (that is, process control) was more important than determining the outcome of a decision. Tyler's research, however, was based in a context in which decisions were made by third parties (judges). To this extent, his conclusions about priorities may not be as relevant for restorative justice processes, which are premised on consensual decision making.

The same point can be made with respect to the elements subsequently identified by Paternoster et al. (1997) as providing legitimacy. These included: representation (playing a part in decision making), consistency, impartiality, accuracy (the competency of the legal authority), correctability (the scope for appeal) and ethicality (treating people with respect and dignity). Restorative justice embodies some of these principles – particularly with regard to respect for victims and offenders. However, it does not meet others. To my mind, this is not problematic because Paternoster et al.'s notion of legitimacy is again derived principally from conventional criminal justice values. Restorative justice involves different values and its legitimacy must derive from these. Important elements, therefore, in providing legitimacy for restorative justice are the inclusion of the key parties, increased understanding of the offence, and its consequences, and respect. Much of the evidence I have cited so far would support restorative justice's claims for legitimacy. And, again, one has to be sceptical about the assumed legitimacy of conventional criminal justice systems, at least for those groups that are marginalized, alienated and socially excluded.

Claim: restorative justice fails to provide 'justice'

As noted earlier, just deserts theorists argue that the sanctions agreed to within a restorative justice framework may not be proportionate to the severity of the offence and are unlikely to be consistent. Such criticisms can be responded to in a number of ways. First, judges in conventional criminal justice processes do not always deal with like cases alike. However, that is hardly an adequate response.

Second, and related to the above point, the different reasons for these inconsistencies are crucially important. Inconsistencies on the basis of gender, ethnicity or socioeconomic status per se – which is what research on conventional criminal justice systems (Hood, 1992; Hedderman and Gelsthorpe, 1997) points to – can never be right.[23] Inconsistencies between outcomes which are the result of genuine and uncoerced agreement between the key parties, including victims, may be.

Third, restorative justice is premised on consensual decision making. It requires all the key parties – the victims, offenders and their communities of care – to agree on the appropriate outcome. The state continues to remain a party to decision making through its representatives – for example, the police or the judiciary – depending on the location of the particular restorative justice process in the criminal justice system. But what is different is that these representatives are not the 'primary' decision makers.

Finally, consistency and proportionality are constructs that serve abstract notions of justice. Ashworth and von Hirsch (1998: 334) refer to desert theory providing 'principled and fair guidance'. But there are a number of criticisms that can be made of this: in particular, the oversimplification of the gradation of offences (see Tonry, 1994 for more details). There are some writers on restorative justice who refer in similar terms to 'uniformity', 'fairness' and 'equity' as means of ensuring that outcomes for offenders are not disproportionate to their culpability (see, for example, Van Ness, 1993; Bazemore and Umbreit, 1995). But, in my view, uniformity or consistency of approach (as opposed to uniformity or consistency in outcomes) is what is required and this is achieved by always taking into account the needs and wishes of those most directly affected by the offence: victims, offenders and their communities of care. Specifically from a restorative perspective, desert theory does not provide outcomes that are meaningful to them. Indeed, desert theory is silent on why equal justice for offenders should be a higher value than equal justice (or, indeed, any kind of justice at all) for victims.

Conclusion

There is nothing wrong with critiques per se: I agree with Schiff and Bazemore (2001: 329) that they can serve a positive function in that they are part of restorative justice's evolutionary process. But critics need to have a good understanding of the essential values of restorative justice and to aim their criticisms at applications that reflect these values. They also need to acknowledge what restorative justice is struggling to combat and replace. After all, as Tracy (1998: 276) writes, we have experienced hundreds of years of the harmful consequences of a retributive justice system that has 'handed down a legacy of oppression against women, people of colour, and impoverished people'. And Delgado (2000: 771) describes the (American) criminal justice system as 'perhaps the most inegalitarian and racist structure in society'. Schiff and Bazemore (2001: 309) are surely right when they state that 'it is one thing to point out that after ten years of full implementation, restorative justice has failed to resolve pervasive justice system problems ... It is quite another to *blame* such longstanding problems on restorative and community justice' (emphasis in the original).

More specifically, this review points to four main conclusions. First, although restorative justice has a long history, its modern format is relatively recent and more time is needed to translate its critical values into good modern day practices.

Second, programmes claiming to be an example of restorative justice must be evaluated so that we can continue to collect information that will either fuel or silence the critics.

Third, this review suggests that both positive and negative spins can be put on the same data.

And, fourth, this review suggests that we have to contrast what restorative justice has achieved and may still achieve with what the alternative has achieved. At the very least, restorative justice offers us a new mode of thinking about crime and justice and a way of challenging conventional justice systems to address its failings. However, it offers much more. There is strong evidence that, at a general level, restorative justice offers more to victims than traditional criminal justice processes – they have high levels of satisfaction with reparative agreements; they have reduced levels of fear; and they seem to have an improved understanding of why the offence occurred and its likelihood of recurrence. There is also strong evidence that, at a general level, restorative justice expects more of offenders than traditional criminal justice processes – they feel involved in the process; they have the opportunity to say what they wanted to; they understand and agree with the decisions made about how best to deal with the offending; they see restorative justice processes and outcomes as fair; and they are satisfied with both these processes and outcomes. Research has also shown that restorative justice processes and outcomes can result in fewer people appearing in the criminal courts and fewer people being sentenced to residential or custodial sentences. This consequently results in cost savings. In addition, research has shown that restorative justice processes and outcomes can impact on reoffending when compared with matched offenders dealt with solely in the criminal courts. Thus, there are many reasons to feel encouraged. Now it is time to present a challenge to the critics of restorative justice: what have conventional criminal justice systems achieved in the last ten years or so? I doubt it is as much.

This extract is taken from 'Critiquing the Critics: A Brief Response to Critics of Restorative Justice', by Allison Morris, in British Journal of Criminology *(42:3, 2002), pp. 596–615.*

Notes

1 See also Ball (2000) who argues specifically that referral orders, introduced in England and Wales in the Youth Justice and Criminal Evidence Act 1999 and intended to reflect restorative justice values, are likely to result in outcomes directly the opposite of those intended.

2 It is perhaps invidious in this introduction to identify certain writers on restorative justice and I may open myself up to challenge by choosing to quote these rather than others. However, these critical works can be taken as 'representative'. The criticisms in them are 'typical' and not individual or idiosyncratic.

3 There is also considerable variation within the different types of conferencing. For example, family group conferences in New Zealand operate very differently from restorative conferencing in the Thames Valley Police Authority (Morris and Maxwell, 2001; Morris and Gelsthorpe, 2000a).

4 Some examples: Levrant *et al.* (1999: 22) refer to restorative justice involving public shaming. At most, restorative justice processes might involve Braithwaite's (1989) notion of reintegrative shaming (and some examples of conferencing are explicitly based on this) but see Morris (2002) for a critique of the relevance of shaming for conferences in New Zealand. Delgrado (2000: 764), who admittedly sees restorative justice only as victim offender mediation, paints the picture of a 'vengeful victim and a middle-class mediator' ganging up on a 'young minority offender'. This is certainly not an accurate picture of conferencing in Australasia (where many of the facilitators are from minority groups) and I doubt very much that this picture reflects current practice in victim offender mediation either where attempts are made to recruit facilitators from local communities. Paradoxically, some commentators paint the opposite picture: they claim that restorative justice is reserved for white middle-class offenders (see, for example, Tracy, 1998: 276; Levrant *et al.*, 1999; Kurki, 2000: 242).

5 Miers, for example, speaking of Miers *et al.* (2001) acknowledged that not all of the programmes included in the evaluation were really examples of restorative justice (personal communication).

6 Kurki (2002: 277), for example, refers to data from Maxwell and Morris (1993), which in her view raise concerns and cites as a finding that 31 per cent of victims felt better after conferencing and that one third felt worse. What Maxwell and Morris (1993: 119–19) actually say is that 39 per cent of conferences with victims in attendance had victims who expressed positive views and that, if one looks at the total number of victims rather than at the total number of conferences, the figure expressing positive views rises to 59 per cent. They also say that although over a third of conferences with victims in attendance had victims who said they felt worse, the figure drops to a quarter if one looks at the total number of victims rather than at the total number of conferences.

7 These lawyers are specially selected for their personality, cultural background, training and experience at being suitably qualified to represent young people. They provide the young person with legal advice generally, represent him or her in court, and can attend the young person's family group conference.

8 A quite different issue not explored in this paper is how lawyers should act in restorative justice processes. In a survey by Morris *et al.* (1997), a few of the youth

advocates who attended conferences seemed to act in a way which was at odds with the principles of the restorative justice (for example, they spoke for the young persons rather than allowing or encouraging them to speak for themselves).

9 In some jurisdictions too, judges play a role in protecting offenders' rights. In court-referred family group conferences and in the court-referred restorative justice pilots in New Zealand, judges receive recommendations from the conferences and it is up to them to decide whether or not to accept them.

10 Again, this is not the place to discuss offenders' interactions with the police, but, in my view, this is a key area for the erosion of offenders' rights and obviously is one which precedes both restorative justice and conventional court processes.

11 Morley and Mullender (1994) estimated that the 'average' victim was assaulted 35 times before calling the police.

12 In practice, violence by men against their female partners is often excluded from restorative justice pilots (as in the current pilots in New Zealand) but there are a few examples of the use of restorative justice processes in family violence cases and these seem to have been viewed positively by communities (as in Hollow Water – see Braithwaite, 1999 for more detail – and in areas of Newfoundland – see Burford and Pennell, 1998 for more detail).

13 There is no reason why restorative outcomes should not seek to do this. Section 4 of the Children, Young Persons and Their Families Act 1989 in New Zealand states that young offenders should be given the opportunity to develop in 'responsible, beneficial and socially acceptable ways' and preliminary analysis of more than 650 cases dealt with by family group conferences there in 1998 (Maxwell et al., 2001) shows that just over a quarter of the young people agreed to get involved in some kind of programme (mainly counselling) and that almost a quarter agreed to some kind of education or training.

14 For example, the number of young people appearing in courts in 1999 represented a marked reduction (of more than two-fifths) over the 1989 figure (Spier and Norris, 1993; Spier, 2000).

15 Dalley (1998: 316) reports that the number of young offenders admitted to social welfare residences declined from 1295 in 1989/90 to 655 in 1992/93. On 4 October 2001, there were 75 young offenders in social welfare residences (Child, Youth and Family Services National Office, personal communication).

16 Six per cent of young offenders sentenced in (all) courts were given custodial sentences (corrective training or imprisonment) in 1999 compared with 3 per cent in 1989 (Spier and Norris, 1993; Spier, 2000). However, the actual number given custodial sentences in 1999 was much lower: 105 compared with 193 in 1989. The more recent penal census (1999) showed that only 12 male prisoners and 1 female prisoner were under the age of 17 (Rich, 2000).

17 Feeling remorse was constructed from a number of variables: feeling sorry for what one had done and showing it; feeling that one had repaired the damage; completing the tasks agreed to; and reporting that the conference was a memorable event.

18 Current ongoing work (Maxwell et al., 2001) is examining whether or not these findings hold good for a larger sample of young offenders dealt with in family group conferences in 1998. Interviews conducted so far show that three quarters of the young people interviewed said that they could understand how the victim felt; two-thirds said they felt really sorry for their offending and more than two-thirds said that they had showed the victim that they were really sorry and that they could see the victim's point of view. In all, more than three-quarters said they were able to make up for what they did and most also felt treated fairly and with respect. Half, however, said that the way that they were dealt with had made them feel that

they were a bad person and more than half felt that they had been treated as though they were criminals. These findings have not yet been related to whether or not the young person was subsequently convicted in the adult criminal courts.

19 See, for example, Umbreit *et al.*'s (1994) comparison of four victim offender mediation programmes in the United States compared with non-mediated and non-referred offenders; the meta-analysis by Bonta *et al.* (1998) of programmes using community service, restitution and mediation compared with programmes without these elements; McCord and Wachtel's (1998) evaluation of young offenders randomly assigned to conferences or to courts; Maxwell *et al.*'s (1999) comparison of 200 participants in two restorative justice pilot schemes in New Zealand with a matched sample of offenders who were dealt with solely through the criminal courts; and Sherman *et al.*'s (2000) comparisons of young people randomly assigned to conferences or to courts.

20 This contrasts with Miers *et al.*'s (2001) findings with respect to a number of restorative justice schemes in England. It is not clear, however, that all of these schemes really met the core values of restorative justice.

21 In the above examples, we might not think it appropriate to give all offenders an equal voice and this would have to be taken into account in trying to achieve a balance.

22 Ashworth and von Hirsch (1998: 303) certainly justify conventional criminal justice practices on the grounds that they displace vigilantism and prevent people from taking the law into their own hands.

23 I acknowledge that desert theorists would not support such inconsistencies either, but I prefer to respond to their criticisms of restorative justice by referring to how sentencing 'is' empirically rather than how it 'ought' to be ideally.

References

Abrahams, R. (1998) *Vigilant Citizens*. Cambridge: Polity Press.

Andrews, D. and Bonta, J. (1994) *The Psychology of Criminal Conduct*. Cincinnati, OH: Anderson.

Ashworth, A. and von Hirsch, A. (1998) 'Desert and the Three Rs', in A. von Hirsch and A. Ashworth (eds.) *Principled Sentencing: Reading on Theory and Policy*. Oxford: Hart Publishing.

Ball, C. (2000) 'The Youth Justice and Criminal Evidence Act 1999 – Part I: A Significant Move Towards Restorative Justice or a Recipe for Unintended Consequences?', *Criminal Law Review*, April: 211–22.

Bazemore, G. and Umbreit, M. (1995) 'Rethinking the Sanctioning Function in Juvenile Court', *Crime and Delinquency*, 41: 296–316.

Bonta, J., Wallace-Capretta, S. and Rooney, J. (1998) *Restorative Justice: An Evaluation of the Restorative Resolutions Project*. Ottawa, Ontario: Solicitor General Canada.

Bottoms, A. (1987) 'Limiting Prison Use in England and Wales', *The Howard Journal of Criminal Justice*, 26: 177–202.

Braithwaite, J. (1989) *Crime, Shame and Reintegration*. Cambridge: Cambridge University Press.

Braithwaite, J. (1999) 'Restorative Justice: Assessing Optimistic and Pessimistic Accounts', in M. Tonry and N. Morris (eds.) *Crime and Justice: A Review of the Research*. Chicago, IL: Chicago University Press.

Burford, G. and Pennell, J. (1998) *Family Group Decision Making: After the Conference — Progress in Resolving Violence and Promoting Well Being*, Vol. 1. St John's, Newfoundland: Memorial University of Newfoundland.

Cant, R. and Downie, R. (1998) *Evaluation of the Young Offenders Act (1994) and the Juvenile Justice Teams.* Perth: Social Systems & Evaluation.

Cavadino, M. and Dignan, J. (1996) 'Reparation, Retribution and Rights', *International Review of Victimology*, 4: 233–53.

Dalley, B. (1998) *Family Matters: Child Welfare in Twentieth Century New Zealand.* Auckland, New Zealand: Auckland University Press.

Daly, K. (2001) 'Conferencing in Australia and New Zealand: Variations, Research Findings and Prospects', in A. Morris and G. Maxwell (eds.) *Restoring Justice for Juveniles: Conferences, Mediation and Circles.* Oxford: Hart Publishing.

Darbyshire, P. (2000) 'The Mischief of Plea Bargaining and Sentencing', *Criminal Law Review*, November: 895–910.

Delgrado, R. (2000) 'Prosecuting Violence: A Colloquy on Race, Community and Justice, Goodbye to Hammuarabi: Analysing the Atavistic Appeal of Restorative Justice', *Stanford Law Review*, 52: 751–75.

Gendreau, P. (1996) 'The Principles of Effective Intervention with Offenders', in A. Harland (ed.) *Choosing Correctional Outcomes That Work.* Thousand Oaks, CA: Sage.

Hedderman, C. and Gelsthorpe, L. (1997) *Understanding the Sentencing of Women.* Home Office Research Study No. 170. London: HMSO.

Hood, R. (1992) *Race and Sentencing.* Oxford: Clarendon Press.

Johnstone, G. (2002) *Restorative Justice: Ideas, Values, Debates.* Cullompton, Devon: Willan Publishing.

Kurki, L. (2000) 'Restorative and Community Justice in the United States', in M. Tonry (ed.) *Crime and Justice: A Review of the Research*, Vol. 26. Chicago, IL: University of Chicago Press.

Latimer, J., Dowden, C. and Muise, D. (2001) *The Effectiveness of Restorative Justice Practices: A Meta-analysis.* Ottawa, Ontario: Department of Justice Canada.

Levrant, S., Cullen, F., Fulton, B. and Wozniak, J. (1999) 'Reconsidering Restorative Justice: The Corruption of Benevolence Revisited', *Crime and Delinquency*, 45/1: 3–27.

Marshall, T. and Merry, S. (1990) Crime and Accountability: Victim/Offender Mediation in Practice. London: HMSO.

Martinson, R. (1974) 'What Works? Questions and Answers about Prison Reform', *Public Interest*, 35 (Spring): 22–54.

Maxwell, G. and Morris, A. (1993) *Families, Victims and Culture: Youth Justice in New Zealand.* Wellington, New Zealand: Social Policy Agency and Institute of Criminology.

Maxwell, G. and Morris, A. (1999) *Understanding Re-offending.* Wellington, New Zealand: Institute of Criminology.

Maxwell, G. and Smith, C. (1998) *Police Attitudes to Maori.* Wellington, New Zealand: Institute of Criminology.

Maxwell, G., Morris, A. and Anderson, T. (1999) *Community Panel Adult Pre-Trial Diversion: Supplementary Evaluation.* Wellington, New Zealand: Crime Prevention Unit Department of Prime Minister and Cabinet and Institute of Criminology.

Maxwell, G., Robertson, J., Kingi, V., Anderson, T. and Lash, B. (2001) *The Preliminary Report on the Achieving Effective Outcomes in Youth Justice Research Project.* Wellington, New Zealand: Institute of Criminology, unpublished.

McCold, P. and Wachtel, B. (1998) *Restorative Policing Experiment.* Pipersville, PA: Community Service Foundation.

McConville, M., Hodgson, J., Bridges, L. and Pavlovic, A. (1993) *Standing Accused: The Organisation and Practices of Criminal Defence Lawyers.* Oxford: Clarendon Press.

Miers, D. (2001) 'An International Review of Restorative Justice', Crime Reduction Series Paper 10. London: Home Office.

Miers, D., Maguire, M., Goldie, S., Sharpe, K., Hale, C., Netten, A., Uglow, S., Doolin, K., Hallam, A., Enterkin, J. and Newburn, T. (2001) 'An Exploratory

Evaluation of Restorative Justice Schemes', Crime Reduction Series Paper 9. London: Home Office.

Mirrlees-Black, C. (1999) *Domestic Violence: Findings from a New British Crime Survey Self-completion Questionnaire*, Home Office Research Study No. 191. London: Home Office.

Morley, R. and Mullender, A. (1994) 'Preventing Domestic Violence to Women', Crime Prevention Unit Paper 48. London: Home Office.

Morris, A. (2002) 'Shame, Guilt and Remorse in Family Group Conferences in New Zealand', in A. Duff and I. Weijers (eds.) *Punishing Juveniles: Principle and Critique.* Oxford: Hart Publishing.

Morris, A. and Gelsthorpe, L. (2000a) 'Something Old, Something Borrowed, Something Blue, but Something New? A Comment on the Prospects for Restorative Justice under the Crime and Disorder Act 1998', *Criminal Law Review*, January: 18–30.

Morris, A. and Gelsthorpe, L. (2000b) 'Re-visioning Men's Violence against Female Partners', *The Howard Journal of Criminal Justice*, 39/4: 412–28.

Morris, A. and Maxwell, G. (2001) 'Restorative Conferencing', in G. Bazemore and M. Schiff (eds.) *Restorative and Community Justice.* Cincinnati, OH: Anderson Publishing.

Morris, A., Maxwell, M. and Shepherd, P. (1997) *Being a Youth Advocate: An Analysis of their Roles and Responsibilities.* Wellington, New Zealand: Institute of Criminology.

Palk, G., Hayes, H. and Prenzler, T. (1998) 'Restorative Justice and Community Conferencing: Summary of Findings from a Pilot Study', *Current Issues in Criminal Justice*, 10: 138–55.

Paternoster, R., Bachman, R., Brame, R. and Sherman, L. (1997) 'Do Fair Procedures Matter? The Effect of Procedural Justice on Spousal Assault', *Law and Society Review*, 31: 163–204.

Pease, K. (1985) 'Community Service Orders', in M. Tonry and N. Morris (eds.) *Crime and Justice: An Annual Review of the Research*, Vol. 6. Chicago, IL: University of Chicago Press.

Platt, A. (1969) *The Child Savers.* Chicago, IL: University of Chicago Press.

Polk, K. (2001) 'Positive Youth Development, Restorative Justice and the Crisis of Abandoned Youth', in G. Bazemore and M. Schiff (eds.) *Restorative and Community Justice.* Cincinnati, OH:Anderson Publishing.

Rich, M. (2000) *Census of Prison Inmates 1999.* Wellington, New Zealand: Department of Corrections.

Schiff, M. and Bazemore, G. (2001) 'Dangers and Opportunities of Restorative Community Justice', in G. Bazemore and M. Schiff (eds.) *Restorative and Community Justice.* Cincinnati: OH: Anderson Publishing.

Sherman, L., Strang, H. and Woods, D. (2000) *Recidivism Patterns in the Canberra Reintegrative Shaming Experiment (RISE).* Canberra: Australian National University.

Spier, P. (2000) *Conviction and Sentencing of Offenders in New Zealand: 1990 to 1999.* Wellington, New Zealand: Ministry of Justice.

Spier, P. and Norris, M. (1993) *Conviction and Sentencing of Offenders in New Zealand: 1983 to 1992.* Wellington, New Zealand: Ministry of Justice.

Strang, H. (2001) 'Justice for Victims of Young Offenders: The Centrality of Emotional Harm and Restoration', in A. Morris and G. Maxwell (eds.) *Restoring Justice for Juveniles: Conferences, Mediation and Circles.* Oxford: Hart Publishing.

Strang, H., Barnes, G., Braithwaite, J. and Sherman, L. (1999) *Experiments in Restorative Policing: A Progress Report on the Canberra Reintegrative Shaming Experiments (RISE).* Canberra: Australian Federal Police and Australian National University, http://www.aic.gov.au/rjustice/rise/progress/1999.html.

Tonry, M. (1994) 'Proportionality, Parsimony and Interchangeability', in A. Duff, S. Marshall, R. E. Dobash and R. P. Dobash (eds.) *Penal Theory and Practice*. Manchester: Manchester University Press.

Tracy, C. (1998) 'Associate Editor's Editorial: The Promises and Perils of Restorative Justice', *International Journal of Offender Therapy and Comparative Criminology*, 42/4: 275–77.

Trimboli, L. (2000) *An Evaluation of the NSW Youth Justice Conferencing Scheme*. Sydney: New South Wales Bureau of Crime Statistics and Research.

Tyler, T. (1990) *Why People Obey the Law*. New Haven, CT: Yale University Press.

Umbreit, M., Coates, R. and Kalanj, B. (1994) *When Victim Meets Offender*. Monsey, NY: Criminal Justice Press.

Umbreit, M., Coates, R. and Vos, B. (2001) 'Victim Impact of Meeting with Young Offenders: Two Decades of Victim Offender Mediation Practice and Research', in A. Morris and G. Maxwell (eds.) *Restoring Justice for Juveniles: Conferences, Mediation and Circles*. Oxford: Hart Publishing.

van Ness, D. (1993) 'New Wine and Old Wineskins: Four Challenges of Restorative Justice', *Criminal Law Forum*, 4: 251–76.

Young, R. (2001) 'Just Cops Doing "Shameful" Business?: Police-led Restorative Justice and the Lessons of Research', in A. Morris and G. Maxwell (eds.) *Restoring Justice for Juveniles: Conferences, Mediation and Circles*. Oxford: Hart Publishing.

Young, R. and Goold, B. (1999) 'Restorative Police Cautioning in Aylesbury – from Degrading to Reintegrative Shaming Ceremonies?', *Criminal Law Review*, February: 126–38.

Appendix A: Declaration of Leuven on the Advisability of Promoting the Restorative Approach to Juvenile Crime

(made on the occasion of the first International Conference on 'Restorative Justice for Juveniles. Potentialities, Risks and Problems for Research', Leuven, May 12–14, 1997)

This declaration has been accepted on May 13th, 1997 by the participants in the business meeting of the International Network for Research on Restorative Justice for Juveniles, among whom Gordon Bazemore, John Braithwaite, Ezzat Fattah, Uberto Gatti, Susan Guarino-Ghezzi, Russ Immarigeon, Janet Jackson, Hans-Juergen Kerner, Rob MacKay, Paul McCold, Mara Schiff, Klaus Sessar, Jean Trépanier, Mark Umbreit, Peter van der Laan, Daniel Van Ness, Ann Warner-Roberts, Elmar Weitekamp, Martin Wright, Lode Walgrave.

In spite of differences in approach and in emphasis, the participants agreed that the text can be considered as a common ground for further elaboration.

Introduction

The aim of this public statement is

1. to emphasise the belief of a substantial part of the scientific world in the potential of restorative justice for offering a constructive response to crime,
2. to encourage political leaders and governmental officials to inform themselves thoroughly about the concept of restorative justice and necessary system changes required to implement the concept properly,
3. to stimulate legal authorities to widen the opportunities for implementing restorative responses to crime, to promote experimenting with new goals and forms of restorative responses to crime, and to encourage policy debate and scientific research.

[. . .]

The potential

1. All over the world, initiatives are being taken that can be covered by the term 'restorative justice'. They lead to an increasing belief of many scientific scholars that restorative justice can evolve towards being a serious alternative in responding to crime. The aim of the restorative approach is to restore the harm done to victims and to contribute to peace in the community and safety in society.

2. The initial success of the approach as documented by scientific research has led to a growing confidence in its potential.

The great majority of the restorative obligations are well accomplished by the offenders. Most participating victims experience a greater degree of satisfaction than those who are involved in more traditional judicial procedures. Offenders generally have less difficulty in understanding the restorative obligations than they have with regard to the punitive or rehabilitative responses. Outcomes in terms of recidivism seem to be positive, though further research is needed to establish this more firmly. When informed realistically about its possibilities, the majority of the public appears to prefer restorative responses to crime.

3. No decisive limits concerning the feasibility of restorative justice have yet been observed.

Many victims of serious offences are also willing to cooperate in restorative processes. Serious offenders can and regularly do comply with restorative obligations. No more threats to public safety have been observed as a result of the restorative experiments than have been caused by any other traditional sanctions or measures.

4. The restorative response to crime is based on a socio-ethical approach which stresses the responsibilities of the parties to find a constructive solution to the crime conflict. The approach therefore offers the potential for more peacekeeping in society as a whole.

5. Optimism concerning initial restorative responses to crime leads to a more general concept of restorative justice. The wider potentialities of restorative justice appear to be very promising though more research is needed to further explore these potentialities.

6. Given that much of the experimentation has been carried out with juveniles and given that public opinion as well as legal authorities generally accept more openness in their reaction to juvenile offending, the following propositions are advanced for the restorative response to juvenile offending.

Ten propositions

1.

(11) Crime should not be considered as a transgression of a public rule or as an infringement of an abstract juridico-moral order but should, in the first place, be dealt with as a harm to victims, a threat to peace and safety in community and a challenge for public order in society.

(12) Reactions to crime should contribute towards the decrease of this harm, threats and challenges. The purely retributive response to crime not only increases the total amount of suffering in society, but is also insufficient to meet victims' needs, promotes conflict in community and seldom promotes public safety. The tendency towards more punitive responses to juvenile crime is therefore counter-productive.

(13) Reactions to crime should consider in full the accountability of the offender, including his obligation to contribute to the restoration of the harm and peace, and his entitlement to enjoy all rights to which all members of the society are entitled. A purely rehabilitative response is often not advisable as it can circumvent the possible accountability of the offender and it may not offer an adequate framework for legal safeguards. It is therefore important that the rehabilitative approach to offenders is voluntary and not judicially enforced.

2.

(21) The main function of social reaction to crime is not to punish, but to contribute to conditions that promote restoration of the harm caused by the offence. It is therefore called restorative justice.

(22) All kinds of harm are susceptible to restoration, including the material, physical, psychological, and relational injuries to individual victims, losses in the quality of relational and social life in the community and declines in the public order in society.

3.

The role of public authorities in the reaction to an offence needs to be limited to
- contributing to the conditions for restorative responses to crime,
- safeguarding the correctness of procedures and the respect for individual legal rights,
- imposing judicial coercion, in situations where voluntary restorative actions do not succeed and a response to the crime is considered to be necessary,
- organising judicial procedures in situations where the crime and the public reactions to it are of such a nature that a purely informal voluntary regulation appears insufficient.

4.

(41) The victim has the right to freely choose whether or not to participate in a restorative justice process. The possibility of such a process should always be offered to him or her in a realistic way. If the victim accepts, he or she should have the opportunity to express completely his or her grievances and to make the full account of any injuries and losses sustained. A refusal to cooperate should not hamper the victims' possibility for indemnity through judicial procedures.

(42) The offender cannot be involved in any voluntary restorative process unless he or she freely accepts the accountability for the harm caused by the offence.

(43) If the victim refuses to cooperate in a restorative process, the offender should nevertheless in the first place be involved in some form of restorative responses, such as contributions to victim-funds and/or community service.

(44) The realisation of a restorative process with the particular victim may not complete the restorative reaction, if the community itself is a party concerned. The offender may be obliged to complete a community service, functioning as a symbolic or actual restoration of the harm done to community.

5.

(51) Within the rules of due process and proportionality and in so far it does not obstruct the restorative response itself, the action towards young offenders should maximally contribute to competency building and reintegration.

(52) The implementation of a restorative process, whether from within or outwith the judicial system, should not limit the availability of voluntary treatment, assistance and support to the juvenile offender and/or his family from agencies operating outside the judicial system.

6.

If concerns for public safety are judged to necessitate the incapacitation of an offender, the offender should nevertheless be stimulated to undertake restorative actions from within his or her place of confinement. These actions can take the form of offering apologies, participating in a mediation programme, and/or accomplishing services to the benefit of the victim, a victim-fund or the community.

7.

(71) Every public coercive intervention, whether or not it is aimed at restorative goals, should only be taken by a judicial instance, according to clear procedural rules.

(72) The outcome of any restorative process should not transgress a maximum which should be in proportion to the seriousness of the harm that has been caused and to the responsibility and the capacities of the offender.

8.

Authorities should make serious efforts to facilitate restorative responses to juvenile crime. These include

(81) remodelling the juvenile justice system in order to enhance the opportunities for restorative responses in and outside the system.

(82) providing the necessary agencies in communities which are equipped to carry out these actions,

(83) promoting the development of adequate methodologies for sound implementation of restorative processes,

(84) creating opportunities for education and training of staff who will be responsible for implementing restorative processes,

(85) promoting scientific research and reflection on restorative justice issues.

9.

In concert with practitioners, scientific research on restorative justice has to

(91) provide scientific feedback on the processes and outcomes of ongoing experiments and practices, and to make suggestions for new experiments,

(92) construct theories which can lead to deeper insight into the ongoing processes, collate the separate practices into a coherent framework and increase the innovative appeal of the restorative approach,

(**93**) contribute to the development of adequate methodologies for implementation of the restorative processes,

(**94**) investigate the cultural and structural contexts currently operating in the judicial system, the community and in society, which together determine the existing opportunities for restorative justice, and to reflect upon possible ways of improving this,

(**95**) develop reflection on the socio-ethical basis of restorative justice,

(**96**) examine the legal context of restorative justice and to make clear in how far legal safeguards are respected.

10.

Although the propositions advanced above focus primarily on responses to juvenile offending only, similar considerations may very well apply to adult offending also.

For more information:

Lode Walgrave
Criminology-K.U. Leuven
Hooverplein 10
B-3000 Leuven
Tel. 32-16-32 52 74
Fax 32-16-32 54 68
E-mail: lode.walgrave@law.kuleuven.ac.be

This extract is taken, with minor abridgements, from 'The Declaration of Leuven on the Advisability of Promoting the Restorative Approach to Juvenile Crime', in L. Walgrave (ed.), Restorative Justice for Juveniles: Potentialities, Risks and Problems for Research *(Leuven University Press, 1998).*

Appendix B: Statement of Restorative Justice Principles

Restorative Justice Consortium

This Statement of Principles derives from a development of an exercise undertaken by the Restorative Justice Consortium to revise the well recognised Standards for Restorative Justice. The Principles will provide the basis for a series of standards in particular settings of practice, namely Adult Criminal Justice, Youth Criminal Justice, Schools, Workplace, Prisons and Neighbourhoods.

1. Principles relating to the interests of all participants

(a) Participation to be voluntary and based on informed choice
(b) Avoidance of discrimination, irrespective of the nature of the case
(c) Access to be available to relevant agencies for help and advice
(d) Maintain access to various established methods of dispute resolution
(e) Processes that do not compromise the rights under the law of the participants
(f) Commitment not to use information in a way that may prejudice the interests of any participant in subsequent proceedings
(g) Protection of personal safety
(h) Protection and support for vulnerable participants
(i) Respect for civil rights and the dignity of persons

2. Principles relating to those who have sustained harm or loss

(a) Respect for their personal experiences, needs and feelings
(b) Acknowledgement of their harm or loss
(c) Recognition of their claim for amends
(d) Opportunity to communicate with the person who caused the harm or loss, if that person is willing
(e) Entitled to be the primary beneficiary of reparation

3. Principles relating to those who caused the harm or loss to others

(a) The opportunity to offer reparation, including before any formal requirement
(b) Reparation to be appropriate to the harm done and within their capacity to fulfil it
(c) Respect for the dignity of the person(s) making amends

4. Principles relating to the interests of local community and society

(a) The promotion of community safety and social harmony by learning from restorative processes, and so take measures that are conducive to the reduction of crime or harm
(b) The promotion of social harmony through respect for cultural diversity and civil rights, social responsibility and the rule of law
(c) Opportunity for all to learn mediation and other methods of non-violent resolution of conflict

5. Principles relating to agencies working alongside the judicial system

(a) Matters to be settled outside the judicial system, except where this is unworkable due to the level of harm done, the risk of further harm, issues of public policy, or disagreement about the critical facts
(b) Avoid unfair discrimination by ensuring that rights under the law are not compromised
(c) Provide a wide and flexible range of opportunities to enable those who have caused loss or harm to make amends

6. Principles relating to the judicial system

(a) Primary aim to be the repair of harm
(b) Restorative requirements to be fair, appropriate and workable
(c) Where a restorative requirement is appropriate, but victims decline to participate, there should be opportunities for community reparation, or reparation to others who have suffered harm or loss
(d) Where a restorative requirement is appropriate, but those who have caused harm or loss decline to participate, community reparation should be enforced
(e) Voluntary offers to repair harm or loss, by those who have caused it, to be valued
(f) Content of restorative meetings to be considered privileged, subject to public interest qualifications

7. Principles relating to restorative justice agencies

(a) Commitment to needs based practice
(b) Safeguarding of legal human rights
(c) Restorative justice practitioners who are seen to be neutral
(d) Restorative justice practitioners who act impartially
(e) Maintaining neutrality and impartiality, restorative justice practitioners should play no other role in the case
(f) Restorative justice agencies making a commitment to keep confidential the content of restorative meetings, subject to the requirements of the law
(g) Participants to be encouraged to keep confidential the contents of restorative meetings

(h) The engagement of weaker parties in negotiation to be facilitated
(i) Upholding respectful behaviour in restorative processes
(j) Upholding equality of respect for all participants in restorative processes, separating this from the harm done
(k) Engagement with good practice guidelines within the restorative justice movement
(l) Commitment by the agency to the use of constructive conflict resolution in general, and specifically in internal grievance and disciplinary procedures, and in handling complaints by clients
(m) Commitment to the accreditation of training, services and practitioners
(n) Commitment to continually improved practice

March 2002

This 'Statement of Restorative Justice Principles' is published by the Restorative Justice Consortium (UK) (see www.restorativejustice.org.uk)

Appendix C: Basic principles on the use of restorative justice programmes in criminal matters (UN), 2000

The Economic and Social Council

Recalling its resolution 1999/26 of 28 July 1999, entitled 'Development and implementation of mediation and restorative justice measures in criminal justice', in which the Council requested the Commission on Crime Prevention and Criminal Justice to consider the desirability of formulating United Nations standards in the field of mediation and restorative justice.

Noting the discussions on restorative justice during the Tenth United Nations Congress on the Prevention of Crime and the Treatment of Offenders, held in Vienna from 10 to 17 April 2000, in relation to the agenda item entitled 'Offenders and victims: accountability and fairness in the justice process'.

Recognizing that the use of restorative justice measures does not prejudice the right of States to prosecute alleged offenders,

1. *Takes note* of the submission of the preliminary draft elements of a declaration of basic principles on the use of restorative justice programmes in criminal matters, annexed to the present resolution;

2. *Requests* the Secretary-General to seek comments from Member States and relevant intergovernmental and non-governmental organizations, as well as the institutes of the United Nations Crime Prevention and Criminal Justice Programme network, on the desirability and the means of establishing common principles on the use of restorative justice programmes in criminal matters, including the advisability of developing an instrument, such as the preliminary draft declaration annexed to the present resolution, and on the contents of this draft;

3. *Also requests* the Secretary-General to convene, subject to the availability of voluntary contributions, a meeting of experts selected on the basis of equitable geographical representation to review the comments received and to examine proposals for further action in relation to restorative justice, including mediation, as well as the possibility of developing an instrument such as a declaration of basic principles on the use of restorative justice programmes, taking into account the preliminary draft declaration annexed to the present resolution;

4. *Further requests* the Secretary-General to report to the Commission on Crime Prevention and Criminal Justice at its eleventh session on the comments received and the results of the meeting of experts;

5. *Invites* the Commission to take action at its eleventh session, on the basis of the report of the Secretary-General;

6. *Calls upon* Member States, building on the results of the Tenth United Nations Congress on the Prevention of Crime and the Treatment of Offenders, held in Vienna from 10–17 April 2000, to continue to exchange information on experiences in the implementation and evaluation of programmes for restorative justice, including mediation.

Annex
Preliminary draft elements of a declaration of basic principles on the use of restorative justice programmes in criminal matters

I. Definitions

1. 'Restorative justice programme' means any programme that uses restorative processes or aims to achieve restorative outcomes.

2. 'Restorative outcome' means an agreement reached as the result of a restorative process. Examples of restorative outcomes include restitution, community service and any other programme or response designed to accomplish reparation of the victim and community, and reintegration of the victim and/or the offender.

3. 'Restorative process' means any process in which the victim, the offender and/or any other individuals or community members affected by a crime actively participate together in the resolution of matters arising from the crime, often with the help of a fair and impartial third party. Examples of restorative process include mediation, conferencing and sentencing circles.

4. 'Parties' means the victim, the offender and any other individuals or community members affected by a crime who may be involved in a restorative justice programme.

5. 'Facilitator' means a fair and impartial third party whose role is to facilitate the participation of victims and offenders in an encounter programme.

II. Use of restorative justice programmes

6. Restorative justice programmes should be generally available at all stages of the criminal justice process.

7. Restorative processes should be used only with the free and voluntary consent of the parties. The parties should be able to withdraw such consent at any time during the process. Agreements should be arrived at voluntarily by the parties and contain only reasonable and proportionate obligations.

8. All parties should normally acknowledge the basic facts of a case as a basis for participation in a restorative process. Participation should not be used as evidence of admission of guilt in subsequent legal proceedings.

9. Obvious disparities with respect to factors such as power imbalances and the parties' age, maturity or intellectual capacity should be taken into consideration in referring a case to and in conducting a restorative process. Similarly, obvious threats to any of the parties' safety should also be considered in referring any case to and in conducting a restorative process. The views of the parties themselves about the suitability of restorative processes or outcomes should be given great deference in this consideration.

10. Where restorative processes and/or outcomes are not possible, criminal justice officials should do all they can to encourage the offender to take responsibility vis-à-vis the victim and affected communities, and reintegration of the victim and/or offender into the community.

III. Operation of restorative justice programmes

11. Guidelines and standards should be established, with legislative authority when necessary, that govern the use of restorative justice programmes. Such guidelines and standards should address:

(a)   The conditions for the referral of cases to restorative justice programmes;
(b)   The handling of cases following a restorative process;
(c)   The qualifications, training and assessment of facilitators;
(d)   The administration of restorative justice programmes;
(e)   Standards of competence and ethical rules governing operation of restorative justice programmes.

12. Fundamental procedural safeguards should be applied to restorative justice programmes and in particular to restorative processes:

(a)   The parties should have the right to legal advice before and after the restorative process and, where necessary, to translation and/or interpretation. Minors should, in addition, have the right to parental assistance;
(b)   Before agreeing to participate in restorative processes, the parties should be fully informed of their rights, the nature of the process and the possible consequences of their decision;
(c)   Neither the victim nor the offender should be induced by unfair means to participate in restorative processes or outcomes.

13. Discussions in restorative processes should be confidential and should not be disclosed subsequently, except with the agreement of the parties.

14. Judicial discharges based on agreements arising out of restorative justice programmes should have the same status as judicial decisions or judgements and should preclude prosecution in respect of the same facts (*non bis in idem*).

15. Where no agreement can be made between the parties, the case should be referred back to the criminal justice authorities and a decision as to how to proceed should be taken without delay. Lack of agreement may not be used

as justification for a more severe sentence in subsequent criminal justice proceedings.

16. Failure to implement an agreement made in the course of a restorative process should be referred back to the restorative programme or to the criminal justice authorities and a decision as to how to proceed should be taken without delay. Failure to implement the agreement may not be used as justification for a more severe sentence in subsequent criminal justice proceedings.

IV. Facilitators

17. Facilitators should be recruited from all sections of society and should generally possess good understanding of local cultures and communities. They should be able to demonstrate sound judgement and interpersonal skills necessary to conducting restorative processes.

18. Facilitators should perform their duties in an impartial manner, based on the facts of the case and on the needs and wishes of the parties. They should always respect the dignity of the parties and ensure that the parties act with respect towards each other.

19. Facilitators should be responsible for providing a safe and appropriate environment for the restorative process. They should be sensitive to any vulnerability of the parties.

20. Facilitators should receive initial training before taking up facilitation duties and should also receive in-service training. The training should aim at providing skills in conflict resolution, taking into account the particular needs of victims and offenders, at providing basic knowledge of the criminal justice system and at providing a thorough knowledge of the operation of the restorative programme in which they will do their work.

V. Continuing development of restorative justice programmes

21. There should be regular consultation between criminal justice authorities and administrators of restorative justice programmes to develop a common understanding of restorative processes and outcomes, to increase the extent to which restorative programmes are used and to explore ways in which restorative approaches might be incorporated into criminal justice practices.

22. Member States should promote research on and evaluation of restorative justice programmes to assess the extent to which they result in restorative outcomes, serve as an alternative to the criminal justice process and provide positive outcomes for all parties.

23. Restorative justice processes may need to undergo change in concrete form over time. Member States should therefore encourage regular, rigorous evaluation and modification of such programmes in the light of the above definitions.

Name index

Subject index